Barbot on

Volun

Edited by
P.E.H. HAIR, ADAM JONES AND ROBIN LAW

ASHGATE

Published by
Ashgate Publishing Limited
Wey Court East
Union Road
Farnham
Surrey, GU9 7PT
England

Ashgate Publishing Company
Suite 420
101 Cherry Street
Burlington
VT 05401-4405
USA

First issued in paperback 2022

www.ashgate.com

Founded in 1846, the Hakluyt Society seeks to advance knowledge and education by the publication of scholarly editions of primary records of voyages, travels and other geographical material. In partnership with Ashgate, and using print-on-demand and e-book technology, the Society has made re-available all 290 volumes comprised in Series I and Series II of its publications in both print and digital editions. For a complete listing of titles and more information about these series, visit www.ashgate.com/hakluyt, and for information about the Hakluyt Society visit www.hakluyt.com.

ISBN 13: 978-1-03-232094-6 (pbk)
ISBN 13: 978-0-904180-33-6 (hbk)

WORKS ISSUED BY
THE HAKLUYT SOCIETY

———

BARBOT ON GUINEA
VOLUME II

SECOND SERIES
NO. 176

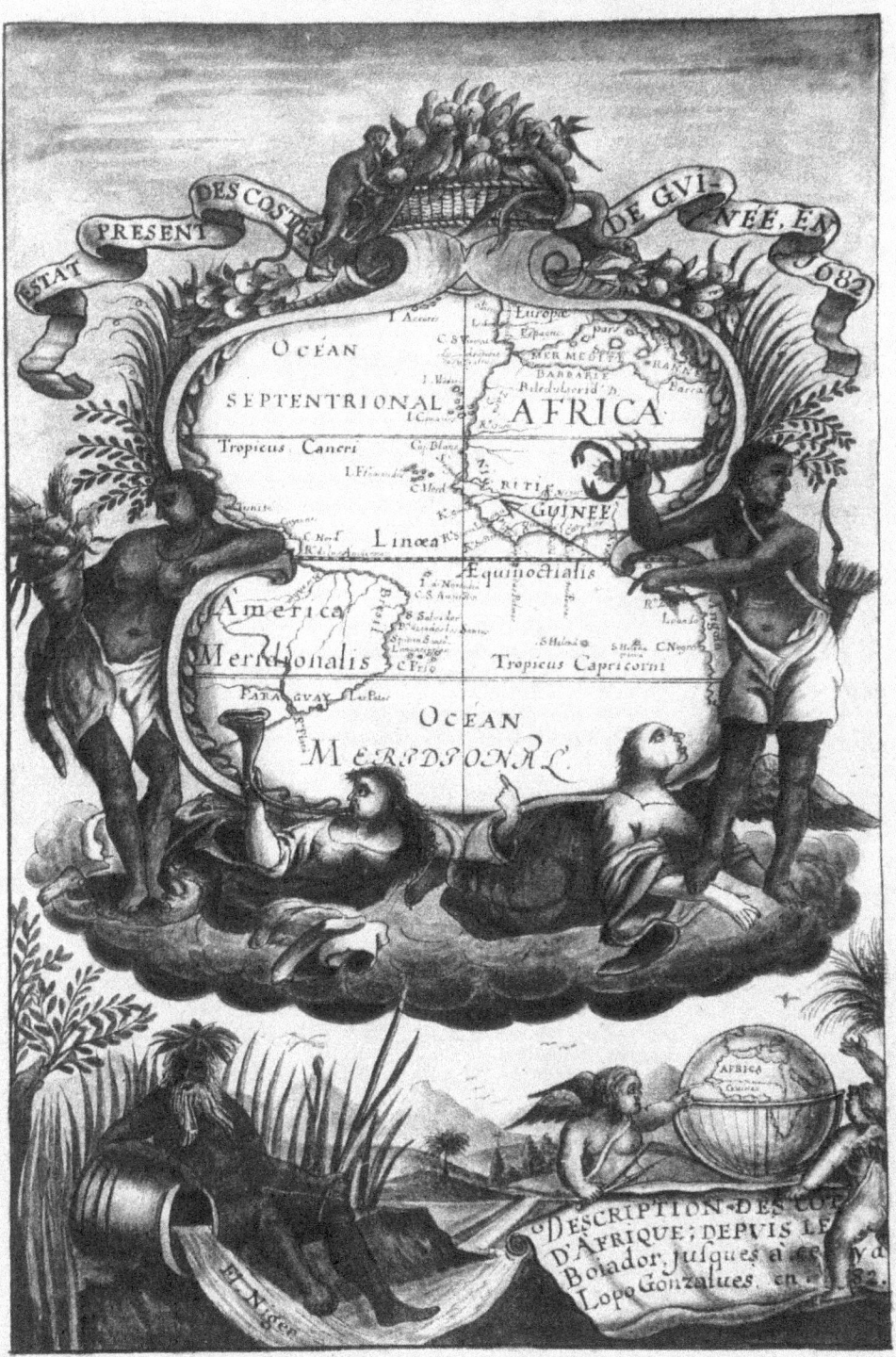

27. Barbot's frontispiece to his French text

BARBOT ON GUINEA

*THE WRITINGS OF JEAN BARBOT
ON WEST AFRICA 1678–1712*

VOLUME II

Edited by
P. E. H. HAIR, ADAM JONES and ROBIN LAW

General editor
P. E. H. HAIR

THE HAKLUYT SOCIETY
LONDON
1992

ISBN 0 904180 33 6
ISSN 0072 9396

Typeset by Waveney Typesetters, Norwich
Printed in Great Britain at
the University Press, Cambridge

Published by the Hakluyt Society
c/o The Map Library
British Library, Great Russell Street
London WC1B 3DG

CONTENTS

Part Two

DESCRIPTION
OF THE GOLD COAST OF GUINEA

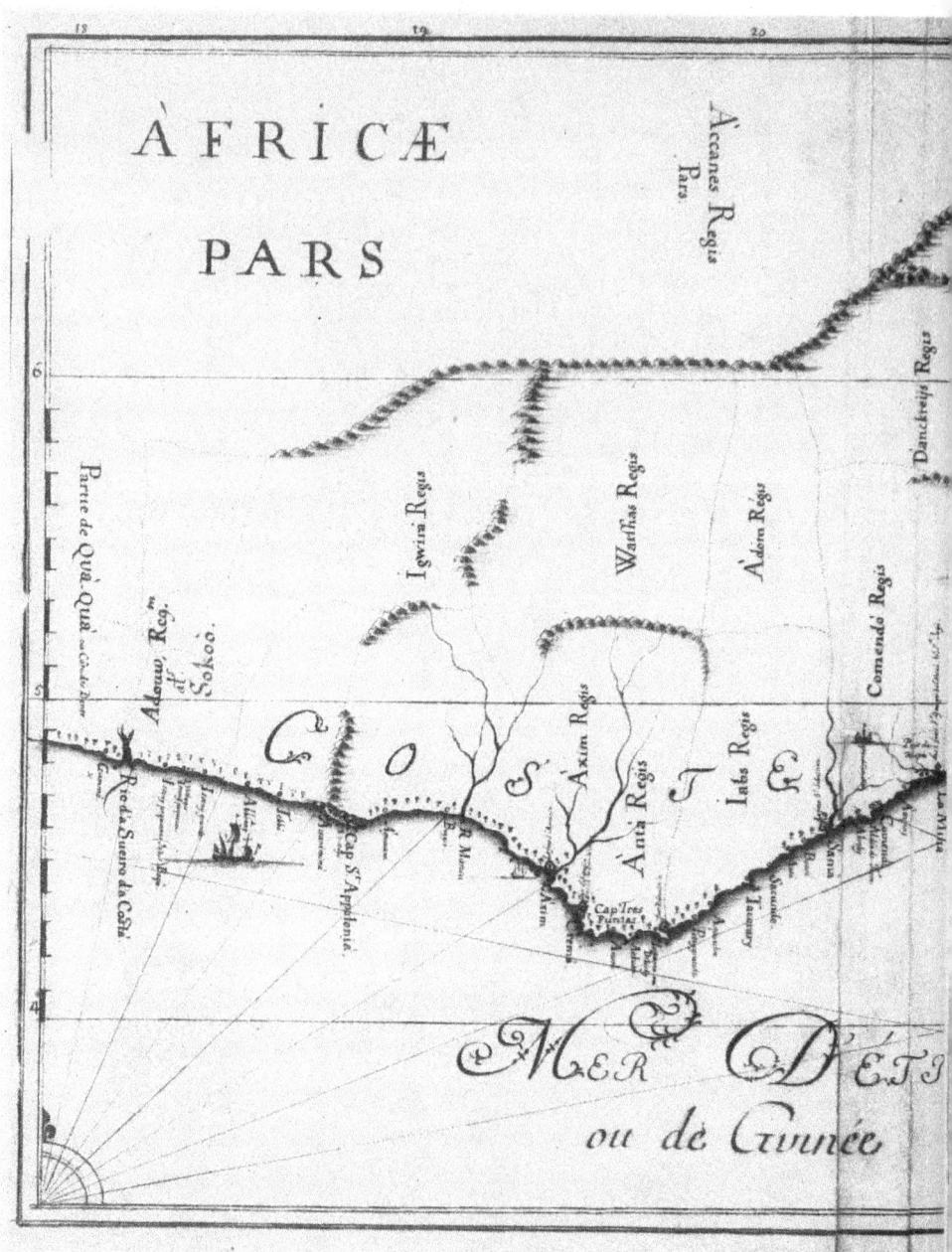

28. Gold Coast

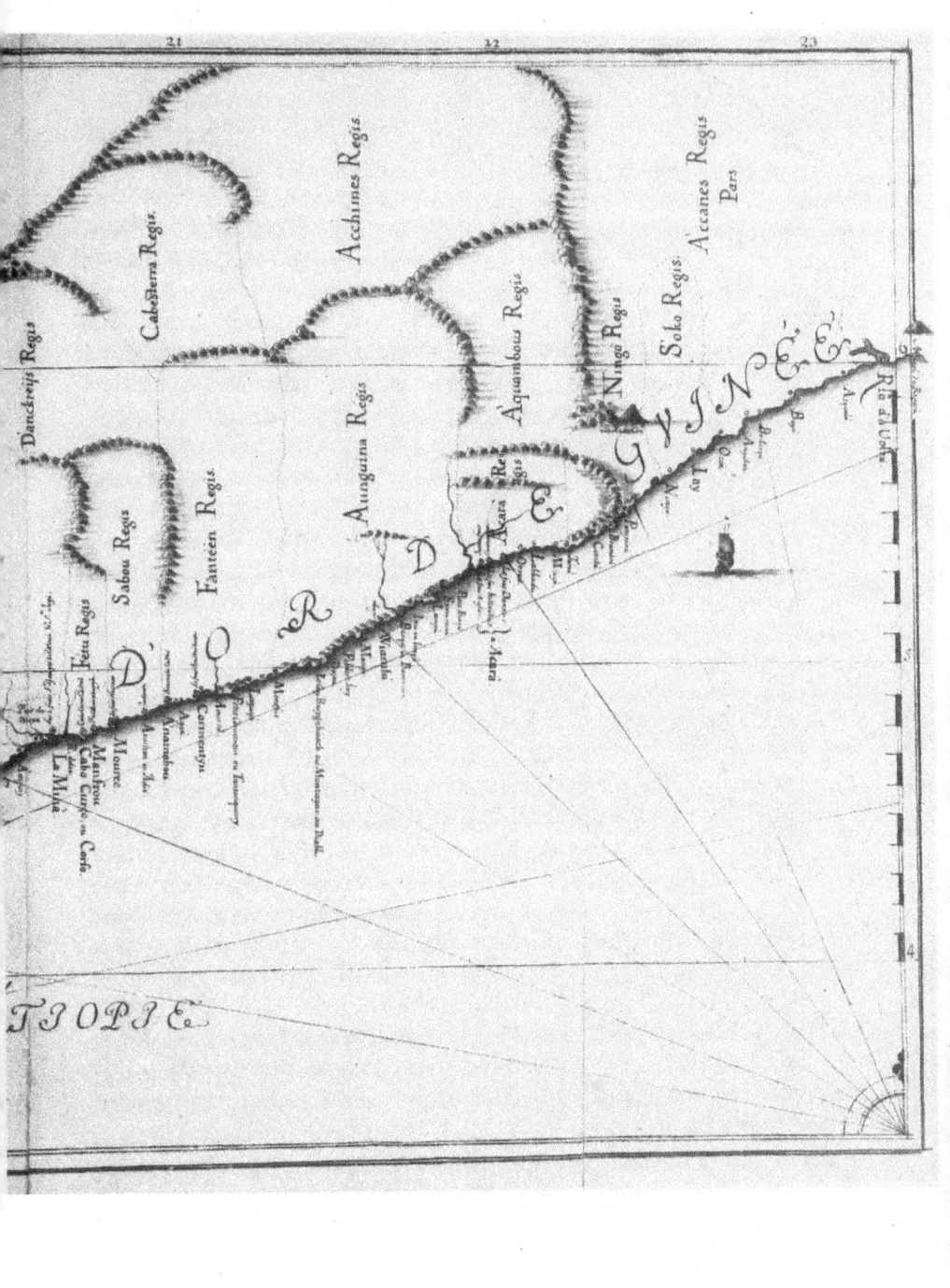

To Mr ∗ ∗ ∗

LETTER 1

Definition of Gold Coast in general.

Sir, You advise me in your letter not to halt when I am making such
excellent progress, particularly at the present time of year. But, Sir,
you do not see what it costs me. Would you yourself like to spend a
complete Spring pondering, rummaging through accounts, and writing, while the whole world savours the sweetness of this new-born
season, savouring it with all the more pleasure because its fine days
follow the most troublesome winter we have had for several years
[*margin:* 1684] ? No sooner have I finished one report than you want
another, and as an encouragement you say that all those I have
already given you, pleasant although they have seemed to you, fall
short of your expectations regarding the one you await, the one on
Gold Coast, since I made a longer stay at this point than elsewhere
[in Guinea]. You, Sir, have good reason to know how ample and
most exact are the scruples that you well know have taken hold of me
by my partiality.[1] I must therefore obey you, the more so as I have
already promised this description, and it would be disgraceful for me
to prefer my repose to the satisfaction of an individual I honour as
highly as you. Here, to start with, I am sending you a map of this
coast, so that you may tell me how you like it. I constructed it on the
spot with great diligence and accuracy. Take the trouble to compare
it with those you have: you will assuredly see a great difference and
much that has been added. I treat Gold Coast as extending from the
Rio da Sueiro d'a Costa to River Volta, although the Dutch regard it
as beginning at Axim and ending at Acra. I think this extension fully
justified, since more gold can be found [in the additional localities]
than other commodities, it only being between Lay and River Volta
that the trade is limited to slaves. I have shown on this map the
principal kingdoms of the interior, but in order not to make the
drawing too confused have omitted a number of small ones which
you will find mentioned in my account, as I was advised to do. Pray
tell me whether you share this opinion. I am, Sir, Your etc.

331

[illustration no. (52), map of Gold Coast, inserted before p. 2/1]²†

NOTES

[1] This obscure sentence may merely refer to Barbot's scruples about how he should compile his text. But alternatively it may indicate that, early in 1685, Barbot was under pressure to renounce his Protestant faith, perhaps as a condition of retaining his employment, and that he was weighing up the circumstances which eventually led him, in late 1685, to leave France.

[2] Among Barbot's main sources, Dapper and Villault defined Gold Coast as beginning at Assinie, and Dapper said it ended at Accra; whereas Marees began it at Cape Three Points but extended it to River Volta (Marees, ff. 3v, 113v; Dapper, p. 63/3; Villault, p. 164). Barbot compromises generously, taking the maximum extent on each side. His map of Gold Coast (reproduced in Baesjou 1988, map 3) was printed with hardly any changes in *1732*, Plate K (p. 148) (which also contains a more detailed inset of the coast between Abreby and Mouree). It gives a large number of coastal features, but despite Barbot having visited localities on the coast, and despite his claim of originality, is largely otherwise, being copied from Dutch charts. It does, however, mark the forts more clearly. When 'on the spot' Barbot doubtless made notes and rough maps (for instance, perhaps the inset mentioned above), and checked and marked up earlier maps, but the present map was compiled, not in Africa, but in France. Cf. *1732*, p. 145/1, which now ends Gold Coast at Lay.

LETTER 2

Definition of the lands and kingdoms which comprise Gold Coast.

You seem so content, Sir, with my map of Gold Coast that I am more than repaid for all the pains I have taken to map this rich country for you, and I should consider myself most happy if the trouble I will take to give you an exact account of it renders you as much satisfaction. I am very glad that you share the opinion of those who advised me not to change this map, but simply to mark on it the principal kingdoms and their boundaries; there are several little states which /p. 2/ you do not see on it and which I will nevertheless mention in this account, but very succinctly, for besides the fact that the interior is too little known for one to speak with certainty about the country, the government and the religion of these peoples, I wish neither to tire out my mind nor to bore yours by a long account. Besides, there is so much conformity in what I know of the manners of these [various] barbarians that I am led to the conclusion that there is also much affinity between all of them in those matters about which I have no [direct] knowledge concerning the practices of those furthest from the coast. Please note that I make use of accurate reports, and of journals written by my friends or by others who have observed at first hand.[1] This, Sir, is my way of giving you a complete acquaintance with this part of Africa; for, in short, you can clearly see that it is difficult for a man who has limited knowledge of the history of the world, and who has a trade to conduct, to be so accurate that nothing of the practice of a country escapes him, given that it is a country where there are few people who can supply him detailed information on all matters, in any depth. As far as possible, I shall approach the task critically, in order that you may not be persuaded to accept as true the imaginative fictions of several travellers, whose writings it would be easy for me to convict of falsehood if I did not fear being too long-winded. Here, then, in a few words, is what I know, and what I believe to contain the most truth.

Gold Coast, which the Portuguese call 'Costa d'Oro' and the Dutch 'Goudt-kust', derives its name from the metal which is found in great abundance in its mines and among the sands of its river. Under the name 'Gold Coast' I include 42 kingdoms and countries along the coast of Guinea and up to 60 or 70 leagues inland about which there is some degree of knowledge. There are thirteen maritime ones – Sakoo, Axim or Atzyn, Warshas or Little Inkassan, Ante or Anta, Guafo or Commendo, Fetu, Sabou, Fanten or Fantin, Aghuwena, Acra, Labade, Ningo and Soko. The 29 others are Igwira, Great Incassan, Incassia, Igyma, Tabue, Adom, Mompa, Wassa, Wanquy, Abramboe, Quyfora, Acanez, the territories of Inta and Ahim, Aqua, Quahoe, Cammanach, Bonoes, Equea, Lataby, Accarady, Insoka.[2] All these countries are situated between 4°30′ and 6°N latitude, some being further South than others; and they extend from 17° to 21° [East] longitude.[3] The extent is about 110 leagues, from the River d'a Costa to River Volta, and the distance around its circumference may be estimated at about 400 French leagues. All these different states, although so flung together and so small in size, are nevertheless each governed separately by kings or lords; and almost all are independent, as I will explain later in this account.[4]

I have shown you, Sir, from the beginning of my description of the coasts of Guinea, that men from Dieppe first discovered the coasts, as far as Grand Sestre, near Cabo das Palmas. If some writers are to be believed, they even founded the Castle del Mina, on Gold Coast, which the Portuguese subsequently seized; others maintain that the latter were always the natural owners of it, and that they alone occupied all of this coast for 150 years.[5] Whatever the truth is, through the changes of time we today find it shared out among several nations of Europe, who have been attracted from all parts by the trade in gold and slaves. This has obliged these nations to build trading posts and forts in several places, to protect their trade and their lives. These trading posts and places of security have all been built either with the consent of the Moorish kings or by artifice and by force, as I shall explain elsewhere; the majority were founded by the Portuguese, but through the chances of war they have fallen into the hands of the Dutch, who are today the nation best established on Gold Coast and on the coast of Angola.[6]

I imagine that you would already like to know the history of these revolutions, but order requires that I report in my separate description of each country the manner in which these changes occurred there. I therefore propose to begin my first letter to you with a geographical plan of all these /p. 3/ kingdoms, with which I shall combine an account of the wars which have occurred in each place and of the manner in which those who possess them today have gained control of them. This, as you may judge, will form the subject of several letters, and after this I shall tell you about the customs and religion of these barbarous peoples. Such is the aim of the work that I have very willingly undertaken in order to provide you with a testimony to the deep feeling which makes me Your, etc.

Additional Passage from *1732*

[p. 147/1–4, on the chartered companies and interlopers]

The Blacks of the gold coast are for the most part very rich, through the great trade they drive with Europeans, both aboard the ships and ashore, bartering their gold, for several sorts of European commodities, of which they make a vast profit up the inland; or through the large allowance they have out of the goods they buy of Europeans, for the account of the inland Blacks, for whom many of these on the coast act as brokers, buying considerable quantities of goods of the interlopers, who resort thither in great numbers from several parts of Europe; but especially from Zealand and France, notwithstanding the severe penalties they are liable to; for if taken by the English or Dutch companies, their factors or agents, their goods are not only confiscated, but a heavy fine laid on them. The cunning Blacks are not deterr'd by all these rigours, knowing how to bribe the companies Laptos, or slaves, who are set to watch them; and thus in the night run ashore the goods they buy of interlopers, or foreigners trading on the coast from Isseny, both by sea and land. For when the roads are clear of robbers, they travel to Isseny and Rio d'Oro to buy their goods, and bring them in by stealth, conveying them up the country without any molestation. They generally have such goods of the interlopers, 25 or 30 per cent cheaper, and perhaps much better, than those the companies' agents sell. By this under-hand trade, they in process of time grow rich, and the company suffers very much. / Few or none of the Blacks are to be trusted, as being crafty and deceitful, and who will never let slip an opportunity of cheating an European, nor indeed will they spare one another; some may their masters, but all do not. Of this, and their laziness, more hereafter. The English Royal African, and the Dutch West-India companies, having the privilege by patent of trading to this coast, exclusive to all others their fellow-subjects; and I suppose the Danish and Brandenburg companies have the same: such of the said nations as resort to those coasts, are liable to seizure of ships and goods, if taken by the ships, or agents, of any of the said companies, within their respective districts on the coast, besides bodily punishments inflicted on the offenders, especially among the Dutch, who have made it death; but that is seldom or never executed, some of the companies officers always finding it their interest to let such go unpunished; as is well known to the Zealanders, who of all the subjects of Holland send most interlopers every year to that coast. / These interlopers generally make use of ships of small burden, and good sailors, well fitted and mann'd, the better to make their escape, or stand upon their defence, if attack'd by the company's ships.[7]

NOTES

[1] There is no clear evidence that Barbot used any journals other than his own in constructing his account of Gold Coast.

[2] The lists of names of kingdoms are from Dapper, p. 63/4–5, with many changes, including variant spellings, partly by miscopying. To produce 13 marine kingdoms, Barbot adds Sakoo and Soko: he adds alternative names for several, especially 'Warshas or Little Inkassan' in error, Warshas being the same as Wassa in the second list. Only 22 inland kingdoms are named: from Dapper's list he omits Atty, Dahoe, Sanquay, Aquamboe, Tafoe, Abora, and Gavi. The names on Barbot's map do not exactly correspond, for instance, it adds 'Danckreis Regis' (= Denkyira), obviously from a Dutch source (conceivably from Bosman, but if so added at a much later date). A similar list of kingdoms is given in a Dutch manuscript source (ARA, Abramsz 23.11.1679).

Cf. *1732*, p. 145/1–3, which adds to each list new or alternative names, all from Bosman, to produce 'fifteen kingdoms along the seashore' and to conclude the inland list with 'the large kingdom of Accanez, which encloses most of the others from the north-west, round to the north-east'; and which also adds material on the maritime towns, also from Bosman, p. 5.

[3] The latitudes are reasonably correct, as is the extent of the longitude East (Barbot counts from the meridian of Hierro in the Canaries). But in 1678–9 he had recorded the longitudes of Assinie as 19°15' and of Axim as already 21°28' (*1679*, pp. 276, 282 – no longitude further East on Gold Coast than that of Axim was recorded), therefore he has revised his longitudes. His map of Gold Coast compromises, by stretching the coast so that River Volta lies a little beyond 23°: his *1732* map avoids the problem by not marking longitudes.

Cf. *1732*, p. 145/3.

[4] Cf. *1732*, p. 145/1, 3, 5–146/2, which, after a discussion as to whether the territories are large enough to be considered 'kingdoms', including a digression on Israelite and Anglo-Saxon petty kings, modifies the previous view, six maritime nations now being 'commonwealths', based on Bosman's four or five maritime 'commonwealths' (Bosman, pp. 5, 12, 57, 62, 164). It also adds lists of products detailed in subsequent chapters.

[5] Based on Villault, pp. 410–29.

Cf. *1732*, pp. 146/3–5, which enlarges by referring to early English voyages to Gold Coast, the material ultimately from Hakluyt, but probably through an intermediate summary; and Barbot now leaves unanswered 'whoever the first discoverers of this coast were, whether French or Portugueses'.

[6] Cf. *1732*, p. 146/4, which embroiders slightly and adds a detailed summary and an attempted up-date, as follows. 'The Dutch have the greatest number of such settlements . . . and next to them the English. The French, Spaniards and Portugueses, have had no settlements on that coast for a long time, and only make some coasting voyages along those parts. The

Danes have two forts; one at Maufro [Manfro], the other at Acra; and the Brandenburgers a fort or strong-house, at the village of Crema, in the midst of cape Tres-Pontas, all of which shall be mentioned in their places'. This is inaccurate in several respects, as the further account shows.

[7] Enlarged from Bosman, pp. 5–6, 421–2, which only refers to the Dutch. *Lapto[t]* was a term used to denote the African labourers (not normally slaves but 'free blacks', *1732*, p. 19/1) who worked for the French company in Senegal, where Barbot learned the term (see Letter 1/6, p. 25); it is doubtful whether it was ever used by others with reference to Gold Coast. 'Rio d'Oro' is a slip for 'Rio de Sueiro da Costa', and the reference to Isseny is perhaps a misunderstanding of Bosman, although Assinie and its vicinity, being remote from the Dutch and English forts on Gold Coast, did attract many interlopers (Phillips 1732, pp. 199–200; Hazewinkel 1932, pp. 250–1; Roussier 1935, p. 7).

LETTER 3

Particular description of Gold Coast, from Rio d'a Costa Sueiro to La Mina, and of the forts at Axim, Boutrou and Sama.

Sir, I shall begin to write you long letters, because I am afraid of wearing out your patience if I make you wait too long for a description which you have asked me for with such urgency; and for this same reason I shall immediately embark on my subject.

[Assinie and Cape Apollonia]

Between Rio da Costa Sueiro and Cape Sta Apolonia, Gold Coast is wholly low and is lined with large trees and several villages, of which the principal are Boqu, Isseny Pequeene, Isseny or Ashny Grande, Abiany or Albiany, Tebbo or Tabo, and Acanimina. Boqu is in the forest, at the mouth of Rio d'a Costa; Isseny Pequeene is on the coast, as are Isseny Grande and three small villages between them. This Isseny Grande was plundered and burnt by the Moors of the country, in 1681.[1] It is situated at the mouth of a river which only flows in rainy seasons, but which then comes from far inland, from the NNW. Abiany and Tebo are in the forest, and can only be recognised by their equal distance of three leagues from each other and by the large number of palm trees along the coast. Acanimina is on a slight hill, about half a league West of Cape Apolonia. [*insert:* From Isseny onwards, you no longer find anything to trade other than gold and slaves.] The coast from Boqui to Acanimina runs

WNW. The interior of the country is mountainous: very good gold is traded there, as well as some ivory and a few slaves. You anchor at 15–16 fathoms, three-quarters of a league from land.[2]

[illustration no. (53), 'Cap Sta. Appolonia', inserted after p. 2]

Cape Sta Apolonia was so named by the Portuguese, because they discovered it on the day of the festival they celebrate under this name. It projects a little to the South, rising into hills and hillocks which present quite a beautiful view, and it can be seen from ten leagues to the West in fine weather. There are three villages at the foot of the highest hill, but it is very difficult to approach, because the sea breaks with very great force, just as it does at Arcanimina and along the coast as far as Isseny.[3] From this cape to River Mancu, the coast runs ENE and East. There are two villages in between (Agumene and Bogio), set among the forests and palm trees, it being a low, flat country.[4] The kingdom of Sakoo is said to end at this River Mancu, and the Kingdom of Atzyn or Axim or Achem is said to begin there. This river is broad and extends far inland into the Igwira country. It is full of waterfalls and rocks, which make it unnavigable; it produces much gold, which the blacks fish for, diving under the rocks and into the waterfalls.[5] The coast as far as that of Axim (in the kingdom of Axim) runs SE and is entirely covered with forest.

Additional Passage from 1732

p. 430/1–2, 5–6, on the French at Assinie]

The chevalier Damon, who had brought over the pretended prince of Assiny in 1701, and was sent with the men and materials to build a fort there, and settle a factory for the African company of France, finding himself, as well as the French court, imposed upon by Hannibal, and not being able to prevail with the true king, to get footing on the continent, but only on a little island near the mouth of Assiny river, set his men to work, and erected a fort with eight guns, to secure the factory he settled there, which the French had for many years before labour'd to accomplish; that being a place where there is a great deal of the purest and finest gold of all Guinea; and having left a factor there with twelve or fifteen French-men, return'd to France.[6] / The Dutch, growing jealous of that new settlement of the French, at so advantageous a place, and the war breaking out with France in 1702, resolved to obstruct it; and to that purpose, as the Paris Gazette of October the 17th 1703, informs us, they equipp'd at Mina four vessels to attack the fort, which the French had built at Assiny; where being landed, they were receiv'd with so much bravery by the Sieur Lavie, the chief factor, that they were forced to retire, with the loss of twenty-five men kill'd, among whom was their chief engineer, and eleven taken prisoners, leaving their canoos behind them.[7] / ... / However, the French being at variance with the natives, and consequently having little or no trade, the company so far neglected their servants there, that in June 1704, perceiving the hatred of the Blacks against them still increased, and having no sort of trade, they imbark'd for France, after having levell'd their factory to the ground. / I had this account from one Porquet of Dieppe, who was then present at the blowing up of the lodge.[8]

[Axim and Gross-Friedrichsburg]

The kingdom of Axim is called Atchin or Atzyn by some. The natives call it Acchem. To its East lies the kingdom of Little Incassan, to the North that of Igwira, and to the South the sea of Guinea, its coasts being nothing but rocks. There are three villages on the seaboard, almost entirely inhabited by fishermen. The river of Axim passes below the village of Achombene, which lies at its mouth, at a place where the land forms a small inlet full of rocks and islets. The coast slopes down to the sea and is entirely covered with large trees; the piece of ground on which the village is situated projects into this bay in the form of a tongue, and rises as a small mound, almost isolated [from the land]. On this mound the Portuguese, in the time of King Emanuel, built a small fort, which commanded the whole of the land and sea around it; but after being harassed by the blacks on several occasions, they demolished it and rebuilt it on the mainland, on /p. 4/ top of a slope against which the sea breaks fairly gently, and which lies right next to the village of Achombene, so as to command it.[9] On 9 January 1642, this fort was taken from them, and it has since remained in the hands of the Dutch (who occupy it to this day), through an agreement between that crown and the West-Indies Company of Holland.[10]

You can see this castle from afar when coming from the West, like a white mark in the midst of the land, which is high and wooded.[11] I send you a view of it with my letter. It is one of the most charming places of this whole coast, and to stay there is most agreeable, for you see a continual verdure there and do not suffer great heat, as it is always in the shade. The landscape is diversified by several species of trees, and particularly palm and coconut trees; you hear incessantly the chirping of an infinite number of different birds, and to walk along the shore is perfectly delightful. But in my opinion nothing equals the view from the platform of the castle, where the eye wanders with pleasure over a vast extent of sea, and, returning towards the land, is pleasantly arrested by a number of islands and rocks which surround it and which, by their situation, leave only a very narrow passage for a longboat to approach the fort.[12] The little island which you see marked A on the plate is the one on which Mr De Ruyter set up a battery of twelve cannon, by means of which he made himself master of the place;[13] the other, marked B, is the one on which the natives place their wives and children when they go to war. Letter C marks the passage between the rocks, by which you go ashore. D is a little freshwater river which supplies the whole village of Achembene and comes from the Igwira country.[14]

[illustration no. (54), the fort 'St Antonio d'Axim']†

The Portuguese gave this castle the name of Sto Antonio d'Axim, which the Dutch still retain. It is necessary to make a wide detour at the foot of the hillock on which it is built, before you find the steps hewn into the rock to go up, for everywhere else it is steep and inaccessible. Its shape is an irregular and extremely confined triangle. /p. 5/ From the landward side you can make out two small bastions. The ramparts are made of local black stone, and are of medium height, but are liable to collapse in the rainy season; and for this reason a limestone kiln has been built, in order always to have ready the necessary materials. They make the limestone with oyster shells, which are found there in great abundance.[15] The garrison is not large, consisting of only one sergeant with 25 whites and as many blacks. There are 22–24 small-calibre iron cannon with some swivel-guns.[16] You enter by a drawbridge which crosses a ditch cut into the rock, eight or nine feet deep, and cover for this bridge is provided by a position (*banquette*) which can accommodate twenty musketeers and two swivel-guns. The interior of the place is narrow and confined;

29. The Dutch fort at Axim, Gold Coast, 1679

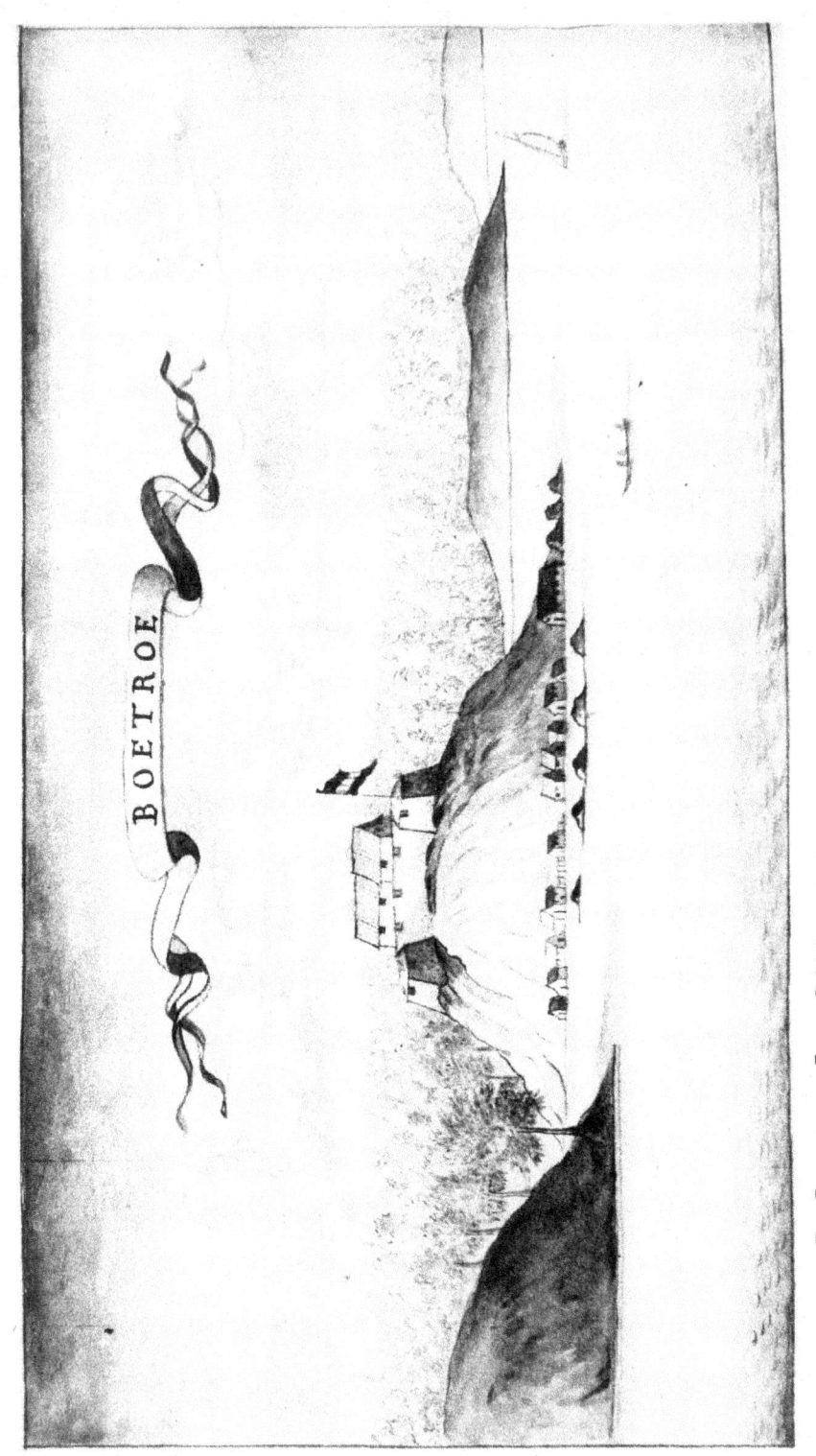

30. The Dutch fort, Fort Batensteen, at Butre, Gold Coast, 1679

the residence of the governor or chief factor, as they call him, is a triangular brick building, suitable enough.[17] [...][18]

The Moors of Axim are for the most part fishermen. They make very fine, large canoes for crossing bars and transporting merchandize. The country is extremely fertile in maize, rice, coconuts, sweet and bitter oranges, limes (*limons*), bananas, water melons, pineapples and many other fruits and salad-plants. You also find there many sheep, cows, goats, poultry and pigeons, with a large quantity of game. The palm-wine there is excellent, and the monkeys are very beautiful and entertaining.[19] The Moors of Axim have the best gold on the whole coast, after that of Igwira and Acra; they collect it in the rivers and on the seashore, taking inconceivable trouble, and consequently they value it highly. [...][20] They pay an eighth of the fish they catch to the Dutch, and are so fettered that they are not free to trade openly on board vessels which do not belong to that nation, for the company at present keeps a fiscal there, just as at the Mina. The village of Achombene has a large population.[21]

The village of Crema is a little further SE, on a slight hill overlooking the country on all sides. Certain subjects of the Elector of Brandenburg built a little fort there in 1682, which has eight or ten cannon. The whole enclosure is of turf, as are the curtains. There is little space for accommodation, and the garrison consists of twenty whites, who are much liked by the blacks because they are newcomers. The whites claim that they will make this fort the seat of their commerce and the entrepôt of their trade on this coast. [*margin:* See the view of the Elector's little fort at Crema on the plate opposite.] From Crema to Axim is three leagues, and from the coast of Axim to that of Apolonia is ten. The currents in the gulf flow along the land.

[illustration no. (55), view of Fort 'Frederickburgh' at Crema, inserted after p. 5]

[*written on the slip containing the illustration*] Sir, one of my compatriots, who made a voyage to Guinea in 1684, inserted in his journal a small profile of the fort which the Elector of Brandenburg has had constructed at Crema for the security of his trade. I have copied the drawing expressly in order to attach it to this description, which will be more complete with it, although this fort has grown considerably since 1684. So you will place this plate at page 5 of the Second Part of this Description. London, 27 March 1688.O.S. [*insert ends*] [22]

Additional Passages from *1732*

[pp. 431/1–3, 6–10, 432/6–7, on the history of the Brandenburg main fort]

I had the following account from a relation of mine, director for his electoral highness of Brandenburgh, at Embden.[23] / In the year 1682 his electoral highness of Brandenburgh sent to the Gold Coast of Guinea two frigates, one of thirty-two guns and sixty men, the other of eighteen guns and fifty men; the former commanded by captain Mathieu de Vos, the latter, by captain Philip Pieter Bloncq; who being arrived in May 1682 at cape Tres-Pontas, landed their men at Montfort-hill, where they set up his electoral highness's flag.[24] / Captain Bloncq, being well acquainted with the natives there, pursuant to the instruction he had from his electoral highness, made so good use of his credit among them, which he had gain'd at several former voyages, that the Caboceiros granted him liberty to build a fort on that hill, and settle a trade with the natives, for his electoral highness.[25] / In order thereto, he caus'd some pieces of cannon to be put ashore there, and set men at work to throw up with all haste, an intrenchment with pallisadoes, whilst others erected some houses; which being furnish'd with goods, provisions, and ammunition, the two frigats returned to Hamburgh, having aboard some Caboceiros, who were immediately conveyed to Berlin, by order of his electoral highness; who receiv'd them very favourably, entertain'd them magnificently for some time, shewed them the grandeur of his court, together with some part of his army; and sent them back to their native country at Tres-Pontas, where captain Bloncq being also return'd at the same time, took upon him the government both of the fort he had mark'd out and begun before he went for Europe, and of the country; and with all due application caused the fort to be finish'd as represented in the cut; mounting thirty-two pieces of cannon on the batteries, and calling it Groote Fredericksburgh, from his electoral highness's name, now king of Prussia.[26] [. . .][27] The walls are thick, strong and high, and within are several fine warehouses and dwellings for the officers and soldiers. / The governor, who stiles himself director general for his electoral highness of Brandenburgh, and of his African company, jointly with the Caboceiros of Pocquesoe, and other neighbouring towns, determine all cases and differences arising betwixt the inhabitants, summoning

them together on such occasions (which meeting they call a Pal-
labra, or council) into the fort, whither immediately those Caboceiros repair; and there decide all causes, civil or criminal, and
their sentences are executed accordingly, with all submission from
the natives; which gives them great credit and authority to the
commander of the fort in that country, being a commonwealth
like Axim.[28] / The chief governor also receives the accounts of the
Brandenburgh factors at Tacrama, or Crema; and at the fort at
Acoba, called Dorothea, at Tres-Pontas, as mention'd in the description; and of those at the lodges at Popo and Fida; which are
all the settlements that nation has on the coasts of Guinea.[29]
[...].[30] / They have only six guns mounted on it [the fort at
Tacrama], to hinder the natives of the adjacent villages from
trading with any foreign ships within the reach of their guns, the
natives being almost intirely under the Prussian dominion. / In
1701, the Prussian agent allow'd any foreign ships to take wood
and water there, for ten pounds a ship.[31] [...].[32] / There have been
seven directors successively, in about thirteen years time, at Fredericksburgh, from about the year 1689 to 1702; which shews how
irregular the Emden company's affairs have been at the coast ever
since. / In what condition the Prussian affairs stand at the coast
since the year 1702, I have not heard; [...].[33]

[p. 455/13–15, 17–18, on a visit by James Barbot to Gross-
Friedrichsburg in April 1699]

Eighth, anchor'd before the Prussian fort, Great Fredericksburgh,
at Tres-Pontas. / The Prussian general receiv'd us at his fort very
civilly, but told us, he had no occasion for any of our goods; the
trade being every where on that coast, at a stand, as well by reason
of the vast number of interlopers and other trading ships, as for
the wars among the natives, and especially that which the English
and Dutch had occasion'd on account of a Black king the English
had murder'd, which must be the king of Commendo before
mention'd in this Supplement, and that the armies had actually
been in the field for eight months, which stopt all the passes for
merchants to come down to the forts, to trade; that it was expected
there would be a battle speedily betwixt them; that the Hollanders, a people very jealous of their commerce at the coast, were
very studious to have the war carried on among the Blacks, to
distract as long as possible the trade of other Europeans, and to

343

that effect were very ready to assist upon all occasions the Blacks, their allies, that they might beat their enemies, and so the commerce fall into their hands.[34] The ninth we came to an anchor before the Prussian fort, Great Fredericksburgh, a very handsome fortress, mounted with about forty guns. The general told me, that six weeks before in his return from cape Lope to Tres-Pontas, he had been assaulted by a pirate, who was forced to let him go, being too warmly received; and that there were two or three other pirates cruizing about that cape and St. Tome.[35] / The Blacks there, through malice, had diverted the channel of the fresh water ashore, to hinder us taking any, of which we complain'd to the Prussian general, who thereupon gave orders to let us have water. / He lent us some of his bricklayers, to set up our copper aboard, for our slaves before-hand.

[Ahanta]

The kingdom of Little Incassan or Warshas begins on the coast at Crema and ends at [blank]. To the West of it lies Axim, to the North Igwira and to the East Ante or Anta. It is made noteworthy by Cape Tres Puntas, so called by the Portuguese because it is made up of three headlands (*pointes*) rising in the form of little hills which project southwards into the sea, at 4°15′N latitude.[36] In the spaces between them are formed two little bays, where there are three villages, Acora, Accuon and Infiama, called 'Dickisky' or 'Dickisco' by the English, after the Moorish captain who governs it. The first village is at the bottom of the westernmost bay, the second is on the slope of the second headland, which looks NE, and the last is in an /p. 6/ inlet formed by the land between Cape Boutrou and Accuon.[37] It is easier to land at the two former than at the latter, because it has, at its entrance, a bar containing rocks that project from the water. Here on my last voyage I lost two men and the boat from my bark, after I had crossed the bar myself when going to see the black *cabesseire* (headman), in order to prevent my crew from being assaulted while taking water. This bar is only difficult during the new and full moon, for in the first and last quarters you can go there in a longboat very easily.[38]

[illustration no. (56), Cape Three Points, inserted after p. 5]

Ships stop mainly in front of Infiama, both to trade and to furnish themselves with water, firewood, maize and fowls, which are available in abundance there at certain times, particularly at the close of the winter season. You pay some small fee to the captain of the village in return for the right to anchor and take water and wood. Sometimes you take them on the coast at Infiama, and sometimes it is necessary to go a quarter of a league into the forest which lies behind it, the whole country being mountainous and wooded.[39]

The kingdom of Ante or Anta begins at the last of the three points of Cape Tres Puntas and extends eastwards along the coast about fourteen leagues, as far as Abroby. To the North it borders on the kingdom of Adom, to the NNW on the kingdom of Mompa, to the West on Little Incassan, to the NW on Igwira and to the NE on that of Tabeu. Its villages on the coast are Boutrou, Poyera or Petrygrande, Pando, Tacorary, S'acunde, Anta, Sama and Maque Jaque, the principal one being Tacorary.[40] Boutrou is situated on a small stream which flows into the sea to the NE of the third point of Cape Tres Puntas.[41] The Dutch had a small fort built for them there by Mr ('le Sieur') Carolof.[42] They call it Badensteein. It is on the summit of a hill which juts out a little into the sea to the East. The place is of little consequence, although it has four bastions; the Dutch company maintains a sergeant and 12–15 soldiers there, under the command of the chief factor.[43] It owes a rent of several ounces of gold a year to the King of Anta, which some call J'abbs and others Gavy.[44] There are only six or eight cannon in this small place, but it overlooks the village of Boutrou or Butry, situated at the foot of the hill occupied by Fort Badensteein. Here is a view of the fort. The little Boutry River washes its base. There are few inhabitants, and it is only of significance because of its being neighboured by the people of Adom and the Moors of the country.[45] The king lives four leagues inland. He is the sovereign ruler. The country is entirely wooded in the vicinity of Boutrou. The gold traded there is quite pure.[46]

[illustration no. (57), Fort 'Badensteyn'] /p. 7/†

Poyera or Petry Grande and Pandos, two villages between Boutrou and Tacorary, are not of great size and are hardly frequented, as they contain only maize farmers and a few fishermen. They can be easily recognized by a large rock which lies in the sea on the coast and is consecrated to their fetish, as is the one in front of Tacorary, where they go to perform ceremonies which will fill you with compassion when I describe the religions of these Africans. I will not give the distance between the places, since this is given to you by the map. [47]

Tacorary lies on a cape which runs SE into the sea, having in front of it several rocks lying below and above water and up to three quarters of a league into the sea, on which breakers are evident. The village is fairly large, and can easily be seen from the sea after one has rounded the rocky cape mentioned above. The Dutch had formerly a small fort that was constructed facing it, on a hill some distance from the village, which the fort overlooked, as it did the country and neighbourhood. [48] [...] [49] There are still a few remains of this fort, and there is a trading post (*loge*), where the Dutch keep a factor, although he is sometimes obliged to abandon it to evade the anger of the natives. Mr Villaud de Bellefonds alleges that this fort was first built by the French, but I can nowhere find any proof of this opinion, and I do not know on what evidence he bases it. [50] You find here [at Tacorary] the finest and largest canoes in the whole of Guinea; they are used for crossing the bars at Juda and Offra, and for transporting their merchandise from one place to another. They are made from a hollowed-out tree-trunk, but have such large stowage space that some can be seen carrying up to ten tons as well as the crew, which consists of 18–20 oarsmen. Vessels destined to buy slaves at Ardra always equip themselves with one, either here or at Axim. The Moors sell them for £400-£600 in merchandise. [51] The Moors of this place are reputed to be very bad people to trade with, and this led to the abandonment of the trading post and Fort Wittsen for several years, according to what I have been told. [52] Vessels can very easily enter Tacorary Bay, where the little River St George enters the sea, about one league from the village, on the eastern side. Some people place yet another village a little to the East of this river, and call it Jabbe. [53] Sacunde is in the other corner of the bay. The English and Dutch have trading posts there, and the French formerly had one. [54] Anta and Boare are two small villages between Sacunde and Sama, the latter lying three leagues East of Tacorary; the whole surrounding country is full of low wooded hills. [...] They trade gold on board vessels. /p. 8/ However, they have been prevented from doing so for some time, being busy defending themselves in wars against Adom. [55]

Sama is built on a hill, and watered by the St George River, which runs at its foot. It extends from there to the seashore, having about

346

200 huts divided into three quarters, one of which lies on the seashore at the foot of this hill and below the cannon of Fort St Sebastien, which the Dutch occupy. [. . .] The fort looks quite pretty from the sea, and they have handled these poor Africans so well that they have reached the point of only doing what the Dutch grant them liberty to do.[56]

[illustration no. (58), Fort St Sebastien, inserted after p. 8]†

This building, which cannot be seen from the sea until one is South of it, and then only looks like a simple white house, is situated very advantageously for trade with the people of Adom and Wassa, who come there to trade. It pays something in the way of tribute to the King of Anta. The Moors of the two aforementioned localities transport the merchandise which they buy from the whites so far inland that they sell it, so they say, to people who live in fortresses, which strongly leads me to believe that they trade among the Arab Moors on the banks of River Niger. You anchor in front of Sama in nine fathoms, muddy bottom, one league out, with the fort to NW-by-West; there are rocks between Sama and Boare which extend almost half a league out.[57] [. . .][58]

Abroby is in a bay, which terminates at Cap de Torres or Aldea de Torres. The village is divided into two quarters, situated within large bordering plains, and having little hills out front. You can easily see it from the roadstead, which is on the inside of the cape. Much maize and poultry, as well as a little gold, are traded there.[59] The whole land of Anta is extremely fertile. [. . .][60] The gold traded there is often adulterated and mixed with silver or copper. For this reason, commerce there is no longer as pleasant as it was when they gave this metal pure and in its natural state, just as it came to them from Igwira and Mompa. Each village has its captain and a *brafo* or governor over everyone, appointed by the king. These people are often at war with those of Adom, as are those of Axim and Incassan. The colour of the stone in this country is reddish.[61]

[Komenda]

The kingdom of Great Commendo is also called Guaffo or Comany by some. [. . ./p. 9/. . .] The villages on the coast are Aitaki or Agitaki, called Little Comendo by others, Cape Aldea de Torres, Abrobe, Lori or Cotabry, and Ampeny, and these occupy 4½

347

leagues of coast, the village of Little Comendo being the largest.[62] The capital, Guaffo, gives its name to the kingdom. It is the residence of the king; it is situated on a mountain, four leagues from Little Comendo. The Dutch call it Great Commendo to distinguish it from the one which is on the coast. This village has at least 400 huts and is full of inhabitants.[63] Little Commendo, where the brother-in-law of the king normally resides, is divided into several small hamlets. To walk through the surrounding countryside is very pleasant, but it is very difficult to land, because of the bar; also, one goes there in the mornings rather than in the evenings.[64] The people are for the most part fishermen or merchants, there being a great trade in gold dust and sometimes in slaves here, for this is the place where the merchants from Acanez most often come to the coast. This village has about 150 huts, situated on the banks of a stream which enters the sea there and forms a small harbour for canoes. Its eastern bank is low and on its western bank is a hill, flat on top, and suitable for building on.[65] L'ory is not large, nor is Ampeny or Ampena, where there lives a man called Coucoumy, a black whom one saw in France, he having been sent there in 1671 by the King of Commendo to offer the coasts of that kingdom for the protection of French commerce.[66] [. . .][67]

The Moors of Comendo like the French much more than they like any other Europeans and, if one is to believe them, would work wonders for this nation. I have never passed this place without being wearied by the proposals they made to me for an alliance. On my last voyage the king sent his second son aboard to serve as a hostage while I was to go to Great Commendo.[68] He particularly wanted to see me to oblige me to lay the foundations of some kind of establishment on the coast, something for which the English and Dutch obtain permission only with great difficulty. Formerly both had semi-permanent trading posts built in stone at Little Comendo, but only that of the English remains there, under the protection of the king, although he does not care to permit them to enclose it with high walls.[69]

The most suitable place for an establishment, in my view, is at Ampeny, on a small point which juts out southwards, where the ground rises a little and the coast at this place forms a little elbow; one can land there in canoes without being greatly inconvenienced by the waves, which break on this point and are sheltered by it from the southwesterly wind.[70] It is, Sir, assuredly the most suitable place

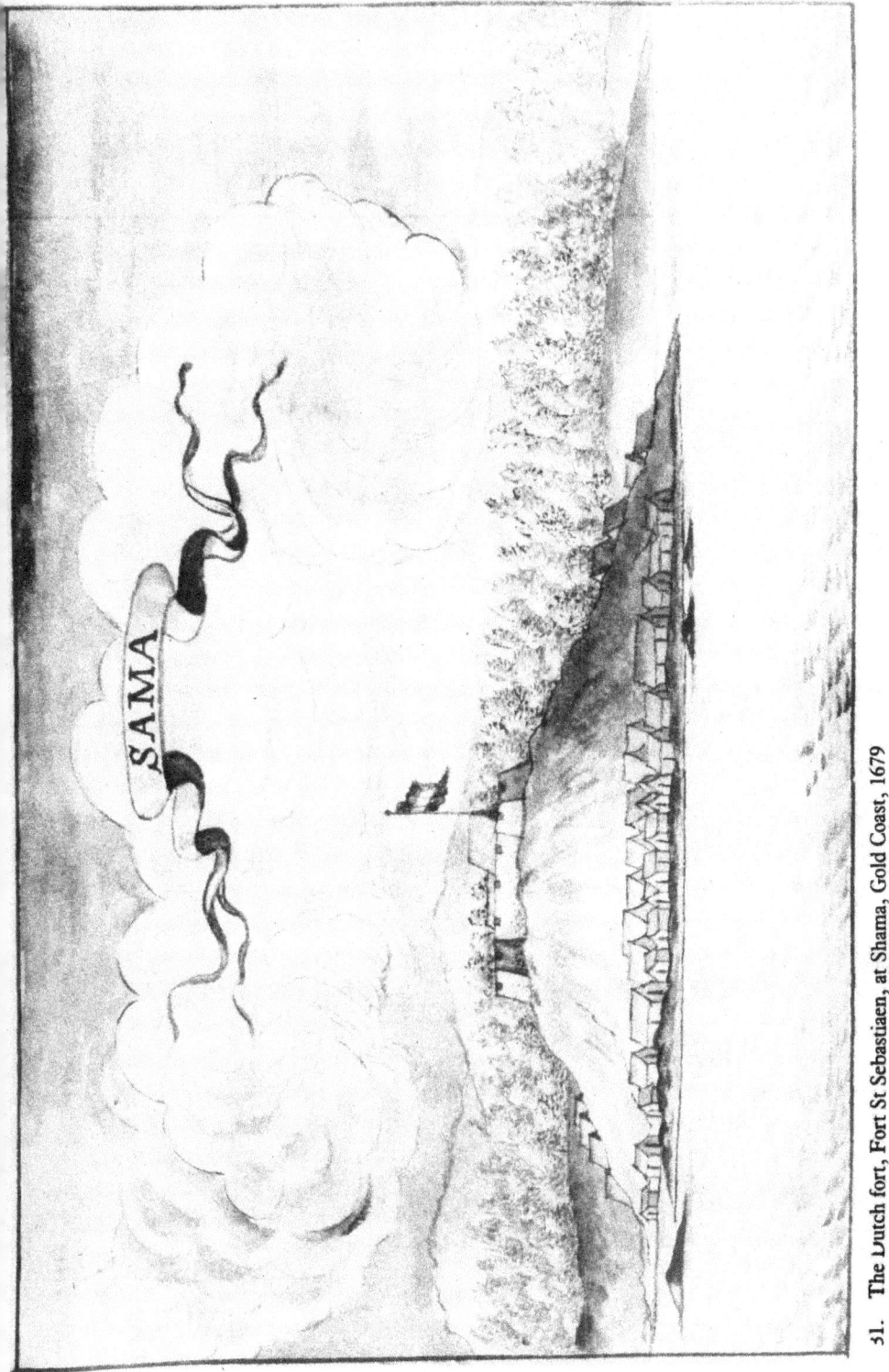

31. The Dutch fort, Fort St Sebastiaen, at Shama, Gold Coast, 1679

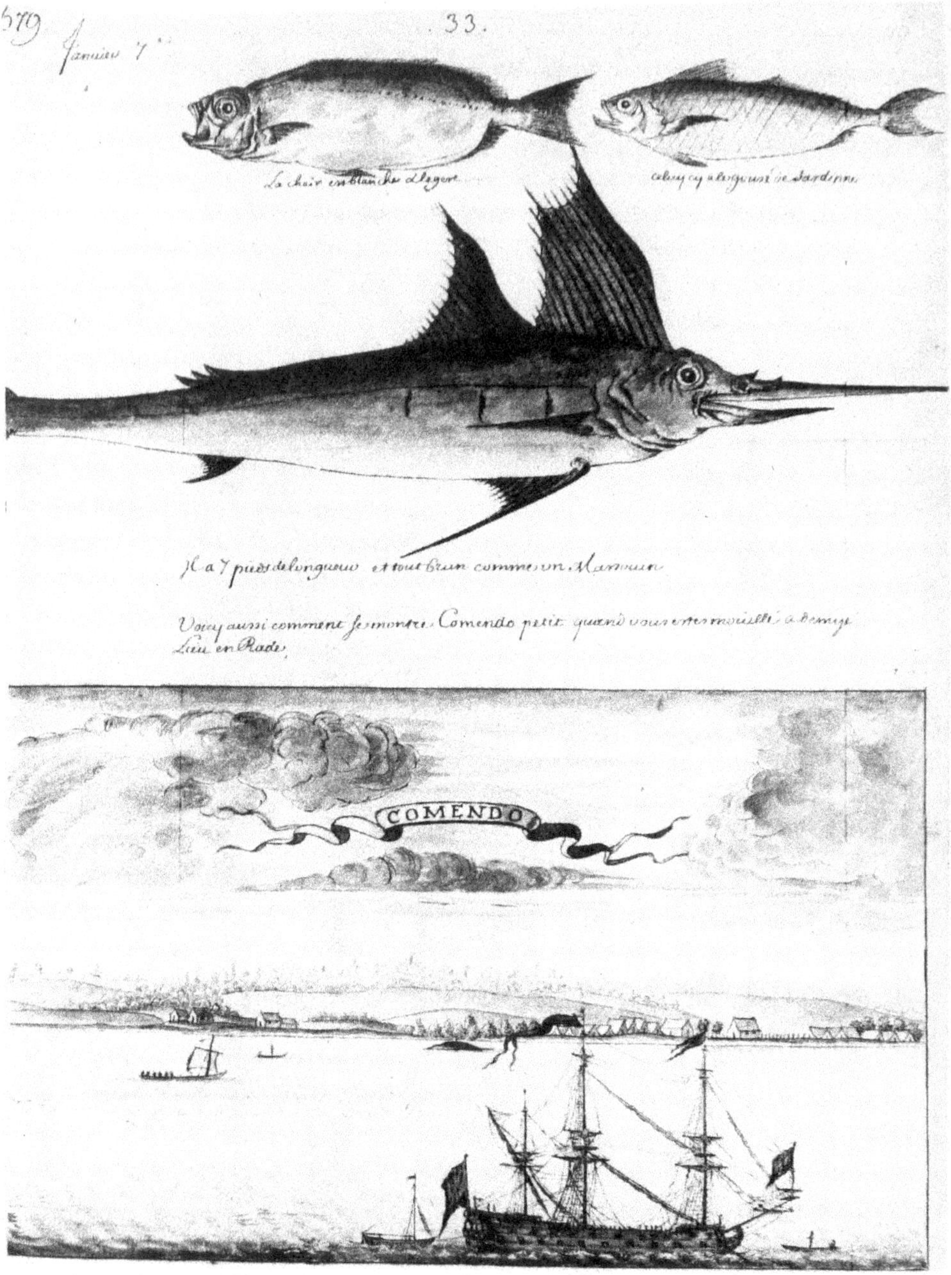

32. 'Comendo' and fishes: a page from Barbot's 1679 journal

on the whole coast at which to build [a fort], both on account of the good quality of the country and of the favourable situation for commerce. It is resorted to by all the merchants of Accanez and of other kingdoms of the interior, and it would also assuredly be a post which would do much harm to /p. 10/ that of La Mina. There the Moors are treated with severity, which has disgusted them, so that they would give themselves to a newcomer without much hesitation, such is their aversion in respect of the Dutch.[71] It would admittedly be better to construct a fort at Cape Aldea de Torres, which is West of Little Commendo, but to land there involves more danger than at any other place. The French formerly had a trading post there, and its four walls are still to be seen at the edge of the most northerly village.[72] Here, Sir, is how Little Commendo appears from the roadstead.[73]

[illustration no. (59), Little Comendo]†

The country behind Little Commendo rises into hillocks, covered with trees, below which lie plains and savannahs, full of fruit trees. The country is densely populated; it is warlike, and the king can put 20,000 men in the field when necessary. The king also has 500 soldiers as his guard.[74] The gold traded here is extremely adulterated, for these blacks are generally deceitful and bad people to trade with, apart from them all being thieves fit to be hanged. I have noticed this even in those whose birth and status ought at least to distinguish them from the others and to purge them of these evil tendencies, yet they are such by nature and weak by inclination.[75] Sir, Your etc.

Additional Passages from *1732*

[pp. 155/9–10, on a gold mine and a brisk slave trade]

The country of Commendo is thought to be very rich in gold mines; and some fancy the king will not have them opened for fear the neighbouring nations, or the Europeans, should attempt to destroy him and his people, or drive them away, to possess themselves of so rich a country. I have often heard some of the natives say, that not far from the promontory Aldea de Torres, there is a very rich gold mine, and that, for fear it should be search'd, they have made a God of that head or hill, which is the only means they can imagine to preserve the mine intire; so great a veneration the Blacks have for such sacred places, that they are sure no person whatsoever will touch it: and if any Europeans should attempt it, they must expect to have all the country about them, and to be massacred if taken.[76] / Here is sometimes a brisk trade for slaves, when the Commanians are at war with the upland Negroes, and have the better of it, for then they bring down abundance of prisoners, whom they sell immediately, at a cheap rate, to some interloper or other, if any be in the roads, to save the charge of keeping and subsisting them. And it once happened, not many years ago, that an English ship riding there, just at the time they return'd from an expedition, wherein they had succeeded, they deliver'd their prisoners to the Englishman as fast as he could fetch them from the shore with his boat; and, in a few days, he got above three hundred slaves aboard, for little or nothing: so great was the number of prisoners they had brought down, that they were glad of this opportunity to dispose of part of them at any rate.[77]

[p. 436/10–11, on the French at Komenda in 1688]

John Bloome's Letter, from Cabo-Corso, to J.B. the 27th of February 1691/2.[78] / In the year 1688 M. Du Casse, came upon the coast with four French men of war, equipp'd at Rochefort, with great confidence to make there several considerable settlements, for the royal African company of France, but especially at Commendo, upon the frequent former invitations of the Aquaffou men, both king and people; in order to cross the Dutch interest at their coast, and in some measure revenge themselves of the insults they had received from the Hollanders at Mina, for many years before; some instances of which you may see in the precedent description, and his people boasted so much before-hand at Rochel, of the great exploits that were to ensue of this expedition, that the people there gave that officer the title of petty-king of Guinea. / Du Casse made an attempt upon Commendo, where he settled a factory, and proceeded farther to Alampi and Fida, on the same design; but a few months after he had sailed from Commendo, thro' the instigation of the Dutch, a war happening against the Aquaffoes, in whose country the French factory stood, the Aquaffoes were routed, their king kill'd, all the French effects pillaged, and the French men, who kept the factory, forc'd to fly to cape Corso castle for refuge: since which time, there have not appear'd any French ships, nor have they any settlement upon that coast.[79]

[p. 439/1–2, on employing trustworthy Europeans]

It will not be amiss to proceed with my Author's account, as an introduction to the transactions of those times, which have caused such considerable damage to the Dutch interest at Mina, as well as at Commendo; and have so much depopulated the fine large town of Mina, now as little, as it was great and famous in my time. It will not only show the uncertainty of sublunary things in general, but be a proper caution to the directors of all African companies whatsoever, to employ in the government of their affairs in Guinea, both by sea and land, men of known candor, probity, understanding, true courage, and experience; attended with modest behaviour; etc. And when they have found any such, not only to continue them much longer in their employments, than is commonly done; but also to grant them such competent salaries, and perquisites, as may content them, and they may not be tempted to commit perpetual breaches of trust, and contrary to their most solemn oaths, and all the ties of conscience, *to make hay, while the sun shines*; as is too notoriously and generally practised. / This I formerly propos'd to the directors of the French African company, at a full board, in Paris; and it was, it seems, better liked than practised; and it is no wonder, that they and our royal African company at London, have not made such advantage of their commerce, as might have been expected . . .[80]

NOTES

[1] In 1678 Barbot passed along this coast and stopped at an unnamed village, mistaken for Assinie but three hours' sailing short of it, where no contacts were made; then at 'Isseny' ('a large village on the coast, heavily populated', the houses described), at 'Abiany', where there was no trade, and at 'Tebbo', where he bought gold from a canoe (*1679*, pp. 276–7). In 1682 Barbot visited Cape Apollonia from the East (see Letter 2/5, p. 18, below) and probably learned there about the 1681 war between Assinie and Abine (attested by a contemporary source, Jones 1985, pp. 37–9). However, his account of the coast has echoes of Villault, pp. 185–6, and most of the toponyms are borrowed. For an attempt to locate the contemporary

toponyms of this coast, including Barbot's, see Baesjou 1988, pp. 14–31 (but note that not all Barbot's borrowings are recognized). 'Assine', 'Abbener or Albine', and 'Taboe' were mentioned by Dapper, pp. 61/4, 63/6; and 'Asbini' (undoubtedly a misreading of the double 's' character on Dapper's map), 'Albiani' and 'Tabo' by Villault, pp. 185–6; while both 'Iseny' and 'Assenee', as well as 'Abenye' and 'Tebbo', appeared on the Robijn/ Roggeveen 1685 map. However, 'Boqu', later 'Boqui', seems to be original, and on his map Barbot identifies it with Little Assinie ('Isseny pequeeno ('Je dis') [not 'Jadis', Baesjou 1988, p. 19] Boqu'); in 1687 'Bocco' (? Mbokrou) was described as belonging to the Kingdom of Issiny (Roussier 1935, p. 7). 'Isseny pequeeno', which Barbot probably thought was the name of his unnamed 1678 village, must surely have been derived ultimately from a Portuguese source but the source and its transmission to Barbot are untraced, whereas 'Boqu' may have been obtained by inquiry at Assinie. Barbot's map also indicates '3 villages pequeene' between 'Boqu' and Assinie – again presumably from an ultimate Portuguese source. Note that the hills backing the lagoon East of River Assinie are today known as the 'Albani Hills', either an explanation or a consequence of 'Albiani'; note also that Barbot's 'Ashny' (as a variant of 'Isseny') indicates an English influence. In 1637 French missionaries visited 'Abiany or Bene' (Brásio 1960, 462); in 1672 the Royal African Company claimed to have factories at 'Ashinee' and 'Abinee' (*CSP Colonial 1669–74*, pp. 412–2); and in 1685 the Dutch company set its limits at Assinie and Abine (Jones 1985, p. 170). In 1671, the distance between 'Assenay' and 'Benay' was given as two leagues (Delbée 1671, p. 369). For earlier and later Dutch references to trading ivory and gold at Assinie and Abine/Abane, see the 1629 map; Leers 1665, p. 298; ARA, Abramsz 23.11.1679, and WIC 124, 7.8.1684; Hazewinkel 1932, p. 250; Ratelband 1953, p. 53; Jones 1983a, p. 104, n. 24.

Cf. *1732*, p. 147/5–6, with a trace of Bosman, p. 491 ('Adouw'). For the French at Assinie, see the Additional Passage at the end of this section.

[2] Barbot's river is Aby Lagoon, which is entered by two major streams, rivers Bia and Tano. In 1687 it was stated that the 'river' at Assinie ran far inland, could be easily navigated, and passed through gold-bearing countries; and in 1694 that Assinie stood 'in a swamp or bog, there being no other swamp between Bassa and it' (Roussier 1935, pp. 7–8; Phillips 1732, p. 200). 'Albiani' and Tabo lay six and ten leagues beyond Assinie, according to Villault, p. 186 (Baesjou's argument that they were relocated further West c. 1681 is not altogether convincing, Baesjou 1988, p. 16). The inserted sentence is possibly a late insertion derived from Bosman, p. 492; but the statement is contradicted immediately below, with a reference to ivory. 'Acanimina' is a corrupted form of a toponym appearing on maps at various points on this coast from the sixteenth century: a village mentioned below and shown on Barbot's map just to the East of the cape,

'Agumane', is perhaps a variant of the same name at an alternative location.

Cf. *1732*, p. 147/6–9, which changes WNW more logically to ESE, and adds: 'At the mouth of this river, and very close to the shore, is a little island, very fit for building of a fort, for the conveniency of the inland trade ... Isseny-grande is famous for its fine gold, which, it is likely, comes from Asiente or Inta, towards the source of the river Sweiro da Costa, in about nine degrees of north latitude; a country rich in gold, and but lately known to the Europeans on the gold coast'.

[3] On 30 December 1678, Barbot anchored and traded at Cape Apollonia, and drew the four hummocks forming the cape, each with a village (*1679*, pp. 277–8; see *Africa pilot* 1967, p. 438); and he visited it for three days in 1682; nevertheless his description partly echoes Villault, p. 187. For the name, see Teixeira da Mota 1950, pp. 265–6.

Cf. *1732*, p. 148/1–2, which adds a reference to 'straggling trees' on the hills, and the following – 'I had here a pretty good trade for gold during the three days I lay before the villages, under the cape'. The drawing of the cape (*1679*, p. 277, the drawing not reproduced) is repeated in *1732*, Plate K (p. 148): the view '1 league from the ENE' in the earlier drawings becomes 1½ leagues and the coast is extended to the left, but the later drawings lack the inscriptions below the villages to the left and right on the original, 'village where we were anchored', 'village of the point'.

[4] The coastline between Cape Apollonia (Beyin) and River Ankobra consists of a wide sandspit, cut off from the mainland by swamps. The location of 'Bogio' ('Bogu' on the Luís Teixeira 1602 map, 'Bogio' in Robijn/ Roggeveen 1685) roughly fits that of the present-day village of Beku.

Cf. *1732*, p. 148/3–4, which incorporates a description of the 'strand' and substitutes 'coco [i.e. coconut] trees' for 'forests', changes based on Bosman, p. 493; it adds a distance ('nine leagues') and a statement that River Mancu reaches the sea 'by Bogio', and also the following: 'there is little or no trade [at the villages]. The shore bending away to east-north-east of the Bight for some leagues, and the Dutch fort bearing E.S.E. the ships trading along the coast commonly steer that course from St Apolonia, from whence the tide runs along the coast to Axim'.

[5] Based on Dapper, pp. 62/7, 64/4, where 'Sakoo' is the name of a king. Sakoo/Soco, on an island in Aby Lagoon, was in fact the capital of the Assinie kingdom (Roussier 1935, pp. 54, 63). But in the 1700s this kingdom's eastern neighbour at Cape Apollonia was said to be, not Axim, but 'Guoumray'/'Guyomray' (Dapper, p. 62/6, 'Jemore'; Labat 1730, I, 248–50; Roussier 1935, pp. 189, 227). Barbot's map of the coast has 'Adouw Regm. als. Sokoo': this rather looks like a late insertion, in which case the first name may be from Bosman, p. 491; otherwise the name is original.

Cf. *1732*, p. 148/4–6, which enlarges considerably on the river, from

Bosman, pp. 4, 11–12, and hence substitutes 'Cobra, or Ancober' for 'Mancu' – hereafter Barbot uses 'Mancu' and 'Cobra' interchangeably for River Ankobra, although this gives the impression that these are two different rivers. Barbot adds a comparison between the beauty of the countryside up this river with that up River Sess and at Whydah.

[6] The English on Gold Coast reported a French attempt to establish a post at Assinie as early as 1687 (OBLR, C.747, 2531, report of 29.12.1687). Barbot relates the history of a French settlement at Assinie 1701–4 in *1732*, pp. 429/4–430/6, mainly drawing on Bosman, pp. 420–1, 492; but the section here given is not from Bosman, the source being presumably the informant mentioned, Porquet. Bosman cites 'the European Mercury for the Year 1701', Barbot adding incorrectly 'printed at Paris': the reference is to *Mercure historique et politique, contenant l'etat present de l'Europe*, published at The Hague, 1701 issue, pp. 319–20, and Bosman's text (in translation) is mainly correct (but 'Syria' should read 'Sirie' and the baptism date 12 not 27 February). For Damon and Hannibal (or 'Aniaba'), see Labat 1730, I, 230–47; *Bull. Soc. His. Paris*, 1911, 194–5; Roussier 1935, pp. xvi, n. 1, xvii–xxx, 53–9, 67, 93–5, 157–63. There are several discrepancies between Barbot's information and Damon's own account. According to the latter, he reached Assinie at the end of June 1701 and persuaded the king to let him build a fort on a 'sort of peninsula' (i.e. the spit running parallel to the coast, West of Assinie), although the king had wanted him to settle on the island of Soco, which was his capital. Damon erected a wooden fort (Fort St Louis) and departed on 23 July, leaving behind thirty men (including officers and priests) under the command of Lavie (Roussier 1935, pp. 95–6, 101–5, 157). To Bosman's account of Hannibal, Barbot adds that another prince of Assinie was carried to France in 1695, the information derived from Froger 1698, p. 47 (*1732*, p. 429/5).

[7] The director-general of Elmina had already made several attempts in 1702 to dislodge the French from Assinie (AGA, 4775, p. 641; Roussier 1935, pp. 222–7; Van Dantzig 1978, pp. 92–3, 99–100). Barbot gives an exact translation of the report in the *Gazette de Paris* of 27.10.1703, but omits that the fort at 'Issigni' was built 'two years ago'.

[8] This account confirmed in N * * * 1719, pp. 39–40. But another eyewitness stated that De Grosbois, the commander of a French fleet, having quarrelled with Africans who came aboard at Assinie, suddenly gave orders for the fort to be evacuated, and the abandoned fort and the property left behind were then seized by the Africans (Roussier, pp. 233–4). For a 1709 attempt by Hannibal to persuade the French to re-establish the fort, see Baidaff 1929, pp. 291–2.

[9] On 1 January 1679 Barbot visited both the fort and the village at Axim, and drew the former, which he described as 'built on a rock which juts into

the sea' between two detached rocks on which the sea broke heavily (*1679*, pp. 278–281): in early 1682 he visited the fort again, and in 1699 his brother's ship passed Axim (*1732*, pp. 148/9, 455/11). But the references here to the kingdom of Axim, the toponym 'Achombene', and the fort are based on Dapper, p. 64/1–4. For the earlier history of the fort, see Lawrence 1963, p. 229; Vogt 1979, pp. 83, 86.

Cf. *1732*, pp. 148/3, 7–8 (with 'Ancete' a misprint for 'Ante'), 148/8–149/3, 149/7, much enlarged from Bosman, pp. 2–7, but also apparently from recollection or the 1681–1682 journal. The description of the village 'under the command of the Dutch fort', the wood behind and the stream running through the village, the 'great number of coco and other trees planted at equal distances among the houses', and the rock-strewn shore fits and may be based on Barbot's drawing of the scene. The decline of the gold trade noted by Bosman is more specifically evidenced, as follows. 'Axim was by European traders look'd upon as the best place for gold, and consequently much resorted to; but declin'd very much in the year 1681, by reason of the long wars that had then been between Anta and Adom, which almost dispeopled the country, and accordingly ruin'd the trade; insomuch that it could scarce be restor'd in ten years to its former condition, as the fiscal of Axim declar'd to me' (*1732*, p. 148/9). For the Anta-Adom wars, see *1688*, p. 6 below.

[10] Based on Dapper, p. 64/2 (partly from Leers 1665, p. 298, where the date is 9 February 1642). For an account of the capture of the fort, see Jones 1983a, pp. 105–6.

Cf. *1732*, p. 149/8.

[11] Two white gable-ends of the governor's house showed up among the trees (*1679*, p. 278).

Cf. *1732*, p. 149/5 ('from some distance out at sea, it looks like a large lofty white house').

[12] Since this description enlarges considerably on what Barbot recorded about his one-day visit in 1679 (*1679*, p. 280), it may rather represent his experience and impressions in 1682.

Cf. *1732*, pp. 149/1, 5, 150/3, which adds that Axim is nevertheless unhealthy, from Bosman, pp. 111–2.

[13] The man responsible for the capture of Axim in 1642 was not Ruyter but Jacob Ruychaver, Director-General of the Dutch settlements in Guinea, 1640–5, 1651–5: Barbot did not name Ruyter in his journal. (And Ruyter did not re-capture Axim from the English in 1665, as stated in Lawrence 1963, p. 229: see Ruyter 1961, pp. 79, 243).

[14] The drawing, with the key, appeared first in the journal (*1679*, p. 282, 'Vue de St Anthonio d'Axem'), and was repeated full-page in *1732*, Plate L (p. 149). The lettering and key were extended in *1732* to indicate 'The

Landing Place', which presumably proves Barbot's assistance with the engraving. But the exact position of the many rocks varied somewhat between the versions, so that the 'only passage' between the rocks is hopelessly confused. Details of the fort, however, varied little.

Cf. *1732*, p. 149/2–3, 6, on the stream and Rock B, which emphasizes the slightness of the stream and inserts Amerindian and Biblical references.

[15] In 1679 Barbot described the fort as follows. 'To enter you must circle round to the rear. You ascend in two stages, each with its guard-post. From there you go down to a kind of lower court, then climb again a third stage to the governor's apartment, built in brick and triangular, laid out very suitably. Leaving this apartment you come out on a platform overlooking the sea' (*1679*, p. 280). The burning of lime at Axim was noted on the Dutch map of 1629 (Daaku 1970, p. 182).

Cf. *1732*, p. 149/4, 9–11, which elaborates that the fort has 'proper outworks', also of black stone, 'low to the sea, because the rock is there high and steep, and much higher towards the land'.

[16] In 1679 Barbot recorded the garrison as one of 40 whites, with as many black slaves, and the guns as eight on each of two sides, firing shots of 4–8 lb., with a SE battery broken down by the rains (*1679*, p. 280). The new figures apparently resulted from Barbot's later visit. In 1679 a Dutch report gave the garrison as a factor, a sub-factor, an assistant, a barber, a 'constable', 12 soldiers, and some slaves (ARA, Abramsz 23.11.1679).

Cf. *1732*, p. 149/9, 11, which clarifies, in respect of two batteries on the land side with 22 iron guns, 'when I was there, besides some pattareroes [small swivel- or salute-guns]', and adds that the fort 'if well stor'd with provisions, may hold out against an army of the natives'.

[17] The references to a drawbridge and covering position are not in *1679*.

Cf. *1732*, p. 149/4, 9–10, which elaborates that 'the gate of the fort is low', that from the 'spur' (i.e. the *banquette*) to the fort are 'several steps cut in the rock', and that the governor's house has, on one of its three fronts, 'on the west side . . . a very small spot of ground, planted with a few orange-trees'. For a ground-plan of the fort in 1657, see KITLV, H65, p. 770; for later and present-day views, Lawrence 1963, plates 60–63.

[18] Omission of one paragraph, on the 'River of Axim' and its gold, from Dapper, p. 64/3–4, and Villault, p. 188.

[19] In 1679 Barbot recorded seeing at Axim all the plants, fruits and animals mentioned (including *gros mil*, if not 'maize' as he states in *1688*, then sorghum, see Letter 1/16, note 46, above), except rice, oranges, limes, water-melons, and hens; and he noted large and small canoes, but without referring to their production for sale (*1679*, pp. 280–1). He later refers several times to the use along the coast of bar canoes from Axim: see note 51 below. For rice as the predominant crop at Axim, see Bosman, p. 7. In the

1690s the garden of the fort had 'China apples, pomegranates, *cassu* [?], pineapples, bananas, water-melons, plantains, and limes' (Tilleman 1697, p. 56).

Cf. *1732*, pp. 149/12, 150/1-3, which includes material on the damp climate of Axim, from Bosman, pp. 111-2, including a statement that maize did not flourish there; hence Barbot drops it from his list.

[20] Omission of the rest of the sentence and another sentence, on the gold trade from or through Igwira, from Dapper, pp. 84/8, 109/6-7. The Dutch map of 1629 stated that the gold at Axim and Abeny was all from Igwira (Daaku 1970, p. 182), a country lying just East of Axim.

Cf. *1732*, pp. 148/9, which substitutes – 'The great plenty of gold brought down hither from the wealthy country of Assine, besides what the mines of Iguira produce, makes a flourishing commerce; and therefore Axim was ... look'd upon as the best place for gold ...' (see note 9 above for the rest of this passage).

[21] In 1679 Barbot noted that the people near Axim paid the Dutch 'one tenth part of their goods' and did not dare to come aboard vessels without Dutch permission (*1679*, pp. 280-1); echoing Villault who had argued that the local Africans were overawed by the Dutch (Villault, p. 188). On Dutch attempts to stop trade with foreign vessels or interlopers, see *Relation* 1674, p. 14; Tilleman 1697, pp. 56-7. The Dutch levied a fish toll at Axim, Shama, Komenda, Elmina and Mouri (Bosman, p. 55; Daaku 1970, pp. 58, 82); but apparently only as previously levied by local rulers and by the Portuguese (Marees, ff. 28v-29, 40, 62v, 103). In the 1690s the village of Axim was estimated to contain about 100 huts and to furnish 300 men with guns (Tilleman 1697, p. 56; Phillips 1732, p. 201).

Cf. *1732*, pp. 148/9, 150/4-6, which drops the reference to Dutch monopoly, refers instead to trade with English and Zeeland interlopers, and adds material on the judicial powers of the Dutch fiscal at Axim, following Bosman, pp. 5-6, 167-72. Barbot concludes that – 'So great is the authority of this factor at Axim ... [and] that post [so] very beneficial ... [that] it is reckon'd the next to the general at Mina: for when the general's place is vacant, the chief factor at Axim succeeds in that employment'.

[22] The description and the drawing evidently refer not to 'Crema' (Takrama), where a small Brandenburg fort was built only in 1694, but to the first and principal Brandenburg fort, Gross-Friedrichsburg, 1½ Dutch miles further NW, whose foundations were laid on 1 January 1683, with six cannon being placed there (Jones 1985, pp. 4, 48-9). Barbot presumably obtained his information (and misinformation) from the Frenchman mentioned in the caption to the drawing. The drawing (reproduced in Jones 1985, plate 9) was not repeated in *1732*. For plans and other drawings of Gross-Friedrichsburg, see Jones 1985. For the chronological significance of this insertion, see the Introduction, note 84.

Cf. *1732*, p. 150/7, which, very curiously, omits any reference to the Brandenburg fort and substitutes the following: 'Three leagues east of the Dutch fort of St Antony, is the hill Maufro [Manfro], and near it the village Pocquesoe, pretty large and populous, one Jan or John being captain of it. The hill is very proper to build a fort on, being close to the first point of cape Tres-Pontas'. The references to Manfro and Pocquesoe are from Bosman, p. 7. In 1679, when Barbot's ship lay off an uncertain part of Cape Three Points, Barbot quarrelled with a 'black captain Juan' who demanded dues (*1679*, p. 283). This may have been the Jan/John mentioned, or the reference may be to the later, better known, John Conny (Daaku 1970, pp. 127–43). Barbot did, however, provide material on Gross-Friedrichsburg in the Supplement: see the Additional Passages.

[23] The relative was Jacques Barbot de la Porte, a senior officer of the Brandenburg company, whose headquarters was at Emden (see the Introduction, note 52). It seems that Barbot obtained information from his relative around 1700, but in 1699 Barbot's brother also obtained information about the Brandenburg forts when he visited Gross-Friedrichsburg. The drawing of the fort which appeared in *1732*, Plate 11 (p. 173) (mistakenly labelled 'the Dutch fort', although showing the Brandenburg flag), together with accompanying plans, was presumably supplied by Barbot de la Porte.

[24] Barbot's relative does not appear to have consulted the first-hand if egotistic account of Von der Groeben, who commanded the expedition, published in 1694. In fact, the two ships concerned, the *Chur-Printz* (with 32 guns and 60 men), and the *Morian* (with 12 guns and 40 men) did not leave Europe till May 1682, and the party landed at Cape Three Points in late December (Jones 1985, pp. 20, 49). 'Montfort' is a European corruption of Amanforo (which, confusingly, was also the name of the hill on which was built the Danish castle further East called, also confusingly, Frederiksborg).

[25] Blonck had made an agreement with three *caboceiros* (headmen) on 16 May 1681, but when he returned two had been killed and their village had been destroyed. The new agreement was signed on 5 January 1683 (Jones 1985, pp. 17–18, 57–8).

[26] The disembarkation of the cannon and the erection of palisades were described in Von der Groeben's account, but the visit of the headmen to Berlin was not mentioned. It seems that in fact only one headman, with a servant, travelled to Europe with Von der Groeben, and it must be doubtful whether he received such sumptuous hospitality (Jones 1985, p. 90, n. 2). Blonck returned to Europe only in 1686 (Schück 1889, I, 147). Barbot's use of the Dutch name for Gross-Friedrichsburg reflects the fact that much of the company's correspondence was conducted in Dutch, many of the senior servants of the company being Dutchmen.

[27] Omission of two paragraphs describing the fort, from Bosman, p. 7.

[28] Pokeso (modern Prince's Town) lay close to the fort. An agreement signed in 1712 between the acting director-general of Gross-Friedrichsburg and the 'caboceers' of Pokeso laid down that all disputes should be brought before the director-general; no new caboceers should be created without his consent; and fines were laid down for theft and murder (Schück 1889, II, 538–40). The agreement mentioned by Barbot appears to be an earlier and perhaps less authoritarian version of the 1712 agreement. The latter was signed by the 'king' of Anta, as well as by a large number of caboceers; but most other agreements made by the Brandenburgers do not mention any such king (other sources only mention a king of Ahanta by c. 1710: Schück 1889, II, 538–40; Hazewinkel 1932, p. 253; Van Dantzig 1980, p. 185). Barbot borrowed from Bosman the references to dwellings, the director-general's title, and the description of Axim as a 'commonwealth' (Bosman, pp. 8, 164).

[29] Fort Dorothea was founded in 1684, and lodges at Popo and Whydah do appear to have existed, at least for brief periods, most probably during the mid 1690s (Jones 1985, pp. 6, n. 27, 81–2).

[30] Omission of a reference to the fort at Tacrama, from Bosman, p. 10: this includes the copying by Barbot of a misprint, the obviously wrong date in the English translation of Bosman, '1674', instead of the original '1694' – proof that Barbot was using the English translation (and that rather unintelligently).

[31] In 1713 Tacrama was said to have four cannon (Schück 1889, II, 550). The date 1701 may indicate that this information also came from Barbot de la Porte. The exact site of Tacrama fort has not been identified.

[32] Omission of material on the forts at Tacrama and 'Acoba' (a copying error for Acoda, i.e. Akwida) and on the conduct of the Brandenburgers, from Bosman, pp. 4–5, 8–10. But Barbot inserts, with reference to the guns at Fort Dorothea, 'my brother says twenty'. James Barbot may have visited Akwida in 1699 (see note 35 below), or he may have obtained this information at Gross-Friedrichsburg.

[33] The date 1702 may indicate that Barbot de la Porte's information on Brandenburg activities was produced in that year. Omission of the rest of the paragraph, an English report that in 1708 the king of Prussia had received an offer from Portugal for the forts at Cape Three Points, taken from Davenant 1709, p. 221.

[34] It is uncertain who the 'Prussian' (i.e. Brandenburg) commander was at this date (Jones 1985, pp. 214–5). The war caused by the killing of the king of Commenda by the English is referred to in Bosman, p. 37, and ARA, WIC 917, Sevenhuysen 15.2.1700: the clause referring to the Supplement must be a gloss by Barbot rather than part of his brother's journal. Later in 1699 the authorities at Gross-Friedrichsburg reported that 'business [is] now

at a standstill, on account of both the war and the lack of current trade-goods' (Jones 1985, p. 215).

[35] For the attack on a Brandenburg vessel, apparently by a vessel privateering on behalf of the deposed English king, James II, see Jones 1985, pp. 211–2. It is not clear why on both the 8th and the 9th the ship is said to come to anchor before the same fort, and it is possible that on the 9th it moved to the second Brandenburg fort at Akwida, although the text seems to continue to refer to the 'general' at Gross-Friedrichsburg.

[36] These three sentences are from Dapper, p. 64/5, and Villault, p. 189, but changing 4°10' to 4°15' (more correctly given as 4°42' in *1679*, p. 282), and adding 'Warshas', an error, since Wassa was an interior territory (Dapper, p. 85/6) – and shown as such on Barbot's map of Gold Coast. In 1679 Barbot's ship watered at Cape Three Points, and Barbot drew the coast, marking the place, '100 steps from the sea', where the water was 'better than that of Sierra Leone but more troublesome to obtain', as his caption stated (*1679*, p. 282, the drawing not reproduced). The watering place is captioned more briefly in the present drawing, and when the drawing was repeated in *1732*, Plate M (p. 150), there was no caption to explain the letter B that indicates the watering place. 'Little Incassa' was noted in the text of the 1629 map, and the Little Incassa people were described as being devoted to the Portuguese at Axim, to whom they sold oyster shells; but the map itself only showed Incassa and Great Inkassa, both of them inland, with 'Little Wassa' on the coast, and Cabo de Tres Puntas as a separate coastal region, West of Anta (Daaku 1970, p. 183 and map 1; Hazewinkel 1932, p. 251). A Dutch map of c. 1660, which showed the district to the East of Cape Three Points in some detail, marked 'Little Incacer' inland, with Axim and Anta 'adjoining' coastal countries (Jones 1985, fig. 7). By the end of the century Anta included Cape Three Points (Bosman, p. 13; Jones 1985, p. 5).

Cf. *1732*, pp. 150/8, 151/2, which adds doubts whether the 'kingdom' of Little Inkassan existed, probably correct doubts.

[37] In 1679 Barbot anchored off and traded at 'Ackuon', which he described as a large village among high trees, to the East of the third headland of Cape Three Points, adding that the houses stood on the slope and top of the hill (*1679*, p. 284). Since Cape Three Points, despite its name, consists of at least seven headlands, it is difficult to tell where he meant. Today the only large village lying just East of Cape Three Points is Akwida, where the Brandenburgers had a fort from 1685 to 1687 and from 1690 to about 1713. But contemporary sources referred to Akwida as Accada/Acada/Accoda/Acoda/Ackeda (Bosman, p. 10; Roussier 1935, p. 8; Jones 1985, *passim*) – all of which are closer to Barbot's 'Acora' than to 'Accuon'. However, 'Acora' might well be the present-day Akrakrom (Akra + *krom*, see below). Both Ackuon and Acora are marked on Barbot's map, but this is insufficiently

detailed and accurate to identify them. In 1679 Barbot next watered at 'Dikiscrom, a seaside village equidistant from Ackuon and Boetroe', paying dues to the local commander or *cabeschier* (*1679*, p. 284). The English claimed to have a factory at 'Dixcove' in 1672, tried to settle there in 1684, but did not actually begin building a fort till 1692 (*CSP Colonial* 1669–74, pp. 412–3; Davies 1957, pp. 247–9; Lawrence 1963, p. 293). 'Dikiscrom' (like 'Akrakrom') perhaps includes Akan/Twi *kurow* 'town', *kuromuni* 'town inhabitant' (note 'his croome', Davenant 1709, p. 219; 'Quashey's Croom', OBLR, C. 745–7 passim; 'parcels of houses, which the negroes call crooms', Phillips 1732, p. 228 – at Whydah but the term perhaps acquired on Gold Coast). The alleged English etymology of 'Dickisco' was presumably 'Dick-(ie)'s Cove'. Barbot visited this locality again in 1682 and may have then acquired the alternative name 'Infiama' (allegedly *unfoema* 'crocodile', Jeekel 1869, pp. 11, 19).

Cf. *1732*, pp. 150/8–9, 151/3, which even less helpfully describes 'Acoba or Acora' as 'at the bottom of the first bay, from the west eastward'; and discusses timber at Acoda, from Bosman, pp. 295–6.

[38] This episode occurred when Barbot revisited Infiama in April 1682 (*1732*, p. 275/4). When water was collected there in January 1679 no difficulties were recorded, presumably because none was encountered by virtue of the higher tide. Yet Barbot later claimed that 'at another time, [I] was like to undergo the same fate myself', although his 1679 journal seems to indicate that in fact he did not leave the ship on this occasion (*1732*, p. 150/10). 'Dix cove is encumbered with reefs . . . At low water, the sea breaks entirely across the entrance' (*Africa pilot* 1967, p. 443). For a contemporary, but perhaps over-optimistic view that landing at Dixcove was easy, see Roussier 1935, p. 8.

[39] In 1676 'corn' was obtained at Dixcove by an English ship; in the late 1680s it was reported that Dixcove was a good place for obtaining wood, water, stone and lime (i.e. oyster-shells); and in 1692 the Englishmen building a fort at Dixcove reported that it might 'prove a good place for corn and at wooding and watering' (Donnan 1930, I, 204; Roussier 1935, p. 8; Lawrence 1963, p. 293 – no source cited).

Cf. *1732*, pp. 150/10, 151/1, which enlarges as follows: 'The water is usually taken from a large pond, just by the strand; but sometimes the sea happens to overflow it, and then fresh water must be fetch'd a good half mile up the land. The wood also is sometimes cut just by the shore, and at other times, an English mile from it, up the country, behind the village, as the Caboceiro thinks fit'. This information too was probably obtained in 1682, since in 1679 Barbot recommended Ackuon as the place to take water. Barbot adds: 'The trade is here but indifferent, as well as at the two above-mentioned villages, the Blacks of Infiama, and the adjacent parts, being almost intractable, of a turbulent, violent, knavish temper, and great adulteraters of gold'. The derogatory adjectives are from Bosman, p. 14, but in 1679 Barbot complained about adulterated gold at Cape Three Points (*1679*, p. 282). At Infiama Barbot once saw a porcupine (*1732*, p. 214/4). The material on the English fort at Dixcove in the Supplement (*1732*, p. 433/1–3) is from Bosman, pp. 14–15, and Davenant 1709, p. 223 (mysteriously and misleadingly headed 'Letters to P.').

[40] The three sentences are based on Dapper, p. 64/6, with 'Petrygrande' added as an alternative to Poyera, but Dapper's 'Takorary or Anten' separated, the latter becoming 'Anta' (the modern form is 'Ahanta'), and the eastern neighbour, Guaffo, omitted. 'Monquironque' was shown East of Takoradi on a Dutch map of c. 1660 and as 'Makayanke' in Robijn/ Roggeveen 1685; while a 1685 document mentions 'Mankajanka' (Jones 1985, fig. 7, and p. 98). For the view that Anta included Akwida and Dixcove, see Roussier 1935, p. 8.

Cf. *1732*, p. 151/4–7, which adds 'Anta, or Hante, as the Blacks call it', names Boesira and Jabs as its western and eastern boundaries, from Bosman, pp. 13–14 ('Boeswa'), 21, and reduces the extent to 'about ten leagues'. Barbot continues with extensive material on the productivity of Anta in crops and animals, including crocodiles and monkeys, all from Bosman, pp. 16–18, except that Barbot adds that 'I carried some [monkeys] to Paris, which were look'd upon as the finest and most gamesome of any ever brought thither'.

[41] In 1679 Barbot's ship lay off 'Boetroe' (Butre) and he drew the 'little fort on a rock', but did not give it a name (*1679*, p. 284). However, his reference to the stream at Butre echoes Villault, p. 189. Butre lies about 5 km NE of Dixcove, which Barbot apparently considered to be part of Cape Three Points.

Cf. *1732*, p. 151/6, which adds material from Bosman, p. 17.

[42] Heinrich Carloff, a native of Mecklenburg, served under the Dutch West India Company in the 1640s. He then entered the services of the Swedish African Company and in 1650 established trading posts on its behalf at Butre and Cape Coast, posts he later transferred to the Danish (Glückstadt) African Company. Barbot was mistaken in thinking that Carloff founded the trading post for the Dutch. But the Butre lodge was soon abandoned and the Dutch occupied the site, or a nearby one (Lawrence 1963, p. 262; Nørregard 1966, pp. 10, 16–17; Jones 1983a, pp. 142–4).

[43] Dapper called it a 'fairly strong fort' (Dapper, p. 65/1). In 1679, when Barbot obtained information from a soldier from the fort, he reported that it had 11 cannon and a garrison of 30 whites (*1679*, p. 285). Since he now changes the number, he presumably obtained further information when at Butre in 1682, including the name 'Badensteein' (more correctly 'Batensteen'). The fort was in poor repair c. 1680 (ARA, Abramsz 23.11.1679).

Von der Groeben, who also visited the fort in 1682, reported that the garrison consisted of 'a factor, an assistant, a corporal, and eight soldiers' and the artillery of four 3-pounders and six 2-pounders (Jones 1685, p. 44).

Cf. *1732*, p. 151/8, which does not mention the garrison, but describes the fort, following Bosman, p. 15.

[44] The toponyms reflect Dapper's 'Jabbe', a town East of 'Anta', and 'the king of Gavi', a neighbouring ruler (Dapper, p. 65/2, 7). For Jabbe/Yabi, see Henige 1975.

Cf. *1732*, p. 151/8, where these toponyms are omitted.

[45] The drawing of the fort was repeated on *1732*, Plate M (p. 150), with the original viewpoint distance changing from one league to 1¼ leagues. The small size of the village was confirmed by Von der Groeben (Jones 1985, p. 44): a decade later it was 'indifferent large and populous' (Bosman, p. 16). For a 1707 drawing of the fort, and for the present-day ruins, see Lawrence 1963, plates 68–71.

Cf. *1732*, p. 151/8, which enlarges – 'it would still be less were it not for the inland Blacks, who now and then resort thither from Adom and other parts, bringing very good gold. In 1682, when I was there, the trade was very dull, because of the precedent war betwixt Adom and Anta, which ended in 1681, but had so dispeopled the towns and villages of Anta, that several had not ten families left in them; but at my arrival, the commerce began a little to revive, by the coming down of the Adom Blacks'. Later in the 1680s, according to another Frenchman, the Dutch made it virtually impossible for French ships to trade anywhere near Butre (Roussier 1935, pp. 24–6). A German visitor implied that the destruction of coastal villages by the Adom people, who lived inland, occurred after the signing of the 1682 Brandenburg agreement, the wars continuing until c. 1690 (Bosman, pp. 16, 23; Jones 1985, p. 47). However, earlier wars between Adom and Anta had occurred (Dapper, p. 110/2; Daaku 1970, pp. 182–3). For the history of Adom, see Henige 1975.

[46] The reference to the king's residence is from Dapper, p. 65/2. If Barbot obtained gold at Butre, it must have been in 1682.

Cf. *1732*, pp. 151/8, which adds – 'and is often at variance with the aforesaid Blacks of Adom; their territories lying in such manner, that they extend between the rivers Sama or Chama and Cobra, distant near twenty leagues from each other, along the coast, and seem to go up the river Sama in a line, and then to turn with a narrow slip away to Cobra' – the extent from Bosman, p. 22. However, the *1732* map repeats the same frontiers for Adom as the *1688* map. References in the Supplement to Dutch sugar-works at Butre and to Badenstein (*1732*, p. 433/4–5) are from Davenant 1709, p. 221, somewhat embroidered, and Bosman, p. 15.

[47] The toponyms are from Dapper and Dutch maps ('Poyera, Pando' in

Dapper, p. 64/6). 'Poyera' may be a corrupt and wrongly located 'Boare', and Pando/Ponde/Pandos most probably represents only an extreme corruption of 'Puntas' (in 'Tres Puntas'). The further reference to the fetish rocks is in Letter 2/26, p. 102, 'rocks and sacred stones, as seen at Boutrou and Dickiskydorp', rocks visited annually by persons from the Ivory Coast seeking protection against storms. The annual visit is from Dapper, p. 62/7–8, but this does not specify individual rocks or locations. Perhaps Barbot saw these rocks in 1682. The reference to the map is unhelpful, since the map fails to mark 'Pandos' and only indicates Boutrou by marking 'Fort Badensteyn'.

Cf. *1732*, p. 152/2, 9 ('maiz or Indian wheat . . . vast rock near the shore'), also p. 309/9, for which see the Additional Passage to Letter 1/31 above.

[48] In 1679 Barbot passed Takorary (Takoradi) and called it a 'large village on the coast' (*1679*, p. 285). But the reference to rocks and a fort (Fort Wittsen) is from Dapper, pp. 64/6, 65/3 – who supplied a double-page illustration of the fort which significantly Barbot does not copy.

Cf. *1732*, p. 152/3–4, which includes material from Bosman, p. 19.

[49] Omission of six sentences describing the English capture and Dutch recapture and razing of the fort in 1664–5, from Dapper, p. 65/4–5.

Cf. *1732*, p. 152/4.

[50] The reference is to Villault, pp. 190–1. But there is no record of French activity at Takoradi before their brief settlement in 1686–7 (Jones 1985, pp. 157–8), hence the ruins which Villault claimed to have seen can only have been those of the razed Dutch fort. By the 1690s 'no visible remnants' of the fort were to be seen (Bosman, p. 20).

Cf. *1732*, p. 152/4–5, which adds that 'the English, Dutch, Danes, Swedes and Brandenburgers . . . all possess'd it successively', partly from Bosman, p. 20. On the Swedes and Danes at Takoradi in the 1650s, see Jones 1983a, pp. 143–4; on the Dutch subsequently and spasmodically, and the Brandenburgers in the 1680s, see Van Dantzig 1978, p. 197 and n. 13; Jones 1985, *passim*. The English had a post at Takoradi in the 1640s and again in 1673 (Ratelband 1953, pp. 153, 248; Davies 1957, p. 247). In the Supplement Barbot reported, 'by many letters I have in my hands', that the Dutch had been 'very industrious to disturb our British settlements at the coast, in a more particular manner since the year 1706', having built a new fort at Takoradi in 1707 (*1732*, pp. 433/6–434/1). But all this information was taken from Davenant 1709, pp. 214–5, 220. The date '1706' is significant, as it signals the notional dividing date between the main text and the Supplement.

[51] This enlarges on what Barbot recorded in 1679, that the bar canoes essential for trading at Ardres, were bought here, for 3–4 ounces of gold (*1679*, p. 286). The '£' is the French *livre-tournois*, not the English pound. A

1673 source confirmed that 'most canoes are made in Ante', i.e. Ahanta (Jones 1983a, p. 254).

Cf. *1732*, p. 152/6–7, which substitutes 'forty or fifty pounds sterling' and adds a size for the canoes, from Bosman, p. 129. For later references to these large canoes, see Letters 2/20, p. 83 and note 41; 3/20, p. 238, below.

[52] Dapper stated that the Dutch and English had formerly sent yachts to Takoradi to trade, but the English had ceased to do so because of the lack of gold (Dapper, p. 109/7). However, the Dutch in 1678 abandoned their lodge at Takoradi (where Fort Wittsen had long before been destroyed) because the local people were trading with 'English, Portuguese and other ships' (ARA, Abramsz 23.11.1679). They reoccupied it again in 1682 and 1684, but for periods of months only, fearing Adom attacks (ARA, WIC 124, 5.1.1684, 10.1.1684, 10.2.1684).

Cf. *1732*, p. 152/4, 8, which states that 'the Dutch have a house there at present, but are often oblig'd to forsake it'. 'At present' may be a late revision, reflecting Davenant 1709, since total abandonment of Dutch trade at Takoradi had been reported by Barbot's 1705 source, Bosman, p. 20. The material on Takoradi in the Supplement (*1732*, pp. 433/6–434/1) is from Davenant 1709, pp. 214–5, with embroidery.

[53] The river's name and the reference to 'Jabbe' are from Dapper, pp. 65/2, 66/7, interpreting Marees, f. 40. In fact, Jabi country lay NE of Sama, and was perhaps a miniature city-state on River Pra (Marees, f. 45v; Daaku 1970, p. 183).

Cf. *1732*, p. 152/8–9, which omits mention of Jabbe and adds that 'the coast affords vast quantities of oysters, the shells serving to make lime . . .'.

[54] In 1679 Barbot's ship lay off Sekondi and was visited by agents from the English and Dutch lodges (*1679*, p. 286); and in 1687–8 another French visitor noted English and Dutch activities (Roussier 1935, pp. 9–10). The English had a lodge here from at least 1672 – possibly with breaks, since a 1679 Dutch report suggested that the English had recently 'crept in' (ARA, Abramsz 23.11.1679) – and they built a small and weak fort, apparently between 1682 and 1685, which was plundered in 1694 and not re-occupied until 1704; while the Dutch built a small fort in the 1690s (*CSP Colonial 1669–74*, pp. 412–3; Donnan 1930, I, 204; Bosman, pp. 18–19; Phillips 1732, p. 203; Davies 1950, pp. 248, 268, 370). But there is no confirmation of Barbot's report of an earlier French lodge.

Cf. *1732*, p. 152/10, which adds a little from Bosman, pp. 19, 108, and states that 'at present the English and Dutch have each of them a strong house', i.e. after 1704. The extensive material on the later history of the English and Dutch at Sekondi in the Supplement (*1732*, p. 434/2–435/7) is from Bosman, pp. 18–19 (but not p. 435/5 as there stated), from Davenant 1709, pp. 200–4, 209, 214, 223, and from the *Gazette de Paris*, 1694. But Barbot begins by stating that the Dutch Fort Orange was erected 'before

1682' which, being incorrect, suggests that he did not revisit Sekondi in 1682.

[55] Barbot applies the name of the Anta (Ahanta) country (and perhaps of its inland capital) to a coastal village. However, the 1629 map gave Anta as an alternative name for Tacorary, and Marees spoke of anchoring at Anta (Marees, f. 40). Much of Barbot's information about Anta derives from Dapper's description of the Ahanta country (whose source was mainly Marees, f. 40–40v). For Boare (Aboadi), see the 1629 map; Jones 1985, fig. 7; Bosman, p. 20; Ratelband 1953, p. 27. The omission is of two sentences on the trade of Anta in palm-wine and gold, from Dapper, p. 66/3, 5, 110/2.

Cf. *1732*, p. 152/1, 11–12, which describes these villages as 'not considerable for any gold trade, unless by accident', and adds material on the 'ravenous appetites' of some natives, and the strategic position of Adom in relation to the gold trade from Igwira and Mompa, from Bosman, pp. 14, 17, 19–20, 25. In the Supplement (*1732*, p. 436/1–9), the 'bloody cruel nature' of the people of Adom is described at length, from Bosman, pp. 22–5.

[56] In 1679 Barbot passed by and drew the Dutch fort at Sama, 'from NW at one league', and also recorded its 12 guns (*1679*, p. 286): the drawing reappeared on *1732*, Plate M (p. 150), the later drawings giving the fort the name 'St Sebastien'. Perhaps Barbot concluded that the Dutch over-ruled the local Africans because in 1679 no canoes came out to trade. The omitted sentences, describing the role of the *brafo* (governor) and the history of the fort from its Portuguese foundation (but not supplying the name 'St Sebastien' or the mention of maize), are from Dapper, pp. 65/7, 66/1. In 1679 the Dutch had a factor, an assistant, a barber and nine soldiers at Shama (ARA, Abramsz 23.11.1679); but in 1682 there were only two assistants (Jones 1985, p. 43). For relations between the Dutch and Shama, and the importance of River Pra ('River St George') as a source of wood, see Daaku 1970, p. 79; Bosman, p. 22; Ratelband 1953, p. 13; and for present-day views of the fort, see Lawrence 1963, plates 73–7.

Cf. *1732*, p. 153/1–2, 4, with added material from Bosman, p. 20.

[57] Barbot's references to Adom and Wassa and to tribute are from Dapper, pp. 66/1, 81/4, 6, 8, 110/1. In 1679 the Dutch at Shama obtained gold from 'Adom, Wassa and Twifo' (ARA, Abramsz 23.11.1679). The reference to the anchorage may indicate that Barbot visited there in 1682. For other anchoring instructions, see Leers 1665, p. 229.

Cf. *1732*, p. 153/3–4, 8.

[58] Omission of one paragraph describing River Pra, from Dapper, p. 66/2.

Cf. *1732*, p. 153/5–7, 9, with additions from Dapper, p. 85/2 and Bosman, pp. 21–2.

[59] Cf. *1732*, pp. 153/10–154/1, which adds material on 'Jabs Country', from Bosman, p. 21, and states that Abroby is 'the only notable place that occurs on the sea-coast, of this little country of Jabs'.

[60] 'Abroby' is 'Aborby' in Dapper, p. 66/9, where 'Aldea de Torres' is given as another name for Little Komenda. The omission is of the rest of one paragraph describing agricultural and marine products of Anta, from Dapper, p. 66/3, with a little embroidery.

Cf. *1732*, p. 151/4–6, 154/2–3, which partly substitutes material from Bosman (see note 40 above).

[61] The gold trade from Igwira and Mompa, and the village *brafo*, are from Dapper, pp. 66/5–6, 84/8, 85/5, 7, and the reddish rock is from Villault, p. 191. But Dapper says that the gold trade had declined because the gold brought from the interior was 'of little importance'. For adulterated gold at Shama, see *Relation* 1674, p. 15.

Cf. *1732*, p. 154/4, which adds material on Anta from Bosman, p. 14.

[62] The information on Great Commendo, including two omitted sentences on its boundaries, is from Dapper, p. 66/7–9, (based on the 1629 map, Leers 1665, p. 300, and Marees, f. 40–40v). Apart from variant spellings, the list of villages is also from Dapper, except that Dapper's 'Aldea de Torres', yet another name for Little Comendo, becomes a separate village called 'Cape Aldea de Torres', and that Barbot adds 'Lori' as another name for Cotabry and omits Dapper's 'Terra Pekine'. (Neighbouring 'Cotobery' on the Robijn/Roggeveen 1685 map is 'dorp' written in a form capable of being misread as 'Lory'.)

Cf. *1732*, p. 154/5–6, which redefines 'the cape Aldea de Torres', inserts 'Oddena or Mina, a little commonwealth between Commendo and Fetu', and changes Agitaki to 'Ekke-Toki', the latter changes from Bosman, pp. 27, 42. Little Komenda became politically independent of the Eguafo kingdom some time before the 1720s (Henige 1977, pp. 11–12): if this occurred before 1710, Barbot was unaware of it.

[63] In 1679 Barbot's ship lay off Little Komenda for two days, during which time Barbot drew the coast and gained a certain amount of information from a Dutch agent and from Africans who came aboard (*1679*, pp. 287–90); and in 1682 he visited Little Komenda again (see note 68 below). But the first three sentences are from Dapper, p. 66/10, and Villault, p. 192 ('four leagues', although in 1679 Barbot reported that Great Comendo lay one league inland).

Cf. *1732*, p. 154/6.

[64] In 1679 the king's brother-in-law, Jan Pietersz, governor of Little Komenda, came aboard: Barbot did not record that either he or any other Frenchman went ashore on this occasion (*1679*, pp. 288–9).

Cf. *1732*, p. 154/7, which omits the references to the brother-in-law and to the walks ashore, divides the village into 'three parts', and adds that 'most of it was accidentally burnt not long ago, which caused many of the inhabitants to settle at Ampeny: much about the time the father of this present king of Commendo died', from an untraced source.

[65] In 1679 Barbot bought gold and slaves at Little Komenda and described it as 'a fairly large town, although it hardly seems so from the roadstead', whose inhabitants were mainly fishermen (*1679*, pp. 288–9) – this last point echoing Dapper, who also stated that the Dutch and English obtained gold there (Dapper, pp. 67/3, 110/3). Barbot's information about 'merchants from Acanez' seems to have been obtained mainly from Olrichs, commandant of Fort Christiansborg at Accra (*1679*, p. 336). The last two sentences, describing the village, are from Villault, pp. 191–2, except that the number of houses is raised from 100 to 150. A French plan, presumably of the late 1680s, shows sections of the village on both sides of the mouth of the river, with (quotes in translation) a 'fort which the English have begun to build' on the West side, a 'hut of the Dutch' on the East side, and a very large 'hut which the French have had built' further East, near the village: the harbour, almost enclosed by rocks, lay East of the river mouth (Roussier 1935, Plate III).

Cf. *1732*, p. 154/7–8, which omits, significantly, 'suitable for building on'.

[66] Barbot's present references to Komenda were influenced by the fact that in 1682 he had been closely involved in semi-official attempts to establish at Komenda a French commercial and military base for the whole Gold Coast: for the background see note 21 of the Introduction. Since French interest in Komenda began in the 1660s, as reflected in Villault's reference to a suitable site for a building, even in 1679 Barbot was aware of the national concern. In his journal he reported as follows. 'This is the place where the late Mr Micheau took the two blacks whom we saw at La Rochelle and who were presented to His Majesty to assure him that their king passionately wished that His Majesty should establish a place of commerce in his territory. I asked Jan Pietersz what had become of these two blacks. He told me that Nunez, the elder, had died eight or ten moons (or months) ago and that Foutou, the younger, was at war at Cormentyn' (*1679*, p. 290). Two ambassadors from Komenda who reached France on 14 April 1672 were received not by the king but by Colbert, and were sent back to Africa with presents. A third, the 14-year-old son of Captain None, alias Captain Obrinone, alias Governor Hoabry Nunno, arrived on 13 June 1672; and it was arranged that he should be taught to speak, read and write French. Later, three years after Barbot's visit in 1682, the king of Komenda, learning of the formation of a new Guinea Company, sent another ambassador, who died on his way from La Rochelle to Paris (Roussier 1935, p. xi; Thilmans and Moraes 1976, pp. 295–7). Presumably Barbot saw the African

envoys at La Rochelle in 1672 (when he was only seventeen); and presumably he learned about Coucoumy when he visited Komenda again in 1682.

Cf. *1732*, p. 154/9, which enlarges, to the effect that Coucoumy was sent 'to the French king, to invite him to send over his subjects to erect a fortress at Commendo, and settle a trade with his subjects; the Commanians having been long much disgusted at the arbitrary power the Dutch of Mina exercise over them upon all occasions'.

[67] Omission of two paragraphs, on local wars and the death of a king of Comendo, the many canoes, and the local products, especially bananas, from Dapper, p. 67/1–4, slightly embroidered (e.g., fish exchanged at Great Comendo for gold).

Cf. *1732*, pp. 154/10–11, 155/3–5.

[68] In 1679 Barbot stated that Jan Pietersz 'repeated the extreme desire they had that the French should build a fort in their land, even offering three or four times to give us one of his people, to go once again [to France] to assure the king' (*1679*, p. 290). In late January 1682, English agents at Komenda reported on the arrival of 'Mons. Berdoe' and stated that the French company 'gives great encouragement to Blacks, alsoe that daily here is expected two Frenchmen . . . a general and merchants goods and materials to settle the gold coast especially to build a Fort at Comenda which by contract has been agreed 10 years agoe, for these people here sent a Black to France whoe spoke to the Kinge himselfe' (OBLR, C.745, James Nightingale, 21.1.1681/2 O.S. = 31.1.1682 N.S.). Later they reported that 'Mons. Ducas comes General with two men of war of 45 gunns apeece and one small frigat and two sloopes to settle upon this coast' (ibid., 24.1.1681/2 O.S. = 3.2.1682 N.S.). But the information about Ducasse travelling to Guinea in 1682 and the imminent fort-building was wrong (Du Casse 1876, p. 54). Some of this information – and misinformation – may have reached the English from Barbot in person. For an agreement between a French agent and the king of Komenda in 1667, the attempts to bring it into operation in 1669 and 1671, and the eventual setting-up of a French post in 1687, see Thilmans and Moraes 1976, pp. 281, 290–4. It appears to be correct that difficulties in operating the agreement arose on the French side and that the Africans remained welcoming to, and even eager for French activity, presumably because the people of Komenda wanted European support against irruptions from neighbouring polities which already had European allies, as symbolised by permanent bases. In 1671 a Frenchman who visited the king at Great Komenda reported that the people there told him that they had 'a French heart' (*Relation* 1674, pp. 15–17). Barbot does not explain why in 1682, although invited to do so, he did not visit the king.

Cf. *1732*, p. 155/1.

[69] The English and Dutch had posts at Little Komenda in the 1670s and 1680s, although not continuously, and in 1679 Barbot met a man who had

formerly spent three years as the Dutch factor at Little Komenda (Delbée 1671, p. 373; *1679*, p. 287). The Dutch post existed in 1679, was destroyed in 1681 by the people of Komenda, and re-established in 1682: the English post was burnt in a 'palm oil fire' c. 1682 and abandoned in 1683, re-established in 1684 and abandoned again in 1687 (ARA, Abramsz 23.11.1679; PRO, T70/367, Cape Coast ledger 3, 18.3.1681/2, T70/11, reports of 2.6.1683, 14.12.1683; Davies 1957, p. 267; Henige 1977, p. 7; Van Dantzig 1978, pp. 36–7). Du Casse, who tried to set up a French post in 1687–8, wrote: 'The Dutch and English have a small store, the kings never having wanted to let them place cannon there ... The Dutch, who were the first established, took up arms and carried war by means of the king of Adom against the King of Commendo, when the English wanted to establish themselves there; ... but since the king persisted in supporting the English, they remained there, although the trouble lasted two years' (Roussier 1935, p. 33). The Dutch claim to a trade monopoly on the Komenda coast rested on treaties signed in 1642, 1659 and 1688 (Daaku, pp. 57, 81).

Cf. *1732*, p. 155/1, which adds that 'the Dutch had one formerly, but were forced to quit the country', and that the people of Comendo particularly disliked the Dutch and 'their hard domination over them' (a cliché of non-Dutch commentators).

[70] The present-day village of Ampeni lies between Komenda and Elmina, and slightly closer to the former. The land does not 'jut out southwards'; but there is an inlet which fits Barbot's 'little elbow'. For another recommendation of Ampeny as a good trading-place, see Phillips 1732, p. 203.

Cf. *1732*, p. 155/1, which introduces the recommendation as follows: 'At my return into France [in 1682], I deliver'd to some ministers of the court, all the memoirs I had taken on this head at Commendo, and my own observations of the most proper place to erect a fortress on that coast, at Ampena ...'.

[71] One advantage of Komenda from a French point of view was that it might serve as a base from which to launch a military attack on the Dutch at nearby Elmina (Roussier 1935, p. 39). Akani merchants did visit Komenda at this date (PRO, T70/11 p. 5, report of 14.12.1683).

Cf. *1732*, p. 155/1, which omits the reference to inland merchants, but adds that a fort at Ampena would allow 'malcontents' at Mina to trade there.

[72] It is not clear why Barbot had second thoughts about Ampeny. The reference to an earlier French post is from Villault, p. 192; in 1671 another Frenchman was shown a house the French had at one time built there (*Relation* 1674, p. 15). There appears to have been a short-lived French trading post at Komenda in the late 1630s and early 1640s (De Jonge 1871, pp. 51–69; Brásio 1960, pp. 582–3; Thilmans and Moraes 1976, p. 290).

Cf. *1732*, p. 155/2, which substitutes 'on the borders of the land of Jabs or Yabbah' for 'west of Little Commendo'.

[73] The drawing made in 1679 (*1679*, p. 291, '1 league to NE') is repeated in *1688* with rather less foreground, and in *1732*, Plate N (p. 134), much extended at the sides: the later drawings fail to mention the viewpoint. Although all the buildings shown are square with double-sloping roofs (as on all Barbot's Gold Coast drawings), a taller building which appears to have windows above a door on the narrower face might be a European lodge.

[74] The first sentence is from Villault, p. 192. The military information, if a borrowing, is from an untraced source.
Cf. *1732*, p. 155/6.

[75] In 1679 Barbot complained of gold mixed with silver offered to him by Jan Pietersz, and noted that the copper pins he was selling were used to adulterate gold; and he believed that he had confirmation of the view put to him by a Dutchman, that the local people were 'shameless thieves' (*1679*, pp. 287–9). Barbot's comment also echoed an earlier complaint about adulteration of gold at Komenda (Marees, f. 40v).
Cf. *1732*, p. 155/7–8, with additions, 'of a turbulent temper', 'brass or silver', 'especially the Crakra gold', echoing Bosman, pp. 81–2.

[76] Probably inspired by a statement in Bosman, pp. 29–30: 'Some miners being sent to us from Europe, they were Order'd to make an Essay at a Hill situate in Commany about half an hour above our Fort Vreden-Burgh ... This Hill was at that Time Dedicated to one of their Gods, tho' there was scarce ever any Talk of any such thing before; but this was really only a Pretence that they made use of to Declare War against us'. See Van Dantzig 1975, p. 214, n. 26.

[77] The episode is dated to 1681, and when repeated in *1732*, p. 271/5, the English ship is stated to be an interloper. In 1679 Jan Pietersz offered to bring Barbot 500–600 slaves if his ship would remain at Komenda two months. But the Dutch governor of Shama said that the people of Komenda could not even provide thirty slaves a month, because they had recently been defeated by the people of Kormantine (*1679*, p. 287). For evidence of the growth of the slave trade at Komenda in the early eighteenth century, see Donnan 1930, II, 110, 186–91. Barbot's assertion that wars provided slavers with prisoners in large numbers and for 'little or nothing' has much influenced a popular interpretation of the history of Afro-European relations in the period of the Atlantic slave trade.

[78] Since Barbot also made use of 'Memoirs' by John Bloome, it is possible that Barbot was the J.B. to whom the letter was addressed – if indeed it was a letter and not part of an official report. Bloome served the Royal African Company, mainly at Accra, between at least 1687 and 1695 (OBLR, C.745–6); and in connection with the 1688 French attempt to settle at Komenda, Bloome was sent to Anashan to prevent any settlement there (PRO, T70/11,

letter of 9.1.1687/8). It is uncertain whether Barbot made Bloome's acquaintance on the coast in 1682, and it is possible that he was put in touch with him much later by Greenhill, the retired Company governor (see note 53 of the Introduction).

[79] For Du Casse, see Du Casse 1876; Roussier 1935, p. xiv, n. 1. After service in Senegal in 1677–9, during which he captured Arguin and cowed the African polities of the Little Coast, and after later service in the West Indies, Du Casse was sent to West Africa in command of the French frigate *Tempête*, reaching Little Komenda on 28 November 1687, where he raised the French flag. The Dutch, who had had a trading post there, withdrew; and it was soon reported that they were inciting the people of Adom to attack the king of Komenda, on whose head the Dutch had allegedly set a price. In January 1688 the English and French withdrew from Little Komenda; and the French trading post was then burnt down. After again receiving promises of protection from the king, Du Casse sent six men ashore to re-establish a French post and sailed on to Whydah. Dutch ships then bombarded Little Komenda; the French post was plundered by Africans from Elmina; and the six men left by Du Casse were induced by the inhabitants of Little Komenda to leave. (This suggests that Little Komenda was already to some extent independent of the Komenda kingdom). Once more the king urged the French to return; and it was resolved that three men should go to Little Komenda to maintain the French claim to the site, but without any possessions except those necessary for their subsistence. Here Du Casse's own account ends (Roussier 1935, pp. 18–24). If the three Frenchmen did go to Little Komenda, they cannot have remained there long, for the Dutch had already made an agreement with the king and elders of Komenda, by which they had 'divested the ruler of any shadow of authority over his coastal strip' (Daaku 1970, p. 81). (Bosman stated that it was in 1687 that the Dutch 'subjected the Commanians, after they had in the War lost their King and most of the Grandees of the Kingdom': Bosman, p. 31. But the date of the king's death was 1688: PRO, T70/11, report of 12.5.1688. For confirmation that the king was killed as a result of his agreement with the French, see Hazewinkel 1932, p. 254.) Du Casse's own account does not confirm his visiting Alampi (Lampi/Alampo/Lampaye, just West of the mouth of River Volta), and merely notes that the English, Dutch and Portuguese bought four or five hundred slaves a year there, but he did visit Fida, i.e. Whydah (Roussier 1935, pp. 14, 24, 80). The reference to Du Casse's reputation at La Rochelle may be not from Bloome's letter to J.B. but from Barbot's French contacts. It may have been Barbot who told the English in 1682 that Du Casse was heading the French naval squadron (see note 68 above), and it is possible that Du Casse, although not participating in the expedition, did have some connection with its formation and aims. If so, Du Casse's reputation at La Rochelle may have dated back to the period when Barbot was resident there.

[80] 'My Author' is Bosman, Barbot having inserted in the Supplement (*1732*, pp. 436/12–442/3), on the subject of Commendo, very long extracts from Bosman, pp. 27–41, so cited, with occasional inserts of material from Davenant 1709, pp. 193–4, 198–9, 219–20, 223, not cited. Barbot also introduces very occasional comment, as in the passage cited, and as follows – 'From this account of Sir Dalby Thomas in 1707 may be infer'd, not only that John Kabes was again become a friend to the company's interest, but also, that the English were then at variance next to a war; but what the issue has been, I do not hear as yet' (*1732*, p. 439/7). It is clear from such comment, and from his total reliance on the printed information in Davenant's 1709 work, that, in the latter years of his life, Barbot had no access to oral information on English affairs in Guinea, apart from what he gleaned from interrogating French prisoners.

LETTER 4

Particular description of the territories and town of Mina. History of the establishment of the Portuguese on Gold Coast.

Sir, I do not know whether my last letter will have wearied you, on account both of its length and of the number of barbaric names it contains. You will admit that it was not open to me to make it more agreeable for you to read /p. 11/ and that I varied it as much as I could with little pieces of history, to lighten your spirit. I assure you that the present letter will be somewhat more pleasant to read, since it deals much less with geography than with historical deeds. If I am not mistaken, I have reached the kingdom of Fetu, which is the eastern neighbour of the kingdom of Guaffo or Grand Comendo, the only country in between them being that of Mina, which resembles a kind of republic. Before describing Fetu, I must tell you something about this little territory of Mina.[1] It is of small extent, being only three leagues in circumference; and the only place it has on the coast is the large village of La Mina, which is situated on a tongue of land below the cannon of the castle, St Georges del Mina, three leagues from Little Comendo.[2] The buildings in this village are closely packed together in the manner of the Portuguese; the streets are irregular, tortuous, and dirty during the rains; most of the houses are of masonry, one or two storeys highs.[3] The village is extremely long, containing about 1,200 huts, with so many people in them that one can reckon almost 6,000 men bearing arms, and there are almost six times as many women and children.[4] It is a low-lying village, situated between the sea and River Benja [. . .]⁵ I have sketched with great precision the view of it which I am sending you. It is only accessible from the western side, for it cannot be reached from the sea because of the surf; the entry to the river's mouth is defended by the castle, which lies to the East of the village, at the end of the piece of ground, and which serves it as a rampart.⁶

[illustration no. (60), view of the town of Mina]

This River Benja leads inland, northeastward for several leagues and then NNE; it is 150 paces wide and 10–11 feet deep at its mouth, where it receives vessels of 100–120 tons, which enter it in order to be caulked and careened there.⁷ [. . .]⁸ /p. 12/ Some say that the word Mina means 'free' in the language of the country.⁹ The castle of Mina is situated at the end of the isthmus formed by the River Benja at the place where it enters the sea.¹⁰ [. . ./13–14/. . .]¹¹

But in the end the time was up for this [Portuguese] nation, more barbaric than the barbarians themselves, and it had to yield this rich country involuntarily to Holland; and the Dutch have taken such revenge for the ill-treatment they had received that the Portuguese, who boast that they were the first to set foot there, now no longer have any place there, and all that remains for them is the glory of having populated it with several animals and decorated it with fruits which were formerly unknown there, as you will see below, in my other letters; for it is time to close this one. I am, Sir, Your etc.

NOTES

¹ The reference to Fetu is from Dapper, p. 67/5. The whole passage is omitted in *1732*.

² Barbot passed Mina in 1679 and drew the forts from the sea (*1679*, pp. 290–4); in 1682 he visited Mina (*1732*, pp. 158/8, 320/6); and in 1699 his brother's ship passed by (*1732*, p. 456/4). In the late fifteenth century the African settlement adjacent to the castle of of São Jorge da Mina (at modern Elmina) had been known as the 'village of two parts' and jurisdiction over it was shared by the polities of Eguafo (Komani/Komenda) and Fetu (Efutu); but by the seventeenth century the village had made itself independent.

Cf. *1732*, p. 156/1, which omits the circumference, but adds that the town is 'by the Blacks call'd Oddena', from Bosman, p. 42, and is so near the castle that the latter 'can throw hand-grenadoes into it'.

[3] This appears to be one of the earliest references to two-storey houses on Gold Coast (and perhaps in West Africa), although the 'tall houses' at Cape Coast mentioned by a slightly earlier source may also have had two storeys (Jones 1983a, p. 202). It is perhaps unlikely that all the houses were 'of masonry', but it was elsewhere stated that 'the Houses are built with Rock-Stone, in which it differs from other Places, they being usually only composed of Clay, and Wood' (Bosman, p. 43).

Cf. *1732*, p. 156/2–3, which now states that 'most of the houses are one story high, and some two', and adds material from Bosman, pp. 42–3.

[4] According to Dapper (p. 75/1), the village could muster 2,000 men in wartime, but in 1688 the figure was estimated to be 4,000 (Roussier, p. 10).

Cf. *1732*, p. 156/3, which explains the number of women and children: 'every man generally keeping two, three, or more wives, as is usual in Guinea'. A recent population estimate for other Gold Coast polities of the period uses a multiplier of eight for household size, rather than Barbot's seven (Kea 1982, pp. 139–40) – both are probably exaggerated, since polygyny cannot have been general. For Elmina's population in the seventeenth and eighteenth centuries, see Feinberg 1989, pp. 83–4.

[5] Omission of the remainder of the sentence and another sentence, on the village's occasional flooding and its wall, from Dapper, p. 74/2–3.

Cf. *1732*, p. 156/7, which omits the flooding but enlarges to 'a strong rock-stone wall . . . iron guns, and a large ditch'.

[6] The drawing made in 1679 (*1679*, p. 291, 'NE of you one league'), with the two forts overlooking the town, 'St Jago del Mina' and 'St Georges del Mina', to the left and right respectively, is repeated in *1688* and in *1732*, Plate N (p. 134). But in both the later drawings the cupola on the tower of 'St Jago' disappears and there are various minor changes to the outline of 'St Georges' – these may reflect changes between 1679 and 1682 (Lawrence 1963, pp. 82, 151), or, just as likely, be mere careless copying. Also, in *1732* 'St Jago' is renamed 'Coenraedsburg' (after Bosman, p. 46) and the direction is now 'NNE about 2 miles'. Whether to the NE or NNE, it must be doubted whether the line of vision would produce the view supplied, with the more eastern fort well to the left of the more western one. (In his journal, Barbot referred to the town running between two heights on which stood castles, whereas in fact the town stood below one fort and was separated from the other by the river: *1679*, p. 290; *1732*, p. 156/8.) In the original drawing, a large number of houses are shown along the shore-line; none of those fully visible is double-storeyed, although some of those further back whose roofs are showing may have been; the houses appear to be of European design, being oblong with two-sided sharply inclining roofs.

[7] Barbot modifies Dapper, p. 74/2: 'Some years ago this river used to be 10 or 11 feet deep at its mouth; but now it is . . . almost dry and cannot be

navigated by yachts which draw more than 4 feet'. Today the entrance to Benya Lagoon has a depth of only 3 feet (*Africa pilot* 1967, p. 452). The sentence is omitted in *1732*.

[8] Omission of seven sentences on the government of the town, from Dapper, p. 75/3–4 (derived from the Dutch map of 1629).
Cf. *1732*, p. 156/4–6.

[9] Source unidentified – there is no such word in any Akan language.

[10] Cf. *1732*, p. 157/6, which enlarges – 'Both the north and south sides are encompassed with the rocky strand and the sea, so that it is accessible only on the west side, which is cover'd by the town of Mina'.

[11] Omission of seven paragraphs on the French claim to priority of discovery and on Portuguese ruthlessness, from Villault, pp. 422–44 (whom Barbot names), and Marees, ff. 104v, 106v–107, with one paragraph, on the 'French battery', from Dapper, p. 68/2.
Cf. *1732*, pp. 157/7, 160/4–164/1, much enlarged, with references to Marmol, Faria y Sousa and Vasconcelos as additional sources on the Portuguese period. Barbot still repeats the French claim to priority but introduces it as what the French 'pretend' – perhaps in the English rather than the French sense of the word, since he also refers the reader to his introduction, which was sceptical of the French claim.

LETTER 5

History of the establishment of the Dutch on Gold Coast. The sieges and capture of the Castle S. Georges del Mina, and of the redoubt S. Jago. Description of the castle before and after its surrender. Present state of the castle and of Fort Coenraedsburgh. Remarks on the government of the natives of Mina.

You are right, Sir, in saying that the rule of the Portuguese on Gold Coast was too rigorous to last long; but how will you judge that of the Dutch, who succeeded them? [. . ./pp. 15–16/. . .][1] Having [captured Mina from the Portuguese and] so happily settled a matter which they had always regarded as an obstacle to their designs, the Dutch applied themselves with all their energy /p. 17/ to subjecting the Moors and making themselves sole masters of the trade of this coast. For this purpose they transferred General Van Ypre from Mourée to Mina, the latter appearing more advantageous for their commerce. They repaired what had been spoilt by the war and by the ravages of time, and fortified and embellished this place to a far greater extent than the Portuguese had ever done, as you will easily be able to judge from the drawings I send you, which are more accurate than any which have hitherto appeared.[2]

[illustration no. (61), St Georges del Mina and Conraedsburg, after p. 17] /p. 18/

It was from this base, Sir, that the agents of this company managed to drive the Portuguese out of Axim in 1642 and, some time later, from all the places on the coast where they had establishments.[3] [. . .][4] In order that the natives should not be able to oppose their designs in any way, the Dutch built forts in several places – Boutrou, Sama, Corso, Anemabo, Cormentin and Acra.[5] By this means they have always kept a tight hand over these peoples, even to the point of levying duties on them and on their kings in some of these places, although in others they are still obliged to pay certain monthly rents to the local kings for the land within their states which they occupy.[6]

All this, however, did not in any way subdue the spirits of these peoples, who love change; nor did it prevent them from doing some trade with other [nations] when the occasion presented itself. They [*margin:* the Dutch] even attacked the [other] Europeans, and caused them every vexation imaginable, passing from casual good nature to even cruelty and inhumanity, as I have myself experienced in some places. This indicates clearly how conscious this nation is of its interests, and how high the profits there must be.[7] But no matter what they do, by this rough and barbaric behaviour they will lose part of what they possess. I am too familiar with the inconstancy of these Africans and the taste that other nations have developed for this trade, not to suppose that sooner or later someone will take advantage of their divisions and drive the Dutch from these possessions, just as they robbed the Portuguese of them. I know that the French have some designs on it, all the more so because of their rights as founders. They see themselves at present favoured by the Moors, especially those of Commendo, who, as I have told you, are weary of Dutch rule. Those of Fetu and Sabou have been groaning under the Dutch yoke for several years, and those of Acra are only waiting for a good occasion to declare themselves. I would even venture to say that those of Axim will not let slip the opportunity if it once presents itself.

But all these discontents do not match what the people at Mina itself loudly testify to. They can hardly refrain from action any longer, and if they had the strength proportionate to their desires, the Dutch garrison would already have been massacred and the castle razed to the ground or placed in other hands long ago.[8] This, Sir, is an incontestable truth; and when I made my last voyage to the coast, General Verhoutert had been hiding behind the walls of the castle for ten months, not daring to go out. [*margin:* Governor of the village of the Mina, together with the castle (1682)][9] What is more, they [the Africans] twice tried to storm this place, but their ignorance of how to lay siege and their lack of leaders experienced in warfare rendered all their efforts in vain. Consequently, despite their large numbers, they are forced to have their law laid down by a handful of people. In this last attempt, eighty Moors were killed, but only four Dutchmen. Every morning during that siege, thirty or forty canoes of these Moors came to Comendo (where I was anchored) to inform me of the complaints of their compatriots and beg me to solicit the King [of France] to assist them.[10] I was obliged to promise this, to rid myself of their importunities; and when, on my last passage to Mina [*margin:* 7 April 1682], I had driven them off my back (at the entreaty of the General), they came to trade there in spite of me. Following their refusal, the General, who was of an impetuous temperament, nearly put me under arrest, one day when I was dining with him, because from time to time people came to tell him that there were always canoes around my brigantine, although at my request a canoe armed for battle, with the fiscal on board, had been sent to drive them away; but it was even worse when, after my return on /p. 19/ board, I told some people whom I found there that I had sold the remainder of my cargo to the General. I was obliged to expel them by force, in order to avoid exposing myself to the anger of this man, who, I believe, would quite promptly have forgotten all the affection he had shown me during the two days he had kept me with him, and would doubtless have confiscated the brigantine.[11] I speak of trade with the General, because they [the Dutch] very often conduct trade with the factors of vessels which are on the coast, when they need some article of their cargoes or when they [*sc.* the factors of ships] wish to sell at a cheap rate, as I did on that occasion, in order not to have anything that could tie me any longer to the coast. These purchases are made in public on the company's account, for when they trade privately they take great precautions and employ much secrecy, since heavy fines are imposed, in addition to the confiscation of the article traded and seized. This is the job of

378

the fiscal of Mina or Axim, there being no fiscals in the other places under the Dutch, the fiscals of Mina and Axim going there when necessary.[12] [. . .][13]

The Dutch have altered it very much and made considerable additions, as I have told you; they have erected a third battery facing the river and the sea and covering the two other seaward batteries which I have mentioned. They have also demolished the barracks which separated them from the landward ones and impeded their communication. In their place they have built a covered passageway, which makes it easier to walk round the castle along the parapet.[14] Access to this place is by nature difficult; for besides the fact that when coming from the sea you have to cross a small bar which breaks at the mouth of the River Banja, the only place where you can disembark is near the bridge which leads to Mount Sto Jago. When going towards the castle, you are entirely exposed to its musketry for more than two hundred paces, and finally you come to the draw-bridge, which is defended by eight cannon and a ditch hewn out of the rock, 20 feet deep and 18 wide, with its portcullis, and four brass pedreroes inside the gate, which is fortified by a very good guard-house. This bridge is also commanded by the musketry on top of the parapet of the castle, which makes it extremely difficult to approach.[15] The inside of the castle is almost quadrangular, with fine store-houses made of white stone and brick around the quadrangle, forming a very attractive parade-ground. The General's lodgings are above: they are reached by a large staircase of black and white stone, defended at the top by two small brass cannon and four brass pedreroes, covering the parade-ground. There is another large guard-house at the top of this staircase, and next to it a great hall which serves as an arsenal. From here, by a little bye-passage, one comes to a large covered gallery belonging to the general's lodgings, which consist of several very well-made rooms, all of which look on to the ramparts. The church, on the other side of these rooms, is quite near and is well kept.[16] It is normally served by a Protestant minister, assisted by a clerk or reader (there being none but Protestants in this fort).[17] The infirmary lies along the /p. 20/ ramparts, facing the mouth of the river; there is space for one hundred sick men, and they are well enough attended to. The stores are large and well stocked. You can see there a large tower, on the same side as Sto. Jago, commanding the redoubt; but since defence at this point is of little consequence, no cannon have been placed on it.[18] [. . .][19]

In short, Mina is built in such a manner that it is more like a very fine castle in Europe than a trading store in Guinea. Today it has 48 fine cast-iron cannon and several pedreroes, with a garrison of 100 white men, not counting the blacks in the company's pay (who know very well how to fire a musket).[20] Furthermore, it is always furnished with all sorts of merchandise for commerce and with enough food to support the garrison for a year, as well as with everything necessary for warfare. The merchandise and wares enter and leave through a gate which leads to the sea-shore, where they are hoisted and lowered by cranes.[21]

The weakness of this place is that it is totally commanded by the redoubt situated on Mount Sto Jago.[22] It amazes me that General Coenraed (who had the redoubt constructed and gave it his name, for it is called 'Coenraed's *burg*') did not foresee that if this redoubt were once captured, it would mean the loss of Mina. If the Portuguese had been consulted at the time this place was conquered, they would have said that it had greatly contributed to the loss of Mina. Nevertheless, the Dutch today maintain Mina in a better condition than ever before and do all they can to make it impregnable. It is surrounded by a double stone curtain and supported by a little square tower with a gun-platform. The curtain is flanked by four small square bastions, mounted with twelve iron cannon. Each side is 24 fathoms long. The curtain is only 7 feet high.[23] The lodgings are comfortable, and the redoubt is entered by a drawbridge over a small dry ditch. The northeastern side lies on the slope of the mountain. A sergeant is posted there with twenty men, who are relieved from Mina every 24 hours.[24] It is easy to walk up to Sto Jago from the side of Mina, there being a road cut in the mountain, which is less steep here than elsewhere; but it is much harder to approach it from Commendo or Fetu. The bridge which connects it with Mina has a break in the middle [to form a drawbridge], both for the security of the place and to let ships pass further up the river in order to refit. At each end of the bridge is a large guard-house, and there is a lifting-device in the middle. There are also large sheds for canoes and maritime stores at the end of this bridge leading to Sto Jago, as well as several small tombs of negro kings and princes, decorated with grotesques and ridiculous figures.[25]

The garden of the general is close to the foot of Sto Jago, on the North side. It is not badly laid out, by local standards, and one can see walks lined with orange and lemon trees, palms, Palma Christi, and several other kinds of trees unknown in Europe. It produces a large quantity of vegetables, herbs, roots, salads and grains from Europe, which are sown there.[26] The freshwater River Utry enters the sea one league East of Sto. Jago. It is unnavigable, on account of the rocks in it: even canoes do not go there.[27] [...][28] /p. 21/

The natives of Mina are all either blacks or mulattoes. Of the latter, there are about two hundred families, and they are baptized and call themselves Portuguese.[29] They all engage either in fishing or in commerce, but the former is their commoner occupation. Every morning four to five hundred canoes, with two or three persons in each, go up to two leagues out to sea to fish. It is a pleasure to see these fleets of little vessels.[30] [...][31] They would be the happiest people on the whole coast were it not for the mortification they receive from the Dutch. At first, they used to assemble in the house of the *brafo* (each village having three men with this title) to discuss matters, and then inform the general of the castle, who ratified their decisions if he approved of them. If he disapproved, they debated the matter again in another assembly, until this general was of the same opinion and approved of their intentions; for this was practised particularly with regard to matters which concerned the republic. But since the Dutch nation has claimed the right to make them entirely dependant on its government, and has treated them as slaves, they have conducted their deliberations among themselves without informing anyone.[32] [...][33]

The natives of Mina are in general strong men and good fishermen (a profession more highly esteemed among them than that of a merchant).[34] They pay one fifth of their catch, raw, to the Dutch general, not without bitterness, for this was the origin of the troubles of 1680 and 1681.[35] They also recast crystal and glass, taking considerable pains.[36] They all live in an abominable state of idolatry and profound ignorance. The mulattoes, however, are a little more enlightened, for they are half Christian, being born from the union of Portuguese men with indigenous black women.[37]

The Dutch general has powers of life and death over all those under his jurisdiction, and so he is greatly feared and respected. He often assumes the position of an admiral. The first three years of his employment are /p. 22/ equal in remuneration, but each year after these three the amount [he earns] increases by a third, which means that those who have been there nine or ten years have been extremely rich when they left (since, moreover, they have large perquisites).[38]

381

All the factors of the other Dutch places on the coast tender their accounts to him and receive their clearances from him; and in the storehouses of this castle are deposited all the goods traded by vessels and fortresses between Sierra Leone and Angola.[39] The principal trade done at the castle is in gold; they buy not less than five or six marks of very pure gold daily. The annual trade of the Dutch in gold is said to amount to 5,000 marks; they are also said to trade 8,000 slaves, whom they are obliged to furnish each year to the Spaniards in Curaçao, and they are paid 101 pieces-of-eight for each one, that is, for each *pièce d'Inde*.[40] This does not include the ivory, wax, cloths and other African manufactures, whose value amounts to large sums of money.[41] This seems to suggest that they make incredibly large profits. Yet we have twice seen this same company reduced to large losses, which may be attributed to the great expenses which it is obliged to incur in maintaining these places on the coast, in America and elsewhere, as well as the number of factors who are in them. Today, having better understanding of everything, they have made extensive reforms, which have made things more satisfactory than when they began. The construction of the forts costs a great deal, and in my opinion this company would be able to meet all its expenses in a short time if it had fewer fortresses and people to maintain.[42] This, Sir, is all I can tell you about Mina; and since this subject is now completed, it is also time for me to finish my letter, which is so long that I am weary from writing it. I am, Sir, Your etc.

Additional Passages from *1732*

[p. 157/1, on the Mina canoe-men]

The Mina Blacks drive a great trade along the Gold Coast, and at Wida by sea, and are the fittest and most experienc'd men to manage and paddle the canoes over the bars and breakings [breakers], which render this coast, and that of Wida, so perilous and toilsome to land either men, goods, or provisions; the waves of the ocean rising in great surges, and breaking so violently on the strand, for better than a musket-shot in breadth one after another; which requires a great deal of activity and dexterity to carry canoos through without being sunk, overset, or split to pieces, and often occasions the death of many men, and considerable losses of the goods.[43]

[p. 160/2, on interlopers]

Having been well acquainted with the general, at the time of my being there, we had much discourse about the French and Dutch interlopers; arguing, whether it were not for the common interest of both companies, French and Dutch, that their ships should, as occasion offer'd seize such ships of either nation, as ventur'd to trade on that coast. We had also the advice of his counsel upon that subject, who thought such a treaty ought rather to be made in Europe, between the directors of both companies, than on the coast of Guinea by their agents.

[p. 168/1, on the profitability of the Guinea trade]

On the contrary, it may be concluded unreasonable to expect any thing but loss for any company, as I did make out to the French African company, who, perhaps, are much the better ever since, for driving their trade by shipping only along the Gold Coast, and in other parts of Guinea properly so call'd, without the charge of such settlements ashore. An instance hereof they have in their trade at Senega, Goeree, and Gamboa, where, tho' the profits, at first sight, seem very considerable, yet by reason of the vast charges in maintaining garrisons, and so many servants there, and in the Caribee islands of America, we have seen the stock of that company quite exhausted, and two or three times successively renew'd. And I am apt to believe, the Dutch West-India company have no great cause to boast of their profit in Guinea, notwithstanding their expences as above.

NOTES

[1] Omission of one paragraph, on early Dutch voyages to Guinea, from Marees, ff. 22v, 45v–46, 105; and seven paragraphs, on the Dutch settling at Mori and capturing Mina, from Dapper, pp. 69/3–72/2.

Cf. *1732*, pp. 164/2–166/7, which adds more of the material in Dapper.

[2] Barbot's French text refers throughout to Mina as 'La Mina' (similarly Englishmen on the coast spoke of 'the Mina': Davenant 1709, pp. 198–201). Apart from viewing the forts from the sea in 1679, and a little information obtained previously from the Dutch commander at Axim, all of Barbot's original, detailed and first-hand information on Mina must have been obtained when he spent two days in the main fort in 1682, as a guest of the

commander. For the first of his two drawings of the forts, see Letter 2/4, p. 11 and note 6, above. The present drawing, not in *1679* but printed as a double page in *1732*, Plate 8 (p. 156), presumably derived from the 1682 visit, although some of the details may have been copied from the earlier drawing. The printed version has minor changes in the main fort (e.g. the smoke from a salute omitted, two instead of three buttresses on an outer wall, an interior building at a different angle), probably introduced by the engraver. The view is this time more satisfactory, being from more or less due East (no viewpoint is stated), thus showing the two forts on opposite sides of the creek, with Conraadsburg higher than the main fort. (The printed version, however, widens the gap between them somewhat, making the higher fort's position less commanding). There were many earlier drawings of both forts (see Lawrence 1963, pp. 82, 97, 110–152, 379 – the comments on the significance of Barbot's drawings not entirely sound – and plates 7–11; also present-day views, plates 2–4, 14–36). But Barbot was almost certainly comparing his later drawing with two illustrations in Dapper, one showing Mina in Portuguese times, the other showing two forts and therefore to be dated to the 1660s (Dapper, between pp. 67–8). Although Barbot certainly up-dated the forts, his viewpoint is fairly close to that of the second Dapper illustration; his drawing has some resemblances to the Dapper illustration and may well have been inspired by it. For Nikolaas Van Yperen, who commanded at Mina 1637–1639, see Dapper, p. 69/3; Ratelband 1953, pp. xlix, li, lxviii; Jones 1983a, p. 105.

[3] Cf. *1732*, p. 166/6, which omits the second half of this sentence. For the conquest of Axim, see Letter 2/3, p. 4 and note 10, above.

[4] Omission of four sentences on how the Dutch established their authority, from Villault, pp. 444–5.
Cf. *1732*, p. 166/8.

[5] This was untrue of Corso (Cape Coast), where the Dutch had merely taken over the Swedish fort for two brief periods (in 1659 and 1663–4). At Kormantin they had captured an English fort in 1665; and at Shama they had bombarded the Portuguese fort in 1640 and then rebuilt it.
Cf. *1732*, p. 167/1, which adds that – 'pretending to the Blacks, they did it to protect and defend them against the outrages and insults of their neighbouring enemies of the inland country, who used often to attack them'.

[6] Cf. *1732*, p. 167/2, which is more specific, being loosely related to Bosman, pp. 55, 166–75 – 'laid duties on their fishery at Axim, Mina, and Mouree', 'proceeded to lord it over them so absolutely, as to take cognizance of all civil and criminal causes, and to assume the power of life and death over them'.

[7] The idea that the profits of the Dutch must be enormous if they made such an effort to exclude competition derives from Villault, p. 445.

Cf. *1732*, p. 167/3, a summary.

[8] For French designs on Elmina in the 1680s, see Roussier 1935, pp. 39–41, 80–1; and for Portuguese designs in the early 1670s, see Brásio 1982, pp. 153–9.

Cf. *1732*, p. 167/4, which summarizes the section in one sentence, omitting any reference to the French, Accra or Axim.

[9] Daniel Verhoutert was Director-General from 1679 to 1682. Barbot had also met him in January 1679, when he was still in charge of Axim (*1679*, pp. 278–9).

[10] Of course 'every morning during the siege' means 'every morning my ship was in the vicinity during the period of the siege' – very few mornings.

Cf. *1732*, p. 167/5–6, which adds: 'all the Blacks coming to complain of the hardships the Dutch put upon their countrymen; keeping some of them for a long time in the bilboes, within the castle, exposed stark naked to the scorching heat of the sun in the day, and to the cold dews in the night. I myself saw three of them in that condition on the land-batteries, show'd me by the then Dutch general; who told me, he had kept them so above nine months, as a punishment for their boldness and treachery, as having been concern'd in the conspiracy of the Blacks of Mina at that time, to surprise the castle of St George, and to destroy it by fire, to which purpose they had actually gather'd a great number of the Mina men; but the intended design, being by him prevented, many of them were fled from the town to other places on the coast, after firing their houses'.

[11] Cf. *1732*, p. 167/7, which tells the same story more clearly. 'Being one morning at breakfast with the general, with whom I was pretty familiar, as being my old acquaintance; he espied through the gallery window several canoos of Mina, which were going aboard my sloop in the road to trade: whereupon he abruptly in a passion said, he would detain me, and seize the sloop, and had effectually done it, but that I desired him to send aboard and inquire, whether I had not left positive orders with the master, to sell nothing to the Blacks; besides, that the fiscal was actually in the sloop, to observe what passed. For his further satisfaction, I sold him the remaining part of the cargo that was in the sloop, for about ten marks of gold; and when I returned aboard, I had much ado to get rid of the Blacks, who were all much dissatisfied that I had sold those goods to the general.' A similar incident occurred in 1684, when the chief factor at Elmina visited a French ship to buy gunpowder, but was told that 'the gunpowder had been bought in such great quantities by a continuous stream of people coming in canoes that the entire stock of the French ship as well as that of a Zeeland interloper also anchored there had been sold' (Van Dantzig 1978, p. 43 – see also p. 47).

[12] A former chief factor at Elmina stated in 1682 that French and

Portuguese vessels sometimes sent boats ashore in front of the castle and conducted trade with people living nearby (Jones 1985, p. 22).

Cf. *1732*, p. 167/8, which replaces this section with an entirely new passage: 'The hard usage of the Mina Blacks, obliges many of them to fly from thence to other parts of the coast, which much lessens the trade of the Dutch; as does the great resort of other European ships on that coast; for I can remember, that some years there have been above fifty trading there, all at one time. Another detriment is occasion'd to them by the many settlements made on that coast, within these fifty years last past; and the Dutch general, at Mina, admits of no Blacks to buy goods, unless they can purchase the value of six marks of gold together.'

[13] Omission of one paragraph describing the castle, derived from Dapper, pp. 68/4–5. Barbot's only addition is the statement that the castle was made of hard brown freestone – 'dark brown' in *1732*, p. 158/2, which modifies this paragraph to take account of Bosman, p. 42.

[14] The later sentences are probably derived from Dapper, p. 74/1, although Dapper says that the barracks were 'made five foot shorter at the rear', not 'demolished'. This passage is omitted in *1732*.

[15] In the early 1640s there were nine brass cannon (Jones 1983a, p. 129). A 'pedrero' (Spanish *pedrero*), in English usually 'patterero', was a light gun or mortar, normally used for salutes.

Cf. *1732*, pp. 157/5–6, 158/4, which omits the reference to the musketry, and adds that the fort is named after St George because the Portuguese landed on his day, and that the eight cannon stood on a redoubt (i.e. the West bastion: see Lawrence 1963, p. 146).

[16] Cf. *1732*, p. 158/7–8, which calls the parade-ground the 'place of arms', and adds that the great hall was 'full of small arms of several sorts' and that the covered gallery was 'all wainscoted, at each end of which there are large glass windows'. Earlier in the century 'the great hall ... was hung with pikes, muskets and similar weapons, and was more like an arsenal than a church' (Jones 1983a, p. 130).

[17] Cf. *1732*, p. 158/8, which substitutes for this sentence – 'and well fitted for divine service; at which I was present on Easter-day 1682 [i.e. 16 April N.S.]'; and adds a sentence from Bosman, p. 99.

[18] Cf. *1732*, p. 158/9–10, which adds – 'The counting-houses, particularly, are large, finely fitted for the factors and accountants, book-keepers and servants, being in all about sixty persons'; but the three sentences that follow are from Dapper, p. 68/2, 4.

[19] Omission of seven sentences on the water supply, from Dapper, p. 69/2.

Cf. *1732*, p. 158/5, which makes several changes, derived from Bosman, p. 42.

[20] The information on cannon may date from 1679, when Barbot was told by Verhoutert that there were 48 cannon, mostly cast-iron, on the two forts (*1679*, p. 291). In the early 1690s a Danish official reckoned that the major fort had 50 large cannon and 150 common soldiers (Tilleman 1697, pp. 65–6).

Cf. *1732*, p. 158/1–3, 6, 12, which adds – 'There is room . . . for a garrison of two hundred men, and several officers', from Bosman, p. 42.

[21] It was noted some decades earlier that goods were 'brought through a water-gate and hoisted up' (Dapper, p. 69/2).

Cf. *1732*, p. 158/11, the first sentence omitted.

[22] Cf. *1732*, p. 159/3, which adds, from Dapper, p. 68/5 – 'so named by the Portugueses, from a little chapel they had built on it, dedicated to St James'. This chapel was later demolished by the Portuguese themselves, but in 1637 the Dutch captured São Jorge da Mina by bombarding it from St Jago (Santiago) Hill. To prevent anyone following their example, they built a redoubt on the hill, which in the 1660s was turned into a full fort. Unlike other Gold Coast forts, its purpose was solely military.

[23] It is somewhat unlikely that Barbot would have been allowed to visit Conraadsburg: in the early 1690s no foreigners were allowed to go there (Tilleman 1697, p. 16).

Cf. *1732*, p. 159/3–4, which omits the reference to Coenraed, and the references to the double curtain, gun-platform, bastions, drawbridge and ditch, substituting – 'a beautiful quadrangle, strengthen'd with four good batteries, the walls twelve feet high, and strong, having four lesser square batteries, mounted with twelve guns' – this from Bosman, p. 46, except for the height and the number of guns.

[24] A Dutchman who had been Director-General at Elmina at the time of Barbot's first voyage wrote at the end of 1679 that Conraadsburg was manned by a sergeant and four soldiers who spent their time 'drinking and whoring' (ARA, Abramsz 23.11.1679). A Brandenburger who visited the coast in 1682, 3, although not Elmina, stated that the fort was in the charge of 'an ensign who has about twenty men under him' (Jones 1985, pp. 54–5).

Cf. *1732*, p. 159/4, which gives the number of men as 'five and twenty men under an ensign . . . in peaceable times'. Bosman, who should have known, was vaguer – 'an Ensign . . . with a good Garrison' (Bosman, p. 47).

[25] Cf. *1732*, p. 159/5–6, which is slightly clearer – ' . . .a large canoo-house, to preserve them from the weather; and a store-house built near it, for the conveniency of ship-carpenters . . . several tombs or little monuments, with abundance of puppets and antick ridiculous figures, which, as I was told, are of some kings, and other notable persons buried there, all adorn'd with imagery and other baubles'. The 'grotesques' were funerary terracotta figures (see Letter 2/28, note 23, below).

[26] Cf. *1732*, p. 159/7–8, which adds an extra detail ('sweet and sour oranges') and a sentence on the gardens, both from Bosman, p. 289, as well as one sentence not in Bosman – 'In the midst of the garden is a large, round, open, and curious summer-house, with a cupola-roof, several steps leading up to it' – this possibly confuses Elmina with Frederiksborg: see Letter 2/6, p. 26, below. It also adds material on Benya Creek, from Bosman, p. 46.

[27] From Dapper, p. 74/4, which allows that it can be navigated also by small ships. The river is Sweet River or River Kakum, which enters the sea near Iture (hence 'Utry'), half-way between Elmina and Cape Coast. Omitted in *1732*.

[28] Omission of three paragraphs, mainly from Dapper, p. 74/5–6, describing how water was fetched from 'Utry River' (also in Villault, p. 449), and on the infertility of the area near Elmina, only the first retained in *1732*, p. 159/1–2. Also omitted is a repetition of Barbot's earlier statement about the population of the village (see Letter 2/4, p. 11 above).

[29] Derived from Dapper, pp. 75/1, 76/1, which refers to 200 people, not families.

[30] In the 1620s the people of Mina were reported to be 'skilful fishermen, greatly outnumbering all their neighbours both in canoes and in people' (1629 map).

Cf. *1732*, p. 156/10, which changes the number of canoes ('seven or eight hundred') and oarsmen ('some two, some three, some four'), adding that they used 'hooks and lines'. It also adds: 'When the fishing is over, and they never fail in the summer season to catch abundance of sundry sorts of good fish, they return to shore about noon, when the fresh sea-gale begins to blow, and carry the fish to market, after having paid the fifth part thereof to the Dutch officers'. Apart from the last clause, this represents material in Letter 2/20, pp. 78–9, below, including an illustration of fishing off Mina (for which see note 9 of that Letter). For material on the canoes, see the Additional Passages.

[31] Omission of two sentences on the early history of the area, from Dapper, p. 74/3.

Cf. *1732*, p. 156/4.

[32] As described by Dapper, pp. 75/3, except that this source stated that if the general disapproved of a decision, the people changed it to suit his wishes. It seems to be incorrect that each village had three men with the title of *brafo* (Akan/Twi, *o-bráfó*). But the exact significance of the title requires further investigation, its political and military implications having apparently varied from place to place and over time (see Kea 1982, pp. 127, 144–5; Jones 1983a, pp. 187, 298; McCaskie 1990, pp. 135–8).

Cf. *1732*, p. 156/5–6, which adds that this 'also was the method they were liable to, when under the protection of the Portugueses', and enlarges on the growing hostility between the Mina people and the Dutch, 'and by degrees, things are come to such extremities between both parties, as I shall hereafter mention . . .'.

[33] Omission of one paragraph and part of a second, on political procedures, from Dapper, p. 75/4. Omitted in *1732*.

[34] Cf. *1732*, p. 156/9, which substitutes: 'The Blacks of Mina are commonly handsome, lusty, and strong men, of a martial courage, and the most civilized of all the gold coast, by the long correspondence they have constantly had to this time with the Europeans'.

[35] The duty on fish was an imposition of African origin, taken over by the Portuguese and then the Dutch: other Europeans had to pay for all the fish they consumed (Jones 1983a, p. 83, n. 217; Jones 1985, p. 88).

Cf. *1732*, p. 156/10, which omits the reference to 1680–81.

[36] Derived from Dapper, p. 75/5 (in turn from the 1629 map and Marees, f. 26), but Barbot uses the term 'recast', which may be significant, since the earlier sources had only stated that European beads (Venetian pipe-beads) were broken and polished before being resold. It is not known when Elmina craftsmen began to grind European beads in order to obtain powdered glass for new beads, to be polished after baking (as still produced in Ghana today). For a study of beads excavated at Elmina, see DeCorse 1989.

Cf. *1732*, p. 157/3, ('melting all sorts of glass, as to give it any shape or figure they fancy').

[37] By this time (half a century after the Dutch conquest of Elmina) there were probably as many Afro-Dutch as Afro-Portuguese. Dutch officials were in fact often concerned lest mulattoes should 'relapse into paganism' (e.g. Van Dantzig 1978, p. 176).

Cf. *1732*, p. 157/4, which elaborates as follows: 'even these are very indifferent new Christians, as they call themselves, their religion being mix'd with much Pagan superstition. The great concern of the Dutch on this coast, as well as of all other Europeans, settled or trading there, is the gold, and not the welfare of those souls: for by their leud loose lives, many who live among these poor wretches rather harden them in their wickedness, than turn them from it. I beg leave to mention this with sorrow, to the dishonour of christianity ! tho' on the other hand it must be own'd, that the nature of these Blacks in general is such, that it is very difficult for well-disposed Christians to convert them, as experience has sufficiently well shown.' Barbot is less dismissive of the mulattoes' Christianity than is Bosman, p. 141.

[38] Cf. *1732*, pp. 156/10, 159/9–160/1, which adds material from Bosman, pp. 96–101, 117. For Barbot's discussion with the governor on a policy towards interlopers, see the Additional Passages.

[39] Cf. *1732*, pp. 159/9–160/3, which expands considerably, following Bosman, pp. 91–2.

[40] The Spanish term *pieza de Indias* and its equivalents in other languages were used in treaties and agreements relating to the Atlantic slave trade to denote a healthy male slave, in prime life and capacity (therefore not originating from certain varying regions of Africa), other slaves being reckoned as fractions of a *pieza de Indias*. For Barbot's own definition of the term, see *1732*, p. 571/2.

[41] Cf. *1732*, p. 167/9–10, which substitutes for this section: 'I was told there, by some of the chief factors, that formerly they used to export thence above three thousand marks of gold yearly, and now, not above two thousand, when the trade is at the best. They also used to export near eight thousand slaves from the whole coast, beginning at Sierra Leona, down to Angola, most of which they delivered at Curassau, whence the Spaniards had them at an hundred and one pieces of eight per head; besides vast quantities of elephants teeth, wax, Guinea-pepper, red-wood, cloths and other goods of the country.' Another Frenchman stated in 1688 that the Dutch at Elmina had formerly bought 2,500 marks of gold a year, but at that date bought only 1,000 marks (Roussier 1935, p. 11). Just over a decade later, Bosman estimated the annual export of gold from Elmina at 1,500 marks (Bosman, pp. 88–90) – this may well have influenced Barbot's figure. For modern discussion of this question, see Postma 1973, pp. 59–60; Garrard 1980, pp. 155–7; Feinberg 1989, pp. 53–8.

[42] Although Barbot's opinion that forts on Gold Coast were unnecessary no doubt owed something to the fact that other nations had them while the French had none, it must also represent something of a change of view since 1682, when he participated in the French attempt to establish a land base on the coast.

Cf. *1732*, p. 167/11, which mentions other expenses: 'the vast expence of so many wars successively against the natives and others; bribing the Black kings, and paying large sums for auxiliaries and spies; presents, tolls, customs'. For Barbot's further comment on the cost of maintaining shore bases in Guinea, see the Additional Passage, where he now states that on return to France in 1682 he had advised against a land base – perhaps a dubious recollection.

[43] This enlarges on a briefer reference to the Mina canoe-men in Letter 2/20, p. 84, below. In 1694 an Englishman visiting Whydah reported 'a croom of negroes, which call themselves Mine-men and assist the Dutch ships that come here in their business' – presumably a settlement of canoe-men (Phillips 1732, p. 228). Barbot also adds material on gold-working (*1732*, p. 157/2), which he here relates to Elmina, but which is part of more general discussions in Letter 2/16, p. 61 (and see notes 12–13) and Letter 2/20, p. 82 (and see note 35), below.

LETTER 6

Description of the kingdom of Fetu, of the town and the castle of Corso belonging to the English, and of the castle of Manfrou belonging to the Danes.

If I took as long, Sir, in describing each village and territory of Gold Coast as I have done in dealing with Mina I should take up a great deal of time and write a fat volume, and your patience would certainly be exhausted. But besides the fact that I seek to be as brief as I can in what I write, what I have to tell you from now on will not provide me with as much material, either because I know less about it or because, since the castle of Mina is the most important locality [on Gold Coast], I saw myself obliged to discuss it in more detail. In this letter I propose to describe the kingdom of Fetu and not to take as long as I have done with the preceding descriptions. [. . .][1]

[Cape Coast]

There are fully 500 huts arranged in streets and alleys, all forming a large village under the command of a single *brafo*, with lieutenants under him.[2] Here is a view of it from the sea, and of the English fort which dominates it at will. This fort or /p. 23/ castle has been built by the English since the last war of 1666. I have told you elsewhere that the Dutch formerly had quite a large fort there, which they had bought from the factor of a man called Carolof, who had had it built when he was in the service of the Danish company.[3] [. . .][4]

[illustration no. (62), 'Cabo Corso Castel', on p. 25]†

Today they call it Cabo Corso Castle. It looks very fine from the sea. Its shape is quadrangular.[5] It is built of locally baked brick and black stone, and is situated on a point which juts out to SSE so that it is only connected with the mainland on its northern side.[6] The rocks in the sea surrounding it make it almost inaccessible, because the sea breaks furiously on them. But it is fairly easy to disembark there in a little bay formed by the rocks on the East side, where longboats enter and are beached on the sand.[7] This, however, does not pose any threat to the castle, which commands this landing place with 16 large 18-pounder iron cannon and with the small-arms of the garrison, these overlooking the bay from the top of walls under which it is necessary to pass to reach the gate of the castle.[8] This gate faces West, and its only strength is its advantageous situation, for it has neither a drawbridge nor a moat, and not even a portcullis. The curtains are flanked by two large towers towards the sea and two demi-bastions towards the land.[9] The walls are high and thick. The lodgings inside the castle are very comfortable and spacious. The barracks look handsome, each having an outdoor balustrade, resembling a continuous balcony. The old apartments are daily being pulled down.[10] The most noteworthy item is the slave-house, which lies below ground. It consists of large vaulted cellars, divided into several apartments which can easily hold a thousand slaves. This slave-house is cut into the rock, beneath the parade-ground, which is large and spacious.[11] There is also a very fine cistern in the castle, capable of holding a hundred tuns of water.[12] In the castle I counted 38 fine pieces of iron cannon and a garrison of 60 white men, excluding the blacks of the country in the company's pay, whose number is far larger.[13] This garrison is clothed in red and maintained at the expense of the Royal Company of London.[14] The only fault of the place is that from all sides except the sea one can look over the SE-facing battery and see everywhere inside the castle. This battery is totally commanded by the Danish fort at Manfrou, which is on a mountain only an 8-pounder cannon-shot away. This consideration makes the English very circumspect towards that northern nation, and they have devoted all their efforts to induce the Danes to cede this fort by mutual agreement; but this has always been in vain. [*margin:* At last the English became masters of Frederixborgh in 168[blank]][15] The castle of Corso and the village are also commanded by three hills lying NW, North and NE of it. These would make it easy for anyone in collusion with the Moors of Fetu to conquer the castle. But the English handle them too well to lose their friendship: on the contrary, this friendship grows daily, because of the presents the English give them and the tribute which they pay punctually each month to the king of /p. 24/ Fetu for the right to keep the castle. Thus in my opinion it would not be as easy to take it from them as it would be to take the castle of Mina [from the Dutch], whose garrison is always at odds with the natives.[16]

The agent of the Royal Company resides at Cabo Corso, where he receives the accounts of the factors of Anamabou, Acra and Ardra, as well as those of their dependent lodges. The trade the English conduct (both at Corso and elsewhere) is in gold, slaves, ivory and

33. The English fort, Cape Corso Castle, at Cape Coast, on Gold Coast, 1679

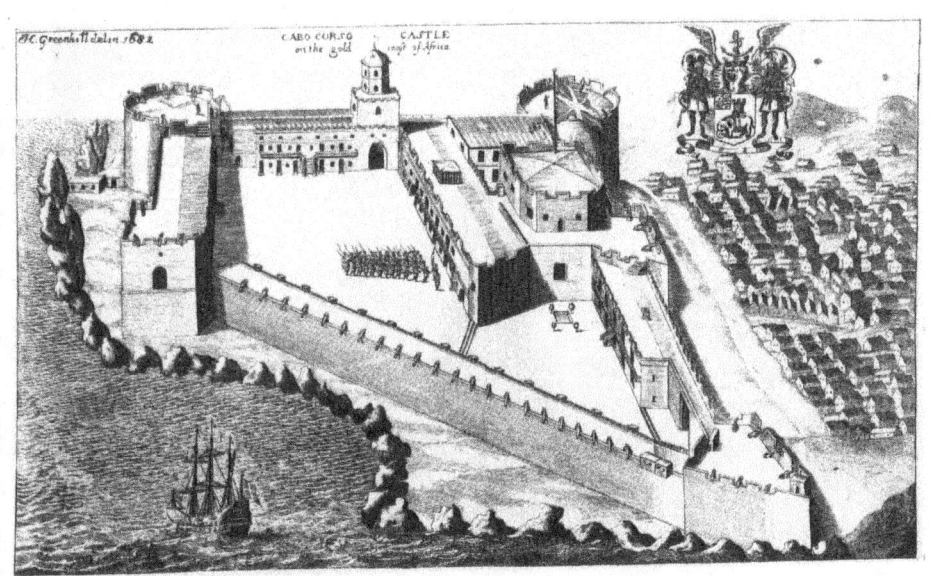

34. Cape Corso Castle, 1682, by Henry Greenhill, engraving of c. ?1690

35. The Danish fort, Fort Frederiksborg, at Cape Coast, 1679

wax. With these the company makes a great profit, not having as heavy expenses to meet as the Dutch.[17]

This [English] nation is always jealous of the honour of its flag, as it demonstrates here and everywhere else where it rules. The cannon alone is not a sufficient salute: they want ships to lower the fore topsail. I have never been so surprised as when, on my latter voyage, I saw the castle, having returned the salute I had made it with five guns, fire at me with ball while I was anchoring in the roadstead, on account of [ours] being a vessel of the King of France. Furthermore, a little vessel of the R[oyal]. Company also fired with ball into my cutwater, apparently for the same reason. I had the moderation to wait till the following day before seeing Agent Greenhill and asking what the reason was. He swore to me that he had express orders from the king and from the company to act thus towards all those who did not salute with the topsail as well as with cannon, and that he did not exempt even his own nation from this. As for the little vessel, he himself did not know why it had taken this step. He had the master of the vessel put in irons and ordered the captain to salute me with three guns the following morning, to make amends. I have thought it necessary to tell you this little story in order that you may remember it if you ever go to that country.[18]

Additional Passages from *1732*

[p. 170/7–8, on the English and other Europeans in Guinea, their vices and health]

The agent general of the English company, who bears the title of general of Guinea from Sierra Leona to Angola, usually resides at Castle-coast, or Corso, where he keeps the great stores and the accounts of the other forts and settlements on that coast; the trade whereof consists in gold, elephants teeth, slaves, wax, red-wood, Guinea cloths, etc. which might turn to considerable profit, were it well and justly managed. But I am apt to believe, want of virtue enough to withstand the temptations of opportunity and importunity of bad example, induces many of the company's servants to make no scruple of breaking the oath they take, not to trade for themselves directly or indirectly any way whatsoever; whereof many instances may be given. This, together with the vast number of interlopers and other foreign ships resorting to the coast every year, deprives the company of the best share of the commerce.

How to remedy it, I leave to the directors of the said company. Certain it is, that few who can live well at home, will venture to repair to the Guinea coast, to mend their circumstances, unless incouraged by large salaries, and that a smaller number of factors [should] be imploy'd, as I have often represented it to the directors of the Royal African company in France; whose trade daily decays, thro' the ill management of their servants in Guinea, who to their own vices add those of the people among whom they live and converse. And they need not go so far to observe the faults of those people to have matter of railing when they come home, considering, that nothing is baser, as Seneca writes, lib.1. *De moribus*, than to object that to another which may be retorted upon one's self. And St Augustin's *Confession*, chap. 10. says, a curious sort of people, to pry into other men's lives, and slothful to mend their own. For none of us Europeans ever go to Guinea, but we are apt at our return to make horrid pictures of the manners and vices of the Blacks.

This must be said, once for all, that the generality of those who look for such imployments, are necessitous persons, who cannot live at home; and perhaps most of them of a temper to improve all opportunities of mending their worldly circumstances, without much regard to the principles of Christianity. For without reflecting on particular persons, it may be said, that what I have here asserted, is sufficiently made out by the irregularity of their lives in those parts; and particularly as to lewdness with women and excess of drinking, especially punch. And it is almost incredible how many shorten their days by such debauchery, and above all, the soldiers and workmen, as well as by ill diet and water, the want of proper remedies and able physicians; and the passing in canoos from one place to another, which has a danger in itself, besides that of the sea. The fondness of their beloved liquor punch, is so great, even among the officers and factors, that, whatsoever comes of it, there must be a bowl upon all occasions, which causes the death of many of them; and consequently the garrison becomes very weak, the survivors looking poor and thin, not only [in the case] of the soldiers, but of the officers and factors, whose countenances are shrivel'd and dismal, through ill diet and worse government; either their stomach or their money falling short, when they have lived there some time. And should we form a judgement of the state of health in Guinea by the number of

English that die there, that country should have a more unhealth-
ful name in England than in France. I am also apt to believe, that
the excessive eating of flesh so natural to the English, is very
prejudicial to them in those parts; as I have often represented to
some of the principal men at cape Corso castle, giving them
directions how to live more regularly, which is certainly more
agreeable to that intemperate unhealthy climate; viz. to abstain
from the black women, to drink moderately, especially brandy,
rum, and punch; and avoid sleeping in the open air at night, as
many when heated with debauchery, do, having nothing on but a
shirt, thinking thus to cool, but, on the contrary, they murder
themselves; for nothing is more pernicious to the constitution of
Europeans, than to lie in the open air, as I have been sufficiently
convinc'd by experience. Therefore I did not only take care to
avoid lying so exposed, but always kept to my bed, as warm as I
could well bear it; and both night and day wore a dress'd hare's
skin next to my bare stomach, for above two years together, which
kept it in good disposition, and help'd digestion very much; tho' I
must own it was sometimes, and especially in the excessive hot
nights, very troublesome, and occasion'd much sweating.[19]

[p. 171/2, on the gardens of the fort]

The gardens belonging to the agent and other officers of the castle,
are at some distance from it, towards the strand, and full of orange
and lemon-trees; but have very few plants and herbs. In the midst
of them is a square summer-house for their diversion. Another
place, much like a garden, but all planted with coco-trees, is the
common burying-place for the garrison and officers.[20]

[p. 172/3–7, on markets, a court, and the export trade]

Besides the daily market I have mention'd to be kept at the town
of Corso, there is a very considerable one at Abramboe, a large
town about twenty-seven miles northward from cape Corso; where
by appointment of the king of Fetu, at a certain time of the year,
is a rendezvous from all parts of his country, for public dancing,
and it is call'd the dancing season, and lasts eight days. An
incredible number of people repair to it from all parts, and spend
all the day, and most of the night, in that toilsome diversion. / At
the same time are decided all suits and controversies, which could
not be determin'd by the inferior justices, in their several districts.

This supreme court is composed of the king of Fetu, his Dey, or prime minister, the Geroffo and the Braffo, with two English factors of cape Corso castle. It is the agent's prerogative to send those agents to that court, and each of them is to have as many suits of clothes as he stays there days, to appear every day in a different suit, which puts the company to three hundred pounds charges yearly. / Aquaffou village is very large, and lies west from cape Corso, being a market where the Blacks buy slaves to be kill'd and bury'd, at the funerals of their kings.[21]

At my first voyage to cape Corso, I had a pretty brisk trade for slaves and gold; but at my return thither three years after, I found a great alteration; the French brandy, whereof I had always a good quantity aboard, being much less demanded, by reason a great quantity of spirits and rum had been brought on that coast by many English trading ships, then on the coast, which oblig'd all to sell cheaply. / There is generally good plenty of gold, but much of it is not pure, especially the Cracra and Feitizo gold.

[pp. 194/9–195/4, on European vices and health, again]

These things consider'd, it is no wonder that the coast of Guinea should yearly consume so many Europeans living ashore; especially if we consider their way of living, being utterly unprovided of what should comfort and nourish them; having wretched medicines, unskilful surgeons, and no support of nourishing diet and restoratives. The common sort at best, can get nothing but fish, and some dry lean hens; and were they able to pay for better, it is not to be had; for all the oxen, cows, sheep and poultry, are lean, tough, and dry; nothing being good but spoon-meats. As for the chief officers, they are commonly pretty well supported with better food; as either having it sent by their friends in Europe, or buying it of European ships that trade on the coast, or else receiving presents of good poultry, salt meat, French and Madera wine, neats tongues, gammons, all sorts of pickles, preserves, fruit, sweet oil, fine flower, choice brandy, etc. with good fresh medicines and restoratives. Besides, they are not oblig'd to be expos'd to all sorts of weather, either to the scorching air of the day, or cold evening-dew; nor to hard labour, or going from one place to another in canoos; or, which is worse, passing over bars, and the breaking of the sea, wherein, as I have said before, there is a hazard besides that of drowning; or if they have occasion to do this sometimes, they are presently shifted and comforted with restoratives: whereas the common sort, especially canoo men, labourers and soldiers, are expos'd to all sorts of fatigues and hardships upon every command, without those comforts and supports which officers have. Besides all this, they are generally men of no education or principles, void of foresight, careless, prodigal, addicted to strong liquors, as palm-wine, brandy and punch, which they will drink to excess, and then lie down on the bare ground in the open air, at the cool of the evening, without any other covering but a single shirt; nay some, and perhaps no small number, are over fond of the black women, whose natural hot and leud temper soon wastes their bodies, and consumes that little substance they have: tho' such prostitutes are to be had at a very inconsiderable rate, yet having thus spent their poor allowance, those wretched men cannot afford to buy themselves convenient sustenance, but are forced to feed on bread, oil, and salt, or, at best, to feast upon a little fish. Thus 'tis not to be admir'd that they fall into several distempers, daily exposing their lives to danger, very many being carry'd off thro' these excesses, in a very deplorable condition, by fevers, fluxes, cholicks, consumptions, asthma's, small-pox, coughs, and sometimes worms and dropsies: of all which diseases I shall say more in another place.

But it is not only the inferior sort who are guilty of this irregular course of life; there are too many of the officers and heads, who, the greater their salaries and profits are, the more eager they are to spend them extravagantly, in excessive drinking, and other vices, never minding to keep something by them to procure fresh provisions at all times for their support. Nay, some of them run so deep in debt, to gratify their disorderly appetites, that their pay is stopped, or made over by bond, before it becomes due; so that several, who do not die there, return home as empty in the purse as they first went out: and it very seldome happens that any make their fortune, except the commanders in chief of forts, who have the best opportunity of laying up; or those who make no account of the solemn oaths they have taken, not to trade for their own proper account, directly or indirectly; which oath is generally administer'd to every person employ'd by any of the African companies in Europe. Yet many of them openly profess they went not thither for bare wages; and I fear the number of such is not small in every nation.

How unwholesome soever the Gold Coast is, the Europeans who do not reside ashore, but are constantly aboard the ships, are nothing near so liable to the malignity of the corrupted and infectious air, provided they be any thing cautious and careful of themselves; and especially if they avoid the frequent opportunities which offer ashore, of hard drinking, and having to do with black women; and if they take heed to shift themselves often aboard, after being wet, or having work'd hard in the hold of the ship: to which purpose most of them wear only a pair of drawers, or thin breeches, leaving the rest of their bodies quite naked. / The sea-breeze, during the day, is a great refreshment to them, notwithstanding the scorching heat then reigning; and the ships generally riding two or three English miles from the shore, the stench of the town, and the mist of the night, is seldom carry'd so far from the land, by the north wind which then blows. Besides, they are much better fed aboard than the common people are ashore.

The natives are seldom troubled with any distempers, because being born in that unhealthy air, and bred up in sloth, and that stench, those things little affect them; and when the tornadoes happen, which are attended with great claps of thunder, flashes of lightening, and violent rain, by them very much dreaded; they keep very close within doors, and under shelter, if possible, being sensible of the dangerous effects on human bodies: or if they cannot avoid being exposed, their skins are so suppled by daily anointing with palm-oil, that the weather can make but little impression on them, the pores being stopped, and not so open as in white men.[22]

[p. 445/4, on a French attack in 1703]

Another inconveniency has appeared at Cabo Corso castle, that in the year 1703, three large ships of the French company of the Assiento, of about fifty guns a-piece, and one of them a Dutch man of war prize, call'd the Medenblick, being trading about cape Corso, and the Blacks not daring to go aboard of them with slaves or gold, the French drew their ships in a line, at about half cannon-shot from the castle, and anchoring there very good, mud and sand, did so warmly batter the castle from that side, notwithstanding its hot firing from the water-battery and turrets, that in less than an hour's time the garrison was forc'd to keep close shelter'd, not daring to appear any longer, to play their cannon.

The commander found himself oblig'd to hang out a white flag for a truce; and to grant to the Blacks of the town, and all others about, to traffick freely with the French, who got thereby a good number of slaves and gold, for their merchandize.[23]

[Fort Frederiksborg]

A quarter of an hour's walk from Corso lies Manfrou, a village to the East of Corso, situated below the cannon of the Danish fort, to the East and West of the hill on which it is built. The advantageous situation of this place makes a stay there quite agreeable and more temperate than at Corso.[24] But there is nothing much to the fort apart from its position, for otherwise it is not really a military strongpoint, having no regular fortifications, but only a confused mass of corners and triangular curtains, and built of such weak material that I was surprised they can resist the recoil of cannon and the heavy rains. You can see three small bastions: the one which is round (in the Moorish manner) faces South towards the roadstead; another faces West, towards Cabo Corso; and the third faces East, towards Fort Mourée or Nassau.[25] I enclose a view of it with my letter, together with the view of the castle at Corso, which I forgot to put in the right place.

[illustration no. (63), 'Frederick-burgh', on p. 25][26]†

The Danes built this fort (which they call Fredericxburg, after the late King of Denmark) with the consent and aid of the Moors of Fetu.[27] [. . .][28] The Danes had a lodge NE of the village of Corso or Igwa, where they kept a factor to trade on their behalf and where they flew the Danish flag. But this house was pulled down eight or ten years ago; and so the Danes have nothing left but Fort Fredericxburg, which, as I said, commands Cabo Corso. Its position is so advantageous that no-one can appear on the parade-ground of Corso without being sighted from Fredericxburg.[29] The lodgings at Frederixburg are made of nothing but clay and a few stones. The Danish general's residence is of the same material, and the only pleasant thing about it is the refreshing SW winds, which prevail constantly on Gold Coast, from 9 a.m. to 9 p.m. every day, but more so on this mountain than elsewhere. Sometimes it is so cold that one is obliged to move out of the wind or put on extra clothes. This great chilliness is apparently what causes so many illnesses and deaths in

399

this garrison, which is more prone [to sickness] than any other garrison [of men] from Europe. It may also be because the Danes, being born in a cold climate where they are accustomed to strong drinks, /p. 25/ make as much use of them here as if they were in the land of their birth.[30] The hill on which the fort stands extends perhaps 300 paces to the summit. It is abrupt and steep in places.[31] The Danish general pays tribute to the king of Fetu, who has a vote /p. 26/ when the nomination of a new general is held. This takes place with great ceremonial on the part of the blacks.[32]

It is very hard to land at Manfrou, on account of the great breakers around the rocks in front of the hill, at whose foot the village is situated. The most favourable place for landing is East of the fort. It is best to anchor one's longboat at a distance from the shore and wait for canoes from the land. The best roadstead for vessels is North and South of the fort in 13–14 fathoms of water, on good holding ground. The English dispute this roadstead with the Danes and claim that it belongs to them, and that the Danes do not really have any roadstead at all.[33] The Danish agent has a very fine garden, about half a mile NE of the fort. It has all sorts of trees, especially orange and lime trees, with a large cupola in the middle, beneath which we were magnificently regaled in 1679 by Agent Witt, who had risen to this rank from that of gunner. There we saw a sort of combat between the Moors, who had come from all parts, armed in their fashion. I will tell you something about this little festival in the proper place. [*margin:* see Letter 23, p. 91][34]

The people of Corso and Manfrou devote themselves more to fishing than to any other occupation. But among them there are many merchants, who go into the interior and act as brokers for the other Moors who live far from the sea.[35]

The trade of the Danes at Fredericxburg is of greater benefit to the factors than to the company, which sends scarcely one ship a year there.[36] This is the only place the Danes have on this coast, having lost their post at Acra, which was sold by a Greek (the only remaining member of the garrison in 1679) to the Portuguese of the Isle du Prince, who still occupied it in 1682. [*margin:* This fort is at present in the hands of the English.][37] I shall give you more details of this in the proper place. Allow me to pause a little for breath, promising that it will not be for long; for I will do everything possible to fulfil punctually the engagement I have made to you, and to testify to you that I am, Sir, Your etc.

Additional Passages from *1732*

[p. 173/2, on the advantages of acquiring Frederiksborg]

A good regular fort, well stored and garrison'd, on this mount, would be almost impregnable, by reason of its natural situation. As it is at present, there is no danger of its being ever reduced by the Blacks. The English at cape Corso must fare very ill, if ever the two crowns of England and Denmark should be engaged in a war; for the Danes can batter the English fort, and utterly ruin it, without receiving any damage themselves, for they intirely overlook and command it. The English Royal African company would do well, if possible, to purchase that fort of the Danes at any rate, and to build there another stronger and more regular, to secure that post from falling into the hands of an enemy; for it would be a sure bulwark to their castle at Corso, as the Dutch now keep their fort Conraedsburg, on the hill of Santiago, for the greater security of their castle of Mina.[38]

[pp. 173/10–11, on the Danish officers]

By what has been said of the business the Danes have on the Gold Coast, it may be concluded their African company makes but a very inconsiderable advantage of it, and that through the unfaithfulness of their servants; for scarce any one, who is sent over from Denmark, as a person of known integrity to the company, as chief or general, lives long on the coast, but is either snatch'd away by a natural death, or by the contrivance of his inferiors, assisted by the Blacks, the better to compass their own designs. Thus it sometimes comes to pass, that a gunner of the fort, or other such mean person succeeds in that post, and so manages affairs according to his small capacity, or rather to his wicked inclination to enrich himself in as short a time as may be; knowing he must shortly be remov'd, or discharg'd by the company, his command being only *pro interim*; or that he may be serv'd by his inferiors, as his predecessor was before, every one endeavouring to make his interest with the Blacks, by large promises of gratuities, if they can once arrive at that supreme post, at any expence of blood and money.[39] / Of the two Danish generals I knew there during my voyages, the first had been the gunner of the fort, the latter, a lieutenant, as he said himself; but others told me he had been the other general's servant, a brisk, bold, daring, well-set man, and very young; both which advanced themselves by the aforesaid means. The first was murdered in his turn; but what became of the other I know not, having left him there, acting the part of a general: yet am apt to believe, he did not enjoy it long. I was told there of an unparalleled inhumanity of his. The book-keeper refusing to comply with him in the manner of keeping the books, he procured some villainous Blacks to accuse him of several misdemeanours and breach of trust, for which he was tried by a set of men, both Whites and Blacks, as is usual there, all of them corrupted. The poor man being thus convicted, and sentence of death pronounc'd against him, was immediately set to make his own coffin, and then shot to death.[40]

NOTES

[1] Omission of nine sentences on Fetu and Cape Coast, three each from Dapper, p. 67/5–6, Villault, p. 195, and Marees, f. 41–41v.

Cf. *1732*, p. 168/2–5, which cites Vasconcelos 1641, and adds material, partly from Bosman, pp. 47–8, 78 (hence the spelling, e.g. 'Ooegwa' instead of Dapper's 'Igwa'), partly from Hillier 1697, p. 687 (repeated in *1732*, p. 443/8). It also adds 'Asiento' or Ashanti to the list of gold-supplying countries, and states that, according to reports received at Cape Coast, the people of the 'Mandinga ... wild and bloody' had a capital, Songo, at 10°N, from which gold reached 'Tombut' (Timbuktu), this last point from a 'modern author', untraced. 'Songo' was known to the early Portuguese and may refer to Begho.

[2] In 1679, when Barbot's ship lay off 'Cap de Corso', now Cape Coast, for a fortnight, he drew the view of the 'castel' (presumably an attempt at the English word), and he visited the English fort several times (*1679*, pp. 291–302); in 1682, on probably a shorter stay, he visited the fort at least once (*1688*, p. 24 below), and in 1699 his brother's ship lay off Cape Coast for three days, sending parties ashore (*1732*, p. 456/5–6). In 1679, Barbot described the houses as 'built English-style, of wattle and clay, some raised up' (*1679*, p. 304). The size of Cape Coast village was said in the 1690s to be such that 'only 400 men with guns can be obtained from it' (Tilleman 1697, p. 74).

Cf. *1732*, pp. 168/6–7, 171/4–172/2, which has instead – 'divided by narrow crooked lanes, along the descent of the hills, appearing like an amphitheatre from the coast. It is govern'd by a Braffo, and one Griffin, a Caboceiro'; and adds remarks on the character of the inhabitants and the local smells, out of context from Bosman, pp. 105, 117, as well as a lengthy description of the vicinity of Cape Coast and its climate, based on Hillier

1697, pp. 692, 699, 701. In 1679 Barbot met the caboceer Griffin, who is also mentioned in English records (*1679*, p. 306; PRO, T70/365, Cape Coast journal, September 1679, 'Paid Griffin two months salary'). For the local political offices at this time, see Kea 1982, pp. 127–8.

[3] Barbot simplifies the history of the fort. Carloff (see Letter 2/3, note 42, above) arranged for a small fort to be built for the Swedish African Company, and building began in October 1653 (ARA, Dammaert journal, 19.10.1653). In 1658 he captured it on behalf of the Danish (Glückstadt) African Company, but in the following year the man whom he had left in charge handed it over to the Dutch West India Company. A few months later, the *dey* of Fetu seized the fort and gave it back to the Swedes. In 1663 it was returned to the Dutch, and finally in 1664 it was captured by the English, with Fetu support. See Jones 1983a, pp. 142–9, 261–4.

Cf. *1732*, pp. 168/8–169/1, expanded.

[4] Omission of seven sentences on the capture of Cape Coast by Holmes in 1664 and the failure of Ruyter to recapture it in 1665, from Dapper, pp. 67/8–9.

Cf. *1732*, p. 168/8, 169/1–2, 5, which expands by embroidering further upon Dapper, but also adds a reference to the 1672 grant of a charter, 'as I shall show in the supplement to this work', from Davenant 1709, p. 86.

[5] It is surprising that Barbot did not comment on the castle's unusual shape, as shown in Greenhill's 'bird's-eye' view (Lawrence 1963, plate 37).† Barbot met Greenhill at Cape Coast in 1682, the year in which the latter's view was most probably drawn: then or, more likely, later, it seems to have passed into Barbot's possession, since it was copied together with Barbot's own drawings, to form a set of undated engravings (see the Introduction, note 165). Barbot's own view of the fort (*1679*, pp. 302–3, 'le chatteau' in the text, 'castel' in the inscription, viewed 'from where we anchored') was slightly modified in the *1688* version, and much more modified in a closer view in *1732*, Plate 10 (p. 169). The earlier change may represent a revision as a result of Barbot's second visit, but the later change has minor features which strongly suggest that it was influenced by Greenhill's drawing. The inscription below the *1688* version, 'bourg de Corso', has '(Oegwa)' clumsily added, a late insertion from Bosman.

Cf. *1732*, p. 169/2, much enlarged, following Bosman, pp. 48–9, and Davenant, pp. 223–4.

[6] In 1679 Barbot noted that the castle consisted of brick and stone (*1679*, p. 301).

Cf. *1732*, p. 169/4–6, which enlarges – 'part thereof being of rock-stone and part of large bricks, which the English make, at some distance from the place'.

[7] Cf. *1732*, p. 169/7: 'a sandy flat, on which the Blacks run their canoos,

403

without danger of splitting'. Today, 'the landing-place is in a small bay under the north-east bastion of Cape Coast castle, behind some rocks, which generally afford good shelter from the sea. During the dry season landing in ordinary boats is frequently practicable' (*Africa pilot* 1967, p. 453).

[8] When Barbot visited Cape Coast in 1679, the battery facing the sea, consisting of eight guns, was not yet completed, but the fort carried 40 guns (*1679*, p. 302). Greenhill's drawing (? 1682) shows 22 guns on the platform facing the landing-place (Lawrence 1963, plate 37).

Cf. *1732*, p. 169/2, which substitutes two sentences from Bosman, p. 49, and a statement about the number of guns, totalling 48, from Davenant 1709, pp. 223–4.

[9] Cf. *1732*, pp. 169/7, which modifies – 'being only defended by the two round flankers on the land-side, and a low small battery, mounted with six pieces of cannon'. A 1694 visitor noted 'four flankers which have a cover'd communication with each other, and are mounted with good guns; and over the tank is a noble battery of fifteen whole culverin and demy cannon, lying low, and pointing upon the road' (Phillips 1732, p. 204). In the 1700s the flankers had 25 guns (Davenant 1709, p. 224).

[10] In 1679 Barbot praised the design of the soldiers' barracks (*1679*, p. 302).

Cf. *1732*, p. 170/1–2, which enlarges: 'well-built of brick, having three fronts, which, with the platform on the south, almost make a quadrangle, answering to the inside of the walls, and form a very handsome place of arms, well paved', also 'a curious continu'd balcony ... with handsome stair-cases on the outside ... Next the agent general's apartment is a large stately hall. There are also spacious storehouses, and counting-houses for the factors and other officers; some of which were not quite finish'd in the year 1682. The then agent Greenhill my very good friend, was diligently employ'd in finishing them'. The arrangements were also admired in 1694. 'As to the soldiers, I believe there are not better barracks any where than here, each two having a handsome room allow'd them ... a fine spacious square wherein 4 or 500 men may very conveniently be drawn up and exercis'd' (Phillips 1732, p. 204).

[11] In 1679 Barbot saw 400–500 slaves paraded on the parade-ground and 'four large slave-holds' in the fort (*1679*, pp. 292, 302). The ventilators of the slave-house are shown on Greenhill's drawing (Lawrence 1963, p. 185 and plate 37).

Cf. *1732*, p. 170/1, which adds that the slaves were 'let down at an opening made for the purpose', and comments: 'The keeping of the slaves thus under ground is a good security to the garrison against any insurrection'.

[12] Cf. *1732*, pp. 170/4, 171/1, which adds that rain-water was collected

from 'the tops and leads of the houses in the castle', and that the company's ships, if not supplied from the cistern, obtained water 'from a large pond, lying at some distance towards the sea, between cape Corso and Mina, the Blacks conducting the boats thither, and rolling the casks backwards and forwards along the paths on the shore among the rocks, at a place call'd Domine'. A 1694 visitor gave a detailed description of the water system, as follows. 'A curious tank or cistern which will contain 400 tons of water, being with great labour cut in a long square out of a rock, and terras'd over, having a convenient pair of steps to descend into it to fetch the water … divers channels contriv'd in the large square conveniently to receive the rain water that pours down from the flankers, and tops of the other buildings in the castle; each of which channels have two conveyances, one out of the castle, and the other into the tank. As soon as it begins to rain, the *Bumbay* (an officer so call'd, whose charge it is) makes the negroe slaves belonging to the castle, stop all the conveyances of the water to the tank, then sweep the castle very clean all over; and after it has rain'd about an hour, and wash'd the castle well, the water for that space running out, and carrying the filth and dirt with it, he opens the channels into the tank, where it runs very clear, and in great quantities … This tank is strongly arch'd over, upon which, by the aforesaid battery, there is a most pleasant walk' (Phillips 1732, p. 204).

[13] In the early 1690s, the fort had 'in all about forty guns mounted, some of them brass' (Phillips 1732, p. 204).

Cf. *1732*, p. 169/2, where the numbers of guns – 13 on a platform, 10 on the battlements, 25 on the flankers, 4–6 in a tower – are from Bosman, p. 49; Davenant 1709, pp. 223–4.

[14] In 1679 Barbot reckoned the garrison was of 80 whites and 200 blacks (*1679*, p. 302). In the early 1690s the number of whites was about 100, and in the 1700s there were '150 gromettoes' (Tilleman 1697, pp. 69–70; Phillips 1732, p. 204; Davenant 1709, p. 224).

Cf. *1732*, p. 170/3, 'about a hundred whites, and near the like number of Gromettoes, with their respective officers', partly echoing Davenant.

[15] The fact that Frederiksborg commanded Cape Coast was noted by Barbot in 1679 and had earlier been pointed out (*1679*, p. 302; Villault, p. 196). The last digit in the date is blank: it should be 5, making 1685. The English had indicated as early as 1679 that they were interested in buying Frederiksborg; and on 16 April 1685 it was handed over to them by the Commandant, Hans Lycke, who had been obliged to pawn it in order to maintain the garrison (Tilleman 1697, p. 75; Nørregard 1966, p. 33). That the reference to the take-over occurs only in an inserted marginal note presumably indicates that Barbot had not heard about the transfer when he wrote this section of the 1688 text. Despite the marginal note, the threat to Cape Coast from Fort Frederiksborg is repeated in *1732*, Barbot mentioning

the transfer of Frederiksborg to the English, with the full date, only in the Supplement, where it is noted in a 1692 letter from Cape Coast, which adds that – 'the royal African company has named it Fort Royal' (*1732*, pp. 169/ 3, 170/5, 445/5). Further material on English activities at and around this fort, in *1732*, p. 445/6–9, is from Bosman, pp. 52–3, and Davenant 1709, pp. 109, 224; neither of these, however, supply the date '1685' for the transfer. Apart from the references in the Supplement, all other references in *1732* (as in *1688*) presume that Frederiksborg is still a Danish fort, which may indicate that the 1692 letter did not reach Barbot before he read Bosman and Davenant, in the mid and late 1700s, when his work was well advanced. The marginal note with an incomplete date either represents a previous, vaguely-dated intimation of the transfer which reached Barbot after completing *1688* – perhaps from James Barbot after his visit to Cape Coast in 1699 – but an intimation forgotten when the English account was being prepared later. Or else it was a very late insertion after seeing the 1692 letter or Bosman – but if the latter, with only a guess at the date.

[16] For presents given in the 1680s to the 'king', 'Dey', 'Fetera', 'Braffo', and 'old Capusheer of Capo Corso', and a monthly rent generally paid to the Dey and not to the king, see PRO, T70/367–369, passim.

Cf. *1732*, p. 170/6, which omits the word 'north' and the last sentence.

[17] This section is somewhat misleading, since the company had probably abandoned Ardra in 1682, and since it is unlikely that any of the trading posts mentioned made purchases of significant amounts of ivory or wax.

Cf. *1732*, pp. 170/7–8, which greatly enlarges on the English company and its servants and on general European behaviour in Guinea – see the Additional Passage.

[18] This episode occurred in 1682, but Barbot had experienced a similar crisis in 1679, when the English fort at Cape Coast threatened Barbot's ship because it had raised and flown a pennant – the French offered as an excuse that they were in the roadstead of the Danish fort but eventually gave way (*1679*, pp. 296–7).

Cf. *1732*, p. 171/3, which omits the first sentence, no doubt to avoid offending English readers, and also the reference to the English vessel, makes the salute 'lowering the topsails down to the tops', and contains extra information, as follows: 'At my last voyage thither, aboard the French man of war Le Jolly, I was not a little surprized after having saluted the castle with seven guns, and being answer'd with five, that, as we were coming to an anchor, they fired three guns at us with ball, one after another, which fell just at the head of the ship. Not knowing the meaning thereof, we held on our course about a mile farther, to Manfrou road, and sent ashore the next morning . . . The general sent word, that if I would come and dine with him, I should be satisfied as to my question. He gave me a noble reception at my landing, the garrison making a lane from the water-side to the castle gate, whither the chaplain conducted me; and the general, with his officers, receiv'd me at the gate, and order'd nine guns to be fired from the flankers. ... The anchoring-place is about two miles from the shore; where agent Greenhil, in the year 1660, made frequent observation, that the variation was 2 deg. 14 min. westerly. It generally flows here S.S.E. and N.N.W. upon the full and change. The water, upon spring-tides, rises about six or seven foot'. The date '1660' is a misprint for 1680 – in 1660 Greenhill was aged only 14.

[19] Barbot was probably writing these comments in the later 1700s, a period when there was lively public discussion in England about the future of the Royal African Company, and he may have been partly inspired by reading Davenant 1709, a summary of which was eventually printed at the end of his account (although Barbot may not have been responsible for this). Yet the comments on the behaviour of the English in Guinea are an enlarged version of references in Bosman, pp. 49–50, 106–7, references to irregular lives, diseased appearance and high mortality, and even the references to English partiality for meat and punch, which otherwise might have been thought to reflect a French refugee's gastronomic discomforts. Three minor references, to canoes, to sleeping shirtless and to the corrosion of iron, are from Hillier 1697, p. 692. There was a grain of truth in Barbot's depiction of Europeans who seek employment in exotic lands as marginal and disaffected persons; and mortality was certainly high among the English in Guinea – 'one man in three died in the first four months, more than three in five in the first year' (Davies 1974, p. 93; see also Feinberg 1974). That drinking and wenching were bad for European health in Guinea was traditional and standard thinking. Overall a certain biliousness in the comments suggests less moral strictness than senescence. As a man from a seafaring community Barbot cannot have been as shocked as he purports to be about the sexual licence of Europeans overseas. Furthermore, his appeal to personal experience is over-done. His own time in Guinea was very limited (the number of nights he slept ashore probably a mere handful), and to boast that he gave advice on healthy living to 'some of the principal men at cape Corso castle', and did that 'often', was a claim that would have received short shrift from his acquaintance, Greenhill, if it had been made while the former governor of Cape Coast was still alive. The 'above two years' Barbot wore his stomacher were mostly spent on the high seas or in the Caribbean, not in Guinea. It may even be doubted whether the advice to the French African company to reduce the number of factors was given, as asserted, 'often' – but in this case, Barbot was reminiscing about a period of his life thirty years earlier, and some nostalgic exaggeration may be forgiven. The reference to Europeans employed as 'canoo men' is curious and may have been a slip.

[20] The description of the gardens is very similar to that of Phillips 1732, p. 205.

[21] The information in this section presumably came from English agents residing at Cape Coast, or formerly resident there. 'Abramboe' may have been identical with the present-day town of Abura (Daaku 1970, p. 64); but more likely it represented the name of a polity lying North of Cape Coast and now known as Abrem. Barbot's statement has been used in recent times by elements in Ghana to support the claim of the Oguaa paramount stool that Abrem has always been subordinate to it (Henige 1973, p. 6) – a claim for which there is little evidence (Jones 1983a, pp. 89, 91, 164–5). The information on Abramboe is repeated in *1732*, pp. 299/6–300/1. 'Aquaffou', if properly transcribed, must refer, not to a place, but to a group of people, perhaps Akan/Twi *o/a-kuàfó*, 'planter/s, farmer/s, especially individual/s excelling in husbandry' (Christaller 1933, p. 267). That slaves intended for sacrifice were kept in one place is plausible – for a whole village of persons under sentence of death, see Rattray 1927, p. 106. The statement about Aquaffou is repeated in *1732*, p. 285/6. A lengthy account of the sacrifice of slaves, in *1732*, pp. 443/8–444/4, is from Hillier 1697, pp. 687–9, as stated, but Barbot changes the date '1687–8' to '1697–8' (for no obvious reason and therefore perhaps a slip) and adds a sentence about human sacrifice in Florida 'according to Mercator'.

[22] This passage reinforces comments in the Letter, enlarged in *1732*, p. 170/7–8 (an Additional Passage, and see note 19 above). While no doubt inspired by Bosman, pp. 49–50, 106–7, it is more original than the previous passage. Bosman in fact argued that the ill-health of Europeans was not due to 'their own Mismanagement'. However, Barbot concludes his discussion (*1732*, p. 195/5) with material from Bosman, pp. 108–9. Barbot's comments on the climate and African responses repeat what he says at many other points in both his texts.

[23] The source of this information, if printed, is untraced, but Barbot may instead have learned about the 1703 French attack from his interrogation of French prisoners-of-war (perhaps those mentioned in *1732*, pp. 414/3, 9, 430/6). For another French attack on Cape Coast in '1704/5', see Davenant 1709, p. 234.

[24] Barbot visited Fort Frederiksborg several times in 1679 (*1679*, pp. 294–305) and again in 1682. 'Manfrou' (now usually written 'Amanful' or occasionally 'Mumford') is today a suburb of the town of Cape Coast. The earliest record of the name, dating from the 1660s, explains it as meaning 'a new country' (Akan/Twi *o-man* 'town', *fófóforo* 'new': Jones 1983a, p. 141). Apparently the hill was deserted until the Danes settled there in 1659. These two sentences are omitted in *1732*.

[25] In 1679 Barbot recorded 12 cannon, of which four were unmounted (*1679*, p. 302), and a Danish document of 1680 stated that the fort had only nine guns (COP, V-gK77, indkomme, April, no. 13, 'specification', 1680),

although it had at one time possessed 24 cannon (Tilleman 1697, p. 75). The three bastions, facing the roadstead, Cape Coast and Fort Nassau, were mentioned by Villault, p. 197; and other sources stated that the bastion facing the roadstead was triangular, not round (Roussier 1935, plate 7; Jones 1983a, p. 149).

Cf. *1732*, pp. 172/10, 173/1, 8, which enlarges slightly – 'being only a pretty large, almost triangular inclosure, . . . with a round flanker towards the sea-side, and two other sorry small bastions to the land, of the same materials as the wall and curtains . . . there are fifteen or sixteen old iron guns, in no good order'.

[26] The drawing made in 1679, from the anchorage (*1679*, p. 303), was repeated fairly faithfully in *1688*, and again in *1732*, Plate 14 (p. 177), except that on the latter it was noted that it was now 'Fort Royal English' and a Union Jack was substituted for the Danish flag.

[27] Frederiksborg was named after King Frederick III of Denmark (1648–70). Omitted in *1732*.

[28] Omission of two sentences, on the earlier history of the Danes, from Villault, pp. 195–6.

[29] The first sentence is from Villault, p. 196. The post at Cape Coast, part of the agreement between the Danish African Company and the Fetu elders in 1659, was destroyed by the English in 1675 (Jones 1983a, p. 140, n. 8).

Cf. *1732*, pp. 170/5, 173/9, which adds a personal reference – 'I have several times from the Danes fort seen the men walking in the place of arms at cape Corso'.

[30] In 1679 Barbot opined that, because of the regular wind, the air was 'very healthy' (*1679*, p. 302). But in June 1679 only six servants of the company on Gold Coast were still alive; and the commandant of the fort whom Barbot met in 1682 had recently reported that the state of the buildings was such that all inside were soaked whenever the slightest storm occurred (COP, V-gK 77, udgaede, October, no. 47; V-gK 78, Lücke 12.5.1681).

Cf. *1732*, p. 172/10, 173/3–4, which elaborates – 'a disorderly heap of old clay buildings, thatch'd, like those of the Blacks, and all out of repair. The Danish general's apartment has nothing in it worth taking notice of, unless it be an old gallery, which has a very fine prospect, both by sea and land'; and further – '. . . of all the European nations, which live on that coast, the Danes lose most men in proportion, tho' settled in the best air; which is ascribed to their ill diet and government, wherein they exceed the English of cape Corso, being often in want of money to buy the most necessary things for their subsistence, and great lovers of hot liquors, which quite spoil their stomachs. It has been observ'd, that Danish women cannot live long there, being commonly subject to a prodigious loss of blood, by a distemper peculiar to their sex; as lately happened to a general's wife, who had not been there a year'. The comparison with the English was derived from Bosman, pp. 49–50.

[31] Earlier sources stated that 'the height of this hill is a good 300 paces, reckoning not perpendicularly but as one walks', and 'the hill is only 300 paces in circumference [and] ... perhaps 100 paces high, and is climbed in a spiral' (Jones 1983a, p. 149; Villault, pp. 196–7). The hill is indeed fairly steep in places and walking by the spiral path it takes an average person about 400 paces to reach the top.

Cf. *1732*, pp. 172/10, 174/2, which enlarges to 'above three hundred paces over, and level at the top ... very steep and high on all sides'; and adds a description of the country behind the hill, based on a more general reference in Hillier 1697, p. 690.

[32] Barbot is the only contemporary source to mention an African having a vote in the election of the commandant. Although it has been stated that in 1659 the then commandant agreed that the caboceers should have a voice in such election, this does not appear in the 1659 agreement (Van Dantzig 1980, p. 46, no reference given; Jones 1983a, p. 262). The Danes did pay tribute or rent: in 1680 it was stated that annually they had to give the king of Fetu 247 guilders in merchandise, the *Day* 444, the *Fettero* 111, the caboceers 15, the captain of the Akanists 22, the captain of Cape Coast 9, and the caboceers of Cape Coast 22 (COP, V-gK 77, indkomne, April, no. 8; July, no. 29).

Cf. *1732*, p. 174/1, which elaborates – 'The Danish company pays a yearly acknowledgment to the king of Fetu, for fort Fredericksburg, and have allow'd a vote in the election of a general to be chosen there upon occasion *pro interim*, when that post becomes vacant. This is the occasion of the great abuses so frequently committed there, and of men's lives being so much exposed; good men being made away, to make room for villains.'

[33] In 1679 Barbot heard of the Anglo-Danish dispute (*1679*, pp. 297–8). In 1664 the English had promised the Danes the right to use the roadstead (COP, V-gK 77, udgaede, October no. 48/3, Holmes/Selwyn to Albrecht 19.4.1664). The anchorage for Cape Coast fort lay to the East 'in 7 fathoms of water, sandy bottom' (Tilleman 1697, p. 74). The rocks directly in front of the hill do make it impossible to land boats there, and nowadays fishing canoes use the beach to the East. As for the anchorage, 'during the dry season vessels can anchor in depths of about 5 fathoms, about half a mile south-eastward of Cape Coast castle ... In the rainy season, when there is usually a long swell, it will be prudent to anchor in a depth of 10 fathoms, about 1½ miles south-eastward of the castle' (*Africa pilot* 1967, p. 453).

Cf. *1732*, pp. 172/8, 173/5–6, the anchorage said to be 'due south from the fort'.

[34] In 1679 Barbot recorded a detailed account of the festival held in a

'walk of sweet-orange trees' (*1679*, pp. 304–5). For a vegetable garden at Frederiksborg, and a similar African dancing display, seen in 1667, see Villault pp. 315–8, 380–1; and for fruit gardens there in the early 1690s, after the fort had passed into English hands, see Tilleman 1697, p. 76; Phillips 1732, p. 209. A contemporary source refers to an equally sumptuous celebration held by the Danish commander in 1682, at a cost of five *bendas*, in honour of the king of Fetu (Sieveking 1937, pp. 51–2).

Cf. *1732*, p. 173/7–8, which contains slight changes – 'a large stately summer house'; 'a mock fight among Blacks, representing their true manner of engaging in battle'; and adds – 'Whether it be usual with the Danes to treat strangers sumptuously, or whether it is only peculiar in those parts, I must own their entertainment was magnificent, and we had sometimes above twenty healths drank at a meal, five or seven guns firing to each of them, according to the dignity of the person'.

[35] Fishing was given as the main activity by Dapper, p. 67/7.

Cf. *1732*, p. 172/9, which adds two additional occupations – 'husbandmen or salt-boilers'. For an earlier, more detailed account of these occupations in this area, see Jones 1983a, pp. 231–40, 243–53.

[36] The fort received hardly any supplies after about 1673, and therefore depended largely on trade with interlopers and Portuguese ships, as well as with a few French ships, such as Barbot's (ARA, Abramsz 23.11.1679).

Cf. *1732*, p. 172/9 – 'Sometimes there is a pretty good trade with the Blacks, as also with the Danes, who having seldom above one or two ships in a year from Denmark, are often in want of many things, either for their own use, or to carry on the trade, in the proper season; and I have my self sold the Danes considerable parcels of goods for gold and slaves'.

[37] For the history of the Danish fort at Accra, see Letter 2/10, p. 37 and notes 8–9, below. The sentence in the margin must refer to Frederiksborg rather than to Christiansborg, and was presumably added at the same time as the previous insertion on the same subject – see note 15 above.

Cf. *1732*, p. 173/9, which changes 'Isle du Prince' to 'St Thome' and enlarges slightly, but omits the reference to the English.

[38] That Barbot wrote in the 1700s this new paragraph and did not revise it before his death in 1712 indicates that he was in a muddle, since Frederiksborg had long since been in English hands (as he should have learned from Bosman), and since it contradicts his statement in the Supplement.

[39] It was correct that the Fetu people were sometimes involved in deposing one commandant in favour of another (e.g. COP, V-gK 78, Lücke, 13.1681). Barbot's 1682 visit took place at a time when the fort's administration had been in total disarray for over a year (COP, V-gK, indkomne, July no. 7, Tetz 22.4.1681; October no. 13, Busch 2.2.1681).

[40] In 1679 the Danish commandant, Peter Witt, sought to rid himself of

his book-keeper 'Conraedt' (Johann Conrad Busch) by sending him on board Barbot's ship, in order to have him transported to the West Indies (*1679*, p. 316). Barbot's account is partly confirmed in the company archives (COP, V-gK 77, indkomne, April no. 21, Thorne 1.4.1680). However, Busch managed to return to Europe and then to Gold Coast, and in 1681 even became commandant of Frederiksborg himself (COP, V-gK 78, Lücke 12.5.1681). Barbot may have combined the story of Busch with that of another officer, or simply improved the anecdote. Witt, who had been appointed in 1678, apparently died in 1680 (Nørregard 1966, p. 236, n. 11). At the time of Barbot's visit in 1682 the commandant was probably Hans Lycke (Lücke), the man who later handed the fort over to the English.

LETTER 7

Description of the kingdom of Sabou and of Fort Nassau at Mourée.

Being ever mindful, Sir, of the promise I gave you, I could not let myself tarry long without again setting to work on the account which I have begun. Having finished my last letter only yesterday, I again take up the pen this morning to write another, a letter about the kingdom of Sabou, which I have mentioned to you. The estates of the king of Sabou are entered between Manfrou and Mourée, two villages about two leagues apart.[1] This country does not extend far, possessing only three villages on the coast, the largest being Mourée, which lies in the middle. The first village, Icon, is three-quarters of a league West of Mourée, on the coast.[2] [. . .][3] [At Mourée] it is very awkward to walk /p. 27/ in the streets, which consist of pointed rocks.[4] Fort Nassau commands the whole of this village, which surrounds it except on the East side, where the sea washes its feet. It was built in 1624 on the orders and at the expense of the States General, in honour of the illustrious Nassau family, and was later given to the company, which possesses it today.[5] [. . .][6] Its present shape is fairly regular. It is defended by 24 iron cannon, and a garrison of 40 white men and some paid blacks, who are very good soldiers, as are all the rest of the inhabitants of this place; and so today this fort is in a position to resist the Moors.[7] It looks very attractive. The lodgings are compact but quite comfortable. The fort is surrounded by a large, wide moat, cut into the rock, with a drawbridge defended by four cannon.[8]

412

[illustration no. (64), Fort Nassau]⁹†

West of the fort, the governor has a garden, which is considered the finest on the coast. The walks are very beautiful, and several very pleasant summer-houses can be seen. It produces all kinds of salads and herbs; but it has the same fault as the garden at Manfrou, namely that the view is restricted on all sides by the neighbouring hills.¹⁰ /p. 28/ [. . .]¹¹

The king of Sabou rules a country of only 6–7 leagues, yet he can raise an army of 2,000 men if necessary. Formerly he always lived on good terms with the Dutch, in order that his subjects might remain obedient, for they paid him tribute only with reluctance. But after the Dutch attained a position where they could lay down the law, this friendship was broken and the inhabitants rose against him. Consequently this king would not be angry if another nation undertook to oust the Dutch, and there is no doubt that he would assist the enterprise as much as he could.¹² [. . .]¹³ My own enterprise is to assure you that I am, Your etc.

NOTES

¹ In 1679 Barbot passed by Fort Nassau, 'one league from Frederiksborg', and drew it (*1679*, p. 305); in 1682 he must have passed it again. The actual distance being only about 4 km, the earlier estimate was more correct.

Cf. *1732*, p. 174/3, which replaces this sentence with a paragraph taken from Bosman, p. 53.

² 'Icon' refers to the hill known today as Akong or Queen Anne's Point, Barbot probably miscopying 'Icom' in Villault, p. 206. Other seventeenth-century sources called it 'Congh' (e.g. ARA, Dammaert journal, 13.5.1653; Van Dantzig 1978, pp. 64, 112–3, 128). The Dutch had a post here from about 1657 to 1659; the Danes set up a post in 1660, which was destroyed by the Dutch in 1661; in the early 1690s the Dutch again settled at Akong for a short period (Jones 1983a, p. 245, n. 479; Tilleman 1697, p. 78; De Jonge 1871, p. 45).

Cf. *1732*, p. 174/4, which gives 'Congo' as an alternative name for Icon and adds material from Bosman, p. 53.

³ Omission of eight sentences on the villages of Sabou and Mourée (Asebu and Mori), from Dapper, p. 76/2–3.

Cf. *1732*, p. 174/3–7, which adds material from Bosman, p. 55.

⁴ Source untraced.

Cf. *1732*, pp. 174/7, 175/6, which adds that 'the best landing-place at

Mouree is at a bay, just under the cannon of the fort, on the E.N.E. side of it; which must be with the help of canoos, as is practised at many other parts of this coast'.

[5] The first sentence is from Villault, p. 206. The fort, named after Maurice of Nassau, Prince of Orange and Stadtholder of the Netherlands 1584–1625, was in fact founded in 1612, but extensive rebuilding took place in 1623–4 (De Jonge 1871, pp. 40–3; Jones 1983a, pp. 80–2).

Cf. *1732*, p. 174/8–175/1, which expands, adding material from Bosman, p. 55, and also the following: 'The English commodore Holmes took this fort from the Dutch, in 1664, as has been before mention'd; but admiral de Ruyter recover'd it from them again in 1665, with the assistance of nine hundred Mina Blacks, sent him by Valkenburg from Mina. He improved the fortifications to the condition here laid down, and garrison'd it with European soldiers, and fifty natives'. This is quite incorrect: Fort Nassau remained in Dutch hands throughout 1664–5, and the first sentence, from Dapper, p. 65/4–5, should refer instead to Takoradi (see Letter 2/3, n. 49, above).

[6] Omission of four sentences on the history and form of the fort, from Dapper, p. 77/2.

Cf. *1732*, p. 174/9, which gives a more precise description of the fort, from Bosman, p. 54, and adds – 'all the works of good black stone and lime'.

[7] In 1679 the fort was reported to be manned by a factor, two assistants, a sub-factor, a barber-surgeon, an armourer, 12 soldiers and 60 male and female slaves, who had their own plantations (ARA, Abramsz 23.11.1679). In the early 1690s it had 22 cannon, the same senior officers, and 'one sergeant, one corporal, ... four gentlemen cadets, one drummer, and 20 common soldiers, besides natives' (Tilleman 1697, pp. 79–80).

Cf. *1732*, p. 174/9, which substitutes a more detailed description from Bosman, p. 54, but retains the figures given here.

[8] Barbot did not visit the fort in 1679, and it seems that he did not go there in 1682 either: hence, for instance, the absence of any information about the anchorage until *1732* (quoted in note 4 above). However, in 1679 he reported that a colleague had visited the fort and found 'that the fortifications are very fine and that it is surrounded by a large moat, with a very fine drawbridge and a palisade' (*1679*, p. 305).

Cf. *1732*, p. 174/9, which modifies, from an untraced source: 'a drawbridge, covered with a gallery to contain several men to scour it, with their small arms'.

[9] The view of the fort drawn in 1679, purportedly as seen at 1½ leagues North-by-NW (*1679*, pp. 305–6), is not the same as the *1688* view, which is from a different angle and has minor differences in the structure of the fort, perhaps representing a revision made by Barbot when passing in 1682. The

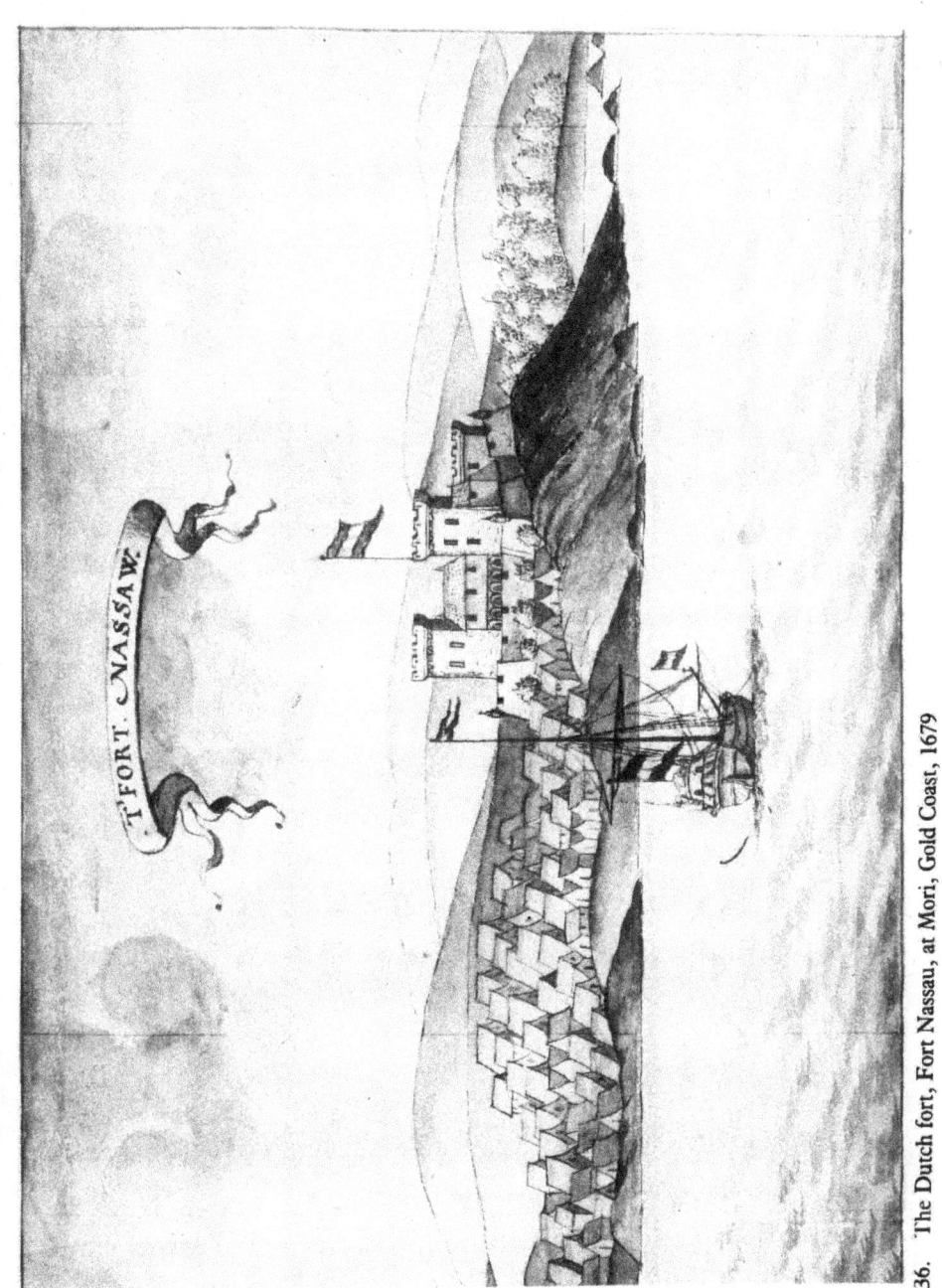

36. The Dutch fort, Fort Nassau, at Mori, Gold Coast, 1679

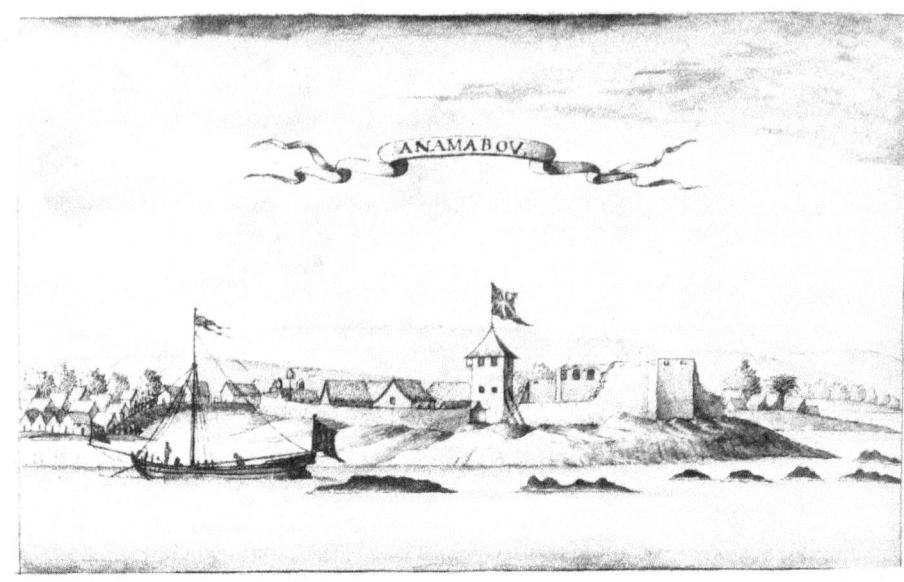

37.   The English fort at Anomabu, Gold Coast, 1679

38.   The English fort at Anomabu, Gold Coast, 1682

latter view was printed as 'The Prospect of Fort Nassaw at Mouree seen from the Sea' in *1732*, Plate 12 (p. 175). But an inset shows a third view 'from the ENE', again from a different angle and with features perhaps closer to the later view, and an inscription reads – 'I have here added this small Prospect of Fort Nassaw to supply some omissions in the other below'. This inset view does not appear to represent or borrow from the views in Bosman, opposite p. 41.

[10] Cf. *1732*, p. 175/2, which makes minor additions: 'summer-houses and seats', 'plentifully stored with trees and plants', 'gardens at Mina and Manfrou'.

[11] Omission of three paragraphs on the country's inhabitants and products, from Dapper, p. 76/4–5 (partly derived from the 1629 map).

Cf. *1732*, p. 175/3, which condenses but add a little information from Bosman, p. 54.

[12] This section is loosely based on Dapper, pp. 76/9–77/2, which refers to the country as '5 miles in circumference', and to the king raising 'about 1, 500 men'. Those who rose against the king were probably inhabitants of Fantyn rather than of Sabou (ARA, Dammaert journal, passim). Apparently Barbot's only reason for thinking that Sabou would welcome enemies of the Dutch was a reference in Dapper to a conflict between the Dutch and the king of Sabou, a conflict probably settled in 1657 (ibid., Dammaert journal, 5.6.1652; De Jonge 1871, pp. 43–6; Daaku 1970, p. 63). In 1665, the king assisted the Dutch against the English, but in the wars of the 1690s played an ambivalent role (Bosman, p. 54: Ruyter 1961, p. 263). Barbot evidently had no first-hand knowledge of Sabou affairs.

Cf. *1732*, p. 175/4, which adds further distortions: 'The inhabitants of Mouree . . . are forbid by the Dutch to pay him any duties: for which reason, that prince will willingly assist any other European nation with two thousand Blacks to beat the Dutch out of their fort'.

[13] Omission of three paragraphs on wars fought by the people of Mori, from Dapper, pp. 76/8–77/1 (partly derived from the 1629 map).

Cf. *1732*, p. 175/5, a summary.

LETTER 8

Description of the kingdom of Fantin, of the castle of Anamabou, and of Fort Amsterdam at Cormentyn.

If my letters to you are short, Sir, it is because I have a headache which absolutely refuses to go away, and which becomes worse the more I apply myself to writing to you. But it is quite fair that I should suffer some inconvenience in recomp^nse for the pleasure I have in corresponding with you. I shall therefore resume my account. The kingdom of Fantyn [...] covers about nine leagues of coast, extending as far as [Cape] Ruygenhoeck.[1] On this stretch it has several villages – Anichan, Nomabo (or Janassia), Aga, Cormentin, Amersa, Little Cormentin, Aqua, Laguyo, Montfort, and several others between this last place and Cape Ruygehoeck which I do not record here as they are little frequented. Fantyn, the metropolis which gives the country its name, is situated five leagues inland, where there are also several villages and hamlets, for this kingdom is heavily populated, being one of the most considerable on Gold Coast.[2] The village of Anichan is about three-quarters of a league West of Janassia or Anamabo, situated on a slight /p. 29/ elevation, two leagues East of Mourée. The Dutch formerly had a lodge here, but the small profit they drew from it and the annoyance caused by seeing that the English had a better post there drove them away.[3] Today there are Englishmen and Portuguese in this country: the former in a hut with several cannon, the latter in a sort of redoubt made of turf, constructed since 1679. The village is not large. I have never done any advantageous trade there and it is not worth the trouble of stopping. The anchorage is between this place and the castle of Anamabo, which can easily be seen from the roadstead, although situated in a dip.[4]

Anomabo, Nomabo or Janassia (all of these are names for the same place) is a large village, just under one league from Cormentin and 2½ leagues from Mourée. It is divided into two parts, one occupied by fishermen from Mina, the other by those of Fantyn.[5] It is difficult to land there at certain times; but generally speaking, it is the best landing place on the whole coast of Fantyn. People often beach their shallops on the sand in between the rocks, which form a kind of large and spacious harbour. The problem is to get past these rocks, but this can be done if you take your time.[6] The surrounding countryside is very pleasant, with a great variety of trees. The best palm wine of Gold Coast grows [sic] there, as well as the largest quantity of maize.[7] You also find many of the little parrots called parakeets: these are the size of linnets and have red heads and tails. Some of them have been seen in France, at the residences of *Monseigneur* and of the Prince of Chartres.[8] A large quantity of salt is also produced there, as well as very fine cotton.[9]

The castle which the English possess there is situated at the place most favourable for landing, in order to defend it better. It is actually no more than one compact main building, flanked by four small brick bulwarks, which are armed with 16 small cannon, almost all being of cast iron. Here is a view of it.

[illustration no. (65), 'Chateau d'Anamabou']¹⁰†

The external walls of this castle are of little importance, consisting merely of a turf circle, 7–8 feet high. Inside it are various lodgings built of the same material, for the paid blacks and the slaves. The English garrison and the commandant occupy the large dwelling-house, and it is here that all the merchandise and provisions are kept. This little castle has been built since 1679, for on my first visit it was merely a confused jumble of huts and stores made of turf, within the same outer wall which /p. 30/ is still standing and which it is proposed to demolish and replace by one made of brick, which would be more apppropriate. The soil is very suitable for baking bricks, and the oyster shells afford excellent lime. There is also no lack of building timber.¹¹

The little village of Aggia lies a cannon-shot further East. The Danes formerly had a fort there, and on its ruins the English have built a small lodge of turf, where they keep a factor and two white men. The Dutch too used to have a hut here, on the other side of the village, which is divided into three small parts, like hamlets, each containing 20–25 huts. This Dutch lodge was fortified by a small outer wall in the manner of a redoubt.¹² [. . .]¹³

This village [of Cormentin] is the most important one on the [Fante] coast, both on account of the number of inhabitants, which almost equals that of Mourée, and on account of its advantageous location. It also used to be the principal trading post of the English, before they made themselves masters of Cape Corso. They built this castle on hard and mountainous terrain, alongside the village, and flanked it with four bastions. Access to it was extremely difficult, both because of the hill, which is almost a bluff cliff, and because the breakers prevent boats from landing on the shore.¹⁴ [. . .]¹⁵ /p. 31/ During the years 1681–2 the Dutch [who took it from the English] entirely changed the shape of this place, making it much more convenient and placing it in a much better state than it had been. Here, Sir, is how it appears from the roadstead.¹⁶

[illustration no. (66), Fort Amsterdam at Kormantin]

As I went inside it on each of my voyages, I had a chance to observe its situation and shape. The Dutch engineer who had been sent there at that time even consulted me on several matters. The fort is strongly built on a high hill, which is escarped and precipitous in several places. It can only be reached by a path cut into the rock of the slope. It is a square fort, flanked by four bastions, of which two are round and two are rectangular. The curtains and all the remainder of the outside wall are of large black stones, mortared with lime (made from oyster-shells). The parapets are fine and large. The interior of the place is compact. At the entrance you find /p. 32/ a parade-ground, on one side of which is a keep, which serves as living quarters and as a store. Above this is a fine platform, from which one can see very far, and on which the flag is hoisted. The fort has 20 cannon and a garrison of 25 white men, not counting the paid blacks. It is called Fort Amsterdam.[17]

The Moors' village called Cormentin lies to the West and North of this fort. The country inland is mountainous and uneven. The village of Little Cormentin or Tantonquerry is a league away, on the other side of the bay, where there is nothing worth noting except the goodness of the air and the fertility of the soil in maize and other natural products.[18] [...][19] Amersa, Aqua, Laguyo, Montfort and several other villages between the last of these places and Ruygehoeck are of little importance. Aqua lies on a small river, two leagues East of Cormentin. The country is flat and low-lying. Ships obtain much corn (*mil*), water and firewood there.[20] Laguyo is two leagues further East, on a rising ground which descends towards the sea. People trade a few slaves and a very small quantity of gold there, but the gold is all adulterated. Montfort has nothing of importance except millet and a few slaves.[21] As for the other small villages which come after it, they are hardly frequented by Europeans, being inhabited by poor fishermen who sometimes come on board ships to sell their fish, as do those of Montfort and Laguyo. There is no need to stop there, although they always boast that the country has much gold and many slaves. They do this in order to halt ships and have the pleasure of selling them fish and a few trifles. Here, and between Ruygehoeck and Acra, the English call more often than any other Europeans. [...][22] /p. 33/ Like those between Axim and here, these peoples speak the same language; at least, those living near the coast do. I shall send you a vocabulary of the most familiar words in their language when I have finished my account.[23] But here I shall end my letter, assuring you that I am [Yours etc].[24]

Additional Passages from *1732*

[p. 176/4–5, on the English and Portuguese at Anishan]

The English have a factory there at this time, defended by two pieces of cannon, and two or three white men, with some Grometto Blacks, and a flag, but very little or no trade. / The Portugueses, since the year 1679, cast up a redoubt of turf for their security, the commander whereof, Laurence Perez Branco, has ten or twelve of his country-men to defend it. His trade consists in tobacco and pipes, Brazil sweet-meats, soap, rum, and such like American commodities; but I cannot imagine what advantage he can make of it, unless he buys European goods of the interlopers, or has them sent from Holland by the Jews, who know how to get Portuguese passes; and such ships, when they come upon the coast, are received, as if they really came from Portugal.[25]

[p. 446/3, on an attack on Anomabu fort in 1701]

It appears to me by Bloome's memoirs, the chief at Anamaboe, with some of the other principals, were so assaulted by the Blacks at the time they attacked the castle, on the 4th of September 1701, that they fled to cape Corso castle naked in their shirts only. The Negroes of Anamaboe are the most turbulent restless people of all the coast.[26]

NOTES

[1] In 1679 Barbot's ship spent three weeks on this section of the coast: he visited the 'little English fort' at Anomabu five times, the English lodge at 'Agga' four times, and the Dutch fort at 'Cormentyn' once; and he made drawings of the forts (*1679*, pp. 305–21). In 1682 he passed along the coast and apparently drew Anomabu again; and in 1699 his brother's ship called at Anomabu and a ship's boat visited 'Anischan' (*1732*, p. 456/7–8). The omission is of two sentences on the countries adjoining Fantyn, from Dapper, p. 77/3. The Fantyn country covered a much smaller area than the present-day Fante country – see the 1629 map; ARA, Dammaert journal, passim; Marees, ff. 42, 47v; Jones 1983a, pp. 84, 92, 95.

Cf. *1732*, p. 175/7–8, 10, which adds material on Fantyn behaviour from Dapper, p. 80/2, and Bosman, pp. 57–9, embroidered.

[2] The first half of this sentence is from Dapper, p. 77/4.

[3] In 1679 Barbot tried without much success to obtain water at 'Achenir (*1679*, pp. 306–7). The English established a post at Anishan (today Biriw in about 1650, but were driven out by people from Sabou (Asebu) in 16. (ARA, Dammaert journal, 8.2.1653). They returned in 1663, but left aga in 1665 (*CSP Colonial 1661–8*, p. 158; Ruyter 1961, p. 263). In 1679 tl 'stone stronghold' built by the English was said to be in a dilapidated sta (ARA, Abramsz 23.11.1679). Barbot appears to be the only source mentior ing a former Dutch post and the statement may well be an error.
Cf. *1732*, p. 176/3, 6.

[4] The English had a factor at Anishan from at least the mid 1680s, yet d not appear to have established a permanent post there until the end of 168' when it was feared that the French would gain a foothold (OBLR, C.745 747, passim; PRO, T70/11 p. 31, Humfryes et al. 9.1.1687/8; Hazewink 1932, p. 256; Davies 1957, pp. 247–8). An English work of 1686 whic mentioned 'a Fort upon a little eminence about six hundred Paces within th Land' was presumably referring to Barbot's 'hut with cannon' (Burton 168(p. 62). Since there was apparently no English post at Anishan by 168. Barbot presumably obtained his information in 1687 or 1688, perhaps fror company acquaintances in England – although Barbot may have intende the text to be read as implying that information collected 'since 1679' wa collected in 1682. In 1679 Barbot saw a Portuguese vessel trading, appa rently at Anomabu (*1679*, p. 307); but his information on the Portuguese a Anishan may well have come from the same source as the information on th English.
Cf. *1732*, p. 176/4–5, which terms the place 'Anican or Ingenisian', th latter term from Bosman, p. 56, and enlarges considerably – see the Additic nal Passage.

[5] 'Janassia' was probably only another variant of 'Anishan', which earlie Dutch sources had referred to as Ayasiang/Ajanassiangh/Ajanesiangh (Ratel band 1953, pp. 79, 191, 201) – hence 'Ingenesian' (note 4 above). Barbo may have been misled by the statement that the English had a fort a 'Janasia' (although this was described as a village between Adja and Ano mabu), in Dapper, p. 80/3, from which the second sentence is derived.
Cf. *1732*, p. 176/7–8, which adds material from Bosman, p. 56.

[6] The reference to good access echoes Dapper, p. 79/3.
Cf. *1732*, p. 176/10, which elaborates slightly: 'The landing at Anamab is pretty difficult, the shore being full of rocks, among which the se sometimes breaks very dangerously. The ships boats anchor close by, and the people are carry'd ashore in canoos, which come out from the town, to narrow sandy beach'. The elaboration may be from recollection, or from James Barbot, who anchored at Anomabu (*1732*, p. 456/7).

[7] In 1689 the Director-General at Elmina stated that Anomabu was 'the principal granary' from which English ships obtained maize (Van Dantzig 1980, p. 116; Roussier 1935, p. 13). In 1699 James Barbot at Anomabu 'purchas'd with much trouble, and at a very dear rate, a quantity of Indian wheat ... We paid three Akies for every chest of corn, which is excessive dear' (*1732*, p. 456/7).

Cf. *1732*, pp. 176/1–2, 12, 177/1–5, which incorporates much material from Bosman, pp. 56–7, but also enlarges considerably on each topic, apparently in the main from recollection (or possibly in part from oral information from James Barbot), as follows. 'The country about this place is full of close hills, beginning at a good distance from the town. There are five together, higher than the rest, which are a good landmark to know Anamabo, from some leagues to the westward.' 'I have there eaten excellent green cabbage; as also Papas, a green fruit, about as big as a little melon, which taste like collyflowers.' 'The maiz or Indian wheat sells there by the chest, at one Akier of gold. The chest contains about three bushels. When there is a great demand or scarcity, it rises to two and three Akiers. In plentiful years and times of peace, it has been sold for ten, and even for eight Takoes of gold, which is not three shillings English.' The reference to cabbages and pawpaws (including the odd comparison with cauliflower) repeats a reference in *1679*, p. 319: this appears to be the earliest reference to the cultivation of the pawpaw (*Carica papaya*) on Gold Coast. The reference to 'times of peace' echoes Bosman, pp. 297–8. For prices of maize, see Letter 2/20, note 40, below.

[8] In 1679 Barbot was presented by the English factors with a dozen 'green and red parrots no bigger than a sparrow', but of the 50 parrots or parakeets he acquired in Guinea not one reached America alive (*1679*, p. 312). In 1682 he apparently again acquired parakeets, some of which reached Europe – 'of the great numbers I used to carry away every voyage, I could save but very few alive when arrived in France' – note 'every' voyage (*1732*, p. 220/6).

Cf. *1732*, p. 176/12, which is more specific in its reference to French royalty when it substitutes – 'parrokeets, about as big as sparrows, their bodies a curious green, and their heads and tails of a most beautiful red; some whereof I carry'd to Paris, to present to some of the blood-royal of France. These birds are sold there for a crown a dozen; but they are so very hard to keep alive, that not one in twenty survives the long voyage to Europe'.

[9] In 1679, Barbot noted cotton bushes (*cottoniers*) at Agga, and at Anomabu 'a great lake which produces very fine salt without any human effort' (*1679*, p. 319). Cotton bushes were uncommon on Gold Coast, and if Barbot saw any they may have been planted by Europeans as an experiment. For salt, see Dapper, p. 81/2. Dutch maps showed several 'salt villages' on this coast (1629 map; Robijn/Roggeveen 1685). Omitted in *1732*.

[10] Barbot's 1679 drawing represented the earlier fort (*1679*, p. 318): the *1688* drawing, followed fairly closely by the printed version, *1732*, Plate 13 (p. 176), represents the rebuilt fort, and therefore Barbot drew the fort for a second time in 1682. Neither drawing states the viewpoint: the *1732* version indicates 'The Landing place', 'The Entry to the Port', and 'The Port within the Rocks'.

[11] In 1679 the English fort, which then had only seven cannon and a garrison of 7–8 whites, was composed of 'turf', but the factor was preparing to rebuild it in brick, using bricks baked on the site by slaves (*1679*, pp. 312, 317). This fort, which had earlier belonged to the Swedes and the Danes, was in 1664 seized by the English from the Dutch (ARA, Abramsz 23.11.1679). The limited detail in Barbot's account of the new fort makes it difficult to decide whether or not he actually visited it in 1682.

Cf. *1732*, pp. 176/9–11, 177/1, which in part substitutes: '... the English castle, lately built there, instead of an old house, which stood there in 1679, the mud walls whereof are still to be seen before the castle. This is ... rather a large strong house, defended by two turrets on the one side, and two flankers on the other next the sea, all built with stone, brick and lime, and seated on a rock, about thirty paces from the strand; having twelve good guns and two pattareroes mounted on it, and commonly garrison'd by twelve white men, and eighteen Grometto Blacks, under a chief factor. The lodgings within are convenient, and there are proper warehouses ... This wall, I was told, would be pull'd down, when the castle was quite finish'd ... The greatest inconvenience there is, that they must fetch fresh water from two leagues distance, by means of their slaves.' Most of this decription closely resembles that in Davenant 1709, pp. 224–5, and may derive from this source, in which case the personal reference in the penultimate sentence, if not fiction, may apply to a 1682 visit. But the final sentence repeats a statement in *1679*, p. 319. Further material on Anomabu in *1732*, p. 446/1–2, 4, is from Davenant 1709, pp. 184–5, 192–3, 206.

[12] In 1679 Barbot four times visited the English lodge at 'Agga' (Egya) and its three white residents, and he described the locality as 'a cluster of five or six small villages, about a musket-shot apart from one another' (*1679*, p. 317). There is no evidence that he visited it again in 1682. The Dutch established 'Fort Good Hope' at Egya in 1647, but it was captured by the English in 1664 and during the Anglo-Dutch war of 1672–4 the English settled there (ARA, OWIC 11, Caarlof 26.10.1647; Van Dantzig 1980, pp. 38, 49, 51). The Danes do not appear to have ever had a post at Egya (COP, TKIA, A 171, P. Klingenberg and H. Carloff 28.3.1659; S. Schmidt 1.5.1658) – probably Barbot confused the Danes with the Dutch. For other references to Egya, see ARA, Abramsz 23.11.1679; Hazewinkel 1932, p. 256; Tilleman 1697, p. 83; Bosman 1705, pp. 57–8.

Cf. *1732*, pp. 177/5–8, 446/5, which elaborates, from Bosman, p. 57, and Davenant 1709, pp. 196–7.

[13] Omission of the remainder of the paragraph and the next paragraph describing the 1664–5 attacks on Egya by the English and the Dutch, concluding with a reference to the English retiring to Kormantin, from Dapper, pp. 79/4–80/2.

Cf. *1732*, p. 177/7–8.

[14] In 1679 Barbot noted that landing was difficult at Kormantin; that the fort, built on a steep hill, was flanked with four bastions; that – 'like a castle' – its outer walls had deep spiked ditches; and that it commanded a large well-populated town on the slope of the hill, partly hidden from the sea (*1679*, p. 319). The first English lodge at Kormantin, built in the 1630s, was burnt down in 1640 (ARA, Abramsz 23.11.1679). Between 1645 and 1647 the English built a fort, which became their headquarters on Gold Coast; but this was captured by Ruyter in 1665, a year after the English gained Cape Coast, and was subsequently held by the Dutch (Van Dantzig 1980, pp. 37, 45–50).

Cf. *1732*, p. 177/10.

[15] Omission of one paragraph describing the 1665 Dutch attack on Kormantin, from Dapper, pp. 78/3–79/1.

Cf. *1732*, p. 178/1–3.

[16] In 1679 Barbot drew 'T'Fort Amsterdam' from the anchorage (*1679*, pp. 318–9) – note that the title is in Dutch. But a considerably revised version appeared in *1688* and this was closely followed in *1732*, Plate 14 (p. 177), the main changes being the loss of the upper part of a tower and the replacement of a pyramid dome by a curved cupola. The set of engravings of Gold Coast forts, perhaps to be dated to the 1690s (see the Introduction, note 165), contains a view headed 'Cormentin or the Fort Amsterdam', but this is so different from both the other views as regards the interior buildings of the fort (they appear unfinished) that either it represents a drawing made at another time (or a deliberate revision), or else there has been confusion with another fort (Lawrence 1963, plate 68b, pp. 248–9 – a discussion of limited validity). Certainly some rebuilding became necessary after 1679 when rain destroyed much of the original fortifications (ARA, Abramsz 23.11.1679). Today the fort still has two rectangular and two rounded bastions, but some of the features have been 'restored' in the present century (Lawrence 1963, plate 66).

[17] In 1679 Barbot noted that the fort had four bastions, with 18 cannon, and was manned by 50 whites, and also had cisterns (*1679*, pp. 318–319). The different figures in the text perhaps relate to 1682, but may be again only guesses, since in 1679 there were in fact only 19 whites at Kormantin (ARA, Abramsz 23.11.1679). In the early 1690s the fort was reported to have 24 cannon and 33 whites (Tilleman 1697, pp. 83–4).

Cf. *1732*, p. 177/9, which substitutes for the latter part: '... strengthened by three small, and one fine large battery, mounted with twenty pieces of cannon; and within is a very large square tower, in the midst of it, design'd to have a cupola on it, where the flag-staff stands. There are very good lodgings, and all offices for the service of the commander and garrison, consisting of twenty-five white men, besides Grometto Blacks. The breastworks are large, and the prospect from the top of the tower delightful, overlooking all the sea and the country. Large convenient cisterns are made in it to hold rain-water. The buildings were not quite finish'd, when I was there last'. The remarks on batteries and cannon are from Bosman, p. 58. The final remark about unfinished buildings may offer an explanation of the apparently unfinished buildings in the engraved view (see previous note).

[18] In 1679 Barbot noted that Fort Amsterdam 'commanded a large and well-populated town on the slope of the hill, partly hidden from the sea', and he passed but did not visit Little Kormantin (*1679*, pp. 318, 320). The name 'Tantonquerry' (Tantumquerry, otherwise Otuan) does not appear in pre–1680 sources. The English maintained a post there from 1701 and built a fort in the 1720s (Bosman, p. 58; Davies 1957, p. 248).

Cf. *1732*, p. 178/4–5, which on 'Great Cormentin' adds material from Bosman, p. 58, and on Little Cormentin comments on the food and drink, repeating material referring to the 'Fantyn' country in general in *1679*, p. 319. Also *1732*, p. 446/6, which quotes the reference in Bosman, p. 58, to an unnamed new English 'fort' – actually the post at Tantumquerry – and in the light of Davenant 1709, p. 225, wrongly interprets it as referring to Shido.

[19] Omission of three paragraphs on local trade, from Dapper, pp. 80/4–81/1. Barbot again confuses Dapper's 'Janasia' (Anishan) with Anomabu. To Dapper's list of goods sold at Kormantin and Mori he adds spirits and glass beads, perhaps influenced by Marees, f. 42v.

Cf. *1732*, pp. 178/5–179/4, which adds to the list 'pewter basons, muskets ... powder, etc.', and inserts lengthy material on Afro-European trading relations at Anomabu and Kormantin, as in the 1660s, from Dapper, p. 80/5, and as more recently, from Bosman, p. 59, embroidered.

[20] 'Amersa' must refer to the Amisa Lagoon, shown as 'R. Amysa' on the 1629 map: 'Aqua' probably refers to Nakwa and 'Montfort' to Mumford. Barbot shows the first two, as well as Laguyo, on his map, whereas no villages are shown in Robijn/Roggeveen 1685. But the names are not noted in *1679*, and none is in Dapper, therefore Barbot probably learned them in 1682.

Cf. *1732*, p. 179/5, which translates *mil* as 'Indian corn' (i.e. maize).

[21] In 1679 Barbot bought four slaves while lying off 'Laguyo, a large village on a hill on the coast' (*1679*, p. 320). The name is not in Dapper or

Robijn/Roggeveen 1685. This is presumably Legu, where the English had a lodge in 1704–5 (Davies 1957, p. 248). Given the l/d sound-convergence in the local Kwa languages, this was probably the 'Dagio' shown on the 1700 Mortier map. The statement of a Dutchman formerly resident on the coast to the effect that 'Ladjuw', where the English and Dutch had had lodges (apparently in the 1680s), was the same as Ruygenhoek must be wrong (Hazewinkel 1932, p. 257).

Cf. *1732*, p. 179/6–8.

[22] Omission of one paragraph on the king of Fantyn, from Dapper, p. 81/2–3. Other sources (and Dapper, p. 80/5) refer to Fantyn not as a monarchy but as a loose confederation led by a *brafo*, here defined as a military commander (ARA, Dammaert journal, *passim*; Bosman, p. 57; Daaku 1970, pp. 166–7; Van Dantzig 1980, pp. 33, 37, 51, 109, 154).

[23] For the list of vocabulary, see Letter 3/14, pp. 193–200, below. Barbot's statement about the extent of the coastal language was based on Dapper, p. 82/2 (derived from Marees, f. 42v); but since he must have had opportunities to test whether it was true, it is perhaps more significant than other borrowed passages. See Hair 1967, pp. 259–60; Hair 1969a, pp. 229–32, 239–40. Today the modern form of the language, Akan/Twi, is spoken, in dialects, broadly where Barbot indicated: see Kropp Dakubu 1985.

Cf. *1732*, p. 179/9.

[24] Cf. *1732*, pp. 179/10–180/4, which at this point adds a section on the 'Acron country' and the village of Apam, neither of which was mentioned by Barbot in *1679* or by Dapper. The material is entirely derived from Bosman, pp. 60–62, 295–6, cleverly disguised: e.g. Bosman's reference to 'the King, who is about seventy years of Age' becomes – 'At the time of my being there, the king . . . was . . . about fifty years of age'. Also on Acron is *1732*, p. 446/7, another passage from Bosman, but here acknowledged.

[25] The sentence on the English may be mere embroidery; otherwise there are echoes of Davenant 1709, p. 224. In the late 1690s a hostile source alleged that the post housed a single Englishman (Bosman, p. 56). The additional information on the Portuguese is more detailed and more puzzling. Could it have been obtained by James Barbot in 1699, when he was travelling in company with a Portuguese vessel?

[26] This passage follows material on the same attack (*1732*, p. 416/1–2), taken from Davenant 1709, pp. 184–5, 206.

LETTER 9

Description of the kingdom of Aunguina.

In my last letter, Sir, I halted at the Devil's Mount (or the Ruyge-hoeck), so called by the Dutch and French on account of the squalls which descend from it; for the land is high and can be seen from far out at sea.[1]

[illustration no. (67), 'Cap Ruygehoeck ou Montagne au Diable', inserted after p. 32]

This is where the kingdom of Aungwina or Augwina begins. [. . .][2] It extends 15–16 leagues along the coast, on which there are several villages and hills: D'ajou, Polders-Bay, Mango, Wimba or New Wiamba, Bercu or Barraccau, J'acco or Innya, Lampa, Succuma, Little Bercu and Koock-broot (a round mountain in the shape of a sugar-loaf, two leagues West of Accra). D'ajou and Polders-bay are of no particular importance.[3] Mango is famous for its mountain, which forms a large cape in the sea. It is called Devil's Mount on account of the sacrifices which the natives make there to that spirit of falsehood.[4] [. . .][5] Wiamba lies in a curve of the coast. The village can be seen on the slope of a hill. The English used to have a stone lodge there, but it was attacked by the Moors of the place in 1679. The factor, who was dangerously wounded, would have risked forfeiting his life, and the lives of his men, had he not escaped with them in the night and reached Cabo Corso, where I saw him arrive, covered in blood and wounds.[6] [. . .][7] Among these Moors [between the Devil's Mount and Accra] you find several who use many French words when speaking to Europeans. This again proves what I have told you, Sir, namely, that this nation [of ours] frequented this part of Africa for a long period without any competitors. This can be seen particularly at Acara and Berqu.[8] [. . .][9] /p. 34/ I have already observed, Sir, that not much trade is done at these places, except at Berqu, where the traders of Acara come when vessels are there. Generally speaking, however, you can find a few slaves, which are bartered for says, sheets, coesveld linen and glass beads. A slave is sold here, as almost everywhere on Gold Coast, for one *benda*, which is two ounces of gold.[10] [. . .][11]

426

This, in substance, is all I can tell you about the kingdom of Aungwina. Allow me to take leave till tomorrow, when I shall deal with the kingdom of Acra and with between there and the Rio da Volta; for I need to reflect a little, in order that I may tell you only authenticated facts. Do not give credit to everything you see on maps and in treatises concerning this coast, for they are the products of ignorance or falsehood. Most travellers have had no scruples about lying, or have taken little care to obtain precise information about what they report. You know my sincerity too well to suspect that I would imitate these authors, and you will not doubt that I devote all possible care to discovering the truth about what I write; for you have already been sufficiently convinced of the desire I have to please you, and of the strong passion with which I am, Sir, Your etc.

Additional Passage from *1732*

[p. 180/9, on Devil's Mount]

It had the name given it by the Portugueses, from the sacrifices the Blacks offer there to the devil, as they pretended; but since we have no instance of any Blacks on the Gold-Coast, that pay any veneration to that evil spirit, we may conclude the Portugueses are in the wrong as to this point. However that is, this mountain is very rich in gold, which the Blacks, after violent showers, gather in considerable quantities, the rain washing it from among the sand. The Dutch gave this mount the name of Ruyge-hoeck, because being very high, they often saw it at a distance, long before they could reach it, in sailing along the coast from east to west; the wind being constantly, most of the year from morning till night at S.W. and a very fresh gale, the tide commonly setting to the eastward, so that it requires much time to turn it up. [12]

NOTES

[1] In 1679, as Barbot's ship passed along the coast between Little Kormentin and Accra, he drew Ruigenhoek, and the ship lay off 'Wiomba' but no Africans were met there, either in canoes or on the shore (*1679*, p. 321); in 1682 he passed along the coast again, several times; and in 1699 James Barbot's ship passed Apam and lay off 'Winniba' (*1732*, p. 456/9). The name 'Ruigenhoeck' (Dutch *ruig* 'rough', *hoek* 'hook, headland – as in Hook of Holland) appears on the 1629 map and in Dapper, p. 81/5 ('Ruige Hoek').

'Devil's Mount', a hill 207 m high lying one km from the sea and known locally as Ejisimanku, was mentioned in 1654 (ARA, Dammaert journal, 30.12.1654, 'Duyvelsbergh'). The view of the cape and hill in *1679*, p. 321 (not reproduced), copied in *1688*, was printed in *1732*, Plate 15 (p. 182). 2. Omission of two sentences on the 'Augwina' (Agona) country, from Dapper, p. 81/4.

Cf. *1732*, pp. 180/5–7, 181/10, which adds material on the country 'in my time' but actually a little from Dapper, p. 82/1, and the rest from Bosman, pp. 63–4.

[3] 'Polders Bay' appears on the 1629 map; and 'Solder-bay' (a misprint), 'Jako' and 'Koxbroot' are in Dapper, p. 81/5–6. Versions of almost all the names appear on the relevant map in Robijn/Roggeveen 1685 (e.g., 'Dayou', 'Biemba', 'Berku', 'Jaco'). 'Koxbroot' ('Cook's Loaf' – in this vicinity early Portuguese sources located 'Pam de Nao', 'Ship's Loaf': Pacheco Pereira 1956, p. 129) is Dampa Hill (at 0°23′W). For 'Wimba' and 'Bercu', see notes 6–7 below.

Cf. *1732*, p. 180/5, 8, which adds that all are 'very dangerous places to land at, the sea rolling and breaking violently along the strand'.

[4] This presumably refers to Mangoadze, and is perhaps derived from Marees, f. 42v: ' . . . the high hill of Mango, on which the Blacks sacrifice to their devil. But no trade is done here'. See Tilleman 1697, p. 84; Garrard 1980, p. 139.

Cf. *1732*, p. 180/9, the Additional Passage.

[5] Omission of two sentences from Dapper, p. 82/1, 3, and three from Marees, f. 42v, on trade, women and natural products (Marees was referring to Winneba, but Barbot applied his statement to 'Mango').

Cf. *1732*, p. 180/10.

[6] In 1679 Barbot noted when lying off Winneba and finding the area deserted – 'two large houses on a bluff by the sea in which the English had resided a month earlier but from which they had been driven by the blacks, as I have mentioned when discussing Corso' – the journal does not in fact mention the episode at the stated point – and he further recorded that 'the blacks murdered the agent while we were at Corso' (*1679*, p. 321). Barbot was at Cape Coast in early January, and later that month the commander at Anomabu visited Winneba, presumably to restore the position (*1679*, pp. 307, 309). The attack on the lodge may have been connected with movements of armies in the vicinity (*1679*, pp. 300–301). The English had a lodge at Winneba ('Wiamba', 'Biamba') 1659–64, 1673–9 and from 1694 onwards (Davies 1957, pp. 247–8; Van Dantzig 1980, pp. 48–9, 51–2). According to a Dane writing in about 1692, it was not the 'Moors of the place' but those of 'Quambu' (Akwamu) who destroyed the lodge (Tilleman 1697, p. 86).

Cf. *1732*, p. 180/11, which adds a little from Bosman, p. 64, but also enlarges on the village, partly from *1679*, p. 321 ('200 paces'), and partly (both loosely and word for word) from Phillips 1732, p. 210. Further material on Winneba, and generally Agona, in *1732*, pp. 446/8–447/5, is, as indicated, from Bosman, pp. 62–4, and Davenant 1709, pp. 194, 217, 225; but the dating of 'Aquamboe' attacks on Agona to 1693 and 1694 is probably a deduction from Phillips 1732, p. 210. The reference to 'Plate 25' indicates the plate of views of forts entirely copied from Bosman's illustrations.

[7] Omission of one paragraph on 'Berqu or Barracou' (Senya Beraku) and a brief reference to 'Little Berqu', from Dapper, pp. 81/7, 82/1–3 (mainly Marees, f. 42v).

Cf. *1732*, pp. 180/12–181/6, which adds a reference to parakeets and a suggestion that a fort be built at Senya Beraku. In fact, the Dutch built a fort there in 1704–6, and the English, who had contemplated settling there in 1695, opened a trading post at Shido, slightly further East, in 1705 (Tilleman 1697, p. 85; Davenant 1709, p. 225; Davies 1957, p. 248; Lawrence 1963, p. 341; Van Dantzig 1980, pp. 155–6).

[8] It is conceivable that Barbot met Africans here who knew a few French words, but more likely that he drew this conclusion merely from the reference to the French having formerly traded at Senya Beraku in Dapper, p. 82/3 (from Marees, f. 42v).

Cf. *1732*, p. 181/4, which omits the claim that the French preceded the Portuguese.

[9] Omission of one paragraph on the coast between Kormantin and Accra, from Dapper, p. 81/6 (based on Leers 1665, p. 30). Barbot adjusted the distances: 'from Cormentin to the Devil's Mount, 12 leagues; from there to Berqu is 9 leagues; and from Berqu to the little river of Acra is 8½ leagues'.

Cf. *1732*, p. 181/7–8.

[10] After the first sentence, this passage is from Dapper, p. 82/3, although the only goods mentioned by Dapper are says and linen. Barbot's retention of Dapper's statement on the price of slaves was a piece of laziness, the value of slaves in relation to gold having changed since Dapper's information was obtained: as Barbot himself had noted, in 1679 the rate of exchange at Accra was one slave for 12 *gros*, i.e. 0.75 *benda* (*1679*, p. 330).

Cf. *1732*, p. 181/9, which adds 'iron and brandy'.

[10] Omission of one paragraph on 'Berqu', from Dapper, p. 82/1.

Cf. *1732*, p. 181/3.

[12] The references to gold and to the Dutch are from Bosman, p. 62; and the following sentence represents Barbot's attempt to explain in navigational terms what Bosman meant. Barbot's conversion to rejection of the notion that Africans worship the devil may reflect Bosman, p. 158.

LETTER 10

Description of the kingdoms of Acra, Labade, Ningo, and Soko, and of Forts James, Croevecoeur [sic] *and Christianburg at Acra.*

Sir, daylight has arrived, and I am barely aware that I have given myself some moments of respite. I would again ask for further delay, if I thought that I could obtain it, but your impatience is too great to grant it. So today I will tell you about the kingdoms of Acra, Labade, Ningo, and Socko, which is the last kingdom of Gold Coast, at least if one supposes, as seems best to me, that Gold Coast extends as far as River Volta.

[Accra]

The kingdom of Acra or Acara is 15–16 leagues in circumference, bounded on the West by Agwana and Anonce, with a little river between them [and Acra], on the North by Aboura and Bonoe, on the East by Labade and Ningo, and on the South by the ocean. As there are only 2½ leagues of coast, there are only three villages on the sea, Soko, Little Acra and Orsaky. The village of Great Acra is 3½ leagues inland at the foot of the mountains which can be seen from the sea.[1] Each of these villages is backed up by a fort; Soko by Fort James, belonging to the English, Little Accra by Fort Crevecoeur, belonging to the Dutch, and Orsaky by Fort St Francis Xavier, belonging to the Portuguese (formerly Cristiernburg, belonging to the Danes). These three places are situated in the compass of 1½ leagues of land, each on a rocky headland extending a little way into the sea, and where landing is difficult, except at Little Acra, where it is easiest to land during the first and last quarters of the moon, although it is always necessary to use bar canoes.[2] The village of Soko is the smallest, not having 100 houses, and those all dispersed. The village of Little Acra used to be very agreeable and convenient, having a fine market, but since the war of 1680 /p. 35/ with the Aquamboes, it is almost all burnt down, scarce 60 houses being left standing. King Fourri, whom I saw there on my first voyage, liked it much better there than at Great Acra. This place was famous for its trade in gold and slaves at the time when it was free for everyone to trade there. Orsaky is also of only small importance today, having, like the previous village, suffered from the fury of the Aquamboes' war.[3]

430

39. The English fort, Fort James, at Accra, Gold Coast, 1679

'T.FORT. CREUECŒVR.

You might reasonably conjecture, Sir, that the trade in gold and slaves might not be good at Acra, since you see three forts there within a league and a half. But in fact, however exhausted and afflicted this little state regularly is by wars and frequent famines, and [however exhausted in supply of exports] by the arrival of many ships, you still find there more favourable despatch than at any other place on this coast.[4] The kings of Acra have naturally always liked the whites, but they could not be persuaded to allow the building of forts. However, the last of these princes, having a more mercenary spirit than his predecessors, allowed himself (38–40 years ago) to give way to the persuasion of the Dutch and Danes, who at first asked only for permission to set up lodges, for a payment of tribute of seven marks of gold a year, and this allowed the Europeans to insinuate themselves among the Moors. They brought things to the point of persuading the Moors that they should allow them to en-close the lodges with walls carrying cannon, because the Moors would then be able to go there under cover from the assaults of the Aquamboes, their irreconcilable enemies. It was by this argument that Fort Crevecoeur was in the end built, and next the fort (James Fort) of the English, who, seeing the great profits of the Dutch and Danes, begged so hard that finally they obtained permission to build the westernmost fort. It is true, too, that these forts have been a great help to the peoples of Acra, because without them, not one would have remained alive during the conquest made by the king of the Aquambous in 1680. The owners of these forts know well how to take advantage of the refuge they have given, for they have the Moors so much in subjection that they absolutely dare not come to the ships without permission of the agents, particularly the Dutch.[5]

These three forts are built in almost the same way, on similar terrain. Here is the appearance of James Fort, which is only half a cannon shot away from Fort Crevecoeur.

[illustration no. (68), 'Le Fort James'] /p. 36/†

It is built of the local stone, on a headland of rocks jutting out into the sea, which beats terribly against it. It is in the shape of a square, flanked by four small bastions. The whole main work is very flimsy. Accommodation is in a keep which rises in the form of a square tower, on which there is platform above the roof and a parapet all around, with embrasures and loopholes. The accommodation is

431

insignificant, and of too weak a structure to resist for long the rains of winter and the shock of the cannon, which are fired fairly frequently there, the English and the Danes being, of all Europeans (so I think), the ones who are fondest of the sound of cannon when diverting themselves. In the fort there are 18 small cannon, and 20 white men of the garrison, with 30 Moors. The village of the Moors is North of this place, distant one musket-shot.[6]

[illustration no. (69), Fort Crèvecoeur]†

Fort Crevecoeur, whose profile is shown here, is half a cannon-shot away from James Fort. It was first constructed as a lodge, as I have told you, and later enclosed with curtain walls flanked by bastions, which were made higher on the occasion of the last war against the Aquambous. This little fort is in a fine situation. It is stronger than the English fort, both in its [outer] structure and in its accommodation, and the fabric itself is more durable. The curtain walls, the bastions and the keep are of local stone. The keep is the same shape as that of James Fort, with the addition of a little dome which serves as an office on the platform, and from which a flag is flown. The parade ground is fairly large for so small a place. The commandant's quarters are neat, convenient and in an airy position. As the fort is built on a headland, it joins the land only on the North side, which, however, is not fortified by any palisade or ditch. This, indeed, is not necessary in respect of the Moors, who do not know how to capture these places and who fall flat on the ground at a cannon-shot. The gateway is on the same North face opposite to the village, and is on the road that leads to Great Acra. It has only one small guardroom and two gates. There are 14 iron cannon and several swivel-guns (*pierriers*) as artillery. The area leading across the rock towards the sea is commanded by cannon and musket fire the most fully. There are only 15 whites and a few blacks to hold the fort.[7] Two places as close as this fort and James Fort would have good occasion to burn powder if there was a rupture between the two parties in /p. 37/ Europe, but here, as in other places, interest takes precedence over reasons of state, and if they go to any expense in time of war, it is to entertain each other, turn and turn about, feet under the table, pipe in the mouth. One reason in particular forces them to dispense with hostile acts. It is this – in order the better to fill their purses, acting in concert for private purchases and sales.

St Francis Xavier is the last fort of all those owned by the whites on Gold Coast. It is at Orsaky, a village one league East of Crevecoeur. I have told you, Sir, that it has been in the hands of the Portuguese for only four years. [*margin:* sold to the Portuguese in 1679 for 7 marks of gold][8] They left the Isle du Prince in two brigantines, and went to Acra, where they learned that there was only a Greek left of the whole Danish garrison occupying the fort. They corrupted this man and made him give them the place for seven marks of gold, of which three were paid cash down and four he was to receive at St Thomas (a bargain for a fort).[9] The Danes at Frédericxbourg have since made various representations to the Portuguese, to the effect that they should give it up by mutual agreement, if they received what they had paid for it. But the Portuguese raised their recompense to 100 marks, to take account of the additions they said they had made there, which the Danes could not pay without seriously incommoding themselves. Hence they run the risk of not recovering it, unless the Danish crown makes it an affair of state.

[illustration no. (70), St Francis Xavier Fort or Fort Christiansborg]†

This fort is approximately the same shape as the others, but I consider it to be in a better state to offer resistance, being bigger and better constructed, the structure being more solid and the bastions and curtain walls higher. The entry has no other defence than a double gate which faces the village of the Moors. The keep is larger and more spacious than at Crevecoeur and in a condition to make a longer resistance. The whole place is surrounded by good curtain walls flanked by their bastions, which the Portuguese have raised three feet, and they have added cannon, making 24 in all at present, all of iron, with several swivel-guns on the keep. They have 45 Portuguese as garrison, since they have no Moors in their service, because the Portuguese are generally hated by the whole of Gold Coast. Several families of Orsaky have changed their residence on account of the Portuguese and the Aquambou wars. These Portuguese have made a large /p. 38/ saltings NE of the fort, from a lake which was formerly the fetish (of Orsaky village) in respect of the harvest and drought. They obtain from it white salt, using the methods employed in Portugal and France. They have built a small chapel in the fort, for the celebration of mass by a black priest ordained by the Bishop of St Thomas.[10] The garrison was in a very bad state when I left the coast at the beginning of 1682.[11] It had put Julian de Campo, its governor, under arrest in the keep, and he was so well guarded that no-one could approach him except the two slaves who served him. I had myself carried by hammock to Orsaky to see if I could give him any help (having known him three years earlier at Príncipe, where he was assistant to the commander at St Thomas).[12] But I could get nothing from the factor who received me at the gate of the fort and who told me it was for the bad treatment he and his companions had received that they had imprisoned the governor. This precise behaviour and the care with which they prevented anyone going near him made me believe that there was something felonious about this man and this garrison. One of our vessels having joined us from Europe at the same time as I was performing my little work of charity, a trumpeter was sent the next day with a ship's agent, summoning them to set him at liberty and let him leave if he wished. This they were willing to do, but he refused, thinking it proper to remain until the Portuguese court gave him orders [to leave]. He gave me letters to this effect, which I took care to have sent on their way when I arrived at the Islands.[13]

The Danes made great profits when they were masters of the place, but this did not all go to the Danish Company. The agents, who rose from the lowest ranks as a result of the frequent deaths that happen there, easily amassed considerable sums of money before orders [restraining them] were brought from Denmark. And since this locality is the final one owned by the whites on the coast, at this point most of the ships get rid of many goods unsuitable for Lay, Juda and Ardres, at very low prices. I could have bought the fort for 30 gold marks at the time when a man named Olrichs was its governor. It is to him that I owe a good part of the information that I have about this coast, for he never refused to explain anything to me. The blacks cut his throat in 1679.[14]

These places draw maize for their subsistence from Corso, Manfrou, Anamabou and Cormentin, because the country is ruined by the continual wars which have caused terrible famines, so that I have seen a chest of maize (about two bushels) sell for 10 *écus*.[15] The country, although dry and infertile, supports many hares, rabbits, squirrels, and Guinea fowl, and a number of hinds, oxen, cows brought there from Labade, and wild boar. Also hens in large

41. The Danish fort, Fort Christiansborg, at Accra, Gold Coast, 1679

S. FRANCISCVS XAVIER

42. The Portuguese fort, Fort São Francisco Xavier, formerly Fort Christiansborg, at Accra, Gold Coast, 1682, engraving of c. ?1690

numbers and some deer and goats, for it is mountainous inland.
Only about three leagues of flat land inland from the coast are
suitable for hunting, the land having little forest. The air is purer
than at any other place on the coast, and the soil is heavy and the
colour of crushed brick. They have hardly any fruit, only yams and
several kinds of beans and peas.[16]

The gold traded at Acra is considered as pure as that of Igwira.
Most of it comes from inland by way of the land of Abonce, and in
time of war you can reckon on 500–600 slaves a year.[17] Gold and
slaves are traded for Coesveld cloth, *Sleysiger Ly-watt* [Silesian
linen], knives, bedsheets, says, perpetuanas, brandy, guns, powder,
glass beads and *contecarbe* [beads]. A slave is reckoned at about a
benda of gold, reducing the goods to the value that they sell for gold.
[.../p. 39/...][18] This will suffice for the kingdom of Acra.

Additional Passages from *1732*

[p. 184/11–185/2, on anchorage at Accra, and the Akwamu con-
quest]

Before I leave Acra, I must warn sailors to weigh their anchors in
the road every two or three days, because the ground being full of
rock-stones, the buoy ropes and the cables are apt to be cut, about
eight or nine feet from the anchor. Thus we lost a sheet-anchor in
that road; and many other ships, before and after me, have had the
same fortune. The fresh S.W. gales, which generally blow from
morning till night, except in the rainy season, cause the seas to
swell high, and the tide setting eastward very rapid with the wind,
ships work very hard on the cables, and render it very tedious and
troublesome to get up the anchor in the day-time; which is much
easier done in the night, the weather being calmer. / In the wet
season the tide sets as the wind and moon rule it; for two or three
days before and after the new and full moon, the tide sets up to the
westward, as it also does after it has blown hard at N.E. and
E.N.E. and the wind returns to S.S.W. and S.W. Then the tide
for twenty-four hours will run upwards against the wind, as has
been found by experience, lying before Corso, Anamabo, Cormentin and Acra.[19] The kings and chief Blacks of Acra were, in
my time, very rich in slaves and gold, through the vast trade the
natives drove with the Europeans on the coast, and the neighbouring nations up the country. These people, in their flourishing

peaceful times, possess more wealth than most of those before spoken of put together; and yet these natives of Acra being much addicted to war with their inveterate enemies the Aquamboes, have been at last overcome by them, and their country ruin'd and finally reduced to a province in the years 1680 and 1681, as has been mentioned in its place.

[p. 448/4, on the village of Soko]

Bloome's Memoirs, chief at Acra in 1693. The village Soko situated under this fortress is also much enlarg'd ever since, by a large number of families of the people of the neighbouring village Little Acra, under the Dutch fort, who have settled at the former, after the devastations of the Aquamboes at the latter, they having burnt most of it; others retired to other places of the coast eastward, as Lampa, Popoo, etc. those Blacks being also, on the other hand, much dissatisfied at the Dutch proceedings towards them. / This town of Soko is at present one of the finest and largest of the Gold Coast, seated on a level ground, and regularly built, and so much increased in buildings and inhabitants since the year 1692, that it has a very considerable trade with the English, to the prejudice of the Dutch.[20]

[p. 448/6–8, on the later history of Fort Christiansborg]

The Danish fort at Acra, when I left the Gold Coast, in 1682, was possessed by the Portugueses; but some time after, the Danes redeemed it for a good sum of money, and settled their trade anew with the natives, and so possess'd it till the year 1693, when the Blacks surpriz'd it in the following manner, expelling the Danes, and keeping possession of it for some time. / *Bloome's Memoirs*. This misfortune of the Danes was occasion'd by the death of several of their garrison, and they having done some insults to the king of Acra, that prince studied revenge, and observing the Danes had much confidence in one Assemmi, a Black who having a great interest in that country, procured them a very brisk trade, he ingaged him to contrive how to surprize the fortress. Accordingly Assemmi made the Danish governor believe he would bring him a considerable number of merchants at once, to buy fire-arms, which they wanted much, and therefore advised him to inhaunce the price, appointing the day when they should come. / On that day accordingly Assemmi brought about eighty bold Blacks along with him, whom the Danes introduc'd into their fort, in hopes of selling them a quantity of fire-arms, and not suspecting the least treachery. When the Blacks had agreed on the price of the goods, and paid the value in gold, they loaded their muskets with powder and ball, which each of them had brought with him, as if they designed to try them; but on a sudden fell all unanimously on five and twenty or thirty Danes, that then composed the garrison, who presently yielded the fort to them. They immediately dispersed the Danes into several parts of the inland country; after which the king of Acra and the Blacks intirely stript it, and took a booty of above seven thousand pounds sterling: the fort was given over to the treacherous Assemmi in propriety, who garrison'd it with his own Blacks, and so settled himself therein, trading with all the European ships that came thither; buying great quantities of European goods of them, and afterwards selling them again to the Blacks of the country to a considerable profit.[21]

[p. 456/10–11, on James Barbot at Accra in 1699]

The fifteenth [of April] we arrived at Acra, and anchor'd about a league and a half from shore. Here we stay'd to the twenty-sixth, trading for gold, slaves, and some few teeth; and diverting ourselves by turns, with the English, Dutch and Danish commanders of the forts; but more intimately with Mr Trawne, the Danish chief, who has his lady with him.[22] / The twenty-sixth, as we worked our small bower aboard, both cable and buoy-rope breaking, we were forc'd to sail, leaving the anchor behind, which was hitch'd among the rocks at the bottom; and having purchas'd sixty-five slaves along the Gold Coast, besides gold and elephants teeth, saluted the three European forts, each with nine guns; and then steered east south-east, for four or five leagues, then south-east by east for twenty-eight leagues, towards New Calabar, to buy more slaves.

[Labadi to the Volta]

The kingdom of Labadde is of so little importance that it does not deserve to be mentioned; but as it forms part of our subject, I must tell you that it is limited on the West by Acra, on the North and East by the kingdom of Ningo, and on the South, at the sea, by about one league of coast. On this coast there are two villages, the first Orsou, the other Labadde. [. . .][23] The country of Ningo, or Nimgo, has to the West Great Accra and Labade, to the North Equea and Little Acra, to the South the sea, and to the East Soko. It extends 15 leagues along the coast, which runs NE-by-East from Labbede to Occa. Beyond Lay [read: Labade] are found the villages of Lesser Ningo (Ningo minor), Tema, Cincko, Brambra, Pompena, Greater Ningo (Ningo major), Lay or Alampey, and Occa, all places with a bar.[24] I will write only of Cincko, Greater Ningo and Lay, which are the most important for trade, as the others are not worth stopping at; but I must say that Tema or Temina was frequented by the Dutch from 1600.[25] Cinko is eight leagues from Acra, and Greater Ningo five leagues beyond Cinko, which has been frequented since the beginning of this century. The land produces fine oranges. The natives devote themselves largely to fishing. They trade with Spice, which is a large inland town. They pay tribute to no king. Their language is different from that of Acra, although they are not far distant from there. They like cloths, as do all the countries between [Acra and] River Volta.[26] I have said that Greater Ningo is further East. Neither this village nor Cinko can be clearly seen from the sea. There are few landmarks to help easy recognition, although Ningo has Mount Redonda (North of Lay) which, when you are NNE of it provides the assurance that you are off Ningo. The Moors, who very often come out in their canoes as soon as they see a ship coming, also provide recognition. Slaves are available here, and a small quantity of gold, in exchange for coesveld and Indian cloths. The people of Ningo also fatten large numbers of cattle, which they sell at Acra and higher up Gold Coast, to which places they carry them in canoes and sell them at 30 *écus* each.[27]

[illustration no. (71), the coast around Lay and Mount Redonda, inserted after p. 38]

The village of Lay is two leagues East of Ningo. The roadstead runs NNE and SSW of Redonda (a mountain which is /p. 40/ six leagues inland, and seems to be very large and in the shape of a sugar-loaf).[28] The coast is wholly white cliffs, broken in several places and covered with trees. Sands appear at the edge of the sea, all the way along, like a nap cloth. You see many palm-trees standing apart from each other. The coast further to the East is lower. The village is situated on the slope of a hill facing North, so that from the roadstead only a few of the houses highest up can be seen.[29] There are many inhabitants, who are good people, but who nevertheless always want to have hostages in their hands and refuse to trade without this precaution. Sometimes many slaves are available, being brought in droves here when the Acquems and the Aquambous are at war, for all the prisoners taken on one side or the other are sold at Acra and Lay, the Aquambous coming to Lay to sell their Accanez prisoners and the Accanez selling their Aquambou prisoners at Acra. Slaves are traded for cowries, says, perpetuanas, coesveld cloth, *Sleysiger-Lywatt* [Silesian linen], knives, glass beads, guns and powder. A man named Santi is the Inspector of Trade for the king of Lay. He arrives to fix the price of slaves going on board, one by one, according to sex and age, and as they are delivered from the mountains he sends them aboard. This greatly facilitates trade, to the extent that vessels have been known to spend 15 days in this place and to have traded for 500 slaves.[30] [. . .][31]

On account of the little trade done there the kingdom of Soko is so seldom frequented that I can tell you about it in a couple of words. On the West it is bounded by the kingdom of Ningo, on the South by the sea, on the East by River Volta. It has four principal villages on the coast, apart from several others unknown to us, and at these much maize is produced. These four villages are Angulan, Briberqu, Baya and Aqualla. The inhabitants of these places are occupied mainly in sowing and cultivating the land.[32] The Accaniz sometimes come to some of these places to trade local cloths (*pagnes*) which they bring there and on which they make prodigious profits. But the difficulty of brigands on the roads causes them to come seldom. They say that the people of Soko know nothing at all about gold and have no use for it. The Portuguese sometimes leave pieces-of-eight in exchange for provisions or Accanez cloths. The country is flat along the shore and raised inland, and wholly covered with forest, including many palms. Slaves can sometimes be found there, they having arrived by River Volta, which I will describe in due course.[33]

I will now work away at this hour, in order to collect and put in order what I have to tell you about the customs, politics, and peoples of Gold Coast, a region I have just described to you briefly. I seek your permission to dispense with writing to you about the hinterland of these countries, since I can only speak about it by repeating a Dutchman who has dealt with several of the kingdoms neighbouring those by the sea and who, in fact, speaks of them only very summarily, which is not to your liking. For you, Sir, want to know about things down to the minutest details. However, if you will be content with this imperfect notion, I will satisfy you at once. I await your reply. Meanwhile, I remain, Sir, Yours etc. /p. 41/

Additional Passages from *1732*

[p. 186/6, on trade at Lay]

The French, English and Portuguese ships ply most at this coast, to purchase slaves and provisions. Notwithstanding the great number of slaves I have mention'd to be transported from these parts, it sometimes happens, when the inland country is at peace, that there are none at all; as it happen'd to me in the year 1682, when having lain three days before Lay, I could not get one, nor was there any likelihood of it at that time, as the afore-mentioned Black Santi told me; and yet, but two months before my arrival there, one of the men of war of our little squadron got three hundred slaves in a very short time, which shews that the trade is very uncertain.[34]

[p. 449/3–4, on the later history of Lay]

Bloome's Memoirs 1701 The kingdom of Lampa or Alampa, is at this time a place where a great quantity of slaves is purchas'd, by the English, French, Dutch and Portuguese, and a cargo of them soon compleated. The Europeans carry thither for trade, almost the same sorts of European merchandize, as serve for the commerce at Acra; but of all the European trading nations, the French have the greatest traffic on that coast, from Ningo-minor, to Ningo-grande and Lay. / This was confirmed to me some years ago by a French officer of the Assiento company, prisoner of war at Southampton, who had made three voyages to Alampoe successively, for the said company.[35]

NOTES

[1] Barbot's ship was off Accra for a fortnight in February 1679 (*1679*, pp. 321–331), and he visited Accra again, apparently for brief periods, twice in 1682, in February and April. James Barbot visited Accra for a fortnight in May 1699 (*1732*, p. 456/10), but Barbot seems to have learned little fresh on Accra from his brother. In 1679 he received much information from Johann Olrichs (Ollricks/Ulrich), the governor of the Danish fort of Christiansborg,

and from his assistant, Peter Valk (COP, V-gK 187, 6.2.1674 'Jan Olrichs'; *1679*, pp. 323, 331, 335). Olrichs provided a 'mémoire instructif' on the coastal trade, and apparently also oral information about African social practices, information which Barbot later incorporated in his account of Gold Coast, although it is uncertain whether the particulars were intended to refer to other than the people of the Accra region (*1679*, pp. 331, 334–41). However, all the information so far is derived from Dapper, p. 82/4–6 (and hence, indirectly, from the 1629 map), with Anonce a miscopying for Abonce (perhaps modern Abese, near Pokoase), apart from the references to 15–16 leagues rather than miles, the little river (shown on Barbot's map), the 2½ leagues, and the view from the sea. Soko (modern Tshoco) and Little Acra represent the two halves of Accra proper, later 'English Accra' or Jamestown, and 'Dutch Accra' or Usshertown (from the later name of Fort Crèvecoeur), districts which did not coalesce until the nineteenth century. 'Orsaky' (probably a corrupt form of the toponym, by miscopying) is modern Osu, the village of Fort Christiansborg, which remained physically distinct until the end of the nineteenth century. The site of Great Accra, near Ayaso, lies in the low hills which are the continuation of the Akwapim range (visible out to sea) rather than 'at the foot' of the hills.

[2] In 1679 Barbot visited, drew and described each of the forts. He noted that, on account of the breakers, landing was extremely difficult at James Fort, a little less difficult at Christiansborg where the Danes used large canoes, and easiest at Crèvecoeur where boats could be used (*1679*, pp. 332–4).

Cf. *1732*, pp. 181/11–14, 184/4, which embroiders and also adds, repeating *1679*, p. 331, that the villages are 'under the cannon' of the forts, yet the forts have little authority over the blacks, this last view to fit Bosman, p. 69.

[3] In 1679, Barbot met Fourri, 'a young man of 22–23', at the Dutch fort; and he records that the king was paid two ounces of gold per month by each fort, and that Barbot's ship paid him with brandy for the right of anchorage. The history of a war with Akwamu, in which Fourri was taken prisoner and his lands were devastated, was narrated by Governor Olrichs (*1679*, pp. 322–4, 331–2). A visit by Barbot to King Fourri is described later (Letter 2/ 28, pp. 109–10, below). According to recent historians (using as part-evidence *1732* but not *1679* or *1688*), the war between Akwamu and Accra was in 1677, when the king of Accra was killed; but a prince, Ofori, fled from Great Accra to Little Accra, where he was overwhelmed by a second Akwamu attack in 1680 (Wilks 1957, pp. 106–11; Daaku 1970, pp. 154–5 – but see Van Dantzig 1980, pp. 190–1). Here Barbot gives the date of an Akwamu attack on Accra as 1680 but elsewhere as 1681 (Letter 2/30, p. 119, below). The penultimate sentence was perhaps inspired by a remark on 'free trade' in Dapper, p. 81/11. All that Barbot states here dates from 1679–1682: for a later view of Soko, see the Additional Passage.

Cf. *1732*, pp. 181/14, 182/2–4, 310/4, 322/1, 5, which adds regarding King Fourri – 'I was there several times with him in 1679. He was a man of a good mien, a great friend to Europeans, but of too restless a spirit, which at last occasioned his ruin, having too powerful a nation to contend with; as were the Aquamboe, who, in conclusion, obliged him to abandon his dominions, as has been said'. Barbot further adds that 'most of the inhabitants of these three villages have left them, since the irruptions of the Aquamboes, and settled themselves and families at Popo near Fida', and notes also 'the great numbers of families that have removed thence to Lay, Popo and Fida, as their king Fourri has done to Fetu, being a near relation to Aben Penin Ashrive, king of Fetu, to deliver themselves from the arbitrary power of the king of Aquamboe, whose soldiers frequently plunder this and other countries; being countenanc'd by their haughty sovereign, who never fails to espouse all their quarrels'. Barbot's view of the devastation strongly influences Kea 1982, p. 139. Dutch archive sources confirm the exile of Fourri at Fetu in 1681, as well as the name of the Fetu king, Ahen Penin Ashrive (not 'Aben' – Akan/Twi ɔ-hene 'chief, king'; -pan(y)in 'male person, adult, elder'), who witnessed the Accra-Danish agreement in 1661 establishing Fort Christiansborg (Wilks 1957, p. 111). This king died on 3 October 1687 (Hillier 1697, p. 687). Barbot may have obtained in 1682 the information about Fourri at Fetu, or he may have heard it from James Barbot or from English informants. Fourri eventually removed to Little Popo, where his presence is first recorded in 1687 (OBLR, C.747, J. Carter, Whydah, 10.5.1687). As regards the relative size of the three villages, in the 1690s a Dane estimated that, in terms of men with guns, Soko ('Sioco') could supply 60, Orsaky ('Ursow') 300, and Little Accra ('Aprag') 500 (Tilleman 1697, pp. 89–97).

[4] Cf. *1732*, p. 182/1, which enlarges, incorporating more material on the effect of the Akwamu wars, from Bosman, p. 69.

[5] The history of how the Europeans, or at least the Dutch, obtained permission to trade at a lodge and then a fort, for a tribute of seven marks, is from Dapper, p. 83/3. It is not clear why Barbot chose a date '38–40' years previously (and why he says this was in the time of the 'last' king of Accra), which, since he was writing most probably in 1684, would make the date c. 1645: in fact, a Dutch lodge existed by 1645, and a Swedish lodge was established in 1652 and became a Danish fort in 1661 (Lawrence 1963, pp. 49, 199).

Cf. *1732*, p. 181/14, which carelessly retains '38–40 years ago', and enlarges by stating that the king accepted money for permission to build a 'stone house' and by adding a description of the Dutch fort, these from a re-reading of Dapper, p. 83/3. As stated in note 2 above, Barbot's view that the Africans were dependent is changed to the opposite, Bosman's view, that the Europeans have 'little authority', although it might be argued that a changed balance had occurred over time as a result of the Akwamu conquest.

[6] Barbot provides the major source on these three forts as they were c. 1680. In 1679 he visited and drew James Fort, and he described it as having two bastions on the seaward side, two towers on the landward side, 18 cannon, and a large town one musket-shot away (*1679*, pp. 322, 331 – 'St James', but in the margin already 'James fort', the usual English form of the name, adopted in *1688*). James Fort was only upgraded from a lodge and given its name in 1679 (Davies 1957, p. 246). In 1682 an English agent at the fort reported – 'Mr Barboate I received ... and treated him with all the civillity I could' (OBLR, C.745, p. 168, Accra, 23.2.1681/2 O.S. = 5.3.1682 N.S.). A visitor in 1694 reported that the rains had washed away clay and plaster and caused one bastion to fall, and that there were about 20 cannon and only 12 whites (Phillips 1732, p. 213). In 1709 it was stated that the fort had 40–50 guns and a garrison of 50–60 whites and 50 gromettoes (Davenant 1709, p. 227). The illustration of James Fort drawn in 1679 (*1679*, p. 332) was repeated with little change in *1688* and again in *1732*, Plate 14 (p. 177).

Cf. *1732*, pp. 182/5–6, 447/6, which adds, as well as 'I saw', passages describing improvements in the 1690s, from Bosman, p. 67. The added passages include statements that since 1682 the 'lodgements' have been raised and the 'dungeon' (i.e., keep) made higher, statements not in fact in Bosman, and it does not appear that they could be deduced from Bosman's crude illustration: they may therefore either be from the source cited next in *1732*, Bloome's 'Memoirs', or else they may have come from James Barbot who visited Accra in 1699.

[7] In 1679 Barbot visited and drew the Fort 'Croevrecoeur'/'Crevecoeur' (*crève-coeur* 'heart-break': note that, as followed in the translation, Barbot consistently declines to mark an accent on *crevecoeur*). He described it as of regular shape, flanked by small bastions, with the town under its ten cannon (*1679*, pp. 322, 331–2). Barbot seems to have obtained additional information about the fort in 1682. In the 1660s it was described in some detail (Dapper, p. 83/3, quoted in *1732*, p. 181/14); and in 1679 an official noted recent improvements to the accommodation, adding that the garrison consisted of an agent, his assistant and six soldiers (ARA, Abramsz 23.11.1679). In 1694 an English visitor noted that it overlooked James Fort and could fire muskets into it (Phillips 1732, p. 213). Surprisingly, a Dutchman said only that, although this fort had more and better guns than its English neighbour, its walls were thinner (Bosman, p. 67).

Cf. *1732*, p. 182/7–8, which enlarges as follows – 'within it a large flat square house, with a platform, and on it a turret with a cupola, on which the Dutch flag is display'd, as at all other forts on the coast, as soon as any ships appear at sea'; and also adds a little from Bosman, p. 67.

[8] Barbot referred to the transfer of the fort in Letter 2/6, p. 26 above, but did not state the date when this occurred, other that that it was after his visit

in 1679 and before 1682. The implication of his present remark is that he is writing this section 'four years' after 1679, that is, in 1683 or 1684.

[9] At Accra in 1679, the day before he sailed for Príncipe, Barbot bought a slave from a Greek working at Christiansborg (*1679*, p. 330).

Cf. *1732*, pp. 173/9, 183/3, which enlarges considerably. 'In 1679, it was govern'd by John Olricks of Gluckstad, a worthy person, with whom I was very intimate: him the treacherous Blacks inhumanly murder'd at the instigation of a Greek, who had liv'd there some years under him. That villain, some time after, sold the place to Julian de Campo Barreto, formerly governor of the island of St Thome, for a sum of money, not exceeding seven marks of gold. Barreto was the same person I had known three years before at Ilha de Principe or the prince's island, in the gulph of Guinea.' In 1679, while at Príncipe, Barbot learned that Campo Barreto was preparing two small ships for Guinea, and since Barbot had gained the impression during his visit to Accra that he could buy the fort for 30 marks – or so he says, see p. 38 above – it is just possible that it was Barbot who put the idea of gaining the fort into Campo Barreto's mind (*1679*, p. 347). But Barbot does not tell us how he gained this impression, or, if a specific offer was made to him, who made it, although he implies that the governor, Olrichs, was involved. There is in fact no confirmation of the involvement of any Greek in either the murder or the sale, and another source stated that the fort was sold for 36 lb. of gold by Pieter Bolt, apparently Olrichs's successor as governor (Tilleman 1697, p. 95).

[10] In 1679 Barbot drew this fort, then occupied by the Danes and called Christiansborg, and he described it as better built and stronger than the others, but with fewer whites and only four cannon and three swivel-guns, and with the town a musket-shot behind the fort: he also described a rain-making ceremony at the lake (*1679*, pp. 332, 335–6). He visited the fort again in 1682, hence the additional information in *1688*. The *1679* drawing of the fort (p. 333) was repeated in *1688* and in *1732* Plate 15 (p. 182), but a building with a cross on the roof was added in the later drawings, to indicate the new chapel. The *1679* and *1732* versions show a Danish flag, but the *1688* version shows, in error, the English flag (a dark cross on a light ground, instead of the Danish light cross on a dark ground). Curiously, only the version in the set of engravings of the 1690s shows a Portuguese flag. The *1688* version gives the fort its Portuguese name, but Barbot has added, presumably much later, 'Christarn-burgh'. Bosman briefly described this fort, and Tilleman who served in it in the early 1690s provided a drawing and a plan as well as a description; but, according to Lawrence, these descriptions differ from that of Barbot – whose drawing is criticized – because the fort was reconstructed in the 1690s (Bosman, p. 68; Tilleman 1697; Lawrence 1963, pp. 201–5). A profile of the fort and nearby coast, and a plan of the fort (not known to Lawrence), were made in 1704 (BL, Add.

MSS 19560, Des Marchais manuscript, p. 41). On the pre-1700 history of Fort Christiansborg, see Nørregard 1966, pp. 57–61 (but note that this authority, while deploying much Danish archive documentation, does not always supply references to other sources, and that he depends heavily on *1679* and *1732*).

Cf. *1732*, p. 183/1–2, which adds that the fort has a guardroom and a 'spur' at the gate overlooking the village, and that the lake is 'parcel'd out into divisions' to make salt, 'as they do at Setubal'. (Had Barbot been to Portugal or was this common commercial knowledge?). Portuguese salt-making at Accra is mentioned again, in Letter 2/16, p. 57 below. Salt from 'Ursow' and elsewhere carried 'great distances inland for trade' was noted by Tilleman 1697, pp. 110–11.

[11] That Barbot 'left the coast at the beginning of 1682' is either a slip or misleadingly worded. He arrived on Gold Coast in January, and visited Accra in February and again in April. However, whereas in February he visited James Fort, and therefore probably Christiansborg, in April he may only have lain off Accra, there being no positive evidence that he landed. Thus, 'when I left the coast' may mean 'when I left Accra after visiting the fort'.

[12] See note 9 above.

[13] The Portuguese occupation of the fort is confirmed by Tilleman 1697, p. 95.

Cf. *1732*, pp. 183/3–4, 407/5, 448/6, which extends the story. Barbot was carried from the Dutch fort; the Portuguese chief factor only allowed him 'to salute [the prisoner] at the window of the room he was confined to above-stairs, from a considerable distance'; the factor's terms for the prisoner's release were that he should travel to Europe with Barbot; Barbot carried a letter to the Portuguese court which he handed over at Príncipe, and Campo Barreto 'sent word . . . he hourly expected a Portuguese man of war from Lisbon'. Barbot adds – 'The Portuguese garrison was then in a miserable condition, in want of all sorts of provision, and even bread; and all the goods in their warehouse did not amount to the value of sixty pounds, as I was told at the Dutch fort'.

[14] Although Barbot's 1679 journal reports contacts and discussion with Olrichs and others of the Danish garrison (see note 1 above), there is nothing about selling the fort – and this statement is not repeated in *1732*. In 1682, Barbot must have been disappointed on arrival at Accra to find Fourri in exile, Olrichs dead, and Campo Barreto incommunicado, but he perhaps also had hopes of obtaining the fort for the French. An English agent, reporting Barbot's arrival at Accra, added that 'the French had great hopes to have bought the fort of the Portuguese but they obteyned not their desire' (OBLR, C.745, p. 171, Accra, 23.2.1682 O.S.). The weakness of the Danes

even after their recovery of the fort in 1683 was shown by their mortgaging it in 1685–9 to the English, and by the Akwamu offer of the fort to the French in 1688 (Davies 1957, p. 249; Wilks 1957, p. 121).

Cf. *1732*, pp. 173/9, 184/1, 3–4, 407/5, where the first reference declares that the Portuguese possess the fort 'now', a careless slip on Barbot's part since his brother had visited the fort in 1699, and since he elsewhere refers to the Danes recovering it – and then losing it again, for which see the Additional Passage.

[15] In 1679, Barbot reported that because of war and a consequent famine, whereas corn (*gros mil*, perhaps maize) cost 1½–2 *aquiers* per chest elsewhere on the coast, it cost as much as 8 *aquiers* at Accra. He also stated that the forts made their bread from corn which they were obliged to obtain from Cape Corso or from 10–12 leagues inland, the wars having made it impossible for the people of Accra to cultivate their lands (*1679*, pp. 324, 334). The price of 10 *écus* per chest, 'after the Aquambou war in 1679', is given again in Letter 2/20, p. 83, below. Possibly the price was higher on Barbot's return in 1682, after further war, and in recollection he confused the two prices. Alternatively he just exaggerated. War was not the only reason for high prices at Accra, since, as Dapper noted, provisions were dear there during annual shortages of food before the harvest (Dapper, p. 82/7). Irregular rainfall and the infertile nature of the soil near the town, owing to blown salt from the surf, together perhaps with pressure of population on the land in the interior, made Accra dependent on food imports at highly fluctuating prices (Tilleman 1697, p. 111); and wars aggravated the situation, by making it particularly difficult for local farmers to go to their rather remote farms. Nevertheless, in May 1693 an English captain obtained 700 chests of corn from the English agent at Accra (Phillips 1732, p. 211).

Cf. *1732*, p. 184/2, 8–10, which has 'ten pieces of eight', and which adds material on wars in general from Bosman, pp. 70–1.

[16] In 1679, Barbot noted that Christiansborg had fresh meat from oxen, cows, pigs, sheep, goats, three kinds of deer, Guinea-fowl and pigeons; and that hunting in the locality was possible (*1679*, p. 334). In 1693, Guinea fowl and deer, the latter '500 at once', were noted (Phillips 1732, p. 211). But the references to cows from Labede, flat land, hares, wild boar, and no fruit but yams, beans and peas, are all from Marees, ff. 43, 66, and Dapper, p. 83/7, 91/2. However, it is correct that livestock was brought from further East to fatten on the grassy plains at Accra (Tilleman 1697, p. 112).

Cf. *1732*, p. 184/5–7, slightly embroidered, perhaps from re-reading Marees (hares killed 'with sticks', but adding 'Europeans take them with spaniels' and their flesh is very insipid). Hares at Accra are mentioned again, in Letter 2/14, p. 52, below. They were seen in 'vast numbers in the sedge and furze' by a 1694 party which included 'Mr Bloome, with a little spaniel' (Phillips 1732, p. 212): it is just possible that Barbot's specific reference to spaniels came either from Bloome's 'Memoirs', which he cites for other information, or else from Phillips's manuscript. Barbot also adds, perhaps from recollection, a reference to another Accra feature. 'It is worth observing, that in the flat country beyond the European forts, there are abundance of ants nests, which those industrious insects have rais'd above the rest of the ground in a most amazing manner, several of them rising like sugar-loaves, three foot high, or better: of which, I shall hereafter speak more at large. These anthills, not improperly deserving to be call'd turrets, look, at a distance, like the salt heaps on the isle of Rhe in France, at the beginning of the salt season'. For further discussion of 'anthills' (strictly termite mounds, still prominent in the Accra plains), see Letter 2/15, p. 56, below.

[17] In 1679, when Barbot obtained about 150 slaves at Accra (or 200, according to *1732*, p. 271/5), he reported the argument that slaves were in short supply there because of peculiar war circumstances, the people of Accra having pledged slaves to their allies, the 'Achenists', or sold them further West on the coast for corn. He also stated that the inland peoples obtained slaves in war, in order to use them as porters in the trade to the coast (*1679*, p. 324). The references to gold from Abonce and to a large number of slaves are from Dapper, p. 82/12, where the number is given as 300. In eight months of 1678, the English fort at Accra bought 166 slaves (Davies 1957, p. 226). In the later 1690s, it was estimated that of 700–800 slaves shipped annually from Gold Coast, the greater part came from Accra; or alternatively, that because of the wars waged by Akwamu, the number of slaves sold at Accra equalled that of the whole of the remainder of Gold Coast (Bosman, p. 70; Roussier 1935, p. 7).

Cf. *1732*, p. 182/1, 184/3, 8–10, which incorporates the alternative view, omits the number of slaves, and adds material on Accra neglect of fishing and salt-making and on the blacks welcoming wars, all from Bosman, pp. 69–70.

[18] At Accra in 1679, in exchange for slaves, Barbot's ship supplied coesveld and various other cloths including nicanees, knives, brandy, muskets, beads, coloured carpets, and agates; and the cargo had also included bed-sheets, perpetuanas and says (*1679*, p. 249). The omitted section is of three sentences, on trading at the inland market of Abonce, from Dapper, p. 83/1, 4. This includes a reference to an efficient taxation system and Barbot adds a moral conclusion – 'You see, Sir, this proves that there are no people, however stupid, who do not have something good about them'.

Cf. *1732*, p. 184/3, which substitutes top-sails and nicannies for *contecarbe*, misprints 'slyziger, lywat', and omits both the statement about the price of a slave and the moral conclusion.

[19] In February 1679 Barbot recorded the loss of an anchor, caused by failure to examine the cable every second day, by the rocky bottom off Accra, and by the high breakers at new and full moon (*1679*, pp. 331–2);

while in April 1699 Barbot's brother also recorded the loss of an anchor at
Accra – see the Additional Passage. In 1693 an English captain who experienced anchorage problems at Accra noted that 'few ships come here but
leave their anchors behind 'em' (Phillips 1732, p. 213). In August 1953, a
survey vessel reported off Accra a persistent south-westerly swell averaging
1.2 m at seven-second intervals on the 10 fathom line and steeper inshore,
with heavy surf breaking at about two fathoms (*Africa pilot* 1967, pp. 460–
1). It is therefore possible that the whole of this passage is based on the
experiences of the Barbot brothers and on what they learned from colleagues
aboard, and was not drawn from some navigational manual, despite the
reference to the rainy season and the fact that neither of the Barbots was ever
on Gold Coast during that season.

[20] Bloome served on the coast as an agent of the Royal African Company
from at least 1687 to at least 1695, mainly at Accra, where he entertained
Phillips in 1694, and was acting chief English agent on the coast for short
periods in 1691 and 1692 (OBLR, C.745–7; Phillips 1732, p. 211; Porter
1966, p. 206). It is not clear what the date 1692 refers to, or when exactly the
'Memoirs' were composed, although apparently after 1701; hence the exact
date of 'at present' is uncertain. It has been argued that the English supported the Akwamú conquest of Accra, presumably to weaken the Dutch
(Daaku 1970, pp. 154–5).

[21] The Portuguese evacuated the fort on orders from Lisbon, and if the
Danes made a payment for its recovery this may have been to the local
African ruler, by now the king of Akwamu (Nørregard 1966, p. 46, source
not stated). In keeping with this updated history, the illustration of Cris-
tiansborg in *1732*, Plate 15 (p. 182) shows the fort with a Danish flag. On the
fort when occupied by Assemmi, see the first-hand account of a visiting
English captain (Phillips 1732, pp. 211–13; also Wilks 1957, pp. 120–21).
As a souvenir of the African occupation, keys of Christiansborg remain
today in Akwamu state treasury (Lawrence 1963, p. 203 and plate 41b).
Barbot continues, in *1732*, pp. 448/9–449/1, with Bosman's account of the
occupation of the fort by local Africans (Bosman, pp. 67–8 – mistakenly
attributed to Bloome's 'Memoirs' in Wilks 1957, p. 136, n. 106). But the
final sentence attributed to Bosman is actually a comment by Barbot – see
note 22 below.

[22] Barbot inserted a comment elsewhere, perhaps borrowed from his
brother's journal. 'The Danish agent that commanded there in 1699, was
one Mr Trawne of Copenhagen, who had his wife there with him; the
gentlewoman being of that fond temper to accompany him to Guinea, and
live with him during his commission, tho' she is of a very good family of
Denmark, and might have been told, that European women run much
greater risks of life in that intemperate climate than the men; as we have had
instances of it heretofore in some Danish ladies, that were soon snatch'd

away by death at this coast' (*1732*, p. 449/1). Johann Trane was commander at Christiansborg 1698–1703 (Nørregard 1966, pp. 62, 64).

[23] In 1679, Barbot travelled no further West along Gold Coast than Accra, and all that his journal says of Labadi is that it lay half a league beyond Christiansborg (*1679*, p. 334). In 1682, he coasted in a brigantine or 'yacht' from Lay to River Volta, and therefore must have sailed from Accra to Lay (*1688*, pp. 2/129–130; *1732*, pp. 186/6, 321/2). But he does not seem to have acquired any first-hand knowledge of the coast East of Accra until he reached Greater Ningo, perhaps because on the earlier stretch of the coast the vessel lay out at sea. The brief account of Labadde, including the section here omitted, is an embroidered conflation of Marees, f. 43, and Dapper, p. 83/5–8, Barbot making the former's wall around the main town a dry stone wall and adding Marees's pigs to Dapper's cows, but also adding maize-growing to the salt-making of his sources. Salt-making at Osu, Labadi, Tesie and Nungwa was recorded in the 1690s (Tilleman 1697, pp. 110–11). In 1665 Labadi was described as a 'small town' (*dorpje*), in 1697 as a 'large town' (Leers 1665, p. 300; Tilleman 1697, p. 97). Orsou is Tilleman's 'Ursow', i.e. Barbot's Orsaky, a village which Barbot has already discussed: as he marks Orsou on his map of Gold Coast, he probably copied it from a map (see next note). Osu may at one time have been part of the state of Labadi: Labadi village is itself now a suburb of Accra.

Cf.*1732*, p. 185/3, where the cows become sheep.

[24] Ningo, Equea, Tema and Cincko are from Marees, f. 43–43v, and Dapper, p. 84/1 (which says that all three coastal villages have reefs), and Pompena is on Dapper's map of Guinea. Apart from Lay and Soko, Barbot says nothing further about the other places he mentions, so he almost certainly read their names from a map. These, and names of villages to the East later cited, appeared on later seventeenth-century Dutch coastal charts, e.g., Roggeveen/Robijn 1685. Lesser Ningo (the earlier Ningo) is modern Nungua; Brambra is 'Prampram' or Gbugbra (where there was an English lodge in the 1720s, Nørregard 1966, p. 96); Pompena is apparently Kpone ('Pompena or Ponni', *1732*, p. 319/8; 'Pumponnee', Donnan 1932, I, 220; 'Ponni', Bosman, p. 326) but if so should precede Brambra; Greater Ningo is Old Ningo or Nugo; Occa, where there was a Dutch lodge later in the eighteenth century ('Okko', Nørregard 1966, p. 108), is unidentified. Barbot's kingdom of Ningo appears to be the kingdom of Ladoku, usually known to Europeans as Lampa. It was threatened by Akwamu from 1679 and conquered in 1702 (Wilks 1957, pp. 113–4, 116–7; for the earlier history of Ladoku, see the references in Kea 1982, pp. 351, n. 8; 354, n. 47; map of the region, p. 68). Barbot is unaware of these moves in *1688*. In the present context, Little Acra refers, not to the village mentioned earlier, but to an inland state, probably Akrade, which occupied an area to the West of River Volta, near modern Kpong.

Cf. *1732*, p. 185/4, which adds that Ningo is called by the French Lempi (misprint for Lampi) and has a ruler called Ladingcour (i.e. Ladoku), from Bosman, p. 327. A recent historian has noted that Barbot speaks of the Aquamboes occupying 20 leagues of the coast and ruling the kings (*1732*, p. 181/11), which certainly refers to the conquest of Ladoku (Wilks 1957, p. 114), but the reference is in fact borrowed from Bosman, p. 64, Barbot merely changing 20 miles to '20 leagues'. The only post–1682 information Barbot gained on this part of the coast was from Bloome's 'Memoirs' – see the Additional Passage.

[25] Misquoting Marees, f. 43v, and Dapper, p. 84/1, the 1600 reference being to Cincko, not Temina: cf. *1732*, p. 185/5, which misprints 1680 for 1600. Barbot echoes Marees's view that the towns further East are of no consequence.

[26] Apart from the reference to cloths, the information on Cinco is directly from Marees, f. 43v, rather than from Dapper, p. 84/1, which mangles it. No modern village called Cinco exists: it may have been situated a little West of modern Kpone, where local traditions point to the existence of a town. The statement about language is of uncertain accuracy. Accra and the villages to the East, up to River Volta, most probably at this date all spoke dialects of Gā-Adangme, as they have done more recently. Today, while Gā and Adangme are considered to be in general to some extent mutually unintelligible, adjoining dialects within one and the other are said to be mutually intelligible (Hair 1969a, p. 246, n. 55; Kropp Dakubu 1985, pp. 195–8).

Cf. *1732*, p. 185/6.

[27] Greater Ningo is not the Ningo of Marees and Dapper, yet Barbot's reference to cattle-trading up-coast echoes Dapper, p. 84/2. Nevertheless, cattle were in fact brought by sea to central Gold Coast from as far East as Lay (Bosman, p. 327 – quoted in *1732*, p. 186/9; Jones 1983a, p. 239). The remainder of the paragraph appears to be original, suggesting that in 1682 Barbot's vessel lay off Greater Ningo.

Cf. *1732*, p. 185/7, with minor changes (e.g., 'thirty crowns a bullock') and the addition of a reference to the gold coming from Quakoe.

[28] Mount Redonda must be Nayo Mountain (400m), which is high enough to be seen from the sea ('a round high hill', Leers 1665, p. 300), although 30 km inland. On the illustration which he drew in 1682, looking NNW from one league off the coast, Barbot showed it as a uniquely prominent hill, but there inscribed that it was ten leagues inland : when printed in *1732*, Plate 15 (p. 182), the same view was now stated to be towards NNE and the inscription noted above was omitted, as well as another indicating a 'remarkable tree for mooring' (that is, the ship was to be moored in alignment with the tree).

[29] Lay is modern Leponguno (meaning 'Lay-on-the-ridge': Wilks 1957, p. 113). D'Elbée sailed past Lay in 1670 but merely noted palm-trees and a lower coast following (Delbée 1671, p. 379). From a few miles West of the village to as far as River Volta is 'an uninterrupted beach' (*Africa pilot* 1967, p. 467).

Cf. *1732*, p. 186/8, where Barbot recollects that 'the best riding before Lay is when mount Redondo bears N.N.W. the ground sandy mixt with very small stones'.

[30] English agents reported the trading of a French vessel at 'Allampo' in mid-March 1682, stating that 'the Frenchman had nothing but bouges [cowries] which the natives wanted to buy corne' and complaining that he had 'clear'd the Towne of slaves'; and again reported, in early April, that 'the French sloope' was there (OBLR, C.746, pp. 285, 286, 293, Allampo, 5.3.1681/2, 6.3.1681/2, 24.3.1681/2 O.S. = 15–16.3.1682 and 3.4.1682 N.S.). These were most probably visits by other vessels of Barbot's squadron, but Barbot's sloop cannot have arrived before late April. Barbot stated that he sailed from Lay to River Volta during the maize-planting season (*1732*, p. 321/2), which may well have extended to late April. The penultimate sentence may alternatively be translated – 'He comes on board to fix the price of slaves, . . .', but Barbot's own translation does not confirm this. The root term Lɛ (Lay) gave rise to the following derivatives and corrupt forms : Lepungono, Laduku ('Old Lay'), La-bi ('children of Lɛ'), Lampi, Alampi, Alampo, Adangme, Adangbe (Wilks 1957, p. 114). A Dutch source stated that in 1692 Lay was 'destroyed by the war', presumably the war with the Akwamu (Van Dantzig 1978, p. 53). This event may have given rise to some migration eastwards, which would explain why later sources sometimes used the term 'Alampo' to describe the coast East of River Volta, around Ketu (OBLR, J. Pearson, Whydah, 3.4.1694; Bosman, p. 329; Phillips 1732, p. 214). Bosman's brief account of the kingdom of Lampi mentioned that the slave trade flourished when there were wars and sometimes 'proves very advantageous, especially about the village Lay' (Bosman, p. 327).

Cf. *1732*, p. 186/1–5, which varies by stating that 'a ship is often furnish'd with four or five hundred Blacks in a fortnight or three weeks', and adds that Santi 'receives goods from the Europeans in proportion to the number of Blacks shipp'd off at each time', and that 'in my time, a good male slave might be bought there from fifty-five to sixty pounds of cauris or shells, and sometimes they advanced to seventy'. For other material on Lay in *1732*, see the Additional Passages.

[31] Omission of two paragraphs, on fishing with baskets at Ningo and Lay, and trade at Spice, from Marees, f. 43v (where the fishing is at Chinka). Cf. *1732*, p. 186/7, 10, the latter paragraph, on river-fishing, being from Bosman, pp. 327–8. Barbot adds that 'these places have been neglected since

so great a trade in gold has been found on the Coast', an inaccurate comment.

[32] Soko and the four villages are named on Barbot's map of Gold Coast (but the villages are shown in a separate unnamed coastal kingdom), and he almost certainly copied them from a Dutch coastal chart (see note 20 above). Briberqu appeared in earlier Portuguese sources as 'Beriqui' (Carneiro 1642, p. 84) and may be 'Tubreku', modern Tobrecu on the Songaw lagoon, where the Dutch had a lodge c. 1720 (Nørregard 1966, p. 95). The other names are difficult to relate to modern toponyms. Angulan may be a misplaced version of Angaw, the lagoon immediately East of the Volta mouth, but Aqualla, which on the charts is located inland, near the West bank of River Volta, is unidentified.

[33] Apart from the description of the coast (confirming the one in Leers 1665, pp. 300–1), there are doubts about the authenticity of the material in this paragraph. The information on cloths, brigands, lack of knowledge of gold, and exchange for pieces-of-eight, echoes Dapper on the far inland kingdom of Insoko (Dapper, pp. 88/16–89/1). But if Insoko was intended by Dapper to represent Nsawkaw in the gold-trading Begho complex, the remark about lack of knowledge of gold was misplaced. Since the Adangme people of the coast in earlier centuries possessed a ritual prohibition on the use of gold, it is possible that Dapper conflated information on two different areas, and that some of his description of Insoko did in fact apply to the coastal area Barbot terms Soko, and perhaps to Ladoku as well (assuming that there was actually a state of Soko separate from Ladoku).

Cf. *1732*, pp. 190/15, 319/6–11 (Barbot now counting Soko in Slave Coast rather than Gold Coast), much embroidered, partly by applying what Bosman says of Lampi to Soko, since Bosman has Lampi running to River Volta and makes no mention of Soko. The following additions may have been based on information obtained in the 1680s and not previously deployed, or they may be merely speculative. 'The Negroes of Volta and Coto likewise come to Soko by sea, when they are inform'd that some European ships make any stay there, and bring some quantities of slaves'. 'Very few of them have any gold, unless it be the Acra, Lampi and Aquamboez Blacks, who are settled among them with their families, of which there are a pretty many; as well as at Lay, Ningo, Cinko, and so to Pompena, or Ponni, westward.'

[34] This late recollection of trading at Lay in 1682 was aroused by reading Bosman, the first part of the sentence echoing Bosman, p. 327. In 1688 a Brandenburg vessel reported that slaves were scarce at 'Laij, Lampe, and Poupou' (Jones 1985, p. 165); and in the same year a French source reported that whereas Lampaye and River Volta had over the past ten years provided 25,000 slaves, they now provided only 5–600 annually, and the English, Dutch and Portuguese bought these (Roussier 1935, p. 14).

[35] In 1709 Davenant referred to an English factory at Lampa or Alampa

(i.e. Lay), whose conversion to a fort had been started but abandoned (Davenant 1709, pp. 225–6): the passage is quoted in *1732*, p. 449/2. The English had resident agents at Alampa between 1701 and 1704 (Davies 1957, p. 249); and the ruins of the projected fort, abandoned allegedly after the local Africans chased the English away, were noted in August 1704 (BL, Add. MSS 19560, Des Marchais MS, p. 42). For the view that 'Alampo coast' slaves were the cheapest but least desirable slaves, see Phillips 1732, p. 214.

LETTER 11

Geographical description of the countries, lands and kingdoms of the interior of Gold Coast.

[. . ./pp. 42–44/. . .]¹

Additional Passages from *1732*

[p. 189/1, on the lingua franca]

Many of them can still speak some few words of Portuguese, and the Lingua Franca they learnt of their fore-fathers, when the Portugueses had the whole commerce on that coast. This Lingua Franca is a corruption of Italian, Latin, French and Portuguese.²

[p. 191/1, on the sources of gold]

All the above-mentioned kingdoms and territories in general, are not so woody, as the country about Cormentin, and the others higher on the Gold Coast, nor so fruitful. . . . Mandinga, Gago, and Tafoe, furnish them with very much [gold] in exchange by goods, or by way of plunder; and these again, besides what their own land produces, receive it from many unknown countries northward, on both sides of the Niger: those places, according to the accounts of all authors and travellers, producing an immense store of gold.³

NOTES

¹ At the end of the previous Letter, Barbot threatened to dispense with an account of the inland countries, since he had no original information on them and could only repeat a Dutchman – he now changes his mind,

although the whole of the present Letter is, as he earlier admitted, derived from one source (Dapper, pp. 84–9, whose major ultimate source was the 1629 Dutch map). In the opening paragraph Barbot acknowledges that he has little to say on this subject other than what he has learnt from his 'Dutch author' or from 'a Moor with whom I have sometimes conversed on these matters'. The latter may be fictitious: Barbot does not appear to have obtained any significant information about the interior of Gold Coast during his two voyages to Africa – merely a legend about a river in the kingdom of 'Ackeny' 60 leagues inland, a branch of River Niger, which received the souls of the dead, and the names of three kingdoms further North (see note 3 below), information possibly from a European informant (*1679*, p. 336). At the end of the letter he remarks that the information which he has gained from the Dutch (i.e. Dapper) differs from that offered by the English, who mention only 18 kingdoms on Gold Coast – a reference probably derived directly or indirectly from the 'eighteen kingdoms of Guinea' noted in *Golden Coast* 1665, p. 4.

Cf. *1732*, pp. 186/11–191/2, 449/6–451/6, which adds, as well as more from Dapper (perhaps via a secondary source), extensive material from Bosman, pp. 72–4, 78. Barbot begins by pointing out the difficulty of obtaining information from the interior, 'none of the Europeans dwelling along the coast having ever ventured far up the land, that I could hear of' – a statement largely true at the time of Barbot's two voyages. But since then he apparently had not learned about David van Nyendael's visit to the Asante capital in 1701–2. At several points Barbot expands slightly on Bosman by referring to 'a modern author' or 'the best geographers' – the reference being almost certainly to the French geographers and the Delisle maps: for instance, misreading Bosman, p. 78, about the extent of Akani territory, he asserts that 'the best geographers' place Gago and Guber 'between the Accanese lands'. In the Supplement Barbot provides additional material on the inland countries, largely from Bosman, pp. 73–9, but also from 'a modern author', probably either one of the French geographers or a Delisle map.

[2] This modifies Dapper's statement about the use of the Portuguese language by Akani traders (Dapper, p. 86/7). Although seaman's lingua franca did contain some age-old Mediterranean elements, Barbot's references to Italian and Latin in the Guinea lingua franca are far-fetched, while the reference to French is dubious: the Romance elements in the lingua franca were of course largely from Portuguese, perhaps entirely.

[3] This vague passage typifies Barbot's embroidery of standard sources on the interior. In 1679 Barbot noted a kingdom of 'Gagor' which neighboured the kingdom of the Acanes (presumably Gao, the name perhaps from a map), and also the kingdoms of 'Meranson' and 'Allance' – unidentifiable names – which lay 200 leagues inland, near the desert, and provided the

most gold in Africa (*1679*, pp. 324, 336). In *1688* and *1732* he followed Dapper and Bosman and abandoned the latter two names.

LETTER 12

General description of Gold Coast. The properties of the soil, the air and the seasons.

At last, Sir, here I am in the most pleasing part of my account of Gold Coast. I hope that you will in the future read my letters with much more pleasure than you did previous ones. /p. 45/ I find my spirit greatly cheered up and liberated, now that I have reached the point of describing the seasons, the fruits, and the various other particulars of this new land. [. . .][1] The soil is rich and of the colour of brick, and is suitable for producing maize.[2] In some places there is sand.[3] [. . ./p. 46/. . .][4] These lands produce a sufficiency of edible products in various places, above all maize, millet (*mil*), rice, *patates* (sweet potatoes), yams, limes, oranges, coconuts, palm wine, *bordon* (raffia palm) wine, bananas, Indian figs and pineapples, but very few of the last three.[5] [. . .] [6] The sea there is extraordinarily rich in fish, and provides salt. The rivers not only contain an abundance of fish, but also conceal in their waters immense treasures, for they all contain gold – some more, others less, according to where their source lies.[7] But I recall that I promised to give you as precise details of these matters as possible. That is what I shall henceforth labour to do, if it pleases the Lord. Yet you will not be angry to have this general idea, which will make you await what is to follow with greater patience. I am always, Sir, Your etc.

Additional Passages from *1732*

[p. 192/2–3, on the seasons]

The English call these two seasons winter and summer, the French the high and the low season; and the Dutch, the good and bad times. The best observation of the time when the rains begin on the Gold Coast, is made by agent Greenhill, who brings it to about the 10th of April. 'This, says he, may be generally observ'd, from fifteen degrees north, to the same number of south latitude, that they follow the sun, with five or six degrees, and so proceed with him, till he has touch'd the tropick, and returns to the like station again.' This he makes out by the following instance, viz. cape Corso castle is in four deg. and fifty-five min. north; about the 12th of April the sun has there about twelve deg. north declination; as at that time the rains begin and continue in that latitude till he has perform'd his course to the greatest obliquity from the equator, and return'd to the like position south. The same he supposes may be understood of other places within the tropicks.[8]

[p. 193/4–194/2, on the harmattan]

An Harmatan will last two or three days, and sometimes four or five, but seldom so long: yet such a one we had, lying off Boutroe, in January 1682. It blew a sharp piercing cold air, no sun appearing all the while; but the weather was thick, close, cold and raw, which very much affected the eyes, and put many into an aguish temper, so violently piercing the naked bodies of the Blacks, that I observ'd many I had then on board, look'd at a distance as if they had been all over strew'd with meal, and shiver'd as in an ague. Nor is it any wonder that the natives, who are used most of the year, and even of their lives, to a scorching air, should be so tender and sensible of a sharp piercing wind, coming so suddenly on them, when the Europeans themselves, who are used to cold climates, can scarce endure it, but are sensible of the effects thereof, tho' close confined to their chambers, with a gentle fire and strong restoratives to keep up the spirits. / The latter end of December, all January, and part of February, are subject to these Harmatans, as the Blacks call them; but January most of all. Those which happen in February, do not commonly continue long; and they are never known before or after the times here mention'd.

During the time of an Harmatan, all persons whatsoever, white or black, without any exception, are obliged, by the sharpness of the air, to keep confined to their houses, or chambers, without stirring abroad, unless upon very urgent occasions: for the air is scarce to be endur'd, because it suffocates, obliging people to draw their breath often, and short; and they are forced to correct the acuteness of it with some sweet oil; without which, it would be difficult breathing as at other times. / This sharp piercing air is as prejudicial, if not more, to beasts or cattle, than it is to men; and certainly destroys many of them in a very short time, if not drawn together betimes into some close cover'd place: which, for this reason, the Blacks generally provide before-hand, being acquainted with the proper season of these Harmatans, and knowing they never miss coming, sooner or later. An experiment was made at cape Corso, of the sharpness of the air, on two goats; which were not exposed to it above four hours, before it kill'd them. Besides, the joints of floors in chambers, and the decks and sides of ships, as far as they are above water, did open so wide, that a caulking-iron could be thrust in deep between the seams, continuing so all the time Harmatan lasted; and as soon as it was over, those joints and seams closed again of themselves, as if they had never open'd.[9] These harmatans generally blow from East to E.N.E., and are the most steady fresh gales that are observ'd to blow, never attended with thunder, lightening, or rain, or at least very rarely...[10]

[p. 194/4–8, on the relative cold of the rainy season, and on the effects of lightning]

This is not at all improbable; for I have met with such cold weather under the line, that one of our men made use of his gloves and a muff he happen'd to have among his apparel.[11] In the good season, I have observed the effect of the corrupted evening air to be such, that in two hours it corrupted a piece of fresh meat, so that the next morning it swarm'd with maggots, as soon as the sun came to shine upon it; and even on woollen clothes, that lay out all night, the vermin would breed: nor could we keep the fish just taken out of the water, sweet above four hours. By this we may guess what effect the air of the high season, or winter, may have on such bodies, and consequently on human nature. Notwithstanding I have before said same thing to the same purpose, I think myself oblig'd here again to warn sailors, that they do not lie down on the decks uncover'd, as they are too apt to do after working hard; or perhaps drinking brandy, punch, or any other strong liquor, which may occasion them to sleep so all the night: for it is ten to one, but that in the morning they will find themselves so stiff and cold, as not to be able to stir from the place; which casts them into fluxes, of which few or none recover. It behoves them therefore carefully to avoid lying abroad, and uncover'd in the night; and masters of ships ought strictly to forbid it, if they value the success of their voyages, many stout and brave

457

men having perish'd miserably after this manner on the coast of Guinea: and thus voyages, which might otherwise have been advantageous, have prov'd destructive to the adventurers, for want of hands to carry the ships home with all diligence, which is a main point towards a good voyage. But of this more in another place.

In September the winds usually blow from the south during the day, driving away the stench up the inland; and the north wind returning commonly at night, carries it off again to sea. This month of September, by degrees drives away the winter season, and generally concludes with fine clear weather, and great heats.

The Gold Coast lying between the tropick and the line, it is easy to guess what dreadful thunder it must be subject to, which is most in the winter season. The lightening is sometimes so frightful, that it really looks as if the world were going to be consum'd by fire. The sheets of lead nailed on the sides of a gallery, over the seams of the ship I was in, were in some places almost reduc'd to nothing; and it is recorded at Mina, that in the year 1651 gold and silver were melted in bags, which remain'd untouch'd.[12]

NOTES

[1] Omission of four sentences, on the relief and natural vegetation, from Dapper, p. 89/2–3. But whereas Dapper described the country as being particularly 'wild' and forested around Elmina, Barbot substituted, more correctly, 'Axim, Sama and Comendo', high forest being more common west of River Pra than near Elmina.
Cf. *1732*, p. 191/3.

[2] Cf. Dapper, p. 89/3, 'mille'. Barbot's reference to the colour of the soil was broadly accurate, the ferrisol and ferralitic soils of Gold Coast, with a high content of ferric oxide, tending to be reddish.
Cf. *1732*, p. 191/4, which modifies the colour to 'pale brick colour'.

[3] Cf. *1732*, p. 191/3 – 'in other places it is also sandy and gravelly, as about cape Corso'.

[4] Omission of seven paragraphs, on the two seasons and the causes, on squalls, prevailing winds and currents during the year (including the harmattan, mistakenly said to be from the ESE – a mistake Barbot follows), on the effects of the climate on Europeans, and on days and nights, mostly from Dapper, pp. 89/4–9, 90/2–4 and Marees, f. 55v, and/or largely repeating points stated earlier about the Guinea climate in general, in Letter 1/5, pp.

12–16 above, with slight modifications. Winter is now said to be April-October; squalls are 'continual' April-June, forming from the SE, East and NE, or sometimes from the North; cold rains fall June to early September and the foul mists appear in August. Barbot adds, as regards the effects, that Africans are better protected against heat because they frequently anoint themselves with palm oil; and as regards the winds and currents, that when in winter these make the journey from Ardra to the equator difficult, 'I noticed, on my latter voyage, that if a vessel headed south-south-east, it merely made an east-north-east course' (cf. *1732*, p. 194/2). Barbot adds to Dapper that the harmattan, which he observed on his second voyage at Boutrou (January 1682), makes the skins of blacks have goose-pimples (*élévé et farineux*). For detailed meteorological evidence on the Gold Coast climate in 1686–1687 from a contemporary, see Hillier 1697.

Cf. *1732*, pp. 191/9–194/8, which enlarges, partly from Bosman, pp. 104–6, 108, 111, a source concentrating on the ill effects of the climate on resident Europeans: for significantly enlarged passages, see the Additional Passages. Barbot adds to Bosman's list of unhealthy places (Butri and Secondi) 'the Danish mount at Manfrou, Wiamba and Acra'. He introduces the section on Gold Coast climate by remarking that he proposes 'to treat hereafter, by way of supplement, of the seasons and monsoons of Nigritia and Guinea in general' (*1732*, p. 191/8), but does not do so.

[5] Although the list echoes Dapper, pp. 90/7–91/1 and Marees, f. 57 and chaps. 34–5, Barbot had seen most of the items (many being recorded in *1679*, pp. 280, 304, 319).

Cf. *1732*, p. 191/4, which begins by noting that the country along the coast is 'most hilly, gradually rising more and more up the inland, till it becomes almost mountainous', and modifies the list (adding 'Indian wheat, millet . . . potatoes . . . bananas, plantains, ananas; but least of the last', and omitting raffia wine). Barbot discusses edible plants and fruits at length in Letter 2/13.

[6] Omission of one paragraph on fauna, from Dapper p. 91/2. Cf. *1732*, p. 191/5. Barbot discusses fauna at length in Letter 2/14.

[7] Cf. *1732*, p. 191/6–7, which is more specific about gold-bearing streams, 'the river Cobra, those of Boutrou, Sama, and others further eastward'.

[8] Presumably the extract is from the 'observations' of Greenhill on the Guinea climate, which Barbot quotes more from elsewhere (*1732*, p. 540/1–5 – given here as Letter 3/20, Additional Passage).

[9] There are traces of Dapper and Bosman in this passage, but it is largely original, Barbot having spent the months of January-March on Gold Coast in both 1679 and 1682. His 1679 journal does not comment on this aspect of the weather. Barbot defines the harmattan as 'a dry north or north-east wind' (in *1732*, p. 193/3), correcting the error of direction in *1688*. On the

harmattan, whose 'cold nights require people to have blankets – a joy to Europeans and a trial to Africans', and whose low humidity causes timber to split, and lips, fingernails and even bare skin to crack, so that barefoooted Africans may find it painful to walk, see Church 1980, p. 22. But Barbot, as usual with climatic references, much exaggerates the ill effects – for instance, Africans would not regularly stay indoors. The Cape Corso 'experiment' was probably reported to Barbot by Greenhill: its end result, or at least the climatic explanation, is somewhat implausible.

[10] The remainder of *1732* p. 191/1, and the whole of 191/2, refer to the reversed currents and squalls which help ships travelling West, and to the prevalent winds and currents which make the journey due South from the coast difficult, repeating points made in either Letter 1/5 or the present Letter (see note 4 above).

[11] This follows a reference in *1732*, p. 194/3–4 to the cold making the ground almost freeze (a false assertion), from Bosman, pp. 114–5.

[12] The penultimate paragraph repeats material in Letter 1/5, pp. 13–14, above: the 1651 reference is from Bosman, p. 112.

LETTER 13

Fruits and plants.

Sir, I think I should begin the detailed account I have promised by discussing maize, rice and *mil*, which are the principal edible crops (*fruits*) of our Africans.[1] [.../pp. 47–48/...][2] Sweet potatoes and yams grow in abundance in many places on this coast, especially at Comendo. These two roots look almost alike in shape and colour. They grow freely in the fields, as turnips do in Normandy. Roast sweet potato has the taste of boiled chestnuts, and when boiled with meat it can serve as a substitute for turnips. It is one of the most delicious foods of this country, and the sweet potatoes are far better than those of America. The Moors make a sort of pap out of them: this is very white and nutritious. Yams are larger: I have seen some which weighed 8–10 lb. They are reddish brown on the outside and extremely white on the inside. Their natural taste is not as pleasant as that of sweet potatoes.[3] [...][4]

Bananas [*sc.* plantains], Indian figs [*sc.* bananas] and pineapples grow abundantly at Axim, in the vicinity of Boutrou and sometimes at Comendo, but they are very rare at other places on the coast. [. . .] This tree [the banana or plantain plant] does not have any branches:

instead it has only about 25–30 large leaves, 5–6 feet long and 12–15 inches wide. [. . .] What is surprising is that the conspicuous trunk, which is sometimes 12–15 feet tall and two feet in circumference, is composed of nothing but these coiled leaves. [. . .] They [bananas/plantains] can be transported very far in the space of 15 or 20 days, and gradually they become ripe. [. . ./p. 49/. . .] Some of the leaves are two ells long and half an ell wide. There is nothing more beautiful than to see them fresh on the tree; nothing more pleasant than to drink, eat and even sleep under them.[5] [. . .][6]

Small limes (*limons*) are very common there. They are the size of a hen's egg and their juice is extremely sour and bitter. At several localities the juice is extracted, [each lime supplying] up to two or three *moids*, as at Axim, Manfrou, Boutrou etc., where it is sold in barrels. It is good for the slaves who are transported, since it protects them against scurvy; and in general all the Moors use it to wash out their mouths and prevent this cruel disease.[7] Orange trees are common too. There are two kinds of oranges – those which are small and very bitter and those which are sweet. The latter are found at Axim and Manfrou, but they are much smaller than those of China, which would grow very well there if brought as saplings. I have also seen fine pomegranates in the garden at Fredericxburg, grown on saplings brought from Europe. They are sweeter than ours but not as large. I have seen and tasted grapes at the same place. The vines bear fruit at all times of /p. 50/ the year, but a bunch never ripens all at once. The vine came from Europe.[8] [. . .][9]

As I believe you know, Sir, palm oil is of great medicinal use and is generally esteemed in Europe, when applied warm, as a treatment for flatulence, chills of the shoulders and dislocation of the limbs. I beg you to excuse me, Sir, from discussing in detail the nature and properties of the various other species of palm trees and the distinctions which are made between male and female. Perhaps I shall have an opportunity to say something about this elsewhere.[10] In some places here one finds sugar cane, 20–22 foot high. It is not as sweet or juicy as that of the Islands of America. There is a little ginger and malaguetta, but the latter is found only seldom.[11]

So much for the edible plants. I shall next tell you about the /p. 51/ animals which are found in this country. Meanwhile I am, Sir, Your etc

[illustration no. (72), plants and trees][12]

461

Additional Passages from *1732*

[p. 199/7–8, on tobacco and garlic]

The Portugueses know how to make their advantage of this people's greediness of tobacco, as do the French, who bring to the coast some quantity of St Domingo tobacco; both sorts being twisted like cords about the bigness of a small finger ... Another thing the French especially bring most to the coast, is Garlick: 'tis scarce to be conceived how greedy the Blacks generally are of it, so that they purchase it at any rate, for fish or even gold; and I can aver I have myself made five hundred per Cent. by it: but not in any quantity. Whether it will grow in this country or not, I am ignorant, as well as concerning onions. It never came to my thought, to inquire into it. But I am apt to think it will not, any more than several other fruits and green herbs common in Europe, which never come there to perfection.[13]

[p. 201/8, on bananas/plantains]

This fruit in many parts of the East and West Indies is eaten instead of bread, roasted or boil'd, just at the time it is come to its full bigness, somewhat before it is quite ripe, or turn'd yellow, as I have my self eaten it thus prepared at the Prince's Island in the bight of Guinea. It eats well also with a sauce made with pimento or malaguetta, salt and lemon-juice, and tastes better than dry bread in France. It is likewise very agreeable stew'd with wine, cinnamon and sugar, and also made into tarts, baked in an oven, or raw, or boil'd into puddings, as I shall more fully observe hereafter.[14]

[p. 202/1–3, on coconut and palm trees]

Here are two sorts of coco-nut trees, the one called, for distinction, the right coco-tree, which shoots up to the height of thirty or forty, or sometimes fifty foot, generally slender and streight, bears its fruit the fourth or fifth year, and lives fifty years and longer. / The branches or leaves are like those of the palm, excepting that the coco-branches are not so long or fit for the uses the other are put to. The leaves are some three, some four fathoms long, and it produces that we call the coco-nut; which, with the outer rind on, is bigger than a man's head. The outer rind being taken off, there appears a shell, some of which will hold near a quart. Within the shell is the nut; and within the nut, is about a pint and a half, more or less, as the nut is larger or smaller, of pure, clear, sweet, and refreshing water, which is very cool and pleasant. The kernel of the nut is also very good; when pretty old, it is scraped or sliced, and the scrapings being set to soak in about a quart of fresh water, for three or four hours, the water being strain'd, has the colour and taste of milk; and, if it stands a while, will have a thick scum on it not unlike cream. This milk being boil'd with any poultry, rice, or other meat, makes a very good broth, and is reckoned very nourishing, and often given to sick persons. Every ship ought to provide a quantity of these nuts, when they can get them, to help their sick men in the passage. The leaves of the trees serve to thatch houses; the outer rind of the nut, to make a sort of cloth, and ropes, rigging, cables, etc. The shell of the nut makes pretty drinking cups; it also burns well, and makes a very fierce and hot fire. The kernel serves instead of meat, and the water therein contain'd instead of drink; and if the nut be very old, the kernel will of itself turn to oil, which is often made use of to fry with, but most commonly to burn in lamps. So that from this tree it may be said, they have meat, drink, clothing, houses, firing and rigging for their ships. But there, through the ignorance of the Blacks, no other advantage is made of them, than what the nut affords, both the kernel and the milk within it being very pleasant, as has been said, when at its full maturity. Whilst the nut grows, it is full of liquor within; but as it ripens, by degrees the flesh or kernel begins to form itself on the inside of the shell; and, by little and little, that white substance grows thick and hard. I present you with my own drawing of this tree, in Plate 17. Letter Q.

The wild coco or palm-trees growing here, bear a fruit which but very few of the Europeans eat, tho' the Blacks do. This tree is very much thicker than the right coco-tree, especially in the middle, where it is of a vast bigness; and what adds to the oddness of its figure is, that the top and bottom are one half smaller. At the top grows a fruit, which seems to be the pith of the tree, and is call'd palm-cabbage, because it has a sort of cabbagy taste, or rather that of bottoms of artichokes; it eats very well, either boil'd, and afterwards put into butter sauce and nutmeg; or raw, with pepper and salt, as green artichokes are eaten. See the figure in Plate 17. Letter O. The branches are commonly about nine or ten foot long, and about a foot and half from the trunk of the tree, they shoot forth leaves four foot long, and an inch and half broad: these leaves grow so regularly, that the whole branch seems but one intire leaf. The cabbage, when it is cut out from amongst the branches, is commonly six inches about, and a foot long, some more some less, and is as white as milk. At the bottom of the cabbage grow great bunches of berries, of about five pounds weight, in the shape of a bunch of grapes; their colour is red like a cherry, and the berries are about the bigness of a black cherry, with a large stone in the middle; and they taste much like English haws. They never climb up to get the fruit or cabbage, because the tree is so high, and there is not any thing to hold by; and therefore 'tis a hard matter for a man to get up, tho' the trunk of the tree is made up outwardly with several knots or joints, about four inches from each other, like bamboe cane, void of any leaves except at the top. [15]

[pp. 203/16, on the uses of palm wine]

All the sorts of the wine aforesaid, provoke urine, and are reckoned very good against the gravel or stone in the bladder; and thence it must be that few or none of the Blacks are troubled with those distempers; and tho' it will soon make a man drunk, yet the fumes of them do not last very long, and cause no headach. It is a great blessing to the inhabitants of these countries, to be so abundantly supplied with very little trouble and charges, with so comfortable and pleasant a drink, which, with the help of bread, fish and salt, subsists most of the people on the coast, together with the nuts and oil the palm-trees furnish them with besides.

[p. 205/7–8, on the use of the kapok or silk cotton tree for masts]

The capot-trees commonly grow to the greatest height and wideness, when planted on moist grounds, and near the sides of river and watry places. / It is very likely there are good large trees, for to make masts, if not for the greatest ships, at least for barks, yachts and sloops. But as yet I have not heard that any Europeans have made any use of them: for had such trees fit for larger or smaller masts been found up the country, it would be a very difficult task to bring them down to the shore, the ways being every where so very narrow and crooked. [16]

[1] This letter is built around the descriptions of edible plants and fruits in Marees, ff. 81–84v, as borrowed in Dapper, p. 90/5–10, and Villault, pp. 380–5. But Barbot incorporates personal observations – in 1679 he recorded seeing on Gold Coast *gros mil*, 'bananas and figs' [i.e. bananas and plantains], pineapples, orange trees, and pawpaws (*1679*, pp. 280, 304, 315, 319).
Cf. *1732*, pp. 196/1–205/10, which adds very extensive material from Bosman, pp. 225, 284–309, but also other material which appears to be original, reading Bosman having presumably jogged Barbot's memory. See the Additional Passages.

[2] Omission of four paragraphs on the named crops, the material from Marees, ff. 56–57, 81v, Dapper, p. 90/6–9, and Villault, pp. 382–5. Barbot's only significant additions are his statements that rice was planted in January and that children sometimes took the grains off maize cobs and heated them on a very warm stone.
Cf. *1732*, pp. 196/1–197/11, with additions from Bosman, pp. 296–9. On *1732*, Plate 16 (p. 200), the illustration of 'The Millet Plant' is from Marees, plate 13, but the illustration of 'The Mangnoc Tree in seed' is probably from a West Indian source (in 1679 Barbot noted 'cassavre ou magnocs' at Cayenne, *1679*, p. 368).

[3] 'Pap' perhaps refers to *fufu*, a flour or paste for cooking made from tubers, although this is normally made from yams or cassava (Jones 1983a, pp. 111, 209). The description of the two tubers, and the remark on their comparison, have echoes of Marees, ff. 83v–84, plate 14 caption. Yams 'sliced like turnips in Limosin' (Villault, p. 381) perhaps influenced Barbot.
Cf. *1732*, p. 197/12–198/10, which modifies the reference to Comendo ('I think at Comendo also, but dare not be positive'), and adds of sweet potatoes that 'their sweetness here exceeds that of the Barbadoes potatoes, so much praised in the Leeward islands of America', and of yams that after being dug up they 'keep sweet for a considerable time'; finally, it adds material, including information on beans, from Bosman, pp. 299–301 (but compares yams with carrots rather than turnips, after Marees).

[4] Omission of two sentences on eating yams, from Marees, f. 84.

[5] The three omissions cover 32 sentences, all from Marees, ff. 82v–84, and Dapper, p. 90/10, except for a digression on Biblical references to banana leaves ('fig leaves') from 'an author I read the other day' on the history of Ethiopia (i.e. Ludolf 1684). But whereas Marees says that a hundred bananas can grow together, Barbot says '50–60'. The reference to Comendo may derive from Marees, f. 40v.
Cf. *1732*, pp. 201/3–9, which adds material from Bosman, pp. 291–2, enlarging slightly, and misleadingly, as follows. 'The pizang, or fig-trees, are common at the coast, and generally known by the name of Banana and fig-

trees; the French follow that denomination after the Spaniards. The English call them Plantans and Banana trees; the Dutch, Baccoven and Banana, to distinguish the two species thereof.' In fact, seventeenth-century writers were not always consistent in distinguishing between the banana (*Musa sapientum*) and the plant producing similar but larger fruit, the plantain (*Musa paradisiaca*). The former was often known as 'bakoven' and the latter as 'banana', with both sometimes sharing the name 'Indian fig' (see Jones 1983a, pp. 225–6). In *1732*, Barbot concludes – 'Having observ'd, in all the relations of the East and West Indies, where the authors have drawn the figure of this plant, that it was not exactly done, I thought proper to present the reader with a true draught in Plate 17, Letter N': the tree, copied from the plantain in Marees, plate 14, appears on illustration no. (72), p. 2/51, below.

⁶ Omission of one paragraph on pineapples, from Marees, f. 83v, and Dapper, p. 90/10, except for the remark that Guinea pineapples are 'by no means as good as those of Dominica'.

Cf. *1732*, pp. 199/10–200/5, with additions from Bosman, pp. 301–4, and a reference to Plate 16 (p. 200), where the pineapple plant (see illustration no. (72), p. 51, below) is an improved copy of the one on Marees, plate 14, perhaps influenced by Froger 1698, p. 77.

⁷ Cf. *1732*, p. 204/8–9, which modifies the geographical reference ('I think there is some made at Axim, Manfrou and Boutry, but not in any quantity'), changes 'wash out their mouths' to 'wash their teeth', extends the use from slaves to 'slaves and sailors', and also adds material from Bosman, pp. 289–90. For the extraction and export of lime juice, see Dapper, p. 90/10; Bosman, p. 290; Jones 1983a, pp. 230–1. Note that lime juice to combat scurvy was given to slaves long before its use was general in the British navy.

⁸ In 1679 Barbot noted sweet oranges and grapes in the garden at Frederiksborg (*1679*, p. 305). For other references to oranges, see Letter 2/3, p. 5; Letter 2/6, p. 26, above; and for a contemporary reference to the two kinds of orange (*Citrus aurantium* and *Citrus sinensis*), see Jones 1983a, p. 112. Barbot appears to have been the first writer to mention pomegranates on Gold Coast: for a later reference, see Bosman, p. 292.

Cf. *1732*, pp. 200/6–201/2, 204/7, 10–14, which contradicts the first sentence (to fit Bosman), adds material from Bosman, pp. 289, 292–3, including some on pawpaws and melons, and also expands slightly, as follows: 'I have eaten grapes in that manner [sc. variously ripe] two or three times, which were pretty sweet. ... The flesh of this fruit [the praecocemelon] is a watry congealed substance, which melts in the mouth as soon as chew'd, and therefore a man may eat a whole melon, without much difficulty. ... You may see the figure of this tree [the pawpaw] in Plate 16, as they are found in the Leeward islands; next to or under which letter, is another sort of papay-tree of that country, much different from the former...'. The illustrations of two sorts of 'Papay Tree' on *1732*, Plate 16 (p. 200) are probably from an untraced source on the West Indies.

[9] Omission of four sentences on green vegetables and herbs, from Villault, pp. 380–1, and a paragraph on the palm tree, from Marees, ff. 21, 84–84v. In 1679 Barbot ate kale (*choux verds*) at Anomabu (*1679*, p. 319).

Cf. *1732*, p. 198/11–14, 199/6–9, 203/1–204/5, which adds, as well as the Additional Passages on tobacco, garlic, and palm wine, the remark that purslane is 'a good refreshment to the Europeans, especially sailors, to make broth; more particularly to the French, who generally are fond of pottage, wherever they go'; and also adds considerable material from Bosman, pp. 224, 285–8, 306–7 (but to Bosman's description of kola Barbot adds that it grows more plentifully in North-Guinea). The palm tree on illustration no. (72), p. 51 below, and *1732*, Plate 17 (p. 202), is from Marees, plate 14.

[10] Palm oil, which has a high carotin content, featured in eighteenth-century trade lists under the heading 'drugs'. For its use as a medicine and as a fuel, see Jones 1983a, pp. 122, 224.

[11] For sugar cane on Gold Coast in general, see Marees, f. 81–81v; Jones 1983a, pp. 227–8.

Cf. *1732*, p. 199/1–5, with additions from Bosman, p. 305, and the remark that the Guinea canes are 'not so sweet nor so full of juice, as they are commonly in the Leewards Islands of America, because, as I suppose, they are not rightly managed and planted as they should be. The country of Anta, as I said before, has the most of that sweet plant, and undoubtedly as the soil is of its nature, the sugar-canes would improve to advantage, if well cultivated' – the reference to the Anta (Ahanta) country being derived from Davenant 1709, p. 31. Since Marees's description of ginger was derived entirely from a work on Asia (Linschoten 1934, II, 89–89v), it is not certain that ginger was known on Gold Coast in the seventeenth century: Müller, Dapper, Bosman and other writers did not mention it and Barbot probably merely copied from Marees. Illustrations of the ginger root and a sugar cane appear on *1732*, Plate 16 (p. 200): the former resembles but the latter differs from the corresponding item in Marees, plate 13.

[12] This illustration is referred to in the epistolary flourish at the beginning of the next Letter, within which it appears. Against an imaginary African scene, of hills and a village, the following plants are drawn and labelled: pineapple, millet, banana, maize, 'palm-wine tree', Indian fig, rice. All are copied from Marees, plates 13–14. An imaginary scene showing animals and African hunting, in *1732*, Plate 17 (p. 202), includes some of the trees (items N, O, and P, unlabelled), as well as additional copyings from Marees (e.g. H).

[13] In 1679 Barbot sold garlic at a good price at Anomabu (*1679*, p. 230). A Twi vocabulary of 1673 included a term for 'onion, garlic', but the term

seems to include a component from Portuguese, perhaps indicating an imported or transplanted item (Jones 1983a, p. 322).

[14] Barbot does not return to the subject.

[15] In 1679 Barbot saw 'coconut trees or wild palms' at Axim (*1679*, p. 281). The passage cited has introductory sentences on each species of tree from Bosman, p. 289, but the remainder is not from any of Barbot's usual sources. Possibly, however, it is from an untraced source on either the East or the West Indies, and the illustration of the Palm Cabbage tree on *1732*, Plate 16 (p. 200), may also be from the same source. The coconut palm (*Cocos nucifera*) is distinguished from the fan palm (*Borassus aethiopum*), which, however, is not in fact the only palm to produce 'palm cabbage', the young shoots at the top of the trunk. Barbot refers to an illustration of a 'wild coco': the tree he indicates, on *1732*, Plate 17 (p. 202), item O, seems to be from Marees, plate 14, where it is labelled 'den Palmitas', but Marees's description (f. 84v) does not match Barbot's. Further, 'The Palm Cabidge als. Cabidge Tree' shown on *1732*, Plate 16 (p. 200), is quite different: this illustration is probably from a West Indian source. Barbot's alleged 'own drawing' of the coconut tree (item Q on Plate 17) appears as an element in a tableau showing men carrying a hammock and crossing a stream on a bridge suspended from four coconut trees. But the tableau, including the trees, is in fact a modified copy (from a different angle and adding the hammock) of part of an illustration in Dapper, p. 102. (Moreover, while the rest of Dapper's scene refers to Gold Coast, the bridge is out of place, being an artefact from the interior of Cape Mount, as later explained in Dapper, p. 103/3).

[16] Following Bosman, Barbot moves from fruit trees to other trees, discussed in *1732*, p. 205/1–10, based mainly on Bosman, pp. 294–6. Apart from the passage cited, Barbot inserts a reference to the 'great canoos made at Axim and Cormentin'.

LETTER 14

Animals that are free-ranging and wild (francs et sauvages).

In the note, Sir, I received from you yesterday evening, you appear to complain that I have not sent you the drawings of some of the plants I discussed in my last letter, and you point out to me that since there are an infinite number of plants in the world it would be helpful to you to have these ones drawn by my hand. Here then is a plate. I will not forget to make you another showing the animals I am going to explain to you in this letter.[1]

I begin with the elephant, as the largest animal. Apart from what I have already stated elsewhere, I will add, Sir, that few of them are found in Gold Coast. [.../p. 52/...]² The land is full of tigers, leopards, panthers, lions and other wild beasts. [...]³ The land nourishes oxen and cows, goats, sheep, pigs, deer, roe deer, boar, fallow deer, hares, agouti (*agoutils*), and other animals not known to us. There are also civet cats, monkeys, cats, dogs, weasels, snakes and insects.⁴ [Also] oxen and cows [...]⁵ [And] goats and sheep [... and ...] pigs [...]⁶ Wild boar are called *cotoccon* and at Mina *porpor*.⁷ There are many hares at Acra. [...]⁸ Civet cats are found at Man-frou. [...] These animals have the shape of a fox and the tail of a cat, their coat being very much speckled in grey and black. [...]⁹ There are several kinds of monkeys. [...] I saw some at Mina and Acra which were as large as a child of twelve and which had a very short tail and a face like the muzzle of a mastiff. [...]¹⁰

[illustration no. (73), hunting of animals, inserted after p. 52]¹¹

These lands have to bear with many snakes (*serpents*). [.../p. 53/ ...] There are places where they worship them, as they worship snakes (*couleuvres*) at Juda.¹² Sometimes crocodiles are found near Acra. The Danes' people there made me a present of a live crocodile in 1679. They had captured it when small two years previously and had always kept it in a barrel – as you know, this is an amphibious animal. Another sort, rather different from the first sort, is called *langadi* by the blacks, and these never enter the water.¹³ There are large lizards. [...]¹⁴. Chameleons are fairly common in certain places. [...]¹⁵.

Cats have been brought here from Europe, as have many dogs. [...]¹⁶ There are no horses. [...]¹⁷ The porcupines here are extremely large and heavy. They much resemble the Zaetta of Barbary, for like them they have quills 20–24 inches long, and are spotted black and white.¹⁸

Some of the spiders seen here are of an astonishing and horrifying size. There are also very large numbers of small spiders.¹⁹ The vipers are larger, longer and more venomous than ours, but otherwise the same.²⁰ Anyone who penetrated further inland would doubtless find many sorts of animals unknown to us. But the great risks one would run inhibit the curiosity of the most daring.²¹ Hence we must limit ourselves to what is best known. Also you must permit me to finish my letter, since it is after midnight and very cold. I wish you as good a night as anyone in the world, Sir. /p. 54/

[illustration no. (74), wild animals][22] /p. 55/

Additional Passages from 1732

[p. 207/2, on the elephant]

This creature is so well known almost throughout Europe, that it will be absolutely needless to proceed to a description of its form and figure; much less to repeat abundance of things reported of its natural docility, wonderful instinct, and many other singular qualities, which naturalists assign it, as well as Indian travellers. That it is capable of performing many surprising motions and actions, has been sufficiently made known in Europe, by such of them as have been exposed to publick view in several cities, as Paris, London, Amsterdam, etc.

[p. 210/2–3, on the crocodile]

I was presented by the Danish general at Acra with a young one alive, being about seven feet long, which he kept in a large fat [vat], and had design'd to bring it over into Europe; but considering the great quantity of fresh water that would be spent in so long a passage, as from thence to the French Leeward islands of America, and thence into France, I order'd it to be kill'd, and some of my men and the Blacks eat it, as a delicate bit. It tasted much like veal, but very luscious, and had a strong scent of musk. / . . . there is scarce any way of killing them but at the head, and so it was we serv'd the young one that was given me at Acra. A stout Black sat astride on the head of the fat the crocodile was kept in, with a large hammer in his hands, and two other Blacks one on each side of the first, holding a couple of iron bars athwart the head of the cask; another Black knock'd out the head of the fat, through which the alligator advancing his head, with flaming eyes, to get out, but being stopt by the two iron bars across, the Black who sat on the head of it, gave him two or three such strokes on the forehead with the hammer, that it died immediately.

470

[p. 210/10–211/2, on civet-cats]

I carry'd some very fine civet-cats into France, which were much admired there, and afforded excellent civet. / These creatures, when very hungry, will prey on any thing that comes in their way, which they can master. I had one at Guadaloupe, which was kept in the next chamber to me: my man having neglected to feed it a whole day, it came into my chamber the next morning, and immediately leap'd at a curious talking parrot of the Amazons river I had brought from Cayenne, laying hold of it by the neck, tho' it was perch'd above six feet high from the floor, and tore the neck quite off before I could relieve it. / I have often observ'd, that these cats will always roll and tumble themselves several times on the flesh they are to feed on, before they eat it; and are so cleanly, as always to ease nature close up in the corner of the cage they are kept in;[23] and when hungry, gnaw the very wood of the cage to get out for provision. They are generally so well known in all trading places in Europe, that I shall forebear adding any more . . .

[p. 211/12, on antelope]

Antelopes are sometimes seen and hunted at Acra, their flesh being very good, and they incredible swift, generally keeping within the the hilly country beyond the European forts. The shape of them is between a goat and a stag, their horns like the goats and buffaloes, lying towards their back, and a little bow'd, but commonly longer than a goat's.[24]

NOTES

[1] In this letter, and in Letter 2/15 on birds, Barbot draws on Villault, on Dapper, and on Dapper's major source for the subject, Marees, incorporating only very limited personal observations or comments of his own. The material is much enlarged in *1732*, mainly from Bosman, but with occasional additional personal observations. In 1679 Barbot noted, but without discussing, cows, goats, pigs, pigeons and turtle-doves at Axim; and oxen, cows, goats, pigs, sheep, three kinds of deer, Guinea-fowl and pigeons at Accra (*1679*, pp. 279–80, 334). Barbot's original information is in general so marginal that it has not been considered necessary to supply references to other sources on these creatures, but attention is drawn to the relevant notes

in Jones 1983a. The drawing of plants and two subsequent drawings of hunting and wild animals (pp. 51, 52, 54) are copied, with only small changes, from illustrations in Marees, nos. 11–14.

[2] Elephants were previously discussed in Letter 1/15, p. 85, above. The present passage is almost entirely derived, the 'few' confirming Villault, p. 375, while material on two methods of killing, a vernacular name, white elephants, and their meat and hide, are from Dapper, pp. 1/15/2, 1/17/2, 91/2; Marees, ff. 64–6.

Cf. 1732, pp. 206/4–208/8, which much enlarges, mainly from Bosman, pp. 241–5, 317–22; but it adds Biblical commentary and more from Dapper, as well as a reference to a discussion on whether tusks are teeth or horns taken from Letter 1/15, p. 85, above. Barbot mistranslates his own earlier material, so that pits dug to trap elephants on their way to drink become traps filled with water.

[3] Omission of three sentences on 'tigers', combining material from Villault, p. 373; Dapper, pp. 91/2, and Marees, f. 65.

Cf. 1732, pp. 209/2–7, much enlarged from Bosman, pp. 245–6, 312–6. Barbot contributes that these animals are 'so frequently carry'd about in Europe to show, that it will be needless to be more particular in their description, most persons having observed that they much resemble a cat, and are bearded in the same manner'.

[4] The list mostly follows that in Villault, p. 373. The agouti is a large rodent found only in America (and reported to Barbot at Cayenne, 1679, p. 368), but the reference is probably to a similar rodent of Guinea, the Cane Rat (*Thryonomys swinderianus*).

[5] Omission of five sentences, from Dapper, p. 91/7 (ultimately from Marees, f. 65), except for a comparative reference to bad pasturage at Cape Verde.

Cf. 1732, p. 215/1–5, much enlarged from Bosman, pp. 235–6, except for the following. 'At my last voyage to the castle of Mina, I presented the then Dutch general with a hogshead of French wine, and a fine cow I had taken aboard at Goeree, which used to afford milk aboard the ship in a tolerable quantity, and was extraordinary well received by him; and in return, just as I was under sail, he sent me four of the country sheep, which prov'd but very sorry meat, even among the meanest sailors'.

[6] Omission of three sentences, from Dapper, pp. 91/7, 92/1 (from Marees, f. 65), but Barbot mistranslates, bringing sheep from São Tomé and feeding goats and sheep, instead of hens, on millet.

Cf. 1732, p. 215/6–12, much enlarged, mainly from Bosman, pp. 236–9, but adding that pork from the French Leeward islands is as good as that of Fida; also the following descriptions which appear to be original. Sheep – 'their horns turn towards the back, somewhat bow'd, and their legs are

somewhat longer in proportion than those of our European sheep'. Pigs -
'they are neither of the shape or bulk of our European swine, being short
body'd and legg'd, and generally all black or spotted; but the sows are very
fruitful, and when with pig their bellies hang down almost to the ground'.

[7] A mistranslation of Dapper, p. 92/1, which states that at Mina *porpor* is
'wild pig' (Akan/Twi *purpu*, perhaps from Portuguese *porco*: Jones 1983a, p.
289) and *kottokko* is 'porcupine' (Akan/Twi *kɔtɔkɔ*). For porcupines, see
note 18 below. For wild boar, or bush-pigs, at Accra, see Marees, f. 43.
 Cf. *1732*, p. 210/9, enlarged from Bosman, p. 247, but adding that wild
boar travel in herds of 3–400 (from an untraced source and contradicting
Bosman, who says that there are few wild boar).

[8] Omission of two sentences from Dapper, p. 91/2; Marees, ff. 43, 66.
 Cf. *1732*, p. 214/11–12, enlarged slightly from Bosman, pp. 62, 249. For
an earlier reference to hares at Accra, see Letter 2/10, p. 38, above.

[9] Omission of five sentences on civet cats from Dapper, pp. 1/21/12, 92/1
(from Marees, f. 66–66v), with the addition of 'especially at Manfrou'. In
1679 at Frederiksborg (i.e., 'Manfrou'), Barbot was given a female civet
cat, which he transported to France and presented to an *intendant* at Rochefort (*1679*, p. 301). In a marginal note in *1688*, the reader is referred to a
previous lengthy description of the civet cat (Letter 1/21, pp. 116–7 above,
here omitted as entirely from Dapper).
 Cf. *1732*, pp. 210/10, 211/1–2, much enlarged, partly from Bosman, pp.
251–2, but with personal observations – see the Additional Passage. The
animal is *Viverra civetta*.

[10] Omission of four sentences, on different kinds of monkeys and how
they are caught, from Dapper, p. 92/2 (Marees, f. 65v), except that Barbot
adds that white-nose monkeys are otherwise grey. The animals seen were
presumably baboons, as seen at Winneba in 1694 by another visitor (Phillips
1732, p. 211).
 Cf. *1732*, p. 212/1–11, much enlarged, under the head 'Apes, Monkeys
and Baboons', the additional material largely from Bosman, pp. 254–6, (but
at p. 212/5 Barbot substitutes 'apes' for 'monkeys' – in fact, Dutch *apen*
means both), with one item (the black streak on the white-bearded monkeys) suggesting a re-reading of Dapper. Barbot adds, in respect of Bosman's
smitten, that 'their heads are the most deform'd, being short, round and
large, not unlike our great mastiffs'; and in respect of Bosman's second sort,
that their tricks include turning a spit (Barbot refers the reader to Letter 1/
16, p. 92 above) and that 'the same is done by another kind somewhat larger,
by the French call'd Marmots, and are the common monkeys, their heads
very ugly and have little or no tail'. He further adds, in relation to the white-
bearded animals – 'I brought one of this sort from Boutroe, which was all
sport and gamesomeness, valu'd at Paris at twenty L[o]uis d'Or for its

tameness and beauty; and I must own I never saw any other like it in all my travels ... That very beautiful monkey or ape I had at Boutroe above mention'd, stole out of my cabbin aboard the ship a case, in which I had a silver-hafted knife, fork and spoon; and opening it, threw each of them, one after another, into the sea, which was then very calm, skipping and dancing about very merrily, as each of them went overboard ... Besides these here mentioned, there are several other sorts of very fine and gentle apes and monkeys, but naturally so tender, that it is a very difficult matter to preserve them alive in so long a passage, as it is from Guinea to Europe, especially considering that our carrying slaves over from thence to America lengthens it considerably'. Barbot's tame monkey with the white breast and beard would be a Diana monkey, *Cercopithecus diana*, although his reference to a white spot on the nose seems to confuse it with various 'Spot-nosed' species, e.g. *Cercopithecus petaurista*. As a pet, the Diana is 'lively, affectionate and very decorative' (Booth 1960, p. 25).

[11] The scene of Africans hunting elephants, deer and hares, and of a feline entering a trap, is basically copied from Marees, plate 11, Barbot adding a ship in the background. All the elements in the scene reappear in a larger scene, in *1732*, Plate 17 (p. 202), as items E, I, L, and M. Other items are from Marees, plate 12 (D, S), Dapper pp. 1/123, 94, 100, 102 (A, F, R, and perhaps G), and Bosman, p. 268 (B and the other E).

[12] The omitted section of seven sentences, on a giant snake, and on 'winged snakes' also seen in Abyssinia and Senegal, is from Dapper, p. 93/3, and Marees, f. 73–73v, although Barbot begins – 'people have assured me'. Barbot refers to 'vipers' separately, a few sentences on. For the snakes at 'Juda' (Whydah), see Letter 3/2, p. 135, below.

Cf. *1732*, p. 213/1–10, much enlarged from Bosman, pp. 273–4, 310–2. Barbot adds – 'All the Blacks in general eat the snakes and serpents they can catch, as a very great dainty; and I have seen French gentlemen eat them at Martinico'.

[13] The last sentence is from Marees, f. 64 (cf. f. 74–74v): the animal is perhaps the Nile Monitor (*Varanus niloticus*) or the Giant Ground Pangolin (*Manis gigantea*), and the name appears to be from Portuguese *lagarto*, 'alligator'. The gift of a crocodile by the Dutch governor of the Danish fort (hence 'the Danes' people' rather than 'the Danes') was recorded in *1679*, pp. 329, 331. But this states that Barbot was offered the animal alive and declined, and that later the governor had it killed and flayed, in order to be stuffed, before presenting it to one of Barbot's companions.

Cf. *1732*, p. 210/1–8, much enlarged from Bosman, pp. 246–7, 253, and also, for legends about American alligators, from Navarette and a missionary source (p. 210/8 and perhaps 210/4). The following may be original: 'They have a great strength in their tail with which they will overset a small canoo. Their most usual food is fish, which they are continually chacing at the

bottom of the rivers'. Barbot adds an extended version of the gift episode –
see the Additional Passage.

[14] Omission of two sentences from Marees, f. 64v, enlarged in *1732*, pp.
213/11–214/1, from Bosman, p. 256.

[15] Omission of four sentences, refuting that the chameleon lives on air and
changes colour at will, from Villault, p. 374, and Marees, f. 75–75v.
Cf. *1732*, p. 214/2–3, enlarged from Bosman, pp. 257–60 and the drawing
opposite p. 248, but with copying errors – 'their eyes [eggs] are about half as
big as those of lizards [birds]'. Barbot adds – 'They live in Guinea five years
or longer, being kept on trees; and some are sent over into Europe'.

[16] Omission of five sentences, on the form of dogs, their non-barking, and
their being eaten, all this from Dapper, p. 91/4–5, and Marees, ff. 64v, 75v,
apart from the remark that the dogs' head has the shape of that of a hare or
a fox.
Cf. *1732*, p. 216/4–7 enlarged from Bosman, p. 239, with the following
addition in respect of the local appreciation of dog-meat: '. . . and therefore
when they go aboard ships, they will offer to buy the dogs they see there. I
remember one of our cabin boys had three Aquiers of gold at Cape St
Apollonia for an ugly one he had kept some time'. The drawing of 'Gold
Coast doggs' on *1732*, Plate 18 (p. 216), seems to be based on the figure of
the dog in Marees, plate 10.

[17] Omission of two sentences from Dapper, p. 92/2 (Marees, f. 65), but
Barbot changes 'one (horse) brought here' to 'two brought from Cape Verde
to Mina'.
Cf. *1732*, p. 216/2, which substitutes from Bosman, p. 238 – but whereas
the English translation of Bosman gives 'Northern Horses' for 'Noordsche
Paardjes', Barbot gives 'Norway horses', which is closer (see *HIA*, V, 253);
hence it would seem that Barbot sometimes consulted the Dutch original.

[18] In 1679, at Adja, Barbot saw a 'Zaita, a kind of porcupine or hedgehog,
similar to one seen at La Rochelle last year. The head is like that of a hare,
except the ears, and the rest of the body like that of a hedgehog', and he
marginated – 'Zaita, a kind of porcupine or hedgehog' (*1679*, p. 317). There
are previous references to porcupines in Letter 1/7, p. 31; Letter 1/21, pp.
115–6, above.
Cf. *1732*, p. 214/4–6, which is largely from Bosman, pp. 249, 311, but
adds, partly repeating material in Letter 1/21, p. 115, above, the following.
'I saw one at Infiama, about two feet high, some being two feet and a half,
and brought over some of its quills, about as thick as a goose's, two spans
long, and some three, according to the bigness of the beast, divided at
distances with black streaks; as may be seen in the figure of this creature,
here inserted [on Plate 17, p. 202]. These are much like the porcupines I
have seen in France, brought over from Morocco.' Barbot visited Infiama

(Dixcove) in April 1682 (*1732*, p. 275). The Crested Porcupine (*Hystrix cristata*) is indeed found in both Guinea and the Mediterranean region.

[19] This echoes Marees, ff. 64, 65v, 74v–75.

Cf. *1732*, p. 222/4–7, which is much enlarged, partly from Bosman, p. 322, but Barbot adds a reference to 'a kind of spiders', taken from Hillier 1697, p. 701, and also digressions on the tarantula in Italy and a spider in South America.

[20] This is probably influenced by Marees, f. 73v 'snakes or vipers (*Aderen*)'.

[21] This is probably inspired by Marees, f. 65–65v, on Netherlanders fearing to go inland lest they be captured by the Portuguese and their allies.

[22] Barbot's illustration is based on Marees, plate 12, but he omits some of the animals (crocodile, tortoise, *languado*, rhinoceros, frog, fox and cranes) and adds others (hare, two kinds of deer, boar, civet cat, dog), naming some of these. He also adds huts and ships to the background and turns a mound into an ant-hill. This illustration is not repeated in *1732*, but some of the animals appear in Plate 17 (p. 202), and the dog is one of two, described as 'Gold Coast doggs', which together with the ant-hill, drawn more crudely, and described as 'A Pis-mire Nest at Akra', appear on Plate 18 (p. 216).

[23] This observation (also in Letter 1/21, p. 116, above) may be original but it echoes Marees, f. 65v.

[24] Apart from the Additional Passages and those passages cited in earlier notes, the remainder of *1732*, pp. 206/4–216/12, is from Bosman, pp. 238, 245, 246, 250–252, 410–411 (the final passage referring to Slave Coast, not Gold Coast).

LETTER 15

Birds [and insects].

If I remember correctly, Sir, I have reached the birds. There are tame ones and wild ones, and almost all of them are different from those we have in Europe. Among the wild ones are eagles of several sorts. [...][1]. There are several kinds of parrots. [...][2] The little parakeets which I have told you about elsewhere are found here in large numbers. [...] Their plumage is a beautiful bright green, half of their head between the beak and the eye is very orange, their tail is striped black, orange and yellow, their beak is white, and their legs are tawny. [...] The sight and sound of many of them together is very pleasing and diverting. [...][3] [...][4] Sparrows are very common and little different from ours. [...] Swallows are smaller and greyer than in France. [. . .]⁵ [. . .]⁶ The cranes and herons are similar to ours. [. . .]⁷

Hens are so abundant in many places that they can be bought anywhere on the coast for less than two *sols* worth of /p. 56/ merchandise [each]. [. . .]⁸ Acra is the only place on Gold Coast where Guinea fowl are still found. You know enough about these. [. . .] There are turtle-doves with beautiful plumage, wood-pigeons or wild pigeons, and thrushes just like the thrushes here. [. . .] In marshes can be seen river woodcock. [. . .]⁹

They have bats, owls, frogs, grasshoppers, and locusts which sometimes inflict great famines on them, for these locusts come from the borders of Arabia and eat up their crops. The locusts have raised the price of Indian corn to 10 pieces-of-eight for a bin of two bushels. The land-crabs are very good to eat, and have the same shape and colour as the Tourelourous of the Caribbean Antilles islands. [. . .] Glow-worms can be seen here in large quantities, and great black flies which give out a light in the night. [. . .]¹⁰ I think there are no larks here, at least I have never heard of any.¹¹

Gnats are a great nuisance in low places and marshes, where many moths and ants of various kinds are also found. A very large sort of ant, with yellow wings, is found especially at Acra. These little insects build houses in the form of pyramids, as you can see from the plate at the beginning of my letter. Surely it is something to wonder at that such a little creature can erect so solidly such a large construction, for it stands from four to five feet high and is built of clay. You have to use a club to knock it down, and then you see into it, and note, with admiration, a thousand compartments and a thousand passages which join them all up. Some are filled with provisions, others with droppings, and others again are intended for their residence. The fields at Acra are covered with these ants' nests, and the ants, who are mischievous and whose bite is painful, spoil all the places where the honey-bees live in their holes, and they eat up the honey.¹² [. . .]¹³ I conclude, assuring you I am, etc.

Additional Passages from *1732*

[p. 220/6–8, on parakeets]

The trading ships on the coast, seldom fail of taking many of these lovely creatures aboard in cages, but they are so tender, that most of them commonly die in their passage to France, England, or

Holland, notwithstanding all the care that can be taken of them. Of all the great numbers I used to carry away from the coast every voyage, I could save but very few alive when arrived in France. The change of climate and food or what I believe affects them most, the cold weather, is insupportable to them. / I also observ'd that the firing of great guns aboard ship, was so dreadful to them, that several of mine would drop down dead at the noise. / These rare birds cannot be taught to pronounce any distinct words in any language, at least, that I did ever hear or know, tho' I took all the pains I could take to teach some; yet there are persons who affirm, they had some who would utter a few words in French, which I will not contradict: but several of them kept together in a cage in good dry hot weather, will make a pretty sweet pleasant natural chanting.[14]

[p. 221/8, 10, on the bite of scorpions]

The most certain cure is to bruise the same scorpion, if it can be catched, on the wounded part of the body; as our chief surgeon cured one of our men at Prince's island, who being at felling of wood, was thus prick'd by a scorpion in the heel. / ... / Another remedy against this sting, and the pain of it, is to stroke the part that was hurt with a child's private member, which immediately takes away the pain, and then the venom exhales. The moisture that comes from a hen's mouth, is good for the same.[15]

NOTES

[1] Omission of eight sentences on two kinds of 'eagles', from Villault, pp. 374–5 (but Barbot begins – 'I saw one of these at Corso ...') and from Dapper, p. 92/6, Barbot adding that the latter kind have been thought to have been the harpies of the Ancients.
   Cf. 1732, pp. 218/16–219/1, with additions from Bosman, p. 266, and a reference to Plate 18 (p. 216), which includes 'A Sort of Eagle at Cabo Corso'.

[2] Omission of two sentences on parrots, from Dapper 92/3, with a mis-translation of 'in het wilt' as 'dans les Déserts'.
   Cf. 1732, p. 220/11–13, which substitutes from Bosman, p. 271, Barbot adding that the birds have 'a few red feathers in their wings or tails' and that there are no green parrots in Guinea eastwards from Gold Coast. Barbot also adds the following. 'Every body knows the young ones are most apt to learn

to talk, and of such the traveller has choice at Prince's Island in the gulph, where they are very numerous, and bought raw and unskill'd for a piece of eight. Of these we had once half a hundred or more aboard the ship, and twice as many monkeys; of both which but a few remain'd alive when we arrived in France'. Barbot visited Príncipe twice, in 1679 and 1682; on the former visit, he noted 'an incredible number of grey parrots' and records buying three (*1679*, pp. 350–1).

[3] The omissions cover seven sentences which mix up Villault, p. 375 (who found the sound of parakeets displeasing), and Dapper, p. 92/4, partly summarising, inaccurately, Marees, f. 67. Barbot states of the cage behaviour of the male and female birds that 'I noted . . .', when in fact what follows is precisely Marees. However, he gives a closer description of the bird's colours and adds that the natives resist the birds' depredations by guarding their fields. He also adds Anamabou and Accra to Dapper's Berku as places where the birds exist in large numbers. In 1678–9, at Anomabu Barbot was given half a dozen green and red parakeets and at Accra 'six of the finest seen on the coast', and he reported that they were 'no bigger than sparrows but cannot be transported to France: of 50 I had not one reached America'; while at Axim he noted that 'an infinite number of little birds of different kinds and colours produced, in the trees around the fort in which they perched, the most pleasing bird-song in the world' (*1679*, pp. 281, 312, 329). Earlier references to parakeets included Letter 1/22, p. 119 (the passage omitted as being derived), and Letter 2/8, p. 29 and note 8, above.

Cf. *1732*, p. 220/2–10, which includes a little from Bosman, p. 271 (but disagrees that the bird should be termed 'Guinea sparrow'), refers to Plate 18 (p. 216) ('I have drawn the figure of a small parroquet'), and adds the Additional Passage.

[4] Omission of one paragraph on the 'Beque-figue' and a little bird eaten alive by the blacks, from Dapper, p. 92/5, or Marees, f. 67–67v.

Cf. *1732*, p. 218/9–10.

[5] The omissions cover three sentences on smaller birds, from Dapper, p. 92/5, or Marees, f. 67v, and Villault, p. 376.

Cf. *1732*, p. 218/11–13, which adds that the natives shoot as well as net birds, from Bosman, p. 264. Since Marees had remarked that birds were seldom shot because of lack of guns, the change perhaps indicates a difference between c. 1600 and c. 1700.

[6] Omission of two sentences on bitterns, mews and ravens, from Dapper, p. 92/8 and Marees, f. 67v.

Cf. *1732*, p. 218/15.

[7] Omission of two sentences from Dapper, p. 92/7–9 and Marees, f. 68.

Cf. *1732*, p. 217/9–10, which largely substitutes from Bosman, p. 265.

Barbot notes the inclusion of a heron on Plate 17 (p. 202), but the bird is copied from Marees, plate 12.

[8] Omission of two sentences on hens and their eggs, from Dapper, p. 91/7, or Marees, f. 65.

Cf. *1732*, p. 217/1–4, which enlarges from Bosman, pp. 239–40, and thus makes hens dear, not cheap.

[9] The reference to Guinea fowl is original, and the references to thrushes and woodcock may be too – unless Barbot has mistranslated the names of certain of the various birds mentioned in Dapper, pp. 91/8, 92/7–9, and Marees, f. 67v – the sources from which the references to turtle-doves and wood-pigeons, and to the other birds mentioned in the omitted sentences, are drawn. In 1679 Barbot was presented with a Guinea fowl at Accra (*1679*, pp. 324, 334); and Guinea fowl were noted at Winneba in 1694 (Phillips 1732, p. 211). Guinea fowl in Senegal were mentioned earlier in *1688* (Letter 1/7, p. 32, above).

Cf. *1732*, pp. 217/7–8, 218/3–6, 8, 14, with additions from Bosman, pp. 263–4, and with additional comment on bushfowl – 'seen no where but at Acra, where they breed a few. Whether they are natural tö the country, or of the breed of cape Verdo-Pintados, I am not certain, but they are fine curious birds, much bigger than common poultry, and delicate meat, if fed properly, as I have said before'.

[10] Apart from the references to corn prices and Tourelourous, the remainder of the passage, including two omitted sentences on bees, is from Dapper, p. 93/1–2, 4 and Marees, f. 68. But Barbot has introduced the term 'glow-worm', and hence duplicated Marees's reference to 'small [not 'large'] black flies', which are in fact glow-worms. On corn prices, see Letter 2/10, p. 38, note 15, above, and Letter 2/20, p. 83 and note 40, below; also Phillips 1732, p. 208 (at Cape Coast); Donnan 1930, I, 200, 204 (at Axim and Dixcove); Jones 1985, pp. 118, 134 (at Gross-Friedrichsburg).

Cf. *1732*, pp. 220/14, 221/2–5, 13, 15–17, which makes the bats and owls 'very large ones'; adds that 'the honey and wax are very good, but not like ours in France' and that the locusts are from 'the desarts of Lybia and Zara'; increases the insects by adding butterflies and beetles; and also adds substantially from Bosman, pp. 272–3, 275–6, as well as a reference to toads from Hillier 1697, p. 699.

[11] This sentence, out of place, is from Villault, p. 376–7: the information is incorrect, since species of larks do exist in Guinea, e.g., *Galerida cristata*.

Cf. *1732*, pp. 217/11–12, 218/1–2, 5–7, 219/2–220/1, which adds substantial material on various other birds, from Bosman, pp. 240, 262–3, 266–7, 269, 271. Barbot comments that there are more 'partridges' at Accra; he follows Bosman in saying there are no 'peacocks', although Marees, f. 67v, and Dapper, p. 92/7, spoke of them – and although they or their equivalents do exist; and he adds that 'Queests' (ring-doves) are also very common in the woods.

[12] The references to moths, and to ants in general (their labours and attacks on bees), are from Dapper, p. 93/1 and Marees, f. 68. But the references to gnats (i.e. mosquitoes) and to ants and ant-hills at Accra, and the drawing of an ant-hill, are not from these sources. Although Barbot may have copied the information on ants from a general work, it is more likely that they derive from his observations at Accra, probably in 1682, as his 1679 journal does not mention ants or ant-hills: see Letter 2/10, p. 38, note 16.

Cf. *1732*, pp. 221/14, 17–222/3, which enlarges from Bosman, pp. 275–7, but also has some original additions – 'there are ... of ants and gnats most prodigious numbers all over the coast: and more particularly at and about Acra, where the country is flat and level'. On gnats, Barbot adds the following. 'The gnats are another inconvenience to the inhabitants in the night-time, especially near the woods and marshy ground. Their sting is very sharp, and causes swellings and violent pains; whence it it easy to conceive, with what I have said of the ants, and the excessive heat of the climate, what a troublesome life people must lead, where 'tis scarce possible to have an hour of quiet sleep; and provisions are but very indifferent.' Barbot also repeats here a passage on 'Cigarras' (cicada), from *1732*, p. 117/1 – see Letter 1/22, the Additional Passage. The drawing of an ant-hill ('which I drew at Acra') on Plate 18 (p. 216) is entitled 'A Pis-mire Nest at Akra'.

[13] Omission of two sentences, on freedom to hunt and the whites' fear to go inland, from Dapper, p. 91/3 and Marees, f. 65–65v. Omitted in *1732*, which concludes its account of insects with a reference to spiders, from Bosman, p. 322, and a long digression on the tarantula in Italy and a similar spider in South America, from untraced sources (*1732*, p. 222/4–6).

[14] The extent to which parakeets could 'talk' was discussed by Marees, f. 67 and Villault, p. 376.

[15] The scorpion episode on Príncipe occurred in 1682 – see Letter 3/11, pp. 180–81, and note 13, below. The omitted paragraph refers to a Mexican cure – Barbot's source(s) for both the alleged remedies for scorpion-bite is untraced. The surrounding material on scorpions and millipedes (*1732*, p. 221/6–7, 11–12) is from Bosman, pp. 274–5 (and the drawing of a scorpion on Plate 18 is from Bosman, plate 11) – but Barbot becomes confused about the millipede's number of legs.

481

LETTER 16

The method of making salt. How gold is gained and how its quality can be known.

Sir, in my last two letters I discussed the animals of these countries, which I ought to have done after discussing the inhabitants, but since I have already reversed the order I had intended to follow, I am going to converse with you regarding their methods of obtaining salt and gold. I begin with salt, which they call *iakin*. Large quantities are made at Anta, Corso, Anamabou, Acra, Labbadi and Sinko, but more at Sinko and Anta than elsewhere, for these provide all the interior lands with it, via the /p. 57/ markets and fairs established at various localities. The salt is made from sea-water which is either boiled over a fire or exposed to the sun in special places. Employing the former method, they boil it once only, in copper caldrons or in purpose-made earthenware pans (this being the method used at all times), and without more ado they obtain thus a white and fine salt.[1] They put it into baskets made of osiers or canes in the shape of a sugar-loaf, and cover them with leaves from the same plants. In this fashion they transport the baskets on the backs of slaves, without having to fear injury to the salt from the rains, or from the heat of the sun which would blacken the salt if it touched it. The salt becomes so hard in these baskets that it takes a hammer to break it. Although the salt has a good enough taste, it will not preserve meat very long in the great heat, but blackens it and gives it an acrid and bitter taste. Their other method of making salt is by filling with sea-water large holes made in rocks, or the crevices they find in them, then leaving the water there for some time, exposed to the great heat of the sun, which draws out the salt from the water without their having more trouble than that of of removing the salt from the spot. This salt is more bitter than the salt made by boiling the water, also much less is obtained. It can be found in rocks all along the coast [where it is made naturally], and it resembles white stones. Salt is made more in December, January and February than at other times, partly because the sun is then at its highest, and partly because this is the season for travelling, and people come to collect the salt and transport it to the interior of these lands, where it forms the chief trade, as I think I have already told you. The English at Corso and the

482

Portuguese at Acra have marshes of the kind we have in France, where they make the salt they need. To be truthful, this salt is much better and whiter than the salt made by the blacks. But enough about salt.[2]

Let us now say something about the gold that can be found in these countries – [discussing it] at least to the extent that we know about this gold. [.../pp. 58–59/...] This method of obtaining gold from rivers cannot alone produce a sufficiently abundant supply for the trade on Gold Coast, from where I estimate that more than 15,000 marks of gold is carried annually to Europe and elsewhere. [*margin*: The Europeans obtain annually 15,000 marks of gold, that is, 525,000 £ worth][3] [...] Gold is always expensive to extract from the earth, as you know well enough, Sir – you who possess accounts of each of the Indies, and especially of Chile, lands very rich in mines of gold and silver. [.../p. 60/...][4] The kings of Fetu and Accanez at one time had each, as their fetish, a lump of gold the size of a bushel. A Dane at Manfrou swore to me that he had seen these, when on a journey he had made to obtain necessities for the fortress.[5]

There, Sir, that is all I have to tell you on the subject of the mines, so let us proceed to the nature and value of the gold. It is necessary that you have this information to serve as a guide for yourself, should the notion take you to visit the places supplying gold, which however I do not advise you to do. No doubt you have been under the impression that this metal has everywhere the same value and purity, given the short distance between the places where it is obtained, but this is an incorrect view you must reject. The gold varies, Sir, not only inasmuch as it is varyingly adulterated by the natives, but also because it naturally differs in the form in which it leaves the mines (although gold from the mines is always more valuable [than adulterated gold]). I distinguish two sorts, the explanation being that the gold is formed in the earth by the great heat of the sun but is dispersed in veins which spread out like [the roots of] a tree, so that the veins which are deepest in the ground produce much poorer gold than those that are nearer the surface and are therefore more intensively heated by the sun and produce the gold in purer form.[6]

The best Gold Coast gold is that traded between Isseny and Axim and at Cape Appolonia, it being largely obtained from the mines of Igwira, and from the rivers which rise there, like the Mancu and Axim. It is always of the standard of 22 carats and sometimes reaches 23 carats, because the inhabitants of these places hardly ever adulterate it. Nevertheless, it is wise to be on your guard, if only to get rid of the sand which always accompanies it. This is done by blowing softly into a little copper basin specially made for this purpose.[7] The gold from Cape Three Points to Saconde is a little poorer, being obtained from the lands of Adom, the difference not being great.

You begin to notice that the gold is adulterated at Saconde, the gold there being brought from the lands of Accanez and Fetu, where it is grossly adulterated. But the deception leaps to the eye, so to speak, at Little Comendo, at Mina, and even at Corso and Mourée, although it is true that the first two places are the most dangerous [to trade at]. I have seen gold not worth 10 *livres* per ounce. There are even Moors whose effrontery is such that they come aboard vessels with just plain copper filings. This is what makes the gold here very bad, apart from the fact that it has already been adulterated by the Accanez who brought it from their countries. The people of Comendo and Mina augment the compound, and both parties are so skilled at it that that you have to be in the know about it in order not to be cheated. I have at times had those Moors who offered me adulterated metal, especially the sort they call *krakra* (the money at Mina), flogged, in order to rid them of their urge to cheat. But they are too habituated to this disgraceful business, for the same men came on board again with the same gold slightly disguised.[8] The gold from Cormentin and Anamabou is worth little more than that of Corso and Comendo. This gold is from Fetu and Accanes. The gold traded at Tantonquerry and from there to Bergu is even worse.[9]

The gold at Accra (which comes from Tafou) is almost the same quality as that at Axim and reaches about 22 carats, as I have had tested at the /p. 61/ Paris Mint. It is traded pure and natural, as it comes from the river or mine. It is only necessary to attend to removing the gravel it is mixed with (either by using little pincers for the stones or by blowing for the sand), a procedure the natives do not bear patiently, since it lessens the weight. This is the form of cheating those here practise.[10] The gold to be found between Acra and Lay, and further on, comes from the coast [further West], the blacks carrying it away from there in exchange for their slaves, cattle and foodstuffs. Hence you must be on your guard here, for the blacks of [Gold] Coast cheat these, just as they do other people, and these blacks may have obtained gold of poor quality, those of them in particular who have no regular use of the metal, as I have told you. [. . .][11]

484

The love they have, as we do, for this precious metal makes them seize any chance to adulterate it in order to increase its value. They are extremely skilled in all the different ways of mixing it with other metals. [. . .]¹² Nowadays they could give lessons in gold-working and filigree, which they do better than the whites on the coast, even although they lack the right instruments and tools. The Dutch also contributed to creating this troublesome situation, by bringing them from Europe certain tools, files, etc, and then other Europeans did the same, until it can be said of all of these, that they handed over the rods that were used to flog them, and that, truly, trickery was reversed on its author, or, as the Italian proverb says, *a fourbo, farbo mezo*.¹³ I would finish this letter here if it had not occurred to me that you would perhaps like to know more about the different ways in which the Africans adulterate this precious metal. There are five methods. [. . ./ p. 62/. . .]¹⁴ [. . .]¹⁵ In sum, Sir, it is easy to distinguish gold, by acid, by the touchstone, by the punch, by the eyes, the teeth or even the nose. These last two methods are useful only for gold mixed with tin or copper. The teeth distinguish the grittiness of tin and the nose the smell of copper, which is always that of the verdigris. [*insert:* You also notice the weight.] I always made use of all these methods as each was appropriate at various times and places, and I never received gold of a standard below 21 carats. I am, until the next letter, Your etc.

Additional Passages from *1732*

[p. 228/8–9, on estimates of gold export

In this manner, all the gold that is yearly exported from that coast to Europe, is gather'd; which if I may credit some very understanding gentlemen, who have lived long there, amounts to 8000 marks, besides what is sent about to other parts of the world. Of this quantity, the Dutch generally have one fourth part, when there is a general peace among the Blacks, and all the passes are open and free. The English have about a fifth or better. The rest is divided among the French, the Danes, the Brandenburghers, the Portugueses and the interlopers of those nations. / Thus we may say, the whole quantity carry'd away from the Gold Coast, amounts to 12000 marks one year with another; which being reckoned at 30 l. sterling per mark, amounts to 240,000 l. sterling, or little less, according as the price is higher or lower in the parts of Europe where it is disposed of.¹⁶

[pp. 232/3–233/4, on how to avoid being cheated in gold dealings]

Another method to prevent being cheated in gold, especially on shipboard, tho' not altogether to be depended on, but only in general, is nicely to observe the behaviour of the Blacks, which I have done myself; for generally a cheat, who knows his gold is false and counterfeit, is very impatient, uneasy and in haste to be gone, under some colour or other, besides he commonly bids a higher price than usual for goods, and takes them in a hurry without too much examination; and if not found out, will paddle away to shore with the goods, as fast as his canoo can carry him. Nay, I have observ'd some of them to stand trembling and quaking, whilst their gold was upon trial; and such their behaviour is a sufficient indication to suspect some fraud, especially when there is a croud of dealers, for then they expect to find the better opportunity of imposing on the purchasers, and then the European factor ought to be nicest in examining every parcel of gold. When I met with any such knaves, and had discover'd the cheat by trial, I always used them very roughly, even to cocking of an unloaded pistol at their breast, or else threatned to throw their false gold over board, which deterr'd many of them from offering the like to me again. On the other hand, a Black who knows his gold is pure and fine, appears always calm, stands hard about the price of goods, and is curious in examining every piece, whether it is truly good in its sort. / There is another sure way to try gold, which may be used by merchants and is very plain, by twenty-four artificial needles, made with alloy of metals from the lowest sort of gold to the finest of twenty-four carats fine, having exact rules for valuing of it, according to the degrees of fineness or coarseness.

I will further add this advice to all sea-fairing men, trading on that coast aboard ships, that when they see many Blacks come aboard together, to trade with gold, they admit but two or three at most, into the great cabbin, or any other part of the ship, at one time, and always keep about them four or five of their own men to be upon the watch, lest the Blacks imbezil any goods; that so they and their goldsmith, if there be one aboard, as commonly there is aboard French ships,[17] may have leisure to examine the nature of the gold: for it is common there for one Black, most of those on the coast being factors or brokers for the inland people, to have twenty or more several small parcels of gold, wrapt up in rags, or

486

in little leather bags, to purchase goods for so many several persons; and those parcels must be all examined one after another, which takes a long time: and if they admit of a croud of Blacks about them, they cannot so well examine all their different parcels, so as to be sure they take none but what is good. Besides that the Blacks, when in a croud, are always prating together. / Take heed of such as come with rush baskets, as I have seen five or six of them together, with every one such a basket, which are generally designed to conceal what they can steal. So those who talk much and make a noise are to be suspected, and it may be observ'd they will never agree to any price of goods; for the Blacks being generally inclin'd [? not] to steal from one another, make much less scruple of robbing the Europeans, alledging for their excuse, that the Europeans are rich and they poor.[18] Therefore they think it a less crime in themselves to rob us, when an opportunity offers, than for an European to steal from them: and in one respect they may be said to be in the right, since Europeans have the law of God for their guide, which commands them not to steal, which is unknown to the Blacks, who have no other law but that of nature. / Another rule I observed, was to keep in the great cabbin, where I used to trade with the Blacks, only one single piece of each sort of my goods, for a sample; and when I had struck a bargain with a Black, I sent him with my note to the storekeeper, specifying the quantity and quality of the goods he had contracted to pay for. / Another method to be used in ships, is severely to punish any Black that has been taken stealing; for tho' the person so served does not perhaps much value a few blows he may receive, yet it is a great disgrace among themselves, not on account of the heinousness of the crime of stealing, most of them being ready enough and well inclined to do the same, when an opportunity offers, but because he is scoffed at by his countrymen for being so unskilful as to be taken in the act.[19] / I have also observed, that those Blacks who had been pretty well drubb'd with a knotted rope's end, were afterwards more tractable and better to deal with; which makes out that they are like spaniels, that the more you beat them the more they love you.[20]

In this manner, as I have said above, our business was done orderly and safely, without trouble, or confusion, and at night I enter'd all my notes in my book of sale, and weighed all the gold I had receiv'd that day in the lump, to see whether it answer'd the particulars for which it was receiv'd, and also caused it to be enter'd in the same book by my under-factor, observing to keep the said gold in separate boxes, that at my return into France I might have the judgement of the officers of the mint at Paris, or elsewhere, to know which of the chief places of trade on the Gold Coast afforded the finest, and which the worst gold.[21]

[p. 235/2, on European fraud]

I shall conclude this long discourse of gold with an observation I often made there; which is, that many Europeans, who so loudly exclaim against the perfidiousness and deceitful nature of the Blacks, in offering false gold in trade, never consider that on the other hand they are themselves guilty of a notorious cheat and fraud, in using two sorts of weights there, the heavier to receive gold by, and the lighter to pay it away again; which is frequently practised by too many, and is a great dishonour to christianity, being contrary to the golden rule, *To do as we would be done by.* Such base dealing rather serves to confirm those pagans in their ill principles, instead of endeavouring to convert them. But self-interest and covetousness, which is called the root of all evil, are vices too common to all the corrupt race of mankind, either christians or pagans. But christians ought to remember the words of St Paul, to the Roman christians in his days, on the like occasion: chap. ii.v. 24. *That for their evil practices the name of God is blasphemed among the Gentiles.* And that *double weights and double measures are an abomination to God.* Levit.xix.36 and Prov.xi.1.[22]

NOTES

[1] The term *jakin* is a version, via *iukenin* in Marees, of Akan/Twi *nkyéne* 'salt'. Barbot's 'at all times' presumably means that the Africans used earthenware vessels before the Europeans brought copper ones, but also continued sometimes to use the former.

[2] The whole passage on salt-making combines information from Dapper, p. 93/5, based on Marees, f. 101v, and Villault, p. 386, with some personal observations. In 1679, Barbot noted a saline at Anomabu and commented on the salt-trade to the interior (*1679*, pp. 319, 324–5); and he may have seen African salt-making elsewhere in 1682, when he was certainly informed about Portuguese salt-making at Accra (Letter 2/10, pp. 38–9 and note 10,

above). Although much of the material is borrowed and some of the additional information may be only embroidery on this, he appears to contribute the references to copper caldrons and earthenware pans, to slaves conveying salt, to the production of salt in rocks, to the travelling season, and to the production of salt by the English and Portuguese. As for the salt-making season, Dapper made it November to January, Villault made it January to March – Barbot compromises on December to February. Villault said that the local salt was better than salt in Europe; Barbot contradicts him ('to be truthful'), inasmuch as he compares salt made by Africans with salt made by Europeans. For African salt-making on the coast East of Accra, see note 23 of Letter 2/10 above; and for an independent account of Gold Coast salt-boiling, see Jones 1983a, p. 244.

Cf. *1732*, pp. 205/11–206/3, which incorporates Bosman, pp. 308–9 (but substitutes 'Acra' for 'Ardra', perhaps a slip), partly by dropping some of the previous material, especially Dapper's salt-making places and the reference to Europeans making salt.

³ The £ is the French *livre*, not the English pound.

Cf. (on the value of the gold trade) *1732*, p. 228/8–9, enlarged – see the Additional Passage.

⁴ Omission of three long separate sections of borrowed material. The borrowed material states that gold, collected as dust or nuggets, is obtained in the interior, either from rivers, by diving for nuggets or panning for dust, both having been washed out of the soil in the mountains by the rains (a point much elaborated by Barbot); or else from mines, part-owned by kings, whose locality is so secret that the coastal blacks only repeat mythical tales about them, including the dangers of working them. Although Barbot in 1678–9 traded for gold all along Gold Coast, and visited the same places again in 1681–2, presumably again trading for gold, in this lengthy account of the gold trade his personal experiences are swamped by material borrowed from Dapper, pp. 93/6–95/5 (in turn borrowed, almost entirely, from Marees, ff. 94v–98v) and from Villault, pp. 387–97. The material omitted includes a drawing of gold-diving (illustration no. (75), on p. 58), entirely copied from Dapper, p. 94.

Cf. *1732*, pp. 227/11–230/8, embroidered, with additions from Bosman, pp. 80–1, 86.

⁵ Entirely a dishonest borrowing from Villault, p. 390, Villault being the 'me'.

Cf. *1732*, p. 230/1, where the deception is extended – '...which he swore to me he had seen and touched; and to what purpose that gentleman should forswear himself, I cannot see'.

⁶ The comparison with tree roots and the notion that deeper gold is poorer are from Marees, ff. 95v–96, hence Dapper, p. 110/10; but Marees argued

that deeper gold is corrupted by silver, so Barbot's notion that the sun creates gold is either original or from an untraced source.

[7] This paragraph combines material from Villault, p. 387, Dapper, pp. 64/3–4, 84/8, 94/1, 111/1, and Marees, ff. 96, 97v (from which the others also borrow): Barbot contributes the copper basin. Barbot goes on to say that he had had some gold from Accra tested at the Paris Mint, but in *1732*, p. 233/5, he extends this test to gold from 'all the chief places of trade on the Gold Coast' – see the Additional Passage.

[8] In 1679 Barbot complained bitterly about the adulteration of gold, not only in relation to Comendo but also when trading near Axim (*1679*, pp. 281–2, 288). However, *1688* echoes earlier extensive European complaints about adulteration and cheating, in Marees, ff. 40v ('Comando the worst'), 95v–97v (a passage which inspired the later references); in Dapper, pp. 98/5, 109/7, 110/10–111/3; and in Villault, p. 392–3 ('especially at Comendo'). For an independent account of gold adulteration and testing, and for earlier references to adulteration, see Jones 1983a, pp. 90, 498–500 and n. 267.

Cf. *1732*, p. 233/6–7, embroidered, and enlarged with the following anecdote: 'Thus a French captain of a man of war, call'd the Tyger, was serv'd, being formerly sent to the coast as a guardship, and brought home about twenty marks of that dross instead of good gold: which shows that gentleman had little or no skill in gold; for had he but observed the bulk of twenty marks of copper filings, as all his parcel was, it would soon have convinced him how notoriously he was cheated, it being well known that twenty marks of such filings will show twice as large, as the same weight of gold, this being so much the more ponderous.' The statement about flogging cheats, embroidered from Marees, f. 98v, is altered to indicate only a single instance.

[9] The references to interior gold and bad gold at Kormantin are from Marees, ff. 41, 42v.

Cf. *1732*, p. 233/8–9, where a wrong translation – 'tho' it also comes from Accanez and Fetu' – contradicts the earlier statement that the gold from those places was bad.

[10] The statement about Accra gold is from Villault, p. 387, enlarging Dapper, p. 111/2; elsewhere Dapper says that Tafoe gold reaches only as far as Mourée (p. 87/11) and that the Accra gold is from Aboera and Quahoe (p. 88/2–3).

Cf. *1732*, p. 233/5, enlarged by adding Quakoe to Tafoe, and altering the standard for this gold to one of between 22 and 22½ carats.

[11] The French of the last included sentence is crabbed, but the meaning given is that of Barbot's own translation, in *1732*, p. 233/10. The exchange of cattle for gold is based on Dapper, p. 83/7 – in Marees's day, the Dutch did not know this part of the coast well. The remainder of a paragraph is

omitted: it moralises that the Africans, not knowing the value of gold before the French and Portuguese arrived, thereafter became proud and haughty; and that when reproached about the low profit to Europeans they retort that gold is the Europeans' god, as proved by the trouble they take to obtain it. All of this is expanded from Villault, pp. 391–2, which is based on Marees, f. 96–96v.

Cf. *1732*, pp. 233/10–234/2, which embroiders but concludes wryly, the Africans observing that, since the Europeans take so much trouble to travel to Africa, 'our country must be very poor'.

[12] Omission of how the Portuguese taught the Africans to mix metals, in order to practise gold-working and to cheat the French and Dutch, a Dutch yarn, based on Dapper, p. 110/8, and Marees, f. 98.

Cf. *1732*, p. 157/2.

[13] The reference to Dutch responsibility is from Marees, f. 98, and the reference to filigree follows Villault, p. 393. The 'Italian proverb' appears to be a condensed and inaccurate version of the saying 'per conoscere un furbo, ci vuole un furbo e mezzo', 'to recognize a trickster requires (you to be yourself) a trickster and a half' (information from Dr Cecil Clough).

Cf. *1732*, pp. 157/2, 230/9, which enlarges, the Africans now 'in general being crafty, knavish and deceitful, and letting slip no opportunity of cheating a European, or one another, rather than fail. A man of integrity, that may be depended on, is among them as rare as the Phoenix'; and the Dutch now accused of selling the Africans 'long brass pins, and silver melted into little bars and wire'. Barbot cites the same version of the Italian saying – with the translation 'Set a thief to catch a thief, or Diamond cut Diamond' – at an earlier point in the English version (*1732*, p. 47/9).

[14] Omission of the remainder of a long paragraph. The five methods are (1) gold outside, silver within, (2) worked gold containing excess copper and tin, (3) tiny gold pieces with copper items added, (4) copper worked into gold nuggets, (5) gold dust with copper scrapings added: all are from Marees, ff. 97v–98, Barbot not limiting himself to the summary in Dapper, p. 110/7–8 or to the brief reference in Villault, p. 392. Barbot embroiders a little, particularly on the specific applications of the tests by eye-inspection, by cutting open, by acid and by the 'touchstone'.

Cf. *1732*, pp. 230/10–232/2, where the earlier material is overwhelmed by material from Bosman, pp. 81–5, to the extent of acceptance of Bosman's view that the test by acid was impractical. However, Barbot's embroidery includes the following significant additions. 'The first sort of false gold is mix'd with silver or copper, and cast into sundry shapes and sizes, which some there call Fetissos, signifying in Portuguese, charms, because that nation gave the said name to whatsoever belonged to the superstitions of the Blacks. You may see them represented in the cut. [*margin:* Plate 7.] These are generally some sorts of toys commonly used there by the women for

491

ornaments, as also by young men, and worn in their hair, or by way of necklaces and bracelets'. (The first part of the sentence up to 'Fetissos' is from Bosman: Barbot's translation of the term is incorrect. For the drawing of 'Fetissos', see Letter 2/26, p. 103, below.) In the case of large lumps 'quite cased with fine gold, within which there is nothing but cast copper or iron ... every piece must be cut clear through with a chizzle and hammer made for that purpose, knives being too weak to do it so speedily' – contradicting Bosman on the use of knives. The blowing test is described thus: 'put it into a copper or tin bason, and winnow it, letting it run through your fingers and blowing hard'. False gold turns acid black (Bosman says green). 'Some people try the Krakra gold by the touch-stone, spreading a parcel of it thinly on a small piece of hard wood, and rubbing it over with a stone; and by the different colours left on it, an expert man may pretty well guess at the quality and value of the gold, by the rule of proportion.'

[15] Omission of one sentence, on detecting cheating by observing the guilty black's behaviour, from Marees, f. 98–98v; much enlarged in *1732*, p. 232/3 – see the Additional Passage.

[16] This enlarges on the statement on p. 59 above. Whoever the 'understanding gentlemen' were, the calculation appears to have been produced by manipulating similar figures in Bosman, pp. 89–91. On estimates of gold exports, including Barbot's, see Garrard 1980, chap. 5.

[17] A goldsmith was aboard Barbot's ship in 1678–9 (*1679*, pp. 309, 313).

[18] The references to baskets and noise are copied from Letter 2/24, p. 94, below, and derive from Marees, f. 53v.

[19] The comment on the punishment of thieves is copied from Letter 2/24, p. 94, and derives from Marees, ff. 54–54v, 89.

[20] Barbot manages to fall doubly foul of late twentieth-century sensitivities by his view of the extreme docility of both Africans and animals.

[21] Barbot's reminiscences on the procedures of trading for gold are valuable, but it has to be remembered that his generalisations are based on somewhat limited experience, gained on only two voyages.

[22] The Biblical references are not exact quotes but paraphrases.

LETTER 17

The natives, of both sexes, [their physique, character and dress,] and their goldwork.

[.../p. 63/...][1] You discover daily that the natives have a splendid mental capacity (*génie*), with much judgement and a sharp and ready apprehension, which immediately understands whatever you suggest.

They have so good a memory that it is beyond comprehension, and although they cannot read or write, they are admirably well-organised in their trading and never get mixed up. I have seen one of the brokers on board trading four ounces of gold with 15 different persons and making each a different bargain, without making any mistakes or appearing the least harassed.[2]

Yet they do not keep their word with whites, and are very skilful thieves, working together in this business and passing very rapidly from hand to hand what they steal, without arousing the least suspicion. The highest in rank are not exempt from this vice. They never rob each other but consider it a virtue cleverly to rob us. Also they are misers, flatterers, drunkards and guzzlers, and they are lazy, jealous of each other and hate each other on the slightest occasion, quarrelsome, slow in paying their debts, and so haughty in all respects that traders who happen to be nobles or officers make their way through the streets of their towns without raising their heads other than to their superiors, and they are followed by a slave carrying a little seat for them when they halt. They speak disdainfully to their inferiors and in a grave tone. True, they greatly respect whites, particularly those employed in the fortresses or on ships, always addressing them with cap in hand. In turn they like to be treated civilly, and this is the best way to gain their favour. What I found most unbearable was that they lie without conscience, over the smallest thing (especially involving theft), but make a great fuss if a white takes anything from them. They hardly ever keep promises to foreigners if it is inconvenient, but keep them to each other. [. . .][3]

Although their forms of dress are completely different from ours, they are nevertheless of interest, and they /p. 64/ make a display in them. However, there is one kind of dress which is very common among both the great and the small, the rich and the poor, and this is always to wear a cloth (*pagne*) (from Holland, Cape Verde or elsewhere) around the waist, a cloth which passes between the thighs and whose ends hang down to the ground, behind and before, or in some instances only to the knees. This is worn in the house or when travelling. But when they go through the streets, they take a length of Leyden serge or *perpetuana*, 2–3 ells in length, which they pass around their neck, above and below the shoulders, like a mantle, and they take a spear (*assegaye*) or a stick in their hand, for the look of things. They go about this way in the village, carrying themselves with gravity and deliberation, and followed by a slave with a little

493

seat. [*margin:* See the illustration on p. 65.] Nobles and merchants distinguish themselves from the common people by wearing larger and richer material, China satin, taffetas, or coloured Indian cloth, worn as a mantle.[4]

They wear their hair in various fashions. Some shave it all off except for a cross the size of a thumb, others leave a crescent shape, others again a circle or several circles. Others again put their hair into plaits and put these in curl-papers. However they do it, each man seeks to arrange it some new way. Plaiting of hair is the duty of wives.[5] Most of them have hats bought from the whites, but others have hats made of straw or of goatskin or the hide of dogs, these skins having been stretched on wooden blocks to dry. Others again have caps of the same materials, and in various shapes for different hair-styles. They attach to them fetish-objects, glass trinkets, goat's horns, or bark of the fetish tree, and some enrich them with small pieces of worked gold, or with monkeys' tails. Slaves go bareheaded.[6]

They adorn their neck, arms, legs and even feet with many strings of glass beads, coral and Venetian *rassade* [coloured glass beads]. I have seen some who had whole bunches of 4 ct. [carat] of this *rassade* hanging aslant from their neck, intermixed with an abundance of their small gold ornaments and bark from the fetish tree, over which they mutter their frequent prayers. They have also on their arms and legs ivory bracelets they call *manillas*, often three or four on each arm. They make these themselves, from elephant tusks brought from Ivory Coast or from the interior.[7] I have specifically prepared for you an illustration showing these little trinkets, so that you may more easily visualise them. Almost all are of gold or of *Conta de Terre*, which is a bluestone from Benin, as costly as gold itself.[8]

[illustration no. (76), ornaments and trinkets][9] /p. 65/†

Liking display, they achieve it. They also take care of their clothes, changing them when they return home and storing them carefully in little deal chests we sell them.[10] They like to have plenty of clothes, and they want the fabrics we sell them to be sound and well conditioned. That, Sir, is all I have to say to complete the portrait of these African men. I will now labour on that of the women, after drawing for you some of these Moors, to satisfy you.[11]

[illustration no. (77), three Gold Coast men]

494

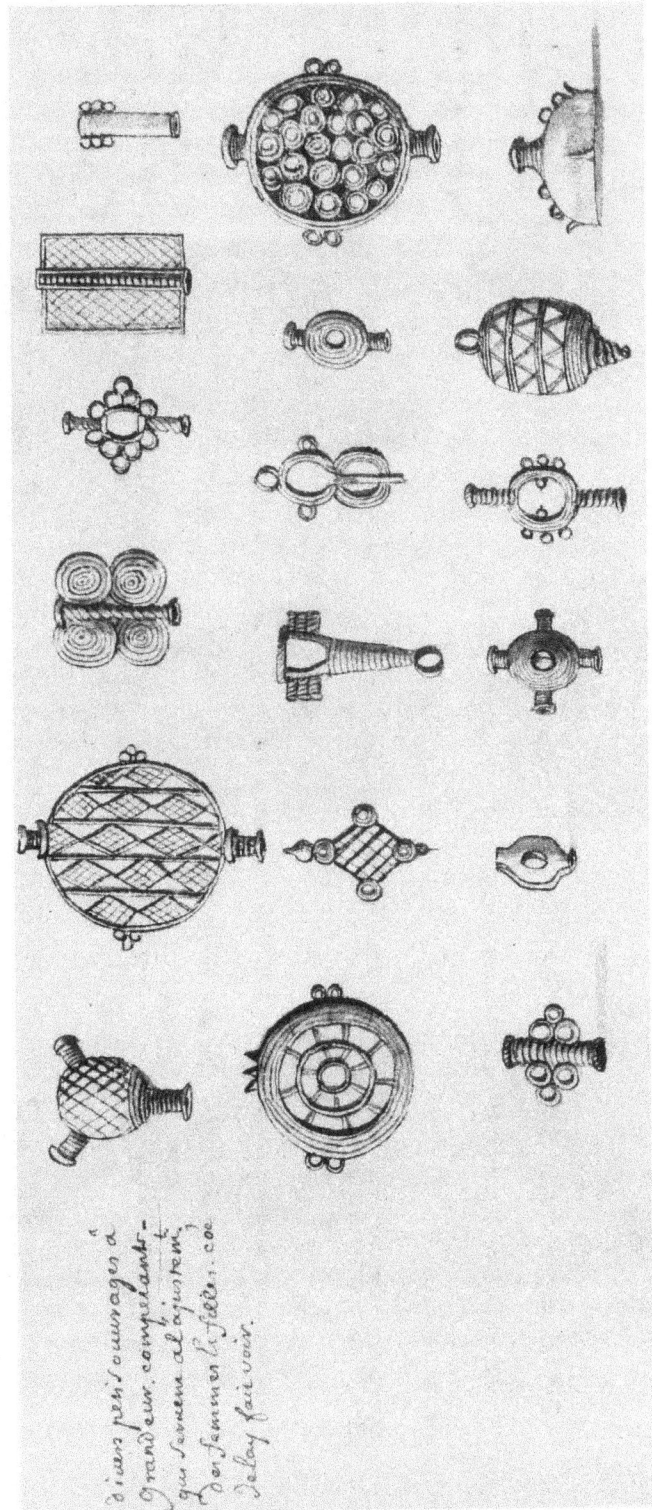

43. Gold trinkets from Gold Coast

44. Heads of Gold Coast men and women

The women/wives of these blacks are in general of a lithe, relaxed and upright build, tending to average size, and decidedly plump, with a fine head, sparkling eyes, an aquiline nose mostly, long hair, a small mouth, beautiful teeth, and a well-turned neck. They are lively in spirit, lascivious and covetous, attached to their house-keeping, great talkers, haughty to their inferiors, fond of eye-catching dress and of their wardrobe, and eager to steal when they can. They take great care of their house and their children, and make their daughters help in house-keeping and cooking as soon as they begin to grow up. They are sparing in their eating, and very clean, inasmuch as they wash themselves daily in the sea or a stream. They keep their heads very tidy. You will see this in the drawing I am sending you, which will spare me the trouble of making a longer description which might bore you.[12] They anoint their hair with palm oil, and decorate it with gold ornaments or red sea-shells and with *rassade*. They often put red or white colouring on their faces, on the brow and eyebrows, and on the cheeks, and they make little cuts on each side of the face. Others have raised marks (*tumeurs*) and pinking (*découpures*) done on their shoulders, breast, belly, and thighs, so that from a distance one might think that they were dressed in pinked material (the men /p. 66/ do much the same). They load their neck, arms and legs with bracelets or ribbons when a ceremony is being held. I saw some at Acra so attired, and they seemed very pretty, their complexion apart, which nevertheless was fine and smooth.[13] [...][14]

[illustration no. (78), three Gold Coast women]

But although some of these African women are very pleasing, among them are some /p. 67/ called *etiguafou*, who have made them-selves public prostitutes, and who are distinguished from the others by their fine appearance and their clothing. These women in particu-lar make a point of always appearing well groomed and they let their nails grow to great length. They dance very well in the fashion of the blacks, and have dancing schools for the young people.[15] [...][16] This very moment I have been called away on urgent business and must conclude against my will. If I have forgotten anything in this letter, I will insert it in those that follow. Meanwhile, believe me, Sir, Your etc.

Additional Passage from *1732*

[p. 238/8, on attractive women at a party]

At a feast the Danish agent made at Acra, to entertain and shew me the pomp of the Black ladies, I saw several of them richly adorned, and could not but own they were very ingenious in dressing themselves, in such manner as might prove sufficiently tempting to many lewd Europeans; who not regarding complexions, say *All cats are grey in the dark*. And indeed there were several genteel persons of that sex, not only curious and rich in their dress, but extraordinary good-humour'd, merry and diverting; which did much attract the eyes, not to mention many lascivious looks and gestures, at which they are very dexterous, and spare no pains or art to allure an European gentleman, thinking it an honour to be in their company, either in publick or private.[17]

NOTES

[1] Omission of two paragraphs, the first introductory (Barbot had intended to write on fishes and fishing but found the subject so extensive it had to be postponed), the second on the physical characteristics of the male Gold Coast blacks, entirely based on Marees, ff. 14–15v, and on the slightly enlarged versions of Marees in Dapper, p. 97/3 and Villault, pp. 213–6 – omitting, however, the references in the Dutch sources to the size of the male organ. In 1679 Barbot merely recorded that Gold Coast men were well built and well proportioned, except those with broken noses (*1679*, pp. 281, 340). Throughout the present letter, Barbot follows closely his main sources and the amount of additional original material based on personal observation is slight. But since he had had some opportunity to observe Gold Coast Africans, his copying a description should indicate that he is deliberately confirming it.
Cf. *1732*, p. 235/3.

[2] These complimentary remarks are not original but follow Villault, pp. 216–7, including even the personal anecdote ('four marcs of gold to 20 persons'), Villault in turn building on Marees, f. 23.
Cf. *1732*, p. 235/4.

[3] In 1679 Barbot recorded many comments on the character of Gold Coast blacks. At some places they were civil and respectful to whites, but maddeningly slow and thievish, while around Anomabu they were honest (*1679*, pp. 283, 285, 289, 318). He summed up as follows: they were mostly extremely rebellious and seditious, thieves, and haters of their enemies, with some

being guzzlers and drunkards too, although others were, on the contrary, very *civilisés*, sober and faithful, 'among whom one could live with ease' (*1679*, p. 339). However, like the complimentary comments, the uncomplimentary ones deployed in *1688* are hardly ever original, at least in their expression, being embroidery on Marees, ff. 15v–17, 53–54; Dapper, p. 97/5, 98/5; and Villault, pp. 218–9. The final two sentences of the passage, referring to blacks urinating like pigs, and to their being expert swimmers, taken from Marees, ff. 15v–16, and Dapper, p. 98/3, are omitted.

Cf. *1732*, pp. 235/4–236/5, which adds material from Bosman, p. 118, and also a brief comment on the worship of idols – 'they have outdone the former Gentiles, whom St Paul describes'.

[4] This detailed description of dress is almost wholly from Marees, f. 17, which distinguishes the waist-cloth and an out-of-doors shoulder-cloth; from Dapper, p. 103/4, which briefly says that all wear a waist-cloth; and from Villault, pp. 219–20, which speaks only of merchants and officers wearing, when out of doors, the waist-cloth and sometimes the shoulder-cloth, both in fine materials. Barbot conflates and embroiders slightly, his only contribution being to vary some of the materials (Marees's linen becoming 'a cloth from Holland, Cape Verde or elsewhere' and 'Leyden serge or *perpetuana*', and Villault's silk, taffetas and fine Indian damask linen becoming 'China satin, taffetas and coloured Indian cloth'), and also to add the stick to the spear. Copying his first sentence from Villault, but making the subject plural instead of singular, he forgets and copies *soit* for *soient*. Serges and *perpetuanas* were fine woollen cloths: see Debien 1979, p. 244; Jones 1985, p. 317. Barbot updates Marees by mentioning Cape Verde cloths, whose arrival on Gold Coast by this date is evidenced in other sources. The illustration, showing three men wearing waist-cloths and one, labelled 'A noble', wearing also a shoulder-cloth, was copied from Marees, plate 2. It was repeated on *1732*, Plate 21 (p. 237), with the two right-hand figures in reverse order and now labelled 'A Cabocero', 'A Fisherman' and 'A Factor', inaccurately, the last two figures being those of a merchant and an interpreter.

Cf. *1732*, p. 237/4–9, where Barbot adds further or alternative descriptions of dress from Bosman, pp. 119–20, and a Biblical reference.

[5] In 1679, Barbot drew a series of six heads (see Letter 1/31, note 35, above), two being those of a Gold Coast man and woman and two more, of a man and woman, almost certainly also Gold Coast individuals. The drawing is reproduced in Garrard 1989, p. 60, whose text notes the gold pendants of the women (but is incorrect in suggesting that one woman is of Assinie, and perhaps also in terming all six individuals 'Akan', two being 'Quaqua' men). A man 'of Corso and Acraa' is shown with plaited hair, and an old man with a single tuft, in the shape perhaps of a crown (*1679*, pp. 275–6, 347). But the *1688* text only slightly enlarges on Marees, f. 16v; Dapper, p. 103/5 (which

miscopies from Marees, giving *kruiz-wijs* for *cruyns-wijs*, so that Barbot has 'cross' for the original 'crown'); and Villault, p. 220 – it omits the horn shape but adds the curl-papers. For men's hair being plaited by women, see Jones 1983a, pp. 204, 216; and for hair-curling, Bosman, p. 119.

Cf. *1732*, p. 236/6–7, which adds material on ornaments of gold and coral in the hair, from Bosman, p. 119, and also additional from Marees, f. 18v, or Dapper, p. 104/2, on combs. Barbot slightly enlarges on combs, giving them two, three, or at most four teeth, 'being like a fork, without a haft or handle', and noting in the margin Plate 21. Only Barbot ascribes combs to men, the original references being to their use by women (as also noted by an earlier source: Jones 1983a, pp. 155, 206); and the reference to Plate 21 is wrong, neither the men nor the women in the illustrations displaying combs. In 1679 Barbot drew three combs with elaborately shaped handles, two of wood and one of ivory, two with five teeth and one with eight (*1679*, pp. 345–6, items 3–5). But the three combs included in the drawing of ornaments and trinkets on the same page, two of these repeated on *1732*, Plate 22 (p. 251) (described as of 'ponderous hard wood', p. 264), are simpler, with two, three and four teeth.

[6] In 1679 Barbot drew three bonnets, of straw, cowhide and goatskin (*1679*, pp. 345–6) – the drawings were not repeated in *1688* or *1732*. The passage is basically from Marees, f. 17, Dapper, p. 103/6, and Villault, p. 220, except for the references to hat ornaments, which appear to be original. A gold hatband, and perhaps a second one, and 'sundry sorts of their gold toys worn as spells' are shown on illustration no. (76), and again on *1732*, Plate 22 (p. 251). For other seventeenth-century descriptions of men's hats on Gold Coast, see Jones 1983a, pp. 86, 113, 196, 204–5.

Cf. *1732*, p. 237/1, 9, with minor additions from Bosman, p. 119.

[7] In 1679 Barbot drew seven bracelets of ivory, gold and copper (*1679*, pp. 345–6, items R–Z), and repeated six of them in illustration no. (76) and again in *1732*, Plate 22 (p. 251) (with a description, p. 264/9). The passage enlarges on Marees, ff. 16v–17, Dapper, pp. 103/6, 104/1, and especially Villault, p. 221. A necklace of miscellaneous materials is shown on illustration no. (76), and again on *1732*, Plate 22 (p. 251): it is described as 'a woman's necklace, of Contas de Terra and Agri, adorn'd with gold spells, and slips of the sacred tree; such necklaces are reckoned there very ornamental, and cost a considerable sum of money' (*1732*, p. 264/7) – but the details are from Bosman, p. 119.

Cf. *1732*, p. 237/2–3, which substitutes 'some of which stand them above a hundred pounds sterling', from Bosman, p. 119; adds that 'these are worn only by persons of great note', as in ancient times, giving Biblical references; and refers to 'silver collars', a mistranslation of *colliers* 'necklaces'.

[8] Dapper referred to women wearing in their hair '*Akori*, a blueish coral'

498

(Dapper, p. 104/2), and Bosman described *Conta de terra* as 'a sort of Coral' and *Agrie* as 'a sort of blew Coral', both very costly (Bosman, p. 119).

[9] The illustration shows some 40 items – gold bracelets, gold beads, combs, a necklace, etc. It contains items, often redrawn, from the 1679 drawing of women's ornaments, ornaments which Barbot said had fallen into his hands and which he had brought away with him (*1679*, p. 339), but also additional ornaments, which he had presumably procured in 1682. Barbot later stated – 'The women wear most of the same ornaments; all of which you will find represented in the cut [*margin:* Plate 21], having drawn them myself for the satisfaction of the curious' (*1732*, p. 237/3) – the illustration referred to is actually Plate 22 (p. 251). The ornaments on this plate include a very few items from the first drawing and more from the second, often redrawn, but also new items. For a redrawing of all of Barbot's gold ornaments, see Garrard 1989, pp. 62–3. The ornaments are detailed later, in Letter 2/20, p. 82, and discussed in notes 37, 41–2. As regards the gold beads, 'similar, and in some cases, identical beads can be found today. Barbot's three illustrations give a remarkably accurate portrayal of the range of seventeenth-century bead types' (p.c., T. F. Garrard, 5.12.1988). Marine archaeologists have recently recovered beads of c. 1700 similar to Barbot's (Ehrlich 1989).

[10] Marees said that the women changed their clothes on returning home, Villault that they used European chests (Marees, f. 19v, Villault, pp. 221–2).

[11] As stated in note 4 above, the illustration is copied from Marees. Although Barbot claims that the earlier section of this Letter refers to Gold Coast men, some of the borrowed material in fact related to women. Cf. *1732*, p. 237/5–7, where Barbot adds material on the dress of Caboceiros and 'the common sort', from Bosman, p. 120, but puzzlingly defines the Caboceiros as being 'from Cape Verde and on the Quaqua coast'.

[12] In 1679 Barbot recorded that, apart from their skin colour, Gold Coast women could be compared with French women for good bearing and fine physical features, apart from the elongated breasts of some when suckling, and also for their good humour and household care, although they were chatterboxes (*1679*, p. 340). Barbot's Dutch sources commented fairly briefly on female physique and character (firm bodies, white teeth, large breasts, firm loins, haughty, unchaste, thievish, clothes-conscious, good housekeepers and trainers of daughters), but Barbot here omits their references to breasts and loins (Marees, ff. 17v–19v, Dapper, p. 98/1). French sources enlarged and embroidered: Villault embroidered the Dutch (Villault, pp. 223–5), and Barbot embroidered Villault. The reference to an 'aquiline' nose is surprising, but was perhaps intended to indicate that the nose was less flat than that shown in caricatures of the negroid stereotype.

The illustration was copied from Marees, one figure taken from Plate 16 and the two right-hand figures from Plate 3: when repeated in *1732*, Plate 21 (p. 237), all of Marees's eight female figures appeared, indicating that the artist copied directly from Marees. But the captions are often inaccurate ('A Merchant's Wife' for a young girl, 'A Woman of the good sort Suckling her Infant' for a woman of the common sort, 'A Woman of the good sort' for an *etiguafou* or prostitute). The noses shown in the illustrations of both men and women are too European in Marees, and grotesquely so in Barbot.

Cf. *1732*, p. 238/1–2, which is briefer but adds 'handsome breasts', and has a trace of Bosman, p. 120, in a reference to an equal love of clothes shown by European women.

[13] In 1679, describing a wedding at Accra, Barbot noted that the bride wore gold ornaments on various parts of the body, and that the girls attending her put red and white marks on her face and body; and he also drew two female heads, one of 'women of Corso and Acraa' and another of a 'woman in her best, her face painted red and white', with lines and patterns apparently in white (*1679*, pp. 337–8, 347). However, the present passage echoes closely Marees, ff. 18v–19, Dapper, p. 104/2–4, and Villault, pp. 224–6.

Cf. *1732*, p. 238/3–5, which includes material from Bosman, pp. 120–1, and enlarges – 'imprinting figures of flowers on their faces, shoulders, breasts, bellies and thighs ... like half-relief, which I have observed in the women of Sestro ... it being all done with hot irons'. Barbot, like his sources, was evidently unaware of the significance in Akan ritual of red and white earth-paints. 'The women fetish themselves with a coarse Paint of earth on their Faces, Shoulders and Breasts, each the Colour they like best' (Atkins 1735, p. 88).

[14] Omission of one paragraph, on the dress of wives of officers and merchants (cloths, purse, bunches of keys, waist-ornaments, rings, platter on head, chest for clothes), based mainly on Villault, pp. 226–8, with additions from Marees, ff. 18–19, and plate 3, and Dapper, p. 104/1–4, all of which are actually on women in general. Barbot varies the cloths a little, and the favoured colours to green and blue, puts *krakra* in the purse, makes the platter pewter or wooden, and adds that their grave demeanour when walking resembles that of Spanish and Portuguese women.

Cf. *1732*, p. 238/6–239/2, which includes material from Bosman, pp. 121, 199, and Biblical allusions to female ornaments, also a passage on a feast at Accra given in the Additional Passage. Barbot's reference to a market woman with a platter 'on the palm of her hand' and 'raised to the height of her head' suggests that he did not grasp the capacity of Africans to carry and balance objects on the head, although he must surely have observed the practice.

[15] In 1679 Barbot spoke slightingly of African dancing, the dancers seeming

more like persons possessed (*1679*, p. 338). *Etiguafou* wearing rings and bells were mentioned by Marees, f. 19, but Villault, p. 228, said *filles de joie* were in no way distinguishable from other women, while Dapper, p. 106/3, provided a lengthy account of how, at Axim, slave women were forcibly and ritually initiated into becoming public prostitutes. Barbot appears to ignore Dapper and Villault at this point, and to attribute to these women the dancing done by all women and the 'houses where young men learn to dance' mentioned by Marees, f. 87–87v, the latter becoming 'schools' in Villault, p. 312. A longer reference to *etiguafou* appears in Letter 2/18, p. 69. The term is not the modern Akan term for 'prostitute' (*aguaman*). Long nails, not of women but of merchants, were mentioned by Dapper, p. 97/3.

Cf. *1732*, p. 239/4, where Barbot says girls are 'put to dancing schools, where they are taught many indecent postures ... It is no wonder that dancing-schools should make women unchaste there, since we see them to produce the same effect in England'. Possibly Barbot's unsympathetic attitude to dancing reflected his religious upbringing, and his later comment the fact that he was now the father of young girls in England. However, apart from Marees, most contemporary European commentators were unsympathetic to African dancing on Gold Coast (e.g. Phillips 1732, p. 210; Jones 1983a, p. 157).

[16] Omission of seven sentences, the first four on the libidinousness of coastal women, learned from Europeans, but their relative infertility, because men, although well-provided by Nature, serve so many women, embroidered from Marees, ff. 14v, 18v–19, and Villault, p. 224: the remaining three sentences, on boys and girls playing naked, and swimming in the sea, whereas interior peoples cannot swim and fear water, from Marees, ff. 13, 93v–94, Dapper, p. 97/6, and Villault, pp. 237–8. In 1679, however, Barbot thought that Gold Coast women were 'very fertile' (*1679*, p. 340).

Cf. *1732*, p. 239/3–5, which embroiders interestingly – 'Few women there have above five or six children, which those who find fault with all things abroad, ascribe to their lasciviousness; though it is not very common in Europe to have above that number, and it may rather be imputed to the mens having so many wives'. It is perhaps Marees whom Barbot is criticizing, since the former blames the 'hot nature' of the women as well as the limited attention of their husbands for their limited fertility.

[17] Although Barbot dined with Olrichs, the governor of the Danish fort at Accra, in 1679, his journal does not record a feast; and perhaps he confused in recollection the Danish feast he attended at Frederiksborg (*1679*, pp. 304–5, 322). The statement that local women considered it an honour to be in the company of European men echoes Marees, f. 18v, but was a commonplace observation.

LETTER 18

Marriage ceremonies and the bringing up of children.

I was obliged, Sir, to conclude my letter yesterday evening sooner than I had intended. I hope you will forgive me, since it was on account of some pressing business. In this letter I am going to inform you about certain ceremonies the Moors practise for their marriages, and about the way in which they bring up their children. There will be quite enough for a letter, despite the fact that the bitter cold of the weather (not the least seasonable) may make me be brief. I state then that, although they allow a man to have as many wives as he can maintain, and although it appears from this (as many have imagined) that they take and discard them as they please (and even sell them as slaves), yet they always have one favorite woman whom they marry with the formalities current among them. These vary on this coast, according to the localities and the people. I shall give as examples some of the commonest and most ordinary. The formalities always favour the man, since the law always makes him absolute master of the woman he marries, who has only such liberties as are granted her by her husband.[1] [.../p. 68/...][2]

A father, having a son whom he finds to be of marriageable age, selects in his village a girl whom he believes to be suitable as a good wife, and having obtained her from her parents, there is paid to the father of the groom the dowry of the bride, which generally amounts to 25 or 30 *livres* in gold, to be used for palm wine and other things for the wedding. A slave is also given, to serve the woman the groom marries. (The dowry is very modest, but even the daughters of kings do not have more). A day is fixed for the solemnizing of this ceremonial arrangement, and when the relatives of the two parties are assembled, the bride promises upon oath to be faithful and obedient to her husband and to have no criminal dealings with any other man. But the bridegroom merely pledges that he will take care of her, that she will be well treated, and that he will keep her in his house until death separate them or until she is divorced or driven away.[3]

Here is what is usually practised at Acra. During the time I was there, a man aged 40 married a girl aged at the most seven or eight. When the day chosen for the wedding ceremony arrived, all the relatives assembled at the home of the girl, where there was good cheer and a loud noise made by their instruments. They danced with great abandon, after which they decorated the bride with certain pieces of goldwork, which they placed in her hair, on her arms, on her neck and on her feet. This done, the black then declared to the priest or *fetissero* who was present that he was taking her as his wife. At night they led her to his house and put her to bed, between two women chosen from among her friends, in order to prevent the bridegroom from consummating the marriage, on account of her tender youth. This precaution was maintained for three days, and then he sent her back to the house of her father, to be brought up there until she was old enough for the marriage to be consummated. I was told that when the time came, all the girls of the place would go to her home in the finest attire imaginable, and that there they would dress her up too, and paint her face, arms and legs in their fashion, in various colours. Then they would lead her in this state to the house of her spouse, he having prepared for her arrival. He would give each of these girls (even if there were fifty of them) half an *acquier* of gold or the value of 50 *sols*, to thank them for dancing all night around the home of the newly wed couple.[4] [. . .][5] There are many other ways of marrying among these people, but I consider it unnecessary to say more – that would bore you and it would go on too long. Instead let us say something specifically about wives. [. . ./ p. 69/. . .][6]

These Moors are not at all as jealous with regard to this kind of [additional] wife as they are towards the first wife (who is like a sultaness); for if they have dealings with another man, they are not subject to any chastisement, nor is the adulterer fined or obliged to pay any civil indemnity. But when it is the favourite wife, it is impossible to exaggerate how passionately they are filled with jealousy and [the desire for] vengeance. If she has had an affair with another Moor, she is repudiated and he is condemned to pay a fine of nine ounces of gold to the king. If it is a white man, the whole penalty falls on the poor unfortunate woman, who, besides being perpetually banished, must pay a fine of one ounce of gold and is sometimes even sold as a slave. When they do not have sufficient proof for a conviction of this crime, they oblige the women to clear themselves by oath, taking what they call the fetish potion.[7] If it is a slave who is their accomplice in this crime, he is slaughtered relentlessly and she is sold. This is particularly the system at Comendo, where despite this harshness one sees many debauched women, because temperament and habit get the better of decency and the penalty which results.[8]

Due to this manner of keeping as many wives as they can, many officers and merchants have 20 or 30, according to their means. Kings and princes have 80 or 100, with an equivalent number of slaves to serve them.[9] [. . .][10] To return to the wives of our Africans, let us see how these little harems are governed. Each woman has in her husband's house a small hut, or at least a cabin (*logette*), whose only furniture is a mat of rushes as a bed and a piece of wood as a pillow; and thither the husband goes to have his frolics with each one in turn. If it happens that a more partial inclination leads him to have more tender feelings towards one woman than towards another, he is obliged to take great care that he enjoys her company without letting the others know, in order to avoid the little upsets which would inevitably occur among them if they came to know of it (although not entirely through a motive of jealousy).[11] You can easily imagine, Sir, that men as voluptuous as these, who have dealings with so many young creatures even more subject to this animal passion than they themselves, are often confronted with long and annoying inconveniences, /p. 70/ when the women they have married (I mean the first they have wed) become aged or infirm. The men attach themselves (with the wife's consent) to their favourite among the other wives. This young beloved woman is then obliged to take over fully the care of the household, and the husband is unable to repudiate her except in cases of adultery. The first wife is entirely divested of the authority she used to have, in order that the younger wife may assume it. Then, if the younger wives have in any way been ill-used by this first wife, they take revenge as they please, and you see them treat her like a mistress treats a slave. They have their husband's money at their disposition, just as the other woman had previously.[12]

[. . .][13] [When giving birth] the women need neither midwives nor female attendants (*gardiennes*), for they deliver with ease and without travail. But women from the neighbourhood who happen to be there give the woman [in labour] all the help they can. This is what I noticed when one of our slaves gave birth on board the vessel, after half an hour in labour. Finally, seeing that she had delivered, she herself carried her child to a tub of sea-water which was at the extremity of the vessel, and washed it there. An hour later she resumed her usual work in the kitchen, which was helping the cook. She kept the little creature all the time on her back, wrapped in an old rag tied around her waist.[14] The men never lie with their wives who have given birth until three or four months later – either because they fear that it would spoil their milk, or because they have sufficient alternatives, having so many other wives.[15]

The children of these African women are all born strong and vigorous. The mothers never apply to them the precautions we take for our children. Having washed them in the sea or the river, they are content to wrap them in a little piece of cloth and then lay them on a rush mat (often even on the ground), where they leave them to sprawl and play as they please for a month or six weeks. After this, the mother takes them and daily carries them, tied to her back, from morning to night, without leaving them, no matter what she does. This manner of carrying them may well in some way contribute to flattening their noses, especially when the women pound maize, which is a very violent exercise.[16] Most of them give the child the teat when it cries, [passing it] over their shoulder. I have seen some [infants] who took it behind in this way with their own two hands and carried it to their mouths, just like a bottle. Furthermore, some of these black women (négresses) have breasts which hang down to their waists, which is very ugly to see, especially on women who are rather old. The children of the rich are not so much subject to these occurrences as are other children, because they are rarely carried on the backs of their mothers, who always keep them at home with them.[17]

Although this manner of rearing such tender little creatures may appear harsh, you rarely see anyone lame, hunch-backed or with rickets. On the contrary, nearly all are healthy, upright, and in full use of their limbs. This leads me to believe that our swaddling and the great amount of attention from our mothers /p. 71/ make us largely subject to great infirmities when we are adults. These people let their infants, from the age of seven or eight months, go around naked, crawling on all fours like little cats, so that they learn to walk and talk before they are one year old. I have seen some who at 13 months could walk quite upright and talk very clearly. I attribute this development to the fact that they are weaned early and then fed simply on coarse foods and on water.[18] Although they behave towards their children so casually, yet they have no lack of tender affection for them. It gives them great pleasure to care for them, and to attach to them various little knick-knacks, to decorate them and make them look attractive. [...][19]

Here, Sir, each mother suckles her own child and each child acknowledges and follows its mother from the time when it is capable of reason. It usually lives with her and is brought up by her till it is eight or ten, either to teach it a trade, or to send it elsewhere or to sell it, as sometimes happens. The whole of the time when the young Moors are with their mothers is for them a time of liberty, for they have no other occupation than to play, to run about and to bathe in the sea or the river. I have seen thousands of them together, playing on the large waves of the surf on the coast, letting themselves be carried on little boards (which they take in order to teach themselves to swim) and being almost like crabs for several moments, until the sea casts them ashore on the sand of its beaches, where, from a distance, they look like little monkeys.[20] [. . ./p. 72/. . .][21]

I have no more to tell you than to say a few words about the way in which these people give their children a name after they are born; and then I shall finish this letter, it being almost an hour after midnight. The names are most often taken from those white people with whom they have the most commerce and whom they esteem most highly. Thus you find all of the men calling themselves Antonio, or Juan, or Pieter, or Claes, or Jacob, or Abraham, or Mattys, etc., depending on which peoples of Europe they live with. At Acra, this is what you see on this occasion [of naming a child]. They assemble the friends they have, and after collecting all the names of those who have gathered together there, they give the infant the name which is most common among them. Quaquou, Adom, Quaw, Corbei and Coffi are the customary names for males; Jama, Canow, Jaba, Aquoaba, Hiro and Accatiaffa the names for females. They have one of these names, together with another taken from the whites.[22] [. . .][23] I can assure you that I too am concluding, being very cold and very much in need of sleep. I am, Sir, Your etc.

NOTES

[1] The material in this letter is based on Marees, partly via Dapper and Villault, but Villault, like Barbot himself, was able to add some personal observations. Favouring the man is inferred from Marees, f. 9v; Dapper, p. 106/6.

Cf. *1732*, p. 239/6, which comments wryly that 'marriages are there concluded without the previous formalities of courtship, disputes about settlement, or nicety about the disparity of persons' – if Barbot was thinking back, perhaps his own marriage had raised these problems.

[2] Omission of five sentences, describing how a young man might take the initiative in finding himself a bride, from Dapper, p. 106/2, Barbot adding – 'Often one sees a peasant marry the daughter of a gentleman'.

Cf. *1732*, p. 239/6–8, which retains only the last sentence, substituting for the remainder from Bosman, pp. 197–8.

[3] Apart from the last two of the bridegroom's pledges, this is from Marees, ff. 9v–10, and Villault, p. 229. The figures given for the 'dowry' represent an attempt to convert Marees' statement: 'The Father gives his Daughter 1½ Peeso of gold and the Mother half a Peeso of gold, making together, by our reckoning, half an Ounce of gold, Troy weight'.

Cf. *1732*, p. 239/9–10, which sets the figure at 'thirty pounds sterling', and is less critical of the imbalance of pledges between the sexes.

[4] Barbot witnessed the ceremony in 1679 and described it at slightly greater length in his journal (*1679*, pp. 337–8). There is only one major discrepancy: in 1679 he wrote that when the marriage was not to be consummated, the women danced all day, not 'all night'. A contemporary source, referring not to Accra but to the area near Cape Coast, stated that 'a young girl ... must sleep in between them [the newly wed couple] and watch out that they do not touch each other for seven days' (Jones 1983a, p. 214).

Cf. *1732*, p. 240/1–2 ('most part of the night').

[5] Omission of one paragraph, describing a marriage at 'Manfrou', from Villault, pp. 229–30, slightly embroidered, the only addition being that at weddings 'one sees many drunkards'.

Cf. *1732*, p. 240/3–6, which adds a reference to royal marriages, from Bosman, p. 193, and a Biblical comparison.

[6] Omission of one paragraph describing why and how men take additional wives, loosely based on Marees, ff. 10v–11, and Villault, pp. 230–2. Marees stated that the husband must give his senior wife 2–6 *engelschen* of gold, which Barbot converts into '4–5 *acquiers*', an *ackey* being the later equivalent of the *engel*, and representing ¹⁄₁₆ ounce on Gold Coast.

Cf. *1732*, pp. 241/7.

[7] Largely Marees, f. 10, although this lacks the statements that additional wives were not punished for adultery and that the senior wife was sometimes sold as a slave.

Cf. *1732*, p. 242/3–5, which largely substitutes from Bosman, pp. 200–1.

[8] Since the Komenda reference was not noted in 1679 (*1679*, pp. 289–90), it probably represents information received in 1682 (for this visit to Komenda, see Letter 2/3, note 68). Omitted in *1732*.

[9] Based on Villault, pp. 232–3, which refers to the son-in-law of the king of Fetu. It was said in 1673 that important men on Gold Coast might have 'ten, fifteen, twenty, thirty, indeed fifty or more wives' (Jones 1983a, p. 213).

Cf. *1732*, pp. 240/10.

[10] Omission of three sentences concerning 'public whores' on the western-most part of Gold Coast, from Dapper, p. 106/3, garbled and embroidered.

Cf. *1732*, p. 246/8–248/2, which adds substantial passages from Bosman, pp. 211–5, lengthy Biblical comparisons, and the toponyms 'Isseny' and 'Awine', which are not in Bosman.

[11] Mostly deduced from Marees, f. 11–11v. The curious last remark is perhaps an attempt to cope with Villault, p. 232, which claimed that wives were not jealous of each other.

Cf. *1732*, pp. 240/7–9, 241/1–4, which shortens the earlier material but adds substantial information on the sexual and economic relationship between a man and his wives, from Bosman, pp. 198–9, 202, 204, 208, as well as a long Biblical comparison.

[12] Loosely based on, or inferred from, Marees, f. 11. Marees's view that a senior wife was rejected when a younger wife received more sexual attention was probably a misunderstanding of the values of the polygynous family. One would have expected the 'long and annoying inconveniences' to include pregnancy and sexual abstinence during lactation rather than old age – perhaps Barbot lost his way in the course of his argument.

Cf. *1732*, pp. 241/5–7, 242/1–2, which adds further information on the relationship between wives, from Bosman, pp. 199–200.

[13] Omission of four sentences on the ease of child-bearing, embroidered from Villault, p. 233 (in turn enlarged from Marees, f. 11v, although Villault did actually attend a childbirth at 'Manfrou'). In 1679 Barbot noted that mothers washed their newly-born infants in the sea or in a river (*1679*, p. 338).

Cf. *1732*, p. 242/7.

[14] It is possible that this refers to a woman who gave birth on board Barbot's ship in January or February 1679 – but who died two days later, 'from the after-birth' (*1679*, p. 338). Villault's personal anecdote about a childbirth (see the previous note) probably inspired Barbot to follow suit. For other early descriptions of child-bearing practices on Gold Coast, see Jones 1983a, pp. 109, 216–8.

Cf. *1732*, p. 242/8–9, which adds that the woman gave birth 'on the bare deck, between the carriages of two guns', and also adds material from another witness of an African childbirth, Bosman, p. 122.

[15] Echoing Marees, f. 12, which however gave the period as 'three months' and did not suggest that this practice had anything to do with the mother's milk – Barbot is perhaps repeating a common European folk-belief. Omitted in *1732*.

[16] A combination of, or compromise between, Marees, f. 12–12v, and Villault, pp. 234–5. The only significant additions by Barbot are the phrase 'often even on the ground' and the reference to pounding maize.

Cf. *1732*, p. 242/9–10, which compares the manner of carrying children with that of 'our gypsies or beggars', a comparison also made by a European contemporary (Jones 1983a, p. 218).

[17] In 1679 Barbot implied that many African women had sagging breasts because they did not wean their babies until they were 12–15 months old, and he commented unfavorably on the sight, like many other Europeans (*1679*, p. 340). (On the alleged denigratory significance of sagging breasts in seventeenth-century iconographic representations of exotic peoples, see Bucher 1977.) The reference to passing the teat 'over the shoulder' derives from a dubious statement in Marees, f. 12, repeated in Villault, p. 235, and in the caption to Marees, plate 3 (which in fact shows a sturdy infant leaning well over the shoulder to suck, a more plausible action). The 'occurrences' (*accidens*) must refer to flattened noses, since the notion that children of rich women were less likely to have flattened noses, because less often carried on the back, was expressed by Villault, p. 235. In 1679 Barbot was a young bachelor, but by the time he wrote his English version the husband of a wife who had borne many children, and his views of the female anatomy were accordingly more sensitive and realistic.

Cf. *1732*, pp. 242/10–243/2, where the mothers feed infants on their backs by 'lifting up the children to their shoulder, and turning the breasts up to them', and where even with long breasts the children suck 'without leaning far over the mother's neck'. And Barbot adds the following. 'Nor is it to be thought strange, those women never wearing any thing to stay up their breasts, which occasions their own weight, especially when full of milk, to extend them; and if we did observe it in Europe, we should find women enough in every country that might do the same.' Also added is a sentence on the period of breast-feeding, from Bosman, p. 121.

[18] Apart from the comparison with European methods of rearing children and the statement about what Barbot saw himself, this is from Marees, f. 12–12v, and Villault, p. 236 ('cats' – otherwise Villault follows Marees). In 1679 Barbot noted the lack of swaddling (*1679*, p. 338).

Cf. *1732*, p. 243/2, which replaces 'coarse food' by 'dry bread', adding that with this diet the African children were 'as well satisfied as ours with all their dainties'. In describing African children as 'nearly all healthy', Barbot ignores, probably because he was ignorant of, the very high infant mortality rate. Perhaps, therefore, he was making a false comparison with the recognized high infant and child mortality rates in Europe – eventually most of his own children died in infancy or childhood.

[19] Omission of one paragraph on protective 'fetishes' worn by infants, from Marees, f. 12v, and Villault, p. 236, followed by Barbot's lengthy reflections on parallels with Roman Catholic practices – 'And do you not think that these poor Moors will rise up some day in judgement on our false Christians, telling them . . . that if, like them, they had had the advantage of

being born among Reformed Christians', they would have rejected their superstitions. Barbot adds – 'I beg pardon for this outburst – I unintentionally entered into this controversy with the gentlemen of Rome, forgive me'.

Cf. *1732*, p. 243/2, which embroiders slightly, and adds a little from Bosman, p. 123, but omits the outburst.

[20] In 1679 Barbot noted his pleasure at seeing 'the thousand natural monkey-tricks' of African children, and added that they had a lively spirit and good judgement, so that anyone who instructed them would not be wasting his time (*1679*, p. 340). The first two sentences in this passage, including the reference to parents selling their children, derive from Marees, f. 13 (for the alleged sale, see Marees 1987, p. 26, note 1), and this also mentions swimming; while the description of children at play, although largely original, was probably inspired by Villault, pp. 237–8, who compared children seen from a distance, not with monkeys, but with 'little devils'. Barbot has made a copying error in the middle of the second sentence, omitting a reference to the father taking over the children from the mother at 'eight or ten'.

Cf. *1732*, p. 243/3, which embroiders and adds, perhaps from recollection, that instead of a board some children used 'bundles of rushes, made fast under their stomach', but omits the reference to the children before and after the age of from eight to ten.

[21] Omission of two paragraphs on the upbringing of children, almost entirely from Marees, ff. 13–14, and Villault, pp. 237–40 (partly based on Marees).

Cf. *1732*, pp. 243/4–244/1, which adds a little from Bosman, p. 123.

[22] In 1679 Barbot noted the naming custom, allegedly at Accra, and gave the African names as Quaquou, Adom, Quavu, Corbé, Coffi, Jama, Canovu, Jaba, Aqueba (*1679*, p. 337). The use of European names echoes Villault, p. 234: for an instance of such practices, see Tilleman 1697, p. 94. The last two African names are from the caption to Marees, plate 3: 'Hiro' represents the modern Twi/Fante word *yere*, 'wife'; 'Accatiaffa' is a misreading of Marees's 'acatiassa', i.e. Fante *akatesia*, 'girl'. Several of the other names are also Akan/Twi (Kwaku, Kwaw, Kofi, Yaa-ma, Yaa-ba, Akwa-ba). Hence it seems likely that the information Barbot received on this subject at Accra, where Gã was spoken, apparently from Olrichs, the Danish commandant, in fact referred to people living near the other Danish fort, Frederiksborg (just East of Cape Coast), where Akan/Twi/Fante was spoken. For other seventeenth-century descriptions of name-giving customs, see Jones 1983a, pp. 88, 109.

Cf. *1732*, p. 244/2–7, which changes the spelling of some African names and anglicizes the European names, adding – 'but that is practised only by those that live under the protection of the forts on the coast', and also adds substantial material from Bosman, p. 209, and classical, ethnographic and Biblical digressions.

[23] Omission of two sentences on circumcision, from Marees, ff. 11v–12, but Barbot fails to specify female circumcision: for circumcision, male and female, see Marees 1987, p. 23, note 3; Jones 1983a, p. 218.

Cf. *1732*, p. 244/8–246/7, which adds that circumcision was practised 'only at Acra', from Bosman, p. 210, also that children were circumcised 'by the priest'; and then continues at length, on the 'Matrimonial State up the Inland' and on single men and women, entirely from Bosman, pp. 202–10.

LETTER 19

Their way of building, the household management of their wives, and their feeding in general.

[...][1] /p. 73/ Generally the houses are dirty, uncomfortable and for the most part stinking, particularly those which have privy-huts (*huttes de commoditez*), from which the great heat causes a very foul air to spread abroad, and this the land wind carries even to the vessels in the roadstead.[2] These houses are located in groups at various points, and thus they form a village, intersected by small streets, very narrow and irregular, leaving a large space empty in the middle, where people hold their market and their meetings.[3] [...][4] The only windows are small holes, and the doorway is so low and narrow that one must virtually bend double to enter. The doorways are closed by reeds woven together, or with a few little pieces of board, suspended by strings instead of hinge-pins, and opening either inwards or outwards, as is wished.[5] [...][6] Every house has in addition two or three small huts. The houses of the rich have seven or eight, each separated from the others, and each used for some purpose – some for wives, others for children, others for kitchen use. Further, each of these [? last] huts has two small rooms, one for preparing the maize and the other as the kitchen. In addition, you see in several of these little cabins (*loges*) slight partitions of canes, reeds or other material. All of the huts are without symmetry or order and are surrounded by a fence of maize-stalks, tied very closely together. Only the main building has its exit on to the street; all the others can scarcely be seen [from outside], for the fences are made as tall as the roofs, in order that passers-by may not look into the

511

courtyard.[7] /p. 74/ [. . .][8] These people are ignorant of the use of paving-stones [in their streets], although the parade-grounds of Corso and Mina have them.[9]

These Africans hardly spend anything on furniture. They limit themselves to what is necessary, and the only things you see in their homes are a few wooden seats, a small chest, a few pots for cooking or drinking, and some weapons hung on the walls. Noblemen have tables and rush mattresses, on which they spread their mats to sleep. The mattresses are an inch thick. Others have simply mats, or a few cattle-hides and skins of other animals, and as a head-rest a small piece of wood, as I have said. The rich use a sort of pillow after their fashion, and a large copper cauldron, for washing themselves without going outside, as the common people do. The whole of this limited household equipment is always in the dwelling-place of the women; for in that of the men you find nothing but their weapons, a seat and a mat, and in that of artisans all the equipment of their profession.[10] [. . .][11] The houses are usually built in 7–8 days, by specialists. The cost never amounts to as much as two *louis d'or*. The materials cost nothing except [the labour of] collecting them, which they do themselves or send slaves to do.[12]

[. . .][13] As soon as it is evening, the women make sure that they have the quantity of rice and maize (in sheaves) that they judge necessary for the following day, sending slaves or their daughters to fetch it from the granaries they have outside the village. (Throughout the year they keep their grain in these granaries or even inside their houses.) At daybreak on the following day they set to work (with their people), beating and pounding the grain in wooden mortars made from a thick tree-trunk, or in holes hollowed out of a rock. They then winnow it, pound it on a stone in order to turn it into flour, and finally beat it again to make it up [with water] (in the same manner as painters make their colours). Following this, they mix it with millet and from this dough make round loaves the size of a hand, which they cook in a large earthenware pot, covered and full of boiling water. This bread is not good, being heavy. The bread they make on well-heated stones is better.[14] [. . ./p. 75/. . .][15] This manner of preparing maize is very laborious. Yet the women do it while singing, and most of them with their children on their backs – all in the blazing sun, which shines perpendicularly on their heads.[16]

They boil fish with salt and malaguetta [pepper], and in the embers they roast yams and sweet potatoes, from which they make a good pap. They dry over the fire bananas, which can take the place of bread. They also eat pineapples, figs, roast maize, rice boiled with chicken or goat, or simply with salt and palm oil. They also use several kinds of legumes, which they cultivate and prepare fairly well. The rich often have the meat of pigs, goats, harts and cows, as well as of a large number of fowls, from which they even make [stock for] cabbage soup, and several other stews which they have learned from the whites and passed on from one to another. Malaguetta is always prevalent in all their stews. In some places the men go so far as to be seated at table and have themselves served like us, but the common people eat on the ground, with their legs crossed, or lying on their sides. You also see some who eat the flesh of elephants and buffaloes.[17] [...][18] With all my heart, I am, Sir, etc.

NOTES

[1] Omission of an introductory sentence.

[2] The phrase about the land wind is from Marees, f. 39–39v.

Cf. *1732*, pp. 253/10, which substitutes – 'the stench of the towns is much more insupportable [than the muddy state of the streets], for ... the Blacks commonly ease themselves in those very lanes, only throwing a little earth upon their excrement, as was injoined in the Mosaical law ... Some of the principal houses there have a small sort of necessary house without for that use, but they take so little care to bury it well when full, that it rather increases the stench, especially in the hot scorching weather ... Add to this the vast quantity of fish kept about their towns rotting for five or six days, as I have before observed they like it best when so putrified; and all together produces such a violent stink, that it is very offensive a ship-board, particularly in the night-time, when the land-breezes carry it off from the shore ...; the ill savour being the more, the greater the towns are'.

[3] The clumsy wording seems to mean that the houses are huddled together in no clear pattern. For a similar contemporary description, see Jones 1983a, p. 139.

Cf. *1732*, p. 252/5.

[4] Omission of twelve sentences, on the larger settlements of the interior, on the lack of fortifications of towns, and on the construction of houses, almost entirely from Marees, ff. 38–38v, 39; Dapper, p. 100/2; Villault, pp. 240–1. Barbot makes a few small additions: 'some houses [on the coast] have flat roofs'; the inside walls are painted 'yellow' (as well as reddish, white or black, as stated by Marees); some are thatched with rice-straw ('thatch' in Villault).

Cf. *1732*, pp. 252/4, 6–253/3, which adds, of European-type houses – 'as I have before observed, at Mina, and some other places on the coast, they are one or two stories high, with several ground rooms ...', and also adds material on the situation of towns, from Bosman, pp. 137–8.

[5] The description of windows, and also the final phrase, are from Villault, p. 242.

Cf. *1732*, p. 253/4.

[6] Omission of three sentences on floors, from Marees, f. 38v.

Cf. *1732*, p. 253/5.

[7] The first sentence and the reference to the height of the fences derive from Marees, f. 38v. For a similar description, see Jones 1983a, pp. 202–3.

Cf. *1732*, p. 253/6, which refers to 'small huts for offices' or 'out-houses', and states that 'most of those huts are divided into two or three parts by partitions' and that 'the better sort of houses are commonly inclosed', but omits the reference to separate rooms for maize-preparation and a kitchen.

[8] Omission of four sentences, on the houses of 'princes and caboceers', and on the poor quality of the streets, from Marees, ff. 38v–39, and Villault, p. 241.

Cf. *1732*, pp. 253/7, 254/1.

[9] Cf. *1732*, p. 254/1–2, which changes 'parade-grounds' to 'markets', and adds: 'Nor are the Blacks at all curious in planting trees in their villages to shade their houses, as they might easily do, except at Axim, where they have many fine lofty trees set about and in the town, which are a great ease to the people against the scorching heat of the sun'. In 1679 Barbot noted at Axim 'many trees before and between the houses' (*1679*, p. 280).

[10] In 1679 Barbot noted that people used as beds reed or straw mattresses, or cloths stretched out on the ground, with a stone or piece of wood as a head-rest (*1679*, p. 340). The first sentence of the present passage is from Marees, f. 39; the sentence on noblemen and the reference to pillows is from Villault, p. 243; the references to weapons, chests, wooden seats (stools), pots and cauldrons are from Dapper, p. 101/3.

Cf. *1732*, p. 254/3, which embroiders but also adds: 'The meaner sort ... lie upon a mat laid on the bare ground, with one arm under their head instead of a bolster, or else have a little block for that purpose'.

[11] Omission of one paragraph on fireplaces, combining Marees, ff. 11v, 58, and Villault, p. 243. Omitted in *1732*.

[12] The first sentence is adapted from Dapper, p. 101/1 ('8 or 10 days', '10 or 12 guilders').

Cf. *1732*, p. 253/8.

[13] Omission of one paragraph on the everyday life of women, mainly from Villault, pp. 244–5 (partly derived from Marees, f. 20), together with

514

remarks on the way women manage their husband's money, inspired by Marees, f. 11, Barbot adding a misleading introduction to the remarks – 'I have a hundred times admired ...'.

Cf. *1732*, p. 254/4–5.

[14] In 1679, at Cape Coast, Barbot noted the two ways of making 'bread', here repeated with minor variations, e.g. 'well-heated stones' replaces 'oven' (*1679*, p. 304). The references to preparing to cook, as well as several other references, are from Marees, f. 20, and Villault, pp. 245–6. Barbot's main additions to these two sources are the references to rice, to slaves and daughters, to mixing maize flour with millet, and to baking bread on warmed stones.

Cf. *1732*, pp. 253/9, 256/6–7.

[15] Omission of three sentences on bread made at Elmina and on 'kankey' (maize cakes), from Marees, f. 20–20v. Barbot misinterprets Marees's statement about Portuguese ships taking bread made at Elmina to Angola, and instead states that Africans eat this bread when travelling to Angola in canoes. Having described *kankey*, he adds: 'I found this kind of cake very good'. For kankies, see Letter 2/20, note 4, below.

Cf. *1732*, p. 256/8–9 – '... a sort of round twisted cakes, call'd there Quanquis ... agreeable enough'.

[16] The first sentence is from Dapper, p. 99/2.

Cf. *1732*, p. 256/9.

[17] This passage contains elements from Villault, p. 247 (fish cooked with salt and malaguetta, recipes learnt from Europeans, people served at table) and from Marees, ff. 20v–21 (legumes, kinds of meat eaten by noblemen – but Marees does not mention pork, the eating of elephant and buffalo meat, sitting on the ground). Other elements appear to be original. In 1679 Barbot noted various fruits and vegetables sold at a market (*1679*, p. 340).

Cf. *1732*, pp. 254/6–9, 255/1–4, which expands the passage slightly – 'They bake green unripe figs' (i.e. 'India figs' or bananas); 'herbs and beans season'd with salt and oil' (not 'legumes'); 'elephant's and buffalo's flesh boil'd'; 'the common sort generally sit ... on the bare ground, cross-legg'd ... or else with both their legs streight under them, and sitting on their heels'. It also adds considerable material from Bosman, pp. 123–4, and a disquisition on the exotic foods of foreign nations, including frogs' hind legs in France.

[18] Omission of two paragraphs on eating and drinking habits, almost entirely derived from Marees, f. 21–21v, with minor additions from Villault, pp. 247–50. Barbot's only significant addition is the statement that when eating, people first 'knead [their food] in their hands into the shape of balls'. For another description of eating and drinking habits, also influenced by Marees, but to a lesser extent, see Jones 1983a, pp. 211–2.

515

Cf. *1732*, p. 255/5–256/5, which adds material from Bosman, p. 125, and describes the eating habits at rather greater length: 'They generally eat very greedily, and after a disagreeable filthy manner, which I could not bear with, when I happen'd sometimes to be treated by any of the prime men; for they use neither table-cloths nor napkins: what meat or fish they dress, is always half-rotten, and most dishes are season'd with palm-oil, which, though pretty good to such as are us'd to it, has a sharpish taste, and a smell very nauseous to strangers. I could not but admire the power of habit and custom in those people, who were wonderfully pleas'd with the most corrupted stinking food, and fed on it most greedily. ... [After throwing food into their mouths] they shake their greasy fingers, as they come from their mouths, over the dishes the meat is serv'd up in.' Barbot recollects his meal at Rufisco (Letter 1/10, p. 53), but also adds lengthy references to drinking habits among the Chinese, Israelites, Romans and Greeks.

LETTER 20

The employments and occupations of the natives. Especially merchants and fishermen [and goldsmiths and canoe-builders]. The fish caught. The Fetish Fish.

I have previously told you, Sir, that these peoples are /p. 76/ very ingenious and capable of various tasks. You will be convinced of this when you have read my letter, for I am going to tell you about the most common occupations among them. I will be writing at greater length than I would wish, but in describing such matters it is not easy to cover a lot of ground in a few words. Among the Moors are persons engaged in various occupations, those at the coasts being mostly merchants, fishermen, goldsmiths, canoe-men, house-builders, salt-makers, roofers, farmers, potters, porters, etc. Each is engaged in his occupation in order to gain a livelihood and even to become rich, since nowadays, having studied us Europeans, they are as ambitious and greedy as formerly they were simple and content with the necessities of life, not even being acquainted with the use of clothes.[1]

[merchants]

Of all their occupations, that of the merchant is the most honourable. [. . .][2] The agents and merchants usually come out to the ships in small, neat canoes paddled by two Moors, they themselves sitting in the middle on a little wooden stool and having beside [each of] them a cutlass, a pipe and a small reed basket to contain whatever

516

they buy on the ship. The gold they are trading is carried in a purse or little box attached to and under their belt, or between their thighs, or around their neck, in order to save it if the canoe capsizes. The gold itself is in several little packets made out of cloth, linen, paper or leather, tied at the top and stowed within the purse.[3] These agents have such a splendid memory that, although nothing is written on the little packets, they know to which person each packet belongs and what they are required to buy with the gold in it. Those who entrust the gold to them weigh it immediately before they set out to board the ships, and should the agents be obliged when aboard to make any adjustment, they take gold [from one packet] to make up another, and keep account. A hundred times I have admired their exactness in this respect, and the care with which all of them check to see if the goods are in perfect condition and of the quality and quantity they normally should be. Hence there often occur serious disputes over the weights used for the gold, certain Europeans using the heaviest weights they can. The Moors have carried out this careful examination ever since they found out, in the last century, that what they bought from the whites was useless and short-weight because they accepted it blindly. Now we think it impossible to overcharge any of them the slightest; indeed, as a result of having been cheated, they have become so dishonest themselves that, far from our being able easily to impose on them, today you must be thoroughly on your guard lest they in turn cheat you. Some of them blow on the scales holding the gold as it is being weighed, to make the pan tip over, while others, when pretending to add gold to make up the weight, hide some away behind their finger nails.[4]

I will indicate to you elsewhere what kinds of merchandise /p. 77/ are sold to them and what they do with them. Those who buy on their own account do not usually sell the goods again until the ships have left, in order to make more gain. They also make much profit on the goods they buy for others, since they hand over the goods to them at a much higher price than they gave for them, or else they hand over short weight. They are so eager for gain that they also cheat their clients (*cometans*) even aboard the ships, either by an understanding with the European factors, or by amusing the clients while someone else in the know does a swindle in any way he can. I have seen some of them aboard a ship in the roadstead at Cors who used to make a profit of two or three *ancres* of brandy in a day and a night, apart from what they were paid by their clients. In daytime they come aboard to deal in slaves and gold, and go ashore with what they decide to hand over to those for whom they have bought the goods, but at night they come back to collect the rest, which they take ashore at places the collectors of royal dues cannot learn about, since they have people in their service everywhere. Or, if they cannot succeed in these ways, they try to steal gold from their clients while it is being weighed, handling it on the pretext of removing dirt or grit, but when the hand is withdrawn their long nails are full of the metal, which they then transfer to their mouth, to their nose, into their ears, or sometimes between their toes.[5] These brokers have even more profit from the *dache*, or present, that the whites generally give them whenever they buy anything. [. . .] Apart from the embarrassment this bad custom causes, it puts up the cost of trade by 5%, and you have to argue all the time with these people about it, they being never satisfied, especially the smaller men who are the greediest. [. . .][6] [. . ./p. 78/. . .][7]

These Moorish merchants do not trade only in gold but also in slaves, whom they bring to the ships in fairly large numbers when there are wars. But in peacetime, as was the case on the whole Gold Coast in 1682, there is little trade in these and they are very dear : they are normally reckoned at from six to eight or nine *poids*. Hardly ever is ivory traded, because such ivory as they have there comes from far inland or from Quaqua or Congo, and because they use it for trumpets, bracelets, and other things they make and use, which means that ivory is dear there. Hardly any wax is available, or at least very little, since they employ it to make candles (whose use they have known for some time).[8]

You can see in this drawing a canoe containing slaves who are to board a vessel, and other canoes arriving to trade gold. In the distance you can see how they upturn the little craft on to some cradles when it reaches the shore.[9]

[illustration no. (79), canoes approaching ships off the coast]†

Additional Passage from *1732*

[p. 261/1, on conveying goods inland]

Those inland Blacks, who come down without slaves of their own to carry back the commodities purchased, hire either free-men or

45. Canoes, with merchants and slaves, off Gold Coast

46. Fishing canoes off Gold Coast

slaves, who commonly live under the forts, at such rates as they can agree upon, according to the distance of the places the goods are to be carried to; which is a considerable advantage to those at the coast, tho' the money is hardly enough earned, those poor wretches having high hills to climb, and bad ways to pass.[10]

[fishermen and fish]

After that of merchant, the trade of fisherman is the most /p. 79/ esteemed and the commonest. Fathers bring their children up to it from the age of nine or ten. Every morning (except Tuesday, which is their Sunday), a very large number of fishermen come out from the land for up to two leagues. There are many of them at Axim, Anta, Comendo, Mina, Corso, Mourée and Cormentin, but more at Comendo and Mina than elsewhere. Some days you can see 300–400 at each place. Their fleets slowly move out one and a half or two leagues with the light land-breeze and on a calm sea, in order to reach the depth they need to fish, and then they disperse, each canoe going its own way to fish without impeding any other. Normally each canoe has two men, one standing up to fish, the other sitting at the extreme rear, in order to steer it and direct it towards what they think are the best places. They always carry in the canoe a cutlass, some bread and water, and live fire on a large stone for cooking fish when they want a meal.[11] From this drawing you can detect, Sir, the pleasure one gains in seeing so many fishermen at work around a vessel at one time. I applied myself vigorously [to sketch them] in these few moments.

[illustration no. (80), fishing canoes off the coast][12]†

They fish in the morning, because this is the time when the fish bite best and also because it is when the land-breeze keeps the sea calm and still. And towards noon they return with the sea-breeze, which increases by degrees and blows so strongly that, if they waited till the evening, they would have great difficulty and danger in reaching land, on account of the violent breakers.[13] Constant practice in fishing makes these Moors very expert in the art, so that they have exact knowledge of the characteristics of each fish and the season of the year to catch it. They have several ways of fishing, both by day and by night. I shall detail these for you. By day, they fish either with lines or with nets made of palm-fibre. They attach hooks

519

to the lines at /p. 80/ varying distances, according to the behaviour of the fish they are proposing to catch.[14] I have seen 20 hooks on some lines and five or six on others, while the normal number is two. Some fishermen attach the lines to their head, fixing them on each side of the head or on one side only, in order to have their hands free to lift the fish aboard and to detect more sensitively the fish biting. You cannot but admire the skill of these men at certain times, as when the fish are biting heavily and they pull out five or six of them at once, very rapidly. Others hold lines in their hands as the canoe drifts along, and others again make the hooks jump along the surface of the water, in the way we fish for bonito.[15] [...][16] They fish also for bonito, dolphin-fish, sucking-fish, large *carangues* with small eyes, and a large fish resembling a shark but darker, which is why they call it *negros* – its flesh is excellent. Here are some of these fish which I have sketched for you from nature, to satisfy your curiosity.

[illustration no. (81), four fish][17] /p. 81/†

Here also you see by itself the sketch of a large fish I saw at Comendo, the Fetish Fish.

[illustration no. (82), the Fetish Fish][18]

Apart from sea-fish, they have many river-fish, but quite different ones from ours, there being any similarity only in the carp and pike. In rivers, nets are used more frequently than lines. These Moors are so untiring in this work that they take very little rest, for after fishing in the sea for part of the day they spend part of the night fishing in the rivers, which is, however, less rewarding. They set up their net (*filet*) on dry land, as we do.[19] [...][20]

But this way of fishing [by standing in the water] is liable to lead to terrible disasters, on account of the large number of those marine monsters, the sharks, who cross the breakers and tear apart those who go out a little too far. Yet these Africans also wage destruction on the sharks, going out deliberately, in order to take them with great harpoons or with lines, to reduce their numbers, and because they sell them at a very good price to the Moors of the interior, who like the flesh when sun-dried. Should it happen that they take a shark of extraordinary size, as many of the sharks in fact are, they help each other to land it, and they distribute it among the people of the village, who eat it in a spirit of hatred.[21]

They also fish among the rocks for various sorts of fish, with implements made for the purpose and like those with which we take conger eels in Aunix. There is one particular kind of fish, called by the English 'King's Fish', which has an excellent taste when cooked and served in butter. They also gather many mussels which are as good as those in England, and such large oysters that two suffice for one man. Since you want to recognize everything as if you were touching it as well as seeing it, I have drawn this plate which will enable you to envisage more clearly what I have been describing to you about the various /p. 82/ forms of fishing from the land. I have forgotten to state that they also fish with cast-nets, and some with scraps of cloth they hold in both hands, between two tides, lifting them up when they see fish in them, but this method is only for little fish. The inland peoples have different ways of fishing from those by the sea. But I think there is no need to say more about the fishermen. Let us turn to the goldsmiths.

[illustration no. (83), ways of fishing][22]

Additional Passages from *1732*

[p. 223/3, on the Fetisso Fish, and on Barbot drawing][23]

At my first voyage, whilst we lay before Comendo, some fishermen, near our ship, took a fish about seven foot long, shaped as exactly represented in the figure. The Blacks call'd it Fetisso, but for what reason I cannot determine, unless it be to express, that it is too rare and sweet for mortals to eat, and only fit for a deity: the word Fetisso, which in Portuguese signifies sorcery, being by the Blacks apply'd to all things they reckon sacred, because the Portuguese gave the name of sorcery to all their superstitions. It was, indeed, a most beautiful fish, tho' the skin is brown and swarthy about its back, but grows lighter and lighter the nearer it comes to the stomach and belly. It had a streight snout, with a sort of horn at the end of it, very hard and sharp pointed, above three spans long; and another small streight horn on the upper part of its mouth. The eyes large and bright, and on each side of the body, beginning at the gills, four longish cuts, or openings. As I remember, the Blacks would not sell it at any rate, but only allowed me the liberty of drawing its figure, as it appears in the cut; and were much amazed to see it so well represented. Nor was that astonishment peculiar to them, for many others there, on the Gold Coast, at Sierra Leona, Sestro river, and other places, very much admired to see me make the figure of any creature upon paper.[24]

[pp. 223/11, 224/6, 15, on other smaller fish]

The sea-toad is a fish of small size, eaten by the common sort of Blacks, the fins of them very curious, as appears by the figure in the cut [*margin:* Plate 18]. The head of it is much like that of a frog, or toad, whence it has the name. ... The machorans, so called by the French, and by the Dutch *Baerd Maneties* [Little Bearded Men], from five pretty long excrescencies, which hang at the end of their chops, like a beard, and on each side of the mouth, just under the eyes, one much longer, as represented in the figure [*margin:* Plate 19]. At the upper fin on its back, and at the under one on the belly, is a long hard sharp horn, the prick whereof causes violent pains and great swellings, as if there were some venomous nature in it, as many sailors have experienc'd to their cost, when accidentally hurt by it; and for that reason many do not care to eat of the fish in the Leeward islands of America, where there is great plenty of them and very large; as also because they feed there among the Manzanilla trees, which produce a sort of poisonous apples, tho' very beautiful, and of a charming red. This fish feeding in America on that fruit, it cannot but be dangerous to eat; but being caught out at sea in Africa, and there being no such trees on the coast, I cannot think it is any way hurtful; besides that experience shows the contrary, they being commonly eaten and found good wholesome fish. Those of the coast of America are generally larger, and mix'd yellow, sky-colour, and brown: the English call it the horn-fish, and when first caught, it seems to groan. ... The Bonito, an excellent fish, is seldom taken there, for it comes not near the shore; but there are prodigious shoals of them playing in the deep sea, and particularly about the equinoctial. See the figure of them as drawn in the plate [*margin:* Plate 18].[25]

[pp. 225/2, 4, 8, 11, 226/1–6, 9–13, 227/1–9, on other larger fish and cetaceans, including the shark, porpoise and flying-fish]

The grampusses, by the French are call'd *Souffleurs*, that is, blowers, or spouters, from their blowing as it were spouts of water out at their nostrils when they rise upon the surface of the sea, holding up their snouts, as I have seen thousands of them together in a shoal, for three of four miles in circumference, either in the gulph of Guinea, or to the southward of the line; which at a distance in calm scorching weather look like huge blocks swimming on the ocean. [. . .][26] They are very swift in their motions, and it is almost incredible how nimble they appear, considering their prodigious length and bulk; and though we often shot at them with muskets, and certainly hit some, we could not perceive they were so wounded as to stand still. [. . .][27]

The Shark, by the French call'd *Requien*, which I have drawn by the life in the cut in the supplement, is an extraordinary ravenous creature. [. . .][28] It is so well known to most sailors, and has been so often described by other travellers, that it will be needless to give a larger account; besides that, the figure of it exactly drawn, as I said above, will give full satisfaction: but for the information of those who have never seen any, I cannot but add, that its eyes, though very small in proportion to the body, and round, look like a bright flaming fire. The jaw-bones or chops are so wonderfully framed or join'd together, that when occasion requires to prey on something that is very large, they can open a mouth of a prodigious width and bigness, within which are three rows, above and below, of very sharp and strong teeth, which at once cut off a man's arm, leg, head, or any other part of the body. It has been observ'd, that missing the bait, it will return three times, though before torn by the hook; and I have been told, that there was found in the belly of one of them a knife and six pounds of bacon. / It does not spawn like other fish, nor lay eggs as tortoises do, but brings forth young as the beasts do, having a matrix, and all the rest like a fish; as has also the seal-fish, which somewhat resembling a small shark, has by some been taken for another sort of them; but when well examin'd, as I have done several times, it appears very different, which may be seen in the cut in the supplement, representing a seal-fish, which the French call *Roussette*, and whereof I shall speak more at large hereafter in the supplement.[29]

To return to the shark: There are every where vast multitudes of them between the tropicks; and more particularly on the coast of Guinea, or [*misprint: read* from] Arguin, on the coast of Genehoa,

523

corruptly call'd Barbary, to the northward of Senega, down to Angola, and farther south, either out at sea or near the shore, all along those coasts; and they are of all sizes, some vastly big, and others small, according to their ages. / Their skins are of a dark brown, almost over all the body, and whitish just under the belly, having neither scales nor shells, but a thick oily fat roughness like shagreen, adorn'd with streaks across very orderly down on each side of the back. It swims incredibly swift, and great multitudes of them usually follow our slave-ships some hundred leagues at sea, as they sail out from the gulph of Guinea; as if they knew we were to throw some dead corps over board almost every day. They are seldom seen far out at sea, unless in a calm, following ships to catch whatsoever is thrown out.[30] / They are commonly attended by a sort of little fishes, about as big as pilchards, but somewhat rounder shap'd, swimming before them, without ever being hurt by those ravenous monsters, which through a particular instinct never devour them, as they do all other fishes they can master. These small ones are called Pilot-fishes, from their swimming before the others; and it is observ'd, that very often when a shark is taken with a hook, and drawn aboard a ship, this Pilot-fish clings to his back, and is taken with him: and I have heard that some sharks have been taken with the Remora-fish sticking to them. / Those days we threw no dead bodies over board, and when the weather was moderate, we diverted ourselves with catching of sharks, with long thick iron hooks fastned to an iron chain, having a large piece of bacon, or stinking meat, for a bait; which way we soon caught some: but in haling them aboard with a rope, or tackle, were always fain to keep clear, because, beside the danger of their sharp teeth, they strike with the tail; which is so prodigious strong, that should it hit a man, it would not fail to break an arm or a leg, if not worse. / No creature is harder to kill; for when cut in pieces they will all move. They have a sort of marrow in the head, which hardens in the sun, and being powder'd and taken in white wine, is very good for the cholick. [...][31] The smaller sharks, of about six or eight feet long, are the best to eat, boil'd and press'd, and then stew'd with vinegar and pepper; which way many European seamen eat it, when they are in want.

To conclude this discourse concerning fish, I shall mention three other sorts. The first is the porpoise, of which there are swarms in this Guinea ocean, and they often appear near the shore. This fish is universally so well known, that I shall not spend much time upon it, having given the figure of it in the cut.[32] / The French call it *Marsouin*. It is wonderful to see how swift they are, and what vast shoals there are of them in the gulph of Guinea, playing about in a brisk gale of wind, and skipping about a ship that has a good run. We one day there struck five of them with our harping-irons, and had leisure enough to view them exactly. / They were about five feet long, and very fleshy, or rather all fat, except the head which is tolerable good meat, being first well salted some days, then boil'd and well season'd, yet it is afterwards uneasy upon the stomach, being too fat and oily. The flesh of their bodies was cut into slices, and after it had lain several days in a strong brine, or pickle, our men hung it up for a time, expos'd to the heat of the sun, and then eat it; but it was still nauseous, the fat being ill-tasted. The ribs and entrails are like those of a hog, bating that they have two stomachs, the one at the end of the oesophage, the other clinging to one side, almost as large as the first; and this last has a little opening, which is the communication between them both. It is full of little cells, like those in the wax, before the honey is taken from it. The duodenum has its rise in the last. / Those fishes, when first laid upon the deck, made a sort of groaning till they expired. Their blood is as hot as that which comes from any beast, and there is a good quantity of it; which is contrary to the nature of other fishes. We took both males and females, each sex having its distinct parts of generation; and they engender by copulation. / The skin is all over like a whale's, of a pitchy colour, and the body round and plump. The snout is pretty long, and in the mouth are rows of very small sharp teeth, looking at a distance like a saw. This fish will not meddle with a man.

The Remora is represented in the cut in the supplement, of which the antients have writ, that it will stop a ship under sail.[33] I shall only speak of its head; the upper part of it is quite flat, with twelve small cuts or dents reaching from one end of it to the other, by means whereof it cleaves fast to any piece of timber or stone, as the lampreys do; so that the whole body hangs down: and hence perhaps proceeded that absurd opinion some men in former ages conceiv'd, that it could stop a ship under sail; some part whereof might be possible, if a sloop or small vessel had a thousand or more sticking to its sides and stern, they being commonly, at full growth, about three foot long or better, for then they might considerably retard the sailing of such a vessel; but it is ridiculous to say they can have any power over great ships under sail, as is pretended. / I observ'd for several days, both in the gulph of Guinea, and about the line, that we were follow'd by great numbers of these fishes, and they appear'd very greedy of men's excrements, which they were continually gaping after as they fell to the water; and therefore the slave-ships are well attended by them in those parts. / They are nevertheless tolerable good meat, when well drest and season'd. The under chop is somewhat longer than the upper; and I believe they engende[r] by copulation, as several other sorts of fish do, particularly whales, sharks, porpoises, and sea-dogs. / The French call this fish *Susset*, or *Remora*, or *Arrete-nef*; the English, the Sea-Lamprey.

The Flying Fish is the third of the three last I promis'd to mention, there being such plenty in those seas, that I shall have occasion to speak of it hereafter; and, for the present, shall only observe, that there are several sorts of it, and refer you to the two figures of the finest I met with in my travels, as exactly represented in the cut.[34] / They are both excellent meat, especially broil'd on a quick fire, and very fine creatures to look to, being about twelve or fifteen inches long. / These, when pursued by the shoals of Bonitos, or other greater fishes, which greedily devour them, take their flight above water; but generally not very high, which is the reason that small low vessels catch more of them than the greater and loftier. They fly as long as there is any moisture left in their wings, and then plunge again in the ocean; and it is no small diversion, in some parts of the ocean, to see millions of flying fishes pursued by the vast shoals of Bonitos in the water; and out of it, assaulted by many large sea-fowl: whereof I will give a particular account in another place, with a draught of the same.[35]

[p. 261/9, on the swordfish]

If a sword-fish, or any other of the greatest bulk, happens to be in the net they have laid in the sea over night, it is certainly torn to pieces; but if the owner of the net has notice of it in time, he desires the assistance of his friends, and two or three canoes go out together, provided with strong harping irons to strike it; and the Blacks being fond of that fish above any other, one of them makes amends for two or three nets torn, by the price it yields.[36]

[goldsmiths]

There are many of this trade at Boutrou, Comendo, Mine, Berku and elsewhere. They learned the art from the Portuguese, as I have noted previously, and have outdone their masters in certain kinds of work, such as cast filigree, chainwork, and drawn gold thread which they make as fine as a hair. To do this, they use tools of their own designing, and their files are better tempered than our own (which may in fact be the result of the water). It is only anvils and hammers they cannot make, and these they normally buy from the Dutch. They make smaller forges than we do, and with the tools they make all sorts of gold objects – breastplates, helmets, bracelets, fetishes, hunting horns, pattens, gold plates, winkles (*burgauds*), collars, and in general all sorts of skull-figures, those of lions, tigers, leopards, oxen, deer, goats, monkeys, and the other animals they honour as fetishes. To sum up, Sir, there is nothing they cannot make in this line, down to hat-bands and buttons. They particularly excel in filigree of the kind that is cast and run through the mould. From my first voyage I brought back a number of objects which have been admired by persons of the highest quality. I drew some of them for you in Letter 17.[37]

[.../p. 83/...][38] Further, it is said of those who neighbour River Niger that gold is so common there that the poorest of the Moors living in that spot can without fuss hand over an *aquier* of this metal for a pot of palm-wine containing only four quarts (*pintes, mesure de Paris*), and two *aquiers* for a fried chicken. And yet for our benefit they like to think of themselves as poverty-stricken, saying (as several of those from the upper country have in fact put to me) that we assemble our merchandise as corn is harvested in a field, without more labour than that of gathering it, because our God is good. Perhaps they also make themselves out to be beggars because they do not wish us to think that their land is so rich, lest this belief encourage us to go there (even though the undertaking involves a thousand perils).[39]

The inland peoples work more at farming than do the others. You have seen [previously], Sir, how they comport themselves and the little trouble they take to farm, and also how weak and lazy their farming is, for although they own land which is rich and fertile, few sow more maize than they think they need to feed them for one year. Hence the great and frequent famines occurring here from time to

527

time, caused by wars, droughts, or insects devastating their crops, as vast clouds of locusts (*sauterelles*) often do. After the Aquambou war in 1679, maize corn cost 10 *écus* a chest at Acra. Their explanation is that they prefer to work little and eat less. It is true that, as I have said, the peoples beside the sea are more hard-working, especially those at Axim, Anta, Abroby, Mouree, Anamabou, and Cormentin, at each of which places at certain times 200–300 chests of maize are available for sale.[40]

Additional Passage from *1732*

[p. 264/6–18, on objects in gold, tools, etc., as shown on Plate 22, lower part, and now listed]

An earthen pot, as they are generally made of several sizes, large and small. / Just under the pot, a woman's necklace, of Contas de Terra and Agri, adorn'd with gold spells, and slips of the sacred tree; such necklaces are reckoned there very ornamental, and cost a considerable sum of money. / 9. A gold hat-band, of curious workman-ship. / From A. to B. sundry sorts of their gold toys worn as spells, or things sacred, and bracelets of six sorts, one of them so long, that it reaches to the elbow; and over them two sorts of flat arm-rings. Under those rings [*read* bracelets] some cast heads of beasts, used also as spells, or holy things, and near the biggest head a gold bracelet, which can be contracted, or extended, as narrow, or as wide as they please on the arm.[41] / Above those rings, a small blowing horn of gold used by the better sort. / 7. A piece of natural gold near an ounce in weight, which I have still by me, being like a piece of a sharp-pointed rock. / 8. A large whilk, or periwinkle, cast in gold filigrene work, a very curious piece. / 6. Two Bousies, or Cauries, East-India shells, which serve for ornaments in necklaces, and go for money at Fida and Ardra. / 4. A great iron pin, with a small semi-circle at the end, like a half moon, which is current money at some places, for a certain value. / 1. Small scales of their making, to weigh gold. / 3. The beans, or pease, with which they weigh gold dust, as has been said before. / 5. Little wooden spoons to put gold into the scales, or take it out, to adjust the weight. / 2. Gold Krakra, which is their small money.[42]

[canoe-making and surf-canoeing]

Those who make canoes generally live at Axim, Ackuon, Boutrou,

528

Tackarary and Comendo, since these lands are forested. They make them from the trunk of a tree, using curved knives. The canoes are shaped like a coffer on the upper parts (*encoffrés par haut*), and flat below [on the floor], the two ends pointed so that they can be easily carried on the shoulders when out of the water. Next they hollow out the trunk with great chisels and apply fire to those parts they cannot tackle with their tools, and finally they smooth it, outside and in, with other small tools, which takes them a long time. However, they make them very light and very neat. The length of the common canoes is 16–18 feet, and the width is 20 inches, but at Takorary and Axim they make canoes 35–40 feet long, five feet wide and three feet in depth, and in these they can easily carry 6–10 tons of merchandise as well as a crew. These are called 'cargo canoes', and the Moors use them to transport their cattle and merchandise from one place to another, taking them over the breakers loaded as they are. This sort can be found at Juda and Ardra, and at many places on Gold Coast. Such canoes are so safe that they travel from Gold Coast to all parts of the Gulf of Ethiopia, and beyond that to Angola. They are moved by paddles or by sail, and travel rapidly on account of their lightness, provided that their crew is reasonably powerful. To tackle the breakers, they have usually 10, 12, 16 or 18 men, according to their size and cargo. War-canoes carry up to 60 men, with their weapons and foodstuffs for 15 days.[43]

The men rowing canoes sit in twos, on benches set across, from the stern [forward]. Each man has a paddle, or oar, this being a pole / p. 84/ three feet long with a portion of board attached at the end and shaped like the iron head of a pike.[44] The man who steers this kind of boat sits at the stern, with a paddle a little larger than those of the others. They hold the paddle in both hands. The men of Mina are the best at manoeuvring these canoes over the breakers without an upset, at least more often than not without one, and you could hardly manage with any other men at Juda and Offra, where the breakers are more dangerous than anywhere else in Guinea. And when it happens that they have been upset in the surf, they are so expert that that they lose little of what has been entrusted to them because it is attached to the canoe, tied to the little bars which cross it at intervals, making it like a sort of pontoon. Most fishermen have little poles in their canoes for the same purpose. The speed with which these people generally make these boats travel is beyond belief, Sir. I am speaking especially of the small canoes, even though they have only two or three rowers. The rear is so low that the sea often washes in there, as well as over the sides which are nearly at water level. One man in the canoe does nothing else but bale out with half a calabash.

I have very often been obliged to travel in either the large canoes or the small ones, as the demands of the trade required me, in order to go ashore, yet I was never once upset. Mind you, I had some alarming moments, sometimes lasting a quarter of an hour, when we were between two swells, waiting for the most suitable time to dash across the breakers, which can only be done at great risk. The rowers know exactly the right moment, which is usually when three large swells have passed by and when those men stationed on the neighbouring rocks shout out to them to come in. Then, Sir, they drive straight at the land with such strength and determination that the canoe appears in sight half-way through the breakers, just as a swell, like a mountain of boiling water, coming from behind, begins to break. This does not prevent the canoe from receiving the spray, and sometimes it is even uplifted to such a height that it seems as if it is being transported through the air between two hillocks of water, and this hides it for several moments from the view of those ashore, causing great perturbation to those unaccustomed to the sight. In this state you are thrown on the beach by the second swell, which carries the little vessel well up, and on to dry land. You then realise the lightness of the canoes, Sir, for they are met by several Moors who run into the water up to their buttocks, in order to unload the notables or the goods aboard, to avoid their being further soaked, for often the canoe, being without protection, fills with water after being beached, its prow being up in the air and its stern low down. All this is even more difficult in the new and full moon [because of the high tides].[45]

So much for landing in a canoe. Now I am going to describe for you how to leave for another destination in a canoe. You get into the canoe on dry land and put the goods aboard the same way. Then the little vessel is pushed into the water by a host of men, who howl like wolves as they hand it over to the crew, who leap in on both sides. They keep the canoe head on to the swell, and swim as far as they can, breasting the breakers. The swell lifts the canoe practically on end, and then lets it drop with a crash, which is terrifying and which scares anyone who has not experienced this before. All goes well if the canoe remains head on to the swell, but if it begins to twist or fails to rise, then it will certainly be overwhelmed by a mountain of water, which often costs the life of those who encounter it and cannot swim sufficiently, or who are torn apart by the sharks. Fortunately one can trust implicitly in the blacks on these occasions, for they take particular care to save everyone.[46] /p. 85/

The sails of these canoes are mostly made of reed mats or [woven out] of plant roots, and their rigging is of palm-fibre twine. They paint their canoes various colours and garnish them with fetishes, behind and before, to keep them safe, as some people do with guardian angels. Most of their fetishes are ears of millet, and the skulls and muzzles of lions and tigers or the dried heads of goats, monkeys or various other animals. Those canoes making long voyages are adorned with a dead goat hung aloft in honour of the fetish.[47] [...][48]

Additional Passages from *1732*

[p. 266/7, on crossing the surf]

When the bar canoos, or any other [canoes of] smaller sizes, are to stand in for the land through the breaking waters, the crew narrowly observes to have the three high surges, which usually follow one upon the back of another, pass over, before they enter upon beating waters. The Blacks, who at those times always wait on the beach, either to succour the canoos coming in, if any accident befals them, or to unlade them as soon as they are safely arriv'd on the strand, give a shout from the shore, which is a signal to those in the canoo, that the three great surges are over; which they can better judge of from the land, as being higher above the water. Then the canoo-men all together, with wonderful concert, paddle amain, and give the canoo such swift way through the beating [? breaking] water, which foams and roars in dreadful manner on both sides, that it is got half way through before the succeeding surges, which commonly rise and swell prodigious high the nearer they come to the beating, can overtake it: and thus the canoo holding that rapid course in the midst of the foaming waves, runs itself at once almost dry on the sandy beach; many of those Blacks, who continually attend there for that purpose, running into the water up to the knees, or middle, before it has touched the ground, and take out the passengers on both sides, whom they carry ashore, though often very wet with the waves breaking into

531

the canoo. After that they also take out the goods, and carry them where commanded.[49]

[p. 267/2, on rowing canoes and swimming]

I have often admir'd the dexterity of the fishermen, when some of them happened to come ashore later than is usual, in the afternoon, at which time the sea-breeze makes the sea swell considerably near the land: I observed how two or three men, in so small, so low, so narrow, and so light a boat, in which he who sits at the stern to steer seems to have his posteriors in the water, could so swiftly carry the canoo through the breaking sea, without any misfortune, and with little or no concern; but this must proceed from their being brought up, both men and women, from their infancy, to swim like fishes; and that, with the constant exercise, renders them so dexterous at it, that tho' the canoo be overturn'd, or split in pieces, they can either turn it up again in the first case, or swim ashore in the second, tho' never so distant from it. The Blacks of Mina out-do all others at the coast in dexterity of swimming, throwing one [arm] after another forward, as if they were paddling, and not extending their arms equally, and striking with them both together, as Europeans do. There, as I have hinted before, may be seen several hundred of boys and girls sporting together before the beach, and in many places among the rolling and breaking waves, learning to swim, on bits of boards, or small bundles of rushes, fasten'd under their stomachs, which is a good diversion to the spectators.[50]

[p. 267/3–4, on Europeans landing and European pleasure-boats]

I would advise those, who are to go ashore, to send their best clothes before them, in a trunk; for I have often spoil'd good apparel upon such occasions, and especially when the Blacks lift a man out of the canoo just when it reaches the beach, as has been said before: for they being always anointed all over with grease, or palm-oil, certainly leave the impression of it on his clothes, wheresoever they touch them, and it is scarce ever to be got out. There every European of any note, commonly wears fine silk, or woollen suits, and often adorned with gold, or silver galoons; according to the post he is in, each studying to exceed another; besides that the Blacks, as well as other nations, show most respect to those who are best dressed.

There is another sort of very fine canoos, of about five or six ton burden, which every commander of an European fort keeps for a pleasure-boat, to pass with his attendants, as occasion offers, from one place to another. The Danish general in my time had the finest of that sort. In the midst of it was a large auning, of very good red and blue stuffs, with gold and silver fringes, and under it hand-some seats, covered with Turkey carpets, and curious curtains to draw on iron rods. At each end of the auning was a staff, bearing a little streamer, and another at the head of the canoo, and under it the Danish flag. These canoos are represented in the cut of the prospect of fort Fredericksburg, at Manfrou near Corso; where is also another canoo, which was for the Danish general's servants and soldiers, which usually attended his own canoo. In the cuts of the castle of St George of Mina, cape Corso castle, and Christiaen-burg at Acra, are exact draughts of the great canoos, used by the English and Dutch to carry goods and passengers along the coast; to which prints I refer, as to the form of the canoos, and the manner of fitting and rigging them.[51]

[p. 268/6, on the small canoe]

This sort of little canoo is exactly represented in its proper form and shape in the print, showing five or six hundred of them abroad fishing, at Mina; and just under it is the other sort of canoo, carrying slaves aboard the ship, both of them differing much from the bar canoos, and those made to perform voyages. The latter is exactly drawn in all its parts, to give the reader a just idea of it, and the way of rowing and steering, and therefore it will be needless to say more of it.[52]

[other trades, royal dues]

I will say nothing here about the trades of house-builders, masons and porters, having said enough about these in my Letter 19. About potters, I will say no more than that they have learned their art from the Portuguese, and that they are skilled in baking clay; for the earthenware vessels they make, although thin are, however, very strong and very suitable for boiling meats. They keep their heat for a very long time. The colour of the clay they use is almost black. There is also little to say about thatchers, since roofs are only an arrangement of leaves or reeds, tied one over another, on large rounded timbers, which they sell in this form in the markets.[53]

533

The people of the far interior are also involved in trade. While many of them work at farming, others make all sorts of hats and caps from skins and straw, and others again make bark cloths, dyed in various colours, which they weave very artistically on small looms, like those at Cape Verde. The people at Isseny and in its neighbourhood also do this very well and produce large quantities.[54]

That, Sir, concludes all that can be said about their various occupations. Now I have only to tell you briefly about the dues their kings exact from these peoples. All are obliged to pay these dues, and do so to a Receiver appointed by the king for this purpose, who is usually assisted by a son or relative of the king, to check that the receipt of the dues is undertaken honestly. These dues are laid on all goods brought ashore, whether fish or merchandise, provided that they are above a certain quantity (below that nothing is paid). The dues are paid either in kind or in gold, usually the fortieth part and [? or] one in five, at the option of the Receiver. The people in the interior do not owe any dues for fishing in rivers, but they do for passing through certain places, 15 *sols* a head when going, with nothing when returning, empty or loaded. Fruit-growers and other peasants bringing their goods to market are exempted from the dues, but if they forget [and carry] their weapons outside the village they are fined 15 *sols*. The Receiver renders his account to the king every three months, accounting for what he has received in gold or in fish (which usually is at the rate of one in five, and the fish is sent immediately to the king, for his household). A fisherman cannot begin to sell what he has caught without permission and without having paid the king's dues, but at sea and in the roadstead he can provide ships with fish, trading the fish for various trifles, knives, fish-hooks, fire-arms, bread, old hats, etc. The Receiver shares fines and goods confiscated, and can take as much fish as he wishes for himself. The king's son does the same.[55] I am, Sir, etc.

NOTES

[1] The occupations are drawn from Villault, p. 319, from disconnected references in Dapper and Marees, and from observation. The final sentence is based on Marees, ff. 22, 25.

Cf. *1732*, p. 258/3–4, which reflects Bosman, p. 128.

[2] Omission of the rest of a paragraph, describing how trading was learned from the Portuguese and why the inland people coming to the coast use

brokers and agents, all from Marees, ff. 22v–23, but embroidered. Barbot contributes disappointingly little to the material on merchants. In 1679, Barbot recorded no details about trading procedures with African merchants, other than noting that at Komenda he found the Africans 'unbearable' because of their delays and discussions (*1679*, p. 288). In fact he traded more frequently with white agents, about whom he also grumbled.

Cf. *1732*, p. 258/5–7, which enlarges on the growth of trade, and where 'I have been told that' means that Barbot read it in Marees, which he appears to have consulted afresh.

[3] The first sentence is from Villault, p. 320, the purse and packets from Marees, f. 23, the rest from observation. A 1693 trader reported that 'the blacks came aboard to trade, bringing their gold in divers little rags, according to the number of those who employ them to trade for them' (Phillips 1732, p. 206).

Cf. *1732*, p. 259/1–3, slightly enlarged (e.g., 'a pipe in his mouth').

[4] The memorizing by the agents, the adjusting of weights, the cheating and counter-cheating, and the long finger-nails are from Marees, ff. 14v, 23–23v, 24v–25, while the impossibility of over-charging by the Europeans is from Villault, pp. 320–1. Barbot's statement that the whites gave useless and short-weight goods 'in the last century' was a patriotic attempt to distinguish between the contemporary French and the earlier Europeans, the Portuguese and Dutch. But for other references to mutual distrust and fraudulent practices in Afro-European commerce on seventeenth-century Gold Coast, see Phillips 1732, p. 198; Jones 1983a, pp. 35, 248–9.

Cf. *1732*, p. 259/3–7.

[5] Barbot elaborates on the descriptions of brokers, interpreters and rowers cheating the 'peasants' who bring gold to the coast, and on hiding gold in the ears, in Marees, ff. 24–24v, 53v, and also on less specific statements in Dapper, p. 98/5. On traders cheating peasants, see Jones 1983a, pp. 34–5, 38–9.

Cf. *1732*, pp. 259/8–10, 260/1, which has clearer details, e.g. 'tho' some of those who imploy brokers to buy for them, are themselves at times present aboard the ships, yet those crafty factors will cheat them to their faces, either in concert with the supercargo, or by amusing them with some flam, whilst another broker or Black, who is in the secret, cuts off some part of the linen and stuff he has bought for them, or alters the weight of what is weighable, or mixes liquors with water'.

[6] The omitted sentences, blaming the Dutch for introducing competition between ships and creating the 'dash', are from Marees, ff. 23v–24, which puts the cost of the dash at 6–7%; while the reference to 'smaller men' is from Villault, p. 392. In 1678–9, Barbot first encountered the dash at Druyn on the Ivory Coast (*1679*, p. 272).

Cf. *1732*, p. 260/2–4.

[7] Omission of two paragraphs, the first describing when the merchants board and leave the ships and how they are received ashore, and the second describing how gold is brought from the interior by armed slaves. Although Barbot must have been familiar with the scene, he adds nothing to Marees, ff. 23, 27, 28–28v, and Villault, pp. 323–4.

Cf. *1732*, p. 260/5–6, 261/2, which has the merchants leaving, at 'eleven of the clock', and elsewhere substitutes material from Bosman, pp. 92–3 – apart from the Additional Passage.

[8] For the price of slaves in 1678–9, see Debien 1979, pp. 248–50; and for the uses of ivory on Gold Coast, see Marees, ff. 16v, 47; Jones 1983a, p. 255. It is unlikely that any ivory came from the Congo. The last sentence appears to be the earliest reference to the manufacture of candles on Gold Coast.

Cf. *1732*, p. 261/3–5, which adds that slaves are carried 'two, three or more aboard together in a canoo', and that in 1682 there was 'almost a general peace', so that slaves were 'two or three pieces of eight a man dearer than on my previous voyage' – perhaps the 'pieces of eight' correspond to the *poids* of the earlier text: for the *poids*, reckoned as two ounces (of gold), see Letter 2/21, p. 87 and note 15, below.

[9] The seascape has an original backcloth of the coast between named places, 'Cabo Corso' and 'Manfrou', with a vessel lying off on the left. But the canoe in the centre is copied from Marees, plate 8, where the occupants are said to be merchants, not slaves. A version of the illustration appeared in *1732*, Plate 9 (p. 156), 'Negro's Cannoes, carrying Slaves on Board of Ships att Manfroe', with the extended coast now named from Mina to Mourée, and more ships in the distance.

[10] On slave-porters, see Dapper, p. 86/8; Kea 1982, p. 254; Jones 1983a, p. 252.

[11] In 1679 Barbot saw more than 300 canoes line-fishing off Anomabu, and he recorded a brief description of the method as seen earlier off Axim (*1679*, pp. 281, 318). In the present passage, the second and third sentences are from Marees, ff. 13–13v, 60v, the position of the men in the canoes repeats Marees, f. 61, and the cutlass and bread are from Villault, p. 325. (Other sources say that the fishermen chewed sugar-cane: Jones 1983a, pp. 112, 233.) The fire for cooking may be original or may derive from the fire for attracting fish at night in Marees, f. 61. (In daytime, fire in the canoe was also useful for lighting tobacco: Jones 1983a, pp. 232–3.) A similar list of fishing towns, a reference to 400–500 fishing canoes at Mina, and the contrary statement that fishermen were more esteemed there than mer-chants, are in Dapper, pp. 75/2, 5, 104/6, 105/1.

Cf. *1732*, p. 261/6–8, with small additions from Bosman, p. 128 (size of canoes, hooks), and the number of canoes increased to 800. Elsewhere

Barbot says of Mina: 'I have often seen seven or eight hundred canoos come out from thence, at a time, for several mornings together, to fish with hooks and lines about a league or two off at sea; each canoo having, some two, some three, some four paddlers. I was so pleas'd with the sight of such a number of canoos thus plying about, that I could not forbear representing them in the print here adjoin'd' ('Plate 9' in the margin, in error for Plate 8) (*1732*, p. 156/10 – see Letter 2/5, note 30 above). This may have been additionally inspired by – 'I have frequently told Five or Six Hundred Canoes which [at Mina] went a Fishing every Morning' (Bosman, p. 43).

[12] The illustration shows the coast between Mina and Mourée, with vessels, but despite what Barbot says about drawing on the spot, the canoes are copied from Marees, plate 9. The redrawn version on *1732*, Plate 8 (p. 156), presents more canoes and a different coastline, from Ampeny to Mina. Since the drawing does not appear in the 1678–9 journal, if any part of the drawing was done on the spot it was presumably in 1682.

[13] Elaborates on Villault, pp. 325–6.

Cf. *1732*, p. 261/8.

[14] Gold Coast fishermen by this date used hooks purchased from Europeans or made them themselves out of imported pins and needles (Marees, f. 26v; Jones 1983a, p. 232).

Cf.*1732*, p. 261/9, which adds a reference to sword-fish from Bosman, p. 130.

[15] The first two sentences about fishing methods contain material from Marees, f. 61–61v, and Villault, pp. 325–6, but in 1678 Barbot briefly described line-fishing (*1679*, p. 281).

Cf. *1732*, p. 261/8, which adds that 'those who stay out later, design to dispose of their fish aboard the ships for brandy, garlick, hooks, and other inconsiderable things; as thread, needles, pipes, pins, tobacco, bugles, ordinary knives, old hats, old coats, small ordinary looking-glasses, etc.'.

[16] Omission of twelve sentences, on fishing seasons and individual fish, all from Marees, ff. 61v–62v, except that Barbot gives alternative names for pike ('bequné') and *korcofado* ('lune').

Cf. *1732*, p. 261/10, which cuts most of the material, but it appears instead in p. 224/2, 6, 11.

[17] Bonito and dolphin-fish were among those described by Marees, ff. 78v–79. The illustration shows four fish, of which a *sardine* and an unnamed small fish were sketched at Komenda in 1679 (*1679*, p. 290), the remaining two being a *nègre* and a *crapaut de mer*. They reappear in *1732*, Plate 18 (p. 216), as the 'King Fish als. Negro Fish, the Comendo Fish of the Taste of Pilchard, a Comendo Fish, the Sea Toad'.

Cf. *1732*, pp. 223/5–224/21, which describes varieties of fish at length, partly following the many scattered references to fish in the present text, including those in this passage, but mainly from Bosman, pp. 277–80, with occasional minor additions, as follows. 'Brazilian cod' is compared with Newfoundland; flounders are not as good as in Europe, a reversal of Bosman, by unintentional clumsy wording; plaice are compared with 'Cabo Verde half-moon' and thornbacks, and lobsters are 'as in the print drawn at cape Verde'; pike are called by the French *Begune* (sic); mackerel are not 'exactly shaped like ours in England; therefore the French call them *Trezahar*; looking as beautiful in the sea, as our mackarel, of a fine emerald green, mix'd with a silver white on the back'; 'Carangoues' are 'of two sorts, the one having large round eyes, and the other small ones, as in the same plate [*margin:* Plate 6]. They have large forked fins on their backs, and very thick forked tails.' For larger contributions by Barbot, see the Additional Passages. Barbot refers to Plates 6, 18–20 (pp. 101, 206, 224), which mainly repeat illustrations nos. 9 (fish taken near Cape Verde), 20, (81), (82), (113), (114), (117). Earlier versions of the drawings of some of the fish appeared in *1679*, pp. 260, 266–7, 290 (the last not reproduced in the printed edition). Barbot's bonito is probably *Parathunnus obesus*; the dolphin-fish is *Coryphaena hippurus* or *equisetis* (Debien 1979, pp. 386, n. 75; 392, n. 172); for *carangues* and *trezahar*, see Letter 1/16, note 57, above. For further material on dolphin-fish, see Letter 3/17, p. 218 and note 6, below.

[18] In 1679 Barbot noted that he saw only one example of this fish, for which the fishermen at Komenda asked three *acquiers* of gold, and that it was seven feet long and brown all over like a porpoise (*1679*, p. 290). The fish, a species of swordfish, may be *Istiophorus albicans* (Debien 1979, p. 388, n. 102). It may be the 'devil's fish' reported in the 1660s (Jones 1983a, p. 235). The drawing, copied from *1679*, p. 290 (not reproduced), appears again in *1732*, Plate 18 (p. 216). For more on this fish, see the Additional Passage.

[19] Inspired by Marees, ff. 62v–63, and Villault, pp. 326–7, but the claim that the same men work on the sea and in rivers is Barbot's and probably wrong, since inland fishing appears to have been normally done by women. The last sentence is obscure – perhaps it refers to drying the net. Cf. *1732*, p. 262/1, which is briefer and omits the last sentence.

[20] Omission of six sentences on night-fishing, from Marees, ff. 60v–61. Cf. *1732*, p. 262/2-3.

[21] Embroidered version of Marees, f. 62–62v. Cf. *1732*, pp. 261/9-10, 262/3-4, which adds material on net-fishing from Bosman, pp. 129–30.

[22] In 1679 Barbot reported that at Cape Coast the Africans collected shellfish such as crabs, mussels, oysters and limpets, and that at Anomabu the oysters were so large that one man could hardly eat two of them (*1679*, pp. 304, 318). He now inserts a few personal references into material on rock-fishing, mussels, and cast-nets from Marees, ff. 62v–63. The references

to the English and England suggest that this section of the account was written after 1685, and may indicate that, although writing in French, he was unconsciously shifting his attention away from a readership in France. Yet contrariwise, when compiling much later his English version, Barbot recollects experiences of his childhood in France (as in the reference from *1732* below). Spanish mackerel (*Scomberomorus tritor*), known in Twi/Fante as *safur*, was also referred to at this time as *ohenn' enám* 'king's fish' (Bosman, p. 278; Jones 1983a, pp. 234, 295). For oysters and rock-fishing, see ibid., pp. 232–3, 238–9. The illustration is copied from Marees, plate 9 (bis, 'La Pescherie de nuict').

Cf. *1732*, p. 262/5–8, which clarifies, including the following changes or additions : 'a sort of iron tool, shaped much like that, with which the country people of Aulnix in France and the isle of Rhe kill congers', 'muscles, as sweet as those of Charon near Rochel', 'oysters . . . commonly tough, and the best way of eating them is boil'd, and then cut in pieces and fry'd'. Also cf. *1732*, p. 223/2 – 'The King Fish, represented in the cut [Plate 18], is reckoned by the English at cape Corso, one of the best fishes in those parts, when in season . . . At full growth it is about five foot long . . . Some call it the the Saffer, and others the Negro, for its black skin. It commonly harbours among rocks, and sometimes comes into such shallow water, that the Blacks, when they go to strike fish at night, with a light, as I have observ'd before, will sometimes kill these with an iron tool, or with a three-pointed harping iron, or morlin' (the omitted material is from Bosman, p. 278). A three-pronged harpoon is shown on Marees, plate 9 bis.

[23] Partly because of the re-arrangement of the sequence of the account, and partly because of the influence of Bosman, material on fishes and cetaceans which appeared in *1688* either earlier, in relation to the western coast of Guinea, or later, in relation to the Sahara and the courses to America, is in *1732* gathered together (as 'fish in the sea of Guinea') and inserted in the Gold Coast section, where it forms a separate chapter (chapter XVI, pp. 222/8–227/9). There is no corresponding chapter in *1688*. The original material in this *1732* chapter is presented here, even though Barbot states that certain items were seen elsewhere than on Gold Coast.

[24] The fish is perhaps the opher, *Lampris regius*. The following paragraph (p. 223/4), here omitted, discusses fish as gods, with references to Biblical and ancient history.

[25] The reference to the machoran's horn, taken from Marees, f. 62v, originally appeared in an omitted section of Letter 2/20, p. 80; the reference to its beard is from Bosman, p. 278. The machoran is a Silurid gen. *Arius* (Debien 1979, p. 386, n. 76). In 1678, when South of Cape Verde, Barbot drew a machoran (*1679*, p. 260), and this was repeated in illustrations no. 9 (Letter 1/7 above) and no. (113) (Letter 3/20 below), together with a drawing of another sort of machoran: both drawings reappeared in *1732*, Plates

19 (p. 224), 20 (p. 224), but the Cape Verde fish was now labelled 'The Cat Fish alias Machoran of America' and the other one labelled 'The Cat Fish of Cape Verde'.

[26] Omission of one paragraph on grampuses, from Bosman, pp. 280, 407–8, although Barbot adds – 'as I could discern at a very small distance, for they would sometimes come within pistol-shot of our ships, in the open sea'. In Letter 3/20, p. 231, below, Barbot mentions *souffleurs* seen on the course to America, perhaps in 1682, since they are not mentioned in the 1679 journal, but does not describe them.

[27] Omission of one paragraph describing how grampuses approach land and drive fish away, from Bosman, p. 280.

[28] Omission of the remainder of this paragraph and the next two paragraphs, on sharks eating dead slaves, largely from Bosman, pp. 281–2. Barbot inserts – 'I have often observ'd, that when one threw a dead slave into the sea, particularly about the mouth of the bay of the Prince's Island in the gulph of Guinea, one shark would bite off a leg, and another an arm, whilst others sunk down with a body; and all this was done in less than ten minutes ...'. The reference is to Plate 32 (p. 536), the original drawing having been made in 1678 when a shark was hauled aboard off Sierra Leone (*1679*, p. 262; see illustration no. (110), in Letter 3/17, p. 217, below). However, the description of the shark that follows the omission is not in *1688* (on p. 2/218, near the end of his text, Barbot says he will describe sharks 'another time'), and may be derived, at least in part, from an untraced source (sharks being described in many accounts of voyages to many parts of the world). The *1679* and *1732* descriptions share only certain details, and the former has the following additional points: the shark was 6½ feet long and very heavy; its stomach contained a cuttlefish, two crabs and a palm-nut; its liver, ¾ of an ell in length, supplied 8 *pintes* of oil; its teeth were like a saw, its jaw two feet wide, some sharks being of a size to eat a whole man; its colour that of the *roussette*; its skin hard and in places a finger thick; its flesh not bad to eat and Barbot ate some (*1679*, p. 261).

[29] The first part of the sentence echoes Bosman, p. 281. The Roussette appears on Plate 32 (p. 536) and is discussed on p. 527/2–3 – see Letter 3/17, p. 218 and note 5, below.

[30] The middle sentence echoes Bosman, p. 282.

[31] Omission of two paragraphs, on the infrequency of sharks on Gold Coast and frequency at Fida and Ardra, and on blacks eating sharks, from Bosman, p. 281.

[32] A marginal note refers to Plate 19 (p. 224), the original drawing having been made in 1679 after Barbot left São Tomé, when two porpoises were harpooned (*1679*, p. 355). Another drawing, on Plate 29 (p. 497), was by James Barbot and shows the 'Sea Hogg, als. Porpoise'. In his 1678–9 journal

Barbot recorded a description less full than that in *1732*, but with the following additional points: some call it the sea-pig, the flesh is black all over, it breathes out a jet of water, it returns if any of the pack is wounded and bleeding (*1679*, p. 355). Although the *1679* illustration re-appears as illustration no. (114), in Letter 3/20, p. 229, below, the porpoise is not described. Note that this drawing has been described as that, not of a porpoise, but of a dolphin of the sub-family *Delphiniae* (Debien 1979, p. 391, n. 165)

[33] The reference is to Plate 32 (p. 536), and the fish is mentioned on p. 527/ 2–4. Barbot's sucker fish or remora is *Echeneis naucrates*: although in 1679 he confused it with the pilot fish, *Naucrates ductor* (*1679*, p. 358), he later drew and recognized the latter.

[34] A marginal note refers to Plate 19 (p. 224), whose two flying fish are those shown in illustrations no. (113), in Letter 3/20, p. 229, and no. (117), in Letter 3/20, p. 233, below, but they are different from the fish drawn in 1679 off Príncipe Island (*1679*, p. 355).

[35] Plate 7 (p. 104) shows birds diving on flying fish, and was copied from illustration no. (116), in Letter 3/20, p. 132, below, with a waterspout added from illustration no. 1, in Letter 1/1, p. 16, above.

[36] This appears to be embroidery of two neighbouring statements in Marees, f. 62v, one on net-fishing, the other on catching sharks.

[37] In 1679, Barbot collected a score of gold ornaments and sketched them, and he stated that he had seen others 'such as *burgauds* in filigree, *éguières* [?], hunting horns, large rings, collars, and hand-guards for swords and cutlasses' (*1679*, p. 339). Barbot's enthusiasm for the goldwork of Gold Coast, exemplified in his drawings of many objects, was largely original and novel. Marees and Dapper said little about gold-working, perhaps because it was less developed earlier: Villault praised the gold-work and Barbot draws a little from this source (Villault, pp. 393–4). However, Barbot was wrong in stating that the art had been originally learned from the Europeans, although certain techniques may have benefitted from contacts with the European goldsmiths who served in some of the forts: for pre–1600 references to gold ornaments and rings, see Hakluyt 1589, pp. 96, 106; Crone 1937, p. 118; Garrard 1980, pp. 107–11. For seventeenth-century references to various objects in gold (hatbands, rings, fetishes, tooth-pieces, chains, animals, etc), and for a brief 1660s account of the techniques, see COP V-gK 187; *Relation* 1674, pp. 20–1; Jones 1983a, pp. 251–2, 267. Barbot says little about techniques, presumably because he did not actually witness African goldsmiths at work. For his drawing of gold ornaments, see Letter 2/17, note 9, above.

Cf. *1732*, p. 157/2 (which relates goldworking only to Mina), and pp. 262/ 9–10, which begins by conflating the *1688* comment on the techniques of the goldsmith with material on blacksmithing from Bosman, p. 128, and otherwise enlarges slightly, to include the following remarks. 'I brought over several pieces of figures, but particularly that of a periwinkle [i.e. *burgaud*], as big as an ordinary goose-egg; which were all much admired at Rochel and Paris, and even by the best goldsmiths. The thread and texture of their hatbands and chain-rings is so fine, that I am apt to believe, our European ablest artists would find it difficult to imitate them. For the satisfaction of the reader I have taken the pains to draw most of the pieces of both goldsmiths and black-smiths work in the cut . . .'. For Barbot's description of his collection of gold objects, see the Additional Passage. For Akan goldworking and Barbot's objects, see Garrard 1989, pp. 44–5, 56, 60, 62–3.

[38] Omission of a passage on gold being so common that women and men wear large quantities and kings give it away, from Villault, pp. 394–5.

[39] Embroidery on Villault, pp. 395–6, which mentions the fried chicken but not the 'Niger' (a northern river, where, in fact, palm-wine would not be the drink). A marginal note explains that the blacks believe that the Europeans grow their merchandise 'like grass': the references to African opinions on European wealth echo Marees, f. 37, and Villault, p. 260. Omitted in *1732*.

[40] This repeats complaints made earlier about farming in Senegal (Letter 1/7, pp. 36–7, above): it also echoes Dapper, p. 105/2 (and for a similar independent, albeit biassed, European judgement, see Hillier 1697, p. 690). Barbot's lack of knowledge of Gold Coast agriculture is a reminder that, as a brief sea-borne visitor, he saw only the marine littoral, and in practice little more than the beaches. The complaint about the cost of maize repeats a remark in Letter 2/10, p. 38, above – see note 15 of that Letter. In 1679 Barbot bought 20 chests (1 chest = 2½ heaped bushels) of *gros mil* on the coast, and complained that it cost 8 *aquiers* a chest at Accra, because of war, against 1½–2 *aquiers* elsewhere (*1679*, pp. 250, 324). The reason for the availability of corn at certain places on Gold Coast was presumably not simply the relative industry of the local people but also favorable ecological and market conditions; for instance, much Elmina maize was consumed locally or kept for Dutch ships.

Cf. *1732*, p. 265/16, which abbreviates, but is less critical of African farmers (despite Bosman, p. 298) and where it is noted that, as in Europe, famine may proceed from other causes than war. Barbot discusses maize prices at length in *1732*, p. 197/3–6, but this is from Bosman, p. 298.

[41] In his 1679 journal, Barbot inserted two drawings, the first drawing of 18 objects brought away from Gold Coast, apparently all of gold, drawn natural size, and therefore very small in reality (so sometimes called 'beads'), all ornaments for women or girls, but not individually labelled or described; and the second drawing of larger objects, mostly of wood or iron, but

including one gold ring. The items are labelled and described in detail (*1679*, pp. 339, 345). The 'petites bagatelles' shown in illustration no. (76) (in Letter 2/17, p. 64 above) are wooden combs and objects in ivory as well as gold objects: the objects are unlabelled and not individually described, but Barbot says, less than accurately, that 'nearly all are worked from gold or from Conta da Terra'. There appear to be about 25 gold objects, most of them ornaments similar to those illustrated in *1679*. Finally, *1732*, Plate 22 (p. 251), engraved by the artist Jan Kip, which is described by Barbot in the Additional Passage, contains some 40 objects which might be of gold. The necklace, hat-band, six bracelets and a manilla bracelet, two arm-bands, two skulls, and a 'periwinkle' can be distinguished, and there remain some 25 of the small gold objects previously illustrated. Because all the items were redrawn by Barbot in *1688* and engraved by another artist in *1732*, and almost certainly sometimes drawn from another angle or side, or with inexact detail, only a minority can be identified with certainty and traced through the three plates. However, if the six bracelets and the manilla of *1732* are the same as those drawn in *1679*, which are described in detail, then only one bracelet was of gold; and the hunting horn described as of gold in *1732* much resembles one described as of ivory in *1679*. Hence the total of gold objects in the engraving is probably about 35. Because of the uncertainty of identification, it is impossible to say precisely how many gold objects are altogether recorded, but it is clear that Barbot drew a large number, particularly of the smaller ones, and that the number illustrated was added to, at least slightly, on each occasion. This makes it likely that Barbot actually owned a proportion of the objects, even when in England, and almost certain that Kip engraved the plate during Barbot's lifetime. As Barbot implies in the *1688* passage, it appears that he collected gold objects mostly during his first voyage. A goldsmith was aboard who perhaps advised and encouraged him (*1679*, pp. 309, 313). For a redrawing of all of Barbot's objects, see Garrard 1989, pp. 62–3.

[42] Two objects to the right of the hunting horn, one perhaps a horse's tail, are not listed. Flat arm-rings worn by women, similar to those in the drawings, were mentioned by Marees, f. 86v. The items listed in the passage but not actually of gold are discussed in the next Letter.

[43] In 1679 Barbot had learned that Takoradi was a centre for canoe-making, especially for the canoes purchased by European ships, and he observed, at sea, large canoes with sails, used, he suggested, by the Dutch to convey goods to Ardra and Benin, and carrying up to eight tons (*1679*, pp. 286, 289, 304). In the present passage the method of canoe-making (clumsily described), and what follows, apart from the references to Juda and Ardra, are from Marees, f. 59v, and Dapper, p. 101/4–103/2, with some embroidery. (Note that the crew of a large canoe must be an odd number of individuals, to allow for a steersman.) For drawings of these canoes, see note

51 below; and for other references to them, see Letter 2/3, p. 7 and note 51, above; Letter 3/20, p. 228, below. For the historical use of canoes in West Africa, see Smith 1970.

Cf. *1732*, pp. 266/1–3, 6, 268/2–4, which enlarges helpfully. The sizes of canoes are different (from 40' x 6' to 14' x 3–4'), perhaps representing a compromise with Bosman, p. 129; the canoes are made from Capot trees, which are 'very porous and soft' (the name of the tree from Bosman, p. 295); the sides are 'somewhat rounded, so that it is somewhat narrower just at the top, and bellies out a little lower, that they may carry the more sail: the head and stern are raised long, and somewhat hooked, very sharp at the end'.

[44] Inaccurate or badly worded, paddles being formed in one piece.

[45] The description of canoes being rowed echoes Marees, f. 58v, but like the rest may be from personal observation. In his 1679 journal Barbot included a useful bird's-eye view of a large canoe, and drawings of a paddle and of a stool used as a seat in canoes (confirming Marees, f. 58v); and he recorded that the rowers sat towards the stern and that seats were placed at intervals forward, 'in order to sail more conveniently without getting wet'. Further, he noted that overturned canoes were quickly righted, and that goods were saved, because in small canoes they were lodged under a slatted 'deck' (*pont à barreaux*). He was warned about the dangerous breakers at Ardra, and he noted that, at Kormentin, pinnaces could not land and instead use had to be made of 'nasty little canoes which can hardly carry two men', but he did not refer to specific incidents (*1679*, pp. 304, 312, 319, 345–6). It was stated in 1671 that certain canoes built on the Ivory Coast were no use as 'bar canoes' because they had rounded bottoms (Delbée 1671, p. 370).

Cf. *1732*, pp. 266/4–5, 7, 267/1, which clarifies, enlarges or changes several points. The rowers sit on 'benches, or boards nail'd athwart the canoo', the paddles are shaped 'like a spade, about three feet long, with a small round handle about the same length' (perhaps from Bosman, p. 129), the rowers 'being excellent swimmers and divers' recover goods from upset canoes (the obscure reference to fishermen and poles may also relate to recovery of goods). Barbot observes that the danger is greater in the months of April to July, as well as at high tides, and especially so at Fida and Ardra, where 'dismal accidents are very frequent, and great quantities of goods are lost, and many men drown'd; whereas at the Gold Coast those things happen but seldom, tho' they use smaller canoos, the landing being nothing near so bad as at those other places. I have gone several times ashore at the Gold Coast, both in great and small canoos, without any ill accident, by reason of the good management of the paddlers, who were all chosen men, and because it was always at the best seasons: yet I must own, that sometimes I escaped narrowly, and wish'd my self elsewhere, being in a small canoo, for a quarter of an hour, or better, waiting between two dreadful waves, and rolling surges, for a proper minute to launch thro' the breaking sea, before Cormentin, which is generally the most dangerous landing-place of all the Gold Coast; in such a manner that it almost made my hair stand up on end with horror. At another place, I think it was Mouree, I ventured to go ashore in the pinnace, and landed pretty well; but the worst was to get off again: to which purpose I hir'd several Blacks, who, with my own men, all swimming with one hand, kept the head of the pinnace right against the rolling waves, but could not prevent my being thoroughly wet.' The description of crossing the surf, being somewhat clearer in *1732*, is given in the Additional Passage. For an earlier reference to the canoe-men at Mina, see *1732*, p. 157/1 – an Additional Passage to Letter 2/5 above.

[46] Cf. *1732*, p. 266/8. This is better put and makes it clear that the rowers jump into the canoe after swimming with it.

[47] Based on Marees, f. 59v, Dapper, p. 103/2, and Villault, p. 325, but slightly enlarged, perhaps from observation, Barbot adding the rigging and the animal heads.

Cf. *1732*, pp. 267/4, 268/1, which adds that 'the European canoes have commonly European canvas and cordage'.

[48] Omission of three sentences, on canoe-making at Agitaki, and on the terms *ehem*, *almadia*, and 'canoe', from Marees, f. 58v.

Cf. *1732*, p. 268/5, which adds that the word 'canoo' comes from the West Indies.

[49] The term 'bar canoos' was introduced by Barbot in *1732*, p. 266/5, for the canoes crossing the surf at Fida and Ardra, *barre* being the term employed in *1688* for the breakers or surf on open beaches, as well as for the breakers marking the 'bar' of rivers.

[50] Based on Marees, ff. 59, 93v–94v, Villault, pp. 237–8, and Dapper, p. 97/6. Note that while contemporary Europeans swam breast-stroke, some Africans swam an over-arm stroke, perhaps a form of the crawl. For a contemporary account of children learning to swim, see Jones 1983a, p. 109. The last sentence repeats a description in *1732*, p. 243/3.

[51] The 'pleasure-boat' first appeared on the drawing of Fort Christiansborg (*1679*, p. 333), but was later transferred to the drawing of Fort Frederiksborg (illustration no. (63), in Letter 2/6, p. 25, above; cf. *1732*, Plate 14 (p. 177) – the second canoe being added). The 'great canoos', sometimes with one or two sails raised, are on drawings of Mina castle (illustration no. (61), in Letter 2/5, p. 17, above; cf. *1732*, Plate 8 (p. 156)); of Cape Coast castle (*1679*, p. 303; cf. *1732*, Plate 10 (p. 169), labelled C, 'A large Canoe of abt. 12 Tuns'; but not illustration no. (62), in Letter 2/6, p. 25, above); of Fort Christiansborg (*1732*, Plate 15 (p. 182), twice, but not on the previous versions (*1679*, p. 333, and illustration no. (70), in Letter 2/10, p. 37, above); and of Cape Ruygehoeck (illustration no. (67), in Letter 2/8,

p. 32, above; cf. *1732*, Plate 15 (p. 182)). Small canoes and European boats appear on most seascape illustrations, the latter being difficult to distinguish, when in the distance, from large canoes.

[52] The reference is to the two illustrations in *1732*, Plate 9 (p. 156). The 'exactly drawn' canoe is in fact copied from Marees, plate 8.

[53] In 1679 Barbot noted potters but did not describe or draw their products (*1679*, pp. 304, 339). Pottery was practised in West Africa for centuries, if not millennia, before the Europeans arrived: that additional skills were acquired from contacts with the Portuguese is not implausible but is unproven. For a contemporary view of Gold Coast pottery, see Jones 1983a, p. 255.

Cf. *1732*, p. 268/8–9, which is slightly enlarged – e.g., 'jugs, pipkins, pots and troughs of various sizes', 'vessels endure the most violent heat' (replaces the reference to keeping their heat), 'the leaves of palm-trees, or of Indian wheat, or rushes'.

[54] This echoes the making of straw hats and dyed bark cloth in Marees, f. 13v, although these activities are there ascribed to girls. Barbot appears to be the only source to refer to the making of bark-cloth on looms, surely an invention: Marees merely stated that the best bark-cloth looked 'as if made on a loom'. For references to making of hats, see Jones 1983a, pp. 86, 113, 196.

Cf. *1732*, p. 268/10.

[55] The substance of this passage on dues is from Marees, ff. 28v–29v, and Villault, pp. 328–30, and the rest is probably embroidery and invention. Cf. *1732*, pp. 274/7–275/3, 261/8, which has 3% instead of one fortieth and one shilling instead of 15 *sols*, and the peasant is fined for *not* carrying weapons. And the reference to fishermen selling to vessels is enlarged (quoted in note 15 above).

LETTER 21

The fairs and markets established on Gold Coast, the way the people there buy and sell, and their weights and measures [and also how their slaves are treated and traded].

[. . ./p. 86/. . .][1] This letter will discuss the fairs and markets of these lands, the way these people sell things, their weights, scales and measures, their money and their way of counting.[2] What you now see follows on my previous letter. These blacks have established markets and fairs at many places in their lands, both on the coast and inland, some of them larger than others according to the locality

546

where they are held. It might be said, indeed, that each village has its own, but at these only the necessities of life and the products of the land are sold. I do not think it useful to pause in order to detail to you all the markets, but I believe it will be sufficient for you if I tell you only about the market at Corso, which is said to be the largest in all Gold Coast, and even the largest in all Guinea.

It is held daily, in a large open space at the end of the town, where the traders of the place and the neighbourhood gather together from daybreak, with those goods produced locally and those obtained from the Europeans. Each trader has his/her own position, the open space being divided up in such a way that all those of the same trade and selling the same goods are placed together.[3] The goods always sold there are the following: sugar-cane, plantains (*bananes*), bananas (*baccovens*), [sweet] potatoes, yams, lemons, oranges, rice, millet, maize, maniguette [pepper], bread, cakes, fish (raw, boiled or fried), palm-oil, eggs, pumpkins, purslane, the beer called *pitou*, fire-wood, roofing material, and country tobacco in untreated leaves.[4] The other traders of the coasts also bring there many kinds of European goods, which they buy from the whites. In the afternoon the peasants arrive with their palm wine and the fishermen with their fresh fish.[5] Most of these goods are retailed by women, who, as I have told you, also have the care of the household. It is women too who buy the goods, for the upkeep of their families. Women are so eager for gain that they come every morning from five or six leagues around to bring in small quantities of goods, and they make their way back after midday, singing and sporting with each other, despite carrying, as well as their goods, often a baby on their back. They exchange their goods for fish or something else, of which they give part to the fetishes they encounter on their way home.[6] Palm wine is the commodity which sells best here, because it is brought to the market at almost the same time as the fishermen and brokers return from the sea, where they have always made some money, which they disburse mainly on this wine, drinking it to excess. This results in most of them becoming drunk before nightfall, but you never see any of them disorderly in the market, the law and order (*la bonne police*) established there keeping everyone well-behaved.[7] The market is not held on Tuesdays, this being their Sunday.[8] Individuals who live in the neighbourhood, and the vessels in the roadstead at Corso, draw great benefit from this market because of the goods to be obtained there. In particular, the sailors get their victuals there, which they buy with pieces of garlic, pins, mirrors, ribbons, firearms, and other trifles.[9] As I have stated, elsewhere there are other markets in several places, and [also] fairs. The latter are held only twice a year, and, within the same territory, never on the same day, lest one prejudice another. As at Corso, all sorts of African and European goods are sold at these fairs, and some of them are attended by crowds of people.[10] /p. 87/

Formerly the Moors in their markets traded goods for goods, but since the Portuguese have passed on to them the making of *kra-kra* (or *Denieros Pey*) which the Europeans thought up to enable them to buy small commodities, these peoples have latterly coined this sort of money to such an extent that today on Gold Coast considerable payments are made in it.[11] I do not remember, Sir, if I have told you that this *kra-kra* is made from gold mixed with a little melted red copper, and then cut up into many shapes a bit like these [*six small ink blobs of varying shapes*] and this size, the commonest shape being squarish. The Acra people have almost none of this money in use among them, but instead have certain little iron pins (*broches*) of the shape and size you see in the margin [*margin: a drawing of a thin pin with a half-moon head, about 4 cm long*] This *kra-kra* money is not counted [but weighed]. You pay with it as with gold dust, if you have bought something worth more than one *acquier*. And if less, either they weigh it against *taccous*, or they take a pinch of it with their fingers, depending how it is thought correct to present it.[12]

Nowadays in many places they have the use of weights and scales. Some make them themselves, others buy them from the whites. The scales they make are not exact, because they are not well hung, having no pointer, but only, in the middle of the beam, which is of wood, a string through which they pass a thumb or forefinger, to hold up the scale. However, they hardly ever are mistaken in using them.

[illustration no. (84), scales and beans][13]

The *taccous* I have mentioned to you are black and red peas. Nine *taccous* make one *acquier*. The interior people make their weights from a yellow, heavy wood, or else they use black and red beans. The coastal people have copper weights, which they cast and mould, then file them down to bring them in line with those of the whites.[14] They have no weights of a *marc* or a pound. When they have weighed

548

out one *benda*, which is two ounces, they begin another. They call 2 ounces one '*benda*'; 1 ounce, '*affa*'; ½ ounce, '*egebba*'; 5 *gros*, '*assuwa*'; 3 *gros*, '*siyou*'; 2 *gros*, '*ensamjo*'; ¾ of a *poids* or 1½ *gros*, '*quientay*'; ½ of a *poids* or 1 *gros*, '*agiraguer*'; ¼ of a *poids* or ½ *gros*, '*mediataba*'. More commonly they say *aquier*, which is divided, as I have said, into nine or ten *taccous*. All these different weights, taken together, make the *marc* one lighter than ours by half an ounce.[15] [...][16]

Linen cloths and other woven or woollen material are measured by the arm-span (*brassée*) which they call *jectam* and which is more than one and a half times ours.[17] Slaves are priced the same way as all other goods, and hence one says – 'so much gold's worth of slaves', 'so much gold's worth of goods'. However, slaves are fairly often traded by the 'piece', for a certain amount of goods, as is appropriate. For instance, three *ancres* of brandy for a young male slave, etc.; one *ancre* /p. 88/ of brandy, one piece of Coesveld linen, and a dozen knives, for a woman; and so on.[18] [...][19]

They have no knowledge of writing or books, unlike those near Cape Verde. They only have certain rules for memorizing, and I have remarked that they forget nothing.[20] They deal between themselves in the language of the country, and with the whites in *langue franque*. However, there are some who speak Dutch or English fairly correctly, and others good Portuguese, which all those on the coasts know something of, which greatly assists trade.[21]

As slaves are, you might say, a form of money among these Africans, I consider it appropriate to say something about them here, before I finish my letter. Slaves are either those who, having no means of subsistence, sell themselves to rich men for life, or those taken in war, or children sold by their parents because they cannot keep them, or, finally, those sold as slaves because they cannot pay the fines to which they have been condemned. But of all these, the largest number are those taken in war or seized in their homes and carried off.[22] The kings, nobles and merchants carry out this trade, excluding the common people.[23] Those among the slaves they keep with them always go about bare-headed. They can also be recognized by their often having on their backs the marks of their wretchedness, being covered with wounds from blows. They have little care taken of them, most of them lacking even the necessities of life. The wives and children of these poor souls are also slaves of those the husbands serve. When they die they are thrown in a ditch. I myself have seen instances.[24]

A good trade in slaves can be found on Gold Coast only when war with those of the interior has broken out and is fierce, as in 1681 when an English interloping vessel took 300 slaves/prisoners (*captifs*) at Comendo, with no more trouble than picking them up on the seashore, since the local people brought them there from the fighting with the Moors of the interior that had taken place the same day.[25] It is not so much the case that this does not happen all the time, as that the local people keep back prisoners so that they can work their lands and carry their goods.[26] On my latter voyage (1682), in all Gold Coast I took only eight.[27] It was a year of misfortune for these blacks, many being taken in war and sold elsewhere. I had some of them on board at Acra whom they came to buy back, giving me two other slaves for one man.[28] It even happened that I bought, at different times and places, a whole family of five persons. I have never seen as much joy as these poor people displayed when they found themselves thus reunited. They could not look at each other without weeping, but despite their tears one could see that that they reckoned themselves extremely fortunate that in their wretchedness they were sharing the hardship and sorrow. I did not care to separate them when I reached the Islands and I sold them to a single master.[29]

I will conclude with a point which may make you laugh. This is, that all the slaves, like most other blacks, believe that we buy them to eat them, as soon as we get back to France. It is this which makes many slaves die on the passage across, either from sorrow or from despair, there being some who refuse to eat or drink.[30] What do you say, Sir ? Do you have the appetite for such a dish ? I am, Sir, Yours etc. /p. 89/

Additional Passages from *1732*

[pp. 270/6–271/3, on the duty of using slaves well]

This barbarous usage of those unfortunate wretches makes it appear, that the fate of such as are bought, and transported from the coast to America or other parts of the world, by Europeans, is less deplorable than that of those who end their days in their native country; for aboard ships all possible care is taken to preserve and subsist them for the interest of the owners, and when sold in America, the same motive ought to prevail with their masters to use them well, that they may live the longer, and do them more service.[31] Not to mention the inestimable advantage

550

they may reap of becoming Christians, and saving their souls, if they make a true use of their condition; whereof some instances might be brought: tho' it must be owned, they are very hard to be brought to a true notion of the Christian religion, and much less to be prevail'd on to live up to its holy rules; being naturally very stupid and sensual, and so apt to continue till their end, without the least concern for a future state of eternal bliss, or misery, according as they have lived in this world. / It must also be own'd, that the Christians in America are much to be blamed in this particular; and more especially the protestants, which I beg leave to take notice of with some concern, take very little care to have their slaves instructed in the Christian religion; as if it were not a positive duty incumbent on them, by the precepts of Christianity, to procure the welfare of their servants souls, as well as that of their bodies. This has been expressly declared by two synods of the protestant churches of France, the one held at Roan, the other at Alencon, in 1637, upon the questions put in those assemblies by over-scrupulous persons, who thought it unlawful, that many protestant merchants, who had long traded in slaves from Guinea to America, should continue that traffick, as inconsistent with Christian charity. The synod thereupon, after a long discussion of the point, decreed as follows: Tho' slavery, as it has been always acknowledged to be of the right of nations, is not condemned in the word of God, and has not been abolished in most parts of Europe, by the manifestation of the gospel, but only by a contrary practice, insensibly introduced; nevertheless, since several merchants trading on the coast of Africa and to the Indies, where that traffick is permitted, acquire slaves of the Barbarians, either in exchange, or for money, the possession of whom they transmit to others by formal sales, or exchange; this assembly, confirming the rule made on that subject in Normandy, exhorts them not to abuse that liberty, contrary to Christian charity, and not to dispose of those poor infidels, but to such Christians as will use them with humanity; and above all will take care to instruct them in the true religion.

But how far most protestant planters and other inhabitants of European colonies in America, are from following such reasonable advice, every person that has conversed among them can tell. There, provided that the slaves can multiply, and work hard for the benefit of their masters, most men are well satisfied, without the least thoughts of using their authority and endeavours to promote the good of the souls of those poor wretches. In this particular, I must say, the Roman catholicks of the American plantations are much more commendable; for at Martinico, one of the French Caribbee islands, all who have been there may have observ'd, that every Sunday morning early there is a mass celebrated in the chappel of the Jesuits, called the mass of the Blacks, as being particularly appointed for those slaves in the island; and every planter, who lives within a reasonable distance of it, is oblig'd to send his Blacks to be present at it, and at other devotions, according to the service of the Roman church. / It is also notorious with what application the Portugueses have indeavour'd, for these two last centuries, to propagate their religion among the Blacks in general, at Guinea, Congo and Angola, by keeping a great number of missioners there, in several places: and even in Brasil, what care they take to instruct so many thousands of Black slaves, as are imploy'd in the service of their plantations, as shall be farther declar'd when I shall treat of those peoples sense or belief of religious worship.[32]

Before I leave this subject I shall mention two principal reasons, to pass by several others of less moment, which protestant planters usually alledge, in the English colonies of America, to excuse this neglect: the first, the great incumbrance it would be to a planter, who has a great number of slaves, some one, others two hundred and more, first to have them learn English, and afterwards to instruct every one of them in the principal articles of the protestant belief, those slaves being generally of a brutish temper, and preposses'd with fantastical superstitious practices of the grossest and most absurd paganism; which, in reality, most of them always adhere to, though they have liv'd ever so long among protestants. The other argument, on which many seem to lay much stress, is, that if their slaves were made Christians by baptism, etc. they should, according to the laws of the British nation, and the canons of its church, immediately lose the property they had before in those slaves; it being inconsistent with the protestant religion, that any of its professors should be kept in bondage for life. But this is a false notion, for neither the laws of the nation, nor the canons of the church of England, nor of any other Christian people in Europe, that I could ever hear of, do discharge any Black slave, that has receiv'd baptism, from continuing so till death. I have in this point had the opinion of very learned English and French divines, alledging one instance of the like case in Onesimus, a Christian slave, in whose behalf St Paul writes to Philemon, his master, in so affectionate a manner, vid. his epistle: by all which it is apparent, that in those times the primitive Christians had many slaves among them, who were also Christians.[33]

To conclude on this head, it may safely be affirmed, that if the protestants were careful to have their barbarian slaves baptiz'd, and well instructed in the principles and maxims of true Christianity, many of those poor wretches would behave themselves much more humanely and dutifully towards their masters and fellow-slaves than they do, for want of such instructions; and consequently we should not so often hear of their mutinying and deserting, as has been known at Barbadoes and other colonies. The maxims of Christianity would doubtless be a curb to their rude temper, and the planters might expect the blessing of heaven on their plantations, as a reward of their charitable endeavours to convert those gross pagans from their deplorable state of depravation in all malice and vileness towards God and man.

[p. 272/2, on slave mortality]

At the end of the supplement to this description, may be seen how I order'd the slaves to be us'd and manag'd in our passage from the coast to the West-Indies; which if it were well observed by other Europeans following that trade, would certainly save the lives of many thousands of those poor wretches every year, and render the voyages much more advantageous to the owners and adventurers; it being known by a long course of experience that the English particularly every year lose great numbers in the passage, and some ships two, three, and even four hundred out of five hundred shipp'd in Guinea.[34]

NOTES

[1] Omission of three introductory sentences.

[2] This list of contents closely resembles the title of a section in Villault, p. 251.

[3] In 1679 Barbot visited Cape Coast town, but his journal does not mention a market there, although later he briefly describes Gold Coast markets in general, with women selling fish, millet 'bread', palm oil and

wine, potatoes, pineapples, bananas, and 'figs' (*1679*, pp. 304, 340). In 1682 he probably visited the town again. However, his selection of this market almost certainly derives from Marees, who has a drawing of the market (plate 4), 'the finest market of all the towns', and Barbot's comment on its arrangement follows Marees, f. 32, and also Villault, pp. 251–2. Although no doubt Barbot did observe some Gold Coast markets, the account of markets that follows is based essentially on Marees, with a little additional from Villault, who was also borrowing from Marees.

Cf. *1732*, p. 268/11–269/2.

[4] The list of goods, longer than that in *1679*, mostly repeats Marees, f. 31v, and also resembles Villault, pp. 252–3 (who stated that the traders were too lazy to put their tobacco into twists). Barbot contributes to the list the five items from pumpkins to roofing material.

Cf. *1732*, pp. 269/2, where the list of goods substitutes earthenware for fire-wood, and translates *baccovens* as 'figs' (i.e. 'figs-of-India') and *gateaux* ('cakes') as *kankies* (Akan/Twi *kankyew* 'cake, boiled maize-bread', Christaller 1933), a term used by Marees, f. 99. For an earlier reference to kankies, see Letter 2/19, note 15 above.

[5] Repeats Marees, f. 31v; Villault, p. 252.

[6] The references to industrious and cheerful market women and the fetishes echo Marees, f. 31v.

Cf. *1732*, p. 269/2, which adds that the market traders are mostly women because they are 'fitter for it than the men, and commonly sharper than they for gain and profit', and that they arrive 'loaded like horses'.

[7] These sentences echo Marees, f. 32, which says that the men lay down their weapons, hence Barbot's 'never ... disorderly'.

Cf. *1732*, p. 269/3.

[8] Marees, f. 31; Villault, p. 255.

Cf. *1732*, p. 269/1.

[9] Enlarges on the remark that the Dutch go to the markets from their ships, in Marees, f. 31v. In 1679 Barbot recorded sailors trading garlic, but to fishermen (*1679*, p. 318).

Cf. *1732*, p. 269/4.

[10] Repeats Villault, p. 255.

Cf. *1732*, p. 269/5.

[11] Basically Marees, ff. 32v, 97v, and Dapper, p. 111/3. Barbot's 'Denerios Pey' (instead of Marees's 'Deniere en Pey') is presumably Portuguese *dinheiros de pais* 'country moneys', that is, small change. *Krakra* is usually explained as deriving from Akan/Twi *kakra* 'small'.

Cf. *1732*, p. 269/6, which omits the Portuguese term.

[12] Enlarges Marees, f. 32v, and Dapper, p. 111/3, with additional from Villault, p. 253.

Cf. *1732*, p. 269/6–7, which is briefer. The illustrations of the *krakra* and the Accra 'pin' reappear in *1732*, Plate 22 (p. 251).

[13] Barbot must have seen these scales, although they are not mentioned in *1679*, yet the description in part closely follows Marees, f. 29, hence Dapper, p. 109/2; and also in part repeats Villault, pp. 253–4; although Barbot omits to say that the pans of the scales are of copper. On scales, see Garrard 1980, pp. 172–3. Scales are not discussed in *1732*, contrary to what is said at p. 269/7. But the scales and beans of the illustration appear again on Plate 22 (p. 251) and are listed on p. 264/15 – see Letter 2/20, Additional Passage, above.

[14] Copper weights, and wooden weights and black and red beans used in the interior, are from Marees, ff. 29v–30, and Dapper, p. 109/3, while red seeds called *tacous* is from Villault, p. 254. The 'yellow, heavy wood' seems to be Barbot's contribution. On weighing by *taku* and *damma* seeds, see Garrard 1980, pp. 173–4.

Cf. *1732*, p. 234/4–5, 10, which adds and adjusts to material on *tacoes* and *dambas* in Bosman, p. 86.

[15] The names (with some miscopyings) and relative values are from Marees, f. 30, except that Barbot substitutes *gros* (an obsolete measure the equivalent of one eighth of an ounce) for *peso*, making two *gros* the equal of one *peso*. The *marc* was eight ounces, and the table makes the *poids* two ounces. The final confusing sentence simply means that each individual weight is slightly less than the weight in ounces given, as Marees stated. On weights and weighing in general, see the detailed study of Garrard 1980, chaps 6–8, and the table in Jones 1983a, pp. 330–1.

Cf. *1732*, p. 234/3–7, which substitutes *ackyes* for *gros* and adds material on 'angels' from Bosman, p. 85.

[16] Omission of one paragraph, on the weights at Accra, from Dapper, p. 109/4, but substituting for 80 *gulden* as the value of a 'large *benda*' the sum of '126 [*sic* – probably £ missing] in our money'. Barbot went wrong in the middle of the table, by missing out the 'small *benda*'. But since the lower weights are correct he cannot have been following the consistently wrong punctuation in the French translation of Dapper, as suggested by Garrard 1980, pp. 256, 272, n. 23.

Cf. *1732*, p. 234/8–10, which substitutes *ackyes* for *engels*, gives the value of the 'large *benda*' as 'worth in gold about an hundred and twenty French livres', and adds a little from Bosman, p. 86.

[17] Repeats Marees, f. 30, and Dapper, p. 109/5, but substitutes 1½ *brassées* for 2 *vadem*.

Cf. *1732*, p. 234/11, which adds a further borrowing from Marees, about strips of cloth used as girdles, but mistranslates as 'woollen' cloth, and adds that they 'have no other measure of that kind, calling it Paw, which is three quarters of a yard English', probably an untraced borrowing.

[18] 'Piece' (originally Spanish *pieza de Indias*) normally meant a prime slave (so that a woman or child was only part of a piece), but Barbot fails to make this clear. Among Barbot's slave purchases in 1679 were instances of the prices he quotes (Debien 1979, pp. 248–9).

Cf. *1732*, p. 235/1, which is abbreviated, Barbot promising to enlarge later, yet on p. 269/7, and again on p. 272/1, he merely refers back to the earlier reference, only adding that the set rate for slaves is 'alterable according to the times'.

[19] Omission of one paragraph on counting methods, derived from Marees, f. 30, including a promise to insert a table of 'their numbers'. In fact, Barbot eventually inserts (Letter 3/14, p. 193, below) both Marees' appendix of Akan/Twi and Adangme numbers (Marees, ff. 127v–128) and his own Akan/Twi numbers, first recorded in his 1678–9 journal (*1679*, p. 341).

Cf. *1732*, p. 269/8.

[20] Echoes Marees, f. 16; Dapper, p. 107/6.

Cf. *1732*, p. 269/8 ('some Blacks of Cape Verde and Rufisco are acquainted with both').

[21] In 1678–1679 Barbot noted that at Tabu, Axim and Komenda the blacks spoke *langue francque* (*1679*, pp. 277, 281, 289). Earlier in the century, the trading language on Gold Coast was 'mostly broken Portuguese or Dutch, and some French too' (Dapper, p. 107/5).

Cf.*1732*, p. 249/3, which enlarges – 'in a sort of Lingua Franca, or broken Portuguese and French'.

[22] Since neither Marees nor Dapper had much to say about slaves and the slave trade, and Villault's comments were limited, the material on slaves is largely original, unlike what has gone before in this Letter.

Cf. *1732*, pp. 270/1–3, which, after two paragraphs on slavery among the ancient Hebrews, the Chinese and Sclavonians, makes more of the kidnapping of children and does not specify parents selling children. Although Barbot dealt in slaves, his experience was limited, and his categories of enslavement are probably not from direct observation, not least since they partly echo Villault, pp. 296–8.

[23] Barbot was probably influenced by the view that only 'those of the highest rank and nobles' were allowed to deal in slaves (at least within the society), expressed in Marees, ff. 86v, 89v, and Villault, p. 296. This prime text for a class-warfare view of the slave trade is a somewhat exaggerated statement, since trading records show many purchases from lesser members of African societies. In 1679, Barbot's recorded purchases on Gold Coast

were half from European agents and half from Africans, some of whom were certainly 'big men'. But slaves were also frequently bought in small numbers without the status of the African seller being always recorded, and the sellers to the resident agents were of course unknown to Barbot (Debien 1979, pp. 248–9). Hence Barbot is probably citing a conventional view rather than making an independent judgement.

Cf. *1732*, p. 270/4.

[24] Enlarges on references to bare-headed slaves and to their families in Villault, pp. 296–8, apart from the reference to seeing unburied corpses, recorded in *1679*, p. 337.

Cf. *1732*, p. 270/5, which adds that 'they scarce allow them the least rag to cover their nakedness, which they also take off from them when sold to Europeans', but omits the final personal reference. Barbot continues by arguing that slaves were therefore better off in America – see the Additional Passage.

[25] Another prime passage for most past writers on the Atlantic slave trade, as expressing the view that warfare was the major factor producing slaves for export. But Barbot states the view as specific to Gold Coast, and it appears to reflect mainly what he was told in 1679 about the recent war between Akwamu and Accra (*1679*, p. 324), so that even if the information was correct the explanation is also time-specific.

Cf. *1732*, p. 271/4–5 (the incident was previously mentioned on p. 155/ 10).

[26] This clumsy sentence reflects comments in the 1678–9 journal on prisoners being retained by Akwamu and slaves being used for transporting goods to the coast (*1679*, p. 324).

[27] Cf. *1732*, p. 271/5, which adds, however, that an additional cause of the shortage was the number of vessels on the coast.

[28] Cf. *1732*, p. 271/5, which introduces the episode differently – 'At another time, I had two hundred slaves at Acra only, in a fortnight or three weeks time; and the upper coast men, understanding I had those slaves aboard, came down to redeem them, giving me two for one, of such as I understood were their near relations, who had been stolen away ...'. This later version is probably more correct in dating the episode to 1679, when Barbot's journal records the purchase of over 150 slaves at Accra but also the ransoming of a single man (not more), in exchange for two others, by a party which had travelled 25 leagues from Cape Coast, producing the comment that 'the son does not sell the father nor the father the son, as some assert' (*1679*, p. 329). Allegations that African parents sold children were common in European accounts (e.g. Marees, ff. 13, 89v).

[29] Cf. *1732*, p. 271/6, which enlarges, so that the family becomes man, wife, three young boys and a girl, acquired during 'my several runs along

557

that coast', and Barbot adds, first, that the sight of the reunion, 'moving me to compassion, I order'd they should be better treated aboard than commonly we can afford to do it', and, secondly, that he sold them at Martinique 'at a cheaper rate than I might have expected had they been disposed of severally', to a planter who promised the family good treatment. This seems to refer to 1679, and Barbot's journal does record a very similar episode, but one involving a pregnant woman bought in the morning, a little boy and a little girl bought in the afternoon, and a husband/father bought several days earlier, probably at the same place – the woman gave birth at Martinique, making the family five, and they were sold to a single master (*1679*, pp. 327). Barbot records in his journal the joy of reunion in similar compassionate and emotional terms, but appears to improve the story each time he tells it. Be that as it may, a husband and wife, bought at Whydah in 1682, possibly by Barbot himself, and certainly conveyed to Guiana on a ship of Barbot's squadron, were sold together and were working together on a plantation in 1690 (Debien/Houdaille 1964, p. 173).

[30] Repeated in Letter 3/2, p. 137, and Letter 3/20, p. 234, below.

Cf. *1732*, p. 272/1, where Barbot adds this. 'And though I must say I am naturally compassionate, yet have I been necessitated sometimes to cause the teeth of those wretches to be broken, because they would not open their mouths, or be prevail'd upon by any intreaties to feed themselves; and thus have forced some sustenance into their throats.'

[31] Discussion of the treatment of slaves from Gold Coast leads Barbot in *1732* to a more general discussion of slave treatment, particularly in America, and hence to an important statement about contemporary Christian attitudes to slavery, here included in this Additional Passage.

[32] For comment on this passage, see note 174 to the Introduction.

[33] The Epistle to Philemon is usually taken to have the meaning Barbot ascribes to it, viz. that it is a Christian duty to treat slaves well but not necessarily to emancipate them. The divines consulted by Barbot may well have included his brother-in-law who was a Huguenot minister in England and his wife's uncle who was an Anglican clergyman.

[34] Barbot concludes his discussion of slavery by noting the master's power of life and death over slaves among the Israelites and Romans (*1732*, p. 272/3-4). He further discusses the treatment of slaves aboard ship in *1732*, pp. 546/1–548/1 – see Letter 3/20, Additional Passage, below.

LETTER 22

European merchandise suitable for trade on Gold Coast and the use the blacks make of it.

Sir, you tell me in your letter, which I have just been given, that you wish me to state all the kinds of European merchandise that are taken to Gold Coast to trade. You then request that I indicate what knowledge these people have of the goods and to what use they put them. That is what I am going to do today, even although I am troubled by a great headache.

Every nation of Europe carries to this coast as many things suitable for the trade as it can from its own country, and it obtains elsewhere, from other countries, such things as it does not have and are nevertheless necessary for a good trade. That is why a French vessel which goes there has generally more brandy, wine, iron, guns, etc. than a Dutch one, because these wares cost less in France. Likewise, for the same reason, the latter has more linen, glass beads, cauldrons, powder, says, perpetuanas, pintados, etc. For the commerce in gold, slaves and ivory, people take from France brandy, white and red wine, rosa solis, firelocks (*fusils*), muskets, gunflints, iron bars, white and black contecarbé, brocaded silk stuffs, shirts, black hats, red floss silk, mirrors, sarsaparilla, fine coral, and glass beads (*rassade*) of several sorts.[1] The merchandise from Holland consists of Coesveld linen, Silesian linen, bed-sheets, Leiden serges in indigo, perpetuanas in green, blue and violet, kings' cloths, large and small annabases made in Haarlem, cloth from Cyprus and Turkey, Barbary carpets (*tapis*), red, blue and yellow cloths, white, green and red Leiden blankets, yellow and red silk stuffs, brass cups with handles, satelas, cauldrons of various sizes, copper basins, Scottish pans, barbers' basins (some chased, others hammered or wrought), brass pots, brass padlocks, brass trumpets, manillas of pewter, brass or iron, tubs, deal chests, dishes, basins with small rims, deep porringers without a rim (pewter throughout), fishing hooks of various sizes, lead in sheets and in the shape of organ-pipes, knives of three sorts, Venetian glass beads (*verrot*) of every kind, sheepskins, cloths from Cape Verde, Quaqua, Ardres and Rio Forcado, akory (blue coral from Benin), a few cowries, long yellow [-metal] pins, small globular brass bells, iron hammers, etc.[2] The merchandise from England, apart from several of the articles mentioned above, includes broad and narrow tapseils, fine and coarse nicanees, various sorts of chintz or indiennes, tallow, red paints, Spanish wine, tobacco, says, perpetuanas (inferior to those of Holland), several kinds of calico, white and blue cotton linen [sic], satins from China, rum from Barbados, flour, and vegetables, etc., which several ships bring to this place from the English colonies.[3] The Danes, Brandenburgers and Portuguese draw the whole of their cargoes from these three nations, having nothing in their own countries suitable for this commerce apart from provisions and silver. The Portuguese bring animals of various species there, as well as cloths which they obtain at São Tomé, Rio Forcado and elsewhere in the Gulf of Guinea, otherwise Gulf of Ethiopia.[4] [.../p. 90/...][5]

All these goods have more or less value on Gold Coast according to the amounts available there, or according to the times of year, as I have fully explained in a little tract on the trade of Guinea.[6] The General of Mina fixes the current prices of the merchandize every year. Several copies are made and given to the factors of the other Dutch places, whose responsibility it is to inform the blacks of the interior.[7] The normal price at the forts is 25% dearer than on board the ships, which sell goods more cheaply in order to reduce the length of their voyage, whereas in the forts people wait for the high season, when the ships have left. In 1682 the gold trade yielded 42–45% for those trading in the roadsteads, all expenses included, although at that time there were 42 ships trading on the coast simultaneously. If there were fewer ships, one could anticipate 60%.[8]

[...][9] The perpetuanas serve to make loin-cloths (pagnes), as do the chintzes or indiennes, the nicanees and the tapseils. Basins and pewter porringers are used to eat from, firelocks and muskets for war, brandy for festivities, knives for the same purposes as us, tallow to anoint their bodies and toes as well as for shaving. They do not use much wine. The hooks are for their fishing; the glass beads, Venetian bugles, and contebrodé constitute ornaments for men, women and children, who wear them in large quantities on their necks, arms and legs, as you have seen. They cure venereal disease with sarsaparilla.[10]

It is possible to trade on Gold Coast in any season, the anchorage being good at all times, except in August and September, when the travados which blow upon the coast sometimes bring about the foundering of any vessels which are (to use a naval expression) not well made fast. One ship foundered at Tackorary in 1679, and another at Comendo. I too thought that my brigantine was going to be lost, off Infiama, where a thunderstorm from the South took us by surprise around midnight and lasted two hours, with inconceivable violence. That was in April 1682. I have hardly ever spent a worse night.[11] I hope that the present one will be kinder to me. I drink to you and am Your etc. /p. 91/

NOTES

[1] Of these many commodities, only seven were not among the cargo on Barbot's ship in 1678–9 (see Debien 1979, pp. 242–6): rosa solis (a cordial), gun-flints, white contecarbé (a type of bead – Barbot's cargo had yellow and black ones), hats, floss silk, sarsaparilla (dried roots of various species of *Smilaceae*, from tropical America) and coral.

Cf. *1732*, pp. 272/5–273/2, which adds 'powder, sheets, tobacco, taffeties, ... linen, paper, laces of many sorts, beads, shot, lead, musket-balls, flints, callicoes, serges, stuffs, etc. besides the other goods for a true assortment, which they have commonly from Holland'.

[2] For explanations of some of these terms, see Debien 1979, pp. 243–6, and Jones 1985, pp. 312–9. All are from Dapper, p. 108 (itself partly derived from Marees, ff. 25v–26), apart from Coesveld linen, Leiden serges (but Dapper has 'Leiden says'), king's cloths, annabases, Barbary carpets (but Dapper has Turkey carpets), silk stuffs, copper cups, satelas, tubs, dishes, cloth from Rio Forcado, cowries, pins, bells and hammers. Many of these new items had played no role in West African trade before the 1670s. The commodities obtained from elsewhere on the Guinea coast testify to some complexity in Afro-European commerce – although Barbot absurdly lists them under 'merchandise from Holland'. In 1679 Barbot purchased cloth from Rio Forcado when at Príncipe (*1679*, p. 246).

Cf. *1732*, p. 273/3, which makes slight modifications: 'Turkey carpets' (as in Dapper); 'silk stuffs, blue and white'; 'brass pins, long and short'. Also it omits 'satelas' and tubs, and adds 'iron bars, ... powder, muskets, cutlaces, cawris, chints, lead balls and shot of sundry sorts, ... strong waters', concluding with the words 'being near a hundred and fifty sorts, as a Dutchman told me' – a reference to Bosman, p. 91.

[3] For a list of merchandise recommended by an Englishman who visited Gold Coast a decade later than Barbot, see Phillips 1732, p. 206.

Cf. *1732*, p. 273/4–5, which changes 'Spanish wine' to 'Canary wine', states that the perpetuanas were 'sack'd up in painted tillets, with the English arms', and adds – 'other strong waters, and spirits, beads of all sorts, buck-shaws, Welsh plain, boysades, romberges, clouts, gingarus taffeties, amber, brandy, . . . Hamburgh brawls, and white, blue and white, and red chequer'd linen, narrow Guinea stuffs chequer'd, ditto broad, old hats, purple beads. Note, That all the iron for Guinea is of the very same size and weight as described in the description of Nigritia; and is called at London by the name of Voyage-Iron, and is the only sort used all over the coasts of North and South Guinea, and in Ethiopia.' These additions were perhaps the result of Barbot's contacts with merchants in England after 1688.

[4] Cf. *1732*, p. 273/6–7, which expands: 'The Danes, Brandenburghers and Portugueses, provide their cargoes in Holland, commonly consisting of very near the same sort of wares, as I have observed the Dutch make up theirs; the two former having hardly any thing of their own, proper for the trade of the Gold Coast, besides copper and silver, either wrought or in bullion, or pieces of eight, which are a commodity also there'. It also incorporates material on the Portuguese from Bosman, p. 89, and credits them (somewhat implausibly) with bringing 'tame cattle' to Gold Coast from Brazil.

[5] Omission of one paragraph on the wariness of African merchants in buying from Europeans, based on Marees, ff. 27v–28, and Villault, pp. 321–2. Barbot adds one sentence: 'They taste the brandy and recognise the ways in which it can be adulterated, but prefer that which is reddish-brown to any other'. For similar remarks, see Jones 1983a, pp. 248–9.

Cf. *1732*, pp. 273/8.

[6] Is Barbot really claiming to have written a tract on the Guinea trade, or is he rather making an elliptic reference to what he has written previously in the present text on this subject? If the former, the tract, whether in French or English, is untraced. But perhaps it was not a published work, only a confidential report to his employers in France.

Cf. *1732*, p. 274/1, which omits the reference to a tract.

[7] The first sentence is from Dapper, p. 108/4. By Barbot's time (and probably before), changes in the current prices were made more often than once a year, in order to respond to new market conditions (for instance, the arrival of interlopers): see Van Dantzig 1978, pp. 37, 40 (documents of 3.12.1682, 4.10.1683).

Cf. *1732*, p. 274/2.

[8] The accounts kept by Barbot on his first voyage (at least those that appear in his journal) are too imprecise to indicate what gain he made on gold purchases: see Debien 1979, pp. 252–3. For an example of the high mark-up at European forts at this time, see the list of goods sold at Gross-Friedrichsburg in 1684, where the anticipated gain on most articles lay between 100% and 200% (Jones 1985, p. 78).

Cf. *1732*, p. 274/3–4, which changes the last words to '60 per Cent or more', adding – 'if a cargo were properly composed, it might well clear 70 per Cent. in a small ship, sailing with little charge, and the voyage directly home from this coast, not to exceed seven or eight months out and home, if well managed'.

[9] Omission of three sentences on the uses to which various types of merchandise were put, from Marees, ff. 25v–26. Barbot changes 'Spanish serges' to 'serges from Leiden and England' and 'rupinsche cloths' (worn as belts) to 'floss-silk and perpetuanas, 4 inches broad'.

Cf. *1732*, p. 274/5–6.

[10] The last sentence is from Marees, f. 88. Pieces of sarsaparilla were steeped in brandy and used as a curative for syphilis.

Cf. *1732*, p. 274/6, which expands: 'French, Madera and Canary wine, are little used by the natives, but commonly bought by the Europeans residing there'.

[11] The first half of the first sentence is from Dapper, p. 109/2.

Cf. *1732*, p. 275/4, which expands slightly ('very good anchorage from one end to the other, except at Acra, where the ground is rocky'), and states that the incident in 1682 took place 'when I made a coasting voyage from Acra, where I left the man of war I was in, to some leagues above cape St Apolonia, at the upper coast'.

LETTER 23

Dances, festivals and feasts in general, and those of these Africans in particular, and the musical instruments they employ.

Sir, I have told you as much as I can about the customs, temperament, occupations and way of life of the peoples of Gold Coast, in general and in particular. I shall now satisfy your request by entertaining you with their dances, recreations, feasts and festivities, both solemn and private, as well as the musical instruments which they use on these occasions.

Generally speaking, both sexes much love dances, songs and melody. The women are so fond of these things that whenever their ordinary occupations give them the slightest respite, they begin to sing or dance. Most of the women do this even while working, as soon as they hear someone singing or playing any instruments. One might say the same in general for all the inhabitants of the southward-lying coasts of Africa.[1] Since time immemorial it has been an established custom among them to assemble every evening in their villages at the market-place, in order to dance and enjoy themselves. The women go there an hour or two before bed-time, dressed up after their fashion and with many small globular bells attached to their legs. The men go there too, dressed up as finely as possible, holding in their hands elephant's tails gilded at the end.[2] The players of musical instruments are stationed at one corner of this market-place, some of them having copper basins, which they beat with a stick, while others have drums of two or three different kinds, upon which they sit astride, beating them with wooden sticks – these drums are made of hollowed-out tree-trunks, covered with the skins of goats or cabrites.[3] Other men have wooden clappers, like those given to cows [to wear as 'bells']; reeds pierced like flutes; a sort of tambourine; an instrument similar to the guitar, with six strings made of reeds; and trumpets of various sizes, made of elephant tusks, with a hole at only one end and producing a sound that is pretty droll.[4] This symphony, together with the voices, produces a somewhat bizarre concert and much noise.

The men and women who are to dance divide into groups of equal numbers, facing one another in couples; and when the dance begins, they approach one another and withdraw in cadence, leaping and stamping their feet on the ground. They snap their fingers and bow their heads together; they talk to one another, loudly, quietly or in whispers; they bring their stomachs close together and sometimes knock their bellies together, while clapping hands at the same time; they move sometimes quickly, sometimes slowly, and sometimes sideways or backwards; they throw their elephant-tails to one another and place them now on one shoulder, now on the other, while uttering certain barbaric and mysterious words.[5] The women have hoops, which they cast upon the ground, dancing around them and lifting them up with the end of their foot as they pass by. Others have little bundles of folded linen, which they lift into the air with their foot and then catch in their hand. And there are some who recite certain verses, singing, to which the others respond in refrain, as if it were a musical choir. Those who have seen these negro dances say that they resemble what we call the dances of the *Filoux* [pickpockets].[6] These Moors take such pleasure in this exercise that they have schools almost everywhere expressly to instruct the young people in it. They have several kinds of dance, depending on the place and the occasion; for there are also some in honour of their fetishes. The kings have a more sedate manner [in dancing] than the others.[7]

I think that I ought to give you an account of a feast that a man called Witt, the General of the Danes, gave in my honour in the garden of Frederickburgh in January 1679.[8] /p. 92/ It began with a sumptuous meal in the fort, from which after dining we descended, in order to go to this garden, which is not far from it. Scarcely had we entered a summer-house in the middle of a walk of orange trees than we were surrounded by more than a hundred Moors, armed from head to foot with assegais, cutlasses, javelins, shields, swords and muskets, with which they made a continual noise, striking one against the other and firing their guns incessantly. They were all dressed up so bizarrely that they looked more like devils than men. When our gladiators had drawn a little aside, we were regaled with a concert of instruments more or less like those I have described to you. Afterwards the General's concubines arrived, followed by those of the other white men at the fort and by several other black women from Manfrou itself, all dressed in their finest attire, and radiant, more on account of the many gold ornaments with which they decorated many parts of their bodies than on account of the vivacity of their complexion. They arranged themselves around us and were served sweet oranges, French wine, palm wine, mum [beer], and brandy. Meanwhile the Moors began to wrestle and fight one another, occasionally breaking into a sort of dance, in which they struck their shields with their cutlasses in cadence, rather like the way in which the *ballet de Mars* is performed at the Opera. At the same time other men kept up a continuous fire with their muskets, shooting at the ground, two at a time, and leaping into the air and making a hundred strange postures, as if they were possessed. It came to the women's turn, and, vying with one another, they showed us that they have many kinds of very curious dances. From time to time the castle answered the salvoes of our musketeers with salvoes of five cannon-shots. At last, as night was approaching, we were conducted to the fort by the whole troop, which walked all the way around the hill in order to give us time to reach the summit, so that we might view more easily the fight which they were about to conduct among themselves. Having divided into two troops, each with its own leader, drums, trumpets and the flag of Denmark, they skirmished for a while, without observing any order. Then, taking their assegais in one hand and guarding their bodies with their shields in the other, they made as if to throw the assegais at one another. Finally, they took their sabres in their hand and struck them against their shields; but the confusion was so great that it was no pleasure to watch. When the fight was over, one group of these fighters conducted the officers to Manfrou, while the other escorted the flag to the fort, where they were regaled with brandy and French wine. This little festivity cost the Danes 4 or 5 *benda* of gold [*margin: or 35 livres of gold*].[9]

These Africans comport themselves in virtually the same manner at the public celebrations, which they hold annually, and on certain days upon the occasion of some victory gained by their nation over their enemies. But then they are even more disguised and more terrifying, for on such occasions some of them wear the skulls and jaw-bones of those whom they have killed in war, which they keep as a memento of their victories. At Accra, among two hundred who appeared before me when I disembarked, I saw one who had 21 of these dry skulls and jaw-bones attached to his cap and his drum, with a large cow's tail hanging behind, trailing to the ground.[10]

These kinds of festivities in particular, and more or less regularly, are always [*sic*] followed by someone being murdered or by some quarrel between the young people, who, having gorged themselves with strong liquor, become (so to speak) mad and inclined to pick a quarrel upon the slightest pretext. Sometimes even several lives are lost, for their wrath cannot be appeased once they are bent on fighting. Admittedly they restrain themselves towards the whites, unless very provoked. Then they lose all respect and have absolutely no regard for their lives. /p. 93/ If they do not fight, they spend a large part of the night running through the villages, shouting and roaring like mad wolves, and carrying terror and dread everywhere.[11] My headache is distressing me. Allow me to close this letter, short though it is. Nonetheless I remain, Sir, Your etc.

Additional Passage from *1732*

[pp. 264/2, 265/2–9, on the musical instruments illustrated on Plate 22]

T. The royal drum, used when a king takes the field and heads his army, adorn'd with spells, shells, and jaw-bones of their enemies slain in battle. The sound of it is not unlike that of our kettle-drums. The body of it is a piece of wood made hollow, covered at one end with a sheep-skin, and left open at the other, which is set on the ground. It is beaten with two long sticks, like hammers, and sometimes round, as in the figure. They also sometimes beat with a streight stick, or with their hands. To be intrusted with this drum, is looked upon [as] an office of honour. ... G. Blowing horns, made of elephants teeth, of several sizes, the biggest of which weigh about thirty pounds; they have a peculiar art to hollow them from one end to the other. At the lower end of them is a piece of rope, black'd with sheep or hens blood, and a square hole, blowing into which makes a preposterous noise, by them reduced to a sort of tone and measure, and alter'd at pleasure. Sometimes the tone is more tolerable, according to their skill. On it are carv'd many figures of men and beasts, and others only the product of fancy. / F. Three sorts of tinkling bells, which make up part of their musick. / E. Two sorts of castagnets us'd in dancing. / D. Two flutes, differing from ours, by having more holes. / C. A sort of cittern, made of a calabash, or gourd, over which is a long narrow piece, made of reeds set close to one another athwart; and over all, four strings, which give the sound, when play'd upon with the fingers, after the manner that the Portugueses touch the guittar; and I am of opinion the Blacks made this instrument in imitation of that. / B. A brass kettle, with two sticks to beat it, in musical manner. / A. Two several sorts of drums, with their sticks, the round one us'd at feasts and in war; the long one also serves sometimes for the same uses, and sometimes in religious worship to honour their deities, or upon other extraordinary occasions. / B. A pair of tongs, with a stick to beat and rattle them, being another of their musical instruments.[12]

NOTES

[1] In 1679 Barbot witnessed dancing when attending a feast at Fort Frederiksborg, and he recorded a brief general description of African dancing – very droll advances and retreats by groups, but wild movements of all parts of the body by individuals, male and female, 'as if possessed'; and he also drew and described a number of musical instruments (*1679*, pp. 305, 338, 345–6). In singling out women in the present passage Barbot was perhaps influenced by Dapper, p. 98/2.

Cf. *1732*, p. 275/5, which enlarges on the enthusiasm of both sexes for dancing.

[2] This is largely from Marees, f. 87, and Villault, pp. 310–11. Marees mentions only horsetails; Villault changes this to 'horsetails or elephant

tails'; Barbot leaves out horsetails altogether – perhaps a significant omission, indicating that these were no longer being imported in significant numbers. Elephant-tails were highly valued and served as fly-whisks, as well as forming part of some men's war-dress (Jones 1983a, p. 124). But they must have become increasingly scarce as the number of elephants in this region declined; hence, by the nineteenth century, if not earlier, they were an important symbol of achieved status.

Cf. *1732*, p. 275/6.

[3] Although Barbot drew percussion instruments in 1679 (see the following note), his description of them derives largely from Marees, f. 87v, and Villault, p. 311.

Cf. *1732*, pp. 264/2–3, 275/6, which incorporates material on drums from Bosman, p. 139, but also describes the royal drum – see the Additional Passage.

[4] The flutes and tambourine are from Villault, p. 311; but wooden clappers are not mentioned by Villault, and Marees merely used this term (*clippels*) for the sticks used to strike copper basins and 'round blocks, cut out on all sides so that air can pass through them' (Marees, f. 87v). While cows in Europe did sometimes wear wooden 'bells', the only kind of clappers recorded in recent times fit Marees's description more closely than Barbot's (Cole/Ross 1977, p. 181). Ivory horns are not mentioned by Marees or Villault in this context, but both authors refer to them elsewhere (Marees, f. 47; Villault, p. 314). In 1679 Barbot drew and briefly described two ivory horns, with 8–10 holes (side-blown, at least in one case), three drums of hollowed wood (two of them covered with goatskin), a clapperless iron bell, and a 'sort of violin [shown with a long neck], with strings made from palm-fronds which they play with their two thumbs, resting the end against the stomach' (*1679*, pp. 345–6). Apart from the last instruments, these all reappear, although sometimes drawn from different angles, either on illustration no. (86) on the following page of *1688*, or in the case of one of the drums on illustration no. (89) on p. 120, and all appear again in *1732*, Plate 22 (p. 251). But the later drawings add a large war-drum and a brass kettle used as a drum (and sticks for all the drums), a third bell, two flutes, a copper basin and sticks, two castanets, a pair of tongs with a stick, and 'a sort of cittern' (replacing the 'sort of violin') – presumably instruments either drawn or acquired in 1682. Barbot seems to have been the only author to describe the 'sort of cittern', four strings over a reed platform above a gourd. But the 'violin' with a long neck was noted before and after his time – see Marees, f. 87v; Bosman, p. 140; Lee 1835, p. 72 (a detailed description); Cole/Ross 1977, p. 181; Jones 1985, p. 88.

Cf. *1732*, p. 275/6, which adapts the instrument now termed a 'gittern' to Bosman, p. 140 ('six extended strings'). For Barbot's *1732* detailed description of these various instruments, see the Additional Passage.

[5] This too is mainly from Marees, f. 87v, and Villault, p. 312, the most significant addition being the reference to physical contact between the dancers and the clapping of hands. Barbot's description of Gold Coast dancing routine may not have been correct in every respect: a contemporary noted that – 'they went to dance by turns, in a ridiculous manner, making antick gestures with their arms, shoulders, and heads, their feet having the least share in the action' (Phillips 1732, p. 201).

Cf. *1732*, p. 275/7, which gives additional emphasis to the erotic aspect: 'men and women running against each other, breast to breast, and knocking bellies together very indecently ... and uttering some dirty mysterious words'. Barbot's disapproving reaction to African dancing, as first stated in his journal (see note 1 above), was normal for an educated European of his period (Jones 1983a, p. 157).

[6] Largely from Marees, f. 87v, and Villault, p. 312; Marees referred to 'straw-whisks' (*stroowiskens*), but Villault changed this to 'hoops' (*cerceaux*). Cf. *1732*, p. 275/8, which again emphasizes the indecency of such behaviour: 'others recite aloud certain immodest verses'.

[7] The sentence on dancing schools is from Villault, p. 312, and derives indirectly from Marees, f. 87v (which referred to such schools as for young men only); and the remainder of the passage is loosely related to Villault, p. 313. Dancing-schools have already been mentioned (Letter 2/17, p. 67 and note 15, above).

Cf. *1732*, p. 276/1, which omits the reference to dancing schools (but see p. 239/4) and adds a reference to the 'Dancing-season' at Abramboe, repeating a reference on p. 172/3 – see Letter 2/6, Additional Passage, above.

[8] In 1679 Barbot recorded at length this event, which took place on 13 January (*1679* pp. 304–5) – see Letter 2/6, note 34, above. Barbot here expands his journal entry considerably, presumably from recollection, sometimes changing details, while the journal mentions several details omitted here: the men's weapons included half-pikes; their shields (*boucliers*, rather than the *rondaches* here) were made of 'straw'; the summer-house (*un grand pavillon*, rather than a mere *cabinet*) was surrounded by lime trees as well as orange trees. The only dances mentioned are those of 'young boys and girls'. Nothing is said about the fort acknowledging salvoes 'from time to time': instead, it is merely stated that after the whole performance the fort 'thanked them with three discharges, which were answered.'

[9] Possibly what Barbot witnessed was the celebration of the anniversary of a military victory (as perhaps hinted at in the next paragraph): hence, perhaps, the mock battle and certain other elements, since these appear in earlier descriptions of such celebrations, which also mention the expense involved (Villault, p. 318; Jones 1983a, p. 199).

Cf. *1732*, p. 276/2–4, which adds a brief description of the war-dress

569

allegedly worn on this occasion, in fact from Bosman, p. 185, and recounts the fighting in slightly different terms – 'divided themselves into two bodies, ... opposite to one another, in order of battle. No sooner were we placed in the long gallery of the fort, from whence we could have a full view of them, but each body began to move towards the other, and skirmished together with fire-arms, ... till it being dark night they left off ...' The equivalent of five *benda* is now given as 'forty pounds sterling'.

[10] The last sentence was probably inspired by Villault, p. 313, which refers to a man wearing a cap decorated with the skulls of those whom he had killed. For the keeping and wearing of skulls and jawbones, see Letter 2/30, p. 119, below; also Marees, f. 45; Villault, pp. 343–4, 357; Phillips 1732, pp. 201–2; Jones 1983a, pp. 199–200.

[11] This passage is loosely based on Marees, ff. 87v–88, which does not explicitly link such behaviour with festivals. The youths referred to by Marees may have been what other seventeenth-century authors called *manceroes*, 'whose activities were very similar to those of the more active members of the *asafo* [township company] in later periods' (Datta/Porter 1971, pp. 290, 293).

[12] Although Barbot is describing his own drawings, perhaps of instruments he actually owned, the description of horns, and the omitted paragraph on 'several sorts of drums', are from Bosman, pp. 138–9. The section concludes (p. 265/10–15) with a digression on Biblical implements.

LETTER 24

The oaths and promises they make to each other, and their method of swimming. Their language and other particulars.

Sir, here is the plate which you requested in your note the evening before yesterday. The reason I did not send it was that I was not in the mood for drawing. It shows you some of the instruments which the blacks use to entertain themselves.

[illustration no. (86), musical instruments] [1]†

My last letter finished at a point which urges me to deal in this one with a few other peculiarities concerning these peoples. I shall begin with the manner in which they make solemn promises to the whites and to their superiors, at least when matters of importance are involved. [...][2] Others cross their two forefingers and kiss them, uttering in Portuguese, *Per esta crus de Dios.*[3] [...][4] /p. 94/

570

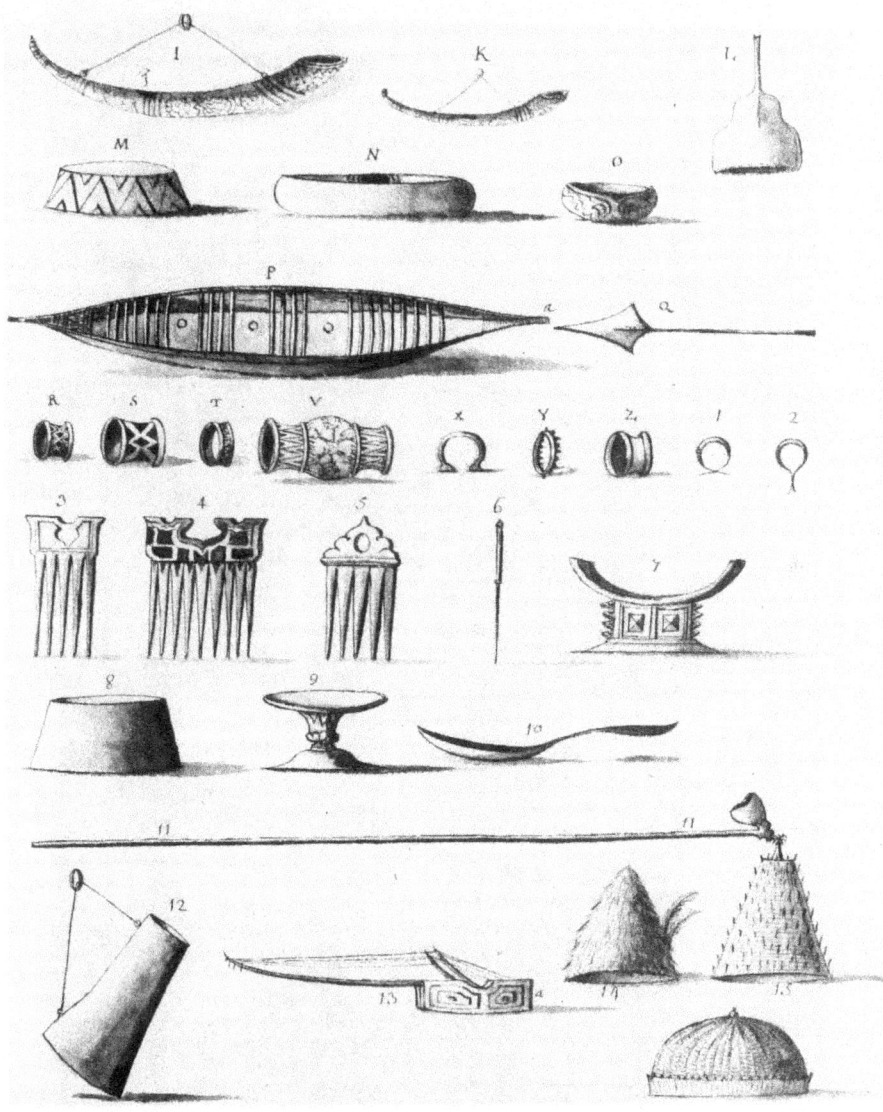

47. Gold Coast artefacts in wood, metal and ivory

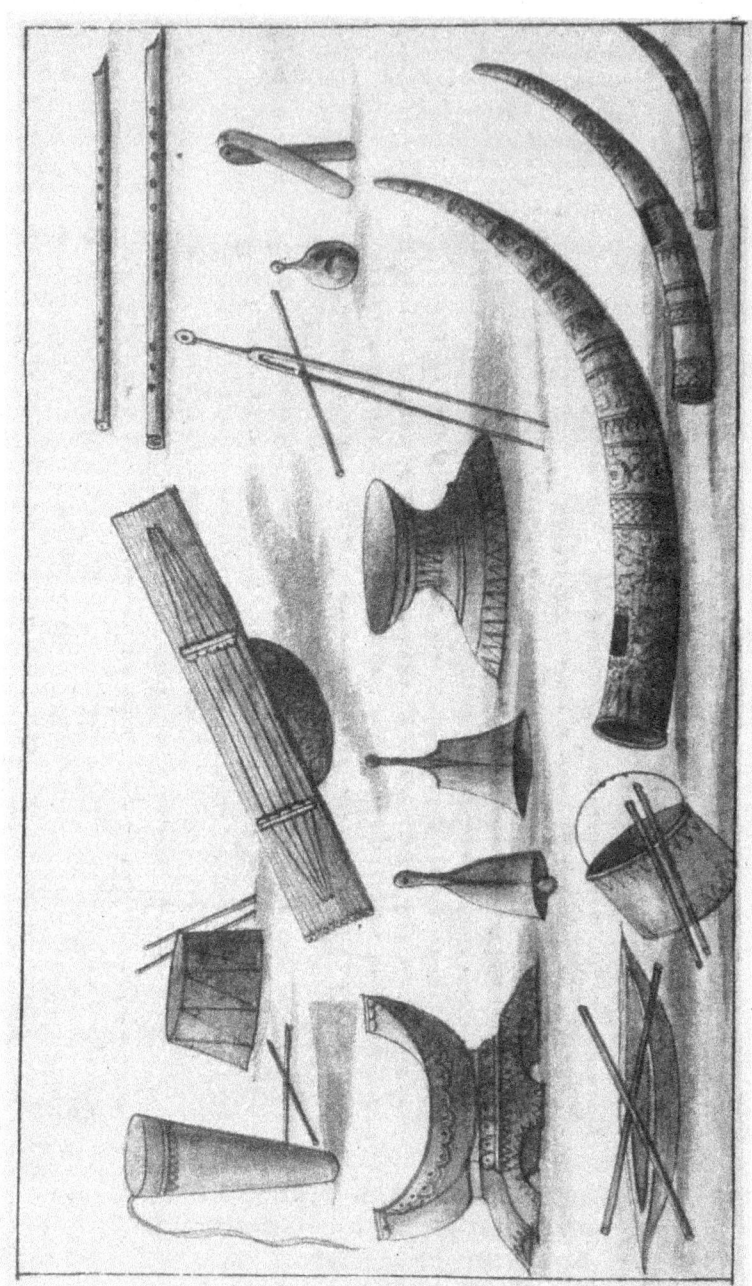

48. Gold Coast musical instruments and other artefacts

I have told you elsewhere, Sir, that there are no thieves more skilled than these blacks. I reiterate this opinion here. You must always distrust them, especially when you see five or six of them coming [aboard] together, carrying reed baskets which they call *akofo*. These kinds of receptacle are [used] to stow away not only what they buy, but also what they steal. You should also suspect those who make a great deal of noise and move around a lot without concluding any transaction. I never let more than two come at a time, or else I kept my merchandise stowed away and only put a few pieces on show. They help one another by receiving the stolen goods and sharing the loot among themselves.[5] [. . .][6] They are so good at righting their canoes when they have capsized that often they save everything in them without losing anything.[7] [. . .][8]

These blacks are by nature not very civilized. Nevertheless, among themselves they make distinctions between one person and another. If they meet one of their friends in the morning, they greet him with much joy and respect, taking each other in their arms, as if they wanted to wrestle; and after releasing each other, they take the two fingers of the right hand – the magister and the thumb – and pinch them [against those of the other person]; then, in letting them go, they make them snap against one another, [which they do] two or three times, bending their head each time and saying 'Auzy, Auzy' twice or thrice (meaning 'Good day').[9] Europeans they greet simply by taking off their hat or bonnet and drawing back one foot, saying 'Aquy, Signor, Aquy, Signor'; sometimes they also take the fingers of the right hand in their accustomed manner.[10]

Although Gold Coast is of small extent in every direction, the people who inhabit it speak various languages, especially between Cormentyn and Acra, where four different ones are found, although these two places lie only 20 leagues apart. The language that is everywhere used most is that of Fetu, at least between Cape Three Points and Cormentyn, as well as beyond, in Anta, although the language of the people there is slightly different.[11] Here I would give you a small vocabulary of the words most used on this coast in the language of Fetu, had I not decided to do so at the end of this work, together with other languages which /p. 95/ I shall join to it.[12] [. . .][13]

From the beginning of my description I have shown you the malignities that these rains bring with them in the high season below the equator, and how they transform into worms and stenches if one does not take care at the moment when they fall upon the earth. In my opinion, this is also the sole reason for so many of the illnesses which overwhelm the Africans and even more the Europeans. Since I have come to this subject without thinking about it, I propose in my first [following] letter to give you an account of the illnesses which prevail most commonly in that country. It will be two or three days before I write to you again, but I hope you will easily pardon me since I am, with all my heart, Sir, Your etc.

Additional Passage from *1732*

[p. 276/5–6, on oath-taking]

I shall now make some farther observations on the same subject, as it is practised in Fetu, either towards Europeans, or among themselves, in things of moment. / Upon such occasions the priest or conjuror erects a pile of small sticks, in the form of an altar, on which he lays a canvas bag, sprinkled with human blood, containing some dry bones of men; to which he adds small pieces of bread, and a calabash or gourd full of the bitter water or drink, so much used among them in religious ceremonies, all of which the priest exorcises, and causes the person to whom the oath is admi-nister'd to swear on it, by Osturé, the name of their chief deity. To which he adds an exhortation for the inviolably observing of the said oath in all points, with a terrible denunciation of a most horrible punishment in case of perjury; and if the person takes an oath to the English, or other Europeans there, he is made to swear on the bible.[14]

NOTES

[1] See note 4 of the previous Letter.

[2] Omission of two sentences on promises made to Europeans, from Marees, f. 55–55v.

Cf. *1732*, pp. 236/4, 277/2. Note that the present Letter, made up of scrappy material, is dispersed among several Chapters of *1732*.

[3] Cf. *1732*, p. 277/1, which corrects *per* to *por*, and adds – 'which is, By this cross of God'.

[4] Omission of one paragraph on the keeping and breaking of promises, from Marees, f. 55v.

Cf. *1732*, p. 277/2, and see the Additional Passage.

[5] The reference to baskets and their use for stealing aboard ship is from

Marees, f. 53v, which undoubtedly inspired Barbot's passage, despite the personal observations.

Cf. *1732*, p. 232/6 – see Letter 2/16, Additional Passage.

[6] Omission of two paragraphs on how to punish thieves and on the term 'Moor', from Marees, ff. 54–54v, 89, and one sentence on swimming, from Dapper, p. 97/6.

Cf. *1732*, p. 233/2–3, 252/1.

[7] The ability to right a canoe was mentioned by Marees, f. 16; but in 1679 Barbot noted that some canoes were designed to retain objects in them if they capsized (*1679*, pp. 304, 345–6).

Cf. *1732*, pp. 259/2, 266/5.

[8] Omission of three sentences on divers, and on swimming and sharks, from Marees, ff. 16, 94, and Dapper, p. 94/1.

Cf. *1732*, p. 267/2.

[9] This type of handshake, which is still practised, is difficult to describe; the best early attempt to do so was probably that of Müller in the 1660s (Jones 1983a, p. 155, and n. 76, which also gives other references). Barbot's description is mainly from Marees, f. 17v, but he adds the reference to 'magister and thumb' and to bending the head, as well as the words 'twice or thrice'.

Cf. *1732*, pp. 257/4–258/2, which adds material on 'civility' from Bosman, pp. 125–7; a Biblical comparison; another greeting originally in Barros 1552, Dec. 1, liv.3, cap. 1, but no doubt through an intermediate source; and the following – 'Inferiors salute their superiors after this manner; they first wet their finger in their mouth, then rub it on their stomach, and that done, present it to the superior', probably from an untraced source.

[10] The reference to taking off hats repeats Villault, p. 219. The greeting 'Aquy' (given as 'Aqui-o' in Letter 29, p. 156, above, on Grain Coast) was probably related to the modern Akan/Twi greeting (*ma-*)*akyé* (Christaller 1933, p. 286). For other contemporary references to this term, see Jones 1983a, pp. 154, 168, 182, 190, 215–6 ('acju'); Roussier 1935, p. 157 ('Aquio').

Cf. *1732*, p. 257/5.

[11] The first sentence is from Dapper, p. 107/4; the remainder represents an interpretation of Dapper, apart from the words 'that of Fetu'. The only other author who referred to the seventeenth-century ancestor of the dialect of Fante-Twi as 'Fetu' was Müller (see note 9 above), whom Barbot did not read.

Cf. *1732*, p. 248/7–249/2, which adds material from Bosman, pp. 130–31.

[12] See Letter 3/14, below, where the vocabulary is merely named as that of Gold Coast. In 1679 Barbot described the language as rather like Bas-Breton, with many gesticulations (Barbot's home district neighboured lower

Brittany): it was spoken rapidly, many words ended in certain vowels, and it included the double consonant /kw/. Barbot had obtained the vocabulary from a slave who spoke Portuguese (*1679*, pp. 340–41).

Cf. *1732*, p. 249/3, which adds – 'if the letters and vowels are pronounc'd as in French, I doubt not but a Black will understand it, when so sounded and expressed. Had I lived any considerable time among them, I had collected a much greater number of phrases and words, to help sea-faring men in their commerce with the natives of the Gold Coast, besides the other languages, in which we can talk to them: for many of the coast Blacks speak a little English or Dutch; and for the most part speak to us in a sort of Lingua Franca, or broken Portuguese and French'.

[13] Omission of most of two paragraphs on work performed by physically handicapped or old people, and on Africans' dislike of rain, from Marees, ff. 57v–58, 89v, and Villault, pp. 294–5.

Cf. *1732*, pp. 256/10, 257/1–3, which adds a reference to Hebrew practices.

[14] Although it has faint echoes of Villault, pp. 279–81, and Bosman, p. 149, this passage is either largely original or from an untraced source.

LETTER 25

The sicknesses of the land, in general. The worms that appear in the flesh, and the manner of curing them. The treatment of the sick.

There is much to admire, Sir, in the constancy and courage which these Moors show in their sicknesses. [.../p. 96/...][1] In the case of the whites, the precautions against colic are to keep warm, never to sleep on the ground, and to keep out of the night-dew (*serein*) and rain. Fresh water and lemons, together with the use many men make of lemon-drinks and punch, are also very contrary [to health]. I kept this regime and found I stayed very fit.[2] [...] Stomach aches are cured [variously]. [...] You must also avoid excess of wine and spirits. I drank no pure wine and only a little brandy, a quarter of an hour after a meal, in order to aid the digestion; in relation to which, a hare-skin on the bare stomach helps very greatly. I always had one on all the time I was in the torrid zones. Excessive use of the local beer and many other alcoholic drinks that are corrupted [by the climate], these being generously consumed in the forts and lodges, contribute even more to this disorder. [...][3]

Many different reasons are put forward to explain why Europeans are more subject to these disorders than the natives. For indeed, out of ten whites who arrive on the coast in good health, six fall ill in less than a month, and invariably two or three of these die shortly afterwards. The natives on the contrary are always robust and live long. Therefore some say that the Europeans, not having been born in this climate, cannot bear its extreme aspects as the natives can, and that the lightning-flashes and meteors continually to be seen infect the air and that the wind spreads the infection. Others say that the cause is the malign vapours arising from the earth and carried by the sea wind from SE to the NE and North. Others again add to these very likely reasons that the Europeans are excessively debauched with women and wine, and I go along with this view – together with the view that our bodies share much of the nature of the climate into which they were born and in which they were bred, this being the result of the food we eat. The Moors being similarly shaped for their own climate, it should be a matter of no surprise that they remain much healthier than the whites, who are out of their element here, if I may say so, and who find everything different, especially the food, which, being almost all of it tainted by the heat, further corrupts the blood and causes these regrettable acts of intemperance.[4] A proof of this truth, Sir, is that the whites are almost as subject as the blacks to certain worms. [.../pp. 97–98/...] I have seen one worm which made almost two turns around the waist of a slave I had on board and which appeared in some places to be between the skin and the flesh. The surgeon drew it out over 3–4 days of treatment, and it looked like a slightly dried-up white sinew. [.../p. 99/...][5] [...][6] The blacks make little of wounds. They are content to treat them merely with herbs they know, allowing them to close up on the piece of iron or the shot within. A slave I had aboard on my first voyage had a tumour in his side three months after embarking. It was treated and three musket balls were drawn out. According to what he said, they had been there since he was shot more than four months before.[7] [...] I am, Sir, Your etc.

Additional Passage from *1732*

[p. 279/4, on the aims of the account]

I fear I shall prove tedious upon every subject I treat of; but my design having been, from the beginning, to omit no particulars of use, or for curiosity, to render the description of the Coasts of Guinea more compleat than any yet published in any language, I shall now enter upon a digression of the various causes, which are thought to breed the worms in men's bodies in that part of Africa.[8]

NOTES

[1] Omission of a long passage on diseases in general, venereal diseases, and headaches. Apart from embroidery, the present Letter derives almost wholly from Dapper, pp. 95/6–97/2, and Villault, pp. 299–309, the latter being slightly enlarged from the former; while Dapper is derived largely from Marees, ff. 88–88v, 98v–100v. The material omitted at various points is derived from these sources. Occasionally the information becomes garbled during this transmission. At a few points, Barbot presents in the first person derived material, e.g., 'I have seen a morsel of meat ...', an anecdote in Villault, p. 305. But he also occasionally adds a point from personal experience. Thus, within the present omission, sarsaparilla as a cure for venereal diseases is stated to be boiled in spirits, rather than in water. For the whole Letter, cf. *1732*, pp. 277/3–280/1, which for once adds very little from Bosman.

[2] The two last sentences are original.

Cf. *1732*, p. 277/7, which adds the following, from an untraced source – 'The Blacks, in case of a violent cholick, drink morning and evening, for several days successively, a large calabash of lime-juice and Malagueta mixt, which seems at first to be contradictory for such distempers, were it not known, that our physicians in France give Limonade for gravellous cholicks'.

[3] Omission of one paragraph, on medicines for cholic. The reference to a hare-skin was inspired by Villault's injunction to cover the stomach at night, to prevent chills, with a padded vest (*chemizette d'ouatte*) or a skin (Villault, p. 300). For Barbot's earlier reference to the health of Europeans, to his own health and to the hare-skin, see Letter 2/6, Additional Passages, and note 19, above.

Cf. *1732*, p. 277/11, which enlarges at some length, mainly embroidery but including the observation that the hare-skin 'made me often sweat wonderfully'.

[4] Barbot enlarges on Dapper, p. 95/6, but in *1732* omits this theorizing.

[5] Omission of almost all the whole of a very long passage on Guinea worms, possible explanations of how and why they affect whites and blacks, and how to deal with them, taken from Dapper and Villault, but derived ultimately from Marees. Barbot adds – 'I recollect that you have previously pressed me to detail the nature of these worms and what engenders them. You have always expressed to me reservations on this last point since the

exact cause is not easy to discover, but as I have now a greater knowledge of this than on my first voyage, I wish to report here what I have learned in these parts'. In fact, he adds very little to his sources. He notes that 'fish cannot be kept free from worms for more than 3–4 hours', and commenting on the view that there were no worms at Accra, adds – 'I believe that the lack of woods and hills contributes to the purification of the air, for this part of the Gold Coast does not have what is inland'. His sources having spoken of the agony caused by worms in the breast and scrotum, Barbot enlarges as follows – 'It has been necessary to tie down men who have had worms in these places or in the penis'. To encourage the worms to emerge, Barbot adds that poultices and fomentations may be applied twice daily. Finally, he adds the anecdote in the text. There is no mention of worms in Barbot's 1678–9 journal.

Cf. *1732*, pp. 278/2–279/2, which adds that 'to prevent this disease' whites should observe the general health injunctions and 'especially abstain as much as possible from the use of women'; and also includes occasional slight borrowings from Bosman, pp. 108–9, e.g., 'at Cormentin and Apam'.

[6] Omission of a short passage on the callousness of the blacks to sick people, from Dapper, p. 97/2. Barbot adds – 'I have several times asked the reason for their hard-heartedness but never had a satisfactory explanation'.

Cf. *1732*, p. 279/8–9, which adds that the blacks 'when sick or wounded, endeavour to appear unconcerned'.

[7] This incident is not mentioned in the 1678–1679 journal.

Cf. *1732*, p. 280/1.

[8] This curious and untypical passage is printed in *1732* within inverted commas, for no obvious reason and perhaps in error.

LETTER 26

The religion of the natives. Their fetishes, sacrifices and priests.

Today, Sir, I propose to converse with you about the religion of these peoples, about their fetishes, sacrifices and priests. Be prepared to laugh at the fantasies you will behold; yet at the same time lament the baleful state of these wretched Africans, abandoned by God to the Prince of Darkness, who is preparing them for eternal gloom; and at the same time join me in blessing this thrice-wise Providence for singling us out in such a favourable manner.[1]

In general it may be said that these people do not, strictly speaking, possess any religion, any more than do those of Guinea. All that they have is a confused, general notion of a Supreme Being who, having created the world, supervises it. Since they have no other knowledge about this whatsoever, they cherish ideas that are altogether strange. However, they imagine two gods in nature – the one white, the other black. The former, whom they call Jan Goeman [*insert:* or Bossum] (which means 'Good Man John'), is in their opinion the god of the whites and is called 'good man' because they say it is from him that we obtain the many fine things we possess.[2] The latter, whom they call *diabolo*, is their own god, because this Spirit of Falsehood heaps misfortune and misery upon them.[3] [. . .][4] /p. 100/ They have such a horror of this black god that they tremble when people speak of him. They attribute to him all their misfortune and lack of success, claiming that those fetishes which they make for themselves in accordance with their whimsical fantasies are totally governed by this Apostate Angel. Several people have thought that those who say that the blacks state that the Devil beats them were pulling their legs, yet if they would take the trouble to come to Guinea, they would soon see that it is a constant truth and that often one hears the blacks shouting and howling in the night. Indeed, they frequently come out of their houses in a great sweat and terror-stricken, their eyes flooded with tears. At Accra some have told me that the Devil often appeared to them in the form of a black dog, and on another occasion also that he spoke to them when they could see no being near them.[5] [. . .][6] /p. 101/

I have told you elsewhere, Sir, that these peoples have fetishes, allocated for various purposes, just as Roman Catholics have their saints. Generally they take them from one of the elements, from forests, rocks, animals, birds, plants, herbs or from a compound, for instance of moistened earth with tallow and feathers, the whole object being covered on top with a small piece of linen.[7] Women possess them in order to have a successful delivery; some of them heal headaches, others fever, others the pox; one is against worms, another against drowning; some are to ensure that a person encounter no thieves on the road or that there be no storm when someone goes fishing or makes a journey; and they give these fetishes a thousand other properties.[8] [. . ./p. 102/. . .][9]

As fetish trees they generally take palm trees. In my view these are the one that most deserve this [recognition], as many of them can be found in this coast, and you also find many of them dedicated to this purpose. All who go past them tear off fibres of the bark, and twist them between their fingers; then, having made a knot at one end,

578

they attach them to their waist, arms or legs.[10] Not content with
turning hills into fetishes, they also believe that this is where other
fetishes reside, because thunder occurs there more often than anywhere else. Furthermore, they have more respect and veneration for
these hills than for other things. They place wine, oil, bread, roast
fowls, maize, etc. around the foot of hills for the sustenance of the
hills. They do the same in the case of the rocks and stones which
they have consecrated, such as those that can be seen at Boutrou and
Dickisjydorp, which have hooked staves and provisions all over
them.[11] [...]12 I have told you that in many places the lakes and
rivers are likewise treated as fetishes.[13] At Accra there is a lake very
close to the Danish fort, where I one day saw a droll ceremony of
prayer to the fetish, in order to bring rain upon the maize, which
greatly needed water. A large band of blacks from the village and its
vicinity went to the banks of this pond, carrying a sheep ceremo-
niously. At the pond the priests cut the sheep's throat in such a way
that the blood mixed with the water in the pond, which was salty.
Then a fire was lit; the flesh, which had been cut into pieces, was
roasted there on the embers; and as fast as it was roasted, they ate it.
Afterwards they took a *pot de gray*, which they threw into the lake,
uttering certain words. I got a Dane who was serving as my interpreter to ask them what they expected of this entertaining ceremony.
They told me that since the lake was a great fetish and a messenger
of the streams and rivers of the whole country, they were imploring
its assistance /p. 103/ and mediation, in order that it might be willing
to take the pot they had given it and go and ask these rivers and
streams for water. They said they hoped that upon its return it
would tip the pot, filled with water, upon their crops.[14] The Portuguese drained this pond and turned it into a salty marsh, which
caused the natives great hardship; and partly on account of this, and
partly also because of the Aquamboes war, the natives abandoned
the place to Portuguese domination, many of them moving to Little
Popo (near Ardra), where they established themselves.[15] [...]16

It is true that it greatly distresses them if one insults the fetishes
[they wear]. Often, indeed, it is necessary to snatch them forcibly;
and even when you order them [to hand them over] it is quite
difficult to succeed. I remember having had in my hand for a
moment the fetish of one of the blacks belonging to the Danish fort
of Acra. The following day this Moor came to the Commandant, in
front of whom he fell upon his knees, his eyes flooded with tears.

He cried out at the top of his voice that his fetish was so enraged at having been desecrated by a white man that he had been very much ill-used by it during the night, because he had allowed this outrage to be committed. And in the morning, after he had made a sacrifice to it and prayed to it in company with the priest, the fetish had told him it must be given a bottle of brandy and two *aquiers* of gold to appease it. This was given to the poor black, who, I believe, would have hanged himself if we had refused, for he firmly imagined that he would have no rest unless this small present were made.[17] The fetish which I had taken from this black [*nègre*] was in the shape of a Bologne sausage and was composed of glassware, beads, herbs, clay, burnt feathers, tallow, and threads of bark from the fetish tree, all pounded and kneaded together. At one end of the figure was a sort of human face, as you can see.[18] This black also had a calabash containing several little stones, bones, pieces of wood, kernels, etc., which served to make known to him the wishes of the fetish, according to the arrangement in which they were found after being tipped out of the calabash.[19]

[illustration no. (86), a fetish object]†

Some people are convinced that these fetisseros or fetish priests are /p. 104/ sorcerers; that they are in communication with the Devil; and that it is through his means that they operate. Whether or not this is true, they are very serious people and lead a prudent life. They vow never to drink palm wine.[20] This office is hereditary within families; there are some families [*insert:* at Comendo] which have held it since time immemorial, which gives them greater esteem among the blacks.[21] [. . .][22] These priests, like all the other Moors, have strange opinions concerning the separation of the soul from the body. Some believe that the soul perishes together with the body, as in the case of animals, some say that they do not know where it goes; and others that people's souls are incorporated into other animals without their essence being changed. I have met some who have told me that the soul goes beneath the ground, where there resides an old man whom they call Bossefou. He examines them carefully, and if the soul has led a good life in the world, he lets it cross a river, having transmuted it into some kind of animal, but if it has acted badly during its life, he hurls it into this river, where it cannot help being drowned and in consequence becomes nothing. All of this resembles the metaphysics of Pythagoras concerning the Acheron of the poets. I believe this

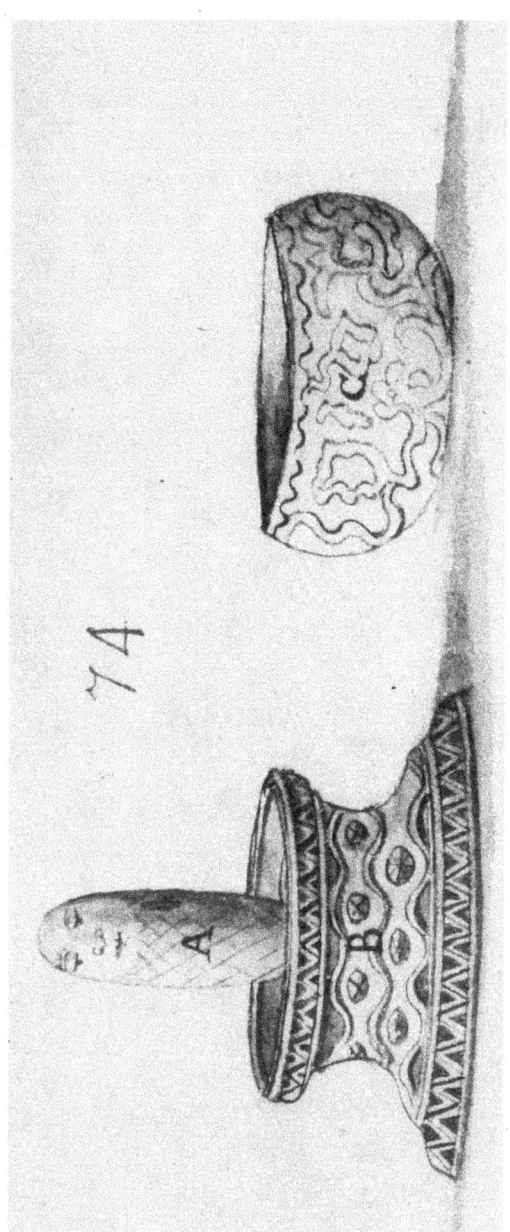

49. Gold Coast fetish object

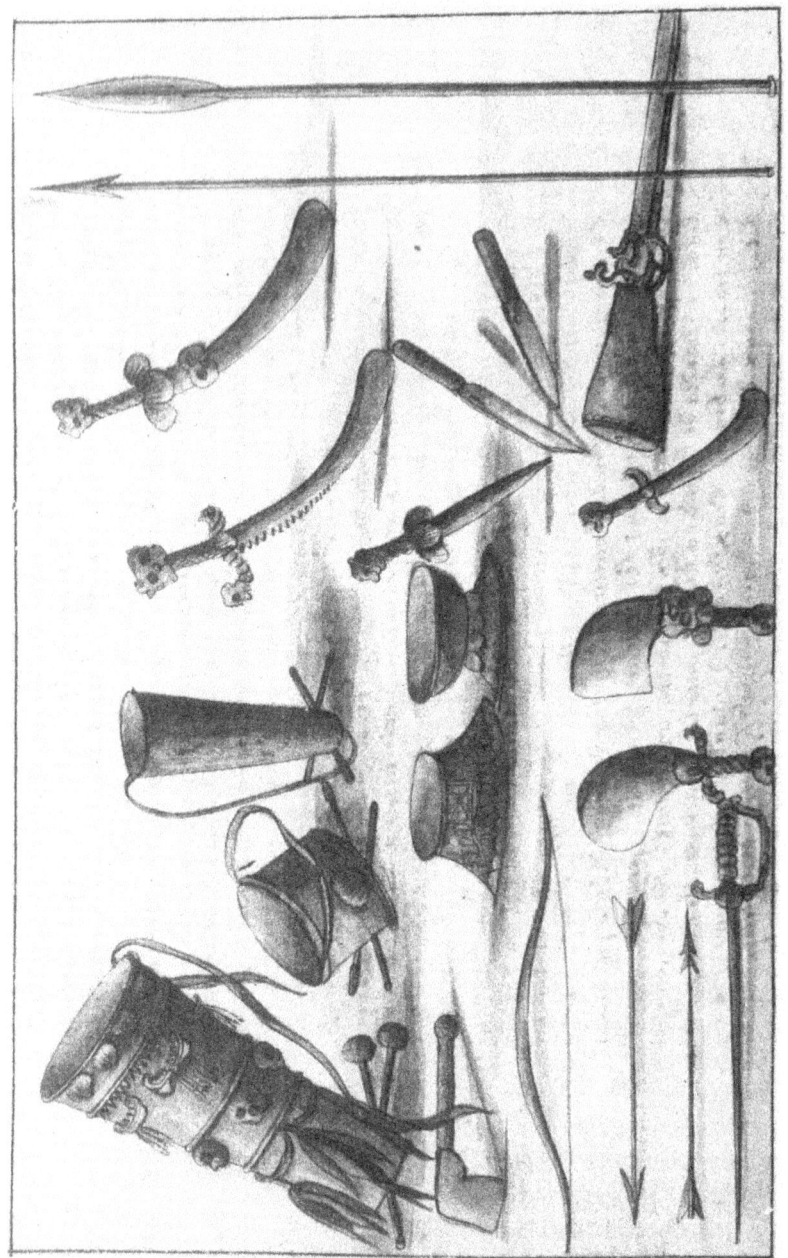

50. Gold Coast weapons

fellow Bossefou resembles the Charon described by the latter.[23] [. . .][24]

Indeed, Sir, although you may tell these people about the Divinity that is looked up to by the works of Nature, Nature being – as you know – the great book for mankind, and although they may at first assent to what you demonstrate to them by palpable evidence, as soon as you leave them for a moment they no longer remember anything; or, if they do retain it, they do so in order to turn it to ridicule among themselves. They lack neither good sense nor memory. I have met several who, having been brought up among Europeans on this coast, were able to answer the catechism of the Bible quite well; they even talked knowledgably about the Creation of the World, the Fall of Adam, the Flood, Moses, and Jesus Christ; yet like the others they live in the superstition of the fetishes. The number of those who renounce fetishes completely is very small.[25] The majority of them have /p. 105/ absurd opinions concerning God. When there is thunder, they say that the noise is that of the trumpets of Jean Goeman, who is amusing himself with his wives.[26] I detest reciting such instances of impiety to you, but am obliged to do so because of your curiosity to know everything. This is the way they conceive of God. They are so frightened of thunder that they convince themselves that unless they were to hide, the thunderbolts would crush them; for they are fully aware that they are not His people and that they are black. One meets few of them who venture to remain out of doors when it thunders; and if taken by surprise in the open country, they do everything possible to reach shelter. According to what I have been told, lightning has killed several of them and injured an enormous number. They are likewise amazed that white people have so little fear of it and take so little trouble to reach shelter when there is thunder or lightning.[27] With this letter I enclose a plate which I have drawn in order that you may better understand how these Moors conduct their fetish-worship. I am, Sir, Your etc.

[illustration no. (87), scene of worship][28]

Additional Passage from 1732

[pp. 317/9–10, 318/4, on certain figures of humans, and on African idolatry]

The Teraphims or Seraphims in Aegypt, were figures having a human head, without a body, arms or other limbs . . . / I have seen such figures at Sierra Leona, Rio Sestro and Mina, as appears in the cuts relating to the description of those countries; and they were set up in the roads, under little huts. ... Those puppets mention'd in the description of Mina, and the idol of the Acra Blacks, there discours'd of, were no other than the resemblance of human heads, without any body or limbs. ... This will suffice to convince some persons who will argue, that the service the people of Guinea do to their idols is not idolatry, in a strict sense, because they do not worship them as gods, nor even the devil himself, though they dread him so very much, as has been said before; for confirming whereof I shall use the words of St Paul, 1 Cor., chap. x. 19, 20 ... Others also have been of opinion, speaking of Jews and Gentiles, that they might attain to life everlasting, without the knowledge of God, the Supernatural Being, and without the knowledge of the immortality of the soul, and of reward and punishment after this life; but Navarette very justly says, that such doctrine cannot be defended or taught by sound apostolical missioners.[29]

NOTES

[1] In 1679 Barbot recorded fairly extensive, albeit selective, information about religious beliefs on Gold Coast, obtained both by personal observation and from the Commandant of Christiansborg, Olrichs (*1679*, pp. 334–7). Some of Olrich's information seems to fit central Gold Coast rather than the Accra district – perhaps Olrichs had previously served in the other Danish fort, Frederiksborg, or perhaps religious beliefs in the two areas had more in common than they do today. Nevertheless, in the present Letter, which generally incorporates fairly typical European attitudes of the period towards non-Christian beliefs (with perhaps a specific trace of Barbot's Huguenot upbringing in the emphasis on predestination in this opening paragraph), Barbot in fact relies almost as heavily as elsewhere upon his normal sources for the region, Marees and Villault. The corresponding chapter in *1732* (pp. 304–18) is very long: in addition to extensive borrowing from Bosman, Barbot incorporates many comparisons with other cultures.

[2] The statements about African lack of religion and about European possessions derive from Villault, pp. 257, 260, embroidering Marees, f. 36–36v, while 'Jan Goeman' represents 'Iuan goemain' in Marees, f. 37. Barbot's attempt to explain this expression (Dutch *goede man*, 'good man') is nonsense: in reality it was an Akan term, *onyankome* (Jones 1983a, p. 176, n. 156). Barbot seems not to have recognized that he himself had collected the

term in 1679, in the form 'Jankomé', glossed then as 'a sort of divinity living on high' but not capable of being invoked (*1679*,p. 334). The term 'Bossum' (*o-bósõm*, Jones 1983a, p. 158, n. 96) was apparently inserted after reading Bosman, p. 147.

Cf. *1732*, p. 304/2–5, which enlarges with references to Virginia, Japan and Plato, also a little from Bosman, p. 146, and which confuses 'Bossum' with 'Bossefoe' (see note 23 below) – but it does correctly stress the diversity of religious practice, almost from village to village.

[3] Apart from the word 'diabolo', this passage is from Marees, f. 36v. But the dichotomy between two gods – one good and white, the other bad and black – was Barbot's own and seems to have rested upon a misunderstanding.

Cf. *1732*, p. 304/4, which embroiders, including – 'from the Portuguese language, Demonio, or Diabro'.

[4] Omission of two sentences, on beliefs of Africans concerning their harsh treatment by God, from Marees, f. 36v.

Cf. *1732*, p. 306/3–8, which replaces this with a discussion of 'Opinions of the creation', from Bosman, pp. 146–7, and a digression on the religion of Madagascar and the Cape of Good Hope, from a named French source (Misson, i.e. Leguat 1708, pp. 289, 297).

[5] In 1679 Barbot recorded that the devil was worshipped and that he beat people (*1679*, p. 337). On fear of the devil, Barbot echoes Marees, f. 36, and Villault, p. 261; and beating by fetishes was mentioned by Villault, p. 282. Despite the personal reference, the last sentence is from Marees, f. 35v, which did not specify Accra. Whereas Müller in the 1660s stated that in the Cape Coast area the devil was believed to have a black complexion and to be accompanied by a black dog (Jones 1983a, p. 159), Barbot's sources stated that he appeared in the form of such an animal (Marees, f. 35v, and Villault, p. 282).

Cf. *1732*, p. 305/1–7, which changes 'totally governed' to 'sometimes overruled', adds material on sacrifices and ghosts from Bosman, pp. 158–9, 161, and also comparative material on America and India.

[6] Omission of six paragraphs on worship and fetishes which attempt to harmonize Marees, ff. 33v–34v, 35v, 37v, with Villault, pp. 257–9, 263, 267, 284. Barbot uses the first person when in fact quoting directly from Marees.

Cf. *1732*, pp. 308/2–309/3, 315/3–4, 6, which changes the first person to 'us Europeans', and adds considerable material from Bosman, pp. 153–5.

[7] The reference to earth, tallow and feathers echoes Villault, pp. 264, 272, 280 (for these ingredients of fetishes, see Bosman, p. 150; Jones 1983a, p. 163). Since Barbot, unlike Villault, refers to a fetish being wrapped in linen, he may have received information on this subject himself, perhaps at Accra.

But the fact that he placed such diverse elements within the single category of 'fetish' indicates that he had a limited grasp of religious beliefs in this region.

Cf. *1732*, p. 309/4–7, which omits the Catholics and adds to the list of what was worshipped – 'the sea, rivers, lakes, ponds, fishes, mountains, trees, plants, herbs, rocks, woods, birds and beasts', items mentioned in a later paragraph of *1688* here omitted (see note 9 below).

[8] Although many of the properties described are not specifically mentioned, Barbot was probably influenced by Marees, ff. 12v, 34v.

Cf. *1732*, p. 317/7–8, which adds material from Bosman, pp. 153–4.

[9] Omission of one paragraph on fetishes of natural objects, mainly from Villault, pp. 265–7 (itself partly from Marees, ff. 41v–42). Barbots's main addition is the remark: 'it is true that they are not so enraged when these fetishes are insulted by a white man, because they say that we are gods, like the fetish; but the Moors are punished by death'.

Cf. *1732*, pp. 309/4–7, 315/9–316/3, which adds material on the Sabbath from Marees f. 33v; material on the Sabbath, sacred groves, etc, from Bosman, p. 153; and a discussion of sacred groves among the Hebrews and others, partly from Jurieu 1704.

[10] Barbot was the only seventeenth-century author to associate the palm-tree (*palmiste*) with 'fetish': he was probably mistaken and was perhaps merely embroidering upon Marees, f. 34v. For beliefs concerning 'powerful' trees in this area, see Rattray 1927, pp. 7–8.

Cf. *1732*, pp. 309/8, 314/4–315/2, which expands – 'especially that sort of [palm tree] which they call Assianam'. Here Barbot was drawing upon a reference to trees referred to as 'Fetisso Dasianam', whose supernatural power could help men to catch more fish, in Marees, f. 34v. As Barbot recognized, the initial consonant in 'Dasianam' must be Portuguese: thus the Akan/Twi term was probably not *daase na nam*, 'thanking for fish', but simply *nsu-nam*, 'fish, when considered as an article of food' (Marees 1987, pp. 68, n. 6; 254). The passage also adds substantial miscellaneous third-hand information on Gold Coast religion, stated in error to be from 'Faria e Sousa' (Faria y Sousa 1698), but actually from Vasconcelos 1641.

[11] Derived from Marees, f. 36, and Villault, pp. 267–8, except for the roast fowls and the reference to Butre and Dixcove. (This is the only instance where Barbot used the Dutch variant of the latter toponym, 'Dick-iskydorp'. Elsewhere he referred to the place as 'Infiama', 'Dickisky', 'Dick-isco' or 'Dikiscrom': see Letter 2/3, note 37, above). If Barbot himself saw hooked sticks at these places, it was probably in 1682, since he did not record them when he visited Butre in 1679 (*1679*, pp. 284–5). Sacred sticks were mentioned with reference to central Gold Coast by two earlier sources (Jones 1983a, pp. 108, 161) and with reference to the coast further East by

two later sources (Rask 1754, pp. 259–60; Rømer 1760, pp. 74–5). In more recent times, however, sticks of this kind do not appear to have played a major role in the religious beliefs of this area. For the sacred rocks, see Letter 2/3, p. 7 and note 47, above.

Cf. *1732*, p. 309/9 (see Letter 1/31, Additional Passage and note 58), which adds that the 'rock deities . . . adorned all over with hooked staves' included 'a vast rock at Tachorary'.

[12] Omission of one sentence on Ivory Coast worship at sea-rocks, from Dapper, pp. 62/8, and two paragraphs on fishes and birds which served as fetishes, mainly from Marees, f. 35v, and Villault, p. 266.

Cf. *1732*, pp. 309/9 (see previous note), 310/5–312/2, which links the Ivory Coast practice with Barbot's own information on 'rock deities' at Butre, Dixcove and Takoradi, probably without justification. Among changes are a reference to the swordfish as 'the English fish of which I have given you a picture', while Villault's description of a wren-like bird is modified from 'black mixed with grey and white' to 'black mixed with grey and brown', and it is stated that many such birds are to be found at Whydah, whereas Villault was referring to central Gold Coast. Barbot also inserts a very lengthy section on 'Idolatry of other nations', including a reference to Navarette's travels.

[13] In Asante mythology the major rivers were described as children of the 'Sky God' Nyame and to varying degrees were 'all looked upon as containing the power or spirit of the divine Creator' (Rattray 1923, p. 146). Among the Gã, for whom lack of water was a common problem, rain was often associated with the god of the lagoon belonging to the town concerned (Field 1937, passim).

[14] In 1679 Barbot noted this ceremony, which he must have witnessed in February. He was more specific about the location – a small, Y-shaped saltwater lake (i.e. lagoon) to the East of Christiansborg, a pistol-shot from the sea. He implied that such ceremonies were held regularly in the dry season, which he said lasted from October to March. He described the pot as an an earthenware one, and offered an explanation of the symbolic meaning: having filled the pot with water begged from the rivers and streams, the deity of the pond was expected to return home and cast the pot upon the earth so that it broke; thus the water would spread out and reach all the crops (*1679*, pp. 335–6). Barbot's description represents the earliest relatively detailed account of a religious practice in the Accra area – for an eighteenth-century account, see Rømer 1760, pp. 49–106; and some twentieth-century parallels may be recognized in the account of Gã religious practices in Field 1937.

Cf. *1732*, p. 310/1–3, which translates *pot de gray* as 'gallypot' (a small pot for ointment, etc.) and introduces minor modifications – 'some ceremonies' were performed after the sheep had been brought to the pond, the Dane 'spoke their language fluently' – and adds material on religious practices at Elmina from Vasconcelos 1641, as well as a digression on Hebrew feasts.

[15] Barbot earlier stated that the lagoon had been the fetish of Orsaky village (Letter 2/10, p. 38 and note 10, above). The draining of the lagoon must have taken place between 1679, when the Portuguese bought Christiansborg from the Danes, and Barbot's return at the beginning of 1682, a year before the Portuguese handed the fort back to the Danes. Salt from Accra was an important commodity in trade with the interior in the late seventeenth and early eighteenth centuries (Tilleman 1697, pp. 110–11; Van Dantzig 1978, pp. 144–5). The reference to a migration from Accra to Little Popo is significant: it is known that the king of Accra, Fourri/Ofori, having fled from Accra to Fetu at some date between 1679 and early 1681, eventually moved to Little Popo, where he founded a dynasty; but apparently he did not do this until after Barbot's second voyage (see Letter 2/10, note 3, above; Letter 3/1, note 16, below). Probably some of his people, however, went to Little Popo earlier than he did – see Bosman, pp. 69, 332; Wilks 1957, p. 111; Van Dantzig 1980, pp. 190–1, 211.

Cf. *1732*, p. 310/4, which is somewhat clearer: 'the Portugueses, when they became masters of the Danish fort there, drained the afore-mentioned pool, in order to convert it into a salt-pit, after their manner'. On the other hand, instead of mentioning the Akwamu war, it refers vaguely to 'the depradations committed by the Blacks at Acra'.

[16] Omission of two paragraphs and part of a third, on fetishes and the immunity of Europeans from magical punishment when they destroy them, mainly from Villault, pp. 268–75, 285, with minor additions from Marees, f. 35.

Cf. *1732*, pp. 312/3, 315/5, which embroiders.

[17] This incident occurred when Barbot was dining with Olrichs at Accra in 1679, and Barbot then implied that Olrichs demanded the fetish from a servant in order to show it to Barbot (*1679*, p. 335). The present passage elaborates. Barbot's fairly sympathetic attitude contrasts with that of his Catholic compatriots, who noted with satisfaction the consternation caused when they desecrated fetishes (Villault, pp. 270–73; Roussier 1935, p. 216).

Cf. *1732*, p. 312/3, which elaborates further, adding that the man claimed to have been 'beaten . . . cruelly' by his fetish during the night and that after Barbot, 'to be rid of his clamours, and rid him of his fears', had granted his request, the man 'went away well satisfied, and in appearance full of joy, carrying the gold and brandy to his priest who 'tis likely reaped the benefit of it'.

[18] In 1679 Barbot described and drew a phallic-shaped object, with a human face roughly marked at the top, which he stated was formed of a mixture of a little piece of gold, pearls or other precious things, ashes from

burned parts of birds, earth, and the whites of eggs; and he drew the object standing upright in a curiously shaped vessel, said to be a reed-basket (but more likely a wooden stand or the lower part of a gourd), with a decorated or carved outer surface, and alongside it, another vessel, a decorated gourd, used in consulting the fetish: he did not state that this fetish was the one taken from the servant (*1679*, pp. 334–5). The description he now gives of the seized fetish repeats the shape of the object, including the face, but the materials are different. The illustration on this page of *1688* is based on the earlier description, but the object now stands within the second vessel – this version is repeated, more crudely, in *1732*, Plate 7 (p. 104) (where the other fetishes shown are mainly copied from Marees, plate 5). The 'stand' appears instead in illustration no. (86) (in Letter 2/24 above). Barbot now omits to repeat what he had noted in 1679 concerning the 'basket', in which a fetish was kept in order to avoid contamination (see Villault, p. 280; Jones 1983a, pp. 162–3, 221). A possible explanation of the change in materials is that Barbot obtained further information on the subject during his later visit in 1682. It will be noted that Barbot now terms the second vessel a 'calabash' – this eliminates the suggestion that the vessel shown is a brass, lidless bowl of Islamic profile (Garrard 1983, p. 30). In Akan culture, objects with protective powers which do not come directly or indirectly from God (Nyame) are called *suman* and are in most cases personal to their owner (Rattray 1927, p. 23). Barbot appears to be the only early author to mention an anthropomorphic element in the shape of these objects.

Cf. *1732*, p. 312/4, which modifies somewhat – 'an antick, rough and misshapen human countenance . . . set up in a painted deep calabash, or gourd'.

[19] In 1679 Barbot noted the method of divination now described, the contents of the gourd apparently being tipped out before the fetish, but the list of items involved was somewhat different – stones, beads, knives, and pieces of wood cut in various shapes (*1679*, p. 335). For similar references to divination, see Jones 1983a, p. 166; Jones 1985, p. 53, n. 98.

Cf. *1732*, pp. 312/4, 313/10, 314/1–3, the latter passages being from Bosman, pp. 150-53 (but 'pipe or horn', a mistranslation, should read 'tray or calabash': *HIA* 1977, p. 249), the divinatory items used in the swearing of an oath being similar to those listed earlier by Barbot.

[20] The reference to communication with the devil may derive from Marees, f. 36. That priests vowed to abstain from palm wine is not mentioned by other authors and is probably incorrect, at least in general, although in recent times every priest must observe the behavioural and dietary prohibitions of the particular god by whom he or she is possessed (Rattray 1927, pp. 42–4; Field 1937, p. 119). Possibly Barbot was influenced by Villault's statement that certain people – not necessarily priests – vowed to abstain from wine (Villault, p. 265; and see Bosman, p. 155; Jones 1983a, pp. 86, 163).

587

Cf. *1732*, pp. 312/5–313/10, 316/4–6: the latter passage dismisses the view that Gold Coast priests were sorcerers, ascribing it to the Portuguese, and adds Biblical references; the former passage, relating to oaths and the use of fetishes, is entirely from Bosman, pp. 148–51, apart from a reference to swearing an oath 'by their parents head or beard', the source of which is untraced. Swearing 'upon the head of someone' is mentioned by Loyer (see Roussier 1935, p. 217), but his book appeared in 1714 – too late to be used by Barbot.

[21] There is no reason to believe that the profession of priest (*komfoo*) was ever hereditary in Akan society. Among the Gã, however, it is true that priests (*wulomei*) were drawn from particular 'houses' (patrilineages). The reference to Komenda may merely be intended to give Barbot's remarks an air of authenticity; but it is possible that he received information in Komenda during his second voyage, when he was involved in attempting to establish a French post there (see Letter 2/3, note 66).

Cf. *1732*, p. 316/7–8, which expands slightly, emphasizing the priests' 'frauds and impostures', probably influenced by Bosman, pp. 151–5.

[22] Omission of three sentences on the influence and clothing of priests, from Villault, p. 275, Barbot changing 'Leyden serge' to 'Leyden or Coesveld serge'.

Cf. *1732*, p. 316/9–317/5, which elaborates further: 'the coarsest Leyden says, or Coesveld linen, which is wrapped about their waists, and hangs down to their legs, with a loose scarf over it' – other details suggest that when writing his English text Barbot re-read Villault. The passage also adds substantial material on 'Banishing of the Devil' and 'Computation of Time' from Bosman, pp. 158–60.

[23] In 1679 Barbot obtained information from Olrichs about local beliefs concerning the afterlife, which he now largely repeats (*1679*, pp. 336–7). But the references to the soul perishing with the body and to people who did not know where the soul went are from Marees, f. 36v. Also Barbot here omits or alters significant details he noted earlier, such as the fact that the river on which Bossefou lived was the 'Combour', situated in the 'kingdom of Ackeny', 60 leagues from the coast, and discharging into the 'Niger', a river watering the kingdom of 'Gagor', a neighbour of the kingdom of the 'Acanes'. (A contemporary source, discussing opinions about the afterlife, referred to 'a distant path behind Accania': Jones 1983a, p. 179.) There does not appear to be a modern river-name corresponding to 'Combour'. The name 'Bossefou' presumably represents a combination of Akan *o-bósōm*, 'deity' and *-fó(o)*, 'person'. It is possible – especially in view of what Barbot goes on to say about African knowledge of the Christian faith – that the 'judicatory' role attributed to Bossefou constituted in part a response to intercourse with the Portuguese. This almost certainly applied to several other features of what has usually been interpreted as 'traditional African religion' (see Henige 1982; Garrard 1984).

Cf. *1732*, pp. 307/1-9, 308/1, which abridges considerably and alters the orthography to 'Bossefoe', and also adds material on the afterlife from Bosman, pp. 156–7, as well as lengthy material on Hebrew and other views of the afterlife (including the supposition that African beliefs had been influenced by Jewish beliefs via the Arabs). Barbot overlooked the striking resemblance between his 'Bossefou' and the 'great Feticheer or Priest' described by Bosman: both lived in a roofless house, yet were sheltered from the rain (*1679*, p. 337); and both determined whether those who had died should have an afterlife. (It has been suggested that Bosman's 'Feticheer' may in a certain sense be identified with Komfo Anokye, the priest who is said to have played a leading role in the founding of Asante: McCaskie 1986, pp. 319–20 – but McCaskie does not discuss Barbot). However, some of the characteristics mentioned by Bosman and Barbot may not have been confined to a single entity: for instance, Asante people say that all houses in the spirit world have no roofs (Rattray 1927, p. 195). For views on reincarnation expressed in this region in more recent times, see Grottanelli 1965.

[24] Omission of one paragraph on the afterlife, mainly from Villault, pp. 260–61, and of five sentences on Christian missions, from Dapper, p. 114/4–5.

Cf. *1732*, pp. 305/8, 307/10.

[25] The reference to local knowledge of Christian beliefs echoes Marees, f. 37v; but Barbot shifts the emphasis from the Old to the New Testament. Like most Europeans, Barbot failed to understand why, on Gold Coast in particular, many people saw nothing contradictory in accepting certain aspects of Christianity while retaining many existing beliefs and practices – a matter which has continued to interest scholars to the present day: see Peel 1987.

Cf. *1732*, p. 305/8.

[26] This sentence derives from *1679*, p. 336, although Barbot modifies the orthography ('Jankomé' becomes 'Jean Goeman') to take account of Marees. Other writers reported that Jankomé was associated with thunder, albeit in different ways (Marees, f. 37; Villault, p. 261; Jones 1983a, p. 178).

Cf. *1732*, p. 306/1.

[27] This passage is loosely based on Marees, ff. 36v–37, and Villault, p. 261.

Cf. *1732*, p. 306/1–2, which adds material on the use of sea-shells as protection against thunder, originally from the Spanish chronicler, Pulgar, but via a stated intermediate source – 'history of Spain ... p. 1202. lib. 22'; and also a reference to the Brazilians.

[28] This illustration is copied from Marees, plate 5.

[29] Barbot concludes this chapter (and the 'Third Book' of the English account), in *1732*, pp. 317/7–318/4, with a 'digression' on 'idolatry in

general', Hebrew, Roman, etc, partly from Jurieu 1704. For the figures at Sierra Leone and Rio Sestro see Letter 1/17, p. 97 and note 11, above, and Letter 1/29, p. 157, above; and for the 'puppets' (terracotta heads) of Mina, Letter 2/28, pp. 112–3 and note 23, below. Barbot's discussion of the evil of idolatry is coloured by the Protestant interpretation of Roman Catholic 'veneration' of images as 'worship' of them.

LETTER 27

Deaths and funeral ceremonies.

You are giving me so little respite, Sir, that I am finding it impossible to keep my account going step by step. You have encountered many things in my previous letters which will no doubt have caused you to smile. Today I have more such episodes in mind because I intend to tell you about death among these peoples and about the ceremonies they perform at their burials. [. . ./pp. 106/. . .][1] They speak to the dead person, sometimes all at once, sometimes in turn, and ask him what reason he had to depart this life, what he lacked in the world, who killed him, and a hundred other such ridiculous questions. [. . .] At Acra, they lie stretched out on the dead person's stomach and they take him by the nose and proceed to ask him all the same questions as those which I have just outlined to you, and they claim that this lifeless person responds to their interrogation by the movement of his tongue, his teeth, his eyes or his lips. [. . ./p. 107/. . .] When the time for burial comes he is borne upon the shoulders of two Moors. [. . .][2] I have told you elsewhere that in several places slaves are not [properly] buried. At Acra I have seen some thrown into a ditch. Where burial is done they are put down only 18–20 inches. This is because it is believed that those who find themselves in such a lowly state are not worthy of the slightest effort being made on their behalf.[3] [. . ./p. 108/. . .]

Poor children [of widows] are reduced to begging [by the system of inheritance]. [. . .] It is only at Acra that the law is less harsh towards the children, since they do enjoy the wealth of their deceased parents, with the exception of royalty, king's sons being excluded and the king's brother inheriting.[4] I should describe to you at this point the ceremonies which take place at the funerals of these African princes and upon the deaths of the nobility in these lands, but I shall reserve it for some other occasion, to include at an

appropriate juncture. I am going to spend the rest of the day producing an illustration of the burials of the ordinary people for you, more
or less along the lines of the description I have given you in this
letter. I remain, Your etc./p. 109/

[illustration no. (88), a burial scene][5]

Additional Passages from *1732*

[p. 282/5, on an unusual burial custom]

The Blacks about the Brandenburg fort at great Frederickstadt
near cape Tres Pontas, have a peculiar custom among them, which
is, to bury their dead in a sea chest, bowing the corps; and those
chests being commonly but four feet, or four feet and a half in
length, and the dead body consequently too long for them, they
chop off the head, and lay it on one side. As soon as the corps is let
down into the grave, the persons who attended the funeral drink
palm-wine, or rum plentifully, out of oxes horns; and what they
cannot drink off at a draught, they spill on the grave of their
deceased friend, that he may have his share of the liquor.[6]

[p. 284/10, on a funeral at Cape Coast]

I will conclude this long account of funeral ceremonies, with two
or three observations; the first, as I was told, by the English agent
general at cape Corso; that being himself present at the obsequies
of a notable deceas'd Negroe woman of the place, the sorcerer, or
priest, made a pathetick speech to the company there present,
exhorting them all to live well; to hurt or cause damage to no
person; to be very religious observers of their promises and con-
tracts, and a deal more of such morality; after which, he made the
panegyrick of the deceased woman, and ended the ceremony, by
throwing on the ground a long string of sheeps jaws, threaded
together, holding one end thereof by one hand, and cry'd aloud,
*Do ye all as the deceased; do ye imitate her; she was very careful,
during the whole course of her life, to consecrate great numbers of
sheep, on occasions of this nature; as these jaws do sufficiently testify.*
Thus many of the people there present, were moved to give each a
sheep; the agent himself not excepted: most of which did turn to
the profit of the crafty priest.[7]

NOTES

[1] In 1679, when at Accra, Barbot was told by 'Mr Olrichs, by two other men in his house, and by two black headmen' about local death rites and burial customs, especially how the dead are interrogated while the corpse is carried around, to find out who was responsible for the death (*1679*, pp. 336–7). Whether the information applied only to Accra or was intended to be more general is uncertain. To this limited information the present Letter adds no additional original information. Instead it is largely based on Marees, ff. 35–35v, 91–93v, with shorter passages from Dapper, pp. 106/4–107/3, and from Villault, pp. 286–294 (although Villault borrowed from Marees and Dapper, he claimed to have himself witnessed a burial, at Frederiksborg). All the omitted passages are from these sources.

Cf. *1732*, pp. 281/2–285/6, which adds or substitutes lengthy material from Bosman, pp. 225–33, and several comparative references, Biblical and ethnographic (to China and the Scythians, the latter stated to be from a French compilation, D.T.V.Y. 1619), but also a few additional personal references. See the Additional Passages, and for remarks in p. 285/1–2 on funerary statues at Mina, see Letter 2/28, note 23, below.

[2] The 1679 account, which does not specify that this happened only 'at Accra', is slightly fuller. The corpse responds by moving a foot, arm, hand or its head, or sometimes by grinding its teeth or moving its tongue, eyes or ears; and when carried responds by falling from its bearers on to the questioner (*1679*, p. 336).

Cf. *1732*, p. 281/10.

[3] Based on *1679*, p. 337, which does not specify that Barbot saw this at Accra. The implication appears to be that the bodies were left to be eaten by wild beasts.

Cf. *1732*, p. 283/2.

[4] The remarks about general and royal inheritance are from Villault, pp. 338–40, 371–2, but the comment on Accra inheritance appears to be original.

[5] In fact Barbot merely copies Marees, plate 17. This illustration is not repeated in *1732*.

[6] The source of this information (curiously stated to be from 'Frederickstadt' rather than 'Fredericksburgh') is uncertain. It is perhaps unlikely to have been Barbot's relative, Barbot de la Porte, whose information was political rather than ethnographic; possibly it was James Barbot.

[7] Although what the 'priest' is alleged to have said is not utterly implausible, it is unlikely that the agent himself understood the language in which the priest spoke and therefore likely that he repeated to Barbot only what an interpreter had told him – and this may have been tactfully adjusted to please Protestant suspicions about priestly motives on the part of the English (and of Barbot).

LETTER 28

Kings and their courts. Their authority and in general everything related to this [royal] attribute.

Sir, it gives me great pleasure to learn that you are not as weary as I had expected of reading letters which consist entirely of very dull matters; for you instruct me not to change anything in the plan which I originally set myself, which was to give you a description in detail of everything there is in these countries. Today I shall converse with you about the kings of this coast, their courts, their authority, etc., and generally about everything that appertains to them or has some connection with them. Although the only king I have seen was the King of Accra in 1679, I possess such reliable reports on Fetu, Sabou and Comendo that I venture to present to you what I have to say as if I had seen it with my own eyes.[1] From what you learn concerning these four African princes you can infer that those of the interior have more or less the same manners and inclinations. As you may remember, I have already stated that in several places the crown is hereditary. At Comendo, the [formal] election is held amidst festivities and rejoicing. The closest relative of the deceased king is [*inserted:* not] crowned, as he is in other states of the vicinity, at Acra and Fetu, the successor being the man who has been the deceased's *Fatairra*, or captain of the guards.[2] At Sabou he is a prince taken from one of the neighbouring [countries] and never from the country itself. The election is made there by a majority vote.[3] [. . .][4]

The king of Acra whom I saw is of short stature and also plump. He carries himself fairly well, but he is fickle in temper and fond of war, which has always gone against him. As a result he has now been despoiled of his estates by the king of Aquambous and has sought refuge with his ally, the king of Fetu. This king of Acra, called Fourri, likes Europeans, as did all his predecessors.[5] I paid him a visit at the entrance to his palace, where I found him seated, surrounded by his courtiers and guards, some of whom were seated as he was, while others were standing. He expressed great delight that I should have come to visit him, and he got me to sit in front of him while he sent someone to find his wives, in order that I should see them and witness his magnificence. His mother /p. 110/ sat on his

593

right side and his favourite wife on his left. The other wives sat behind them or at the sides, cross-legged, and all the remainder of those present stood around in a semi-circle. Then a large pot of palm wine was brought and placed between this Moorish prince and myself. With this he regaled me a few moments later, making excuses for not being provided with more substantial things with which to entertain me, saying that I had taken him by surprise.[6] His attire consisted merely of a simple gown of cloth like the cloths of Cape Verde, all the rest of his body being bare. The lords of his court and the women appeared to me fairly elegant by local standards, but were by no means as richly dressed as those of Fetu and Comenda, where everything sparkles with gold ornaments and glass beads, and where there may be as many as 200 guards, especially in the case of the king of Comendo or Guaffo, who is called Inchero.[7] The palace of Fourri seemed to me scarcely finer than the other houses of the village. The kings are wont to seat themselves each day towards nightfall at the entrance to their houses, dressed as finely as possible and wearing many pieces of goldwork and glass beads. Most of them even place themselves there in the afternoon, and this is how they spend their days during peacetime.[8] Sometimes you see a king lying there [with his head] in the lap of one or other of his wives, while they are busy examining his head and removing the lice. There are few evenings on which they do not hold a dance. The guards spend most of the time firing their muskets; they are either slaves or hired men. Some are employed within the palace, others outside.[9] The palace of King Inchero is large and spacious, but smaller than that of Fetu, which is considered the most extensive.[10] [. . .][11]

Since the common people may have as many wives as they can maintain, it is easy to convince oneself that the kings have a large number of them. The king of Comendo has 80, all of whom live inside the palace in separate apartments, where they are maintained in a magnificent manner. It is to them that the revenues levied in kind are sent. They never go out except in a hammock, and rarely on foot. It is incredible how much they scorn all other women of the common people and with what pride they walk.[12] [. . .][13]

The kings's children are instructed in various callings, although they are maintained from the revenue of the state as long as their fathers are alive. The reason for this precaution is that since the crown is not hereditary, after their father's death they suddenly find themselves toppled from the throne into the dust, from wealth to poverty; so that then they are /p. 111/ happy to have their own means of subsisting without difficulty. What they have earned during the life of their father, the king, often provides for their marriage after his decease. As a result we see the children of these kings in many forms of employment on this coast – some as merchants, some as fisherman and others engaged in warfare.[14] At Comendo, however, they have one prerogative: they enter public office, and some of them become *Faterra*, or captain of the bodyguard of the king who has succeeded their father. Thus, if this king dies while they are still alive, they themselves become king, because *Faterra* is the rank closest to the throne.[15] I was told that virtually the same practice was followed in Acra, and that in Fanteen, Fetu and elsewhere the children were given important posts in the army, placed in charge of towns or employed in collecting dues from the merchants and peasants, in order that they might earn a more decent living.[16] Many are also given to the whites as hostages, guaranteeing the safety of their forts, for which they pay tribute. Others are likewise given to neighbouring kings for affairs of state, and this is worth a great deal to them in gifts and gratuities.[17] Moreover, those among these kings' children who are engaged in trade do not pay any dues or tolls. Only when they abandon themselves entirely to debauchery are they looked upon with ridicule and contempt by everyone, and then they lose all their prerogatives.[18] [. . .][19] /p. 112/

[At royal funerals] each person is allowed to bring those presents that he wishes to give the deceased to a place in the forest, where the slaves come to receive them in order to bury them with the deceased king, in order that he may live in the same abundance in the other life. These presents consist not only of victuals, clothing and gold, but also of many slaves of both sexes, who are sacrificed and placed in the same grave as the deceased, in order that they may serve him wherever he shall be. If I am to believe the people of Comendo, no high-ranking person among them dies without them slaughtering 60 or 80 slaves (of both sexes and every age), and for a king they kill two thousand.[20] [. . .][21] In truth, Sir, these are great inhumanities! To recall them fills me with horror. [. . .][22] Mausoleums . . . [for important individuals are built and] in addition, they are accustomed to decorate these with a large number of clay busts representing men and women, designed in a fairly jolly manner. These busts are painted in various colours and garnished all over with coral and fetishes. At Mina, on the road leading from the castle to the garden,

I saw several such mausoleums, for *brafos* and officers, including one for a relative of the king of Fetu, which had /p. 113/ between 35 and 40 of these busts, displayed on the posts and in a semi-circle in the midst of the fetishes. All around them were several pots of palm wine and meat, together with leaves and branches from fetish trees.[23]

As soon as the funeral of the deceased king is concluded, people think of making a new king. Usually it is the brother or – failing that – the closest relative of the deceased king whom they elevate to this honour, except in Sabou, where they choose strangers. The coronation ceremony of this new prince consists more in great rejoicing on the part of the people than in any kind of formality. On that day he is taken from the place where he was shut up from the moment when his predecessor died (it being customary among them thus to confine those who are to occupy the throne).[24] [...][25] I have forgotten to mention in the appropriate place that the children of the deceased king's sister are enthroned, if this king's brother has none.[26] This is all that I had to tell you about this subject. I remain, Sir, Your etc.

Additional Passages from *1732*

[pp. 287/5–6, 290/2, on Guinea kings, modern avarice, and moral pride]

The people of Guinea are ignorant and unpolished, and the dominions of their princes so inconsiderable, that they scarce deserve the title of kings; for which reasons there is no drawing of what is there practised into a consequence, or making comparisons between them and polite and potent monarchs of other parts of the world. ... The first men were rude and unpolished, latter ages are doubtless grown effeminate and luxurious; this excess puts us upon all contrivances to satisfy our appetites and desires, and we range all the world to satisfy our extravagant inclinations. / This it is that prevails on so many thousands to expose themselves to all the dangers of the merciless ocean, which swallows such numbers continually, and as it inriches some, so it impoverishes others, either by shipwrecks or pirates, or other accidents; besides the unspeakable toils and hardships those who escape best are expos'd to. This is really an extravagant effect of avarice ...; yet so vain is our nature, that we condemn the poor Blacks because they labour at home, and at the same time deride them as slothful, because they are strangers to many of our superfluous

596

toils; nay, so great is our pride, that the most brutal sailor values himself above the best of these Guinea kings. / This digression is already grown too tedious, though very short in respect of what might be said upon this subject, and may perhaps be not unacceptable to some who have so much good-nature as not to run down all nations, and to believe that all ages have been guilty of their follies, as well as this we live in.[27]

[p. 290/8, on the *Fataira*]

The Fataira, or captain of the guards, is always a man of great note among those people, as being particularly intrusted with the king's person, and always attending him in his expeditions, by which he is rais'd so high, as to be sometimes advanced to the throne, upon a vacancy, as has been said before.[28]

NOTES

[1] In addition to what he writes about Accra, Barbot supplies a little original information about the king of Eguafo ('Guaffo' or 'Comendo'). In 1679 he appears to have learnt very little about Eguafo (*1679*, pp. 287–90); hence this information came either from some unpublished French source or – more probably – from his own observations during his second voyage. His source for Fetu was Villault, who had even less eyewitness experience of Gold Coast kings than had Barbot (Villault, pp. 331–2). The other principal source for this Letter is Marees, whom Barbot presumably regarded as a source for Sabou, although it is unclear how much of Marees's material in fact refers to this part of Gold Coast – and Marees too probably relied mainly on hearsay for this topic. For a modern study of political organization on Gold Coast in the seventeenth century, see Kea 1982, chapter 3.

[2] In these sentences the sequence of thought is weak, the reference to 'hereditary' being followed by an unhereditary example; the punctuation may be a slip, thus affecting the references to the localities; and the insertion of the negative may represent second thoughts. Later (p. 111), Barbot appears to be saying that the *Fatairra* succeeds, not only at Komenda, but also at Accra: for the *Fatairra*, see the Additional Passage.
   Cf. *1732*, pp. 285/9–286/3, which enlarges, first by noting that – 'Commendo, Fetu, Saboe, Acra, and others, are governed either by hereditary or elective kings. Axim, Anta, Fantin, Acron, and others, are commonwealths', following Bosman, pp. 163–4. It adds a digression on variant titles for rulers, and interprets the French passage differently, not mentioning Comendo and attributing the *Fatairra* to Accra and Fetu. Finally, it claims

597

that – 'in Fetu they will also sometimes break through the constitution . . . and elect a subject no way related to the king', this exception being deduced from a single example supplied by Hillier 1697, p. 688, to which Barbot adds his own explanation – 'the Blacks having a conceit, that some men among them are blessed with such extraordinary gifts and prerogatives by their deities, that they are capable of doing things beyond the common course of nature'.

[3] A loose interpretation of Marees, ff. 47v, 49.

Cf.*1732*, p. 286/2, 7, which on elections substitutes material on contested elections, from Bosman, p. 285.

[4] Omission of one paragraph on royal power and the need for a king to be generous, derived almost entirely from Marees, f. 47; Dapper, pp. 112/4; and Villault, pp. 334–6.

Cf. *1732*, pp. 286/9–287/1, 291/6–7, which expands, adding – 'these kings having little or nothing of their own, besides what was left by the former, which sometimes is not very considerable. It is perhaps the consideration of this great charge, which moves some of those who might be chosen in course, according to the custom of the country, to relinquish their right, chusing rather to live private, than be obliged to be so expensive in treating of their subjects.' Also added is more about royal poverty, from Bosman, pp. 188–9. The reference to the 'great charge' derives from the statement of a source that in 1687 the 'Dy' of Fetu refused to accept the kingship (Hillier 1697, p. 688).

[5] Barbot's 1679 meeting with King Fourri was very briefly noted in his journal, which merely stated that the king regaled the visitors with palm wine (*1679*, p. 322). For the earlier and later history of Fourri, see Letter 2/10, note 3, above. The reference to Fourri's predecessors who 'liked Europeans' is probably an inference based on a statement to the effect that the king of Accra took care to remain on good terms with all Europeans by not favouring any one nation, in Dapper, p. 82/8.

Cf. *1732*, p. 291/8–9, which cuts most of the comment on Fourri, but adds introductory material on visiting in general, from Bosman, p. 189.

[6] The reference to Fourri's mother is significant. Sources on Gold Coast before the nineteenth century hardly ever mention either the king's mother or the *ohemmaa* ('queen mother', not necessarily the same person). Yet Fourri's mother may have played a significant political role after the destruction of Great Accra in 1677. In the mid-eighteenth century she, rather than Fourri, was commemorated as the founder of the Little Popo dynasty (Rømer 1760, p. 120).

Cf. *1732*, p. 291/9.

[7] Barbot had evidently forgotten that in Letter 2/3, p. 10, he had estimated the number of the *Eguafohene*'s guards at 500, rather than 200. For a

detailed discussion of 'the *Ahenfo* and their retainer military organizations' on seventeenth-century Gold Coast, see Kea 1982, pp. 134–6. Although Kea's figures deserve to be treated with caution, they suggest that in this period rulers of polities such as Eguafo/Comendo and Fetu had several hundred guards or retainers, the majority of whom would have had firearms. The description of the king's clothing tallies with the remark that even men of high status wore only a cloth hanging from the waist to below the knees, in Dapper, p. 103/4. Other sources, however, mention kings who wore much more clothing (e.g. at Fetu in the 1660s, Jones 1983a, p. 182). The name Inchero does not occur in other published sources.

Cf. *1732*, p. 291/10, where Barbot adds that his information on the kings of Fetu and Comendo was supplied at Accra in 1679 by 'the Dutch commander of the fort Crevecoeur, who bore me company at that visit'. If so, his informant was Nicolaes Sweers/Sweerts, who later became Director-General (see Roussier 1935, p. 26). But neither the name Inchero nor any estimate of the number of guards is to be found in the 1679 journal. Since Barbot is unlikely to have retained these in his memory, it is probable that he received this information in 1682, when he was anxious to obtain information about Komenda (see Letter 2/3, note 68).

[8] The last two sentences are loosely based upon Villault, pp. 333–4 and Marees, f. 48.

Cf. *1732*, p. 292/1, 6–7, which embroiders.

[9] The reference to dances is from Villault, p. 334; and the description of guards was probably influenced by Marees, f. 48, although in Marees's day guards had no firearms and saluted the king by playing ivory horns instead. (By the 1660s horns and firearms were both used: Jones 1983a, pp. 182–3).

Cf. *1732*, p. 292/6–7, which modifies the first sentence, omitting the lice, and adds material on royal drinking in the market-place, from Bosman, pp. 189–91.

[10] As far as Komenda is concerned, this statement may be original. But the reference to Fetu is based on Villault, p. 335, whose account of the king's 'palace' is unconvincing. Müller, who – unlike Villault – went there himself, reported: 'The king's courtyard and houses are of very poor quality, being built like other common courtyards and houses in Fetu' (Jones 1983a, p. 182).

Cf. *1732*, p. 292/1–2, 6 ('we call them palaces, whereas they are but a cluster of cottages or huts').

[11] Omission of one sentence on the Fetu palace and one paragraph on royal processions, basically from Villault, p. 335, with a reference to musical instruments probably based on Marees, f. 47. Whereas Villault stated that a king was carried by slaves 'on their shoulders', Barbot interpreted this as meaning 'in a hammock'. Only two earlier sources, both of the period 1660–

599

1670, mention the use of hammocks for travel on Gold Coast (*Relation* 1671, p. 17; Jones 1983a, p. 186); but in 1679 Barbot noted their use (*1679*, p. 290). It is possible that they were uncommon before the second half of the seventeenth century, although in other parts of West and West-Central Africa their use is recorded much earlier. Palanquins are not specifically recorded in any pre-nineteenth-century source for Gold Coast.

Cf. *1732*, p. 292/2–3.

[12] Both Marees and Villault reported that a king's wives lived in separate 'apartments' within the palace (Marees, f. 48; Villault, p. 336). Here too Barbot interprets Villault, by assuming that if king's wives were generally carried this meant that they travelled in hammocks; yet Villault was probably doing little more than paraphrasing Marees, who stated that when such women went out 'they lean on the shoulders of other women who serve them and are their slaves'. Barbot's statement on the number of wives of the king of Comendo (the *Eguafohene*) seems to be original and sounds plausible. No other seventeenth-century author tried to estimate the number of a Gold Coast king's wives, but in the 1660s it was stated that many men of high status had 10–50 wives, and Villault was told that the son-in-law of the King of Fetu had 40 (Villault, p. 232; Jones 1983a, p. 213).

Cf. *1732*, p. 290/3, which gives the number as 'eight' (presumably a misprint for 'eighty') and conveys the misleading impression that the sentences which follow (derived from Marees and Villault) all refer to the *Eguafohene*.

[13] Omission of four sentences on royal wives, from Villault, pp. 336–7 and Marees, f. 48. Barbot's sole addition is a comment on the jealousy prevailing between the wives of a king: this was presumably not based on any first-hand information.

Cf. *1732*, p. 290/4, which expands on this, stating that in order to outdo their co-wives, women loaded themselves 'with all sorts of ornaments, corals, gold rings, and other toys, [so] that they are a perfect burden to them'.

[14] This section represents mainly an embroidered version of Marees, ff. 48v–49, and Villault, pp. 337, 339. Several other seventeenth-century observers commented similarly on Gold Coast succession practices, noting that the children of a king (and of high-ranking officials) were in a much more precarious position than their European counterparts (e.g., Dapper, p. 107/3; Jones 1983a, pp. 259, 266–7).

Cf. *1732*, p. 287/4, which omits this passage, substituting a sentence from Bosman, p. 192, on the poverty of some kings and their offspring.

[15] Little is known about royal succession in Komenda/Eguafo at this time, but it seems unlikely that the sort of arrangement described by Barbot – if it in fact existed – operated as smoothly as he implies. In the early 1640s the

Eguafohene quarrelled with his brother and arranged that his son should be made king before he himself died (Jones 1983a, p. 123). On other occasions, political divisions threatened the unity of Eguafo: thus, a long civil war took place in the 1690s, and eventually two independent polities emerged.

Cf *1732*, p. 287/4, which abridges.

[16] While the reference to public office and army posts is from Villault, p. 339, the remainder of this sentence is probably mere speculation.

[17] The second sentence is based mainly on Marees, f. 45v (partly echoed in Villault, p. 339). The practice of Gold Coast states giving hostages to the European forts lying within their territory is documented in many seventeenth-century sources (e.g., Van Dantzig 1980, pp. 35, 61, 97–8, 255).

Cf. *1732*, p. 287/4–290/2, which adds material on princes and princesses, from Bosman, pp. 192–3, and then adds a very long digression on the dignity of humble labour, even for royalty. See the Additional Passage.

[18] The statement on exemption from dues is from Villault, p. 338, and the reference to debauchery is loosely related to Villault, p. 340.

Cf. *1732*, p. 287/4, where the latter is omitted.

[19] Omission of two paragraphs and four sentences on the collection of revenues and on royal festivals and funerals, derived almost entirely from Marees, ff. 47v–48, and Villault, pp. 340–5.

Cf. *1732*, pp. 283/10, 284/1, 287/2–3, 292/4–5, which retains most of the material on funerals and festivals and adds Biblical comparisons, but substitutes material on revenues from Bosman, pp. 191–2.

[20] The reference to victuals, clothing, gold and slaves being placed in the grave is from Dapper, pp. 106/4–107/1. The rest of this section appears to be original, but presumably Barbot did not himself witness such a funeral.

Cf. *1732*, pp. 283/11–284/6, which incorporates material on human sacrifice from Bosman, p. 231, and Hillier 1697, p. 688–9 (the latter referring only to executions, although suggesting that sacrifices might be performed in a similar manner); but omits the reference to Comendo.

[21] Omission of nine sentences on human sacrifices at funerals of kings and caboceers, from Marees, f. 93, and Dapper, p. 107/1.

Cf. *1732*, p. 284/7–9, which adds further material from Bosman, pp. 231–2.

[22] Omission of three sentences on burial goods and the erection of a 'mausoleum', from Villault, pp. 345–6.

Cf. *1732*, pp. 284/2, 285/1, which largely substitutes material on the same subjects from Bosman, pp. 231–2.

[23] This passage provides important evidence on Akan funerary terracotta figures – a subject of recent research by archaeologists and art historians. Most of the thermoluminescent age-estimates for the terracottas that have

hitherto been analysed range from c. 1600 to c. 1800. Apart from Barbot, only three authors before the mid-nineteenth century provide original information on this subject. Marees, having described how the heads of people sacrificed at a royal funeral were placed 'around the Sepulchre and Grave' of the deceased king, added: 'All his Nobles who used to serve him are modelled from life in earth, painted and put in a row all around the Grave, side by side' (Marees, f. 93v). Müller, seventy years later, in a reference to graves in general rather than to those of kings alone, reported – 'They also make male and female figures out of clay and paint them red and white. They are supposed to represent the deceased' (Jones 1983a, p. 258). Barbot had evidently read what Marees had written on this subject, and he probably borrowed the term *brafo* from Dapper (e.g., Dapper, p. 75/3); but most of his remarks derive from what he himself observed at Elmina in 1682. As he indicated earlier (Letter 2/5, p. 20 and note 25, above), he saw these 'tombs ... decorated with grotesques and ridiculous figures' near the road connecting the two Dutch forts at Elmina. Particularly valuable is his description of the way in which the figures were arranged.

Cf. *1732*, p. 285/1-2, which introduces slight modifications ('thirty or more figures of human kind, each set up on a post in a semicircle, in the center whereof, were several idols encompassed with pots of palm-wine, and dishes of meat, covered with branches and leaves of the consecrated tree'); and also incorporates a few remarks on 'earthen images' from Bosman, p. 232 – it may be significant that Bosman's statement referred not to Elmina but to Axim.

[24] The first part of this section is based on Villault, p. 347, but with one major addition: Villault referred to the king's successor merely as his 'closest relative', without mentioning his brother. The last sentence may represent mere conjecture, but could also be the earliest reference to the 'confinement' of a new chief – a form of *rite de passage* which helps to emphasize the change in his status. In some Akan states, a chief, immediately after being placed on the stool, must spend a period ranging from one to three weeks shut up in a room, often the one where the blackened stools of his predecessors are kept (Welman 1930, pp. 82–6).

Cf. *1732*, p. 286/4, which incorporates a sentence from Bosman, p. 133.

[25] Omission of three sentences and one paragraph, on the election of kings, mainly from Villault, pp. 347–50. Barbot's only significant addition is his statement that the festival held at the beginning of a king's reign lasted eight days, whereas according to Villault it did not last more than four or five days.

Cf. *1732*, p. 286/4–6, 8.

[26] This sentence seems to be original and suggests that Barbot was dimly aware of the matrilineal emphasis in Akan society. Several other sources recognized that a ruler's children, being considered as belonging to their

mothers' matrilineages rather than to his lineage, could not succeed him (Marees, f. 49; Villault, pp. 338–9; Jones 1983a, p. 184). Bosman too, when dealing with inheritance of property, wrote that 'the Brothers and Sisters Children are the right and lawful Heirs' (Bosman, p. 203). Yet elsewhere Bosman reported that 'the dignity of the king or captain' descended 'from father to son' (p. 133) – a curious remark, which has been interpreted as referring merely to the leadership of *asafo* companies, although it is difficult to see how Bosman could have meant this. Those Europeans who attempted to define the 'rules' of succession in terms of particular relatives misunderstood the nature of political legitimacy in Gold Coast society. The limited seventeenth-century evidence we possess suggests that while in principle a chief was supposed to come from 'that particular kindred branch of the clan to which the Stool belongs' (Rattray 1929, p. 84), in practice this rule was often set aside. Barbot's comment is omitted in *1732*.

[27] Was the reference to those impoverished by marine ventures intended to indicate Barbot himself?

[28] This paragraph is the only original part of a long section on 'Great officers' (*1732*, pp. 290/5–291/5), the rest of which is from Marees, f. 48v; Hillier 1697, pp. 687–8; and Bosman, pp. 194–5, with much embroidery. The term *Fatairra* (otherwise *fitiro*, *fetera*, etc) was derived from Portuguese *feitor* 'manager'. It occurs in many sources relating to Fetu or Komenda in the second half of the seventeenth century. One source considered it as synonymous with 'Ojcammi' (i.e., *o-kyeame* 'linguist' or spokesman of a chief), other sources indicate that these two offices were in some cases distinct (Jones 1983a, p. 185; Henige 1982, p. 12; Van Dantzig 1980, p. 60, n. 114). It has been suggested that in the 1660s 'the *fetereship* was established as an office separate from the *okyeameship*' (Kea 1982, p. 127); but the evidence for such a change is weak.

LETTER 29

The way in which justice is administered, both civil and criminal.

[.../p. 114/...][1] Adultery involving the first wife is also severely punished. [...] At Comendo an ear is cut off the woman's accomplice and he is obliged to pay a fine of four goats and the same amount in gold /p. 115/ as the woman had for her dowry. The private parts of slaves are cut off if they were party to the crime. [.../p. 116/ ...]

603

NOTES

[1] Apart from the reference to Komenda, this Letter is based on Marees, ff. 49v–53 (even when Barbot writes – 'on m'a dit'), and on the slightly enlarged but not altogether accurate version of Marees in Villault, pp. 364–72. Barbot embroiders considerably and revises some statements, for instance, by applying general punishments to particular crimes. The apparently original statements that fratricide is always punished by death and that adulterous women may sometimes pay a fine divided between the king, his nobles, and the husband, are probably only inferences from the sources or misunderstandings of them. But the statement that the relatives of an escaped criminal may have their property confiscated and may themselves be sent into exile 'a white stick in hand' is, if genuinely original, from an untraced source. The topic of justice is not discussed in Barbot's extant journal, but the Komenda reference may represent information obtained on the second voyage.

Cf. *1732*, pp. 299/1–304/1, which on pp. 299/6–300/1 repeats the information on p. 172/3–4 (an Additional Passage in Letter 2/6 above), and adds considerable material from Bosman, pp. 164–77, as well as some embroidery. Chief justices now 'make the circuits; much as it is practised in England at the assizes', and the moral comment includes the remark – 'but what can be expected from men of so loose and depraved minds and principles, besides contradictions and absurdities ?'.

LETTER 30

The nobility and their prerogatives. Method of making war. Peace, etc.

Sir, you have already made me write at such length that I do not think I have much left to tell you about these peoples. I shall now discuss the nobility and its prerogatives, the manner in which the kings make war, the weapons they use and [how they make] peace.[1] This, I believe, will conclude the description of this coast. If possible, I shall do it in a single letter. [. . ./pp. 117–118/. . .][2] [About armies] I shall, however, say nothing of my own. I have never been an eye-witness of their armies, although I could easily have done so if I had had time to absent myself from my business for three or four days in 1682, when I was off Acra. The Aquambous and Ackkems were then encamped about 12 leagues inland and were ready to join battle, each having an army of 10,000–12,000 men, according to what the Dutch factor told me.[3] [. . ./p. 119/. . .][4]

The people of Axim [during wars] deposit their wives on a rock

604

which lies half a league out to sea. This places them out of reach of the enemy, even if the latter gain control of the countryside, for the Moors of the interior are not accustomed to use canoes at all and are very afraid of the sea.[5] People who live under the protection of Europeans on the coast deposit their wives in the forts, to which they themselves retire when they can no longer withstand the enemy. Not one of the inhabitants of Acra would have escaped in 1681 if Fort Crèvecoeur had not opened its doors to them and scattered with its cannon the most ardent of those who pursued them after the former had lost a battle.[6]

The king himself generally goes with his army, being followed by his usual guards. Sometimes it also happens that he gives the command to a lieutenant general, who has under him officers of various ranks. The guards then remain near the king. The general always carries a white staff in his hand as a mark of dignity. All the officers wear on their heads a certain kind of helmet-shaped hat made of elephant or buffalo hide, decorated with the skulls and jawbones of those they have killed in the wars they have fought. Others have hats which are simply decorated with red and white shells and goats' horns, as fetishes, or hats made of lion or crocodile skin, in the shape of a morion, covered all over with maize cobs, red feathers, cockerels' or parrots' feet, or merely with monkeys' heads. In their left hand they carry a large shield, made of the skin of an elephant, cow or tiger, and lined on the inside with goatskin. They have an assegai in their right hand, and at their side a very broad sword. They stick two knives in their girdle, which often consists merely of leather, or of a piece of linen, and which they leave hanging down behind them like a tail (not wishing to have anything which might encumber them in battle). Each of them also wears a necklace of little pieces of carved ivory or the tusks of sea-horses [hippopotamuses]. A slave follows them, wearing a sword at his side and carrying a bow and arrows in his hand. The common people equip themselves for war in various ways. Some have muskets or firelocks and a sword at their side: such people generally go at the head of the army. Others have assegais, arrows, swords, bill-hooks or knives.[7] [. . .][8] Most also have shields, three foot long and six foot broad, slightly curved in the middle. These are made of rushes or maize stalks and covered with the skin of goats or cattle. Inside they are bound with strips of copper or iron, to support the rings through which the arm is passed. Those of persons of quality, as I have said, are made of the skin of elephants, crocodiles, tigers or buffaloes, with a strip of iron or copper, 12 thumbs broad and 21 long.[9]

The assegais, bows and arrows are of several kinds. Common assegais are mounted with iron at the end in order to balance them when they are thrown. They have scarcely two foot of bare wood. The bows /p. 120/ are small and made of a very beautiful wood. The string is made very skilfully from tree-bark. The arrows are either of light wood or of reeds, with a barbed iron tip. [...][10] They feather these arrows with leaves. Their quivers are of goatskin or of rushes covered with other skin. They carry them on their backs.[11] [At least one sentence apparently omitted in copying.] These [blacksmiths] are the people who make the spears, cutlasses, swords, hatchets and bill-hooks which they use in war. The bill-hooks are back to front, as you see in this illustration. The hilt is decorated with strips of copper, iron or gold and there is always the head of a monkey attached. The cutlasses cut both ways. Some are serrated near the hilt, in order to saw what they cannot cut. The scabbards are of dogs' or goats' skins, decorated with a large red shell, which they esteem highly. The hilts are usually of beaten gold or the skin of a fish, which is of higher value among them than gold itself.[12] [...][13] Their trumpets are all made from elephant tusks, hollowed out as far as the end and decorated on the outside with grotesque figures in relief. The hole through which they blow is either in the middle or at the end, according to the different sounds they are intended to produce. Only nobles may possess them.[14]

[illustration no. (89), weapons and other objects][15]†

Those who live under the protection of the whites always carry into battle a flag of the nation which defends them. In this circumstance each *brafo* leads his band of men (which is of no great number, although some bands are larger than others) to the place /p. 121/ of rendezvous. But they always march in confusion, without order or discipline, shouting and singing. They carry with them provisions for eight or ten days, consisting of maize and a few dogs and goats. As they are ignorant of how to encamp, they have neither rules nor order in camping: they are all jumbled together and they sleep in the open air, without huts or tents. When the armies meet, they incite each other to battle. As they charge, they utter terrible cries and howls.[16] Now they throw their assegais and shoot off their bows, while covering themselves with their shields against the enemies' arrows. They also fire many shots with their muskets, which they handle quite well – at least those living near the coast do. It is said that the people of Comendo, Mina and Fetu fire these weapons more frequently than the whites themselves. They continually leap and caper while shooting. They are good marksmen with these muskets and assegais, with which they make an outlandish display, as well as with their cutlasses and knives.[17] [...][18] They decapitate those who have died and cut off the chin and lower jaw of those whom they have taken alive, thus leaving them to die, exhausted and in torment. A Moor from Comendo boasted to me that he had torn off the jaws of twenty-three men on a single occasion: he laid them on the ground, cut their face from the ears to the mouth and then, with his knee on their stomach, tore the jaw off with his two hands and left them to perish miserably, wallowing in their blood. There are some who cut open with their bill-hooks the bellies of pregnant women, beginning at the womb, in order to take out their babies and crush them against the heads of their own mothers. The hatred of these Moors varies according to who their enemies are. For example, those of Comendo have fairly frequent wars with several of their neighbours; but if these fall into their power they do not treat them as mercilessly as they treat the people of Gufo and Accanes, of whom they have long been irreconcilable enemies and with whom their conflicts have more the appearance of a butchery than of a battle; for their hatred goes to the extent of them eating one another's flesh and of carefully keeping the skulls and jaws of those they have massacred, which they place on their drums and on the doors of their houses.[19] If they spare the lives of some of them, it is in order to sell them to Europeans in order that they may be transported. This, as I have told you elsewhere, is a heavy penalty among them.

After winning a battle, they do not retire to their homes. If there is anything worth plundering in the country of the enemy, they enter it, spreading terror and dread everywhere, burning and pillaging villages and laying everything waste. After this they set out for home, sending ahead of them the tokens of their victory and carrying the heads of those enemies who have died in battle /p. 122/ on the points of assegais and spears. Upon their return home, they hold great festivals to celebrate the glory of their nation and rejoice in their victory. These festivals sometimes last 15 to 20 days, according to the importance of the war they have fought. They produce some

of their enemies in chains, in order that these may see their magnificence and in order to taunt them all the more in their misery. In addition
to holding these special festivals immediately [after such victories],
they hold [similar festivals] every year on the same day.[20] [. . .][21]

The blacks who come to terms with Europeans, after having had
some disagreement with them, likewise give their children or close
relatives as hostages, as can be seen particularly at Mina and at
Corso. Even the kings sometimes offer themselves in person, as the
king of Fetu did at Corso in 1681. He was aged about sixty and ruled
over a large country, enjoying the respect of the other kings of
Guinea; yet he came and gave himself as a hostage to the English
agent, half a cannon-shot from Cabo Corso Castle. He did this on
account of eighteen slaves who had run away from the fort to the
village of Corso, where they had been hidden by the inhabitants
(who were not willing to hand the slaves over, even when a summons
was issued). In the end it was decided in the castle to force them,
using cannon. Thereupon these black inhabitants rebelled all the
more, and an army of 700–800 of them set out to attack the castle.
The English were obliged to fire on these rebels, who lost 50–60
men, while the English lost several of their own people. This obliged
the king of Fetu to intervene on behalf of his subjects, for whom he
had become surety to the English [*margin:* against all violence]; for
he had promised to deliver up any white or black deserters from this
fort, no matter where in his kingdom they might flee to. Accordingly
this prince, with twelve of his guards, advanced as far as a fetish tree
which stands half a cannon-shot from the castle. He remained there
eight whole days, in order to conjure up the fetish so that it might
reveal to him where these deserters were and, at the same time, to
convince the English that he had no part in the action of his subjects.
He boasted that he would not leave that place until he had entirely
settled the trouble, and this indeed happened; for he came to terms
with the agent of the Royal [African] Company and the alliance was
renewed by both sides. While he was under the fetish tree this king
was fed by the English. He was then wearing a coat (*justaucorps*) of
black velvet.[22]

This, Sir, is all I have to tell you on this subject, and it concludes
what I was to describe to you concerning the practices, customs,
religion and government of the peoples of the Gold Coast of Guinea.
Although the rulers are all petty sovereigns, they consider themselves nothing less than great monarchs. I would be much obliged if

608

you would be so good as to tell me how /p. 123/ you have found this description, and in particular my last letter. I bid you goodnight and am most passionately, Sir, Your very humble servant.

Additional Passage from 1732

[pp. 263/2, 3, 5–8, 10–264/1, 264/1, 4–5, on weapons and tools]

K. Is a javelin or spear, with a quiver full of arrows, the javelin having a ring in the middle to fasten it to their body when they travel. / L. An Assagaya, a Moorish word used in Portuguese, and thence taken by the Blacks, being a long dart, to be cast at a distance, with another sort of quiver, and three arrows in it. The quiver they hang about their shoulders, at a leather thong, or belt, as mark'd Y. These darts are commonly about two yards long, and pretty large, the end pointed with iron, like a pike, and some of them cover'd with iron a span or two in length. This weapon serves them instead of a cymiter; that holding their shield in the left hand, they may the more conveniently dart it with the right; for they have commonly some body to carry it after them, when they cannot well hang it on their shoulders. ... / L.O. A small dart to be cast by hand, about a yard long and very slender. / O. Razors, with which they shave their beards. / N. Three different sorts of swords or cymiters, with iron or wooden hilts, or a monkey's head cast in gold, and look'd upon as sacred, or a spell. ... / M. Another sort of cymiter, part of the edge whereof is made like a saw, to saw off the bones of their enemies. The pommel is the muzzle of a beast, cast in gold, for an idol or spell. ... / P. A Ponyard, or Bayonet, after their manner. / Q. A round ax, with a blunt edge on the one side. / R. an ax of another form; both these for husbandry. / V. An ax of a third make, to hew or fell timber. / S. A shield or buckler of dress'd leather, used by the Blacks of note in war, or on festivals; or when they visit others of an equal rank. ... / S. Another sort of shield, made of osiers or bulrushes, for the common sort of people. / 4.4. Two sorts of tools for tillage. / W. Such a musket as they buy from Europeans. ...[23]

NOTES

[1] This Letter is based on Barbot's regular sources, Marees, Dapper and Villault, but includes information collected in 1679 and 1682. In 1679 he

609

drew and described (and perhaps collected) weapons, but his journals says litle about warfare (*1679*, p. 344); in 1682 he collected information about recent wars and perhaps saw soldiers and other weapons. The material in this Letter forms part of Chapters 19, 20 and 23 in Book III of *1732*, these Chapters having much added from Bosman, pp. 23–4, 132–42, 178–87, as well as references to the Old Testament, South America and medieval France.

[2] Omission of four paragraphs and part of a fifth, on the nobility and ennoblement ceremonies, and on the origin or wars, the former subject derived almost entirely from Dapper, pp. 113/3–114/4, or from Dapper's source, Marees, ff. 85v–87, and the latter subject from Marees, ff. 44, 46. Barbot's only additions are the following sentences. 'The only prerogative of this estate is to do commerce without paying duties, which is often of no use to them because they lack the means' – probably a misinterpretation of Marees, f. 86v, or Villault, p. 352. 'He [the newly created nobleman] is taken around on the shoulders of four slaves, who carry him on a stool, while two other slaves go underneath him to support his feet' – probably a piece of intuition. 'Those ennobled for some significant deeds which have contributed to the wellbeing of the kingdom are generally given the leading offices of state, after the relatives of the kings' – a loose interpretation of Villault, pp. 352–3.

Cf. *1732*, pp. 249/4–252/3, which adds material from Bosman.

[3] In February 1679, at Accra, Barbot obtained information from a Dutch agent about a war between the 'Aquambou' (Akwamu) and their western neighbours the 'Achenists/Ackenists' (the 'Ackkems' or Akim) (*1679*, p. 324). For this war, which, if Barbot has remembered the date correctly, was apparently continuing in 1682, see Wilks 1957, p. 117.

Cf. *1732*, pp. 294/9–252/3, with added material from Bosman, pp. 132–7, 142.

[4] Omission of seven sentences on the origins of wars – a somewhat elaborated version of Villault, pp. 353, based in part on Marees, f. 45.

Cf. *1732*, p. 292/8–295/1, which adds a Biblical comparison and considerable material from Bosman, pp. 178–81.

[5] The remark about the refuge rock repeats a statement in Letter 2/3, p. 4, above. On women and children being sent to refuges in war-time, see Marees, f. 45; Jones 1983a, p. 198.

Cf. *1732*, p. 294/2.

[6] The reference to refuge in Fort Crèvecoeur repeats a statement in Letter 2/10, p. 35, above, but there it was implied that all three Accra forts gave refuge. Following the Danish loss of Fort Christiansborg in 1679, the Akwamu managed to conquer Accra the following year (Wilks 1957, pp. 109–11). A similar episode occurred on Gold Coast in 1683, when a Brandenburg fort took in refugees and drove off the enemy (Jones 1985, p. 54).

Cf. *1732*, p. 294/3, which mistakenly gives the date as 'sixteen hundred and eighty-seven'.

[7] Barbot's description of war apparel and weapons is based on Marees, ff. 44v–45, largely followed in Dapper, p. 111/4–5, and Villault, pp. 354–6; it is often embroidered, but the additional detail about apparel and weapons (e.g. some of the decorations worn on caps) may be based on his own observations. In 1679 he witnessed a festival at Fort Frederiksborg where the Africans were armed with 'muskets, assegais, half-pikes, cutlasses, javelins and straw shields'; and he drew and noted a bow and arrows, decorated cutlasses, a four foot 'zagaye' or throwing spear, a long slightly-curved knife worn in an elephant-hide sheath at the belt, and a 'tiger'-skin cap decorated with red shells as worn by a war-captain (*1679*, pp. 305, 344–6). Other seventeenth-century sources disagreed as to whether Gold Coast kings went into battle (Jones 1983a, pp. 67–8, 197). For other accounts of war apparel and weapons, see Bosman, p. 185; Jones 1983a, pp. 193–7 (and see Plate 1 for a 1641 drawing of weapons).

Cf. *1732*, p. 295/2–3.

[8] Omission of two sentences on war-paint, from Marees, f. 44v.

Cf. *1732*, p. 295/3–4, which adds comparative material.

[9] In 1679 Barbot did not draw any shields. His description of them resembles Marees, f. 46v, but he varies the size slightly and adds the references to maize, copper, and the special skins used for shields of persons of quality.

Cf. *1732*, p. 295/5, which abbreviates.

[10] Omission of one sentence from Marees, f. 46v, on poisoned arrows.

[11] In 1679 Barbot drew a bow three or four foot long, with a string of fibres (*racinnes*), which he added was 'little used'; and two arrows, a three-foot one of cane, and one half the length, without an iron tip but poisoned (*1679*, p. 344). An earlier source confirmed that bow-strings were made of tree-bark, but stated that arrows were feathered with dog's or cat's hair, and that quivers were made from the skin of a 'tiger' or 'wild cat' (Jones 1983a, p. 194). By the 1690s bows and arrows were 'not much in vogue', presumably because of the increased use of firearms (Bosman, p. 186). For the listing of weapons in *1732*, see the Additional Passage.

[12] In 1679 Barbot drew two cutlasses, one a sheathed cutlass with the skull of a leopard or monkey on the top of the scabbard, the cutlass having a serrated portion of the edge 'to saw the bones of their enemies when they cannot cut through them' (*1679*, pp. 344, 346). For other descriptions of this weapon, see Marees, f. 46; *Relation* 1674, p. 17; Jones 1983a, pp. 95, 194, and note 293. See the Additional Passage.

[13] Omission of two sentences on drums, from Marees, f. 47.

Cf. *1732*, which adds material from Bosman, p. 139.

[14] In 1679 Barbot drew two ivory-tusk horns, indicating on one the mid mouth-hole, and he stated that they came in five or six sizes and were played eight to ten together (*1679*, pp. 345–6). His description of horns was influenced by Marees, f. 47; but he was the first writer to observe that some horns had a mouth-hole at the end. For other references to horns, see Bosman, pp. 138–9; Jones 1983a, p. 255.

Cf. *1732*, which adds the Bosman material.

[15] In *1732* Barbot provides lengthy descriptions of the individual weapons – see the Additional Passage.

[16] The description of marching armies has traces of Marees, f. 45, Dapper, p. 112/2, and Villault, pp. 354–6, but has additional details perhaps learned by Barbot in 1682. For a similar description, see Jones 1983a, pp. 197–8.

Cf. *1732*, p. 295/6–296/1, which adds material from Bosman, p. 182, and a reference to the French *oriflamme*.

[17] The first sentence is from Villault, p. 356, derived from Marees, f. 45, but the reference to muskets is from Dapper, p. 112/1, their possession by Africans being less common in Marees's day. In 1679 Barbot said that the blacks in the forts had been taught to use muskets, which they did skilfully but without taking careful aim (*1679*, pp. 338–9).

Cf. *1732*, p. 296/1.

[18] Omission of two sentences on frenzied behaviour in battle, from Villault, pp. 356–7.

Cf. *1732*, p. 296/1.

[19] Barbot enlarges on, and perhaps embroiders, references to killing prisoners, cutting off their jaws, eating parts, and displaying heads as trophies, in Marees, f. 45, Dapper, p. 112/3, and Villault, p. 357. The reference to 'Comendo' and 'Gufo' (Eguafo) is a slip, since these were alternative names for the same state, although there were already tensions between the port of Little Komenda and the rest of the state. According to another source, the dead or dying were decapitated but prisoners were only enslaved (Jones 1983a, p. 198).

Cf. *1732*, p. 296/2–6, which adds material from Bosman, pp. 23–4, and lengthy American comparisons. Barbot does not allow his tone to be modified by Bosman, pp. 180–1, which argued that Gold Coast wars did not result in many battlefield deaths.

[20] The statements seem to be original but are perhaps mere deductions. For plundering an enemy country, and triumphs displaying human heads, see Jones 1983a, pp. 198–200. For a festival celebrating a successful battle, see Villault, pp. 314–18.

Cf. *1732*, pp. 297/1–198/1, which adds material from Bosman, pp. 24, 182–3.

[21] Omission of two sentences on peacemaking ceremonies, from Villault, pp. 358–9.
Cf. *1732*, p. 298/2.

[22] Cf. *1732*, p. 298/3–4.

[23] Although all these weapons and tools are illustrated in *1732*, and although the earlier drawings evidence that Barbot had seen most of them, the omitted portions of his descriptions (of 'swords', shields, and muskets) were copied from Bosman, pp. 263–264, and his description of the 'assagaya' has traces of the same source. It is likely therefore that a few of the items added in the *1732* illustrations had not been seen or collected by Barbot on Gold Coast, but were instead either copied from illustrations in other sources or else drawn to match the Bosman descriptions (or in the case of one shield and the poniard even the description in Marees, f. 46–46v); and also that the configuration of one or two items was adjusted by Barbot or the artist to match Bosman. Also omitted here is a digression on Biblical references to the 'cymiter or cutlace'. The items added in *1732* are a second bow of a different shape (lower X.), the quivers (L.), the small dart (L.O.), a fourth cutlass (middle N.), the shields (S.), and two 'tools for tillage' (4.4.). One shield appears to be copied from Marees, plate 6, and the other from Dapper, plate on p. 466; the second bow resembles the bow shown on many of Dapper's plates, e.g., that on p. 100; and the tools are the wood-gouging tools shown on Dapper, plate on p. 102. (Dapper's plates also show assegais, cutlasses and quivers, but it is not obvious that Barbot copied these.) The spear has a ring added (this is not in Bosman). The items drawn and described in *1679*, pp. 344–6, which reappeared on illustration no. (89) (*1688*, p. 120, above) – this lacks a key or individual descriptions – were the following: the 'assagaya', described as four foot long and tipped like a halberd; the two arrows (see note 11 above); and a serrated cutlass (see note 12 above); but the animal skull which was formerly said to decorate the sheath is now on the handle of the weapon. Omitted on the illustration were the bow, the sheathed cutlass, and the knife; but the following additional items appeared: the razors, two extra cutlasses, a pointed weapon with a European-style handgrip, the 'ponyard', the axes, and the musket – these being presumably items seen or collected in 1682 (unless the poniard derived from Marees, plate 6 – it is not obvious that Barbot copied at this stage from Dapper's plates). With the exception of the knife and the pointed weapon, all of the above items appeared or reappeared in *1732*.

613

Part Three

DESCRIPTION
OF THE COASTS OF GUINEA
from Rio da Volta to Cape Lopo Gonzalvez

LETTER 1

Description of Rio da Volta, Lay, Monte da Raposa, Great Popo and Little Popo, the coast to La Praya, and Juda roadstead.

Sir, you flatter me greatly in your last letter, when you thank me for the trouble I have taken in describing to you that part of Guinea commonly called Gold Coast ('Costa d'Oro'). I am very pleased, Sir, to have contributed to your pleasure, and I am very willing to set about beginning a third description, as you so earnestly ask me in your letter [*margin:* in order to complete the Description of the Coasts of Guinea]. I will make use in my usual fashion of the reports I have, and of my own observations; I will employ here, as in the other descriptions, the same order and the same style, beginning with the situation of the land and finishing with its properties. What I have to ask from you is not to hurry me as you did during my last description; for you make me commit a thousand mistakes, in language as well as in orthography and punctuation.[1]

The land in the neighbourhood of Rio da Volta is low, with steep hills in the interior of the country, bays of fine sand at the sea, and almost everywhere nine fathoms' depth at one league from the shore. The country is open, except that a few leagues East and West there are many palm trees planted at equal distances from each other. The interior of the land is covered with dense woods and thickets.[2] This river is not easy to recognize from the sea, unless you are within a league of it, when you see the breakers which come out of it and a small wood on the eastern side, by which it can be known. Its mouth is blocked by an island in the middle of the channel, which makes the land appear continuous from two or three leagues away, but from the top of the mast you see the river running to the North, in a very wide bed. I noticed something there which will perhaps surprise you as much as it did me, namely, that having anchored with my brigantine in front of this river, in 18 fathoms of water with a muddy bottom, and at North-by-NW, the currents drove me during the night to the North, from 18 fathoms to 13 in less than five hours, although by their nature the currents ought to have carried me to the South as violently as they issue from the river, which is so violently that fresh clear water is found in the sea at ten fathoms.[3]

617

[illustration no. (90), map of the coast between River Volta and Cape Lopez and of the Gulf of Guinea with the islands of Príncipe and São Tomé, inserted before p. 129]

The coast from Lay to here runs East-by-SE – I should say East and East-by-NE, and sometimes East-by-SE – for 16–18 leagues; [but] the Dutch maps reckon it NE and NE-by-East for 10 or 11 leagues. /p. 130/ This is what obliged me to make an accurate map. It is much more trustworthy than any you can find, mark my words! Nevertheless, use your eyes, and your knowledge of navigation, if you ever go to these places! What forced me to make the map is that I coasted along this land at six or seven fathoms, which gave me an opportunity of noticing many things which one does not see in a large vessel, because these always keep some 10–12 leagues out in the open sea in order to avoid a bank of sand which the Dutch maps suppose to exist to the East of its mouth. This is why I say that a vessel can go along the coast from Lay to here at 1¼ to 1½ leagues out, at the furthest. There is a small bank of sand to the East of River Volta, which these same Dutch maps omit, but it is not dangerous and not extensive; the entrance of the river is by the shore of this bank on the East side.[4] Those who have been there have assured me that there is yet another bank in the mouth, upon which the sea breaks a great deal, forming a bar there, but I believe that this is only the case for the entrance from the West; the rarity of visits there means that it is spoken about with uncertainty. I know on good authority that the interior of this river is full of falls and rapids – the General of Mina told me that if I attempted to enter there with my brigantine, I would infallibly lose it. But this was rather to scare me, he believing that I intended to make a discovery of the trade that can be done there. For he himself told me some time afterwards (without thinking) that he sometimes sent boats there which brought him slaves and cloths, which the natives buy from the Abyssinians and Nubians, whose neighbours they are, the river coming down to the sea from very far in the interior of the country. It makes its way [inland] towards the NNE. He showed me some of the cloths, which resemble the borders of needle-tapestry. It must be the case, however, that the trade is unprofitable and the river difficult to operate, since the Dutch have no establishment there, as they do everywhere else where trade is good. The Portuguese, who have only trifles for their trade, come there often enough to collect some slaves, some ivory, and the maize which is abundant there. I have been assured that gold is little known among the Moors of the country.[5]

From Rio da Volta to Cabo Montego, or Monte do Raposa, the coast runs ESE for 3½ leagues. The village Hova is at about 2½ leagues [from River Volta], and it can be recognized by a large wood, very bushy and elevated, to the NE. The sand brought up in the sounding lead is as fine as that of an hour-glass. Going East from Cabo Montego the coast forms a great bay (*renforcement*) ten leagues from point to point, as far as Cape St Paolo. This has in its neighbourhood the village Quila, known by a small thick wood and above it three palm trees: the bottom there is of fine sand. You never see blacks coming out of it [sc. Quila], because the sea breaks continuously on the land there, and the Moors in that locality are more savage than elsewhere. The land around this bay is broken in several places, and from Rio da Volta onwards the interior is marshy (this gives it the appearance of a lake, with a little river [emerging] near the middle [but] without any outlet to the sea, which you can recognise by the trees on the East bank, [? a lake] with several small islands).[6] The remainder of the coast from Cabo Montego onwards lies ENE, displaying a country with few thickets, level and open – apart from the cape itself. At that point a gap can be seen, resembling a river, the land being on the one side low and open, and on the other a little elevated, with a small wood and some land showing behind it. Round houses can be seen on the shore, from which canoes hardly ever come out to ships, these Moors having little commerce with the Europeans. The village of Bequoe is also in this neighbourhood.[7] It is asserted that the king of these lands is a great landholder, very politic, and powerful in numbers of people; which makes him dreaded by his neighbours. He resides ordinarily in a town which is said to be /p. 131/ larger than Paris, and as populous. His principal care is to police his state well, and to keep on good terms with his subjects.[8]

From Cape de Monte to River Tary or Popo, which the maps mark as Terra Gazelas or Anegada, the coast runs NE, for about five leagues, being flat land, with some trees and thickets here and there.[9] Tary or Popo is a village 12 leagues from Ardra. It is divided into three parts, which are on the mouth of the river, as you will see from this detailed map. [10]

[illustration no. (91), map of Popo Lagoon]†

Popo is easy to recognize, when you come from the West, by the flags which the Moors of the place hoist. The coastal shore is very easy for a bar canoe [to approach].[11] Little commerce was done here formerly, when it was under the authority of the king of Ardres, who obliged the inhabitants to bring their slaves to Ardres, in order to exact duties on them. But since they were freed from his dominion some years ago one sometimes manages to do a fairly considerable trade there for slaves (*captifs*), in exchange for cowries, iron, glass beads, linen (*toilles*), etc. The trade is ordinarily done with the king of the country.[12] This prince is a tall, well-shaped man, and he has in his manner something better than the general run of the Moors. He wears a long robe of brocade and a straw hat.

The blacks who are subject to him love and respect him very much. It is a maxim among them that the king always eats alone. The king's palace is large. His apartment is in the remotest part, so that you have to cross three low courtyards, each of which has a body of guards. In the last courtyard is the tent which serves as a room for the court. This prince has some very beautiful wives, and he always has two of them near him to fan him. The king's greatest pleasure is to smoke, and to talk either with his nobles or with his wives. These wives are maintained in the palace. /p. 132/ They are fed on beef, mutton, fowls, potatoes, and rice.

In 1682 the king of Popo was at war with those of A Monte and of Juda, who forced him to make peace with the latter when he was on the point of losing his territories, and the two came to an understanding and made an alliance against the king of Monte.[13] It is said that the people of Popo are thieves by profession, particularly when they are a little drunk, for then they plunder and carry off everything without caring what happens. This is what makes people reluctant to establish trading lodges there, and explains why nowadays they have found it convenient to undertake trade with the king, as practised at Juda and Ardres. The Moors here, like all the others in Guinea, defer blindly to the opinions of their priests, whom they call *Domine*, and who are all dressed in long white robes, with a crooked stick in their right hand. Vessels trading at Popo are obliged to give presents to the priests, in order that they encourage the Moors working the bar [of the river] to set out. For the Moors are convinced that if the priests are well paid they will pray to the fetishes to make the sea favourable, and then the canoes will not be upset. Another custom here is that these priests throw sand on the heads of embarking

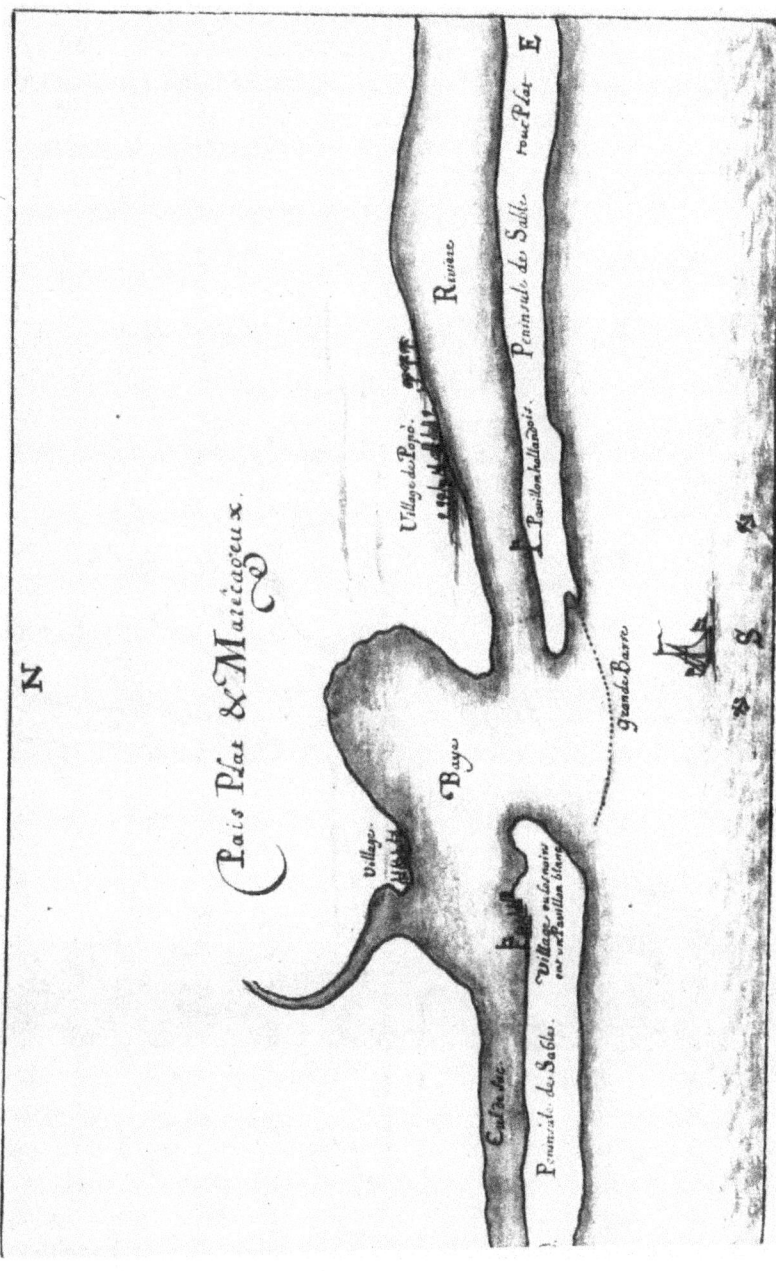

51. Popo Lagoon

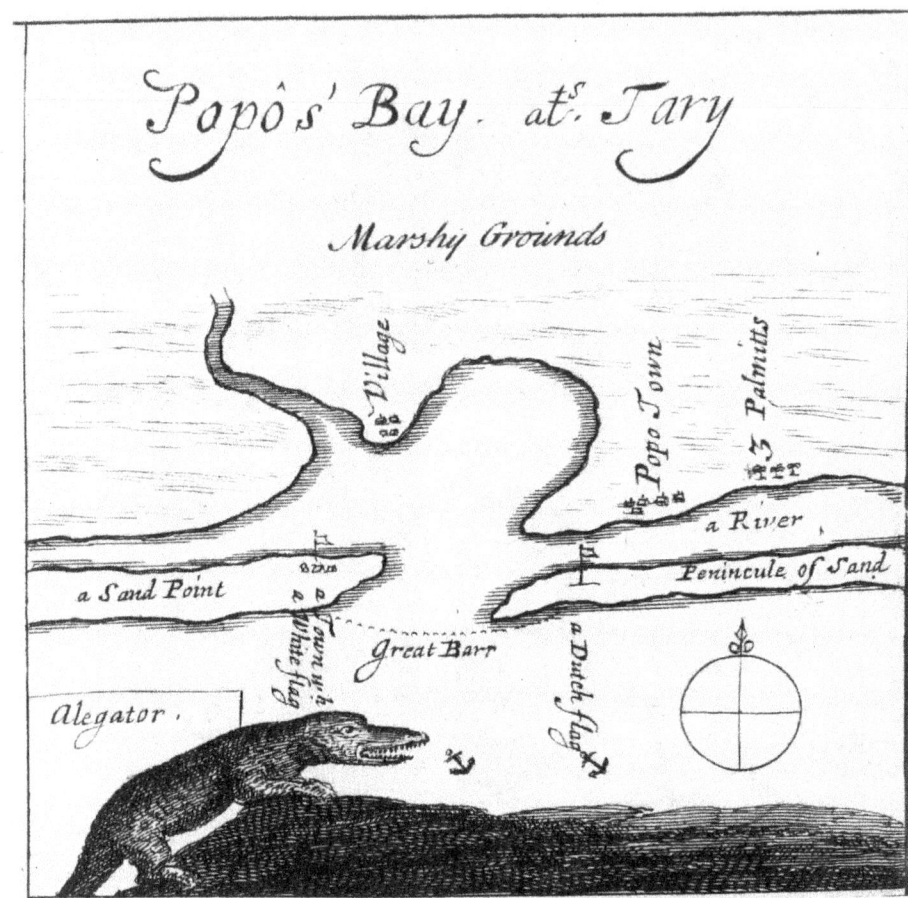

Popô's Bay. at. Tary

Marshy Grounds

Village

Popo Town

Palmitts

a River

Penincule of Sand

a Sand Point

a Town w.th a White flag

Great Barr

a Dutch flag

Alegator.

52. Popo Lagoon – printed version

slaves, to stop the fetish from overturning the canoes in the surf of the bar.[14] The houses in these places are of the same form and style as those of Cape Verde. The interior country abounds in fruit, fowls, cattle, etc. Towards the sea it is all marshy and flat, which led the Portuguese to call it Terra Anegada [Drowned Land]. The Dutch always have an agent there, and a lodge, who/which hoists the flag of that nation when some vessel passes by.[15]

From Popo (Great Popo) to the cabin (*case*) at La Praye, where the flags of France and England are hoisted alternately, is reckoned five leagues ENE. The village Ooy is between Little and Great Popo, a quarter of a league East of a little river which discharges itself into the sea.[16] It is at this Praye that the French Compagnie de Guinée has a lodge within the territories of the king of Juda, this lodge being at rather less than a league from the sea-shore. The country is flat and wooded. The village of Coulainba lies between Popo and this lodge, being located, with some others, on the banks of a stream which goes from Popo to the East, parallel to the sea-shore, within a musket-shot of the sea. This stream passes on to Jackain, where it loses itself in the earth. Its waters are muddy, and it is fordable everywhere.[17] In order to identify clearly the roadstead at La Praye when coming from the West, after leaving Popo you must sail close to the land, until you see five or six large trees, standing separately and forming a sort of bower, and then the flag-pole which is on the sands, quite close to a small house, around which several canoes can be seen. As soon as you are to the South of this flag-pole, you must drop anchor, this being the best holding point, for further to the East there are rocks under the water which can chafe the cables. You can also fire off a cannon as soon as you are three leagues East of Popo, to warn the Company's servants, so that they can send some-one there to raise a flag.[18]

Some persons have believed that this country was one of the dependencies of the King of Ardres, and especially Mr D....., who says that Ardres borders on the East with Benin, and on the West with the river of Tary, or Popo; but he had inaccurate reports, for between Popo and Ardres you find the kingdom of Juda and the kingdom of Torry. Juda marches in the West with the kingdom of Popo, and extends along the sea as far as Torry, a stretch of 4½ leagues. Torry is a small state, with only one village on the sea, called Foulaan, its entire extent being within a circumference of four leagues; nevertheless, it is completely independent of its neighbours,

621

although inferior in all respects. For Ardres, although /p. 133/ of small extent on the coast (since it possesses only the area from Torry to Benin), occupies much space in the interior, extending in the North to the kingdom of Oyeo, which can be found at 15°N; and it is very powerful in numbers of people, as I will tell you elsewhere. The kingdom of Juda has in truth only a circuit of 12 or 15 leagues, yet it is also very populous. It is this last kingdom which I must deal with in the next letter I write to you. The failing light obliges me to finish this letter, by declaring that I am always, with great affection, Sir, Your etc.[19]

Additional Passages from *1732*

[p. 319/1–5, on Slave Coast]

In the former book, which was all of the Gold Coast, I laid down its extent along the shore, from Rio de Sweiro da Costa, to Lay, in the Lempi country. / In this fourth book, I am to treat of the Slave Coast, so call'd by the Europeans, because the whole trade there consists in slaves, and gold purchased merely by chance, in an inconsiderable quantity. / The sea-faring Europeans extend this Slave Coast, to Rio-Lagos in Benin, where it loses its name; the adjacent coast being that of Great Benin; and beyond it the coast of Douwerre stretching to cape Formozo towards the south; and from this cape to Rio del Rey, east; and thence compassing south, as far as cape Lope-Gonzales beyond the Aequator, forms the gulph of Guinea or the Bight: thus stretching in the whole three hundred and fifty leagues in a bow from Volta, the best part whereof, at least as far as the Camarones river at the bottom of the gulph, might be well accounted the Slave Coast, as affording vast numbers of slaves in trade, especially at new and old Calabar, and so on to Rio del Rey. And for the same reason, the tract of land along the sea betwixt Lay and Rio da Volta, might as well be reckon'd a part of the Gold Coast, the country affording now and then some little gold in traffick: and it was on that account that in my original French manuscripts, and in the map, or chart annexed, I made the Gold Coast extend from Rio de Sweiro da Costa, to Rio da Volta; looking upon that its true extent, and assigning two famous large rivers for its limits. / But this being of very little or no consequence, and our English and Dutch sea-faring people reckoning it otherwise, I relinquish my former opinions, and submit to theirs, because it is chiefly for them I write; and now enter on the subject of the Slave Coast, commonly reputed to extend from Lay to Rio Lagos. / This Slave Coast comprehends the coasts of Soko, Coto, Popo, Fida, and Ardra, the subject of the following description.[20]

[p. 322/7, on rats in ships]

If this [employment and rewarding of cats] is effectual to destroy rats, it may be very useful aboard ships, where we are commonly so much pestered with that mischievous vermin: for they pilfer and carry away any thing they can come at, even breeches, stockings, etc and will often bite men in their cabbins, and foul on their faces; nay, they are even so large and so bold, that they have assaulted my grey and blue parrots in the night, kill'd some, and almost eaten them up, tho' the ship I was in was new from the stocks for the voyage.[21]

NOTES

[1] Omitted in *1732*, which substitutes a new introduction, defining Slave Coast – here given in Additional Passages. Barbot sailed along this section of the Guinea coast in April 1682; but a major source is D'Elbée's account of a 1670 French voyage to Ardres. (Note that whereas Letter 2/30 ends on p. 123 of the manuscript, the present Letter begins on p. 129. Apart from a List of Letters, pp. 127–8, here combined with the previous unpaginated Lists, the intervening pages, containing titles and a map, are unpaginated.)

[2] This passage is paraphrased from D'Elbée, who was in fact describing not 'the neighbourhood of Rio da Volta' but rather the coast from Biamba, West of Accra, to River Volta (Delbée 1671, pp. 378–9).

Cf. *1732*, p. 319/12, which adds the suggestion that River Volta 'was so called by the Portuguese for its rapid course and reflux', from Bosman (p. 328), and also the information that 'its spring, according to a very modern author, is in the kingdom of Akam, bordering southward on that of Gago, in nine degrees north latitude, running thence through the country of Tafou, in which are said to be mines of gold; and so downward south, through that of Quahou, Aboura, Ingo, and others', information which corresponds with that in the 1700/1707 map of Africa by Delisle, probably Barbot's source here.

[3] Barbot was presumably carried towards the shore by the sea tide: 'when passing the entrance of the River Volta, allowance should be made for the indraught of the flood tide' (*Africa pilot* 1967, p. 468). The first sentence

corrects D'Elbée, who had written that 'River Volta is easy to recognize by the breakers in front of the mouth, which bring into sight a long bank, and a little water above it, a small wood along the river, the mouth fairly wide, the entrance on the eastern side' (Delbée 1671, p. 379). Despite Barbot's opportunity for personal observation, much of the detail seems derivative: the references to seeing the river from the mast-top and to fresh water at ten fathoms' depth are both from Dapper, p. 115/1, the latter reference in turn derived from Leers 1665, p. 301.

Cf. *1732*, p. 320/1–4, which terms Barbot's vessel a 'yacht', and incorporates additional material from Bosman, pp. 328–9, hence withdrawing the assertion that the mouth of the river was blocked by an island 'as the Dutch maps have it'.

[4] The map, inserted at the beginning of Part 3, was not repeated in *1732*. Derived from Dutch maps, it covers large sections of coast unvisited by Barbot, but is valuable because he marked on it the daily track of his 11-day voyage from Whydah to Príncipe 'in a brigantine of 15 tons in April 1682, the season of *travados*'.

Cf. *1732*, p. 320/5, 321/2, where the material is much rearranged, the line of the coast being given as 'east by north, and sometimes east by south', the criticism of Dutch maps being extended to include English, and the detail being added that as Barbot sailed along the coast 'we saw several fires all along it from Lay to that place; it being then the sowing season for Indian wheat' – it was late April 1682.

[5] The phrase 'those who have been there . . .' perhaps alludes to a reference to a 'reef' before the mouth of River Volta in Dapper, p. 115/1, actually derived from Leers 1665, p. 301 – Dapper himself never visited Africa and it is not clear that Barbot ever thought he did. Barbot's contemptuous opinion of the trade of the Portuguese was shared by Bosman, who noted that they had difficulty in getting slaves 'by reason they are loaded with such sorry Goods' (Bosman, p. 334). Evidently there had not yet developed the local taste on Slave Coast for Brazilian tobacco, which in the eighteenth century was regarded as giving Portuguese traders an enormous competitive advantage (Verger 1968a, pp. 28–34).

Cf. *1732*, pp. 320/6–321/1, which adds the name of the Dutch governor of Elmina, Verhoutert (Director-General 1679–82), and the detail that Barbot spoke to him 'in the month of April, and consequently the fittest season of the year for passing up it in a yacht'. The reference to 'the fittest season' appears to derive from Bosman, p. 328, which stated that River Volta was passable with canoes only before the rains – 'but twice in the year, and that betwixt April and November' (an error in the English translation, the original Dutch indicating rather that the river was passable 'mostly before April and November', *HIA* 6 (1979), 273).

[6] Much of this material is from Dapper, p. 115/3–4 (abbreviated from

Leers 1665, p. 301) – the coast running ESE from Rio da Volta to Cabo Montego for 3½ leagues (three miles in Dapper), the bay on the coast after Cabo Montego 10 leagues across (ten miles in Dapper) with its broken coast and marshy interior, and the river with no outlet to the sea marked by trees on its eastern bank. The names 'Monte da Raposa' and 'Cap St Paolo' were probably borrowed from Dutch maps (e.g. Robijn/Roggeveen 1685) which took them from earlier Portuguese sources. But the description of the villages of Hova and Quila and of a 'lake . . . with several small islands' between River Volta and Cape St Paul appears to be original. Barbot's geography is extremely confused here, although some of the confusion is derived from his sources. The 'Cabo Montego' of Leers and Dapper seems in fact to be merely an alternative name for Cape St Paul (actually about 18 miles/29 km East of the Volta, rather than the three Dutch miles, or 12 English miles, of Leers), and not a separate headland; while contrariwise 'Monta da Raposa' was evidently a distinct locality between River Volta and Cape St Paul, probably to be identified with a 'grove . . . in the form of a conical hill' 3.2 km East of River Volta still recognized as a landmark today (*Africa pilot* 1967, p. 468). The great bay extending from Cabo Montego ten Dutch miles (40 English miles/64 km) across was thus to the East (or rather NE) of Cape St Paul rather than to the West. It is also clear from the Leers account that the small river with no outlet to the sea was not in fact 'in the middle' of this bay, but beyond it to the East; it seems, in fact, to be identical with the 'gap, like a river' which Barbot refers to in the next paragraph (in material taken from D'Elbée – see note 7 below). The name 'Eva', which seems to correspond to Barbot's 'Hova', is given to a place between River Volta and Keta in some early eighteenth century ships' journals (Mettas 1978, nos. 96/1718, 99/1718, 118/1719, 121/1719–20): these names may represent modern Woe, in the vicinity of Cape St Paul. 'Quila' (so also in *1732*) is probably an error for 'Quita', i.e. Keta, about 8 km beyond Cape St Paul; while the lake West of Cape St Paul is evidently the Keta Lagoon.

Cf. *1732*, p. 321/3–5, which misleadingly translates 'renfoncement' as 'bulging', and interpolates a brief paragraph beginning 'This is the kingdom of Coto . . .', from Bosman, p. 329 – since 'Coto' represents Keta, Barbot's identification is correct, despite his failure to realize that Bosman's name was merely an alternative form of his own Quila/Quita. The dangerous surf off Keta was also noted by Bosman, who observed that it discouraged the inhabitants from fishing in the sea (Bosman, p. 330). Nevertheless, trade between Keta and the Europeans began shortly after Barbot's visit in 1682; an English ship is recorded to have loaded slaves at 'Quitto', i.e. Keta, in 1683 (OBDR C.745, letter of John Winder, Whydah, 24.6.1683). By Bosman's time, c. 1698, Keta was trading regularly in slaves with the Europeans, but evidently still not on any great scale (Bosman, pp. 330–1).

[7] With the exception of the mention of the village of Bequoe, this passage is entirely derived (Delbée 1671, pp. 380–1). However, D'Elbée begins his account by referring to the coast 'from River Volta to Cape d'Amonte', and Barbot alters this to 'the rest of the coast from Cabo Montego', thus creating the impression that 'this Cape' is Cape Montego, whereas D'Elbée was in fact referring to Cape Monte, a quite different locality further East. (*1732* clears up this confusion by amending 'the rest of the coast from Cabo Montego' to 'the Coto coast, from cape St Paolo, to cape Monte'.) Cape Monte, in Portuguese 'Cabo do Monte', was probably a headland, now lost through erosion but recalled in local tradition, in the vicinity of Kpeme, about 65 km along the coast from Cape St Paul (Law 1987, p. 339). D'Elbée's gap 'like a river' just East of Cape Monte is clearly identical with the 'small river, blocked at the mouth and stopped up with sand,' which was described by Leers 1665, p. 301, and hence by Dapper, Robijn/Roggeveen 1685, and by Barbot himself (despite some confusion) in the previous paragraph (see note 6 above). Leers places this river 'over 13 miles' (52 English miles/84 km) sailing beyond Cabo Montego (Cape St Paul), which if it was located just East of Kpeme would be only a slight exaggeration. The reference is probably to River Haho, which runs into Lake Togo behind Kpeme, and whose valley forms a vista visible from the sea. The intended meaning of the phrase 'in this neighbourhood' is somewhat obscure, but on his map Barbot places 'Bequoe' midway between Cape St Paul and Cape Monte: this location (as well as the similarity of names) suggests that it might be identified with Be (nowadays incorporated into the modern city of Lomé), about 37 km NE of Cape St Paul and 30 km West of Kpeme. Cf. *1732*, p. 321/6.

[8] Paraphrased from D'Elbée (Delbée 1671, p. 381). It is not clear to which kingdom D'Elbée's informants meant to refer, but possibly it was Tado in the interior, which was recognized by the Houla people of the coast as their traditional cradle (see Law 1987, p. 346 and n. 35). Cf. *1732*, p. 321/7–11, which omits this material and substitutes an account of the kingdom of Coto, or Keta, adapted from Bosman, pp. 329–31: this presumably implies that Barbot believed that D'Elbée's kingdom was Keta, but no other evidence suggests that Keta had ever controlled territory as far East as Cape Monte.

[9] The passage begins awkwardly with a reference to Cape Monte, which Barbot has failed to mention by name earlier (see note 7 above). The main source here is D'Elbée, who sailed from Cape Monte to a neighbouring kingdom called Thary or Tary, situated on a river of the same name, before proceeding to Allada (Delbée 1671, pp. 381–2). Barbot's phrase 'River Tary ... which the maps mark as Terra Gazelas or Anegada' echoes D'Elbée's 'River Tary, marked on the maps Terra', and the final phrase describing the land is taken verbatim from D'Elbée. The names Terra (das) Gazelas and

Terra Anegada appear on Portuguese and later maps of this coast (e.g., that in Marees), while a brief account of the village (but not the river) of Popo had been given in Dapper, p. 115/4–5. Barbot here adds only the distance from Cape Monte to River Tary and the identification of Tary with Popo. The actual distance from Cape Monte (if this was at Kpeme) to Popo (i.e. Great Popo) is about 18 miles/30 km, rather than Barbot's 15 miles (5 leagues). The 'river' of Popo is the outlet from the inland lagoon to the sea nowadays known as Bouche du Roi (a corruption of Portuguese *bocca do rio*, 'mouth of the river'), near Great Popo. D'Elbée's use, followed by Barbot, of the name 'Tary' with regard to this place is problematical. 'Tary' and Popo are marked as separate places on Sanson maps ('L'Afrique' 1655, 'La Guinée' 1656), and it seems clear that Sanson's 'Tary' is in fact to be identified with the small state of Tori, between Whydah and Allada, which Barbot himself describes later under the name 'Torry' (p. 132 below). A river, or a branch of the coastal lagoon system, did indeed flow by Tori, and it may well have been called 'River Tary' in the seventeenth century, but in recent times this has had no direct connection with the lagoon at Popo. It is possible, however, that in the seventeenth century the Popo and Tori lagoons were connected, and that D'Elbée might therefore have heard the lagoon at Popo referred to as 'River Tary', and erroneously concluded that this was also the name of the town. At any rate, it seems clear that Barbot was correct in identifying D'Elbée's 'Tary' with Popo (for further discussion, see Law 1987, pp. 351–2). But the suggestion of D'Elbée, followed by Barbot, that the name 'Tary' was identical with 'Terra' on contemporary maps was wrong. Terra (das) Gazelas ('Land of Gazelles') and Terra Anegada ('Drowned Land') are Portuguese descriptive terms, having nothing to do with the name of the kingdom of Tori, and D'Elbée was misled by the superficial similarity of names.

Cf. *1732*, p. 321/12–322/7, which alters 'the river Tary ... Anegada' to 'little Popo', and adds a lengthy section on Little Popo adapted from Bosman, pp. 331–5. This includes a reference to rats, which leads Barbot to insert a digression on feeding warm milk to cats in the Hebrides in order to stimulate them to attack rats, but he also adds a reference to rats on Guinea ships – see the Additional Passage. While Barbot does not here distinguish very clearly between Little and Great Popo (see note 16 below), in *1732* he decided that the port five leagues East of Cape Monte was Little Popo, and that the bulk of his detailed information related to Great Popo, further East again. In fact, Little Popo (modern Aneho) is only about 8 km from Kpeme, the probable location of Cape Monte.

[10] The distance of 12 leagues (36 miles) from Tary to Ardra is taken from D'Elbée (Delbée 1671, pp. 381–2), while Dapper had given the distance from Popo to Ardra as eight miles (Dapper, p. 115/5) – this slight degree of coincidence doubtless encouraging Barbot to identify the two (see previous

note). Barbot's map and most of the information on Popo which follows it are original, being presumably based on information gathered in 1682. Barbot's is the earliest detailed map of the Popo area: it appeared again, entitled 'Popôs' Bay als. Tary', in *1732*, Plate 7 (p. 104), with a drawing of an 'alegator' added. The distinction on the map between the village South of the lagoon and the 'village of Popo' on the North bank corresponds to that in recent times between the coastal town of Great Popo (or Houlagan) and the royal residence of Agbanakan in the interior. The river running into the lagoon from the interior is presumably River Mono, although in recent times Agbanakan has been situated West rather than East of River Mono. It is noteworthy that the outlet of the river is shown as immediately East of the coastal village, whereas nowadays Great Popo is some 5 km from the outlet of Bouche du Roi, though it is reported that the latter is 'subject to frequent change' (*Africa pilot* 1967, p. 477).

Cf. *1732*, p. 322/8, which substitutes for the distance between Popo and Ardra that between Little Popo and Great Popo, given as about five leagues (15 miles), and adds that the river of Popo was 'by the Portuguese called Rio do Poupo'. The distance between Little and Great Popo is probably taken from Bosman, who gives it as four (Dutch) miles (16 English miles) (Bosman, p. 335); the actual distance is rather less, about 13 miles/21 km. The Portuguese toponym was probably taken from the Mortier map.

[11] Barbot's map marks a 'village where the Blacks have a white flag' to the West of the channel giving access to Popo, and a 'Dutch flag' to the East.

Cf. *1732*, p. 322/8–11, which incorporates this information into the text, at the same time attributing the raising of the Dutch flag to a Dutch lodge at Popo (see note 14 below), and adds material describing the paucity of habitations at Great Popo and its wars with Whydah, from Bosman, pp. 335–6.

[12] The account of the people of Popo being obliged in former times to send their slaves to Ardra so that taxes might be levied is taken from D'Elbée, but the rest of the passage is original (Delbée 1671, p. 382). Barbot's account of Popo's rebellion against Ardra rule might be merely an inference from the contrast between the independence of Popo at the time of his own visit in 1682 and the situation reported in 1670 by D'Elbée; but some later writers independently report that Great Popo (and allegedly also Little Popo) had formerly been subject to Ardra (Labat 1730, II, 8, 12, 284; Roussier 1935, p. 14).

Cf. *1732*, p. 323/1–2, which expands the vague note about all trade being done with the king into the observation that 'all trading ships there commonly adjust the price of slaves on the one side, and of European goods on the other, with the king of great Popo', and it also incorporates additional material from Bosman, pp. 336–7.

[13] The allusion to events in 1682 is original, the information presumably

having been gathered by Barbot in that year. It is not immediately clear which state is referred to here under the name 'A Monte'; in *1732* Barbot identifies it with 'Coto', i.e. Keta (p. 323/8), whereas a contemporary report describes those attacking Popo at this time as 'robbers' from 'Lampi' (ARA, WIC 1024, J. Bruyningh, Offra, 11.3.1682). Corroboration of a conquest of Popo by Whydah is provided by Bosman who relates that the king of Whydah had deposed the king of Great Popo in favour of his brother, but that the latter had subsequently rebelled against Whydah and defeated a Whydah invasion (Bosman, pp. 335–6). In 1693 another European found Whydah at war with Great Popo (Jones 1985, p. 184).

Cf. *1732*, p. 323/7–9, where Barbot repeats Bosman's account of the wars, but without relating it to his own observations in 1682.

[14] The reference to drunken thieves is from Delbée 1671, p. 383, otherwise the passage is original. The term 'domine' is not, as Barbot appears to suggest, an indigenous title, but is the Dutch word for a clergyman (*dominee*).

Cf. *1732*, p. 323/3–6, which expands the vague note about doing trade with the king, as at 'Juda' (i.e. Whydah) and Ardra, into the statement that the Europeans 'have the king adjust matters of commerce betwixt him and his subjects, being bound to make good any irregularities of this kind [sc. theft] to each party; in imitation of the practice used at Fida and Ardra'.

[15] For Terra Anegada, see note 9 above. The last sentence describing a Dutch lodge at Popo is clearly derived from D'Elbée (Delbée 1671, p. 382), and is implicitly contradicted by Barbot's own earlier observation that the thievishness of the inhabitants of Popo discouraged Europeans from maintaining lodges there (p. 132 above). It is possible that D'Elbée found a Dutch lodge at Great Popo in 1670, since there is a record of one there in the 1660s (Van Dantzig 1980, p. 262). But it is unlikely that it was still functioning when Barbot visited in early 1682, since it is said to have been destroyed by 'Lampi' raiders in 1680 (Kea 1986, p. 130, n. 57; ARA, WIC 1024, unsigned letter, Offra, 29.12.1680). A new factor dispatched to the Dutch lodge in Allada in July 1682 was instructed to investigate the advisability of re-establishing a lodge at (Great) Popo but this was not effected until 1688 – and the lodge was abandoned again in the 1690s (Van Dantzig 1978, pp. 24, 31–2, docs. 14, 23–4; Bosman, p. 335). Barbot's map of Popo Lagoon does show a 'Dutch flag' displayed on the beach at Popo (see note 11 above), and in *1732* he explicitly states that this was connected with the Dutch lodge there (*1732*, p. 322/9). But it seems likely that his memory was at fault, that the Dutch flag in 1682 was in fact raised by the local people, and that his report of a Dutch lodge at Popo is merely a phantom echo of D'Elbée's earlier account.

Cf. *1732*, pp. 322/8–9, 323/10.

[16] Here Barbot belatedly and inadequately distinguishes between Great

and Little Popo, and indicates that it is Great Popo which he has been describing. This is the only point in the text where Barbot makes the distinction, although his map clearly marks 'Petit Popo' and 'G. Popa' separately. The casual way in which Barbot introduces the distinction, so that it reads like an afterthought to the main account of Popo, suggests that he did not learn of the existence of two Popos when on the coast in 1682 but only after his return to Europe. The existence of the separate towns was referred to in a Dutch report of 1659 (Kea 1982, p. 222). But Little Popo was evidently of limited significance until it was occupied by refugees from Accra, displaced by the Akwamu conquest of that kingdom in 1680 (Bosman, p. 332 – see Letter 2/10, note 3, above). Since in his *1688* discussion of Accra Barbot does not refer to this movement to Little Popo, it is possible that it occurred after he visited the district in 1682: the presence of Forri, the king from Accra, seems only to be evidenced in 1687 (OBLR, C.747, J. Carter, Whydah, 10.5.1687). The earliest reference in print to the existence of the two Popos seems to be that of Van Keulen 1683, p. 10, copied by Robijn/Roggeveen 1685, p. 26, very probably Barbot's source for this information. The identity of the village of 'Ooy' is uncertain: its location between Little and Great Popo, as well as the similarity of names, suggests that it might be modern Agoue, which is otherwise apparently unrecorded before the nineteenth century.

Cf. *1732*, p. 323/11, which omits the detail about the flags (it is incorporated, in a slightly different form, in a later passage, p. 324/3: see note 18 below), and makes the following changes. The name 'La Praye', a French version of the Portuguese *praia* 'beach', which is applied in *1688* not only to the roadstead in the kingdom of Whydah but also (following Delbée 1671, p. 385) to the roadstead of Ardra (see p. 139 below), is applied in *1732* solely to the latter, substituting in this passage and in others relating to Whydah the term 'the port of Fida'. By altering 'between Little Popo and Great Popo' to 'betwixt both places', Barbot now gives the impression that Ooy is between Great Popo and the roadstead of Whydah, but this is probably a clumsy piece of rewriting rather than a deliberate emendation. Finally, he adds that 'the coast [is] almost inaccessible by reason of the mighty surf', possibly an echo of Bosman, p. 337.

[17] 'Juda' is the usual French form of the name Hueda (Whydah); but in *1732*, probably under the influence of Bosman, Barbot systematically substitutes the Dutch form 'Fida'. It is clear that Barbot himself actually visited Whydah in 1682. Curiously, this is nowhere specifically stated in the text, but Barbot's map of the Gulf of Guinea (p. 129 above) marks his course from 'la Rade de Juda à l'Isle du Prince' in April 1682, and an allusion in *1732* (p. 453/11) to conditions at Whydah 'in my time 1682' also implies that he visited there, as do a number of other allusions to Whydah (e.g. Letters 2/3, p. 7; 2/20, p. 83). In a later passage (p. 133), Barbot attributes the French

lodge at Whydah not to the Compagnie de Guinée but to the Compagnie du Sénégal: in fact, it would have been the latter company which was in occupation in 1682, the reference to the former company (formed in 1685) representing an up-dating at the time of writing *1688*. 'Jackain' (more usually 'Jakin') was a coastal settlement in the kingdom of Ardra, corresponding to modern Godomey (see Law 1987, pp. 353–4). Jakin had been described as situated on a river (Dapper, p. 115/6), but Barbot's statement that this was the same river as that which runs along the coast from Popo, i.e. the coastal lagoon, is original. The further statement that this river 'loses itself in the earth at Jakin' probably alludes to the appearance of a sandbank blocking the lagoon at the western end of Lake Nokue, close to Jakin, during the dry season (Law 1983, p. 321 and n. 3). The village of 'Coulainba' does not appear to be mentioned in any other published source, but an anonymous and undated (? c. 1714) manuscript description of Whydah refers to a western province bordering Popo called 'Oueneba', which is probably a version of the same name (AANAO, Dépôt des Fortifications des Colonies, Côtes d'Afrique, ms 104, 'Relation du Royaume de Judas', p. 30).

Cf. *1732*, pp. 323/12–324/1, which omits the reference to the French lodge, alters 'within a musket-shot' to 'about a quarter of a mile', and makes the following other changes. It modifies the geography somewhat, placing Coulainba still on 'the river Tary, which runs down from the Ardra country, through Fida, to the ocean at Great Popo', i.e. the coastal lagoon, but placing Jakin on a separate river. This follows Bosman (p. 362 bis), who had likewise distinguished the river running from the Popos to Whydah from that running by Jakin; but although Barbot seems to have taken this as contradicting his own information, more probably it merely reflects awareness of the barrier separating the lagoons to the East and West of Jakin to which Barbot himself had alluded. It adds – 'All the above-named villages properly belong to the country of Fida, and are not easily perceived from the sea, but from the top-masts of ships, when sailing near the shore'.

[18] Cf. *1732*, p. 324/2–3, 6, which reduces the number of trees to four or five, notes that the flag raised by the French factor is white, and adds that Barbot believes that the English factor likewise raises a flag for English ships calling there, 'the staff being common to them as it happens' (see note 16 above). It also adds material on the dangers of landing through the surf mainly from Bosman, pp. 337–9, a reference to the danger of being 'devoured by the monstrous sharks, which swarm amongst the swelling waves of the ocean' echoing Bosman, p. 281, and the information that the rowers employed in the bar canoes 'for the most part, are Mina blacks, the most skillful of all the Blacks' (repeating Letter 2/20, p. 83, above). For a 1694 reference to the employment of Gold Coast canoemen at Whydah, see Phillips 1732, pp. 228–9; and for later references, see Smith 1970, p. 517.

[19] 'Mr D. ....' here is D'Elbée, who does indeed state that the kingdom of

Ardra bordered on the East with Benin and extended in the West to River Tary (Delbée 1671, p. 557), Barbot himself contributing the indentification of Tary with Popo (see note 9 above). Despite Barbot's reference to 'several people', the only other earlier source to discuss the extent of Ardra in any detail, Dapper, in fact says the same as Barbot, since he makes Ardra begin East of 'Foulaen' and states that the people of Foulaen defy the authority of the king of Ardra (Dapper, pp. 115/6, 120/4). Barbot seems somewhat uncharitable to assume that D'Elbée is merely wrong, ignoring the possibility that the extent of Ardra authority had shrunk since his day (as he had suggested in the case of Popo: see note 12 above). Some later sources do in fact report that Whydah had formerly been subject to Ardra (Du Casse 1688, in Roussier 1935, p. 14; N * * * 1719, p. 111; Labat 1730, II, esp. 61–74). Barbot's 'Torry' is clearly the small kingdom of Tori, between Whydah and Ardra. As noted earlier (note 9 above), the name had appeared in the form 'Tary' in earlier sources, including D'Elbée's erroneous application of it to Popo (as followed by Barbot). Barbot seems not to have realized that his 'Torry' was a version of the name earlier reported as 'Tary', but his information on this kingdom is clearly original, presumably based upon enquiries at Whydah in 1682. The case of 'Foulaan' ('Foulaen' on p. 139 below) is more complex. The name itself is probably derived from Houla, or Pla, originally applied to Great Popo, and then by extension to settlements which traced their origins from that town and which were located along the coast to both West and East. The toponym 'Foulaen' is applied in earlier sources to a place on the coast between Popo and Ardra (e.e. Dapper, pp. 115/6, 120/4). But it is apparently not recorded independently in any later source, and in the 1860s it was 'impossible to find' (Burton 1864, I, 150). The town might well have been destroyed in the late seventeenth century, but it is also possible that it was known later under a different name. It is an attractive suggestion that 'Foulaen' is a version of the name 'Pelleau', which Barbot himself gives (Letter 3/2, p. 133 below) to the seaport of Whydah, more commonly known as Grehue (Verger 1968b, p. 37). Barbot, however, clearly regarded 'Foulaen' as a distinct place East of Whydah, within the kingdom of Tori, a location which suggests identification with modern Avrekete (Person 1975, pp. 717, 720). It is unfortunately uncertain whether Barbot's own references to 'Foulaen' are purely derivative (from Dapper), or reflect information obtained orally in 1682: his statement that Foulaen was the seaport of Tori looks like a piece of original information, and tends to support the view that Foulaen was a separate place East of Whydah, but it is possible that it merely represents an attempt by Barbot to harmonize his own information with the earlier sources which had mentioned 'Foulaen'. Given the fact, however, that the name Houla/Pla might have been applied to virtually any coastal settlement, some confusion among different places seems very probable: for further discussion, see Law 1987, pp. 349–351.

The statement of D'Elbée, followed by Barbot (and independently supported by Bosman, p. 244), that Ardra bordered Benin in the East, is presumably to be explained by the fact that at this period Benin rule extended West along the coastal lagoon as far as Lagos, and possibly beyond (see Letter 3/3, p. 139, and note 5, below). The statement that Ardra is extensive in the interior, and borders in the North with Oyeo (i.e. Oyo) at 15°N, is taken from D'Elbée (Delbée 1671, p. 557), Barbot adding only the detail about the populousness of Oyo, which is perhaps an inference from the numbers of slaves from Oyo on sale at Whydah (see Letter 3/2, p. 136 below). The promise of further information on this point is not redeemed, although Oyo is twice mentioned later (pp. 136, 139).

Cf. *1732*, p. 327/3, which omits the mention of 'Mr D. . . . .', substitutes for 'the kingdom of Oyeo, which is at 15 degrees' 'the kingdom of Ulkamy, . . . which is under ten degrees north', and adds that 'Ulkamy, according to a very modern author, borders northward on the country of Lamtem, which reaches some way to the kingdom of Guber, and that again to the Sigismes lake or the Niger'. The 'very modern author' seems here again (see note 2 above) to be Delisle's 1700/1707 map. The kingdom of 'Ulkamy' had been described by Dapper as a large kingdom East of Ardra and NW of Benin (Dapper, p. 121/5, copied in Letter 3/4, p. 149, below). The name seems to represent Olukumi, a name sometimes given to Yoruba-speakers, and presumably designates the Yoruba generally, or some section of them (Hair 1969a, pp. 233, 248–9). Barbot's substitution of 'Ulkamy' for Oyo presumably implies that he thought the two were identical: this seems plausible enough, inasmuch as Oyo was at this period the most powerful of the Yoruba states (see Law 1977).

[20] As a result of this change of mind, Barbot reorganized his material, placing his description of the kingdom of Soko, which in *1688* is included at the end of his account of Gold Coast, now at the beginning of his account of Slave Coast. He had not used the term 'Slave Coast' in *1688*, although he did use the similar term 'Captives Coast' ('Cativos Kust') (Letter 1/18, p. 100, and note 2). His adoption of 'Slave Coast' almost certainly reflects the influence of Bosman, apparently the earliest published source to employ the term, Bosman having made Gold Coast end at 'Ponni' (Kpone), East of Accra, and beginning his description of Slave Coast at the kingdom of Lampi (Ladoku), with its coastal port of Lay (Leponguno) (Bosman, pp. 6, 66, 326). Barbot's statement that gold was purchased on Slave Coast only 'by chance, in inconsiderable quantity' was in fact no longer quite accurate by the time he was writing, since Portuguese traders had begun to import Brazilian gold into Whydah, and in 1707 English traders initiated a substantial trade in the sale of slaves to the Portuguese in exchange for this gold (Verger 1968a, pp. 49–51).

[21] It is not certain to which of Barbot's voyages this incident relates, or which ship was 'new from the stocks', but it may be noted that he records purchasing three parrots on Príncipe in 1679 (*1679*, p. 350).

LETTER 2

Description of the country of Juda and the trading posts (loges) *of the French and English. History of the establishment of the French post by Carolof, and the agreement regarding water and wood, etc. The king of Juda, his person, court, palace, fetishes and government. The natives in general. The cannibals among them. The slaves they make and the scorn of these captives for death. The burial rites of the blacks of this district. The reciprocal oaths they take. Their character and occupations, etc. Bouges or cowries, the money at Juda and Ardres, and their way of counting cowries. Women of the land. The nobles, etc.*

The country of Juda, Sir, is very densely inhabited, and there is hardly any land uncultivated, which makes it fair and pleasant. It abounds in maize, rice, millet, and generally in all the crops that there are on Gold Coast. Thanks to the good pastures, many sheep, oxen, cows, red deer, fallow deer, pigs, and fowls are also found there, and these provide food for the natives as well as for the whites. You also see there many small horses. Palm wine and *petaw* beer are plentiful there, this last drink being better than that which they make on Gold Coast. The water from the springs is fine, good, clear, and light.[1]

What is bad in such a good country is that, along the whole coast and from there to half a league in the interior, it is all swamp, and this makes staying at Juda very dangerous for the Europeans. The vapours which the sun draws from the swamp are spread over the whole country by the winds, causing many illnesses among the whites, and so you find hardly any man coming there who does not die after a certain time, or who [at least] is attacked by violent stomach aches, which degenerate into congestion of the brain, with a severe burning fever. Some die of it, others resist it, but it has been noticed that certain of the latter after spending a long time there in good health have had long and troublesome indispositions at sea on the way back to Europe. In fact, most of them die of flux of blood from the liver, or of raging colics, which are attributed to the rawness of the fruits and the freshness of the water at Juda. It is said that the beer which they make there also contributes much to it.

That is why it is necessary to be extremely temperate over all these things, to eat little and often, to take strong drinks with moderation, not to expose oneself to the evening damp or to the sun, to avoid the rain as much as one can, not to give oneself to the violent exercise of hunting, and to keep oneself covered at night because it is cool and damp.[2]

The lodge of the Compagnie du Sénégal and the lodge of the English stand a little beyond the swamp, three quarters of a league from the edge, at the approach to a wood, and near to the village of Pelleau. You have yourself carried there in a hammock on the shoulders of two blacks, who are relieved from time to time, since there are three fords to pass where the water is up to the neck. These Moors are very skilful at this form of transport, for when they are in the water up to their shoulders they carry the hammock and its load raised on the palms of their hands, a third man putting himself between them to support on his head the bottom of the hammock, so that it does not touch the water.[3]

The French lodge at Juda was built in 1671 by a man named Carolof, with the consent of the king of Juda and of Prince Bibe, who permitted him not only to build it and to carry out trade there, but also to traffic in the country of the king of Ardres. The part of the latter country fronting the sea, having been in revolt, had recently placed itself under the protection of these two princes; and this also put a stop to the trade in slaves (*captifs*), who no longer came down to Offra, a village on the river of Ardres. /p. 134/ Here is how the establishment was made. The Compagnie des Indes Occidentales, intending to make an establishment at Ardres, in 1669 sent [. . .] Carolof as Agent General. [. . .] The king of Ardres received the presents with great pleasure, and caused an announcement to be made of freedom of commerce for the French at Offra, in return for the accustomed duties which the Dutch had been paying him for 20 years. This favour drew upon the French the hatred of the Flemings, who did all they could to obstruct this establishment. Finally they quarrelled over the flag. The agent [at Offra], Marriage, complained about it to the king of Ardres, but as this prince was deriving heavy duties from the Dutch, he conducted himself in such a way that he gave satisfaction to both parties without however reaching any decision in this respect. At this time he sent Mateo Lopez, the royal interpreter and one of this prince's ministers, in the capacity of ambassador to the king [of France]. [. . .] He was shown the fine

635

sights of Paris, where he was showered with civilities by the Company, with whom he signed a treaty of commerce. [. . .] Finally he embarked again at Le Havre, on the vessel *St Georges*, which was commanded by Carolof and he got back to Ardres on the first of October in the year 1671.[4]

This ambassador wanted the presents that the king was sending to the king of Ardres to be delivered into his hands, in order apparently to appropriate them, as was afterwards known, but the agent had orders to present them himself to the Moorish king. This refusal annoyed the ambassador, who muddied the affairs of the French at the court, which obliged agent Carolof to take other measures while he waited for an opportunity to see the king of Ardra. (The king was at that time occupied with a civil war, which had caused him a great deal of trouble, because it blocked the passage of the river by which slaves are brought down to Offra, so that in fifteen months only 200 slaves had succeeded in reaching Offra, and this had caused five Dutch vessels to return empty to Mina). Carolof had previously done some trade at Popo, and even while the black ambassador was aboard his ship he had established a small lodge there. He did this with the consent of the king of the country, with whom he had agreed a payment, to cover all duties, of 28 slaves for each French ship coming to trade there, whereas at Offra he was paying 100 slaves. The agent went from there to Juda, where the king received him very well and promised him not only to trade with the [French] nation, but also to have a particular regard for it. All these events obliged him therefore to turn towards Juda, and to ask for nothing more at the court of Ardres, and so to take back to France the presents he had on board. He therefore abandoned the lodge at Offra, and came to Juda where he re-established it. He did this all the more willingly because in the circumstances of the time it appeared that he would do a considerable trade in slaves at Juda. For the roads from Savi to Ardres were open, and by these roads many slaves were being brought down to Juda, this also providing a means whereby the king of Ardres could punish his rebellious subjects, by directing the trade through a different route than the one following the river which passes to Offra.

This was the way this lodge was established.[5] /p. 135/ The Compagnie du Sénégal, having taken over the rights of the Compagnie des Indes Occidentales, maintains an agent there, together with a few whites and a cleric as chaplain. This Company is obliged to pay the value of 25 slaves to the king of Juda for the right to trade of each vessel, and also for permission to obtain water, wood and provisions, and equally for the goods which are disembarked at La Praye. These are afterwards carried by blacks to the lodge and this costs another five or six slaves, with the same again for the bar canoes.[6]

It is with the king that you do the trade (as I have said), and no-one has any right to trade until at least after the king has opened the trading. If he is not trading for himself, he sets the price for the goods for the whole cargo of the vessel, in such a way that you have no more bargaining to do. This prince ordinarily does more trade than any of his subjects, and you go to see him as soon as you arrive. He usually resides at Savy, one league from the French lodge. You give him an account of the goods you have, and out of these he reserves what he himself needs, settling, for instance, the price of a slave at an *alcoves* of cowries, which is 50 *galinas*, weighing about 60 lb. (the blacks call it a *guinbotton*, and it represents cowries to the number of 4,000), or 15 bars of iron, for everything is reduced to these two sorts of goods, as I shall show you hereafter. When the price is agreed, you have the goods brought from the vessel to the lodge, where after the king has taken what he wants of them, next the other lords and Moors of the country supply themselves with what they need. After that, all of them, king and subjects, send their slaves on board, as soon as they arrive from the interior of the country. Or if the weather is not fine, they are kept in 'trunks' (*en troncs*), which are made like barns, until the bar is navigable, which sometimes takes 10–15 days.[7] The bar here is very dangerous in all weather, throughout the year, except in the months of January, February and March, which is the good season of those countries.[8]

Water for ships is obtained in wells situated between the shore and the stream running from Popo. You bring the casks on board, across the bar, by hauling them on board three at a time. The water of these wells is not bad, given that it is so close to the sea.[9] The Moors of the country sell fire-wood, which they collect in the forests in the interior. It consists merely of small stumps of osier and other bushes.[10]

The king of Juda is in the habit of offering many favours to the senior officers of the vessels which come to trade in his lands and who go to see him; for not content with entertaining them well in his manner, he shows great liberality to the populace on those days, and if I can believe the Moors, some of these visits cost him 150 slaves.[11] This prince is today 36–38 years old, and is tall and of fine bearing, betokening spirit and great judgement. He is usually clothed in the Arab fashion, in a robe of violet taffeta. It is believed that he possesses considerable treasures, and that although he rules over only a small country, he nevertheless has a large population under his control. He keeps more than 200 wives, and a large number of foot-guards. The prince is very superstitious and a slave of his fetishes, of which the palace is full. The palace has a double guard of musketeers in front of the main gate, which is defended by four small iron cannon. [12]

The fetishes of this king, like those of the people, are all made of wood or earth, and are large and white, and shaped like puppets. An infinite number of them is placed in special places on the roads, as happens with Saints in Italy and Spain. On the roads you also find /p. 136/ thatched huts (which they call Case de Dios [God huts]) where they keep snakes, which they [seize and] shut up inside the huts whenever they encounter them on their travels. They have a particular veneration for these animals, and especially for the red ones. I must repeat that they have a quite peculiar veneration for these animals, since they worship them like so many deities, praying to them and offering them sacrifices, and displaying before them the fetishes they have made, as if they wished to sanctify them by letting these crawling deities see them. The service they give the snakes varies according to the nature of these animals, for there are different sorts. The red snakes are the most common there, and for this reason they honour them more highly. When a snake by chance enters the house of a Moor (which happens quite often), he goes to find one of the priests of the place, so that the priest can seize the snake and put it in the nearest Case de Dios; and when they are asked where they are taking the snake, they say that the god they are holding will direct them. They never pass in front of these Cases de Dios without going in to salute the deities which they shut up in them. Most of them even consult them about what they must do to remain always in their favour. Since each of these huts contains an old Mooress, whom they maintain to serve as a priestess, and who feeds herself in that place on the meats and fruits each person brings there daily, she replies in a deep and deliberate voice (like the Sybil of old), telling one person to refrain carefully from sleeping with his wife during certain days and certain times, another never to eat the flesh of hens or oxen or sheep, and yet another never to drink palm wine or beer – telling them, in short, to abstain from such and such things, which the poor idolaters observe religiously, for they imagine that if they behaved differently God (*Dios*) would make them die.[13]

The king is absolute master of justice, which he has administered by his principal officers in those places where he cannot administer it himself. The people very much respect these magistrates and call them *fidalgues*. It cannot be adequately expressed how far they carry their reverence and submission in respect of the king, whom they never dare to look in the face but always prostrate themselves on the ground at his approach. It is a custom among these blacks that if any one of them is detected in a theft, it enhances the reputation of the person who finds him if he kills him on the spot, cutting off his head and private parts, and bringing them to the king's palace. Here the dead man's relatives come to look for them, if they have the wherewithal to pay the fine which is due to the king for them; if they cannot bear this expense, then the head, etc. are sold, and – if I can believe some of them – eaten.[14]

An attempt has been made to persuade me that they are cannibals, and that at a place a league from Savy, where a market is held, at a time of intense famine they had slaves fattened, who were then sold, either alive to be butchered and eaten, or dead and cut into pieces for the same purpose, the heads being also displayed on the market stands, so that those who were buying these meats would know if they were young or old, man or woman. I do not give entire credence to what I report at this point from hearsay.

Nevertheless, Sir, truly there must be something in it. For all the slaves from these places, especially those whom we transport to the Islands of America, including those from Oyeo and Benin – irreconcilable enemies of those of Ardra – firmly believe when they are embarked that we have bought them to have them fattened in our own country, so that we will be better able to sell them when they are more suitable to be eaten. This causes them (at least several of them) so much sadness that they obstinately refuse the sustenance which can keep them alive, /p. 137/ and so they allow themselves to die, whatever one does to reassure them on the point. This leads me to make another remark to you, which is that these blacks in general regard death very stoically, being completely Pythagorean, like those of Gold Coast. This is what makes them, without caution but with steadfastness, rush into the most dangerous circumstances. The women have the same spirit and the same resolution. On my 1679 voyage, a black woman of Aquambou, being unable, as she wished,

639

to nurse a small child which she had, and having further got it into her head that we were taking her and her child to eat, threw herself one day, unnoticed, into the sea, leaving her child on the mast-strut (for we were then at the Equator 200 or 300 leagues from land). A moment later she was seen, and a canoe was sent to her rescue, after half an hour's work getting it into the sea. She gave us to understand that she had done everything she could to make herself drown, but that she had not been able to succeed in this, nature obstructing her destruction and making her, in spite of herself, employ the swimming ability and buoyancy she had acquired [earlier in life]. But let us return to the subject of justice under the king of Juda.[15]

A black accused of a crime without there being sufficient proof, is obliged to swim across a river which (according to what they believe) has the virtue of making him drown if he is guilty, be he the best swimmer in the land, and which contrariwise preserves the lives of those [innocents] who have never learned to swim, with the result that anyone who successfully reaches the other bank is solemnly acquitted. But if the accused is drowned in the river, they take the body and have it broiled in a cauldron, and they eat it, out of abhorrence and horror for the crime he had committed. The king's wives and intimates are often exposed to this test, on simple suspicion of adultery. Unless they deem themselves innocent, they never expose themselves to swimming across the river; and if they confess in good faith, they are [only] repudiated or made slaves. These Moors have yet another sort of test with regard to accusations, this being really, Sir, a sleight-of-hand trick, in which by the arrangement of certain things they claim to prove innocence or guilt.[16]

They bury their dead with many signs of mourning, but after the funeral they keep open house for five or six weeks. The dead are usually interred in the hut where they died, because they have no cemeteries or special [burial] places. They observe several ceremonies after death, including attaching to the feet of a black bird (of a kind known to them) some specially-made fetishes; then they put this bird on the grave of the dead man, together with a large pot of water, and they dance around the grave singing, until the grave is level with the ground, for at first they raise the earth as we do. They also cut the throats of many slaves and wives, in honour of the dead, especially kings, whom they say ought to possess greater glory in the other world than in this! This brings it about that at the moment of the death of kings all the courtiers can be heard expressing a wish to be able to die with him. But I am convinced that, in reality, they withdraw the offer as soon as they can.[17]

I will also tell you something of what they practise among themselves when they make one other a solemn promise. They call this ceremony 'drinking God' (*boire Dios*). They make two small holes in the earth, into which they [each] let some of their blood drip, and after having diluted the blood with a little of the earth, the two drink as much of it as they can. By this means they enter so strongly into one other's interests that whatever happens to [either of] them, good or ill, is common to both. That is why they reveal to each other whatever they think, and whatever they hear, /p. 138/ whether said for good or ill, imagining that the least relaxation in this respect will make them die suddenly.[18]

The men and women of Juda are generally large, industrious and strong, and a little less black than those of Gold Coast.[19] They make their principal occupation going to war whenever they have an opportunity. In time of peace they cultivate their lands in such a way that you see none empty or unoccupied, which makes this little country have available cheaply an abundance of all the things necessary for life. They work the fields by hand and in furrows, as in several places in France.[20] In war their only weapons are bows and arrows, spears, cutlasses, swords and muskets. In campaigns they are led by *fidalgues* and captains.[21]

The women make many objects from maize straw, which they ornament and decorate with cowries, taking the place of pearls and rubies.[22] These cowries are the silver and money of the country. I do not know, Sir, if you are aware that these cowries (*bouges*) are collected in the Maldive Islands in the Indies, where they are called *cauris*. They are in fact small white shells, as big as a hazel-nut, and a little longer. [*footnote:* Postscript. These 'bouges' or *cauris* are carried from the Maldives to Cochin and Goa, instead of to the East, and are distributed to the colonies of the Dutch and English, who bring them to Europe.][23] The Moors here pierce through all the cowries with a nail, and make from them strings of 40, which they call in Portuguese *toques* and in the local language *cenre*; and five of these *toques* make a *galine*, which is 200 cowries and is called a *fore*. They like these shells so much that they prefer them even to gold (which is in little use here since it comes from Gold Coast), and this has made some of the blacks say that a handful of cowries is worth as much as an ounce of gold. Further, among themselves they reckon a

641

man's wealth by so many *alcoves* of cowries, very much as they say in some parts of Holland, 'he is worth so many tons of gold'.[24] Slaves represent another form of wealth among them. Since the slaves are brought from places where they work a great deal, they are much more suitable for the colonies in America than any other sort of blacks. They are also highly valued in the Sugar Islands, where the work is hard and slaves from Cape Verde are not suited to it.[25]

As throughout Guinea, each individual man in Juda has as many wives as he can maintain.[26] The wives have the care of the house-keeping. Food and drink are prepared there as elsewhere. Wives serve their husbands at their meals, and always on their knees, at least the wives of the nobles always do so. These women are clothed more decently and prettily than those of Gold Coast, and they have some very beautiful local cloths, some Indian cloths, and some of white satin or brocade.[27]

The nobles have guards at their doors while they take their meals, and these have the task of firing salvoes of musketry from time to time, to honour them and because they are very fond of this noise, as well as the noise of cannon. The king of Juda has four pieces of cannon before his door, as I have said, and Captain Bibe has one at the village by the sea, which he frequently exercises. There is also one at the Company's lodge.[28]

In several of these blacks I have observed, Sir, much docility and decency, with a foundation of judgement and spirit. The nobles vie with one another in all sorts of ways to outdo the commonalty.[29] I say nothing to you here about several other peculiarities of these people, but if you please, what I shall say later about the people of Ardres will make up for it, since they closely resemble each another in all points.[30] I am, Sir, Your etc. /p. 139/

Additional Passages from *1732*

[pp. 338/11–339/1, on the trade in cowries]

[The cowries are]... then brought over to Europe, more especially by the Dutch, who make a great advantage of them, according to the occasion the several trading nations of Europe have for this trash, to carry on their traffick at the coast of Guinea, and of Angola, to purchase slaves or other goods of Africa, and are only proper for that trade, no other people in the universe putting such a value on them as the Guineans, and more especially those of Fida

642

and Ardra have long done, and still do to this very day. And so, proportionably to the occasion the European Guinea adventurers have for those Cauris, and the quantity or scarcity there happens to be of them, either in England or Holland, their price by the hundred weight is higher or lower. I can give no reason why they are usually sold by weight, and not by measure. / These Cauris are of many different sizes, the smallest hardly larger than a common pea, and the largest, as an ordinary walnut, longish like an olive; but of such great ones there is no considerable quantity in proportion to the inferior sizes, and are all intermixt, great and small. They are commonly brought over from the East-Indies, in packs or bundles, well wrapp'd, and put into small barrels in England or Holland, for the better conveniency of the Guinea trade.[31]

[pp. 339/8–340/2, on the Lingua Franca, local African languages, and trade goods]

Another thing of great advantage to trade with them is, that most of the Fida merchants can speak either something of the Lingua Franca, or of some other European language, but more especially French, which some few are very perfect in, through the long intercourse they have had with us: and herein the French have some advantage over the other Europeans trading there, that their language is near allied to that Lingua Franca, or broken Portuguese.[32] / However, for the facilitating of commerce with those and the Ardra Blacks, I have taken the trouble to collect some of the most familiar words and phrases of those two nations, which are annex'd to the vocabulary of the Guinea Blacks most common language, in the supplement to this volume, the Fidasians using the same languge as those of Ardra; by which, as well as their uniformity of manners and practices, it seems they were formerly one and the same nation.[33] / It would be proper here to insert the several sorts of European goods, with which we drive our trade there to purchase slaves; but the same sorts of goods being us'd in the slave trade at Ardra, I refer to the description of that kingdom, and of the trade we have there with the natives.[34]

[pp. 453/5–7, 10, on forts and factories after 1682]

A few years after I left the coast of Guinea, in 1682, the French abandoned their lodge at Fida, because of the changes that happened in the affairs of their African company; and several years after that, a new African company being established in France, they settled a factory at Fida,[35] as have also the Dutch, who in my time had none there, only one at Offra in the Ardra country;[36] and according to the following memoir, those factories are turned into forts, as well as the English lodge.[37] Refl. p. 34.XIV. Whidah is a fort about one hundred yards square, belonging to the English . . . It stands about three miles from the water side, between a Danish fort at Acra, to the westward, and two forts belonging to the French and Dutch, within half a mile. / About four miles from Whidah, in the king's town, the company have a factory house, a place of very considerable trade; but it is a wretched place, as well as all other European settlements, to live in, by reason of the adjacent swamps, whence proceed noisome stinks and such swarms of mosquettoes or gnats, as plague men night and day in an intolerable manner. From the English factory to the king's town is four miles, through very pleasant fields, full of India and Guinea corn, potatoes, and ignames in great plenty, of which they have two crops in a year, and along the roads there are several villages. This was in 1693 and 1694.[38] ... / The Brandenburgers have also a factory at Fida, since the year 1684.[39]

[pp. 453/11–454/2, on the rulers of Whydah]

The same king that was at Fida in my time 1682, was still vigorous in 1701, and then about fifty-two or fifty-three years of age; but as brisk and sprightly as a man of thirty-five.[40] / I have been told by a French gentleman, prisoner of war at Southampton, that this king of Whidah died in 1708, and that his death occasioned a civil war there. One of the principal natives of the country, aspiring to the succession, got together an army of twelve or fifteen thousand men, of his party, to oppose the former king's son, then about twenty-eight years of age; but the young prince being supported by the English and French, who lent him about two hundred European soldiers or marines, soon forced the disturber to retire, and was afterwards with the general consent of the people in-throned; and near one hundred and fifty of the principal rebels, who had been taken, were sold as slaves to the French of the Assiento, and most of them carried to Martinico and sold there. The young man distributed about one hundred of them among the French and English, who had so generously assisted him to ascend the throne of Whidah, and gave other presents to the men that

644

were upon the expedition.[41] / That prince is a great favourer of all Europeans residing or trading in his country, but least of the Portugueses; tho' they are allowed a lodge there, as well as the others.[42] Those factories or lodges are now all inclosed with high mud-walls, like fortresses, and each of them has some cannon, more or less, to defend it, with a small garrison, besides factors and servants, which the former king allowed of upon the pressing instances of our European chief factors there, as the only way to prevent their said factories being robbed and pillaged, as they had been often before by the natives, notwithstanding all their watchfulness; which occasion'd frequent disputes and contests among them.[43] / This new king administers very impartial justice and will not suffer any European factor to abuse, or incroach upon another, but will have them all live in unity.[44]

NOTES

[1] For Barbot's visit to Juda/Whydah in April 1682, see Letter 3/1, note 17 above. The reference to maize (together with a reference to maize in neighbouring Tori, Letter 3/3, p. 139 below) provides the earliest evidence for the cultivation of this plant on Slave Coast. Barbot also interpolates (in Letter 3/3, p. 140 below) a reference to maize when repeating an earlier account of Allada which refers only generically to *mille* (Dapper, p. 116/3). For a discussion of the date and significance of the introduction of maize, see Wigboldus 1986, esp. pp. 343–4 (which, however, overlooks Barbot's evidence). Contemporary European visitors to Whydah regularly commented on the density of the population (e.g., Bosman, p. 339) and the abundance of provisions (e.g., Phillips 1732, p. 221); and occasionally on the local beer, favourably (ibid., p. 217).

Cf. *1732*, pp. 327/4–5, 328/6–330/9, which substitutes a lengthy account of the population, agriculture and fauna of Whydah, from Bosman, pp. 339–40, 362, 389–394, with the additional remark that the sea there lacked fish because of sharks.

[2] Cf. *1732*, p. 328/1–2. Contrariwise Bosman asserted that the local water caused illness and that in consequence beer was drunk instead (Bosman, p. 392).

[3] The name 'Pelleau' seems not to occur independently in any other source, unless the name 'Fulao' or 'Foulaen' in earlier accounts is a version of it (see Letter 3/1 above, note 19), and in the 1860s the name was 'now unknown' (Burton 1864, I, 81). The more usual name for the port of Whydah was Grehue (hence 'Gregory', 'Gregoy' or 'Griwhee' in eighteenth-

century sources), and this name was certainly already current in Barbot's time, occurring in the form 'Agriffie' in an 1681 document (OBLR, C.745, John Thorne, Offra, 4.12.1681; Law 1987, pp. 349–51). The English factory at Whydah noted by Barbot probably did not belong to the Royal African Company, an attempt by the company to establish one there in 1681 having proved abortive, and the attempt not succeeding until July 1682 (OBLR, C.745, John Thorne, Offra, 19.8.1681; C.746, Accounts, Whydah, July-October 1682). However, an interloper called Petley Weyborne had meanwhile formed an illicit establishment in 1681, and Barbot's reference is presumably to this (ibid., C.745, J.Thorne, Offra, 4.12.1681; Davies 1957, p. 121). It is noteworthy that Barbot makes no mention of a Portuguese factory reported to exist at Whydah in 1681 (by Thorne, 4.12.1681), but in late 1682 another report stated that the Portuguese factory was empty, there being only a single Portuguese in the kingdom (*Analecta* 1915, p. 358). For similar accounts of transport by hammock in Whydah, see Jones 1985, p. 190; Phillips 1732, pp. 214–5.

Cf. *1732*, p. 324/6, embroidered.

[4] For the several omissions in this paragraph, see below. The 'Prince Bibe' associated with the king of Whydah in 1671 was perhaps identical with the 'Captain Bibe' mentioned by Barbot later (p. 138) and by sources of 1682 and 1694 ('Captain Bibbee', OBLR, C.746, Accounts, Whydah, July-October 1682; 'Capt. Biby', Phillips 1732, p. 228). Barbot's account of the 1671 defection of the coastal area of Ardra, including apparently the coastal port of Offra, to the protection of Whydah is supported by a 1688 report to the effect that Offra had two viceroys, appointed by Ardra and Whydah respectively, implying a dispute for control there (Roussier 1935, p. 15). In 1692 the king of Ardra induced an army from Little Popo to attack and destroy Offra (Bosman, p. 332; Van Dantzig 1978, pp. 35–6). But in 1698 Whydah and Ardra were still disputing possession of the town, each attempting to appoint its own viceroy (Bosman, p. 398). Barbot's account of the arrival of the French at Ardra in 1670 and the mission of the envoy to France, including the omitted material, is derived, being summarized from a lengthy account in Delbée 1671. However, Barbot's following account of the return of Carolof and Lopez to Ardra and of the move of the French to Whydah is original. Barbot earlier referred to a 'Sr. Mariage', in connection with a voyage up River Senegal (Letter 1/10, p. 61 above): this may have been the same M. Marriage who was a commercial agent at Allada c. 1670, and may indicate that Barbot had a direct or indirect contact with an informant who could have been the source of the additional information.

Cf. *1732*, pp. 324/7–325/4, which omits the reference to Prince Bibe.

[5] For Offra, at this period the principal coastal port of the kingdom of Ardra, see Letter 3/3, note 8, below. 'Savi', as Barbot explains later (p. 135 below), was the residence of the king of Whydah, some miles inland: other

sources gave the name in the form of 'Sabee' (Snelgrave 1734, p. 2) or 'Xavier' (Labat 1730, II, 42) – the modern form is Savi. Cf. *1732*, p. 325/4–7, slightly shortened. Note that Barbot in this section uses the term *captifs* rather than *esclaves* to indicate slaves, perhaps to suggest that they were mainly prisoners-of-war.

[6] In contrast to his naming the Compagnie de Guinée in the previous letter, Barbot here attributes the French lodge at Whydah to the Compagnie du Sénégal, commonly known as the Compagnie d'Afrique, which in fact occupied the lodge in 1682. A chaplain for the lodge was first appointed in 1681: two letters survive written by the first chaplain, a Capuchin, Father Celestin de Bruxelles, one written at Dieppe prior to embarcation for Guinea in September 1681, and one written from Whydah in November 1682, the writer referring to himself as 'Aumônier de la Compagnie Royale d'Afrique et Missionaire Apostolique demeurant à Juida dans l'habitation de François' (*Analecta* 1915, pp. 327, 357–9). Other accounts of customs and dues at Whydah record a total of payments of only 13½ slaves (Phillips 1732, p. 227); or of £100 'in Guinea value, as the Goods must yield there' (Bosman, p. 363v).

Cf. *1732*, p. 325/8–9, which adds a comment on the cheap but heavy portage at Whydah, from Bosman, p. 343, and alters and enlarges slightly, as follows – '. . .keeps there a chief factor and a Recolet friar . . . and has only one iron gun at the gates, for salutes, when occasion offers'.

[7] The promise of further information presumably refers to the discussion of cowry enumeration which is given later (p. 138). Barbot's cowry calculations seem seriously confused (Hogendorn/Johnson 1986, p. 192, n. 39). He later explains that a *galina* (perhaps from Portuguese *galinha* 'hen') is 200 cowries (p. 138), so that 50 *galinas* would be, not 4,000, but 10,000 cowries. Yet, in his vocabulary of the Whydah language (Letter 3/14, p. 193), he gives the term for the unit of 20 *galinas*/4,000 cowries not as 'guinbotton' but as 'guinbale', while 'guinbaton' (sic), meaning apparently 'five *guinba*', is equated with 100 *galinas*, or 20,000 cowries. Of these three alternative figures – 4,000, 10,000, 20,000 – the highest is supported by the stated equivalent weight of 60 lb., since cowries were conventionally reckoned at 400 to the lb. (ibid., pp. 7, 114). The unit of 20 *galinas*/4,000 cowries was usually called a 'cabess' (from Portuguese *cabeça* 'head') (Labat 1730, II, 40, 114; Atkins 1735, p. 113; Smith 1744, p. 187). The term 'alcove' (from Portuguese *alcôfa* 'basket of woven material, as used for carrying, for instance, *galinhas*') may have represented a unit of 100 *galinas*/20,000 cowries, but seems otherwise unattested – the unit was later called a 'sack' or 'bag' (Hogendorn/Johnson 1986, pp. 118, 121). Barbot's price for a slave, 60 lb. of cowries or 15 iron bars, may be compared with Allada prices of the mid-seventeenth century, 100 lb. of cowries (Dapper, p. 118/3) or 10 bars (Leers 1665, p. 312), and of 1681, 72 lb. of cowries or 12 bars (PRO,

T.70/20, 15.1.1681). This would seem to indicate that slaves were significantly cheaper at Whydah than at Allada, at least in cowries if not in iron bars. But if this was so in 1682, the relative cheapness of Whydah did not last, since in 1683 it was complained that prices there had been raised to 25% above those at Offra (OBLR, C.746, John Thorne, Offra, 28.1.1683). By 1694 slaves at Whydah cost 100 lb. of cowries or 14 iron bars (Phillips 1732, p. 227). For similar accounts of the negotiation of prices and the preference given to the king of Whydah, see Phillips 1732, pp. 217–9; Bosman, pp. 363v–364v.

Cf. *1732*, pp. 326/1–327/1, which translates *troncs* as 'a booth or prison built for that purpose, near the beach'. (Another visitor to Whydah spoke of 'a trunk for slaves' and 'the captain of the trunk' (Phillips 1732, pp. 215, 218): the term 'trunk' with this meaning is not recorded in *OED*, but is probably related to the following nautical terms – 'trunk' a watertight loading shaft in a ship, hence 'trunk-cabin' and 'trunk deck'.) Barbot adds considerable material on prices, the selection of slaves, the loading time for ships, the supply of slaves at Whydah and the credit system, all from Bosman, pp. 338, 343–4, 363–4v.

[8] Cf. *1732*, p. 326/7. The dangers of the Whydah bar were well known: 'in April, May, June and July, the surf of the Sea is so violent, that according to the Proverb, he ought to have two Lives who ventures' (Bosman, p. 337, corrected translation).

[9] Cf. *1732*, p. 328/3–4, with additions from Bosman, p. 392.

[10] Cf. *1732*, p. 328/5.

[11] Cf. *1732*, pp. 333/13–334/1, which adds material from Bosman, pp. 363, 366–7, a source which also noted the king's 'continual presents to the Europeans'.

[12] The king met by Barbot appear to have been Agbangla, who died in 1703 at an advanced age (see note 40 below). The same man was described in 1694 as 'about 60 years of age ... of middle stature, and spare, his hair and beard grey, his aspect but very ordinary and mean' (Phillips 1732, p. 228); and c. 1698 as 'aged some Years above fifty, but as vigorous and spritely as a man of five and thirty' (Bosman, p. 360). Similar accounts of his clothing were given in 1693 and 1694 – 'a toga of red velvet, and, on his head, a turban of white linen', 'his head was tied in a roll of coarse calico, and he had a loose gown of red damask to cover him' – but c. 1698 he was 'very magnificently Cloathed in Silk, or Gold and Silver Stuffs' (Jones 1985, p. 94; Phillips 1732, p. 216; Bosman, p. 365 bis). Later sources steadily increase his number of wives, to 700 (Jones 1985, p. 191), to 3,000 (Phillips 1732, p. 219), and to 4–5,000 (Bosman, p. 344). Other accounts suggest a less 'superstitious' character: Father Celestin in 1682 reported that although the king could not be won for Christianity, this was due to his practice of

polygamy, and that 'he does not care which God his subjects worship', while Bosman suggested that he was cynical about the cult of the snake-god, and sought to reduce the expense of offerings to it (*Analecta* 1915, p. 358; Bosman, pp. 369–70). Later visitors shared Barbot's uncomplimentary view of the Whydah palace, one describing it as 'built of stone and clay, surrounded by a wall and thatched with reeds and rushes', another as 'the meanest I ever saw, being low mud walls, the roof thatched, the floor the bare ground, with some pools of water and dirt in it' (Jones 1985, p. 191; Phillips 1732, p. 216). In 1694 the king owned six iron cannon, kept in a building near the palace (ibid., p. 220).

Cf. *1732*, pp. 333/13–336/4, which raises the number of wives to 'about three or four hundred', reduces the royal guard to 'a few soldiers', and describes the palace more fully as 'only a heap of little clay houses, or huts, enclosed'; and it incorporates very considerable material on matters relating to the king, from Bosman, pp. 360–3, 365–6.

[13] Europeans visiting Whydah in the 1690s noted 'little figures of clay about their houses' and 'thousands of idols' (Phillips 1732, p. 224; Bosman, p. 161). These ubitiqous images 'like puppets' (i.e. humanoid) were probably statues of the god Legba, which in this district were commonly placed outside houses or in streets leading out of the towns (Argyle 1966, p. 188). Nearly every European visitor to Whydah remarked upon the snake cult (e.g., *Analecta* 1915, p. 329; Gonzales 1902, p. 467; Phillips 1732, p. 223; Snelgrave 1734, pp. 10–12). Phillips stated that the sacred serpents were black, while Bosman, supported by Snelgrave (if the latter was not borrowing), described them as 'streak'd with White, Yellow and Brown' (Bosman, p. 380); on this, Bosman was the more accurate, the snake worshipped being the royal python, called locally Dangbe.

Cf. *1732*, pp. 333/9–10, 340/3–345/4, where the snake cult material is embedded in extensive material from Bosman, pp. 368 bis–386, with digressions on comparative religion from Jurieu 1704.

[14] The 'magistrates' were elsewhere described as 'the Viceroys, here called Phidalgoes or Governadors ... these in the King's absence and in their Viceroyalties, command as arbitrarily and keep up as great State as the King himself' (Bosman, p. 361v). Later writers also noted the custom of prostration before the king (Jones 1985, p. 195; Bosman, p. 365v). Barbot's account of the harsh punishment of theft in Whydah contrasts with later complaints of the prevalence of theft there and the indulgence of the authorities towards it (e.g. Bosman, pp. 348–50). For cannibalism, see note 15 below.

Cf. *1732*, p. 334/8, 10, which loosely refers to justice, the 'fidalgos' ('which is a Portuguese word, signifying men of quality', a correct definition), and respect for the king, but not to the punishment described; and *1732*, pp. 337/3–338/3, on the administration of justice, which is from Bosman, pp. 357–9.

[15] For allegations of cannibalism by a people of the interior, the Dahomians, see Snelgrave 1734, pp. 41–2, 52. But this seems to be a conventional accusation of inhumanity rather than proof of a local practice. The reference here to Oyo and Benin as 'irreconcilable enemies' of Ardra is probably an echo of D'Elbée, who observed that the king of Ardra was frequently at war with Oyo and Benin (Delbée 1671, p. 558). However, it is quite possible that Barbot found Oyo and Benin slaves on sale at Whydah – at least one slave from Oyo was taken to French Guyana in a ship, *La Perle*, which formed part of Barbot's squadron in 1682 (Debien and Houdaille 1974, p. 173) – and perhaps Barbot was given to understand that these were war captives taken by Ardra. As regards the view that Europeans ate slaves, Bosman also referred to 'a parcel of Slaves, which come from a far In-land Country, who very innocently perswade one another, that we buy them only to fatten and afterwards eat them as a Delicacy' (Bosman, p. 365). Barbot refers again to this fear of the slaves in Letter 3/20, pp. 234–5. The 'mast-strut' or 'channel' (*porte-haubans*) is a timber projecting from the ship's side abreast of the mast to widen the basis for the shrouds: the implication is that the woman jumped from this strut. But the anecdote seems muddled – if she thought the baby was to be eaten, why did she not take it with her in her suicide attempt ?

Cf. *1732*, p. 327/2, which omits the illustrative case of the Akwamu woman.

[16] The obscure reference to 'sleight-of-hand' (Barbot's own translation is 'a juggle', and he adds 'as practis'd at the Gold Coast, by their priests') perhaps refers to divination by casting palm-nuts, for which see Maupoil 1943.

Cf. *1732*, pp. 337/10–338/3, which modifies the account of the river ordeal to imply that nobody was ever found guilty, following Bosman, p. 359. Barbot does not, however, accept the view that adultery with wives of the king or great men of Whydah was punished by death, as stated in Bosman, pp. 357–8.

[17] For a fuller description of a royal funeral in Whydah, see Labat 1730, II, 74–7.

Cf. *1732*, pp. 333/8, 336/5–6, 338/6–8, which adds material on other customs at the death of kings and others, from Bosman, pp. 353, 366–366 bis.

[18] For this practice of a blood pact, see Hazoumé 1938. 'Drinking god' is an accurate translation of the indigenous term, *vodun-nu-nu*, a term which seems to be given for 'oath' in Barbot's Whydah vocabulary, in the form 'bodou-houy' (Letter 3/14, p. 198 below).

Cf. *1732*, p. 338/4–5.

[19] Cf. *1732*, pp. 330/10–331/4, considerably expanded with material on 'courteous behaviour' from Bosman, pp. 340–2.

650

[20] The reference to Whydah agriculture repeats information on p. 133 above.

Cf. *1732*, p. 331/5–7, which repeats only the last statement (but revising it to 'as we do in many parts of England'), and embeds it in material on occupations derived from Bosman, pp. 342–3.

[21] Cf. *1732*, pp. 336/7–337/1, which substitutes a longer account of weaponry (with the addition of throwing clubs) and warfare, from Bosman, pp. 394–6.

[22] The manufacture of baskets by the women of Whydah was also noted in 1694 (Phillips 1732, p. 220).

Cf. *1732*, p. 331/7, which notes that women 'make sundry sorts of hampers, baskets and other like utensils, with the straw of Indian wheat, which they carry to market to sell', within material on woman's work from Bosman, pp. 342, 344.

[23] Apart from the term 'cowries' and the reference to the English, the references to the Maldives, Cochin and Goa are from Dapper, p. 118/3 (as noted in Hogendorn/Johnson 1986, p. 173).

Cf. *1732*, p. 338/11, which states instead that cowries are 'as big as small olives', and adds material on the cowrie trade, for which see the Additional Passage.

[24] For the contradictions in Barbot's cowry arithmetic, see note 7 above. The Portuguese term *toque* means basically 'touch' but has many other meanings, including that of English 'toque' (i.e. bonnet), however none of the meanings appears to fit the present use. In Barbot's vocabulary of Ewe (Gbe), *cenre* appears as 40 (i.e. *kande*). For similar accounts of cowry enumeration at Whydah, see Phillips 1732, p. 228 (where *fogge* is a misprint for *togge*, i.e. *toque*); Labat 1730, II, 40, 114; Atkins 1735, p. 113. Barbot's reference to the import of small quantities of gold dust from Gold Coast is confirmed by gold being listed among the goods suitable for the Allada trade (Delbée 1671, p. 448 – but gold is omitted from the list when borrowed in Letter 3/3, p. 142 below), and by a recommendation of an English factor that gold should be purchased on Gold Coast for re-sale at Whydah (OBLR, C.745, John Carter, Whydah, 11.11.1686). This trade must have ceased, since towards c. 1698 it was noted that there was no gold in Whydah and the people were ignorant of its value (Bosman, p. 350; Roussier 1935, p. 82). However, from 1707 large quantities of gold reached Whydah from Brazil (Draisé de Grandpierre 1718, p. 169; Snelgrave 1734, p. 89; Verger 1968a, pp. 49–51). The statement that 'a handful of cowries' was considered worth an ounce of gold is rhetoric, since in fact an ounce of gold was conventionally equated with 16,000 cowries (Hogendorn/Johnson 1986, p. 134).

Cf. *1732*, p. 339/2–5, which omits the Dutch reference and begins – 'At Fida and Ardra, where ... they are most fond of them, they either serve to adorn their bodies, or as current coin'. It also adds what Barbot has stated earlier (p. 135 above), that an *alcoves* (sic) is 50 *galinas*, or 4,000 cowries.

[25] According to a contemporary source, the slaves most in demand in the West Indies were those from Gold Coast, although those from Whydah were preferred to those from Angola, and those from 'Alampi' (Ladoku) 'are accounted the worst of all' (Phillips 1732, p. 214).

Cf. *1732*, p. 339/5–6, which has added material on slaves being brought from far in the interior and on slave mutinies aboard ship, from Bosman, p. 363 bis, and the following statement. 'To prevent which [sc. mutiny], it is necessary to observe exactly the directions I propose to give in the supplement to this book, both for managing slaves, and subsisting them properly in their transportation at sea; as also for preventing their revolt and mutiny.' The reference is to material which in this edition is given as an Additional Passage to Letter 3/20.

[26] Other European visitors suggested that polygamy was practised on a larger scale at Whydah than elsewhere in Africa (Bosman, p. 344; Phillips 1732, p. 219; Draise de Grandpierre 1718, p. 170; Snelgrave 1734, p. 3).

Cf. *1732*, pp. 331/8, 333/11, 332/10–333/4, which adds material on fertility, adultery, prostitution and circumcision (including female circumcision), from Bosman, pp. 214, 344, 346–7, 353. On female circumcision Barbot added – 'as I have observed it to be practised in north Guinea'. But in *1688* he only referred to male circumcision in Senegambia (Letter 1/10, p. 59), and only mentioned female circumcision when borrowing from Dapper's Kquoja account (Letter 1/26, p. 144 – omitted here). It is perhaps unlikely that Barbot was aware of the practice when in Guinea and since men are rigorously barred from the female initiation rites (even today) almost certain that neither he nor any other European literally 'observed' the ceremony.

[27] Cf. *1732*, pp. 332/6–9, 333/5–6, which adds material more critical of women's dress, and references to men's clothing and going bare-headed, from Bosman, pp. 350–1. On deference kneeling, see Bosman, p. 341.

[28] The king's cannon and Prince (Captain) Bibe have been mentioned earlier (pp. 133, 135 above). A contemporary source reported that when a Whydah chief travelled he was accompanied by ten or twelve men with guns 'making great huzzaings according to their way, and firing along the road; and when arrived at the journey's end they fire a volley, which is the utmost of his grandeur' (Phillips 1732, p. 215).

Cf. *1732*, p. 333/7, which omits the references to specific cannon.

[29] Cf.*1732*, pp. 330/13–331/4, which substitutes a much longer account of the civility of the Whydah people, from Bosman, pp. 341–2. But in *1732*, pp. 331/9–332/5, Barbot gives a less favorable impression of the Whydah people, by repeating at length statements about their dishonesty and thieving, from Bosman, pp. 348–50.

[30] Cf. *1732*, p. 338/9.

[31] This additional material on the European end of the cowry trade probably reflects Barbot's continued contacts with people involved in the African trade after 1688: the material has been described as 'a largely accurate overview' (Hogendorn/Johnson 1986, p. 47). The importance of cowries in the Allada trade was stressed earlier by Dapper, p. 118/3.

[32] This passage is preceded by material on the keeping of accounts by Whydah traders and followed by material on the Whydah calendar (*1732*, pp. 339/7, 340/2), all from Bosman, p. 352, a source which noted that the king 'understood a little Portuguese'. It was reported in 1704 that Captain Assou, the Whydah chief who dealt with the French, 'spoke French without having left the country, having learnt it in our factory' (Doublet 1883, p. 254).

[33] Although Barbot does not in this Letter mention his vocabulary of the language 'common to Juda and Ardra', he presents the vocabulary later, with other vocabularies, in Letter 3/4 (pp. 193–201). In *1732* the vocabularies are not given, as stated, in the Supplement, but at the end of the main text (*1732*, pp. 414–20). Whydah did, indeed, have traditions of a common origin with Ardra, and had formerly been subject to it: see Letter 3/1, note 19.

[34] See below, Letter 3/3, note 9. The final paragraph of the chapter, *1732*, p. 340/3, on the reckoning of time, is from Bosman, p. 352.

[35] This passage is from the section on Fida/Juda/Whydah in the Supplement, a section which includes material acknowledged to be from from Bosman (*1732*, p. 453/2–4, 9; Bosman, pp. 337, 365), and unacknowledged material (*1732*, p. 453/6) from Davenant 1709, p. 226, as well as a mysterious borrowing from Phillips 1732 (see note 38 below). In the passage cited, Barbot oversimplifies a complex story. The French lodge at Whydah still existed at the time of Du Casse's visit there in 1688, but had been abandoned by the time of D'Amon's voyage in 1701 (Roussier 1935, pp. 14, 106). According to D'Amon, the French lodge had been destroyed by raiders from Popo: this was probably in 1692, when an army from Little Popo sacked Offra, destroying the Dutch lodge there, and also attacked Whydah (Van Dantzig 1980, p. 73). At least for some time after 1692 there was still a French factor resident in Whydah, but he lived no longer at the coastal lodge but in the capital, Savi, where he was met by visitors in 1693–4 (Phillips 1732, p. 222; Jones 1985, p. 190). But evidently the French presence had lapsed by the time of D'Amon's visit in 1701; D'Amon then requested permission from the king of Whydah to reoccupy the lodge at the coast, but the king required the French to reside instead in the capital. A French agent was established in the capital by the time of Doublet's visit in 1704 but Doublet's party then constructed a fortified lodge at the coast (Doublet

1883, pp. 253, 255–6). Thereafter, until the Dahomian sack of the Whydah capital in 1727, the French had both a fortress at the coast and a lodge in the Whydah capital (Labat 1730, II, 42–3, 106–7). Barbot's reference to 'the changes that happened in the affairs of their African company' is obscure: it may allude to the failure of the Compagnie du Sénégal in 1684/5, but neither the implied date nor the explanation for the abandonment of the Whydah lodge seems correct. The reference to the establishment of a 'new African company' possibly alludes to the reorganization of the 'Compagnie de Guinée' (formed 1685) as the 'Compagnie de l'Assiente' in 1701.

[36] The Dutch originally moved to Whydah after the destruction of their factory at Offra by the Little Popo invaders in 1692, but continuing military pressure from Little Popo obliged them to withdraw from Whydah in the same year (Van Dantzig 1980, pp. 73–4). In 1698 Bosman had a lodge built for the Dutch in the Whydah capital (Bosman, p. 365 bis; *HIA*, 7 (1980), 285–6). But this was apparently not continuously manned: in 1699 Bosman found that possession of it had been usurped by the French, whom he had to evict (ibid., pp. 288–9). Continuous occupation apparently dated from 1703, when a new Dutch lodge was built at Whydah (Van Dantzig 1980, pp. 75–6).

[37] The 'memoir', the source of the following paragraph in *1732*, here largely omitted, is Davenant 1709, p. 226 (i.e. *Reflections...*, p. 34, item XIV), but Barbot abbreviates 'within half a mile each of the other, to the eastward of it'. The reference to a Dutch fort is mysterious: the account of Des Marchais, probably relating to 1704–8, states that the Dutch had only a factory at the Whydah capital, having been refused permission to build a fort at the coast, and this is corroborated by the fact that in 1726 the Dutch sought permission to build a lodge 'where the other nations have their forts' (Labat 1730, II, 42–3, 106–7; Van Dantzig 1980, p. 221).

[38] 'About four miles ... considerable trade' is borrowed from Davenant 1709, p. 226; but thereafter, with minor verbal changes and the addition of the phrase 'as well as all other European settlements' (possibly influenced by Bosman, p. 365 bis) and of the dates, the material represents a passage from Phillips 1732, p. 216 – although applied wrongly to the inland factory rather than to the coastal one. Since Barbot cannot have seen this work in print, it must be supposed either that Phillips's manuscript, which was in the hands of the publishers from c. 1700, was shown to Barbot, or else that an editor inserted the reference after Barbot's death in 1712: see the Introduction, pp. xxix–xxx.

[39] Earlier in the Supplement (*1732*, p. 431), Barbot states, on the authority of a relative in Brandenburg service, that the Brandenburgers had lodges at Popo (in this case, Little Popo) and Whydah. The existence of a resident Brandenburger factor at Little Popo is corroborated for 1687 (OBLR,

C.745, John Carter, Whydah, 17.5.1687), but there is no clear corrobora-
tory evidence for a Brandenburger lodge at Whydah. A 'shelter' referred to
c. 1698 appears to have been a temporarily occupied lodging rather than a
permanent factory (Bosman, p. 374; Van Dantzig 1980b, p. 288). Since it is
improbable that there was a Brandenburger lodge in Whydah as early as the
1680s, Barbot's date, 1684, should probably read 1694 (Jones 1985, p. 6).
The lodge was presumably abandoned early in the eighteenth century since
no later source refers to it.

[40] For '1701' Barbot is citing Bosman, p. 360; but in fact Bosman's three
visits to Whydah seem to have been in 1697, 1698, and 1699 (Bosman, pp.
329, 334, 337–8, 389, 398).

[41] Barbot was mistaken in believing that the king who died in 1708 was
the man he had met in 1682. In fact, Barbot's king, Agbangla, had died in
1703, while the king who died in 1708 was his successor, Aisan (Akinjogbin
1967, pp. 35, 39–40). Huffon, the king who succeeded in 1708, was even
younger than Barbot's informant stated, being about thirteen, and the
challenge to his succession was based on his unsuitability as a minor (*ibid.*,
pp. 37, 39). Another account of the royal succession of 1708 indicates,
against Barbot's informant, that the European troops were landed simply to
protect the Europeans in Whydah, and did not intervene in the fighting
(AANAO, Dépôt des Fortifications des Colonies: Côtes d'Afrique, ms 104,
'Relation du Royaume de Judas', p. 36).

[42] The existence of a Portuguese lodge at the Whydah capital in this
period is corroborated by the account of Des Marchais, probably describing
conditions c. 1704–8 (Labat 1730, II, 106–7). But it had apparently been
abandoned by 1716, when it was explicitly stated that the Portuguese had no
lodge there (PAN, C6/25, 'Mémoire de l'Estat de Pays de Juda et de son
Négoce'). A permanent Portuguese presence was re-established only in
1721, when a fort was built at the coastal village of Grehue (Verger 1968a,
pp. 132–9).

[43] The English lodge was fortified with flankers in 1692, against the threat
of war with France, and its defences were strengthened with a moat in 1694
(OBLR, C.747, John Wortley, Whydah, 26.1.1692; Phillips 1732, p. 215).
The French fort was built in 1704 (see note 35 above), and the account of its
construction confirms that security against thefts was the official justification. However, despite what Barbot implies, neither the Dutch nor the
Portuguese at this period had fortified lodges in Whydah. Des Marchais,
describing the situation c. 1704–1708, noted that the Dutch had been
refused permission to build a fort at the coast and that the Portuguese,
although they had been granted a site for a fort, had not built one (Labat
1730, II, 43). A Portuguese fort was eventually built, but only in 1721
(Verger 1968a, pp. 132–9).

[44] The Whydah authorities had long sought to impose peace on the Europeans trading in their kingdom: as early as 1681 it was noted there that 'the Blacks will have noe striving one with another but will have all ships trade that come' (OBLR, C.745, John Thorne, Whydah, 4.12.1681). At the instance of the king of Whydah, a formal treaty guaranteeing the neutrality of the port at Whydah was signed in 1703 by the French, Dutch and English agents there, and this was renewed on several subsequent occasions, including 1708 (Davenant 1709, p. 313; Davies 1957, p. 274; Van Dantzig 1980, p. 149). For the text of the treaty, see Labat 1730, II, 107–13.

LETTER 3

Description of Tary, of the kingdom of Ardres in general, and of the coast from La Praye to Little Ardres. How one recognizes it from the sea. How to anchor there. The town (ville) of Jakin and the market-town (bourg) of Offra. Great Ardres, the residence of the king. His palaces. Other towns and market-towns of the kingdom of Ardres. The general climate of the land. Its products. The great lords of Ardres. Their houses in general, and their diet. Their settlements, public markets, and trading places. Royal and other dues. The European goods suitable for this trade. Rules to follow in carrying out this trade. The Europeans established there and their differences. The late King Alkemy and his policy. The reply he gave to a Dutch commercial agent. The present king, and everything concerning his person and character. How to travel in his states. The audiences he gives, and what happens at these events. The Great Marabou at Ardres. The general character of the people of Ardres and their way of making war. The slaves they gain in these wars. Their civil and criminal justice. Their religion and their marabous or priests.

In my last letter I told you, Sir, that Tory was a small state of four leagues' extent, between the sea and the countries of Juda and Ardres. Foulaen is the principal village of this little territory. The only remarkable thing about it is the abundance of maize and provisions which you find there. It stands on a small river which comes from the interior of the country and which discharges itself into the sea at two leagues from La Praye. The inhabitants of this place are for the most part accustomed to commit robberies and thefts on the roads, directed against those of Little Ardres, who are incapable of resisting them.[1]

The states of the king of Ardres begin very close to Foulaen.[2] It is these states that I shall tell you about today. You will remember, I am confident, that you have given me permission to make use of the reports that I have from several foreigners of honest worth who have a complete knowledge of those countries which I have not seen myself.[3] The states of the king of Ardres are not very extensive towards the sea (where he possesses about six leagues of country, from Foulaen to Little Ardres) but they go very far into the interior of the country, widening towards the North, where they border upon the kingdom of Oyeo, and in the East upon the kingdoms of Ulkami and Benin.[4]

The coast stretches some nine leagues to the East between La Praye, where the staff of the Compagnie du Sénégal reside, and Little Ardres, the land being low and wooded in several places. It is everywhere flat and level, except that the coast rises as it approaches Little Ardres, forming three small hillocks close to each other, on a headland which creates a large bay. This is the place where the ships drop anchor in order to trade at Ardres, and it is also this bay which receives the river that comes down from Great Ardres to Offra and from there to the sea. This river separates the countries of Ardra and Benin, and its water is a little salty.[5] [. . .][6] The villages of Offra and Little Ardres are 2½ leagues apart, on the /p. 140/ same river. Located at Offra are the lodges of all the Europeans who trade in these countries, and who live like the natives under the command of a fidalgue. The Dutch and the English have two considerable lodges there; that of France has been abandoned, and transferred to Juda by the Sieur Carolof, as I have shown you in my previous letter.[7] [. . ./pp. 141–142/. . .][8]

[illustration no. (92), Africans saluting each other, inserted after p. 140][9]

The Dutch do more trade at Ardres than any of the other Europeans, followed by the English; and their normal places of trade are at Little Ardres and at Offra. From these they take slaves, cotton cloths, and blue stones (called *accory*, and very highly valued on Gold Coast). The largest trade is in slaves, who are exchanged for cowries, which the Moors like very much, and which form the money of all the countries from Popo to Gabon. It is almost impossible to trade there without them. For a slave at Ardres you usually give half of the value in /p. 143/ cowries, and the other half in trade goods. If cowries are dear in Europe (as happens sometimes) you only give a third or a quarter of the value, and the rest in the following commodities: iron bars (the round ones are worth nothing here), long fine coral, satins from China, gilded leather, white and red damask, cloths (*pagnes*) from Cyprus, red cloths (*draps*) with wide borders, cups of red copper, copper bracelets, glass beads from Venice in several colours, agates, gilded mirrors, serges from Leyden, platilles linen, Moreas, salamporis, chintz on a red base, broad and narrow tapseils, blue cannequins, broad cloth called Guinea cloth, narrow of the same, double cannequins, French brandy in ankers and half-ankers, liqueur wine, black Codebec hats, red and white Italian taffetas, cloths of gold and silver, knives called bossemans [boatswain's], armoisin silks striped with white on a flowered base, brocade sewn with gold or silver, white flowered satin, Indian armoisins, damask napkins, firelocks, muskets, powder, large margriettes, large crystal ear-rings, broad gilded cutlasses, taffeta scarves, large parasols, pieces-of-eight, and copper bells made in the shape of pyramids. All these goods are suitable also for Benin, Rio de Lagos, and throughout the Gulf of Ethiopia as far as River Gabon.[10]

Here, as at Juda, it is necessary to arrange the price for the trade with the king. It is a rule to be followed that, as soon as you arrive on this coast, the agent should go to ask the fidalgue of Little Ardres to take you to an audience with the king.[11] [.../p. 144/...][12] From start to finish, all the duties you pay come to 70, 75, or 80 slaves, whereas at Juda, as I have shown you, you pay only from 32 to 35 slaves. As you see, this is a great saving for the English and French who have lodges there; the English, indeed, have another one at Offra, but the Dutch, as the earlier traders, gain over them in goodwill, moreover there are few years when they do not take from this country nearly 3,000 slaves. The Portuguese also did much trade at the beginning of this century.[13] It is not that these people do not esteem the French a great deal, the late King Alkemy or Tezy having had much respect for the [French] king. [.../p. 145/...][14]

The king who is reigning today is the son of this Alkemy of whom I have just spoken to you. He is very absolute and very respected in his states, his subjects not speaking to him except with their faces to the ground. Only the Great Marabou has the right to speak to him standing up, he being the second person in the kingdom and also the first minister in both spiritual and temporal affairs. There are no kings in these regions who are more respected than those of Benin and Ardres. This prince has sovereign authority in all respects –

taxes, employment, justice, peace, war, everything depends absolutely on him. The natives as well as foreigners owe him tribute, and this tribute is by head and very onerous.[15] [.../pp. 146–148/...][16]

There you see, Sir, how each people has its own peculiar maxims, and how it has pleased the Supreme Wisdom to harden the hearts of several million souls to serve Error and the Devil, who, according to what they say, beats them often. I do not know the truth of this, but it is certain that you often hear people howling and crying in the night. This is the only reason why they worship him, through the fear of his cruelty, painted in the colours of a red dragon (as St Augustine says). This is also done by several peoples of the discovered world, the Chinese, and a world of savages in the Orient and America.[17] [...][18] Allow me take some rest, since I have produced a really long letter. I am, Sir, Your, etc.

NOTES

[1] Barbot never visited 'Ardres' (Allada), but he appears to have gained some information about the locality, and particularly about trade there, when at Whydah. It was not in fact in his 'last letter', but in Letter 3/1 that Barbot had described Tori. This passage repeats information given there, and adds the references to maize, the river, and robberies. The last reference is deduced from Dapper, p. 120/4, on whose map of all Africa (his map of Guinea curiously shows less information on this area) Foulaen had been depicted as just East of a small river running from the interior into the sea (as on other maps of the period, e.g. Sanson 1656). But the information about maize seems original (see Letter 3/2, note 1, above). The depiction of Foulaen as on a river running into the sea was a misunderstanding, since the coastal lagoon at this point has no access to the sea (and appears never to have had). In 1732 Barbot acknowledges the error, placing Foulaen instead on 'the river Torry which runs almost east and west, to Great Popo', i.e. the coastal lagoon (Letter 3/1, note 9, above). For 'Foulaen' see Letter 3/1, note 19, above; and for 'Little Ardres', the principal coastal village of Ardra, see note 5 below.

Cf. 1732, pp. 345/5, 9–11, which substitutes the name 'Fida' for 'La Praye', alters the distance to 'scarce three leagues', and adds that the maize and other provisions were cultivated 'to drive a trade with foreigners'.

[2] This is Dapper, p. 115/6.
Cf. 1732, p. 345/11.

[3] Barbot indicates that he has no first-hand knowledge of Ardra, which indeed proves to be the case. His sources for what follows are not in fact

'several foreigners', but rather one foreigner (Dapper) and one fellow-countryman (D'Elbée). Omitted in *1732*.

[4] Barbot elaborates on the account of the extent of Ardra given earlier, in Letter 3/1, pp. 132–3. The information about Ardra's extent and borders with Oyo and Benin is from Delbée 1671, p. 557, but the information that it also borders with Ulkami in the East is added from Dapper, p. 121/5. (For Oyo and Ulkami, probably alternative names for the same place, see Letter 3/1, note 19, above.) Also from Dapper is the distance between Foulaen and Little Ardra (five miles in Dapper, p. 115/6). Barbot amends these earlier accounts by reducing the coastal extent to a mere six leagues, ending in the East at Little Ardra: Dapper had given its extent as 12 miles, ending at Acqua (perhaps Apa) seven miles East of Little Ardra, while D'Elbée had claimed an extent of 40 leagues (Dapper, p. 115/4; Delbée 1671, p. 557). For Barbot's belief that the kingdom did not extend East of Little Ardra, see the following note.

Cf. *1732*, p. 346/12, which adds the phrase, 'some making it to border on the west upon Rio da Volta, and at east on Benin, enclosing Fida and Torry on the north side, and will have it extend at north and north-west to Oyeo, a large and populous country, and to other potent kingdoms situated towards the Niger'. This addition seems to derive from the 1700/1707 map of Delisle (see above, Letter 3/1, notes 2 and 19), which had shown Ardra extending West to the upper River Volta, North of Whydah, and bordering in the NW with 'Gago', which Barbot may have misidentified with Oyo.

[5] The first section ('The coast . . . to trade at Ardres') combines material from Dapper, p. 115/6 and Delbée 1671, pp. 384–5, Barbot contributing only the distance from La Praye to Little Ardres. The later description of the river likewise appears to combine information, this time from Dapper's text (which described Little Ardra as on a salty river) and from his map (which shows a river running from the interior to the West of the Ardra capital, down to the sea West of Jakin), with Barbot only adding that Offra is on this river, and that it forms the boundary between Ardra and Benin. 'Little Ardra' is the coastal village where the European traders landed (D'Elbée's 'La Praye', 'Great Ardra' being the inland capital), probably corresponding to Adunko (Godomey-Plage), about 23 km East of Whydah (Person 1975, p. 721, n. 1). The account of a river running from the Ardra capital to the sea is problematical: a 'Rio de Ardra' had been mentioned by a 1602 source (Marees, f. 113v) and a river running to the sea was shown on later maps (e.g. Sanson 1656), but in recent times there has been no outlet from the coastal lagoon in this area. If the river was not a mistaken reference to the lagoon, it is possible that in earlier times an outlet existed (perhaps West of Cotonou, East of Adunko) which has since silted up (see Law 1987, pp. 352–3). Barbot's statement that this river formed the boundary between Ardra and Benin is difficult to interpret. Benin rule at this period certainly

extended West along the coastal lagoon as far as Lagos, as Barbot himself later reports (Letter 3/4, p. 148), and traditional evidence suggests that it extended even further West, since certain towns (Ado, Ipokia, and Idole) on the North bank of the lagoon in the area of Badagry are said to have been founded from Benin (Law 1983, pp. 331–2). It is therefore entirely likely that Allada territory marched in the East with that of Benin, as Barbot (and before him D'Elbée) stated. However, this boundary must have been well to the East of Little Ardra. Dapper had stated that Allada territory extended some seven Dutch miles (45 km) East of Little Ardra to 'Acqua' (Dapper, p. 115/5), probably Apa, on the southern bank of the lagoon near Badagry; and this is corroborated by a report of 1715 which describes Apa as a province of Ardra (Law 1983, p. 332, n. 58). If Barbot was told in 1682 that Ardra was separated in the East from Benin by the river which ran by Little Ardra and Offra, his informants probably meant to refer to the coastal lagoon, which would indeed have separated the Ardra dependency of Apa to the South of the lagoon from the Benin colonies of Ado, Ipokia and Idole to the North. Cf. *1732*, p. 345/6.

[6] Omission of three paragraphs, describing the roadstead at Little Ardra and the town of Jakin (Godomey), from Dapper, p. 115/6–7, and Delbée 1671, pp. 385–6 – Barbot contributing only the obvious identification of Dapper's Little Ardra with D'Elbée's La Praye. Cf. *1732*, pp. 345/7–8, 346/1–4, 6, much rearranged.

[7] This description of Offra is basically from Delbée 1671, p. 388, except that Barbot alters the distance from the coast to Offra from 2 to 2½ leagues, and adds the reference to the river (see note 5 above) and the information about the French lodge (given at greater length in Letter 3/2, pp. 133–4, above). Bosman was to conflate Little Ardra and Offra (Bosman, p. 398), but Barbot was certainly correct in distinguishing them, Little Ardra having been described as on the sea-shore (Dapper, p. 115/6) whereas Offra was located two leagues inland (Delbée 1671, p. 388). 'Offra' (a version of the ethnonym 'Pla', Letter 3/2, note 19), said to have been just East of Jakin, was destroyed in 1692 (Law 1987, pp. 353–5). When Barbot wrote in the mid 1680s, his information about the European lodges at Offra was already out of date, since the English had followed the French in transferring their establishment to Whydah c. 1683 (Davies 1957, pp. 229, 250). The Dutch lodge, as noted earlier (Letter 3/2, note 36, above), was also abandoned after the destruction of Offra, so that Barbot's repetition of this information in *1732* was even more out of date. After the destruction of Offra its commercial role in the area passed to neighbouring Jakin, and when the Europeans again established lodges in Ardra territory in the 1710s these were at Jakin rather than at Offra (Berbain 1942, p. 52; Akinjogbin 1967, p. 53). Cf. *1732*, p. 346/5, which omits the reference to the French lodge.

[8] Omission of 20 paragraphs, describing Great Ardra, the towns of Jojo

and Ba, the climate, agriculture, marriage and burial customs, and markets, derived entirely from Dapper, pp. 115–21, and from Delbée 1671. Cf. *1732*, pp. 346/7–348/9.

[9] Barbot's drawing of Africans greeting each other with elaborate salutations is based on an illustration in Dapper, p. 117, which by its placing presumably relates to Ardra. But Barbot re-locates the main figures, and adds, in the lower right-hand corner, a waterway and the prow of a small European vessel apparently moored to the bank, with a seated man smoking a pipe and a little canon pointing ostentatiously inland. This is the only one of the several illustrations borrowed by Barbot from Dapper in which he makes substantial changes, but his point in making the revision is unclear.

[10] This passage is modified and elaborated from Dapper, p. 118/3–4. Dapper having mentioned only the Dutch and Little Ardra, Barbot adds the references to the English and to Offra – perhaps from Delbée 1671, pp. 388–9, rather than from original information. In the section on cowries, Dapper had said that normally a third of the price was paid in cowries but that when these were dear other goods were given instead; whereas Barbot says that normally half was given in cowries, but that when these were dear this might be reduced to a third or a quarter. Barbot's list of trade-goods is partly from Dapper (almost all of Dapper's list, with a few modifications or slips), and partly from Delbée 1671, pp. 448–9 – with omissions (e.g. gold dust). But it also adds the following original items: glass beads from Venice, agates, serges from Leyden, platilles, moreas, salamporis, tapseils, Guinea cloths, liqueur wine, muskets and powder. Barbot takes from D'Elbée, and misapplies, the comment 'the round ones are worth nothing', which in D'Elbée is a gloss on 'long coral'. It is possible that Barbot's list, despite its borrowings, nevertheless reflects his own experience in 1682, but at Whydah rather than at Ardra. In his account of Whydah Barbot does not supply any list of goods imported but remarks that he will not deal with certain matters relating to Whydah which are duplicated in the case of Ardra (Letter 3/2, p. 138); while in *1732*, p. 340/3, he more specifically refers readers wishing to know about goods traded at Whydah to his account of Ardra. According to a 1694 account, the goods most in demand at Whydah were cowries, brass basins (which the local people cut up for bracelets), blue paper sletias, cambricks or lawns, caddy chints, broad chints, coral, rangoes, iron bars, powder and brandy (while sayes, perpetuanoes, knives, old sheets, pewter basins, muskets etc. were 'in low esteem' – meaning that they fetched low prices), and that 'if a cappashier [chief] sells five slaves, he will have two of them paid for in cowries, and one in brass' (Phillips 1732, p. 227).
Cf. *1732*, pp. 348/10–349/1, which erroneously expands the obscure remark 'the round ones are worth nothing' into 'the round or square bars will not do', explains that brandy is sold in 'sixteen gallon rundlets' as well as in ankers (i.e. 10 gallon measures), and alters some of the items, substituting

'canary and malmsey' for 'liqueur wines', 'beads from Rouen' for 'mar-griettes', coral for crystal ear-rings, and silk for taffeta scarves.

[11] Neither Dapper nor D'Elbée states explicitly that prices were fixed with the king at Ardra, although the latter implies something of the sort, noting that after the king and leading chiefs had bought what they wished, trade was open to everyone, 'but all at the same price, the rate of everything being fixed, and all the goods valued at a certain price' (Delbée 1671, p. 439). Barbot is here again probably drawing upon his own experience at Whydah (see above, Letter 3/2, p. 135). However, the detail about the agent asking the fidalgo for an audience with the king is probably generalized from the experience of Carolof in 1670, as reported by D'Elbée, rather than based on any new information (Delbée 1671, p. 388).

Cf. *1732*, p. 349/2.

[12] Omission of the remainder of the paragraph and the following 11 paragraphs, giving details of various duties and payments for services at Ardra, derived entirely from Dapper, pp. 119–20, (derived in turn from Leers 1665, pp. 308–12) and from Delbée 1671, pp. 439–40.

Cf. *1732*, pp. 349/2–350/3.

[13] It was earlier stated that Carolof in 1670 was paying 100 slaves in duties for each ship at Ardres, but that the French in Whydah paid only 25 slaves per ship, plus 5–6 slaves for porters and another 5–6 slaves for canoes (Letter 3/2, pp. 134–5). As noted (note 7 above), the English lodge at Offra, although it still existed when Barbot was at Whydah in 1682, had in fact been abandoned by 1688 when he finished writing his account. The estimate of 3,000 slaves exported per year referred to 1670, being from Delbée 1671, p. 436; exports in the 1680s were probably higher, Dutch slave exports from Ardra being estimated by a contemporary at 4–5,000 annually, and English and French exports from Whydah at around 15,000 (Roussier 1935, p. 15). The Portuguese had traded at Ardra in the early seventeenth century, although not to any great extent, by the 1620s only one or two ships calling each year (Marees, f. 113v; Cordeiro 1881, I, 27). Yet it is odd that Barbot speaks of Portuguese trade there merely as a phenomenon of the past, since by c. 1680 the Portuguese were certainly again attempting to trade on Slave Coast (see Letter 3/2, note 3).

Cf. *1732*, p. 350/4–6.

[14] Omission of the remainder of the paragraph, dealing with the relations of the French with King Alkemy of Ardra in 1670, entirely from D'Elbée.

[15] Barbot's knowledge that the king reigning in 1670 had died derived presumably from oral information gathered either on his voyage in 1682 or subsequently. But the references to the king's subjects' respect and the Grand Marabou are from Delbée 1671, pp. 427, 434. The last two sentences, however, appear to be original.

Cf. *1732*, p. 350/7–11, which adds that 'captains' with titles are also known at Cape Verde.

[16] Omission of the remainder of the paragraph and the following 16 paragraphs, describing the officials of the Ardra court, audiences with the king and other officials, the army, the education of royal children, the origins of slaves, criminal justice, religion and burial customs, all deriving from Dapper, pp. 119–21, and D'Elbée.

Cf. *1732*, pp. 350/11–353/7, which incorporates a brief section (pp. 351/8–352/1) describing invasions of Ardra by an interior kingdom, taken from Bosman, pp. 396–8, Barbot merely adding the suggestion that the invaders were 'the Oyeos and Ulkami' (for whom, see Letter 3/1, note 1, above).

[17] Barbot contributes this passage on devil-worship to the earlier accounts of Ardra religion. The idea of the Devil beating people at Ardra seems to be original to Barbot, but he had earlier recorded the same notion in relation to Senegal and Gold Coast (Letters 1/10, p. 54 and note 11; 2/26, p. 100 and note 5): D'Elbée heard howling and crying at night at Ardra, as did Phillips at Whydah later, but both understood this to be the sound of a religious rite (Delbée 1671, p. 446; Phillips 1732, p. 223).

Cf. *1732*, p. 353/4, which omits the references to the Supreme Wisdom and St Augustine and adds that the people of Ardres believe that the Devil beats them 'as the Gold-Coast people do'.

[18] Omission of one paragraph on the king's knowledge of Christianity and the Portuguese language, taken from Delbée 1671, p. 443.

Cf. *1732*, pp. 353/8–354/1, which adds the following observation. 'To conclude with what concerns religion, it is as morally impossible to convince the people of Ardra of their erroneous, gross paganism by human ministry, as it is to convert all other Blacks, for reasons already given; unless providence would effect a prodigious change in their nature, by its infinite irresistible grace'.

LETTER 4

Description of the coast from Rio de Lagos to Benin. Lake Curamo, Ichoo Island, and Curamo village. The kingdom of Ulkany or Alkomy. Limits of the kingdom of Benin. Descriptions of the River of Argon, Gotton village and the town of Benin. The king's palace. Products of the kingdom in general. Rivers, etc, and natives of Benin, etc. Women and girls. Laws of these blacks. Their funerals and forms of inheritance. Maxims to observe when trading with them. The goods the Europeans export from Benin. The European goods suitable for trading there. Benin cloths. Public markets called Dia de Fero.

Since, Sir, you tell me by your letter that you want an entire and complete account of the whole of Guinea, and that it does not matter to you whether I work from good reports or from accounts already written, I have translated from the Dutch [*margin:* Mr. Dapper] the description of the kingdom of Benin, the kingdom which comes next after the kingdom of Ardres. Since this [Dutch] nation has more intercourse with Benin than any other nation in Europe, I have reached the conclusion that I will be able to present this description to you as representing what is nowadays best established and known about these lands. Apart from some elaboration in the description of the coasts and some improvement of the maps, there will be nothing in it from me.[1]

From the River of Ardres to the mouth of the River of Lagos, so called in Portuguese because it issues into a lake, is reckoned ten leagues. Hence, counting from the River of Ardres to the place where Rio de Lagos actually issues into the sea must be 20 leagues, shore to shore. Rio de Lagos has a bar at its mouth, almost closing it except in the eastern corner, where the river has its channel. This channel only admits boats with great difficulty, because of its rolling waters and the breaking of the sea. The river is joined near a village on the eastern bank by a small stream coming from the West. The river makes its way inland first to the North, then to the NNW as far as a bend, after which it goes to the East as far as the village of Curamo, located on the North bank. From there it again makes its way North, leaving to the East a great lake, into which it discharges itself, and which /p. 149/ the Portuguese call by its [*sic*] name, Lago de Curamo. The lake is bordered towards the sea by the large island termed on the maps Ichoo, and this is one of the dependencies of the kingdom of Benin.[2] At Curamo they make many cotton cloths, and these are highly valued on Gold Coast. The Dutch, who transport many of them there, profit considerably, because they alone do the trade in them, using brigantines and bar-canoes, which can travel back and forwards rapidly.[3] [. . .][4]

The River of Argon (or Benin) cuts through a great part of these countries in its passage. It joins the sea by a very wide mouth, having nine or ten feet of water in the middle of the channel, which makes it suitable for small vessels. Its main stream receives several small rivers, especially one which comes from the Lake of Curamo. This means that, by this channel, from Rio Lagos to the River of Argon is only a journey of 25 leagues, whereas along the coast it is 50. This little river is also called Argon.[5] [. . ./pp. 150–155/. . .][6]

665

Additional Passage from *1732*

[p. 354/2, on the approaches to the Benin river]

We commonly reckon about fifty-five leagues in a direct course east and by north, from the road of Little Ardra, to Rio Fermoso, which is Benin river, call'd also Argon river; being the usual course the Hollanders take to enter that river, to carry on their trade in the kingdom of Benin. But the English and Portugueses enter it another way; that is, at the channel of Lagoas, which begins at Cape Lagoas, distant about eight or ten leagues east from Little Ardra, from which cape, the coast runs in a semicircle to Rio Fermoso aforesaid, on the north side; and the lands Ichoo, or Curamo islands, lie opposite on the south of it, all along at some distance, forming thus all together the Lagoas channel that leads to Benin river, which channel at some places, and for several leagues together is no broader than a large river, especially from the cape Lagoas aforesaid and the south-west point of the largest of the Curamo islands to the river Lagoas, which runs from the opposite north country into the Lagoas channel: the shore on either sides from the cape and the Curamo islands, being low and shallow water, with sands along, as it is also on either side of the said channel from Rio Lagoas, to Rio Fermoso in Benin; only the channel there in some parts is very wide, according as the north or main shore is distant from the south side shore, made up of the low flat islands of Curamo. But the right course in that channel to Benin river, is on fifteen and fourteen foot of water all along from west to east; as is likewise the other channel east of the Curamo islands, which, as I have hinted, is the proper channel used by the Dutch; and both large and deep enough for brigantine sloops and other small craft commonly made use of by the aforemention'd European nations driving some trade at Benin; among whom the Hollanders have the greatest share.[7]

NOTES

[1] Omitted in *1732*. Barbot's avowal of unoriginality in his description of Benin is repeated at the beginning of Letter 3/5 below: 'Since I am doing no more than following my Dutch author, I am much readier to give you my letter than when I have to draw on my own resources'. Letters 3/4–5 on Benin are indeed basically a translation of Dapper, pp. 121/3–131/4, the only

additional material occurring in the early paragraphs of Letter 4 describing the coastal area.

[2] The lagoons around modern Lagos are described somewhat confusingly. Barbot correctly points out that 'Lagos' is from Portuguese *lago* 'lake or lagoon'. The longer of the alternative distances between Rivers Ardra and Lagos (20 leagues) corresponds approximately with the distance given by Dapper, p. 121/3 – 16 miles. The basis for Barbot's alternative computation is obscure, but comparison with the subsequent paragraph (p. 149) on the distance between Rivers Lagos and Benin suggests that the shorter distance is intended to be that by the inland lagoons. Dapper had referred to the existence of an inland waterway and canoe-borne communication connecting Ardra and River Lagos (Dapper, pp. 115/8, 116/4; repeated in Letter 3/3, pp. 140 (omitted above), 142); and Barbot in 1682 may have been given this estimate of the distance by this route. The account of the Lagos channel and the course of the river as far as Curamo which follows is from Dapper, p. 121/3, except that Dapper had placed Curamo on the South bank. Barbot's own map of this coast also places Curamo on the South bank, which suggests that 'North' here may be simply a slip. However, the map in Robijn/ Roggeveen 1685 shows both Curamo on the South bank and 'Caran', which seems to be a variant of 'Curamo', on the North, and it is possible that Barbot had seen this or a similar map and was left uncertain where Curamo belonged. (The reference in *1732*, p. 354/2–4, seems to reflect continuing uncertainty, the village of Curamo being placed on the North side but the name 'Curamo' being also applied to the land to the South.) Curamo/Caran appears to represent 'Korame' or 'Ikurame', a name which is attested in recent times as having been applied by Benin sources to Lagos Island (Law 1983, p. 330, n. 46): in fact, Lagos lies to the South of the main channel, but since there is also a small channel running between Lagos and the coast the confusion is understandable. The account of the course of the river beyond Curamo, including the Lake of Curamo (i.e. Lagos lagoon) and the island of Ichoo, reproduces information from the maps in Dapper (occurring also in earlier maps, e.g. Sanson 1656), although not incorporated into Dapper's text. Barbot adds only the statement that Ichoo was a dependency of Benin. 'Ichoo' represents Eko, the usual indigenous name of Lagos. The land to the South of the lagoon does not in fact form a single island, but rather a series of islands divided by creeks, Lagos/Eko being the most westerly of these islands (Barbot corrects this in *1732*, referring to 'the lands Ichoo, or Curamo islands'). Barbot's knowledge that Eko was subject to Benin appears to be original. Although Robijn/Roggeveen 1685, p. 27, had reported that 'Caran', i.e. Lagos, was subject to Benin, Barbot clearly did not realize that this report related to Lagos. It is conceivable that Barbot merely inferred Benin rule over Lagos from earlier accounts of the extent of Benin and Ardra rule: D'Elbée had stated that Ardra marched in the east with

667

Benin, and Dapper had placed the eastern boundary of Ardra about eight miles west of the Lagos River (Delbée 1671, p. 557; Dapper, pp. 115/5, 121/ 3). But since Barbot offers new information about the boundary between Ardra and Benin (see Letter 3/3, note 5, above) it is likely that his knowledge of the subjection of Lagos to Benin is original also, and probably derives from his enquiries at Whydah in 1682. Lagos was already subject to Benin by 1603 (Jones 1983a, pp. 24, 40).

Cf. *1732*, p. 354/2–4, which substitutes a much more detailed description of the area, based on the map of the Bight of Benin in Robijn/ Roggeveen 1685 (a source it is curious he did not follow more closely in *1688*).

[3] Based on Dapper, p. 121/4, except that Dapper had stated merely that cloths were available at Curamo, Barbot adding the reference to brigantines and bar-canoes. It is likely that the cloth sold at Curamo was in fact manufactured elsewhere, probably in Ijebu to the North of the lagoon (Law 1983, p. 334). The reference to 'brigantines and bar-canoes' is probably not based on new information: if not merely an intelligent guess, it may be derived from Dapper's account of Dutch trade up River Benin (Dapper, p. 123/3, 'Jachten en Sloepen').

Cf. *1732*, p. 354/3, where the material is incorporated into the longer account of the lagoon area derived mainly from Robijn/Roggeveen 1685. But Barbot adds the following: 'The Portuguese geographers place Ciudade de Jubu, or city of Jubu, several leagues inland of this river'. The reference is clearly taken from the Mortier map (1700), which had placed the city of 'Jubu' on the inland continuation of 'River Lagos' North of the lagoon. Mortier's information on 'Jubu' derived, via Portuguese maps and Figueiredo 1614, ultimately from Pacheco Pereira, writing c. 1508 (Pacheco Pereira 1956, p. 131, 'Geebu'). 'Jubu' is Ijebu, the kingdom on the northern bank of the lagoon; its capital, Ijebu Ode, is some 30 km North of the lagoon, and approachable by canoe by River Ona which runs into the lagoon. Barbot also refers, again following Robijn/Roggeveen 1685, to a town called 'Jabum' situated on the north bank of the lagoon. 'Jabum' is also Ijebu, although Barbot evidently failed to recognise the name as a variant of the one given earlier. Robijn/Roggeveen's knowledge of Ijebu, like Mortier's, seems to have come, via Figueiredo, ultimately from Pacheco Pereira: the different locations of the town deriving merely from alternative interpretations of the description of it as on 'River Lagos'. To compound confusion further, Barbot also refers to Ijebu under yet a third name, again without realizing the identity: 'Jaboe', described as a kingdom neighbouring Benin (Letters 3/4, p. 149 above; 3/5, pp. 155, 162 below; cf. *1732*, pp. 356/6, 369/ 2, 376/1). On Ijebu see also Law 1986, p. 254.

Cf. *1732*, p. 354/3.

[4] Omission of three paragraphs on the kingdom of Ulkamy (see Letter 3/1

above, note 18) and the extent of the kingdom of Benin, taken from Dapper, pp. 121/8–122/2.

Cf. *1732*, p. 356/2–3, 6–7.

[5] Based on Dapper, p. 123/3, where the river is called 'Arbo', but Barbot alters the coastal distance from 18 miles to 50, and adds the information about the inland communication and distance and also the information that the small river is also called Argon. This seems to reflect some knowledge of the use of the inland lagoon waterway between Lagos and Benin, perhaps obtained orally in 1682, or possibly merely inferred from maps which showed the route.

Cf. *1732*, pp. 354/4–355/1, which substitutes a more detailed account of the entrance to River Benin combining material from Robijn/Roggeveen 1685 and Bosman, p. 426: it also gives a longer distance, of about 40 leagues, from Curamo on River Lagos to River Benin by the inland route.

[6] Omission of the rest of Letter 3/4 (and of all Letter 3/5). The remainder of Barbot's account of Benin (pp. 149–62) is simply translated from Dapper, pp. 122/1–132/4, with some rearrangement of the material. Repeated in *1732*, pp. 355/2–376/4, which adds a great deal of material from Bosman, pp. 426–68, and digressions which include several Biblical and American references (e.g., pp. 364/2, 5, 8, 11, 371/2), a reference to the 'prime court ministers in England' (p. 368/6), and an attempt to relate Benin to classical Ptolemaic geography (p. 356/6).

[7] The direct distance from Ardra to River Benin may be influenced by Bosman, p. 426 (50 miles), while the detailed geographical information on the Lagos channel comes from Robijn/Roggeveen 1685 (as does most of *1732*, p. 354/3–4). But the information that English and Portuguese traders were approaching Benin through the Lagos channel is original. It is, however, most likely incorrect. No other source suggests any such trade at this period: the Dutch in 1716 are recorded to have prospected the use of the Lagos channel to approach Benin, but concluded that the bar at the mouth of the channel made it impracticable (Ryder 1969, pp. 157–8). It is more probable that European traders in Ardra had dealings with African traders who had come through the lagoons from Benin, as a French report of 1715 suggested (Law 1983, p. 338).

LETTER 5

The king of Benin, his power, wars and fetishes. The election of new kings. Their deaths and burials. Their religion and priests.

[.../pp. 156–162/...][1] They offer the Devil [...] even their own children, as do those in Lybia and most of the savages of America. I am reminded of the lines below written by a learned man [*margin: Mr Drelincourt*] after long reflection on the new aspects of the Two Worlds (the Indies and America) and after observing so many of the peoples in those parts given up to this dreadful ritual.

> The new Discoveries grieve my heart,
> in a New World I see only the Old –
> the ancient race of Adam, slave to false gods,
> rebellious against its Creator, object of His wrath.[2]

I trust you will forgive all the moral comment I am led to make from time to time, for truly there is much here to make us think. [. . .]

NOTES

[1] Omission of the whole Letter, apart from the final personal material, the contents being entirely derived from Dapper – see note 6 of the previous Letter. The introductory paragraph includes the following remark. 'It is also true that I have a great desire to finish this business very soon, whatever pleasure I have in contributing to your satisfaction, [since] I feel little by little my blood warming up; but to return to the matter in hand . . .'. Does Barbot's over-heating refer merely to his enthusiasm to finish the account? Or was it written in the light of his personal circumstances, perhaps in 1684–5 as he was facing persecution in France and making up his mind to escape?

[2] From Laurent Drelincourt, *Sonnets chrétiens sur divers sujets*, Niort, 1677, 'Sur la découverte du nouveau monde'. Drelincourt (1626–1680) was the father of Charlotte Suzanne, whom Barbot, when he inserted these lines in his account, was probably courting (they were married in 1690).

LETTER 6

Description of the kingdom of Ouwerre or Forcado; and of the sea-coasts between Cape Formosa, where the Ethiopic Gulf begins, and Rio Réal or Calbary. The trade there. The natives.

[. . ./pp. 163–164/. . .][1] There is nothing of importance as regards trade on the whole of this coast [from River Forcados to Cape Formoso], although there are some quite large rivers, like those of Lamos and Dodo. Although one does not have much experience of this coast, one assumes nevertheless that there is no great fortune to expect there by way of trade, which is all done at Rio Forcado. The Portuguese and Dutch have wandered up and down this coast without saying anything about it, which makes it quite clear that they have received no encouragement; for if there was anything profitable there these two nations, and especially the latter, would frequent it much more, which they do not do today.[2] [.../p. 165/...]

NOTES

[1] Barbot never having visited the district, this Letter is based on Dapper, pp. 132/8–134/14, and most of it is therefore omitted. It concludes with a promise to produce the next Letter 'tomorrow'.

Cf. *1732*, pp. 376/5–379/9, which inserts a passage on Capuchin missionaries, stated to be from Merolla (presumably seen in Churchill 1704, I, 744), a reference to an alleged classical identification ('Derbici Aethiopes'), and a statement with respect to Ouwerre cloths – 'I have still half a dozen by me' (these being probably the remainder of the fourteen 'cloths from Rio Forcado' bought by Barbot in 1679 at Príncipe, *1679*, p. 353). It also adds navigational material – see note 2.

[2] The names of the rivers are not in Dapper and are from maps (e.g., 'Rio das Ramas ofte Lamas' in Robijn/Roggeveen 1685). Barbot marks these names on his map of the Gulf of Guinea.

Cf. *1732*, pp. 378/4–5, 379/3, 7–8, which adds the following of the Portuguese and Dutch: 'all they get, is some few slaves in Sangama river, and cape Fermosa, and so along the same river[s], which are to be seen from the sea, betwixt that cape and New Calabar or Rio Real: but it is not worth while for a ship of any considerable burden to stop for them, as I shall further show hereafter'. Sangama is modern Sengana Creek, North of Cape Formoso; but Barbot's map of the New Calabar district wrongly gives 'Sangama' as an alternative name for River Sombreiro (*1732*, Plate 27, p. 463). Of Cape Formoso he adds that it 'may be seen from the westward, being upon twenty-three or twenty-four fathom water; but it is not easily discerned farther off at sea, the coast running from south-east to the north-west. The charts make it angular'. (The last point certainly applies to the map in Robijn/Roggeveen 1685.) The reference to difficulty in sighting most probably came from James Barbot, whose ship sailed by Cape Formoso in 1699 (*1732*, p. 457/14 – see Letter 3/7, notes 42 and 43, below). Barbot also adds: 'At all the above mentioned rivers small ships may anchor, and try their fortune, for getting some slaves, and elephants' teeth; but the most probable is the Sombreiro'. This probably also came from James Barbot and represented information he acquired from the traders and pilots he met at

New Calabar (*1732*, p. 463/4). Finally, Barbot adds some slight navigational information on a few of the rivers – this may have been read off the map in Robijn/Roggeveen 1685, or come from an untraced nautical guide, or also have been collected by James Barbot.

LETTER 7

Description of the countries and territories of Calbary [New and Old Calabar], *Cricke, Moncko, and Bany; of everything between them and Rio del Rey; and of the trade.* [followed by '*An Abstract of a Voyage to New Calabar River*' in 1699–1700 by James Barbot]

[.../pp. 166–167/...][1] From Rio Loitomba to the river of Oudt Calbary (otherwise Calborgh) the coast runs East-by-SE for 18 leagues, the land level and wooded. My author says that there is no river between the two, yet, Sir, I have six different maps which all mark another river they call Rio Conde or Rio de Conde. You will please bear in mind what I have stated, for I cannot assure you of the truth of these maps. What matters is that even if this Rio de Conde is in the position where the maps place it, at least there is no trade to be done there, for I note no Portuguese or Dutchman who mentions it.[2]

The English do their principal trade more in Calbory or Oudt Calbary than elsewhere, and they do more there than do any other Europeans. They take 500–600 slaves from there annually, but do so very slowly, for the vessels sometimes stay 8–10 months in the river, lashed to trees. Furthermore, you cannot imagine the inconveniences they suffer from the malignity of the air, something the Dutch have not been able to endure (for they hardly ever go there to trade), not to speak of the long time it takes to reach Cape de Lopo [from Old Calabar], the currents always rapidly bearing towards Camarones, which troubles not only the crews of the ships but also the captives being transported. I met (on my first Guinea voyage), when below the line, an English flyboat which was making for Prince's Island. It had traded 300 blacks [*nègres*] in Calborgh in a 10 months' stay; already it had thrown more than 100 who had died into the sea, and its crew was so weak that it had no more than five men to run the ship. It seemed that this vessel would not deliver in America 100 live slaves. It was bound for Nevis.[3]

The monkeys of Calborgh are very beautiful and highly valued.[4] I am, Sir, etc.

Additional Passages from *1732*

[pp. 379/10–380/3, on sailing directions for New Calabar, the supply of provisions, and the seasonal weather]

From this last river [Rio Sombreiro] to Foko point, being the west head of the Rio Real, or Calabar river, and by others Calbarine river, is but [blank] leagues eastward; and from Foko point to Bandy point east, four leagues, which is the breadth of the entrance or mouth of Rio Real, or New Calabar river, which is navigable, without much trouble, for ships of three hundred tuns, or more, if they be large flyboats; as I shall farther demonstrate in the supplement to this volume, and give [a] true chart thereof, setting down the anchorage and passages as exactly as possible.[5] / The road before this river, which is the eighth river from cape Fermosa, is a hard sandy ground, with five, six, seven and eight fathom water, without the breakers, which lie athwart the mouth of that river, before the two small islands; and the true channel is at Bandy point, north and south at four and three fathom and a half deep, at slack-water; and being come within the breakers, you must steer to the westward almost to Foko point, and afterwards to the north, to the road of Foko town, between the main and [the] little island before it, about two English miles distance.[6] / This island is pretty high, and serves as a mark from the sea, to know the river. Very few ships go as high up as New Calabar town: for it is much better to ride at Foko, which is not so much molested with the mosquettoes as New Calabar town.[7] / A small ship may very well venture upon the channel at Foko point, with the tide, and sail so near the shore as to speak with the Blacks on the land. But, as has been observ'd, Bandy point is the deepest channel at slack water.

The town of Foko is some leagues up the river, on the west side of it, and that of Bandy on the east side, opposite to Foko; and there being several other villages and hamlets dispers'd along the river on the east or west, all inhabited by a very good civiliz'd sort of Blacks, any man may safely venture to trade, either for slaves, elephants teeth, or provisions.[8] / Those of Foko will supply us with fresh water and wood. The water is there taken out of a pond near the town, which keeps well at sea; whereas that which can be had at New Calabar is nothing near so good.

They will also supply us with yams and bananaes [*sic*], at

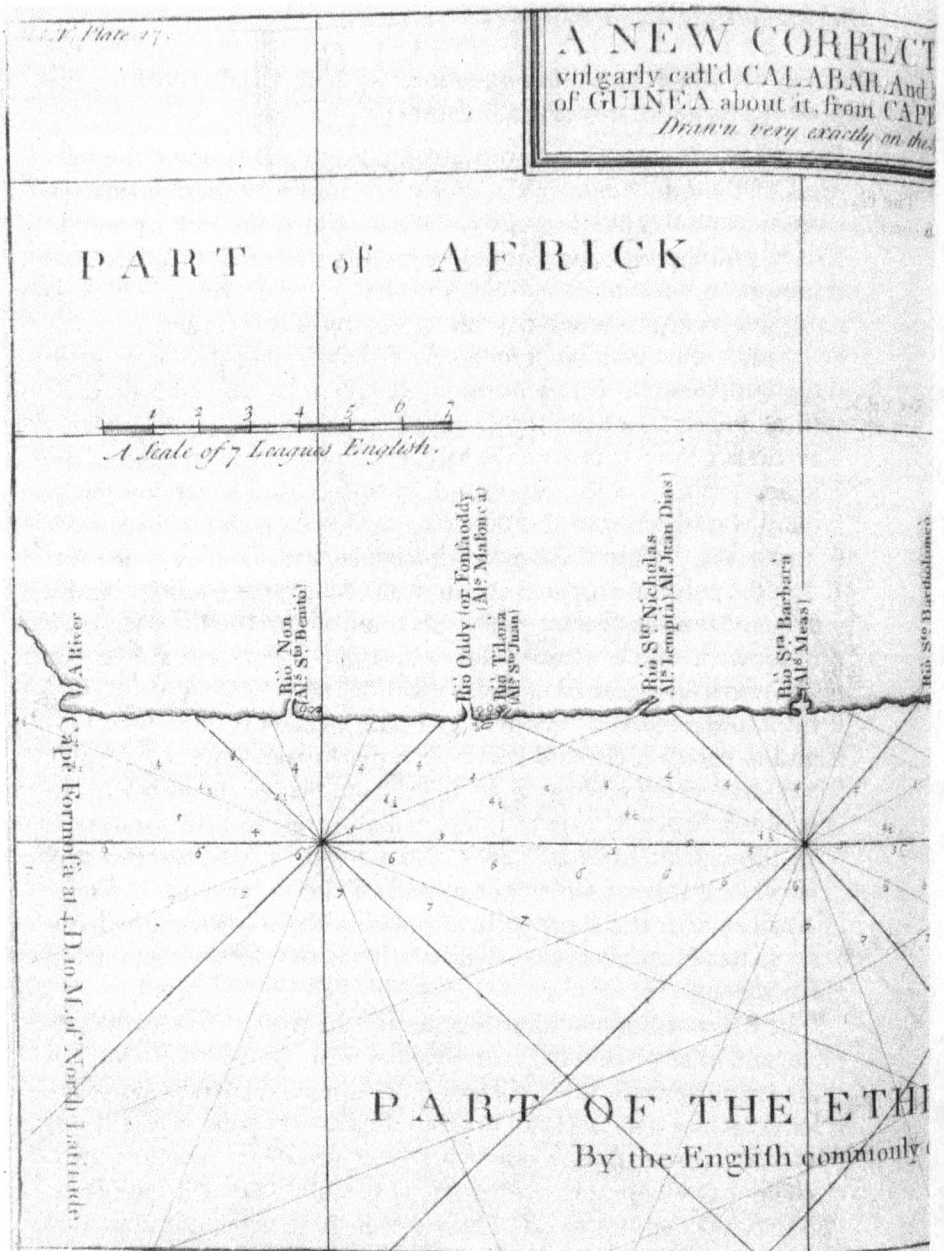

53. Map of the New Calabar district, as surveyed 1699

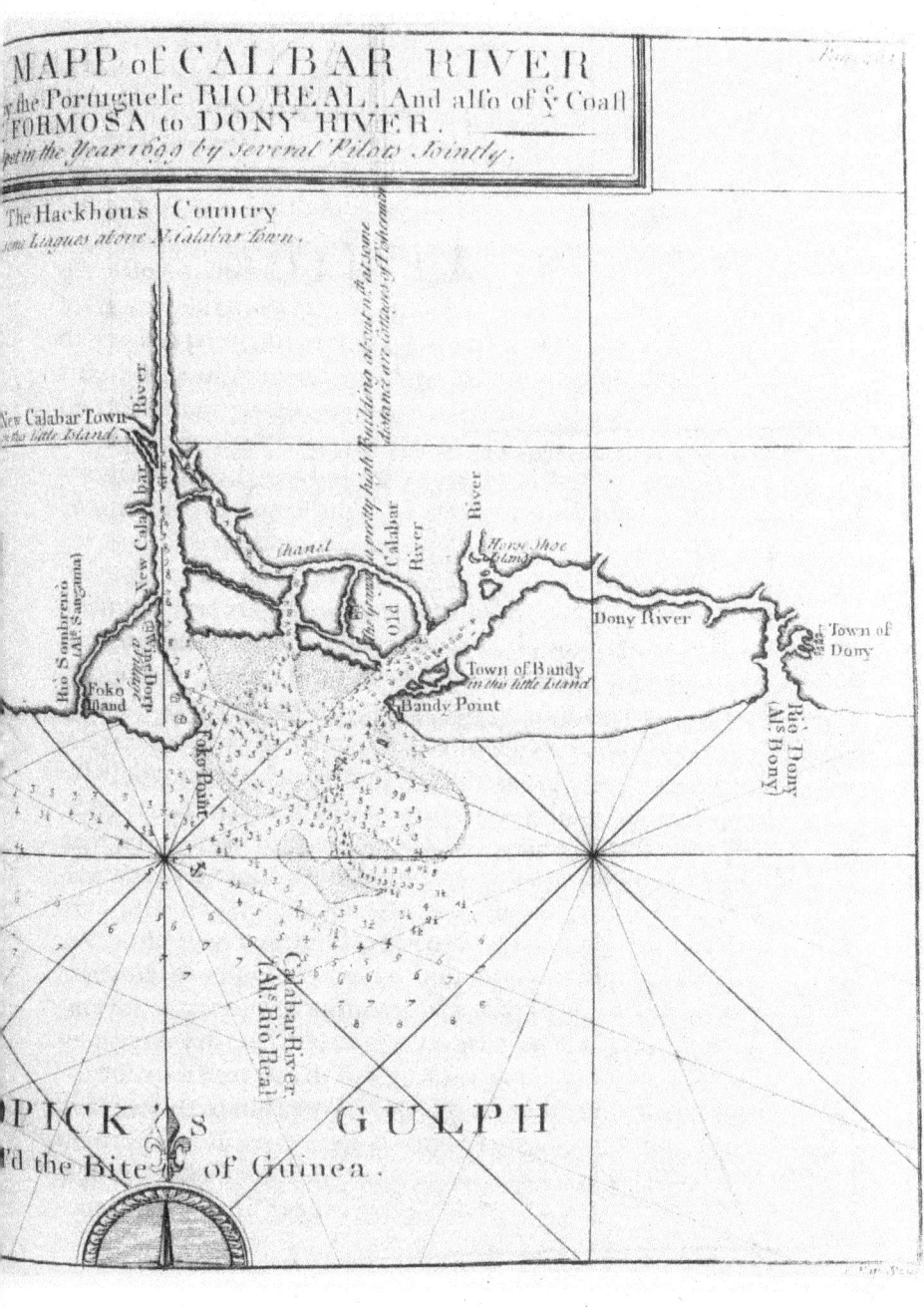

reasonable rates, at the proper time of the year; but in August and September, and so on to March, those eatables grow very scarce, and dear among them: insomuch that some ships have been forced to fall down to Amboses, and Camarones river, in May and June, to buy plantains, which is a sort of banana dried, yet somewhat green, and is a food well lik'd by the natives; thus spending a month or five weeks in that voyage, and afterwards turning up again to the westward, to New Calabar, to purchase their cargo of slaves. To avoid this long delay at that time of the year, it is much better for a ship bound to this place from Europe, to stop in his way at cape Tres Pontas, at the Gold Coast; or at Anamabou on the same coast, to buy Indian wheat or corn there; the Calabar slaves being generally better pleas'd with food of their own country, than with any of Europe, except horse-beans, which many like pretty well, boil'd with pork or oil, but especially those we purchase at the Gold-Coast, as shall be hereafter observed.[9]

The yams, which are the chief of their subsistence, are not fit to be taken out of the ground, before the months of July and August; and therefore most European travellers account those two months, as also June and May, for the best season of the year, in Calabar river; because of the continual rains which refresh and cool the air, and give the natives an opportunity to apply themselves wholly to commerce, up the land, for getting of slaves and elephants teeth; and are consequently the fittest time for us to purchase slaves with expedition, and less hindrance and fatigue: but more especially in August and September, though the months of June and July are somewhat troublesome, because of the lightning and thunder, then very frequent and terrible; but the daily great rains do abate the heats very much. / We reckon the months of October, November and December, the worst season, because of the dry scorching heat of the sun, and the thick fogs, which are there frequent, so that it is not possible to see from one end of the ship to the other.[10] / It is also to be observ'd, that yams at Bandy point are nothing near so good, nor so lasting as those we have from Foko, or New Calabar town, where the soil seems more proper for their production.

[pp. 380/9–381/1, on Bonny]

As to Bandy point, which is the eastern head or cape of the mouth of Rio Real; it is discernable enough from sea, by a tuft of high trees, over-topping the wood which covers all the coast about it. That tuft of trees the Portugueses call *The lanthorn*, or Fanal: which must be well observ'd steering into the river, as well as the islands lying at the entrance to it; the true channel being near this Bandy point, north and south, in four and three fathom and a half at slack water.[11] It is usual there, when the Blacks of Bandy town spy a sail coming in, to send aboard a canoo with pilots, who speak a little either English, Portuguese, or Dutch, to convey it safe into the river of Bandy; which, when open'd, or in view on the larboard side, is to steer north-east, with the tide, which is very swift, and thus come to an anchor before the town of Bandy, or Great Bandy, lying two leagues east with Bandy point. Ships that come to anchor in the road before the town, in fourteen or twelve fathom of water, usually give a salute of three, five or seven guns, according to the bigness of the ship, to the king of Bandy; the Blacks being very fond of such civilities, and it contributes much to facilitate the trade.[12] / The town of Great Bandy, consisting of about three hundred houses, divided into parcels, stands in a marshy ground, made an island by some arms of the river from the main: it is well peopled with Blacks, who employ themselves in trade, and some at fishing, like those of New Calabar town, in the inland country, by means of long and large canoos, some sixty foot long and seven broad, rowed by sixteen, eighteen or twenty paddlers, carrying European goods and fish to the upland Blacks; and [they] bring down to their respective towns, in exchange, a vast number of slaves, of all sexes and ages, and some large elephants teeth, to supply the Europeans trading in that river. Several of those Blacks act therein as factors, or brokers, either for their own countrymen, or for the Europeans, who are often obliged to trust them with their goods, to attend the upper markets, and purchase slaves for them ... [13]

[p. 381/2–4, on the trade in the river, and Barbot's plan for his book]

Of all European nations that frequent this river and the adjacent parts, the Dutch have the greatest share in the trade; the English next, and after them the Portugueses, from Brasil, St. Thome and Prince's islands; and all altogether export thence a great number of slaves yearly to America, besides a considerable quantity of good elephants teeth, and abundance of provisions.[14]

This would be a proper place to enter upon the description of the slaves, and trade of elephants teeth, with the natives, and of the European goods that are used commonly to purchase them, as well as provisions, together with the methods to carry it on successfully; as also, to speak of the customs, tolls, manners and religion of the Blacks of Foko, New Calabar, Fougue, Bandy and Dony, this last being about ten leagues up in Bandy river, towards the east, and the conveniences of driving the trade, by the several rivers having a communication with Rio Real, etc.[15] But I will follow the plan proposed to myself in writing this description of North and South Guinea, and give as good an account of those vast countries, as I could gather from the year 1678 to 1682, during which time I made two voyages thither; after which, by way of supplement, I will add the most remarkable changes and alterations that have happen'd there till the year 1706, as collected from credible travellers, who have been there from time to time: and shall therefore refer the particular description of the trade in Rio Real to that place where I design to insert an abstract of the journal kept by my brother James, in his voyage to that river in the year 1699, aboard the *Albion* frigate; a ship formerly belonging to the British government, then call'd the *Dover-Prize*, which some merchants of London and I bought of the commissioners of the navy in 1698, and fitted out for New Calabar, with twenty-four guns, sixty men, and a cargo of two thousand six hundred pounds sterling: my said brother and one Grazilhier going joint super-cargoes, and purchasing five hundred and eighty-three slaves in two months time, which they carried to Jamaica. / The journals of those two persons, which are in my hands, being exact and curious, I thought more proper to refer them to the supplement I promise, as being transactions of a much fresher date than my own voyages, and later instances of the trade of that river, and of the manners of the inhabitants, etc.[16]

[p. 382/8–9, on Andoni]

S. Domingo river, So call'd by the Portugueses, and by others Laitomba, falls into the Aethiopian gulph, about five leagues east of Bandy point, which is at the mouth of Rio Real. The town Dony, or Bony, stands on the east side of it, is large, well-peopled, and trades in slaves and teeth with the Europeans, by means of Bandy river, which has a communication with it, and by means of those rivers, the Dony people drive their trade up the land, to

676

purchase slaves and teeth. / I might here enlarge upon the description of this town and country, and of the manners and religion of its inhabitants; but my brother's journal mentioning several particulars thereof, I refer that to the supplement.[17]

[p. 382/10–12, 383/4–5, on Old Calabar river and its trade]

... The Dutch call this river Oude Calborgh, and the English, Old Calbary.[18] The true channel for large ships is on the east side, in three fathom and a half water; and the right road in it is near another river, call'd Cross river, coming from the north-west into it, above the place call'd Sandy-point; below which, at the mouth of Old Calabar river, are two villages at a distance from each other, call'd Fish-town and Salt-town; the Blacks of the former being fishermen, and of the latter salt-boilers.[19] / On the east side of Old Calabar river just at the mouth of it, is another little river running up north, and then east to Rio del Rey, through which ships may pass safely, and so makes an island of the coast that lies betwixt it and Old Calabar. In the midst of the entrance of Old Calabar river lies a small oval island, flat and low, called Parrot's island, which makes two channels to enter it; the best being, as I have said before, on the side of Bennet's river; the other channel is between that little island and the Salt-town, on the main; but it has a bar almost athwart it, extending from Salt-town to very near the west point of Parrot's island, leaving only a narrow passage close to that island, six or seven fathom deep.[20] / Thus by all the beforemention'd remarks this river is easily known from sea, and as easy to be navigated by large ships. It is well furnish'd with villages and hamlets all about, where Europeans drive their trade with the Blacks, who are good civiliz'd people, and where we get, in their proper seasons, as at New Calabar, all sorts of eatables, yams, bananas, corn, and other provisions for the slaves, which we barter there, as well as elephants teeth, and I believe have the greatest share of, of any Europeans.[21]

The most current goods of Europe for the river of Old Calabar, to purchase slaves and elephants teeth, are iron bars, in quantity, and chiefly; copper bars, blue rrgs [sic: ?], cloth, and striped Guinea clouts of many colours, horse-bells, hawks-bells, rangoes; pewter basons of one, two, three and four pounds weight; tankards of ditto of one, two and three pounds weight; beads, very small, and glaz'd, yellow, green, purple and blue; purple copper armlets, or arm-rings, of Angola make; but this last sort of goods is peculiar to the Portugueses. / The Blacks there reckon by copper bars, reducing all sorts of goods to such bars; for example, one bar of iron, four copper bars; a man slave for thirty-eight, and a woman slave for thirty-seven or thirty-six copper bars.[22]

[p. 383/7, on a trading vocabulary]

It may perhaps not be altogether useless to insert here a few words of the Old Calabar language. *Yo*, Give me. *Tata, bobob*, Speak. *Singome*, Shew me. *Fai-fay*, To truck. *Yong-yong*, Good and fair. *Qua-qua*, Linen. *Basin*, Basons. *Yallo*, Beads. *Labouche*, A woman. *Negro*, A Black. *Cokeriko*, Chickens. *Cakedeko*, Tomorrow. *Cakedeko singo*, After tomorrow. *Machinche*, Yesterday. *Singo me Crizake*, Shew me the like. *Singo me miombo*, Give me some strong liquor. *Kinde nongue-nongue*, Go sleep. *Chap-chap*, Eat. *Foretap*, All. *Meraba*, Water.[23]

[p. 383/8, on the need for navigational care and the disastrous 1697 voyage to New Calabar]

To conclude this chapter, I would advise such as are to carry ships of considerable burden into the rivers of New and Old Calabar, besides observing the before-mention'd directions, to sound the proper channel and depths with boats, before sailing in the ships; and to make all due remarks, as prudence requires: as also to take the advantage of some of the natives for the channels: and afterwards to examine if it be so, with the boat or pinnace; also to observe the tides, winds and depths, and the situation of the lands and banks; and, if possible, to be even so curious as to make particular charts or draughts thereof; and of the rivers for the present and future uses, for themselves and posterity. The neglect of this in most sea-faring men, even those who have had education, is much to be lamented among us; very many spending their whole life in travelling from one part of the universe to another, and very often to and from the same places, who nevertheless are not able to shew what use they have made of their time, in any observations of this sort, that may be serviceable to posterity, as well as to themselves.[24] Had this been practised in former generations, and even in this present, since navigation is become so familiar to the meanest capacities; and such multitudes of men have visited, more than once, the best parts of the known world,

678

several of them having been at many coasts, harbours and rivers; we should be now better furnished with exact maps and charts thereof, and many ships and men had been saved who have perish'd, in all parts of the world, through the ignorance of the commanders, or through their own neglect: an instance whereof I have, at my own cost, in the Griffin frigat, which some adventurers of London and myself had fitted out in 1697, for New Calabar river; and after a very prosperous voyage and trade, in three months exactly from the Downs to that river, having in that space taken in three hundred and fifty slaves, was miserably cast away on that bar, coming out to proceed to Jamaica, in the best weather that could be wish'd, through the neglect of the officers, and for want of taking due observations of the channel, and not having sense enough, when the ship had but gently touch'd undamag'd on the skirt of the bar, to cast anchor there, and knock out the heads of all the water-casks to lighten her. But all the crew got into the long-boat, and run ashore at Bandy; leaving the ship with all her sails out, and all the slaves in her, to be tossed to and fro for three days in the channel, till at last it was split in pieces, after the king of Bandy had sent several canoos aboard her, which took out all the slaves, and the best part of her rigging and utensils for himself: being amaz'd and much surpriz'd at the conduct of our people, most of whom died there, and some few, after three months stay in misery among the Blacks, got their passage in a Portuguese ship over to St. Thome, and thence afterwards to England. It was a great surprize to the adventurers to hear of their arrival here, when we expected letters from Jamaica, with an account of the ship's arrival there with a good cargo of Blacks; which was no less expected there by many of the planters, then in great want of Blacks, who at that time yielded forty pounds a man.[25]

[p. 413/4–5, on defects of the Mortier map]

... Another mistake in the Portugueses is very gross, not only in the shape and form they give to Rio Real, which is New Calabar river, so very different from the new draught of it, inserted in the supplement to this volume, which was taken with all possible exactness in the year 1699, as is there expressed; but also in this, that from cape Fermoso to the said river Real, they take notice of four rivers only, viz. to begin from the said cape at east, Rio de S.

Bento, Rio de S. Yldefonso, Rio de S. Barbara, and Rio Pequeno; and this last they represent not properly as a river, but as a little bay, or bulging in an island; whereas it is certain there are seven rivers, at a distance from each other, all of them running down from the inland country of the continent into the ocean, through visible channels or mouths, as represented and particularly named in the said new draught of Rio Real. / Nor does the Portuguese map take the least notice of the three high islands of Ambozes, situate between Rio del Rey and Rio de Camarones, nor of the little island Branca ... Which gives us ground enough to think that nation was not thoroughly inform'd of the true position of the coast of the gulph of Guinea, at the time their map was drawn, or that the draughtsmen made it barely on the credit of persons who were in an error as to those particulars.[26]

[p. 465/2–5, on trading at Old Calabar in 1698]

The ship Dragon traded there in April, for two hundred and twelve slaves, men, women, boys and girls, the ship being but a hundred tuns burden; a hundred and two men, from forty to forty-eight copper bars per head; fifty-three women, from twenty-eight to thirty-six of the same; forty-three boys, from twenty to forty bars; and fourteen girls from seventeen to thirty, according to their age and constitution, for the following goods. / Iron bars seven hundred and seventy-one; copper bars four hundred and fifty-two; rangoes seven hundred and thirty; beads five hundred and forty-six pounds, four pounds making a bunch; pewter tankards fifty-two; basons N°.1. thirty-six; N°.2. twenty-six; N°.3. forty-two; N°4. forty-seven; linen two hundred and twenty yards; knives ninety-six; brass bells, N°.1. eight hundred and forty-one; N°.2. sixty-two; N°.3. sixty-nine; N°.4. fifty-six. These goods reduced to copper bars, as follows. [In] Copper Bars One Bar iron 4 One bunch of beads 4 Five rangoes 4 One tankard 3 One bason, N°.1. 4 The other numbers less in proportion. One yard of linen 1 Six knives 1 One brass bell, N°.1. 3 The other numbers less in proportion.

Purple copper armlets, made at Loanda de S. Paola in Angola, are a very good commodity here and at Rio del Rey; and the Portugueses carry a great quantity of them.

Paid for provisions here. Forty baskets of plantains, sixty copper bars. Twenty copper bars to duke Aphrom for game. Sixty to king Robin for the same. Twenty to captain Thomas, at Salt-Town, for the same. Twenty to captain Thomas at the watering-place, for the same. Twenty to Mettinon. Forty to king Ebrero. Forty to king John. Twenty-four to king Oyo. Seventeen to William king Agbisherea. Seventeen to Robin king Agbisherea. Twelve to duke Aphrom. Thirty to old king Robin, at the watering-place.[27]

[James Barbot's voyage]

[pp. 455/2–465/1, 'An Abstract of a Voyagé to New Calabar River, or Rio Real, in the year 1699. Taken out of the Journal of Mr. James Barbot, Super-Cargo, and Part-Owner with me, and other Adventurers of London, in the Albion-Frigate, of 300 Tons and 24 Guns, a Ten *per Cent*. Ship.'][28]

The thirteenth of January 1698–9, we sail'd from the Downs. [. . .]**[29]** / Twenty-fifth [of February], we anchor'd before Sestro river; there we staid till the twentieth of March, getting in wood, water, rice, malaguette, fowls, and other refreshments and provisions, etc. / King Pieter was still alive and well; we got but very few elephants teeth, because very dear. / Twentieth of March, sailed from Sestro river.[30] [. . .]**[31]**

Eighth [of April], anchor'd before the Prussian fort, Great Fredericksburgh, at Tres-Pontas. [. . .]**[32]** The general told me . . . that there were two or three other pirates cruizing about that cape [Cape Lopez] and St. Tome. / On the tenth a small Portuguese ship anchor'd by us, the master, a Black, said he had been but three weeks from St. Tome, and that about three months before he saw there four tall French ships coming from the coast of Guinea, loaded with slaves, mostly at Fida, one of them commanded by Chr. Damou. Those ships were sent by the French king with a particular commission, to purchase slaves in Guinea, to indemnify the freebooters of St. Domingo, for their pretensions to the booty taken formerly at Cartagena by Mess. De Pointis and Du Casse, in lieu of money; and thereby ingage them to return to St. Domingo, and push on their settlement theré, which they had abandon'd; it being agreed to sell them the slaves, at no more than two hundred and fifty livres, per each Indian piece at St. Domingo, which accordingly had made them return to their settlements there. Those ships had been forced to give near fifty crowns apiece, at

Fida; slaves being then pretty thin at that place, and in great demand.[33] ... /p. 456/ ... / The Portuguese master begg'd our protection to convoy him safe to cape Corso, in his way to Fida, fearing the Hollanders at Mina, who, whenever they can, force all Portuguese ships to pay them a very high toll, for the permission of trading at the coast.[34] / We have abundance of our men sick, and several already dead, the weather being intolerably scorching hot, and we can hardly get any provisions for them, but a few goats very dear: we had from the Portugueses, one goat, one hog, and seven chickens, for five Akies in gold.[35] / Here we perceiv'd that above an hundred pounds worth of horse-beans, we had bought at London, for subsisting our slaves in the voyage, were quite rotten and spoil'd, for want of being well stowed and looked after ever since.

On the seventeenth of April, we were before Mina castle, and found seven sail in the road, three or four of them tall ships; among which two frigats, each of about thirty guns, and a hundred and thirty men, cruizers at the coast; who had taken three interlopers of Zealand, one of which carried thirty-six guns, who having made a brave resistance, the commander was to be tried for his life. One of the frigats having been already two years at the coast, was ready to return home, with a thousand marks of gold.[36] / The eighteenth, anchor'd at cape Corso road, where we rid by two English ships, on eight fathom, muddy sandy ground; the Portuguese vessel in our company was set adrift, his cable breaking; and sending his boat to weigh the anchor, in very boisterous weather, from south-west, the boat overset, and three of his men were drown'd. / We found no corn there, every body telling us it was very dear at the coast. / On the twenty-first, we set sail, saluting the castle with seven guns, and anchor'd at Anamabou; where we purchas'd with much trouble, and at a very dear rate, a quantity of Indian wheat, and sold many perpets, and much powder: we paid three Akies for every chest of corn, which is excessive dear; but having lost all our large stock of horse-beans, were forc'd to get corn at all rates.[37] Here the Blacks put a great value upon perpets, in painted wrappers; oil-cloths with gilt leads, with large painted arms of England. / The tenth [of May], we sent the boat to Anischan, at east, for fewel; and bought her loading of billets at three Akies for each hundred, very dear wood. The eleventh, we sailed, and the twelfth pass'd by Apong, a Dutch fort, very advantageously situated; came to anchor at Winniba, an English fort, and went ashore.[38] / The fifteenth, we arrived at Acra, and ... stay'd to the twenty-sixth ... [then] steered ... towards New Calabar, to buy more slaves.[39]

The twenty-seventh, latitude observed five degrees four minutes north, moderate weather, the wind at south-west by west, being followed by our small sloop under sail; and at night it blew so hard, that to keep her company, we put out the fore-sail and two top-sails only. / The twenty ninth, we guess'd we were near cape Fermoso, slow sail, because of our sloop having very rough sea, an heavy gale and rains. / The thirtieth, had sight of land, south-east by east of us, and came within two leagues of it, in ten fathom muddy sand, the sea carrying to land apace. Guessing we had run already near one hundred and ten leagues from Acra, and perceived then, that we miss'd cape Fermoso, which we expected to have seen at north of us; that the tide had drove us about fifteen leagues north-west of it, in the gulph of Benin; which was a mighty surprize, as well as a disappointment of our voyage to Calabar. Our sloop not being able to work it up, so well as the ship, because of the rough sea and high south-west and south south-west wind, [we] were forc'd to come to anchor in seven fathom, muddy ground, in hopes of a land-wind, to favour us to the southward: this was on the thirtieth of May.[40] / The thirty-first, we cast anchor again about a league and a half from land, at four degrees fifty minutes of our observation. This day the tide very swift, to northward, at half a league an hour; the land lying north and south, very low, flat, and all over woody: by our guess, since we sail'd from Acra, we thought to have gained thirty leagues southward; and consequently to be in a proper latitude for cape Fermoso; and in all this time we had but two observations, the weather being continually gloomy, and great rains. This day we reckoned to be fifteen leagues north north-west of cape Fermoso, /p. 457/ wind high at south south-west, the tide at north. [...][41]

Those who say the navigation in Guinea is very easy at this time to the month of August, are strangely mistaken, and ought to carry a double quantity of anchors; for the sea is most days very high, and the wind at south south-west very fresh, blowing on the land; accompanied with very heavy long rains, which strain upon a ship continually when at anchor; and the ground is very stony, or rather rocky, in many places, as at Sestro, Axim, Tres-Pontas and Acra. / It is also thought that the heavy showers of rain abate the surges of the sea; but we find the contrary: for during the five weeks past, we have had continually a high sea, dismal dark, and very cold days and nights, being as raw a cold as in the channel of England in September: our sorry sloop is properly the occasion of our misfortune and retardment. [...][42]

The sixteenth [of June], rain, [we] set sail, steering south-east on eight fathom, and nine at eleven a-clock; we reached cape Fermoso, which is not easy to be known. Coming from the north-west at two o'clock, we pass'd by Rio Non, stearing easterly; at four pass'd by Rio Oddy, in seven fathom; at six at night anchored in six fathom, north north-east and south south-west of Rio Tilana, or St. Juan. / The seventeenth, sailed east along the shore, on six and seven fathom; at nine, we had Rio St. Nicholas, at north; at eleven, Rio St. Barbara; at one o'clock, pass'd the river St. Bartholomew; at half an hour after two, Rio Sombreiro; and at three we came to an anchor, betwixt the latter and New Calabar river, on five and a half fathom muddy sand, by guess north and south off Foko point.[43]

The eighteenth, by day-break, we sent our long-boat with three men to sail to land for intelligence, and bring some Black to pilot us into Calabar, together with samples of some merchandize; we spy'd a ship in Bandy river, as much as we could see it. The tide running eastward at ten, we moor'd our ship about four leagues from shore, supposing we must lie there, and drive our trade in the river with our sloop and long-boat, thinking it impossible to find a proper channel, to carry so tall a ship in, drawing fourteen foot and a half water.[44] / The nineteenth, we sent one of the pilots in the pinnace to sound the bar; he returned at seven at night with much trouble, the wind and sea being so high. The twentieth, lay still, expecting the return of our long-boat from the river. The twenty-first, at day-light, our warp broke, which was moor'd at south-east, because it had blow'd very hard all night, from south south-west, and south-west by south, and the ebb very strong, the weather very cold. We find, as the Portuguese master had told us at Tres-Pontas, the month of June hereabouts to be a Diablo, as he express'd it. / The twenty-second, rough sea at ebb-tide, wind south south-west; we are much concern'd for our long-boat not returning aboard.

The twenty-third, moderate clear weather, wind south south-west. At eleven o'clock we spy'd a boat near the bar; but being come aboard at one, found it was a great canoo with nine Black rowers, besides /p. 458/ other Blacks, and the master of our long-boat, who reported that on the twentieth, being near the bar, and not possible to get out, he dropped his grappling, and a few hours after the rope broke, and was forc'd thus back to Bandy river, leaving on it a buoy-rope. / The king of Bandy, William, had sent us two or three of his pilots in the canoo, with certificates of several English masters of ships they had piloted formerly safe in, some of them drawing thirteen foot water; in case we were desirous to carry the frigat into the river.[45] / Our man reported, that the ship we could see within the river was English, commanded by one Edwards, who had got his compliment of slaves, being five hundred, in three weeks time; and was ready to sail for the West-Indies; and that he would spare us an anchor of about eleven hundred weight, which rejoiced us much. / He reported farther, that as soon as the Blacks could see our ship off at sea, they immediately went up the river to buy slaves, besides a hundred and fifty that were actually at Bandy town when he left it; and that king William had assured him, he ingag'd to furnish five hundred slaves for our loading, all lusty and young. Upon which, we consulted aboard with the officers, and unanimously agreed to carry up the ship, if possible, for the greater expedition.

On the twenty-fourth, early, the weather being fair, the wind south-west, according to that resolution we set all hands to get in our sheet-anchor, the only one we had; but it being so deep stuck in mud, could not bring it up; which put us to our utmost efforts. But whether the anchor was so deep in the mud, or among rocky stones, I cannot say, the ship pitching violently two strands off, our cable gave way, tho' it was a new one; which caused us immediately to chop it off, and then to wind on the warp, on which we had fastened a buoy, being an iron-bound hogshead. / At one in the afternoon, weighing our anchor, our warp broke, and with precipitation obliged us to chop off our cable, to get under sail to save the ship, as well as our persons if possible, at this time in great consternation, having thus lost all our anchors, the head at south-east, to endeavour to weather the breaking on the bar. / Thus we sail'd south south-east and south-east, better than an hour and a half, about two leagues from the place where he [*sic:*

? we] had lain at anchor; and having brought Foko point to north-west by north, and north north-west, and Bandy point to north by east about five leagues from us, we stood to north-west by north, and north west, for some time, running on five and a half, five, four and a half, and four fathom and a quarter; and all the while with the lead in hand to sound the depths. At three o'clock being about three leagues from the points aforesaid, we fell on a sudden on three and a half, and continu'd so for a while; then came to three, and two and three quarters fathom, and finally to two and a half. All then thought the ship lost, as often touching on the ground a-stern, especially the third stroke was very violent; but then, by providence, happening to set all our sails, the ship passed over and got in well, and by degrees found two and three quarters, three, and three and one quarter fathom, for above a league's course, the bottom being very uneven, three or four foot difference, more or less, at each lead cast. Thus sailing for two hours from three to four, and four to three fathom, we suddenly came again to two and a half, and the ship touch'd ground very slightly; but the sea being smooth, receiv'd no harm. At about five o'clock, we got the opening of Bandy river, and the sight of captain Edward's [sic] ship, riding before the king's town; at which moment we steer'd north-east, directly for the said river: three quarters past six brought Bandy point east and west, with a swift course of flood. The moon-shine served us to get the same tide to an anchor on fourteen fathom, before Bandy town, on a small anchor of three hundred weight, the only one we had left, and which we had at Anamaboe from an English ship; but that anchor being too light for so heavy a ship, and the tide so very strong, it required a long time, the ship driving, before it took hold of the ground sufficiently. Captain Edwards sent us soon after, a small anchor of six hundred weight, for that night only, till he could spare us his large anchor, as he had promised, which is very providential in the extremity we are reduced to; and after the dangers of shipwreck, from which we are now so happily preserved. Our Black pilots were properly of no use in our distress, pleading they never were sensible of so shallow water at the bar; and that it was at the nip tide, and at low water too, that the ship has pass'd over so luckily.[46]

Captain Edwards seeing from a great distance, the danger we were in, through the ignorance of our blind pilots, who had mistaken the right channel, came out immediately in his pinnace, to assist and show us the proper channel: to that effect he stood to leeward of us, thinking we apprehended his meaning, to steer towards the pinnace, which he kept there for a mark for us, the bar being there not above half a mile of high ground, and yet at least three fathom water; whereas the channel we got through, is better than three miles and a half of bar: but we supposing the tide had driven him there, /p. 459/ took no notice of his design, and so proceeded, as above related, amidst many dangers and difficulties. But had we, as he said afterwards, when we had brought the two points, or capes of the river, to east and west, steer'd immediately north, and north by east, instead of running to north-west by north, and north north-west, as we did then, we had got in lieu of three or three fathom and a half at best, five, six, seven, and soon after eight fathom channel, at the place where he stood still with his pinnace.

On the twenty-fifth in the morning, we saluted the Black king of Great Bandy, with seven guns; and soon after fired as many for captain Edwards, when he got aboard, to give us the most necessary advice concerning the trade we designed to drive there. At ten he returned ashore, being again saluted with seven guns: we went ashore also to compliment the king, and make him overtures of trade, but he gave us to understand, he expected one bar of iron for each slave, more than Edwards had paid for his; and also objected much against our basons, tankards, yellow beads, and some other merchandize, as of little or no demand there at that time. / The twenty-sixth, we had a conference with the king and principal natives of the country, about trade, which lasted from three o'clock till night, without any result, they insisting to have thirteen bars of iron for a male, and ten for a female slave; objecting that they were now scarce, because of the many ships that had exported vast quantities of late. The king treated us at supper, and we took leave of him. / The twenty-seventh the king sent for a barrel of brandy of thirty-five gallons, at two bars of iron per gallon; at ten we went ashore, and renewed the treaty with the Blacks, but concluded nothing at all, they being still of the same mind as before.[47] / The twenty-eighth, we sent our pinnace up the river to Dony, for provisions and refreshments; that village being about twenty-five miles from Bandy. Transacted nothing with Blacks of Bandy all this day. / The twenty-ninth, had three great jars of palm-oil, and being foul weather, did not go ashore.

687

The thirtieth, being ashore, had a new conference, which produced nothing; and then Pepprell, the king's brother, made us a discourse, as from the king, importing, He was sorry we would not accept of his proposals; that it was not his fault, he having a great esteem and regard for the Whites, who had much inriched him by trade; That what he so earnestly insisted on, thirteen bars for male, and ten for female slaves, came from the country people holding up the price of slaves at their inland markets, seeing so many large ships resort to Bandy for them; but to moderate matters, and incourage trading with us, he would be contented with thirteen bars for males, and nine bars and two brass rings for females, etc.[48] Upon which we offered thirteen bars for men, and nine for women, and proportionably for boys and girls, according to their ages; after this we parted, without concluding any thing farther. / On the first of July, the king sent for us to come ashore, we staid there till four in the afternoon, and concluded the trade on the terms offered them the day before; the king promising to come the next day aboard to regulate it, and be paid his duties.[49] / We took a large shark, which was given to the Blacks of Bandy to feast on. Our pinnace returned at night from Dony, brought a slave for ten bars of iron and a pint tankard; and a cow and a calf, which cost a hundred and fifty rings.

The second, heavy rain all the morning. At two o'clock we fetch'd the king from shore, attended by all his Caboceiros and officers, in three large canoos; and entring the ship, was saluted with seven guns. The king had on an old-fashion'd scarlet coat, laced with gold and silver, very rusty, and a fine hat on his head, but bare-footed; all his attendants shewing great respect to him: and since our coming hither, none of the natives have dared to come aboard of us, or sell the least thing, till the king had adjusted the trade with us.[50] / We had again a long discourse with the king and Pepprell his brother, concerning the rates of our goods and his customs. This Pepprell being a sharp blade, and a mighty talking Black, perpetually making sly objections against something or other, and teazing us for this or that Dassy, or present, as well as for drams, etc. it were to be wish'd, that such a one as he were out of the way, to facilitate trade. / We fill'd them with drams of brandy and bowls of punch till night, at such a rate, that they all, being about fourteen with the king, had such loud clamorous tattling and discourses among themselves, as were hardly to be endured.

Thus, with much patience, all our matters were adjusted indifferently, after their way, who are not very scrupulous to find excuses or objections, for not keeping literally to any verbal contract; for they have not the art of reading and writing, and therefore we are forced to stand to their agreement, which often is no longer than they think fit to hold it themselves. The king order'd the publick cryer to proclaim the permission of trade with us, with the noise of his trumpets, being elephants teeth, made much after the same fashion, as is used at the Gold Coast, we paying sixteen brass rings to the fellow /p. 460/ for his fee. The Blacks objected much against our wrought pewter and tankards, green beads, and other goods, which they would not accept of.

We gave the usual presents to the king and his officers; that is, / To the king a hat, a firelock, and nine bunches of beads, instead of a coat. / To captain Forty, the king's general, captain Pepprell, captain Boileau, alderman Bougsby, my lord Willyby, duke of Monmouth, drunken Henry, and some others, two firelocks, eight hats, nine narrow Guinea stuffs.[51] / We adjusted with them the reduction of our merchandize into bars of iron, as the standard coin, viz. / One bunch of beads, one bar. Four strings of rings, ten rings in each, one ditto. Four copper bars, one ditto. One piece of narrow Guinea stuff, one ditto. One piece broad Hamborough, one ditto. One piece Nicanees, three ditto. Brass rings, ditto. / And so pro rata, for every other sort of goods.[52] / The price of provisions and wood was also regulated. / Sixty king's yams, one bar; one hundred and sixty slaves yams, one bar; for fifty thousand yams to be delivered to us.[53] A butt of water, two rings. For the length of wood, seven bars, which is dear; but they were to deliver it ready cut into our boat. For a goat, one bar. A cow, ten or eight bars, according to its bigness. A hog, two bars. A calf, eight bars. A jar of palm-oil one bar and a quarter. / We paid also the king's duties in goods; five hundred slaves, to be purchased at two copper rings a head.[54] / We also advanced to the king, by way of loan, the value of a hundred and fifty bars of iron, in sundry goods; and to his principal men, and others, as much again, each in proportion of his quality and ability. / To captain Forty, eighty bars. To another, forty. To others, twenty each. / This we did, in order [for them] to repair forthwith to the inland markets, to buy yams for greater expedition; they employing usually nine or ten days in each journey up the country, in their long canoos up the river.

All the before regulations being so made, the supper was served. It was as comical as shocking, to observe those people's behaviour at table, both king and subjects making a confused noise, all of them talking together, and emptying the dishes as soon as set down, every one filling his pockets with meat, as well as his belly; especially of hams and neat's tongues, falling on all together, without regard to rank or manners, as they could lay their hands on it. / After having drank and eat till they were ready to burst, they returned ashore, being again saluted with seven guns.

On the third, the king returned aboard, to see some samples of all our goods, as he said; but it was only a pretence, for instead of that, he fell a drinking and eating all the while, and returned to town with his company, being saluted with three guns. / The fifth, the king sent aboard thirty slaves, men and women; of which we pick'd nineteen, and returned him the rest. / The sixth, the king came aboard with four slaves, which, with the nineteen others of the day before, made twenty-three, for which we paid him two hundred and forty-seven bars, three of the women having each a child. We allowed him for twenty-four heads, in specie, a hundred and twelve bars, in Rangoes ten bars, in beads forty-six bars, in copper fifty-one bars, and in Guinea stuffs twenty-eight bars.

Thus from day to day, from this time to the twenty-ninth of August following, either by means of our armed sloop making several voyages to New Calabar town and to Dony, to purchase slaves and provisions; and by the contract made with the king, and his people of Bandy town, and circumjacent trading places; we had by degrees aboard six hundred and forty-eight slaves, of all sexes and ages, including the sixty-five we had purchased at the Gold Coast, all very fresh and sound, very few exceeding forty years of age; besides provisions of yams, goats, hogs, fowls, wood and water, and some cows and calves. As for fish, this river did not afford us any great quantity, which was a great loss to us, being forced to subsist the ship's crew with fresh meat from land, at a great charge, it being here pretty dear, and most of our salt meat being spent, and [we] have but [enough] for three months more of sea-bisket left in the bread-room. Several of our sailors are tormented with cholicks, and some few dead.[55]

On the thirteenth of July, captain Edwards riding at Bandy point, in order to put to sea, after he had sold us an anchor of

690

eleven hundred weight, with one cask of beef, some deals and tar, etc. we sent our two mates and six men, in the pinnace, aboard him, to be rightly informed of the bar, for our going out when ready loaded.

Mr. John Grazilhier's voyage from Bandy to New Calabar in Rio-Real, in our sloop.

The twenty-second of July, I sailed with a little cargo, for Calabar town. At six at night I anchored before a village called Bandy, situated in the north north-west part of the isle of the interlopers, where the Portugueses usually trade for slaves. On the twenty-third, I set sail with the tide of flood, and about twelve at night came to anchor in Calabar river, and fired a pattarero, but no man came from shore.[56] /p. 461/ / The twenty-fourth I came before the town of Calabar, and fired three guns, to salute the king; after which, I made him the usual presents of one cask of brandy, and a barrel of powder, with a hat; to the duke of Monmouth a hat; to the duke of York a piece of linen cloth; and to captain Jan Alkmaers another piece: these four being here the principal Blacks, who claim presents, before we can trade.[57] And having adjusted the price of slaves and of our merchandize, I presented them also with a hat, a firelock, and a coat. Then the king caused the permission of trade to be proclaimed at Bandy, viz. Twelve bars a man, nine a woman, and six a boy or girl.

The twenty-fifth, I got fifteen slaves aboard the sloop, all young people. / The twenty-sixth. This morning above forty great canoos parted from Calabar up the river, to purchase slaves inland. At noon I sent the sloop back to Bandy, to deliver aboard what slaves I had bought here, and staid ashore at the town, to expect her return with goods, to carry on the trade here at the return of the canoos from above. / The twenty-seventh. Heavy rain all this day: about nine at night the canoos return'd with a great number of slaves. / The twenty-eighth, I got eight slaves. Were our ship here, she would get slaves much faster than at Bandy; the Calabar Blacks being but two or three days out and home, to purchase them at inland markets: whereas the Bandy people, lying much lower, by the sea-side, are eight or ten days out and home, to get them down.

The twenty-ninth, the sloop arrived, and immediately I went back to the ship at Bandy towards night, with forty-four slaves; notwithstanding it rained all the day and this night. / The thirtieth, I came to Foko point, distant five leagues from Calabar, north and south. / The thirty-first, early I sailed, the wind at west south-west, and arrived aboard the ship, at Bandy, about ten. To avoid the banks which lie north of this point, we steer'd east for half a league, and afterwards north-east, coasting the breaking of the sea to windward, in three, and two fathom and a half at low water, to the interlopers island; where we were careful to avoid a bank running out thence about a league. In our course to the point of Bandy, and from it to the town, [the channel] is ten fathom deep all along.

The same night I returned to Calabar in the sloop, with a fresh cargo, taking Mr. Barbot with me; and arrived there the first of August at night. / The second of August, we got forty-three slaves, and the same night went for Bandy, leaving Mr. Barbot at Calabar to trade; lodging his goods in king Robert's house. / The third, I arrived aboard. / The fourth, early I returned to Calabar, in company with a Portuguese ship, and arrived there at night. Mr. Barbot had thirty slaves ready, which I took in, and sailed immediately to Bandy on the fifth early. The Portuguese ship anchor'd before Calabar.

Thus we navigated the sloop to and fro, from Bandy to Calabar, till we had our compliment of slaves. At some trips, when the winds were contrary, and too high, we steer'd our course from Bandy to Calabar through the channel betwixt the long narrow island that lies to westward of the road, where there are some cottages of fishermen, who often brought us fish aboard ship. On the north side of this channel stands a timber building, which is seen as far off as the shore there. The beforementioned island is much higher than any lands. This building is like a barn at a distance; and about it, not very far, are some hamlets for fishermen.[58] Mr. Barbot says, he once was in that barn, and observed there twenty-five or thirty elephants heads dried, set up all round the house on boards, which are the idols of the country, the Blacks resorting thither to pay their religious worship. [59]

In the interval, saith Grazilhier, I made some voyages to Dony, as did Mr. Barbot, in our long-boat; at the second of which, on the eighth we came at night to Dony, and caused my goods to be carried to the king's house, being a man about forty-five years of age. On the ninth I got three slaves, three cows, and one goat, all for fifty-seven bars, the cows at eight bars a-piece, and returned

692

aboard; but by reason of the bad weather could not reach Bandy till the tenth in the morning, when Mr. Barbot arrived also, a little before me, in the sloop, from Calabar, with thirty-seven slaves.

Description of Calabar. [*margin:* Barbot's journal]

The town is seated in a marshy island often overflow'd by the river, the water running even between the houses, where there are about three hundred in a disorderly heap. The king's is pretty high and airy, which was some comfort to me, during the time I staid there. / The land about the town being very barren, the inhabitants fetch all their subsistence from the country lying to the northward of them, called the Hackbous Blacks, a people much addicted to war and preying on their neighbours to the northward, and are themselves lusty tall men.[60] / In their territories there are two market-days every week, for slaves and provisions, which the Calabar Blacks keep very regularly, to supply themselves both with provisions and slaves, palm-oil, palm-wine, etc. there being great plenty of the last.[61] /p. 462/

King Robert is a good civil man, about thirty years of age. / Every evening they club together at one another's houses, by turns; providing two or three jugs of palm-wine, each of them containing twelve or fifteen gallons, to make merry; each person, man and woman, bringing their own stool to sit on. They sit round and drink to one another out of ox's horns, well polished, which hold a quart or more, singing and roaring all the while till the liquor is out. / Their common food is yams boil'd with fish and palm-oil, which they reckon dainty fare.

Whilst I was at the town, they show'd me a considerable quantity of elephants teeth, very large, but so very dear, they would have turned to no account in Europe.[62]

Every house is full of idols, as well as the streets of the town. They call them Jou-Jou, being in the nature of tutelar gods. Many of them are dried heads of beasts, others made by the Blacks of clay and painted, which they worship and make their offerings to.[63] / Before the king goes aboard a ship newly come in, he repairs to his idol house, with drums beating, and trumpets sounding, all his attendants bare-headed. There he makes abundance of bows to those puppets, begging of them to make his voyage prosperous; and then sacrifices a hen, which is tied alive by one leg to the end of a long pole, and has a brass ring on the other leg, leaving the poor creature in that condition till it starves to death. / Every time their small fleet of canooes goes up for slaves, and when they return, they blow their horns or trumpets for joy; and the king never fails, at both those times, to pay his devotions to his idols, for their good success, and a short voyage. [. . .][64]

The Blacks here are generally inhuman, treacherous, very thievish, and false to the most solemn engagements. I could observe no curiosities there, but only some shells I brought to London with me, and their weapons, made by the Hackbous Blacks, and such other things which I have represented in the cut here annexed. [margin: Plate 26][65]†

There is a prodigious number of monkeys and apes about Calabar, but not handsome [ones]. They have also blue parrots. The natives give three or four monkeys for an old hat or coat, taking much pride to dress themselves in our sailors old rags.

Description of Dony [margin: Barbot's journal]

On the twenty-fourth of July I went to Dony, distant about twenty-five miles from Bandy road, along the river, in the long-boat, and arrived there at four in the afternoon. The king being then gone to Bandy-point with some slaves, to sell to our people aboard, I staid for his return, and employ'd my time in walking about the town; and observed the country about it to be all overflowed, being a low swampy ground, cut in many places, with small rivers running into the great one of Dony. / It has plenty of cattle, hogs and goats, and a prodigious quantity of palm-wine, which is their usual drink. The cattle is small, especially cows.

I lay that night in the king's house, near his idol-house, which they call Jou-Jou, and are kept there in a large press, full of the skulls of their enemies killed in war, and others of beasts; besides a quantity of human bones and other trash, some of them moulded with clay, and painted as at Calabar.[66] They are so superstitiously bigotted, that any person whatever, who offers to touch any of those things with his hand, is sure to be severely punished, and in danger of his life. / Besides those idols, they worship bulls, and a large sort of lizards, called Gouanes in the French Caribee islands, as their prime gods; and it is not less than death to kill them.[67] Most of these Blacks are circumcised, and show great reverence to their priests or Marabous; and whensoever they kill any beasts for their own eating, they reserve the entrails for their idol gods,

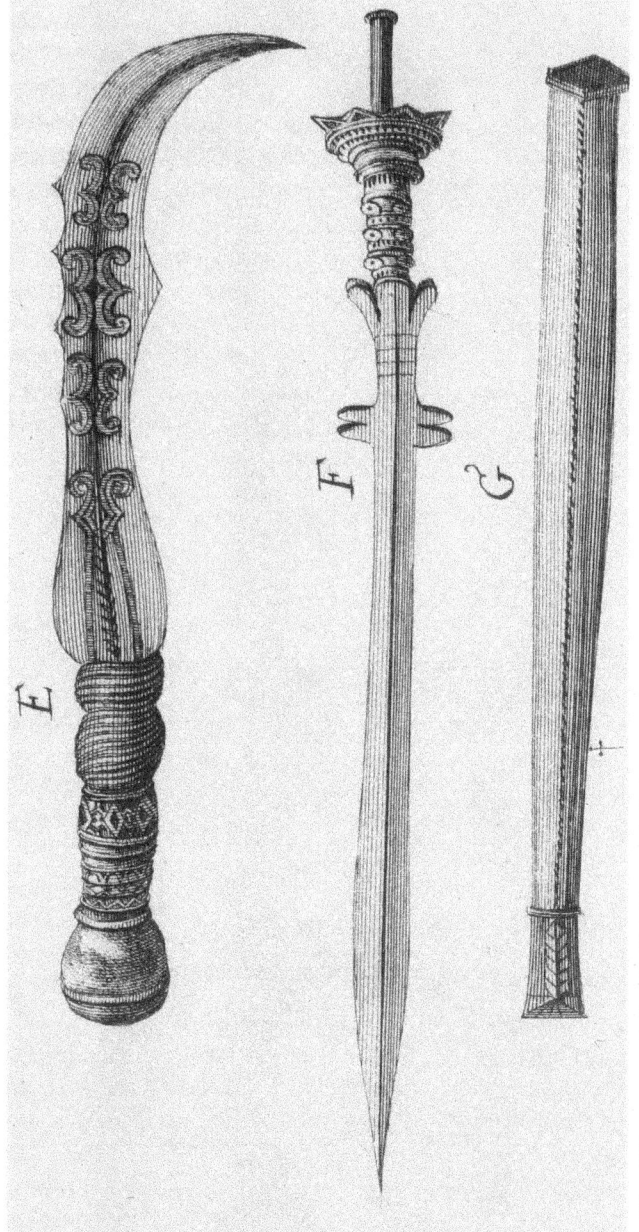

E   F   G

54. 'Weapons made by the Hackbous Blacks'

Veüe de l'Isle du Prince de 2 Lieuës suiv L'Islot a Palmiste etant a E.S.E. 2 Lieüe de Terre

L'Islet a Palmiste

55. Principe Island

which they lay on the little altars erected in many places to their honour.

On the twenty-fourth the king returned home, and obliged me not to go away till next day, to give time to the people to bring down their cattle from the country, it being the chief occasion of my voyage to get some there: yet the next day I could get but three cows, and three goats, the former at eight bars a-piece. About noon, on the twenty-fifth, I sailed for Bandy with these cattle.

The king of Dony is a very good-natur'd civil man, speaks Portuguese, and seems to have been instructed by Romish priests, who are sent over from time to time, from St. Tome and Brazil.[68] The first time he came aboard our ship, which was on the seventh of July, we presented him with a hat and a firelock; he invited us to traffick at his town, and we promised to send now and then some of our goods thither.

John Grazilhier's voyage to Dony in 1704.

Mr. Grazilhier told me he was once hunting of elephants at Dony, in the moon-shine, with the king, and above an hundred Blacks, armed with muskets, cutlaces, lances and saws, etc. They saw several elephants come near them about eleven at night, who were /p. 463/ going to the river to drink, some of them were monstrous tall and large; but the Negroes durst not attack any, those animals making such a dreadful noise, that he was frighted at it. / When the Blacks happen to kill an elephant, they cut him in pieces, and divide the flesh among all the town's people, who approve of it as good food, and have a natural hatred for this bulky creature; which does them much mischief, sometimes entring their villages, and overturning twenty or thirty houses, and killing all such of the inhabitants as are not nimble enough to make their escape betimes.

The river of Bandy falls into that of Dony: the mouth of this latter being to the south-ward of the town, discharging itself into the great ocean. This town is divided into three parcels.

[James Barbot's journal][69] The town of Great Bandy is seated in a little island, much as that of Calabar, being a marshy swampy ground, and somewhat larger, but like it in buildings, and the inhabitants of the same manners, temper and religion, so that it will be needless to say more of them; but I proceed to some general observations concerning the river of New Calabar and the trade there.

695

Whilst we were by degrees taking in our compliment of slaves at Great Bandy, our mates, with the assistance and advice as well of captain Edwards, and the Portuguese master that lay there by us for a time, as of some of the most experienced native pilots of Bandy town, employed several days in our pinnace and canoos, to sound the channels, and depths of the bar and banks, that lie athwart the river's mouth, betwixt Foko and Bandy point, with all necessary exactness and caution; and drew a map thereof, and of the rivers of New Calabar and Dony, which is here annexed, for the benefit of sea-faring men trading thither. [*margin:* Plate 27][70]

It is customary here for the king of Bandy to treat the officers of every trading ship, at their first coming, and the officers return the treat to the king, some days before they have their compliment of slaves and yams aboard. Accordingly, on the twelfth of August we treated the king and his principal officers, with a goat, a hog, and a barrel of punch; and that is an advertisement to the Blacks ashore, to pay in to us what they owe us, or to furnish with all speed, what slaves and yams they have contracted to supply us with, else the king compels them to it. At that time also such of the natives as have received from us a present, use to present us, each with a boy or girl slave in requital. According to this custom we treated the Blacks ashore on the fifteenth of August, and invited the Portuguese master to it, as also the Black ladies; the king lending us his musick, to the noise of which we had a long diversion of dances and sports of both sexes, some not unpleasing to behold.

On the eighteenth, being fair weather, we sent the sloop to look for an anchor, which captain Edwards had left behind, near the bar, at his going out, his cable having broke; and at the same time to sound the skirts of the bar, and set marks. On the nineteenth, towards night, the sloop returned, not being able to find Edward's [sic] anchor, but found a channel pretty wide, that runs south-east, where there is no less than three fathom, and three and a half at low water, and not above two foot of fall; which rejoiced us very much, being near the time of our departure. / On the twenty-second, we let fly our colours, and fired a gun, for a signal to the Blacks, of our being near ready to sail, and to hasten aboard with the rest of the slaves, and quantity of yams contracted for.

On the twenty-sixth, came in a Zealand interloper of sixteen guns and forty men, in two days from Prince's Island last, with a west south-west and south-west by west wind; and from Zealand in March before, having traded at the Ivory and Gold Coast, and thence gone to St. Tome to set his effects there ashore in trust, came hither to look for teeth; and thence was afterwards to proceed to traffick along the coast of Gabon, Congo and Angola, for more elephants teeth.

We got an anchor of about eleven hundred weight of him, for our sloop, with her masts, tack-sails, etc. A high extortion, if ever any was; for we could have got four hundred pieces of eight for the sloop at St Tome: but necessity forced us to comply to so hard a bargain, in the condition we were reduced to, having but one only small anchor left us in so tall and rich a ship. [71] And accordingly, on the twenty-eighth we exchanged the sloop for the anchor, with the Zealander, and at six in the evening we sailed from Bandy with the tide of ebb, and a south-west wind, tacking and working the ship down, keeping constantly near the shore of Bandy-point, to avoid the banks that lie west of it, on which are some rocks; and at ten at night we dropped anchor within the said point, in nine fathom water, having Foko-point west by north of us, and that of Bandy at north-east, about half a league from land, and two English miles from the breakings of the sea, through which are several passages of channels. The channel at south-west and north-east of Bandy-point is sound, there being fifteen to sixteen foot at low water; but being very narrow, it cannot be well sailed through, unless with a land wind; and at this time of the year such /p. 464/ are very rare. Wherefore we resolved to get out the next day through the channel that stretches to south-east; which is wide, and much more easy to sail in with the south-west wind now reigning. / On the twenty-ninth, at break of day, we set sail, the weather fair, and little wind from south-west, we tack'd three or four times with the ebb. At seven in the morning we came near to the breaking, the point of Bandy then being at north north-east, about a mile from us; and Foko point west north-west, sounding six, five, four and a half, then three and four and a half; four, three and a half, and three fathom and three quarters. Having brought Bandy-point to north by east, we got three and a quarter, three and three quarters, and three fathom on the skirts of the bar; Foko-point being at west north-west, and Bandy-point north by east, half east, we found four, and then five fathom water.

It is to be observed, that there are two high grounds or bars to pass over; the first is betwixt two shoals of a breaking sea, where, when you have got Bandy-point at north-east, and Foko-point west north-west, there is no danger at all to range the banks of the south-west very close, the better to make sure the channel; which also is the deepest, for there you have four, four and a half, and five fathom. Coasting along the said bank for some time, and having got the same aboard, steering south south-east for a while, to weather the breaking sea at larboard; and then proceeding to the south-east by south, until you bring Bandy-point to bear north; then, in a very short time you'll get three and a half, three and a quarter, three, three and a half, three and a quarter, three and three quarters, etc. for a mile's course. And when Bandy-point bears north, somewhat west, you are past the dangers, and may boldly steer south by east for a time; for so then you'll come on three and a half, three and three quarters, and somewhat farther four, five, six and seven fathom. / By this course it is easy enough to carry a ship out or into this river. / To carry a ship in, as coming from Foko-point, on five and four fathom and a half, at east and east by south; and having brought Bandy-point to bear north, and Foko-point to west north-west in four fathom, if you have an ebb, you must anchor, if the ship draw above ten foot water: and at the beginning of the flood sail again, steering to north north-west, which carries you directly betwixt the two banks, ranging that which lies at west; the bottom there being level, flat, hard sand.

We were assured here by the natives, they had never seen so tall a ship, drawing near fifteen foot water, get into their river: and really it is almost a miracle we escaped so well, and so narrowly at our going in, as has been observed before.[72]

Mr. Grazilhier, who, since his voyage in the Albion frigat, has made three more thither, commander of English and Dutch ships, assur'd me at Southampton in 1705, that the Dutch then made nothing of fetching slaves from Calabar with ships of three or four hundred tuns burden, that nation having now the greatest trade there of any Europeans, as well for slaves as for elephants teeth; and that by the knowledge he has acquir'd, by often sailing to new Calabar river, he will carry in a ship of six hundred tuns, without any danger, having found a passage of between four and a half and five fathom at the lowest water. / In October 1700, he sail'd from the Downs directly to this river, in two months time, in a little

English ship, where he purchased two hundred slaves at twenty-
four and twenty six bars a man, and proportionably for a woman,
because of the great number of ships, sometimes ten, or more
together, that were then trading, which quite drain'd the upper
markets; and arriv'd at Barbadoes in April following. He has since
made several voyages in the service of the Dutch, being of late
married and settled in Holland.[73]

In 1703, or 1704, the price of slaves at Calabar was twelve bars
a man, and nine a woman. / The slaves got there, says he, are
generally pretty tall men, but washy and faint, by reason of their
ill food, which is yams at best, and other such sorry provisions. A
very considerable number of them is exported yearly from that
river, by the Europeans; he having, as has been said above, seen
there ten ships at a time, loading slaves, which is the reason the
price of them varies so much, being double some years to what it
is others, according to the demand there is of them; the natives
being cunning enough to enhance the price upon such occasions.
He computes there are also exported from thence yearly, from
thirty to forty tuns of elephants teeth, all very fine and large, most
by Dutch ships. / The most current goods to purchase slaves at
New Calabar, in 1704, were iron bars, copper bars, of which two
sorts, a great quantity, especially of the iron; rangoes, beads
goosberry-colour, large and small, Indian nicanees, little brass
bells, three-pound copper basons, and some of two pounds;
Guinea stuffs, ox-horns for drinking cups, pewter tankards great
and small; blue linen, blue long beads, or pearls, spirits, blue
perpets a few.

Mr. Grazilhier told me farther, that in the months of July,
August and September, he observ'd the breaking of the sea did
rise, /p. 465/ and pitch from fifteen to twenty foot high, all about
the mouth of New Calabar river, and without it, over the banks of
the bar; which is a good mark to all such ships as design to enter
it, being so shown the danger. But it is quite otherwise during the
following six months of October, November, etc. when the bar is
cover'd with seven, eight, and nine foot water, and no breaking
seen; wherefore the more caution must be used in sailing in. He
added, that in the months of August and September, a man may
get in his compliment of slaves much sooner than he can have the
necessary quantity of yams, to subsist them. But a ship loading
slaves there in January, February, etc. when yams are very

699

plentiful, the first thing to be done, is to take them in, and afterwards the slaves. / A ship that takes in five hundred slaves, must provide above a hundred thousand yams; which is very difficult, because it is hard to stow them, by reason they take up so much room; and yet no less ought to be provided, the slaves there being of such a constitution, that no other food will keep them; Indian corn, beans, and Mandioca, disagreeing with their stomach; so that they sicken and die apace, as it happened aboard the Albion frigat, as soon as their yams were spent, which was just when it anchor'd at St. Tome, after a fortnight's passage from Bandy-point, at Calabar. Besides, those poor wretches, the slaves of New Calabar, are a strange sort of brutish creatures, very weak and slothful; but cruel and bloody in their temper, always quarrelling, biting and fighting, and sometimes choaking and murdering one another, without any mercy, as happened to several aboard our ship; and whosoever carries slaves from New Calabar river to the West-Indies, had need pray for a quick passage, that they may arrive there alive and in health. To that purpose I would advise, so to order matters at Calabar, as to be in a condition to proceed directly to cape Lope, and not to St. Tome, or Prince's Island. All the ships that loaded slaves with the Albion frigat at Calabar, lost, some half, and others two thirds of them, before they reach'd Barbadoes; and such as were then alive, died there, as soon as landed, or else turn'd to a very bad market: which render'd the so hopeful voyage of the Albion abortive, and above sixty per cent of the capital was lost, chiefly occasion'd by the want of proper food and water to subsist them, as well as the ill management of the principals aboard.[74]

NOTES

[1] Omission of 13 paragraphs on Rio Réal. Barbot never visited this stretch of the coast, which contained two main trading localities, New Calabar and Old Calabar. Most of this letter, being about Rio Réal or New Calabar River, is extracted from Dapper, pp. 135/1–138/1 (with errors, e.g. Dapper's 'Moko' is mis-spelled in Barbot's Letter title). But the trade at New Calabar by 'the whites, especially the Dutch' is changed to trade by 'the English, Dutch, Portuguese and French' – perhaps a paraphrase rather than new knowledge. Barbot wrongly interpolates material from the account of

an Englishman who had an adventure among cannibals, as told in Watts 1672 (but the spelling of personal names suggests that Barbot used the summary of Watts in Burton 1686, pp. 62–71 – in any case note the early use of a source in English); the experiences mentioned in fact occurred on Cross River, further East, at Old Calabar, a locality discussed later.

Cf. *1732*, pp. 380/3–8, 381/5–7, 382/1–7, which is embedded in considerable new material – see the Additional Passages. As Barbot makes clear elsewhere (p. 465/4), his map of the district and by implication the detailed sailing directions in *1732* represent information from his brother who visited New Calabar in 1699: the text of James Barbot's account appears above. Barbot also refers to a disastrous English voyage to New Calabar River which he helped to finance in 1697 (p. 383/8, see the Additional Passage) and subsequent voyages there by John Grazilhier in 1700 and 1704 (pp. 462/8, 464/7). It may therefore be presumed that the new material came predominantly, if not exclusively, from accounts of these voyages and hence relates to the period 1697–1704. Barbot adopts the name 'New Calabar' to distinguish the locality from 'Old Calabar' (Dapper's 'oudt Kalbarien'/'oude Kalborgh') to the East, a usage found in Bosman, p. 399, and other sources of the period (although in fact the name 'Calabar' was first documented, in 1517, for a village on Rio Réal: Teixeira da Mota 1977, p. 23, correcting Hair 1969a, p. 234). Of the village 'captains' of the area, Barbot adds that 'such chiefs or captains are now generally allow'd the title of kings by the Europeans, all over Guinea, as has been before observ'd, but are at best such kings as the two and thirty that Joshua defeated at once, mention'd in holy writ'.

[2] The first sentence derives from Dapper, p. 137/3. 'Rio Conde of [or] Andoni' was noted in Robijn/Roggeveen 1685, pp. 28–9, and on the accompanying map: Barbot's difficulty was caused by the fact that 'Conde' was another name for Dapper's 'Loitomba'.

Cf. *1732*, p. 382/9, in Additional Passages below.

[3] For the incident of the English ship, see *1679*, pp. 353–4, which is fuller. 'Poisonous air' was noted at a 'Calbares' river in 1683 (Jones 1985, p. 56). Although Dapper failed to mention any trade at Old Calabar, the English were trading there by at least 1668 (Watts 1672; Latham 1973, p. 17).

Cf. *1732*, p. 383/1–3, which omits the first two sentences, possibly because the information was out of date, trade having increased, but adds the translated name of Barbot's ship, *The Sun of Africa*. As regards turn-around times for slave-ships in the Niger Delta, despite the reference to a 10-months stay, in 1699 James Barbot's ship spent only 3½ months there – exactly the same period as the average for Liverpool ships in the 1790s, hence perhaps indicating that the development of an efficient interior commercial network began early (Anstey and Hair 1976, pp. 146–9).

701

⁴ In 1679 Barbot bought monkeys, which were 'quite difficult to get', at Príncipe – perhaps he learned that they came from Old Calabar (*1679*, p. 353). In the 1640s chimpanzees were being imported to Mina from Old Calabar (Jones 1983a, p. 126).

Cf. *1732*, p. 383/6: a 'prodigious number of monkeys and apes', deemed 'not handsome', was noted at New Calabar by James Barbot (p. 462/10).

⁵ The earliest navigational directions for the common estuary of the New Calabar and Bonny rivers, although of c. 1500, were copied in seventeenth-century Portuguese guides, but were modified in Dutch guides (Pacheco Pereira 1956, p. 145; Carneiro 1642, pp. 90–1; Leers 1665, p. 304). However, on the grounds that the depths were not constant, no directions were given in Robijn/Roggeveen 1685, p. 28. The earliest detailed map of the estuary appears to be a Dutch manuscript map of 1638 (Ratelband 1953, p. lxxxiv), perhaps followed by a map in Robijn/Roggeveen 1685, inset on 'Paskaert van de Gout Cust en Boght van Benin'. The chart of the estuary and rivers to which Barbot alludes (*1732*, plate 27, p. 463) seems to be largely original and is more detailed, particularly in soundings, with a wider stretch of the coast included, and it formed the basis for his navigational directions. Entitled 'A new correct mapp of Calbar River . . .', it was 'drawn very exactly upon the spot in the year 1699 by several Pilots jointly', as explained in detail in James Barbot's journal (p. 463/4, see the Additional Passage). Its most important detail is the inscription in the interior, 'The Hackbous Country is some leagues above N. Calabar Town' – the earliest naming in print of the Igbo people (Hair 1969a, p. 235).

⁶ 'Foko' ('Fokké' in Dapper) is Ifoko, on the West bank of the mouth of Rio Réal, a settlement which was politically subordinate to Elem Kalabari, or New Calabar (Jones 1963, p. 64; Alagoa 1972, p. 139). While adding a classical reference allegedly to the inland peoples of the region, Barbot later refers to 'Ofoco . . . a city several leagues inland', according to 'Portuguese geographers' (i.e. shown on the Mortier map), without recognizing that this is Ifoko wrongly located (*1732*, p. 381/8). 'Foko Point' is now known as Fouché Point; and the two islands in the river, of shifting size and location, as Deadman Island ('doot Eylant', in the English version 'dead Islands' [sic], Robijn/Roggeveen 1685, p. 28 and map) and Yellow Island (*Africa pilot* 1967, p. 543).

⁷ That ocean ships anchored off Ifoko, the up-river navigation being by yacht, was implied by Dapper, p. 135/2; and the same procedure was standard later (Jones 1963, pp. 38, 82).

⁸ 'Bandy' ('Bany' in Dapper) is Ibani, or Bonny. Barbot gives much greater prominence to Bonny than did Dapper, p. 135/6, which depicted New Calabar as the more important centre of trade in the earlier period.

⁹ The clause about the food for slaves is clumsily punctuated, 'but

702

especially . . .' referring not to the horse-beans just mentioned, which were brought from Europe, but to 'food of their own country', notably the 'Indian wheat' which was indeed 'purchase[d] at the Gold-Coast' (see *1732*, p. 547/1). In 1699, after a supply of horse-beans brought from England became rotten, James Barbot was obliged to buy maize at Anomabu, finding it very dear (*1732*, p. 456/3, 6). However, Niger Delta slaves preferred yams to the extent that 'no other food will keep them', maize and other foods 'disagreeing with their stomachs' (*1732*, p. 465/1). The excellent yams of New Calabar river were noted two centuries earlier (Pacheco Pereira 1956, p. 147).

[10] An allusion to the harmattan, a very dry wind from the arid North, which produces a dust haze on the coast. A little further East, at Old Calabar, 'during the harmattan season (December to March inclusive) the river is at times enveloped in a dense haze lasting a week or more' (*Africa pilot* 1967, p. 571). James Barbot only spent from June to September 1699 in the district, so the information about the weather in the other months of the year probably came from Grazilhier who, on later voyages, spent more time there (*1732*, p. 464/7, 11).

[11] No doubt the Portuguese term *fanal* ('beacon, lighthouse') came from the Portuguese captain who helped to prepare the map in 1699 (*1732*, p. 463/ 4). 'Bandy point' is now called Field Point, and is identified by a radar tower (*Africa pilot* 1967, p. 542).

[12] For pilots and salutes at Bonny in 1699, see *1732*, pp. 457/16, 458/1, 459/1, etc., in the Additional Passage.

[13] 'Great Bandy' ('Groot Bany' on the Robijn/Roggeven map), or 'Grand Bonny' in later sources, refers to the principal settlement and royal residence of Bonny, as opposed to its dependencies. For earlier accounts of the canoes and canoe-borne trade, see Pacheco Pereira 1956, p. 147, and Dapper, p. 136/2, 3, 7, although neither specifies trade in fish or ivory. The reference to Europeans advancing goods to African traders on credit, apparently the earliest reference to the 'trust' system later standard in this region (Jones 1963, pp. 96–7), may be drawn from James Barbot's journal (p. 460/10–11). The omission is of material on the provenance of slaves and on Belli, taken from Dapper, pp. 135/4, 136/6, although not in *1688*.

[14] Barbot omits the French, whom he had included among the traders in *1688*, and adds the references to ivory and provisions.

[15] 'Fougue' is almost certainly a variant of 'Foko'. 'Focke' on the Robijn/ Roggeveen map can be read 'Foche', and the modern 'Fouché' can be traced back to an earlier 'Fouchee' (Jones 1963, p. 140).

[16] This informative and significant, yet also inaccurate and misleading statement is discussed in the Introduction (pp. xxxi–xxxii). Barbot's treatment of this region of the coast does not conform to the 'plan', since material relating

to 1697–1701 is not limited to the Supplement but included in the main text. James Barbot's purchase of slaves 'in two months time' involved a stay in New Calabar river of actually 3½ months. The text of the journals, as abbreviated and conflated by Barbot, appears above.

[17] The trading place of Andoni was mentioned, together with its slave trade, but was not actually named, in Dapper, p. 137/2, the information being repeated in *1688*. Whereas Dapper's name for the river was Rio Sante Domingo or Loitomba, it was named 'Rio Conde *of* [or] Andony' on the map in Robijn/Roggeveen 1685, whose 'R. St. Domingo' was only a creek off Rio Réal. 'Dony' was visited by James Barbot and Grazilhier in 1699, and again by Grazilhier in 1704 (*1732*, pp. 461/4, 462/18).

[18] For the name, see note 1.

[19] This is new information, there being very little on Old Calabar river in Dapper, p. 137/3, or in the text or map of Robijn/Roggeveen 1685, p. 29. The information most probably came from a 1698 voyage to Old Calabar casually mentioned by Barbot later (p. 465/2). 'Old Calabar' is modern Calabar. Sandy Point is still so named (*Africa pilot* 1967, p. 563); 'Salt-town' was evidently the salt-making settlement later known as 'Tom Shotts', on the western bank of the mouth of Cross River, and Fish Town was named on an 1820 map (Latham 1973, p. 50 and map).

[20] 'Parratt Island', so named by at least 1668 (Watts 1672), continues to have this name; 'Bennet's river' was presumably the eastern channel earlier unnamed. The incorrect clause, 'as I have said before', probably indicates that Barbot is extracting material from an unpublished account.

[21] 'We' evidently means the English. European trading at Old Calabar began only after 1650, with the English apparently predominating by the 1690s (Latham 1973, pp. 17–18).

[22] On the copper currency of Old Calabar, see Latham 1973, passim. Comparison with *1732*, p. 465/2, suggests that the price for a man slave, given as 'thirty-eight', is a slip for 'forty-eight'.

[23] This vocabulary, a mixture of bad Portuguese and elements from apparently various African languages, notably Efik (the correct 'Old Calabar language') and certain Bantu languages, is discussed at length in Hair 1992. Presumably a 'trader's vocabulary', perhaps for general use on a wider stretch of the coast (if not so muddled as to be useless), it is unclear which of his informants collected or assembled it and then supplied it to Barbot.

[24] This passage commends in advance the survey of New Calabar River in 1699 shortly to be described (*1732*, p. 463/4), and hence the map Barbot publishes (Plate 27, p. 463). It is perhaps inferred that Barbot had instructed his brother to make the survey, which he may well have done, after the disaster of two years previously Barbot now goes on to describe. The passage

also implicitly commends Barbot's own 'observations', made at various points, and hence his book.

[25] In 1699 James Barbot's ship had to manoeuvre slowly and with great caution to overcome the difficulties presented by the sand-banks at the bar of the river, both in entering and in leaving, although this was partly because the ship drew unusual depth – see his account above, pp. 457, 463.

[26] This passage reflects Barbot's growing (and justified) disillusionment with the Mortier map, and perhaps some awareness that it was based on very much earlier sources. The omitted section complains that the map shows a string of nearly 50 off-shore islands 'between the coast of Ardra and Rio del Rey', the islands representing, at the best, merely land cut off by channels joining rivers; and also that Cape Formoso is shown wrongly as being at 5°N, instead of at 4° 10'N.

[27] This is the only reference to the *Dragon* and its 1698 voyage to Old Calabar. 'Game' in the list of provisions is almost certainly a miscopying of 'yams'. The authority of the overall ruler of Old Calabar, the *obong*, being limited, the term 'king' was regularly applied to a range of chiefs, including the heads of the three component communities of Creek Town, Old Town and New Town (later Duke Town) and even to heads of 'wards' within them (Jones 1956, pp. 126–7; Latham 1973, pp. 49–50). Most of the names of 'kings' in this 1698 document can be identified with those of 'chiefs' attested in later sources. 'Aphrom' (normally 'Ephraim' in later sources) represents Efiom, the name of the ruling lineage of New Town, the title 'Duke Ephraim' being that of the head of the Duke ward, the dominant section of New Town during the eighteenth and nineteenth centuries. The name 'Duke' may derive from Abraham Duke, an English captain recorded as trading at Old Calabar in 1663 (PRO, T70/1222 'Calculation of cargoes exported, 1662–1699'). The 'Duke Aphrom' of 1699 may be identified with Efiom Okoho, according to tradition the founder of Duke Ward, since this man's grandson, Edem Ekpo, is recorded to have died in 1786 (Latham 1973, p. 11). Probably 'king Robin' was the head of Old Town, since later holders of this office had the same name (ibid.), while 'king John' appears to have been a title later applied to the head of the Ambo ward of Creek Town. 'Captain Thomas, at Salt-town' was probably the chief in later sources called 'Tom Salt' or 'Tom Shotts', and 'king Ebrero' was probably the same as 'the king of that place, called Jabrue' in 1704 (Snelgrave 1734, introduction; Latham 1973, p. 49, which also notes 'Dick Ebro' in the 1760s). 'King Oyo' was presumably the head of the Eyo ward of Creek Town, commonly called 'King Eyo' in later sources, even although local tradition holds that this ward was founded much later, the alleged founder being Eyo Nsa, alias Willy Honesty, who died in 1820 (ibid., pp. 46–7) – Barbot's evidence suggests that the tradition has been telescoped and that the ward's origins pre-date Eyo Nsa. The two chiefs described as 'king Agbisherea' were

705

probably the leaders of Ibibio communities in the hinterland of Calabar, since 'Egbosherry' was the name normally applied to the Ibibio during the eighteenth and nineteenth centuries (ibid., p. 50). For comparable details of African traders, commodities and prices at Old Calabar two generations later, see Hair 1990b.

[28] Despite what is said in the title, the printed account of this voyage includes material from a second journal, that of John Grazilhier, joint 'super-cargo' or trader with James Barbot, although this relates only to trading after arrival in New Calabar River. 'Abstract' indicates that John Barbot has extracted daily entries from the two journals, as proved by gaps, for instance, there are no entries between 13 and 23 March; and he almost certainly also abbreviated some entries. A few entries in James Barbot's journal are in the present tense, indicating that they were written up more or less on the day, but others were clearly written up at fairly long intervals, presumably from the ship's log or private notes; while it is possible that the journal was totally recast after the return to England in order to produce a more continuous account, perhaps at John Barbot's request. It is also noteworthy that this journal, unlike Grazilhier's, employs 'we/us' but hardly ever 'I/me', which may again indicate rewriting by James or John, or both. Indeed, it is almost certain that some degree of rewriting of both journals was done by John Barbot at least once, if not twice – and his paraphrasing may have included changing both tense and person. 'Ten per cent' traders were those traders independent of the Royal African Company who were permitted to trade under an act of 1698 modifying the Company's monopoly, subject to the payment to the Company of a duty of 10% of the value of goods exported.

[29] Omission of brief entries up to 25 January (p. 455/3–7): the islands of Madeira and Palma and capes Verde and Mesurado were sighted, and 'we built up our sloop on our deck'.

[30] On James Barbot at River Sess, see Letter 1/29, notes 1, 2, 9.

[31] Omission of brief navigational entries up to 8 April (p. 455/9–11), the ship passing St Andrew's River and Axim.

[32] For James Barbot at this fort, see Letter 2/3, Additional Passages (p. 455/14–18), being the material here omitted.

[33] For 'Damou' read Damon, although curiously the same error appeared in Loyer 1714: for the journal of Damon's 1698–9 voyage, see Roussier 1935, pp. 71–89. The term 'crown' was normally used to translate the French *écu* of three *livres* or francs, conventionally taken at the time to be equivalent to five shillings sterling, making the price of a slave therefore £12. 10s; but Damon records the price of a slave at Whydah as about 50 *francs*, which gives the much lower price of £4. 3s. 4d. James Barbot later indicates that the Portuguese captain supplied him with information about sailing conditions at New Calabar River (p. 457/19 below).

[34] The Dutch West India Company claimed, by virtue of the Dutch-Portuguese treaties of 1641 and 1661 recognizing Dutch sovereignty over the former Portuguese possessions in West Africa, the right to exclude the Portuguese from trading there, and required Portuguese ships to call at its headquarters at Elmina and pay a duty of 10% of the value of their cargoes in return for permission to trade (Verger 1968a, pp. 40–46).

[35] The dearness of corn at Cape Coast and Anomabu further East on Gold Coast is also mentioned subsequently. Scarcity of provisions may have been due at this time to the disruption of trade by wars – hens and corn, abundant and cheap in peace-time, becoming scarce and expensive in war-time, according to a contemporary (Bosman, pp. 240, 298). The same source stated that hens cost 4s. 6d for four in peace-time and double that in war-time, that a full-grown goat cost 12–13 shillings, and a hog of 90 pounds' weight £3 sterling (ibid., pp. 237–40). By buying provisions from the Portuguese ship, James Barbot seems to have obtained them relatively cheaply, since five ackies of gold was equivalent to only 25 shillings sterling.

[36] The 'interlopers of Zealand' were Dutch private traders infringing the monopoly of the Dutch West India Company. (One of the these ships was later met at the New Calabar River: p. 463/9). The total gold exports of the Dutch company were estimated at 1,500 marks, or £48,000, annually (Bosman, p. 6).

[37] In the 1690s, the price of corn on Gold Coast was normally 5 shillings for 1,000 stalks (yielding 5 bushels) in February, rising to £1 before the main harvest in August, giving a price of between 4 and 16 shillings for a 'chest' of 4 bushels (Bosman, pp. 297–8); and in April 1693 corn was bought at Cape Coast for 1½ ackies, or 7s. 6d., per chest (Phillips 1732, p. 208). By comparison, the price of 3 ackies or 15 shillings per chest does seem 'excessively dear'. But the price of corn was driven up by 'the great number of English Slave-Ships which yearly come to this Coast; for these not being as well victualled as we [the Dutch] are, they are obliged to buy Milhio, which yearly carries off many Thousand sacks' (Bosman, p. 298).

[38] 'Anischan' is presumably Anashan, but as this is West of Anomabu, 'east' must be a miscopying. 'Apong' is Apam, between Anomabu and Winneba.

[39] For James Barbot at Accra, see Letter 2/10, Additional Passages (p. 456/10–11), covering the material here omitted. On Gold Coast the ship had acquired 65 slaves, 'besides gold and elephants teeth'.

[40] Cape Formoso, the SW point of the Niger Delta, and East-by-SE of Accra, had to be rounded in order to travel further East. This navigational error cost the voyage over two weeks' sailing time, since the ship was able to work its way South to reach Cape Formoso only on 16 May.

[41] Omission of brief navigational entries up to 9 June (p. 457/1–7).

Because of hazy weather and rough seas the ship lay often at anchor, but eventually lost its sheet-anchor and was unable to recover it, so that it had to proceed with only one anchor.

[42] Omission of brief navigational entries up to 16 June (p. 457/10–13), the ship sailing and anchoring in rough weather. On 12 June they were 'in sight of a river', presumably Rio Sangama, the river immediately West of Cape Formoso, a river mentioned in *1732*, p. 378/4 – see Letter 3/6, note 2.

[43] The names of these various rivers between Cape Formoso and the New Calabar River are shown on the map of the river (*1732*, plate 27, p. 463), where they seem to have been copied, in corrupted variants, from a map similar to that in Robijn/Roggeveen 1685. River Nun is actually West of Cape Formoso, but Barbot and the maps equate it with 'Rio S. Bento' or River Brass, of which 'Rio Tilana, or St. Juan' was perhaps an eastern creek; 'River Oddy' is perhaps Odema Creek; St Nicholas, St Barbara, St Bartholomew and Sombrero rivers have still the same names (Teixeira da Mota 1950, pp. 296–300; *Africa pilot* 1967, pp. 521–2, 541–2).

[44] It is later claimed that no ship with so deep a draught (now said to be 'near fifteen foot') had entered the river before (p. 464/5). But Grazilhier on a later voyage discovered an alternative channel by which ships of up to 600 tons, twice the size of the *Albion*, could safely enter (p. 464/5–6).

[45] For an unlikely identification of King William, see note 48 below.

[46] 'Several do say that the depths do not remain constant, and that the second time they find them contrary to the first' (Robijn/Roggeveen 1685, p. 28).

[47] 'Treaty' here evidently means 'negotiations' rather than 'agreement'.

[48] This speech is italicized in *1732*. 'Pepprell' ('Captain Pepprell' in a later passage) is clearly a version of Perekule or Pepple, the family name of the kings of Bonny in the late eighteenth and the nineteenth centuries. Although sometimes explained in modern Bonny tradition as derived from 'pepper', the name was probably taken from Nicholas Pepperell, an English captain trading at Bonny in 1663 and 1679 (PRO, T70/1233, 'Calculation of cargoes exported, 1662–1699'). According to Bonny tradition, the first King Pepple was a wealthy trader who was called to the throne when the reigning king, Awusa, proved unable to finance a war against neighbouring Andoni: the 'Pepprell' of 1699, however, although influential, was clearly not king, and the family's accession to the royal office must therefore have occurred later than 1699. It has been suggested that 'Captain Pepprell' was the man who later became the first King Pepple, and that 'William' was the King Awusa whom he replaced, but since a ruler who died in 1830 is said by tradition to have been a son of the first King Pepple, this seems impossible – unless the traditional genealogy is telescoped (Jones 1963, pp. 105–7; Alagoa/Fombo 1972, pp. 10–11).

[49] Subsequently Grazilhier negotiated at New Calabar a slightly more favourable price, 12 bars for men, 9 for women (p. 461/1). In earlier times, slave prices in the river were reported in copper bars, the Dutch in mid-century paying 14–15 copper bars for a 'good slave' (Dapper, p. 136/1); and an English ship in 1678 paid 36 copper bars for a man and 30 for a woman (Davies 1957, p. 230). The ratio of four copper bars to one iron bar is given later (p. 460/5), thus the price of 12–13 iron bars, equivalent to 48–52 copper bars, represented a further substantial appreciation of slave prices over time. For details of slave prices in this area in 1700–1704, see p. 464/7–9 below.

[50] The formal 'breaking' of trade by the king or his representative, prior to which nobody was permitted to trade, remained standard practice at Bonny into the nineteenth century (Jones 1963, p. 135). For a similar practice at Whydah, see Letter 3/2, p. 135, above.

[51] Apart from Pepprell, the only chief who can be tentatively identified is the 'Duke of Monmouth', this being possibly an alternative name for the head of a Bonny 'house' usually called 'John Africa' but claiming a common origin with the 'Duke Monmouth' house of New Calabar – see note 57 below.

[52] For the local currencies of the area, see Jones 1963, pp. 92–4; Northrup 1978, pp. 159–64. It was earlier stated that imported copper bracelets formed the currency of New Calabar, although pieces of iron of a shape 'like a sting-ray' were used in 'Moko', that is, probably among the Anang Ibibio, North of Bonny (Dapper, pp. 135/9). The currency of iron bars reported in 1699 was therefore apparently an innovation of the later seventeenth century. The equivalence of one iron bar to 40 copper 'rings' remained standard, the rings forming the small change in local markets. The item 'Brass rings, ditto' makes no sense and must be garbled.

[53] The distinction between 'king's yams' and 'slaves yams' presumably refers to a superior and an inferior variety of yam.

[54] For customs duties at Bonny, later usually called 'comey', see Jones 1963, pp. 94–6.

[55] One of the few points where the present tense appears.

[56] Portuguese trade from Príncipe to New Calabar was noted in 1698 (Roussier 1935, p. 85): the traders were 'interlopers' inasmuch as they were breaching the monopoly claimed by the Dutch West India Company. The village of Bandy was presumably a dependency of the town of Bonny. A 'patterero' (Spanish *pedreiro*) was a small gun used mainly for salutes.

[57] The only chief listed who can be identified is the 'duke of Monmouth', 'Duke Monmouth' being attested in later sources as an alternative name for the New Calabar 'house' otherwise called 'Black Duke' (Jones 1963, pp. 134, 218–9). This house and the 'John Africa' house at Bonny (see note 51 above) claimed a common origin from the house of Owerri Daba, an early

king of New Calabar: the references here, providing evidence for the existence in 1699 of houses called 'Duke of Monmouth' at both Calabar and
Bonny, represent an important chronological indicator for the reconstruc-
tion of New Calabar history, since they show that the reign of Owerri Daba
and the split in the houses had occurred before that date. The king of New
Calabar in 1699, called 'Robert' in later passages, cannot be identified, but
was presumably one of the kings of the Endeme dynasty which is said to
have ruled between the time of Owerri Daba and the accession of the
Amakiri dynasty during the eighteenth century.

[58] The settlement of fishermen is presumably Ayama, which was known
to later sources as 'Fish Town' (Jones 1963, pp. 70–1). The 1699 map marks
a building on an island between River Bonny and New Calabar River and
adds the following inscription – 'The Grange a pretty high Building about
nth. at some distance are Cottages of Fishermen'.

[59] This information from James Barbot may have reached his brother
orally, rather than from a journal. The shrine was probably that, at Peter-
side, of Ananaba, a goddess connected with fertility and war. Since Bonny
worship in the nineteenth century involved a cult of the leopard, but not one
of the elephant, it is possible that the elephant skulls were merely trophies
and not objects of religious veneration (Jones 1963, pp. 42 and n. 14, 71).
For Bonny cults, see notes 66–7 below.

[60] The 'Hackbous' of the interior are undoubtedly the Igbo. 'Hackbous',
repeated on p. 462/9, may be a miscopying of 'Hickbous'. See note 5 above.

[61] 'Two market-days every week' probably alludes to a four-day cycle of
periodic markets, common in Igbo country (Northrup 1978, pp. 149–51).

[62] Despite this negative assessment, a Dutch ship arrived in the river
seeking ivory (p. 463/9), and by the 1700s substantial exports of ivory from
the area had developed, according to Grazilhier (p. 464/6).

[63] The brief account of New Calabar religion in Jones 1963, p. 70, does
not mention any worship of animals. Note 'Jou-Jou': the earliest reference to
juju cited in *OED* is from the late nineteenth century.

[64] Omission of one paragraph (p. 462/8) on the sacrifices of the Indians of
Virginia, obviously inserted by John Barbot.

[65] The 'I' of this paragraph appears to conflate James Barbot, the collector, and John Barbot, the illustrator and author. Plate 26 (p. 462) shows
three, or perhaps four, sea-shells, obverse and reverse, labelled A to C and
H, and three weapons apparently of iron, labelled E to G, but there is no
key. Shell C seems to be the same as a shell collected on Príncipe in 1679
(*1679*, p. 353), leaving only two or three shells from the New Calabar River.
The weapons represent the first artefacts from Igboland known to have been
collected and illustrated, and it is unfortunate that they do not appear to
have survived. Their size is difficult to estimate from the drawings, but one

seems to be a dagger, its scimitar-like blade having intricate patterns on the face, and its elaborate handle perhaps having a carved ivory element in its rings of decoration, while the second is more like a sword with an elaborate handle containing rings of decoration and a hand-guard (surely copied from a European model). The third object, badly drawn, is plainer and may or may not be of iron; it appears to be a long baton with a handle at one end and a square block at the other, and it may be itself either round or square; curiously, it has a tiny cross hanging from it, and whether it is really a weapon is uncertain. The importation to the coast of iron objects from the Igbo interior is noteworthy: in the nineteenth century, iron implements manufactured by Awka smiths were traded widely within Igboland (Afigbo 1973, pp. 84–5). The plate also contains a small profile of 'The English Isld. Redonda at abt. 5 Leagues distance' (one of the Leeward Islands in the Caribbean, seen by Barbot in 1679: *1679*, p. 379), and the illustration of 'A Sturgeon 6 Foot Long Caught in South[amp]ton River', copied from the penultimate page of *1688* (p. 288).

[66] In the present century the shrine of Oyubolo, the national deity of Andoni, was described as containing some 2,000 skulls (Alagoa 1972, p. 164). Eighteenth- and nineteenth-century sources describe a similar display of skulls at Bonny, at the shrine of Ikuba (see the next note). This has produced the argument that, since James Barbot referred to the collecting of skulls only at Andoni, it must have spread to Bonny during the eighteenth century, thus reflecting a brutalization of society caused by the Atlantic slave trade (Alagoa 1972, p. 154; Isichei 1973, p. 53). But given the unsystematic and fragmentary nature of James Barbot's ethnographic information, the argument from silence is unconvincing.

[67] The worship of the iguana deity, Ikuba, at Bonny is well attested in later sources, and the cult is said to have been introduced at an uncertain date from Andoni (Jones 1963, p. 71). The silence of the 1699 witnesses is a tenuous basis for believing that the cult had not yet reached Bonny, and tradition may well be right in suggesting that it was established there at a much earlier date (Alagoa 1972, p. 154; Alagoa/Fombo 1972, p. 6).

[68] The reference to Christian missionary influence in Andoni is signifi-cant. In 1691 the Capuchin mission in São Tomé received a letter from the 'King of Calabar' requesting a visit (Brásio 1985, doc.99). Whether there was any response is not clear, but it is possible that the letter had in fact come from Andoni rather than from New Calabar or Bonny.

[69] The previous section represents oral information supplied to Barbot by Grazilhier, but thereafter the text returns to James Barbot's journal (with some editorial comment in the first person inserted into the first sentence), although this change is not signalled in *1732*. For elephant-hunting by

Africans in the Niger Delta in the 1890s (the ivory going north, perhaps as in earlier centuries), see Hair/Pratt 1963.

[70] See note 5 above.

[71] This statement presents a difficulty, since the purchase of an anchor of eleven hundredweight from Captain Edwards was noted earlier (p. 460/16). The discrepancy may be due to the omission of part of the journal.

[72] With the exception of an extract on the price of provisions at São Tomé (p. 465/6–466/2 – an Additional Passage of Letter 3/12 below), and a summary of the description of the course from New Calabar to São Tomé (p. 541/8) an Additional Passage of Letter 3/20 below), this concludes the material from James Barbot's journal. There is therefore no account of the voyage of the *Albion* to America, and then to England, after leaving the New Calabar River. For more on this voyage – which produced probably the most detailed account of a slave-ship, in any century of the Atlantic trade, arriving at an African port, dealing with African traders, and embarking slaves – see note 74 below.

[73] Although Barbot refers to three voyages made by Grazilhier since the 1699 voyage, the detailed information given alludes explicitly to only two, in 1700–1701 and 1703–1704. On the 1700–1701 voyage Grazilhier called at Anobom (p. 466/4 – an Additional Passage of Letter 3/12), on the 1703–1704 voyage he visited Andoni (p. 462/17–463/2 above). The statement that the Dutch 'now' have the greatest trade at New Calabar implies that this represented a change, presumably since the 1699 voyage, although the intended emphasis may be on the increase in their trade specifically in slaves. However, the Dutch had been the principal traders in New Calabar River at an earlier date, in the middle of the seventeenth century (Dapper, p. 136/1).

[74] The references to extremely high mortality of slaves in 'all the ships', some losing one half, others two-thirds, has much influenced historians of the Middle Passage: Barbot has earlier given a more general reference to high mortality (p. 272/2, Additional Passage, Letter 2/21, above). Yet Barbot may well be over-generalizing, in order to make the *Albion* losses seem less exceptional: certainly the losses quoted were well above average. The argument of the passage is somewhat confused, inasmuch as the difficult circumstances of New Calabar are invoked as a sufficient reason for the losses in respect of 'all the ships', but in the case of the *Albion* 'ill management' is blamed. (If the 'I' of this final passage is John Barbot, as seems so, then, oddly, the complaint about 'the ill management of the principals aboard' would appear to indict Barbot's own brother.) The *Albion* did undoubtedly suffer considerable losses. It left Guinea with 648 slaves (p. 416/18), 65 purchased on Gold Coast and 583 at New Calabar (p. 381/3) – according to Barbot, but the departure figure allows for no deaths during the period of three months since the first slaves were bought, which is implausible. (Another English ship,

sailing from New Calabar in 1678, lost 55 of its 352 slaves before leaving the African coast: Davies 1957, p. 231.) Barbot eventually states that the *Albion* 'lost above three hundred slaves in the passage from St. Tome to Barbadoes; and the two hundred and fifty that survived, were like skeletons, one half of them not yielding above four pounds a head' (p. 547/5, an Additional Passage, Letter 3/20 below). Note that, if 648 slaves left Guinea and only 250 reached America, almost 400 died, rather than the 'above three hundred' mentioned, the difference presumably being the number of those who died between New Calabar and São Tomé. Note also that Barbot earlier gave the destination of the *Albion* on leaving New Calabar as Jamaica (p. 381/3), but in the passage just quoted has the ship arriving and disembarking its slaves at Barbados: perhaps there was a change of mind en route.

LETTER 8

Description of Rio del Rey and of the land between there and Camerones. The trade.

[.../pp. 168–169/...]¹

NOTES

¹ This Letter of 13 paragraphs is entirely from Dapper, pp. 137/4–138/10. Where Dapper states that the inhabitants of some islands are 'the most crafty/the worst (*slimste*) and often sail to the mainland', the 1686 printed French translation interprets this to mean that they go there to earn a living (Dapper 1686, p. 317), but Barbot interprets it, probably correctly, to mean that they raid the mainland. If Barbot composed this passage after 1686, it confirms that he was not following the printed French translation of Dapper, but making his own translation from the Dutch.

Cf. *1732*, pp. 384/1–386/3, which omits a reference to a chief called Sansom (borrowed by Dapper from Leers 1665, p. 313), embroiders throughout, and enlarges as follows. References to a fishery, a middle channel, and villages on both banks appear to come from a nautical guide, since they appear in Robijn/Roggeveen 1685, p. 29, and on the accompanying map. Other references, to the Dutch trading at Rio del Rey 'in yachts sent from Mina on the Gold Coast', and to the trade-goods including 'iron bars, ... bloom-colour beads or bugles, and purple copper armlets or rings, made at Loanda in Angola, and presses for lemons or oranges', may be from the commercial knowledge of Barbot himself or of his trading acquaintances, or may be mere guesswork – the last item looks suspiciously like a misunderstanding or misinterpretation.

LETTER 9

Description of Rio Camerones and of the coast of the Ethiopic Gulf between there and Gabon on the equator.

[.../p. 170/...][1] Rio Anger or D'Anger is fairly frequently visited by the Dutch, /p. 171/ who trade there in wax, ivory, and a few slaves. The English also go there sometimes. [...] It is precisely at [0°]60′ N. The inhabitants are always at war with each other, even although they have only one king. This diverts them from the trade, which is principally in ivory, and which is exhausted in three or four days. This is a general rule throughout Guinea as far as the ivory trade is concerned, eight to ten days in any locality being sufficient to collect all there is available, so that one might as well leave after that, without being delayed by the promises of the blacks, who always claim that more is coming. To trade in the river of Gabon, I mean that of Anger, you anchor your ship off Isle de Corisco and go into the river with a well-armed sloop, to trade from it out of chests.[2] [...][3]

Around this island [of Corisco], the sea is as calm as a mill-pond. You can careen a vessel here very easily, in 3–4 fathoms of water, on a clean bottom and close to the shore. Shoals to the SSE appear at low tide, the tidal rise and fall being considerable. The currents travel SSE-NNW. [...] Some say that the soil on this island will only support cucumbers, which grow very well here.[4] It is a fact that only 30–40 Moors, under a chief, are the island's inhabitants. They live near the NE point of the island, one league from the place where you obtain wood and water. They have some difficulty in bearing with the malignity of the air. In 1679 the commander of Mina sent there a colony of 40 men, who then built a strongpoint of turf and placed some guns on it, in order to protect themselves from the insulting behaviour of the Moors, who are as wicked as the air is bad. These new inhabitants had already raised some crops of foodstuffs, but then sickness took hold in their residence, daily carrying off some, and when the 40 were reduced to 23, who were themselves half-dead, they razed their fort and returned to Mina. According to the plan put to the commander, this colony was undertaken because it would be possible to grow there maize and various other crops, and bearing in mind, moreover, that the settlement would be in a position to supply provisions to

714

ships of that nation which found themselves there while on the return voyage to Europe. Otherwise the ships would have to seek out Isle du Prince, St Thomé or Cap de Lopo, a procedure delaying many vessels, which sometimes even fail /p. 172/to make these localities because of the winds and currents. / Remember, Sir, that when in need you will find in this island good water, wood, and plenty of game.[5] [. . .][6] I am obliged to stop at this point. I am, Sir, Your etc.

Additional Passage from *1732*

[pp. 387/6–7, 388/3–4, on the maps consulted]

From Rio de Boroa to Rio do Campo is fifteen leagues, in which space the Portuguese maps I have by me, made by the king of Portugal's command, set down four ports or villages, which no other European nation takes any notice of. . . . Only one modern English chart of this gulph hints something at this last port. . . / The same English map also mentions thereby, two round hills at some little distance of the coast. . . But the Dutch charts mention no places at all betwixt the rivers. . . . / [I am] obliged in this place to observe, as to the situation of the entrance of Rio de Angra, that the Dutch charts are different therein from the English; for the Hollanders do not only suppose the river to flow into the the sea of the bay, full south-west, . . . but also place the mouth of it, quite on the north side of the great bay, where the English place a little unknown river . . . / Another observation which occurs naturally on the same subject, is, that the Portuguese map I have already made mention of, places the mouth of Rio de Angra in the same latitude as the English does, that is, in the south angle of the bay, but makes it look full west; . . . but 'tis very probable the Dutch charts, being very ancient, are either ignorantly or wilfully mistaken, and rather the latter than the former; for we find by a multitude of instances, that they, for fear other European nations may rival them in the trade of the gulph, have thought fit to conceal from the publick view, the true exact map of that coast, which they have so long frequented; and to expose only such as are very deficient in the position of places.[7]

NOTES

[1] Omission of nine paragraphs, on River Cameroons and its peoples, and the coasts to the South. Barbot never visited this region; hence, with the

exception of two passages, the whole of this Letter is based on Dapper, pp. 138/11–140/1, and on two lesser sources. The compass directions and distances between localities are taken from a nautical guide, all being found in Robijn/Roggeveen 1685, pp. 30–31 or on the accompanying maps, while material on islands off the coast is from Marees, f. 119–119v.

Cf. *1732*, pp. 386/4–389/7, which, apart from the Additional Passage given below, embroiders considerably and adds a handful of alleged classical geographical references.

[2] Most of this passage on 'Rio Anger' (Rio de Angra, that is, Rio Muni and Corisco Bay), including all the omitted sentences, is derived from, or inferred from the printed sources (Dapper, Marees, the maps). But the references to wax and slaves, to the English trade, to the trading from a sloop, and to the general speed of ivory trading, appear to be original and, if so, presumably derive from an English informant. Barbot's map of the coast shows Corisco Bay in some detail, with Rio de Angra in the NW corner, whereas the map in Robijn/Roggeveen 1685 shows it in the SW corner. For earlier Dutch trading in Corisco Bay, see Jones 1983a, pp. 26–8, 68–70.

Cf. *1732*, p. 389/3–4, which apart from much embroidery, also revises the latitude to 2°N, incorrectly.

[3] Omission of two paragraphs, from Dapper, discussing Corisco Island.

[4] The first four sentences are partly inferred from slight references to reefs and careening in Robijn/Roggeveen 1685, p. 31; the omitted sentence, about the roadstead, is from Dapper, p. 139/14; and the reference to cucumbers is from Marees, f. 119v. But the references to tides and currents appear to be original. The island was called *corisco* (Portuguese for 'lightning flash') because of the storms there, so the calm waters were not always evident.

[5] The account of the 1679 Dutch settlement on Corisco is certainly original, Barbot presumably having obtained it from Verhoutert, the Dutch Director General at Mina, when he visited there in April 1682 (see Letter 2/5, p. 18 and note 9, above). A Dutch source of c. 1700 gave a rather different account of Dutch activities: 'At Great Corisco our Company had some Years past a setled Trading Lodge; but it lying too far distant, and not turning to a very great Account, we left it and have not been there since' (Bosman, p. 399).

Cf. *1732*, pp. 388/2, 3, 5, 7, 8, 389/1, which incorporates further references to Corisco in Bosman, p. 399, and also enlarges slightly on the description of the island, perhaps in part from a map, but certainly in part from Dapper, p. 389/14 (or from a source following Dapper, e.g. Du Plessis 1700, mentioned in *1732*, p. 390/4).

[6] Omission of two paragraphs, from Dapper, on islands in Corisco Bay and on the local language and customs.

[7] Barbot's 'Portuguese map' is the 1700 Mortier map of the region, which

716

his references exactly fit. It was in fact this map which drew on 'very ancient' sources, whereas the Dutch charts were mainly based on sources of c. 1650. The English map is probably that in the *English pilot* of 1701, which is only a redrawn version of the Robijn/Roggeveen map. Barbot's distinction between the Portuguese map and the later ones was well founded, the Portuguese map being on the whole less detailed and accurate as well as earlier, but his distinction between the Dutch and English maps was misleading, the differences being only the result of miscopying. Thus, when Barbot says at another point that the English map represents the coast differently from the Portuguese map (*1732*, p. 387/9), his reference to the English description exactly fits the map in Robijn/Roggeveen. Another comparison of the three map sources appears in *1732*, p. 389/7. The term 'Dutch charts' may or may not include the small map in Bosman, drawn c. 1700 but based on the earlier charts, which happens to show this coast fairly clearly.

LETTER 10

Description of Rio Gabon, and of the lands from there to Cap de Lopo Gonsalvez at the equator.

Sir, today I am to tell you about Rio Gabon and the lands between it and Cabo de Lopo Gonsalvez, where Guinea ends, and where I will conclude my description. [.../pp. 173–176/...][1] Cape Lopo is almost always uninhabited, having only 18–20 small huts for those residents of Olibatta who come there when there are any ships in the bay, in order to sell them the water and wood they need. They also bring a little wax and ivory, which they trade for knives (*bosmans*), bars of iron, and sheets, also a few other trifles. The wood is all cut into two-foot billets and a sloop can be filled for one iron bar. You also pay to the Chavepongo of the village a small due for anchorage and for water. The water is obtained in a large muddy marsh near the point of the cape. The water keeps well at sea and is better than that obtained on Isle du Prince and much better than that obtained on St Thomé.[2] [.../pp. 177–178/...][3]

I promised to describe Guinea to you, as exactly as I could. I believe that this is what I have now done, so I hope that you are satisfied with my punctual performance and that you will take account of my compliance with your wishes. I earnestly hope, Sir, that you have indeed gained some pleasure from reading my letters, as you have always indicated to me in your notes was the case. My commitment to you in this respect is now over, yet here is something which in good will I will add. I am preparing to provide you with a close description of the four Portuguese islands in the Ethiopic Gulf, otherwise the Gulf of St Thomas. These islands are too large and too near the continent to ignore, and their location in the gulf is such that it is almost impossible to navigate in this sea without having cause to halt at some of them (especially S.Tomé or Isle du Prince). This then, may it please you, will take up two letters, and these will follow as soon as possible. I am, Sir, etc.

Additional Passage from *1732*

[p. 396/1, on cam-wood]

The cam-wood is the king's peculiar trade there, and all sold by him at about twenty-five or thirty shillings per tun, according to the prime cost of the goods given for it in Europe, and sometimes not above twenty shillings per tun; he undertaking to provide by a certain time forty or fifty tun thereof, provided we lend him axes and saws to cut it down, eighteen or twenty leagues up the river of Olibatta, whence he conveys it at his own charge to the sea-coast; the country thereabouts having large forests of that sort of wood, the best whereof is that which grows on swampy grounds, being very hard, ponderous, and of the best red; whereas that which grows on high dry grounds is much lighter and pale. The better sort is at London esteemed near as good as the Sherbro cam-wood.[4]

NOTES

[1] Omission of 19 paragraphs on River Gabon and Pongo Islands, their navigation, peoples, social customs, trade and government, and on the topography of 'Cabo de Lopo Gonsalvez', i.e. modern Cape Lopez, including illustration no. (93) on p. 174, showing inhabitants of Gabon, the figures copied from Marees, plate 20, with minor background changes. In March 1679 Barbot's ship passed within three leagues of Cape Lopez (*1679*, p. 354): in 1682, although his own ship did not approach the cape, another ship of the same squadron called there briefly, to take in wood and water, but there is no evidence that Barbot obtained any original information about this locality from the crew, other than that they could obtain no provisions (*1732*, p. 573/1). His account of the Gabon-Cape Lopez region is therefore almost wholly derivative, being based mainly on Dapper, pp. 140/2–142/1

(p. 141 misnumbered '133'). Dapper drew on Marees, ff. 119–23, and Leers 1665, p. 314: untypically Dapper did not at this point use Davity 1660, which to Marees had added Brun 1624 (see Jones 1983a, pp. 71–3) as well as Marees's source, the important account of a Dutch visit to the cape in 1594, collected by Paludanus and printed in Linschoten 1596, ff. 3–5v. But Dapper also incorporated much original material, presumably of c. 1650. Barbot, however, also took occasional references directly from Marees, whose material was either from the 1594 visit or from another Dutch visit c. 1600. Barbot's summary of these sources abbreviates them but with few errors and little embroidery. The only derived material not from Dapper or Marees consists of coastal descriptions and navigational directions, and these appear to have been read off maps, particularly 'Paskaart van Gabon, Loango en Congo' in Robijn/Roggeveen 1685 (or a very similar map), with perhaps very occasional additions from the accompanying text in a nautical guide.
    Cf. *1732*, pp. 390/1–399/5 (for details, see note 3 below). For studies of this region in this period, see Patterson 1975, chapter 1 (which wrongly attributes the Linschoten account to 'D.R.' and cites Barbot uncritically), Bucher 1975 (not always sound on the sources and their transmission), and Gaulme 1981, esp. pp. 101, 172–9 (which correctly queries Barbot).

[2] This passage builds on Dapper, p. 142/1, 3, but adds elements which may be original information rather than embroidery – 18–20 huts, wax, bars of iron, knives, details of wooding and dues, the source and quality of the water. A marginal note in Barbot's 1678–9 journal stated that at Cape Lopez – 'One can easily obtain water, very good water, and trade with the blacks for wax in return for knives. See "exposition d'un voyage de Guinée"' (*1679*, p. 354). No printed *exposition* supplying a reference to Cape Lopez wax exchanged for knives has been traced (see the Introduction, note 71). Barbot's other additional details, if genuine, must have been obtained from an informant. Huts, trade in iron, and 'good fresh water' were earlier noted by Brun (Jones 1983a, p. 72) For 'Olibatta', a settlement on one of the mouths of River Ogooué, see Jones 1983a, p. 71, n. 163; Marees 1987, p. 241, n. 12; and for an English vessel cleaning and provisioning at Cape Lopez as early as 1677, see Donnan 1930, I, 231.
    Cf. *1732*, pp. 395/5–8, 11, which expands and alters, from Bosman, pp. 412–3, and Montauban 1696, p. 382 (a new source for Barbot – Montauban visited Cape Lopez in 1695 and his lengthy account was not available in English: Gaulme 1981, pp. 172–9). Barbot also enlarges on the trading, as follows – 'The great number of ships I have said resorts thither yearly, makes a pretty brisk trade for cam-wood, bees-wax, honey and elephants teeth ... all of which Europeans purchase for knives call'd Bosmans, iron bars, beads, old sheets, brandy, malt spirits, or rum, axes, the shells call'd Couris, annabas, copper bars, brass basons, from eighteen-pence to two

shillings a-piece; fire-locks, muskets, powder, ball, small-shot, etc.'. Again, if genuine and not merely embroidery, the additional information must have come from an informant, perhaps Grazilhier (see Letter 3/7, note 1, above). For the cam-wood, see the Additional Passage.

[3] Omission of eight paragraphs on Cape Lopez climate, government, food, dress, weapons, and religion, also a Gabon vocabulary, derived as stated in note 1. The whole account of Gabon and Cape Lopez is considerably enlarged in *1732*, pp. 390/1–399/5, partly by embroidery, but mainly by adding further material, most of it borrowed from Bosman, pp. 404–12, and Montauban 1698, pp. 381–94. Barbot also adds further coastal descriptions and navigational directions, partly from the 'Portuguese map', i.e. Mortier, partly from 'the English, French, Portuguese and Dutch charts I have by me', the English charts being those in the English version of Roggeveen/ Robijn or the copies in the *English pilot* (and perhaps also the map in the English version of Bosman). Barbot's original material, apart from the Additional Passage, consists mainly of very slight additions, including references to sucking-fish on the coast (noted further out to sea in *1679*, p. 359), 'coast trading vessels' from Gold Coast at the cape, 'long pepper and purslain' among available provisions, the views of 'modern geographers' on political boundaries, the way of rowing canoes compared with that of 'the Sierra-Leona Blacks', and ports, rivers and trade immediately South of Cape Lopez. From untraced sources are digressions on promiscuity in Peru and Portuguese ships being mistaken for birds. The following more relevant passage, most likely borrowed, has not been traced. "Tis hardly to be believed what a multitude of parrots there is; for sometimes they fly over the country in such numbers, as really seem to darken the air: they soar not extraordinary high, and may be easily shot, being good meat stew'd or boil'd, especially the young ones ...' (p. 398/2). Barbot concludes the section by announcing his intention to comment further on the various charts and also to supply a set of vocabularies. A profile of the cape is included on Plate 23 (p. 395), 'The Sight of Cape Lopo Gonsalvez att S.S.W. abt. 5 Leagues' showing a long, low, featureless, wooded headland. This drawing was not included in *1679* or *1688*, which raises doubts whether Barbot drew it himself: however, James Barbot in 1699, on passage from New Calabar to America, is unlikely to have approached the cape since his ship visited S. Tomé. For a poor contemporary profile of the cape, see Phillips 1732, p. 231.

[4] This passage, relating to Cape Lopez, supplies original information, almost certainly from one of Barbot's commercial acquaintances in London, Barbot having considered participation in the Sherbro cam-wood trade in 1698 (*1732*, p. 429/3). He had referred to the trade earlier (see note 2 above) and drawn attention to the English term for the timber (*1732*, p. 388/6). The forests of the region were mentioned by all earlier sources; a redwood dye for

body paint was noted in 1594 (Linschoten 1934, p. 7); in the 1600s, at Rio de Angra (Rio Muni), 'red trees like Brazil wood trees' suitable for fine carpentry were reported and a Dutch ship bought 'red sandalwood' (Jones 1983a, p. 26 and n. 28; Marees, f. 119v); and Dapper correctly gave the local term, *takula*, for the tree (*Pterocarpus soyauxii* or *Pterocarpus tinctorius Welw.*) (Dapper, p. 139/13). But Barbot's reference appears to be the earliest to an extensive and well-organized timber trade.

LETTER 11

Description of the island of Fernando Poo and the island of the Prince [Príncipe], in the Gulf of Ethiopia.

[. . .]¹ The inhabitants [of Fernando Po] are Moors like those of the continent opposite and apparently of the same kind as those of the Camarones.

Prince's Island (in Portuguese, Ilha de Principe) did not receive its name because a Portuguese prince discovered it, as /p. 179/ some claim, but because its revenue at one time was set aside to pay for the upkeep of a prince of Portugal.² It lies at 1°50′N, 34–35 leagues from the continent and at [blank]°[blank]′E, 30 leagues NE-by-N of St Tomé. It is a little smaller than Fernando Poo.³ You can see by its appearance from out at sea, which I have drawn very carefully, that it is extremely hilly, the hills steeply sloping on the South and East sides, so that it can be detected from 20 leagues away.⁴

[illustrations nos. (97) and (98), on p. 179, and nos. (99) and (100), inserted after p. 180, Príncipe Island]†

The main roadstead is on the East and in order to reach land there safely you pass between the island and Palm Island (a large round rock a cannon-shot's distance to the South, tree-covered like the island, the trees here chiefly palms, hence its name). You can pass within pistol-shot on either side without finding the bottom. There are two more rocks, small and flat ones, to the South, two leagues from land, where large numbers of birds nest, and another one to the North of Palm Island, this time close to land. You begin to find bottom to the East of this rock, and a little to the North of it, 30, 25 and 20 fathoms, with a bottom of sand, pebbles and shells. The roadstead is in the bay which faces East and is exactly at 1°30′. The

721

bay stretches WSW /p. 180/ for about one league, or a league and a quarter, beginning at the headland marked by the rock called Munster Rock. You can anchor there in 4–5 fathoms of water, on a muddy bottom. Small ships can go to the end of the bay, in front of the redoubt on the starboard side of the entry.[5]

This little fort is built of turf, with a palisade and 8–10 small canons very poorly set up. This minor entrenchment serves as the residence of the Portuguese governor, the buildings being all of wood, faced and roofed with boards. The garrison has a strength of 30–35 men, most of them Portuguese mulattos.[6] The town, or 'Povacaon', of Sto Antonio reaches to this little fortress, only a little stream separating them. The stream runs NNE, descending from the mountain where it has its source. The Povacaon is so situated that it faces the bay. It contains 250–300 houses, all of local wood and faced with boards like those in Holland. There are two main streets running parallel, and all the houses along these streets have balconies and lattice windows as in Portugal, which makes a good impression on the spectator. Each street ends, both at the East and at the West, in a small stream, and both streams run into the bay at the foot of the fort.[7] Two large churches serve the place, one dedicated to St Anthony, whose name the town bears, the other to the Mother of God, the former being at the West of the town and the latter at the East, the two facing each other.[8]

The countryside lying behind and around the town is all hilly and wooded, thus drawing to it the rain and storms very common here. Clouds often cover the hills, and thunder-storms are so frequent and so drastic that they make one tremble, since the caves and chasms echo the noise and make it terrifying. You might think that all this inclement weather would make the air impure and unhealthy, yet this is the locality within the Gulf where a sick man recovers most rapidly, and indeed where those from S. Tomé and the other islands are brought in order to recuperate most successfully.[9]

The land is very fertile and produces in abundance oranges, lemons, bananas, coconuts, sugar-cane – sugar itself being made here (albeit a very dark kind), rice, manioc, some vine plants, very many cabbages, salad-plants, vegetables of all kinds, pawpaws, good tobacco (better than that of Brazil), maize, millet, cotton (from which they make various goods), melons and pumpkins. They roast the bananas when green and eat them instead of bread. The flour from manioc they call *farinha de pau* or 'wood flour'. The forests contain large numbers of the flower we call *belle de nuit*.[10] The Portuguese inhabitants grow these products on their plantations in the hills. They have slaves to work the land. They also rear many kinds of animals – pigs, sheep, goats and the largest hens in Guinea. They sell all these provisions to the Europeans who come there for refreshment and to careen their vessels.[11]

Every ship pays 40 pieces-of-eight, either in cash or in merchandise, in duties to the Governor, in return for permission to water, collect wood and anchor.[12] The best place for watering is in the bay itself, where various torrents fall headlong into it from the hills around about. The water is excellent – yet very dangerous if too much is drunk without letting it stand for some days, as several ships have experienced, mainly in relation to the slaves. Firewood can be obtained anywhere you wish, for the forests come down to the sea, and the wood is very easy to cut. Sometimes scorpions are encountered /p. 181/ whose sting can cause nasty consequences. One of my crew was stung there (on my latter voyage), but fortunately there happened to be present a Moorish slave who seized the animal and crushed it over the wound, which was already beginning to swell up greatly. The man was cured before nightfall.[13]

The bay is also very rich in fish, the same kinds being caught there as in Guinea. There are many fish of the kind called 'Coffres de Mort' because they have flat underbellies and a sharp edge on their back, with two little horns. Here is a drawing of some of these fish.[14]

[illustrations no. (101), two fish, Orfie and Le Coffre de Mort][15]

The sea around this island and particularly in this bay nourishes an enormous number of sharks which are extremely dangerous, since some of them are so extraordinarily large that they can swallow half a human body. I say this, having seen it with my own eyes.[16]

You can hardly imagine how many monkeys (*singes*) one comes on in the woods on this island. They are ugly and they stink, as also do *marmots* (small monkeys). There are even larger numbers of grey parrots with red tails, who make a noise in the woods that goes right through your head. The natives catch both these creatures in snares. The monkeys have red fur and some of them have very amusing monkey tricks. The parrots are good eating. These are the sorts of parrots easiest to teach and they quickly learn to speak distinctly.

There are also many wood-pigeons, turtle-doves and several other varieties of birds, some unknown to us.[17]

The inhabitants are nearly all black (most of them being slaves). There are only 15 or 16 families of true Portuguese, and 50–60 mulatto families, although there are reckoned to be 3,000 souls in the island. All are Roman Catholics, but of the most superstitious sort. They consider St Anthony of Padua so much of an idol to worship that they swear only by him and – I may go as far as to say – place their hope only in him. They are never seen without their paternoster, their Agnus Dei, and their large rosaries around their necks. At certain times they hold processions at night by the light of many small lamps which they light on the balconies of their houses – which makes a pleasant sight. These lamps are orange skins filled with palm oil and with cotton [as a wick].[18]

The Moorish islanders are evil, the mulattos hardly any better, and even the whites are not too reliable. The last always carry a sword and a dagger at their side or in their hand. The Moors have only a knife on their hip in the manner of the peoples of Gold Coast, and wear only a simple cloth, to cover what honesty forbids to be seen. However, all these islanders are, in general, /p. 182/ less savage and cruel than they were at the end of the last century, when they massacred indiscriminately all those who fell into their hands. The Dutch experienced the consequences of so doing, among them Captain Olivier van Noort in 1598. This admiral, having set out from Holland for the Indies, was carried by the currents to this island, whose inhabitants came down to the shore to meet his men, showing them friendship, and under this guise they persuaded several of the crew of the boats to go to see their fort, where they slaughtered them without pity.[19]

On my latter voyage, one of my men was stabbed in the back with a knife by a black which he thought would cost him his life. But cannon were fired against them for two hours until they all gained the hills, and finally, on my return, I made peace with the Governor, Don Sebastien de Vaz, because all this had occurred in my absence.[20] It is not safe to put too much trust in them, for their poverty and their wicked disposition carry them into crime despite themselves. The best of all the islanders is a man called Antonio Soarez, who is Serjento-Major in the fort and with whom we lodged while revictualling.[21]

The women are much more agreeable than the men. The women

of the mulattos generally have a good figure, and to foreigners they are not markedly unkind. They dress in the Portuguese style and follow that way of life, being always shut up indoors and only coming out in order to go to mass, even then being veiled and followed by an old female on whom they lean.[22] The church service is taken by two Moorish priests, one of them ordained by the Bishop of Lisbon, the other by the Bishop of S. Tomé. As these two are the greatest idolaters in the world, it is surely enough to make anyone weep to see the expressions of superstition that they inculcate in these poor peoples. The whole of their religious worship is confined to a blind faith in rosaries, paternosters and the miracles of St Anthony.[23]

The islanders are sold pieces-of-eight, brandy, hats, shoes, all sorts of made-up linens, narrow and broad ribbons of various colours, taffeta and out-of-date brocade, thread in striking colours, gloves, white linen cloth, silk stockings, small images of saints that can be illuminated, old wigs, and spices. These goods are paid for with local products, which are reckoned at a set price in money. An *alquier* of manioc is charged at the rate of one *écu* and an *alquier* of rice at one *écu* and a half.[24]

I have unwittingly gone on at length in this description and perhaps it has bored you. However, I thought you would be well-satisfied to learn in detail about this country in case you ever find yourself there. I shall very soon conclude. In the last century the Dutch did what they could to become the rulers of this island. One of them called Cleerhagen began the construction of a fort at the southern point of the bay, but the people of St Tomé caused him to abandon the project. That is why the Portuguese thought it fitting to build a small fort near the town of Sto Antonio. To begin with, it was only a little redoubt made of turf, with a palisade. Also, since that earlier time, the Dutch go more often to Cap de Lopo and St Thomé than to Isle du Prince. I too hold that a ship requiring only water and wood should go straight to Cap de Lopo. I am, Sir, Your etc.[25]

Additional Passages from *1732*

[p. 401/3, 5–6, on the use of manioc]

. . . many also make it [sc.: bread] of the meal of the Mandioca root, which is only the tender part of the stumps or stalk of

725

Mandioca, a sort of bush, bearing long sharp-pointed leaves, five together in a cluster, at each end of the stalks, or small branches, as represented in the print [*margin:* Plate 16], of which there grow infinite quantities, if well cultivated.[26] These stalks they beat very well, and then dry in ovens, so that with a little more pounding they are reduced to a sort of coarse meal, very crumbly. When reduced to that, the Portugueses call it *Farinha de pao*, that is, flower, or meal, of wood. It is by many eaten by itself, dry, carrying it so in their pockets; but the more general way is to soak and knead it, with fresh water, into dough, and afterwards bake it on large iron or copper plates into thin round cakes, and so it serves instead of bread; which when new, is tolerably nourishing, and agreeable, tho' somewhat insipid; but when stale, is sorry food. The meal will keep good a long time, and is proper for long voyages. . . . / This is very remarkable in the Mandioca , that the sap or juice of the stumps is a cold and quick poison; and therefore all those who commonly use the meal of it, are very careful to press out that malignant juice, when they first prepare it, beating the plant quite flat, and then drying it in hot ovens. / Of this sort of plant every inhabitant of the island always takes care to have a sufficient stock in his plantation, not only to serve his own family at home, but to sell to the ships of their own nation and foreigners, which resort thither from the coast of Guinea in their return to Europe, or to America, either to careen, or to take in refreshments and provisions, as also for wood and water, of which more hereafter.[27]

[p. 402/5, on two fishes and a shellfish]

The one is a little fish, broad and quite flat under the stomach, and as sharp as the edge of a knife, on the back; with two short, thick, hard-pointed horns, on the head, just over the eyes, which are pretty large, and very round; and of that sort many are brought over into Europe, dried, and are called by the French *Coffre de Mort*. The other is a long fish like an eel, with a long snout, looking at a distance like a flute, the skin of its body of a darkish brown, spotted all over on each side, with two long rows of fine blue round specks, which is very good to eat. Among the variety of shells our people found there in the bay, as they fished every day with drag-nets, they presented me with an extraordinary large one, near eighteen inches long, much resembling a muscle, being all over grrnish'd [*sic*] on the upper side with a sort of hollow prickles, as the figure represents in the print [*margin:* Plate 23]; the meat whereof was very good and sweet, two or three being enough for any man at a meal.[28]

[p. 403/1–2, 8, on an episode in 1682 and two Portuguese officers]

At my last voyage to this island, I came thither in a yacht from Fida, to join our little squadron of three frigats, which were gone before me; I found our people at open hostility with the town, on account of our serjeant-major, who had been assaulted by a Black at the beach, and was very dangerously wounded in the back with a knife; which so incensed the commander in my absence, that he very rashly and inconsiderately moor'd two of the frigats, within reach of the town and fort, and fired so briskly for two hours together on both, that all the inhabitants and garrison fled to the hills, and had I not come in good time, he would have done them much mischief. But I set all things to rights, by an excuse to the Portuguese governor, Don Sebastian Vaz, my old acquaintance, promising that the directors of the French company should punish that officer, when returned to France, for his rashness in doing himself justice for the Black's having assaulted our serjeant-major so treacherously, before he had required it of him. / That governor is a gentleman of good fashion, and very courteous to strangers; besides him, I knew the major of the garrison, who is a good-natur'd man; all the rest are not to be regarded or trusted. / The major of the fort is the properest person to apply to and whom I employed to buy all our provisions; which he performed with a great deal of honesty and good husbandry . . .[29]

[p. 403/8–9, on trade at Príncipe and provisioning in the islands]

A small cargo well sorted, to the value of four hundred crowns, in all the above-mentioned goods, and of the cheapest sorts, will sell very well there, in exchange for provisions of the product of the island; but not for money, that being generally little known among the inhabitants, or at best, but little of it in the hands of a few of the principal men, who drive a little coasting trade about the gulf and Gold Coast of Guinea, making up the cargo of their sloops, of tobacco, sugar, some eatables, etc, of the growth of their planta-tions, and of some remaining goods of Europe, fit for that trade, which they sometimes get of Europeans, touching there in their return home, in exchange for necessaries of their voyage.[30] / We paid a crown for an Alqueire of Mandioca flower, which is very dear, the Alqueire being but a little above a bushel Winchester measure; and a crown and a half for one of rice; a crown for an hundred of coconuts: oranges, lemons, bananas, and all other fruits, plants, or poultry, are very cheap; and all of them useful and necessary in slave-ships especially, because they cure and preserve the slaves, as well as the ships crew, at sea, when duly administred to them, during their tedious passage to America. I would advise all persons trading to Guinea, not to neglect taking such refreshments, either there, or at S. Tome: for cape Lope and Annobon cannot afford them so good, the water of St Tome not agreeing so well with the slaves ... For tho' it seems to be a great expence to get it in a sufficient quantity, for so many men as are generally on board a slave-ship, yet the good it does them all, countervails the charge; it saves the lives of many slaves, and keeps them healthy, in a much better condition, and fitter for a good advantageous market in America: for this reason, few of the French ships trading to Guinea, miss touching, in their return from that coast, at one of those Portuguese islands ...

NOTES

[1] Omission of three paragraphs. Other than the sentence that follows, and the distance and direction from the mainland probably read off a map, Barbot's account of the island of Fernando Po (today renamed Bioko) is entirely from Dapper/*Eylanden* 1668, p. 71/3–5. In 1698 a Frenchman suggested establishing a French base on Fernando Po (Roussier 1935, p. 86–7). Cf. *1732*, p. 399/6–9.

[2] Unlike his account of the other islands of the Gulf of Guinea, Barbot's account of Príncipe is based largely on personal knowledge. His ship called there for eight days in March 1679 and his journal contains a fairly lengthy description of what he saw and learned at the main town, Santo António. In April 1682 he visited the island again, for at least several days, reaching it with some difficulty (*1732*, p. 541/5 – see Letter 3/20, note 9, below), but then having time to draw a view of the bay and town of Santo António. Barbot was encouraged to rely on personal knowledge since his normal sources, especially Dapper, had little to say about this island. The view of the naming of the island that Barbot corrects was that of Marees, f. 9, repeated by Dapper/*Eylanden* 1668, p. 72/1; he probably collected the alternative view from a general geography.

728

Cf. *1732*, p. 399/10, which reverts to the first view, probably influenced by Faria y Sousa 1698, p. 304.

[3] Echoes Dapper/*Eylanden*, p. 72/1, but varies the figures, probably from reading a map. In 1679, Barbot put the island at 2°4'N, and said it could be seen, in fine weather, from 25 leagues (*1679*, p. 351). Cf. *1732*, p. 400/1, which adds references to the discoverers of the island, from Vasconcelos 1641 and Faria y Sousa 1698 (as in *1732*, p. 11/5), and to its exact size, repeating information in *1679*, p. 351 (but changing the width from 4 to 5 leagues); and concludes – 'some of the mountains appearing like tables, and others peaked, like pyramids or steeples'. Barbot's map of the island, in *1732*, on Plate 24, p. 400, is an enlarged version of the island as shown on his general map of the Gulf of Guinea in *1688*; but whereas the general map follows contemporary maps, the map of the island has additional details, particularly in relation to the main coastal features, and these appear to derive from Barbot's personal knowledge.

[4] The 1679 journal contains two drawings of the island, and two more were added in *1688*, representing drawings made on Barbot's second visit (as stated, *1732*, p. 400/1). (i) 'Veue de l'ille' when lying 20 leagues ESE, with an inscription to the effect that a dome-shaped feature to the extreme left is not separated from the main island (*1679*, p. 351, noted but not reproduced); repeated as 'Veue de l'Isle du Prince de 18 à 20 Lieues E¼SE', but with the features reversed (*1688*, inserted after p. 180); repeated as 'Princes Island at E¼SE distant abt. 18 Leagues', in *1732*, on Plate 24, p. 400: (ii) 'Ille du Prince veue de la mer E.N.E. 6 à 7 Lieues', with inscriptions A-D, referring to the main island, a small island (Palm Island) described as twice as large as Diamond Rock at Martinique (see *1679*, p. 373), two islets 3–4 leagues out which nevertheless seem close to the 'diamond' when approached from the sea, and the passage to the roadstead between the 'diamond' and the main island at 18–20 fathoms and half a league from the island (*1679*, p. 301, noted but not reproduced – in the manuscript it occupies the margin of p. 89, up and down the page); repeated on a larger scale and from a viewpoint slightly further West, as 'Veue de l'Isle du Prince de 2 [sic] Lieues L'Islot à Palmistes étant a ESE 2 Lieues de Terre', an inscription indicating a channel of 18–20 fathoms up to the land between Isle à Palmistes and the main island (*1688*, between pp. 180–181); the original repeated as 'The Sight of Prince's Island at E.N.E. about 6 Leagues distance from Sea', and a statement indicating a passage outside Palmito Island (*1732*, on Plate 23, p. 395); the *1688* view repeated as 'The Prospect of Prince's Island abt. 3 Leagues distance', with an inscription indicating 'a passage for the biggest Ships' inside 'Palmitt Isld.' (*1732*, on Plate 23, p. 395): (iii) and (iv) 'Veue de l'Isle du Prince de [blank] Lieues', 'Veue de l'Isle du Prince de [blank] Lieues au [blank]' (*1688*, p. 179), two rather crude views from slightly different directions, with the high land to the left.

In 1679 Barbot's ship sailed almost round the island, and he noted that it could be recognized by two sharp peaks resembling steeples. (An earlier visitor referred to 'very high rocks like high towers', Jones 1983a, p. 73). At least one of these peaks is shown, in a precipitous landscape, on all the drawings, while all except (i) in the journal appear to show Palmito Island to the right, which according to Barbot's map (*1732*, on Plate 25, p. 400) indicates views taken from the West, broadly correct. But the stated distances and exact directions in Barbot's various drawings and versions are impossible to reconcile.

[5] Barbot did not describe the anchorage in such detail in *1679*, p. 347; and a briefer account appeared in Robijn/Roggeveen 1685, p. 30. Munster Rock is shown on Barbot's map of the island.

Cf. *1732*, p. 400/2–3, which elaborates slightly ('Palm Island may be seen at a great distance west, copling up like a hay-reek'), and adds a toponym from the Mortier map of the Gulf of Guinea, Ilha de Caroco.

[6] In 1679 Barbot's ship exchanged a gun salute with the fort, where the governor lived; but at this date Barbot described the fort even more scathingly – 'a poor thing, having only seven very badly set up canons, no walls or bastions, only a little wooden bridge over a stream' (*1679*, pp. 347, 352). Dapper had a brief reference to a low breastwork and five four-pounders (Dapper/*Eylanden*, p. 72/2). In 1607 it was said that the fort was of wood because the island lacked stone and lime (Brásio 1955, p. 382).

Cf. *1732*, p. 400/4.

[7] Based on the description of the town in *1679*, p. 352, where the number of houses is given as 350–400 and reference is made to the view of woods, hills and a wooded peak 'more than two leagues high' – the highest peak is actually at 920 m. 'Povacaon' is Barbot's version of Portuguese *povoação* 'settlement', but since the term was for long used as a name for the chief settlement on São Tomé, this may be a slip by Barbot.

Cf. *1732*, p. 400/4, which adds a drawing of the town. This 'draught of the town of St Anthony, taken from the middle of the bay' shows a wide bay, high wooded hills and a small town near the shore, and the two churches and the fort are marked. Since this drawing does not appear in *1679* or *1688* it is possible that Barbot drew it for *1732* from memory. For a drawing apparently of the same bay and settlement a century earlier, see *Begin* 1645, (Olivier van Noort, between pp. 2 and 3).

[8] In 1679 Barbot mentioned four churches, not two, but only named the church of St Anthony, said to be the cathedral (*1679*, p. 352).

Cf. *1732*, p. 400/5, which adds that the two churches are 'decently adorn'd' and that there are two chapels.

[9] Cf. *1732*, pp. 400/6, 401/1, which adds that the town itself is unhealthy,

and that gun-shots also re-echo – in 1679 Barbot's ship and the fort saluted each other with three shots each (*1679*, p. 347).

[10] The first sentence partly echoes Dapper/*Eylanden*, p. 72/3–4, while coconuts, bananas, much rice, a little maize, manioc and *farinha de pau* (a term still used) in large quantities, pawpaws, and a little tobacco, but not sugar, were noted in *1679*, p. 351 (note that in a footnote '*cocos*' were defined, too loosely, as *noix de palme*). Presumably the other products were noted in 1682. The flower is the 'Marvel of Peru' (*Mirabilis jalapa*).

Cf. *1732*, p. 401/2–5, 402/9, which adds 'two sorts' of oranges and lemons, 'European grain', purslain, and ' a prodigious quantity of palm-wine, which is very excellent' (repeating *1679*, p. 351); also adding that there is least of 'Indian wheat', i.e. maize, and that the 'fine purple flowers' have this name in French 'because they have a charming freshness in the morning, and seem almost withered in the day-time'. Finally, Barbot adds a long passage on the use of manioc: see the Additional Passages at the end of this letter. Elsewhere Barbot states that he ate cooked bananas, and manioc 'without mishap', at Príncipe (*1688*, p. 2/187; *1732*, p. 201/8).

[11] Some echoes of Dapper/*Eylanden* 1668, p. 72/3, but Barbot had noted the animals and farm slaves (used by some Portuguese, they themselves being 'extremely lazy') in *1679*, p. 351. For ships provisioning at Príncipe, see a 1683 comment in Jones 1985, p. 57. In 1698 a visiting Frenchman reported that the Portuguese used Príncipe as a collecting point for slaves brought from the mainland in small vessels (Roussier 1935, p. 85).

Cf. *1732*, p. 401/6–7 (the first paragraph in Additional Passages above), which adds that the hens 'well fed are pretty good and sweet; and sell [in] abundance to sea-faring men, especially to the French, who above all other Europeans touch there very often with slaves: the English and Dutch generally furnishing themselves at cape Lope, or St. Tome or Annobon, according as the strong tides of the gulph, which commonly flow eastward do drive them'. It concludes with a reference to why the Dutch do not visit Príncipe, from Bosman, p. 400.

[12] In 1679 Barbot's fellow officers met the governor and were allowed to water and to collect wood: dues are not mentioned, but before the ship left the governor demanded and was refused a quantity of powder (*1679*, pp. 347, 349, 350).

Cf. *1732*, p. 402/1, slightly enlarged from the journal.

[13] In 1679 60 barrels of water were obtained in one day, working on each side of the bay, while four men cut wood at another locality; and the water was highly praised (*1679*, pp. 349, 351).

Cf. *1732*, pp. 402/2–3, which adds from the journal the 60 barrels, and also some new minor details about the exact locations of watering and wooding: it also enlarges on Barbot's second thoughts about the quality of the water, as follows. 'The water is extremely sweet, but so very cold, that kept till six or eight days, it is apt to breed the cholick or pains in the stomach; especially among the slaves, if they drink much of it at a time, as I found by experience in the Emerillon', i.e., in 1682. He also states that the scorpion episode (the sailor now stated to have been stung in the heel) took place 'at my last voyage in the Emerillon man of war'.

[14] In 1679 some of the crew fished in the bay with drag-nets, and Barbot recorded their catching a large shellfish, 'a mixture of an oyster and a mussel, with little tubes on the top, reddish flesh', as well as the two fish now to be described – he made drawings of all three (*1679*, pp. 349, 353, 355).

Cf. *1732*, p. 402/4, which enlarges – 'only I observed among them [the fish] two different and extraordinary species, which are seldom seen at any other of those parts, that I know of; for which reason, I drew them as near the life as my skill would permit, and caused them to be inserted in the cut which gives the prospect of the town St. Antonio [*margin:* Plate 24]'.

[15] Drawings of two fish in *1679*, p. 356, repeated here, were repeated again on *1732*, Plate 24, p. 400, with an added cross-section of one fish. The original inscriptions read as follows (translated). 'Orphie. The sailors call it "orphie". Its scales are brown and spotted with blue circles. Its belly is white and slimy like that of an eel. Has a rat's tail. Many here and good eating.' 'This little fish is drawn natural size. Has a head like that of a pig with two horns, flat under the belly. The Dutch call it "coffre de mort" because it is wide and flat under the belly and narrow and sharp on the back.' The later inscriptions are briefer, but the *1732* version states that the 'orfie' is 18–20 inches long, and the fish 'Call'd by the French Cofre de Mort' is drawn 'of natural Bigness', at 12 cm long. For lengthier descriptions, see the Additional Passage. The drawing of the upper side of a sea-shell in *1679*, p. 353 (not reproduced) was not repeated in *1688*, but appeared in *1732*, Plate 23, p. 395, captioned 'Large Muscles', and again on Plate 26, p. 462, without a caption, in each case together with a drawing of the lower side, perhaps indicating that Barbot had preserved the actual shell.

[16] In 1679 Barbot noted sharks in the bay and witnessed them seizing bodies of dead slaves thrown overboard, in one instance cutting the body of a youth in two (*1679*, pp. 349–51).

Cf. *1732*, p. 402/6, where the shark makes 'but one mouthful of a young boy'. However, earlier Barbot had remarked that 'when we threw a dead slave into the sea, particularly about the mouth of the bay of Prince's Island in the gulph of Guinea one shark would bite off a leg, and another an arm, whilst others sunk down with the body; and all this was done in less than two minutes; they dividing the whole corps among them so nicely, that the least particle of it was not to be seen, not even of the bowels' (*1732*, p. 225/ 8 – but some elements in this passage are copied word for word from Bosman, p. 282).

[17] In 1679 Barbot noted 'incredible' numbers of monkeys and grey parrots and bought some of each; but the further details are not in the journal (*1679*, pp. 350–51).

Cf. *1732*, p. 402/7–9, enlarged in details – 'apes and monkeys ... long, brown, reddish hair ... sold there to foreigners, at a piece of eight each, in exchange for haberdashery wares, or old linen rags, or sailors clothes, especially old hats, which the natives much covet ... snares, or gins, set on the trees ... learn to talk and whistle'. Curiously, the parrots become 'blue, with fine scarlet tails', perhaps out of deference to Bosman, p. 271, 'all the parrots here ... are blew'.

[18] In 1679 Barbot noted that the inhabitants were all mulattos or blacks, some originating from Angola, others from Brazil, apart from a few whites from Lisbon, and that they spoke three sorts of language, Portuguese, *neigre*, and that of the Creoles of the country; as regards religion, he merely noted that all the slaves were baptized and very superstitious, as they had learned from their masters (*1679*, p. 352). The numbers of whites and mulattos may have been an updating of figures in Dapper/*Eylanden* 1668, p. 72/4. St Anthony of Padua was Portuguese and is known in Portugal as St Anthony of Lisbon – hence the name of the town on Príncipe. For official instructions to clean the streets before religious processions, see Castelo Branco 1970, pp. 101, 175, etc. Women of Príncipe wearing only a loincloth but with large strings of religious beads around their necks were shown on a drawing of c. 1600: *Begin* 1645, (Olivier van Noort, between pp. 2–3).

Cf. *1732*, pp. 402/10, 403/3, 6–7, which adds that 'the Blacks, both freemen and slaves, call themselves Christianos Novos, that is, new Christians, or converts', but omits the important specific reference to Portuguese Crioulo, substituting, after Portuguese, 'two or three languages of their own'. On the local Crioulo, see Morais-Barbosa/Ferraz 1975; Bal 1979.

[19] In 1679 Barbot noted only that it was not wise to stay ashore after dark, because most of the inhabitants were untrustworthy – having a wicked countenance and being as poor as Job, they were given to robbery and violence, in particular small groups of them seizing the hats of visitors, as he had learned from experience (*1679*, p. 352). The hat-stealing is not mentioned in *1688*. Barbot's reference to Dutch experience is not from Dapper. For Europeans having their hats snatched by Africans elsewhere in Guinea, see Almada 1984, chap. 9/20. For Olivier van Noort's visit to Príncipe, see *Begin* 1645, (Olivier van Noort, pp. 2–3).

Cf. *1732*, pp. 402/10, which restores the hat-stealing, but now even in daytime.

[20] A clearer and more detailed account of this episode was supplied in *1732*, p. 403/1–2 – see the Additional Passages.

[21] In 1679 Barbot's ship dealt with António Soares de Novais, 'a very

honest man', who was in fact a member of the town council of Santo António (*1679*, pp. 349, 350; Castelo Branco 1970, pp. 23, 29).

Cf. *1732*, p. 403/2, 8.

[22] In 1679 Barbot noted that the women were shut up, but that some, although swarthy, were well made and had a good appearance – they walked lightly but with dignity, and came out only on great feast days (*1679*, p. 352).

Cf. *1732*, p. 403/4–5, which distinguishes between the Portuguese women who are 'very civil' and the mulattos who are 'much kinder'; and it adds the following sentence. 'They eat after the Portuguese fashion, and have in the middle of their rooms, even above stairs, a large square hearth, to boil and dress their victuals, and scarce a chair or stool to sit upon, but only a few pewter or wooden utensils and earthen-pots, with sorry poor beds, for all the furnitire of their houses.' Barbot had earlier stated – 'I have seen many such hearths in the middle of the Portuguese houses in Prince's Island' (*1732*, p. 129/1).

[23] In 1679 Barbot noted merely that two black priests, ordained by the Bishop of Lisbon, officiated at the cathedral church of St Anthony (*1679*, p. 352).

Cf. *1732*, pp. 400/5, 403/6).

[24] In 1679 Barbot's ship paid for provisions with brandy, cloth, glass beads, hats, old shirts, 'etc' (*1679*, pp. 351, 353).

Cf. *1732*, p. 403/8–9, which makes the payment for provisions solely to António Soares de Novais, and adds to and elaborates on the list of goods, as follows: 'coarse and middling hats . . . old and new shoes . . . several sorts of striped and plain coloured silk . . . the islanders being fond of all that is gaudy, and of pieces of eight' – but omits the statues of saints. It continues with a passage on the trade of Príncipe and provisioning in the islands, for which see the Additional Passages above.

[25] Barbot repeats a reference to the fort (see p. 180) but now implies that changes may have taken place since he last saw it, in 1682. The brief Dutch conquest of the island was in 1598, under Juliaan Cleerhage and Gerard Strybos (Marees, 1912 edition, pp. lxii-lxiii). The source of Barbot's information on the Dutch conquest is untraced.

Cf. *1732*, p. 400/4 ('the latter end of the last century', in relation to the century repeating *1688* in error), which also has traces of Bosman, pp. 399–400.

[26] This clumsy description of manioc (later more commonly known in West Africa as cassava) appeared in a footnote in *1679*, p. 351, and was probably copied from a botanical work. Plate 16 (p. 200) includes what appears to be an original but inept drawing of 'The Mangnoc [*sic*] Tree in Seed'. It is not the same as the drawing of a manioc plant in Nieuhoff's

account of Brazil, in Churchill 1704, II, 135, which Barbot had most probably seen. It is notable that Bosman, describing the mainland coast in the 1690s, nowhere mentions manioc (but see Jones 1985, p. 76): the earliest mention of manioc in Africa appears to be in relation to Angola in the early seventeenth century (Jones 1983a, p. 47).

[27] On his first voyage Barbot noted manioc and its meal both at Príncipe and in America and he referred to the poison in the plant (1679, pp. 351, 368 'cassavre', 373). Dapper had earlier noted manioc at Príncipe (Dapper/ Eylanden, p. 72/3), but Barbot's exposition of its preparation and use surprisingly does not draw on Dapper's detailed account of manioc in Angola (Dapper, pp. 227/4–228/2), nor does it draw on Nieuhoff's very full account of manioc in Brazil (Churchill 1704, II, 133–5). The omitted section of this passage refers to manioc in Brazil and on the Amazon, and Barbot mentions manioc again in his account of localities in America, sometimes repeating part of this passage (1732, pp. 552/9–10, 564/4–5, 661/8). He may have observed the processing of manioc at Príncipe, but alternatively his description may have been drawn from one of his sources on America. Elsewhere he records the use of manioc on slave ships (1732, p. 547/1).

[28] The first fish is not the real orphie but Fistularia tabaccaria; the second fish is 'poisson-coffre', Ostracion tricornis; and the shellfish is Pinna rudis (Debien 1979, pp. 391, n. 161; 392, nn. 166–167).

[29] Three ships set out from Whydah, probably in April 1682, but it seems that the Jolly, the largest vessel and probably the ship of the expedition commander, failed to reach Príncipe, instead touching at Cape Lopez before sailing on to Martinique (1732, p. 573/1). Barbot, following after in a sloop or 'yacht', found the two vessels firing on the town, and it seems that he took charge of the situation. As senior agent of the company he perhaps outranked the ships' commanders, but even if so, he presumably took charge only in the absence of the commander of the Jolly. Barbot implies that he had met Sebastião de Vaz, his 'old acquaintance', on his first voyage, but the governor of Príncipe in 1679 was Tomé da Silva d'Acosta and the journal does not mention Sebastião de Vaz (1679, p. 347).

[30] In 1679 Barbot reported that two little ships were being fitted out by Campo Barreto at Príncipe for the Guinea trade (1679, p. 347). According to a Frenchman in 1698, the Portuguese of Príncipe conducted a coasting slave trade in 'four or five small boats of 50–60 tons' (Roussier 1935, p. 85).

LETTER 12

Description of Isle S. Tomas [São Tomé], on the equator.

Sir, I shall devote the whole of this letter to an account of the /p. 183/ island of St Tomas or St Thomé.¹ [. . .]² The extraordinarily fertile land there incited the Portuguese to claim it for their country and to fortify it, making it into a colony. [..]³ From the South this island appears to be high land, sharply pointed in some places and rounded in others. On the East side it drops down to the sea. Here is a view of it from nine or ten leagues to the South.⁴

[illustration no. (102), 'Isle St Tomas']

You pass Islettes d'el Cabre [Goat Islets] and some others situated towards /p. 184/ the SE, in 12 fathoms. The coast is clear of obstructions and can be closely traversed in order to reach the roadstead in the bay. You anchor at the NE point in three and a half fathoms at low tide and five at high, with a sandy bottom, the fort to the SE and two little islands a league and a half away. The roadstead lies NE and SW. The best place to slip anchor is to the South, because the wind nearly always blows from that direction.⁵ [. . ./p. 185/. . .]⁶

The forms of colic here are very severe, as are head-aches, and these disorders are treated as in Guinea. They are so violent that they can kill a man driven to distraction by them in a matter of three or four days. Their cause can be attributed either to the voluptuous lusts of black women or to a chill caught when too hot. Some hold that the consumption of too much sugar or coconut-juice is responsible, others that the evening dew or not wrapping up at night are to blame. Hence, Sir, it is as well to guard against all such acts, for you would scarcely believe how many men from the various nations who go there have perished, and how many still die each day. Those on the ships – by that I mean those who remain on board – are much less exposed to the diseases rife there, as the sea air is far less noxious than the land.⁷ [. . ./pp. 186–188/. . .]⁸

A small river which flows into the sea near this fort [at the town of Povoação] supplies it with the best water on all the island and the most suitable to be transported thence on a long voyage – still and all, not healthy water, for we [have to] draw it at night rather than in

736

the daytime because then the stream is full of slaves and animals who come there for necessary purposes and who throw into it all sorts of dirt. This river also goes through part of the town.[9] [.../p. 189/ ...][10]

Additional Passages from *1732*

[p. 406/5–6, on watering slave-ships]

The fort ... is supplied with water by a little river that falls into the sea, and is the best water in all the island, and the most proper for ships for long voyages, if taken in the day-time: but being then always full of slaves, and beasts resorting from all parts of the town for water, and to wash themselves, and often ease their bodies there, and throw in all sorts of filth, we are obliged to fill our casks in the night, when it is free from all that nastiness which makes it less agreeable to our men and slaves, being perhaps too raw, as it comes from the hills, till warmed by the sun: for it appears by experience, that the water at Prince's Island and cape Lopez proves much wholesomer for our slaves and ships crews at sea. Tho' this of St. Tome keeps pretty well in casks, after it has once stunk, and is recovered. / I would advice such as resort thither to victual their ships, to water in other places in the island, or in the middle of the town, through which the river runs, tho' it will cost double the labour and charges. For it is so essential a point, that the water taken aboard in slave-ships should be of the very best and cleanly, that it often contributes very much to save or destroy whole cargoes of them, according as it is good or bad; and rather than to run a risque, I would advise them to go to cape Lope, Prince's Island, or Annobon for it; because many ships have lost the best part of their compliment of slaves by that water, in their passage from thence to America.[11]

[pp. 465/6–466/2, on prices and dues]

The principal person to be made use of there, in 1699, to contract for provisions, etc, was one Raphael Lewis, an eminent Portuguese merchant; but at the time when the Albion frigat was there, all sorts of provisions were excessive dear, and European goods very cheap, as for instance. A thousand ears of Indian wheat four pieces of eight, or four Akies. Pease two Akies a bushel. Farinha da Pao, or Mandioca meal, two Akies and a half a bushel. A

737

hundred coconuts one Akie. A middle-sized hog, four Akies; the largest, six pieces of eight. An ox, twelve pieces of eight, and a very poor one eight. One Alkier of beans, one Akie, at that time, by reason of the great drought. / The prices of European goods were, One piece of sayes, ten Akies. Perpets, four Akies and a half. Beads, three bunches two Akies. Proportionably for other goods, being scarce the first cost in Europe. Note, that an Akie of gold is valued there at one piece of eight. / The Albion frigat paid the following dues in 1699. To the governor for anchorage forty-one Akies. To the captain of the sea, one Akie. To Raphael Lewis, for his commission, ten Akies. In all fifty-two Akies.[12]

[p. 466/3, on a 1709 French attack on the island]

Paris Gazette, November 9, 1709. We have received advice, that the sieur Parent, commanding four frigats, armed for privateers, after having taken the English fort in Gambia river, in Africa, and a ship loaded with Black slaves, afterwards sailed thence to the island of St. Tome, belonging to the Portugueses, and had taken the town and the castle, defended by above three thousand men well armed, took there a great booty, and carried away thence six ships of several nations, richly laden.[13]

NOTES

[1] Barbot does not claim ever to have visited São Tomé Island, but in April 1682, as his ship passed by, he made a drawing of it. His account of the island is largely based on Dapper/*Eylanden* 1668, pp. 73–80, which he paraphrases and also embroiders at points, and he adds a few sentences from Villault, pp. 401–5. Despite Dutch accounts of post–1600 visits to the island and their occupation of part of it during the 1640s – producing material in Dutch on the island, including that in *Begin* 1645 (Wybrandt van Waerwijck, ff. 3v–4, with map, translated in *Receuil* 1702–6, II, 564–8) and in Leers 1665, pp. 314–8 – Dapper's account is mainly traditional and outdated. (Dutch ships were unwelcome at the island by the 1660s, because of the earlier Dutch depredations: Villault, pp. 401–2.) Thus, apart from the Leers material, Dapper follows closely Davity 1660, pp. 629–634, which in turn is largely based on the excellent account by an anonymous Portuguese pilot who visited the island in the 1530s and 1540s (as first published in Ramusio 1550, I, 125–9). Barbot's occasional errors of translation include *water-zucht* 'dropsy' translated as 'flux de sang' (*1732* 'bloody flux'), which makes more sense but is inexact; and the cure is given as palm-oil instead of

coconut-oil. Some of the minor additions are mere verbiage or attempts to relate the information to earlier material, accurate or inaccurate (e.g., the date of discovery is given as 1452). A few sentences are not from any traced printed source (Barbot does not draw on the account in *Relation* 1674, pp. 21–2). Probably Barbot collected oral information, and conceivably one of his informants was Julião de Campo Barreto, a former governor of the island, with whom Barbot had some contact at Príncipe on his first voyage (*1679*, p. 349; *1688*, Letter 3/10, p. 2/38; *1732*, p. 407/5). In September 1698, Barbot's brother's ship, after sailing from Calabar, called at São Tomé to provision; and Grazilhier, an officer on this voyage, may also have called at São Tomé during three later voyages out of Calabar, before he talked to Barbot in 1705 (*1732*, pp. 464/6, 465/1). Both men may therefore have provided Barbot with further information for his revision. Barbot does not at this point borrow from Phillips 1732, pp. 232–3.

[2] Omission of one paragraph, on the position, size and name of the island, from Dapper/*Eylanden* 1668, p. 73/5–6. Barbot's map of the Gulf of Guinea shows the equator running through the southern tip of São Tomé – which is in fact correct – but an inscription below states that this is an error, since the main church at Povoação is exactly on the equator.

Cf. *1732*, p. 404/1–2, 5, which adjusts the size to 15 leagues by 12 leagues, and refers to the drawing of the island on Plate 23 (p. 395).

[3] Omission of one paragraph describing how the island was settled by deported Spanish Jews and black women from Angola, the essence of the account from Dapper/*Eylanden* 1668, p. 75/3, but much enlarged with inaccurate embroidery, probably inspired by Vasconcelos 1641, pp. 304–6.

Cf. *1732*, p. 404/5–7, which adds a digression on the expulsion of the Jews from Castile, stated to be from Faria y Sousa, p. 304 (the pagination identifying the work as Faria y Sousa 1698).

[4] A similar verbal description of the island seen from the sea is in Delbée 1671, p. 464. The view, 'Isle St. Tomas de 9 à 10 Lieues au Sud', drawn in 1682, was repeated in *1732*, Plate 23 (p. 395), as 'The Prospect of the Island St. Tome from the South about 10 leagues distance'. A profile of São Tomé at 7–8 leagues N-by-NNE taken in 1705 appears in the journal of Des Marchais (BL, Add. MSS 19560).

[5] The source is not Robijn/Roggeveen 1685, p. 32, which is in fact much fuller, so may have been an informant. For an English ship anchoring in the same locality in 1694, see Phillips 1732, pp. 231–2.

Cf. *1732*, p. 405/1, which changes the reference to low and high tide to one to small and large ships.

[6] Omission of eight paragraphs, on the rains and streams, useful plants, including sugar-cane, animals, unhealthy climate and diseases, all from Dapper/*Eylanden* 1668, pp. 74/2–5, 75/1–3, 76/1–2, 77/3, 78/1–3, 5–6. Barbot

739

adds to the plants ginger, beans, and 'trees which distil water, as in Hierro Island in the Canaries'; and to the description of São Tomé as an earthly paradise, 'like St Helena'; also adding that the amount of sugar produced 'is reckoned at 100,000 *arrobas* per year', and that Europeans are cured from dysentery with quinces, fruit or jelly.

Cf. *1732*, pp. 405/2–406/1, 408/9–11, 409/1, which is more tellingly expressed ('thick stinking fog'), inserts a reference to cattle (Barbot makes them black cattle) and adds a paragraph on excessive blood-letting, both from Bosman, p. 414. Barbot also enlarges on the reference to St Helena. On the disease of *bichos no cu* ('creepy-crawlies up the gut'), he substitutes a long passage mainly derived from Dapper's reference to it in Angola (Dapper, p. 224/6–8), but introduced as follows. 'The disease call'd *Bichos no Cu*, is also very common there, both among Whites and Blacks; the nature of it is to melt or dissolve men's fat inwardly, and to void it by stool, which 'tis likely is occasion'd by the insupportable heats. The French call this distemper Gras fondu, that is, melted grease, being in effect a sort of dysentery . . .'

[7] Only the last two sentences are original, the rest being from Dapper/ *Eylanden* 1668, p. 75/3, and Villault, p. 408.

Cf. *1732*, p. 408/4–8, which adds a passing reference to small-pox and another to a nickname for the island, 'Dutch Churchyard', the latter from Bosman, p. 414.

[8] Omission of 17 paragraphs, on the seasons, the sugar industry, useful plants (some repetition here), cloth-making, pests, the inhabitants and their food, the town of 'Povason' (see Letter 3/11, note 7, above) and its fort, almost all from Dapper/*Eylanden* 1668, pp. 73/7, 74/1, 6–7, 76/2–3, 77/1–4, 78/1–8, 79/2. Barbot omits May from the months of 'spring'; and adds that, like the local sugar, 'sugar candy from France only keeps for a short time', also that he has eaten manioc on Príncipe, and that the weaving is done by 'the women in particular'. Further, he decreases the number of houses at Povoação from 1,500 to 800 (Villault gave the number in 1667 as 500, Villault, p. 403), but adds that they occupy an area half a league around – both may be slips. He adds the following passage – 'Today the fort possesses 30 cast-iron cannon, of from 8lb. up to 48 lb. shot. Since the expedition of the Vice-Admiral, when even the churches were sacked and ruined (an unpardonable crime according to the people here), no Dutchman is allowed to enter'. This is from Villault, pp. 402, 405, except for the number of cannon, which Villault gave as 60. (In 1694 the fort had only twenty old guns, Phillips 1732, p. 233).

Cf. *1732*, pp. 406/2–5, 408/1–3, 409/2–8, with small changes: discussing the sugar industry, the number of mills is increased from 54 to 60, 'which all together make every year about fifteen hundred tuns of brown sugar, better than what is made at Prince's Island', although better white refined sugar is imported from Madeira. Barbot also adds, in relation to Povoacão, that 'the

Portuguese say, there are above five thousand such houses about the country, six miles round the town'. Discussing the inhabitants, Barbot adds that 'the commonalty of all those mungrel people, especially of the Mulattos and Blacks, are treacherous villains, very thievish, insolent and quarrelsome on the last occasion; and some without any'. Despite the racial discrimination, this is so commonplace an opinion of foreigners that Barbot may have based the statement on mere supposition. But for a similar unfavorable opinion expressed by a German in 1683, see Jones 1985, p. 56.

[9] This passage was probably inspired by a reference to watering in the same river in 1667 and the water being the best in Africa, keeping a whole year, in Villault, p. 400–1. But Barbot adds a contrary view, presumably that of an informant – for an enlarged version of this passage, see the Additional Passage.

[10] Omission of ten paragraphs, on the houses and churches of Povoação, taxes, governor, imports, and religion, and also on the neighbouring islands of Cabres and Rolhes, mainly from Dapper/*Eylanden* 1668, pp. 73/7–8, 79/3–8, 81/1–2. Barbot adds to the list of imports fustian, thin shoes, hats, shirts and 'all sorts of cheap silk materials which are out of fashion in Europe'; adds Brittany to the provenances; and substitutes that the dues from a slave-ship are three slaves at 40 *écus* each, and 7–8,000 *reis* to recompense the officers and custom officials (for customs dues in 1683 and 1694, see Jones 1985, p. 56; Phillips 1732, p. 233). A reference to black priests and choirboys, supported by royal revenue, is from Villault, p. 403. Discussing the churches, he adds that the church of Our Lady of the Conception is 'larger and more splendid than it was before the Dutch ravaged it' and that the church of St Anne was rebuilt in 1667 and 'is the same size as St Sauveur in La Rochelle but far more beautiful'. This mingles the names supplied by Dapper with statements by Villault, pp. 402–3 (hence '1667'), the latter including the statement that the unnamed cathedral church is 'as large as S. Mederic in Paris, but finer' – which Barbot varies by referring to a La Rochelle church. Referring to governors in general, Barbot adds that 'most are officers who were injured or lost their wealth while serving the crown of Portugal, and they are sent to these territories to recover it' – which may be based on information from Campo Barreto, or may be mere supposition, wholly or partly.

Cf. *1732*, pp. 404/3–4, 406/7, 407/1–7, which adds the depths of the channel between 'Rosas Island' and São Tomé (perhaps from personal knowledge), adds hooks to the imports, adds a reference to monasteries from Bosman, p. 415, and building on a vague reference in Bosman, p. 415, also adds that the island is visited by 'often above one hundred and fifty sail of all nations and sizes' (in 1698 another Frenchman reported that, according to the port registers, 74 ships had visited the island in six months, Roussier 1935, p. 85). Referring to Campo Barreto, Barbot adds that he was 'the Portuguese general that was there, at my first voyage to the gulph ... whom I saw since at Prince's Island, and afterwards at Acra' (see Letter 2/ 10, p. 38, above). This is misleadingly worded, since when Barbot met Campo Barreto at Príncipe in 1679, during, not since, his first voyage, he described him as the former, not present, governor of São Tomé (*1679*, p. 347). Julião de Campo Barreto was in fact governor of São Tomé and the subordinate islands 1673–7 (Castelo Branco 1970, p. 20).

[11] This passage, taking off from the *1688* statement about drinking water, appears to be original and was probably obtained from an informant. Barbot's emphasis on the quality of the water is in accord with the modern view that slave-ship mortality was closely related to change in diet and exposure to unfamiliar organisms in drinking water (the local pollution of water supplies being a commonplace in tropical Africa), although of course there was as yet no scientific explanation of the latter causation. As Barbot implies, the crews might be similarly affected, and indeed much mortality within contemporary Europe is now known to have had the same causes. An English captain who watered at the same locality in 1694, also at night for the same reason, suspected that the subsequent mortality was due to the water (Phillips 1732, p. 232).

[12] This passage relates to James Barbot's voyage in 1699.

[13] See Letter 1/12, note 20, above.

LETTER 13

Historical notes on Isle S. Tomas [São Tomé]. Description of Isle Annoboan [Anobom].

[.../pp. 190–191/...][1] The island of Annobon or Annoboon received its name from the Portuguese who discovered it on New Year's Day. It lies at 1°46'S and 26°[blank]'E, 36 leagues SSW from St Thomas and 58 SSW from Cape Lopo. Some Dutch maps situate it at 1°30' and some at 1°50'.[2] It is approximately five leagues in length and circular in shape, appearing when seen from the sea like a very tall, rounded mountain. It is surrounded on virtually all sides by rocks and breakers, rendering the approach to the bay extremely difficult.[3] [...][4]

[illustrations nos. (94)–(96), 'Isle Annobon', inserted between pp. 176 and 177][5]

The roadstead is situated in the North of the island, slightly towards the East, providing good anchorage in 25 fathoms of water and on sandy ground, one quarter of a league from land. The tides flow swiftly from the South between March and June, and the winds at that time of year come from a SW or WSW direction. There is another roadstead for ships in the NW tip of the island, although this is a foul place and one full of breakers, with the bottom at 32 fathoms.[6] [...][7] All the ships that call at Annoboon are able to replenish their water here and obtain wood, tamarinds and an amount of provisions, these goods being obtained by trading old clothes and other goods of little value for them with the inhabitants. Tamarinds are excellent for combatting scurvy.[8] [.../p. 192/...][9] Please remember, Sir, that when you leave this island to head westwards you will always find the winds unfavorable, hence it is necessary to beat up to windward until you reach 3° South, when without fail you will encounter the SE or ESE winds which will carry you along for a good distance.[10] I was about to close at this point but it has occurred to me that I have forgotten to describe the small island of Branco or Caracombo – I mentioned this locality in my ninth letter, on p. 170. [...][11] There, my task is accomplished, Sir. I hope that you will be satisfied with my detailed account. I shall now go and relax, by helping at our grape-harvest, to which everyone around is flocking. I shall not forget, however, that I have more important information yet to give you. I am meanwhile, Sir, Your etc.

Additional Passages from *1732*

[p. 412/15, on feeling cold in a tropical sea]

The reason why the air seems so cold, I am apt to believe is, that having been so many months together under a scorching air along the coast of Guinea, and coming on a sudden into an open air, where we have continual fresh gales, it is not surprising that our bodies are so pinched with it, as to make us say it is extremely cold; though perhaps, were it possible to transport any person in an instant from Europe into that latitude, he would find the air very hot, when we coming from Guinea say it is, and really feel it very cold.

[p. 466/4, on Anobom in 1701]

[*margin*: Grazilhier's journal] In 1701 there were above a thousand

Blacks in the island, on the several Portuguese plantations, to cultivate all manner of Guinea provisions, and breed small cattle, which turns to a very good account to the proprietor, who is a Portuguese lord, that owns the island. There we got in abundance of water, wood, hogs, goats, tamarinds, Mandioca, meal, Guaiavas, oranges, lemons, etc. The island produces a very great quantity of cotton. We anchored on the north side of it.[12]

NOTES

[1] The account of two Dutch attacks on São Tomé, in 1610 and 1641, is entirely from Dapper/*Eylanden* 1688, pp. 75/3, 80/2, with occasional slips (e.g. 35 instead of 36 cannon).

Cf. *1732*, pp. 409/9–411/7, which considerably enlarges on the 1641 Dutch operations by including an account of the conquest of Angola, enlarging on Dapper, pp. 240/2–242/3, from an untraced source.

[2] The first two sentences are from Dapper/*Eylanden* 1668, p. 72/5, but changing 1°50' to 1°46', and 25 and 35 miles into 36 and 56 leagues. Barbot is not following Delbée 1671, pp. 463–4, which gives different figures again for the latitude and distances. Barbot's map of the Gulf of Guinea does not reach to Anobom, which actually lies at 1°24'S, and is almost due West of Cape Lopez.

Cf. *1732*, p. 411/8, which alters all the figures, to 1°45'S, 26°E, 35 or 36 leagues, and 58 leagues – the direction corrected to WSW; and adds that the island 'appears at sea as represented in the print', marginated 'Plate 23' (see note 4 below). Anobom became a Spanish possession in 1777, and hence has been latterly known as 'Annobon'.

[3] The size, and the last sentence, are from Dapper/*Eylanden* 1668, p. 72/6 ('5–6 French miles'), but the appearance may derive from Delbée 1671, p. 464 ('a little, very high mountain, round like a hat') or may be original. Barbot does not claim to have landed on Anobom. In March 1679 his ship passed the island, out of sight of it, but he obtained from a colleague who had been there the following brief account: a high and arid terrain, 3–4 leagues in circumference, lying in 2°05' (not the 1°28' of maps), settled in a few places by Portuguese mulattos, good for watering and obtaining manioc meal, goats, pigs, fowls and other provisions (*1679*, p. 356). In May-June 1682 Barbot must have passed within sight of the island, since he made three drawings of it, the views being along a course South of the island, travelling probably East to West. The details he supplies about anchorage at the island, unless they were obtained from a nautical guide, raise the possibility that his ship actually called there, but it is perhaps more likely that he obtained them from a colleague, as he had done on the previous voyage.

Cf. *1732*, p. 411/9, which enlarges slightly, with a phrase about the governor from Bosman, p. 417, and a toponym from the Mortier map that shows the island.

[4] Omission of five paragraphs, on the streams, plants and animals, taken from Dapper/*Eylanden* 1668, p. 72/7-8 ('some people would have it that . . .' = Dapper states).

Cf. *1732*, p. 412/5-9, 11-13, which often adds or substitutes material from Bosman, pp. 415-6, and ends with a reference to the Dutch occupation of the island, from Bosman, p. 417.

[5] Three views of Anobom, the island lying seven leagues to the NNW, an unstated distance to the North, and an unstated distance to the NE, in each case the island a fairly featureless mountain rising from the sea. Only the first view appeared in *1732*, on Plate 23 (p. 395). Drawings of Anobom showing Dutch attacks on several occasions and an ambush of a French landing-party, all c. 1600, are in *Begin* 1645, (Sebald de Weert, f. 14v; Wybrandt van Waerwijck, f. 4v; Joris van Spilbergen, f. 12v; Cornelis Matelief, f. 5).

[6] The details of the roadsteads may have come from an informant or an untraced nautical guide (but are not from Robijn/Roggeveen 1685, p. 33); also Barbot may have borrowed a reference to a NW anchorage at 32 fathoms from Delbée 1671, pp. 463-4.

Cf. *1732*, p. 411/9-11, which changes June to September, and continues with a passage about visiting ships from Bosman, p. 415.

[7] One paragraph omitted, on the settlement and residents of Anobom, from Dapper/*Eylanden* 1668, pp. 72/8, 73/1, but Barbot adds, from an untraced source – 'Today there are nearly 30 Portuguese families and 300–400 slaves to be found here. These families live in a large village at the locality of the roadstead which has a turf wall around it.'

Cf. *1732*, pp. 411/11, 412/3.

[8] Cf. *1732*, p. 412/10, which adds – 'a sort of small nuts called by the French, *Nois de medicine*'. Barbot later recommends that ships sailing from Whydah head for Cape Lopez, because the winds prevent them from reaching São Tomé, 'and if provisions grow scanty, then to make for Annobon island, to get that there' (*1732*, p. 541/7).

[9] Omission of three paragraphs, on dress, religion and government, from Dapper/*Eylanden* 1668, p. 73/2-4.

Cf. *1732*, p. 412/1-4, which substitutes for the remarks on religion and government those of Bosman, pp. 412, 417-8, and adds remarks about the seductive women from Bosman, pp. 416-7.

[10] Cf.*1732*, p. 412/14, which adds that some ships travelling from Anobom to Gold Coast encounter cold weather, this being from Bosman, p. 419. Barbot adds – 'a truth which I have experienced myself in the months of

March and April, when several times I passed the equinoctial line to and fro in my return from Guinea, and have seen our surgeon-major use a muff in the night-time'. He continues as in the Additional Passage.

[11] Omission of four paragraphs: the description of the island, its women, and a Dutch visit, is from Dapper/*Eylanden* 1668, p. 81/3–4. But Barbot locates the island more precisely, 'between Rio Borbo and Rio Borra virtually at the mouth of the river called Sto. Benito'. The island and the named rivers are shown on Barbot's map of the Gulf of Guinea, but the island is placed near the mouth of 'R. Borra' and some distance away from 'R. S. Benito', as in Robijn/Roggeveen 1685, p. 30. 'Ilha Branca', if it ever existed, must have been an islet in a river mouth.

Cf. *1732*, pp. 387/2–5, which however calls the island 'Branca or Baracombo' (a miscopying of Dapper's 'Caracombo') and now locates it 'about two and a half leagues distant from the continent'; and adds that certain birds there are the same as the weaver-birds at Sestro (*1688*, Letter 1/29, p. 152, above). Elsewhere Barbot complains that 'the Portuguese chart', i.e. Mortier, does not 'take the least notice of . . . the little island of Branca, lying close to the continent of the gulph, opposite eastward to Ilha de Fernando Po, near the river Borea, or Da Borea' (*1732*, p. 413/5). The map in Bosman shows 'Ilha Branca' much as Barbot's map does.

[12] 'Mandioca, meal' should read 'Mandioca meal'. It is clear that by 1700 Anobom had become a regular source of provisions for ships crossing from Guinea to America, as stated by Bosman, pp. 400, 415.

LETTER 14

Little vocabulary of some of the more common phrases and words among the Jaloffes, the Foules, the blacks of Gold Coast, and those of Juda and Ardres, in alphabetical order.

Sir, I believe that you will not be put out /p. 193/ by my sending you today some brief vocabularies of the most common terms used among the Jaloffi, the Foulles, the people of Gold Coast, and those of Juda and Ardres. I have arranged them alphabetically, to spare you the trouble of having to sort out a term when you want it. I begin with the two chief languages among the peoples who inhabit the coast of Nigritia, between Cape Verde and Gambia; I continue with the language most used on Gold Coast; and I conclude with the one common to Juda and Ardra. I would have given you another, that of the Quabes Monou, who occupy the banks of River Sess and the neighbourhood, but unfortunately I have mislaid my record of it.[1]

[.../pp. 194–200/...]² This, Sir, is all that I have been able to put together of the commonest phrases and words among the Moors of Nigritia and Guinea. Perhaps they will be of some use to you. I am, Sir, Your etc.

You will remember that I have finished my task, and thus the description of this part of Africa, from River Volta to Cape Lopez. And therefore I hope that you will no longer have any cause for complaint against one who will be, Sir, Ever Your etc. /p. 201/

NOTES

¹ Cf. *1732*, pp. 413/6–414/1, where Barbot adds perceptively – 'I fear the pronunciation of the English alphabet may cause some difficulty to render the pronunciation as intelligible to the natives of those different countries, as it is when spoken by a Frenchman, according to whose pronunciation I writ this vocabulary'.

² Barbot's vocabularies of the Wolof, Fula, Akan/Twi and Ewe languages are among the earliest substantial vocabularies of West African languages recorded in extant writing, and are indeed the earliest in the case of two of the languages. When they were collected c. 1680, and even when they eventually appeared in print in 1732 (*1732*, pp. 414–20), they represented a novel and therefore significant contribution to contemporary knowledge of Black Africa. However, Barbot intended them merely to be of practical use, particularly to visiting sailors and traders, as evident from some of the select phrases. The Gold Coast vocabulary was collected in 1679 (*1679*, pp. 341–4), the others were collected in 1681–2; but in neither instance did Barbot detail the mode of collection. The Gold Coast vocabulary may have been written down by Barbot himself from the mouth of an African informant, but the others were perhaps repeated to Barbot by Frenchmen serving in Guinea who had some knowledge of the relevant languages, perhaps even being passed on in writing. Barbot added a Gold Coast vocabulary borrowed from Marees, ff. 125–9, but if he did not see Marees before 1679 it cannot have been this which inspired his first effort. The terms were rearranged in *1732* to put the new English glosses in alphabetical order, but the copying of the African terms from *1688* (or the subsequent proof-reading of their printed version) was done carelessly. For the complete vocabularies, together with attempted identifications of the terms and phrases in the modern versions of the same languages, see Hair 1992.

DIRECTIONS

for the courses to be taken when going to and returning from Guinea, either directly or by way of America; and how to control the slaves carried to America. Together with a brief description of the coasts and islands encountered on this course and certain others in America.[1]

LETTER 15

Rules to observe when undertaking a voyage to Guinea. The course that must be taken on leaving France. Description of the islands of Madeira, Porto Santo and the Canaries that can be seen on this route.

Sir, permit me to say, since I have not been in contact with you for some time, that apparently the more I do to satisfy you, the more you draw me into further work and labour. I have spent one whole year in writing and assembling notes in order to describe to you a vast region, and now when I thought I was quit, you resume and strongly press me to give you directions for sailing a ship to Guinea and back. [.../p. 202/...][2] You are sufficiently knowledgable concerning the despatch and equipping of vessels, and their fitting out with the things necessary for such a voyage. The voyage is an easy one, for once you arrive at the latitude of the Canaries, which is not difficult for a good pilot, there is always a following wind, but never are there gales, and good anchorages are everywhere, so that a new ten-inch cable can always hold a ship of 400 tons on the coasts of Nigritia and Guinea. From there to America, a sloop can make the crossing as safely as the main ship itself, the seas being so calm, and the storms of brief duration. However, to satisfy you and to provide an orderly description, I will state first that the success of these voyages depends entirely on the time of year and the seasonal weather – if not strictly for the actual trade, at least for the preservation of those aboard the ships – although it does seem that nowadays time and weather are disregarded, love of gain exercising more influence than that most precious commodity, health. It is absolutely necessary to leave not later than 10–15 September in order to have the longest spell of good weather on the coast, and, after the time spent in trading, in order to reach the American islands by the end of April (the sugar-making season). Then the vessel can be carefully loaded before hurricanes start up, and can be back in Europe before the Michaelmas storms. Carried out to this time-table, a voyage to Guinea can be undertaken without hazard, fatigue and inconvenience, with at all points good fair weather, that is, on leaving Europe, during the voyage to the coasts of Nigritia and Guinea, when crossing the equator on the passage to the American islands and coast, when in the islands, and on the return passage. The severe storms off Bermuda will be avoided, as will the Michaelmas storms off Europe.[3]

To sail from Europe to Guinea, once you are 25–30 leagues West of Cape Finisterre in Galicia head South-by-SSW straight to Grand Canary, or SSW to Madeira. Some pass between Lanzarote and Fortaventure, others coming from Madeira or otherwise from the North, pass to the West of Palma – I leave this to your discretion. We Frenchmen, coming from the coasts of Poitou, Brittany and Guyenne, usually sight the Coast of Galicia, that is, Cape Finisterre, then we head for [Grand] Canary. I reckon this is the safer route, having sailed each.[4] But as you seek from me not so much directions for this course as a description of the coasts and islands encountered on it, I shall labour at this task, in order to serve your need. [. . ./pp. 203–206/. . .][5]

[illustrations nos. (104)–(106), views of the Canary Islands, inserted after p. 204][6]

[illustrations nos. (107)–(108), views of the Canary Islands, inserted after p. 206][7]

Teneriffe . . . is chiefly remarkable for the mountain of The Peak. I have seen it very distinctly from 35 leagues to the East, which can be done only rarely, it being /p. 207/ almost always covered in thick clouds hiding half its height, otherwise I am assured it would be visible from 40 leagues out at sea. [. . ./pp. 208–209/. . .][8]

NOTES

[1] These 'directions' were repeated to become the Second Book of the *1732* Supplement, being so listed on p. 422 and beginning p. 523/1.

[2] Omission of two sentences, repeating what the letter is to contain. The

implication that Barbot had written the previous part of his text in only twelve months is probably part of the epistolary fiction.

[3] Cf. *1732*, p. 523/1–2, which inserts a useful note on Barbot's 1681–2 voyage, as follows: '...Michaelmas storms; the sad effects whereof I sufficiently felt in October 1681 aboard the *Jolly* man of war. Having sail'd from Rochel road on the seventh of October for the coast of Guinea, and after we had sight of cape Ortegal in Galicia, we met with such a violent storm from the south-west, and variable, that we were sixteen days tossed up and down in the bay, the sea running mountain high, and dreadfully breaking into our ship, which spoil'd abundance of our provisions, and much disabled us in our sails and rigging. However, being a strong ship, we kept sea; but our passage to Senega river lasted forty-eight days: whereas, in a former voyage begun a fortnight later, we made our passage in twenty-four days'. It also enlarges slightly, the Bermuda storms being 'in August' and the Michaelmas storms 'on the coasts of Britany and Poictou in October'.

[4] Cf. *1732*, p. 523/3–4, which resolves the contradiction regarding Cape Finisterre; and also the slight ambiguity in the autobiographical reference, by stating: 'At my first voyage I passed betwixt Fuerte Ventura and Great Canary; and at the second, betwixt the former and the main land of Africa; and thereby had the opportunity of drawing the prospects of Lancerota, Graciosa, Fuerte Ventura, Great Canary, Teneriff and Gomera, as in the print here annex'd, for the advantage or satisfaction of travellers'. In October 1678 Barbot's ship, after leaving La Rochelle, sighted Cabo Penas in Asturias and Cabo Ortega in Galicia, and Barbot inserted drawings of the two capes in his journal (*1679*, p. 257, the drawings not reproduced); thereafter the ship headed for the Canaries. In October 1681 the second voyage sighted Cabo Ortega (previous note). The 'safer route' is therefore to sail through the Canaries.

[5] Omission of 13 paragraphs, apart from the two sentences supplied from p. 206, these paragraphs dealing with the island groups of Madeira and the Canaries, as do completely pp. 209–217. Barbot sailed through the island groups in 1678 and 1681, and his brother and nephew did the same in 1699 and 1700. The nephew called at Funchal in 1700, but there is no evidence that any of the Barbots ever landed on the Canaries or that our author landed on Madeira. Hence the lengthy description of the various islands of these groups in *1688* – considerably abbreviated in *1732*, pp. 523/4–525/7 – is almost entirely derived from earlier printed sources, mainly Dapper (*Eylanden* 1668, pp. 91–103, including citations of Dapper's sources, e.g. Purchas, Gramaye), but also 'nos Géographes d'Aujourd'huy' (p. 204) and specifically 'la Nouvelle Géographie de Samson fils' (p. 215). Barbot states that he is supplying a translation of an account of the ascent of the Peak of Tenerife in Sprat's *History of the Royal Society*, and remarks to his fictitious correspondent: 'As you are curious and often leaf through my books, I should not be

surprised if you have come upon it' (p. 207). This might be thought to imply that Barbot had owned the book, and therefore before leaving France had read English books; but in fact Barbot's translation is not from the English but from the summary of the book in Dapper. The translation is omitted in *1732*. Apart from inserted autobiographical references, the only non-derived parts of this section are the illustrations, drawings of the islands made from out at sea. Similarly, in *1732* only the additional illustrations are original. James Barbot junior in April 1700 produced two drawings of the Madeira group, one of the islets, 'Las Desertas', ESE of Madeira, the other of Funchal town and road (as stated at *1732*, pp. 523/5, 524/5), and these appeared in *1732*, plate 28 (p. 497), where the islets are wrongly stated to be NE of Madeira. In May 1700 he produced drawings of Gomera and Palma in the Canaries which appear on the same plate (as stated in *1732*, pp. 497/ 3, 523/5). A modern profile of Ilhas Desertas (*Africa pilot* 1967, p. 595) suggests that the 1700 drawing is not very exact.

[6] Three illustrations are given. (i) 'Veue des Isles, Alegranca et l'Ancerote (2 des Canaries) veues de 5 lieues au S.E. de vous'. On 6 November 1678 Barbot sighted Alegranza and Gratiosa islets off the NE of Lanzarote, and produced a drawing (*1679*, p. 258, not reproduced) on which the above is based: another version appears on *1732*, Plate 31 (p. 523). While the profiles are the same, the labelling varies: the original lacks the reference at point E to 'Lobos' but point D is described as the corner of Gratiosa. Barbot apparently sighted these islands again in 1681, hence another view of Lobos, Lanzarote and Gratiosa, the islands in line: illustration no. (107), repeated on *1732*, Plate 31 (p. 523). (ii) On 7 November 1678 Barbot sailed between Fuerteventura and Grand Canary and made drawings of each (*1679*, p. 258, not reproduced), on which were based 'Veue de Grand Canarie de 5½ á 6 lieues 0.¼S.O.' (5 leagues on the original, which has additional land to the right and additional labelling, points followed in the version on *1732*, plate 31, p. 523); and 'Veue de Fortaventura de 8 lieues au N.E. L'Isle Canarie à O.S.O.' (ENE on original), which has an abrupt break in the land to the left, apparently an erasion not corrected, this not being repeated in the version on *1732*, Plate 31 (p. 523). The profile of Fuerteventura is accurate: see the profile in *Africa pilot* 1967, p. 598.

[7] Two illustrations are supplied, of which the first has been described in the previous note, at (i). On 7 November 1678 Barbot sighted the Peak of Tenerife 25–30 leagues to the East (*1679*, p. 258, not reproduced), or 35 leagues (*1688*, p. 206), or 45 leagues (*1732*, p. 524). On his *1679* drawing was based 'Veue du Pic de Tenerif de 35 lieues au N.O.', where '25' has been altered to '35'; which is repeated, with the enlarged distance, on *1732*, Plate 31 (p. 523). The labelling on the *1732* version includes an original comment – 'appearing as a thin cloud'. In *1679* a marginal note stated that others had seen the Peak from 60 leagues but Barbot did not repeat this

claim. His drawing is realistic and a great improvement on the fantastic illustration in Dapper (*Eylanden* 1668, p. 94), although the height of the Peak at the stated distance is still much exaggerated.

[8] Cf. *1732*, p. 524/14 – 'I have seen it plain at forty-five leagues distance'. For Barbot's drawing of the Peak, see the previous note.

LETTER 16

Specific description of Teneriffe. History of a journey made by an Englishman to the summit of the famous Peak of this island. Interesting remarks on this peak by another Englishman. Features of this island, its land, vines, dews. Pleasing description of the Guanchios who live there. Views of Samson junior on The Peak and other miscellaneous features of the island. The fish in the sea.

[.../pp. 210–216/...][1] The sea runs high between these islands on account of the SW wind, but fortunately the wind hardly ever prevails in this part of the ocean. From the straits to here, there is fishing for dolphin-fish, sharks, flying fishes, sea-dogs and tunny-fish.[2]

NOTES

[1] Omission of 38 paragraphs, represented by *1732*, pp. 524/15–525/6: see Letter 3/15, note 5, above. The dripping tree of Hierro, described at length in *1688*, in *1732* is said to be 'since known to be a fable and therefore not worth mentioning'.

[2] Cf. *1732*, p. 525/7, but reading 'I have observed that' and 'we had always good sport, catching...'.

LETTER 17

Further course from Europe to the Saharan coast, and the fishes taken there.

[...][1] Angra da los Rivos, or de las Rivas, lies 21–22 leagues South of Bojador. [...][2] The sea on this coast breeds vast number of the fish known as snappers (*parques*) and mackerel (*sardes*). We hove to in 45 fathoms and in less than two hours brought 80 of these fish aboard on a line. Among them were some dog-fish and another large and very fine fish called a 'captain'. Snappers and /p. 217/ mackerel are salted like cod (*le cabilau et la morue*). The Portuguese and

752

Spaniards fish for these regularly and take them to the Canaries, Madeira and other places. Here you see a drawing from life of these three kinds of fish.[3]

[illustration no. (109), four fish]

Later we took a good number of these fish when off Sete Montes, which lies just nine leagues South of [Angra de] Las Rivas or Ruivas, in 40 fathoms, a stony bottom with small sea-shells. Like cod, these fish never come up to the surface of the water and have to be sought on the bottom. For bait we used a herring or a piece of meat, and the first fish caught became bait to catch others. The hooks and lines used must be fairly strong.[4] I have already mentioned to you dolphin-fish (*dorados*) and sharks, many of which are taken in the seas of these parts. Here is a drawing of each.[5]

[illustration no. (110), two fish] p. 218/†

Dolphin-fish and sharks are caught in a different way, the former with a fish-gig or harpoon, the latter with a shark-hook, a heavy iron fish-hook, baited with a large piece of pork fat. I will not go into details about these creatures, since they are well known. I shall simply say that the dolphin-fish is the most beautiful fish in the sea, so that the sailors call it 'the dauphin of the sea' and further that it has been given the name '*dorado*' [gilded] on account of the beauty of its skin, which seen in the water appears a pleasing mixture of silver, gold and blue. Its flesh is good eating. As for the shark, you will know, Sir, that this monster of the deep is very dangerous. It tears to shreds anything it comes up against. But I will say more about this in another place. About the dog-fish we took here I will make only one point. They were mostly females, each carrying two young which, when they were taken out of their mother's belly and thrown into water, swam around vigorously as if they had been born at full term. I make this point to confute those who claim that no fish carries young or reproduces other than by means of laying eggs. You will see presently that whales and porpoises also carry their young.[6]

In this climate the air is always hot and heavy. In daytime you sail towards the land until you reach 20 fathoms, and head back towards the sea all night as far as 40–50 fathoms, assuming that the wind is SW as it was on my latter voyage. You sail parallel with the coast if the wind is North or NE.[7] Around about here (on my latter voyage) a fish passed alongside the vessel and very close to it. It was 7–8 feet long and much as drawn here. [*margin:* some call it the hammer (*marteau*), others *demoiselle*]. Some think it to be the uranoscope of the Ancients, so-called because it always looks at the sky. I saw another one of these alongside the vessel on the Coast of Guinea, and another again at La Rochelle, near the light-house.[8] The sea here is full of small whales, grampuses and a vast number of porpoises and flying-fish. This is the case in all the tropical seas.[9]

[illustration no. (111), the hammer fish]

Angra de Cavalos lies 7 leagues South of Sete Montes. [. . .] Rio Ouro is 15 leagues from Angra dos Cavalos. [. . .] Cape Olaredo is at the mouth of the river. [. . ./p. 219/. . .][10]. Angra de Gonzalo de Sintra is 20 leagues further on and is a great bay. I have fished (here too) for snappers and 'captains', in 30 fathoms, the bottom fine sand, grey and muddy, the best bottom for the latter fish.[11] [. . .][12]

Additional Passages from *1732*

[p. 526/8–9, on the dolphin-fish]

The French sailors call it improperly the dolphin: the name of dorado was given it by the Spaniards or Portugueses, from the fine polished, enamell'd, transparent gold colour of its scales about the back; so wonderfully intermix'd with shining, bright, silver, and emerald green specks, which I have endeavour'd to paint as near to nature as I was capable, in miniature; and have those originally by me still. The tails and fins are of a fine gold colour, and the belly like silver, when in its element; it soon changes aboard, as we observe the same sudden alteration in the mackarels in Europe. The dorado scales in the night-time look of a fiery colour, the flesh of the beautiful fish is very firm, white, and of an excellent relish, especially broiled on brisk wood-coals cut in slices, about two inches thick, and salted for an hour or two. There are two sorts of doradoes, and of either male or female, of very different size and colour: that which I drew after the life, was a cock-dorado, near five foot long; which, as I was told by old travellers, is the longest it grows to. / The doradoes of the American seas differ from those of the African, in that their head is longer pointed, whereas those of Africa are generally flat nosed and round; and for that reason, in some respects not so pleasing to the eye. This fish is no thicker than our salmon: the other sort varies from this, in that the two extremities of its jaws stretch a little further out, and that the specks instead of a fine deep emerald green, are of a lively azure, on a gold ground. Both sorts are very delicious . . .[13]

[p. 527/12, on the custom at crossing the Line and Tropics]

About this latitude, just in passing the tropick of Cancer, is observed an ancient custom, common to all European sailors; which is, that those who have never been under the tropick, are obliged to give the ship's crew a piece of money, or something to drink, from which no man is excused. If any man happens to be so great a miser as to refuse paying of this duty, the sailors, dressed like officers, carry him bound before a tribunal, on which a seaman is seated in a long robe, representing a judge, who examines him, hears what he has to say for himself, and then pronounces sentence; which is, that he be three times ducked in the sea, after this manner: The person condemned is tied fast with a rope, and the other end of it runs through a pully at the yard-arm, by which he is hoisted up, and then let run amain three times under water. It is seldom that some one fails to give the company this diversion. The same is practised with the utmost rigour in passing the line.[14]

[p. 528/13, on a view by Barbot of the Saharan coast]

I have annexed an exact draught of the prospect [margin: Plate 32] of the coast of Gualata, from cape das Barbas to cape Carvoeiro, that coast stretching from north-east by north to south-west by south. At about the middle of that distance lies a long narrow island, call'd Pedro da Galla, which looks swarthy at a distance, and cannot well be approach'd nearer than two leagues . . .[15]

NOTES

[1] Omission of three paragraphs on Cape Bojador and the surrounding coast, mainly from Dapper, p. 1/369/6–10. Barbot sailed along the Saharan coast in 1678 but the only sightings recorded in his journal are of land around Cape Barbas and of capes Carvoeira and Blanc (1679, p. 259): see the Additional Passage. However 1688, followed by 1732, records fishing off

Angra dos Ruivos and Angra de Gonzalo de Sintra, further North; and *1732* additionally refers to the coast from Bojador and to soundings North and South of Rio de Ouro. These later references may indicate that on his 1681 voyage Barbot sailed close to the coast for a greater distance than he did in 1678. Barbot's account of the coast is lengthy, with many historical references, both in *1688* and in *1732*, pp. 525/8–529/2, but is largely derived, principally from Dapper, pp. 1/369/10–370/4, and from Dutch nautical guides. Only passages unambiguously derived from personal observation are hereafter noted.

² Omission of one sentence. Barbot adds in *1732*, p. 528/5: 'From cape Bojador to Rio do Ouro we observed the coast in many places to be all high cliffs, some grey, others whitish, and the country, as far as we could discern from our top-mast heads, barren, dry, scorch'd, and red sandy ground, overgrown with shrubs and reeds, but could neither see men, houses, nor beasts, in all that tract of land.' See a similar description in *Africa pilot* 1967, p. 244, with profiles on pp. 610–11.

³ Earlier sources supply many references to the sea-fishing off the Saharan coast, which was particularly practised by Portuguese and Spanish fishermen, as indeed it still is today.

Cf. *1732*, p. 526/4–5, which does not translate *pargue* and *sarde* but enlarges – 'caught above a hundred with lines and hooks', 'the captain is the best meat of all, being very white, firm and savoury: the head of it is much like that of the French Rochet-fish, but not red, being of a bright brown, and ugly to look at'. Barbot adds that the 'captain', which he now describes as one of 'two sorts of the Sardes', is said to be known as the 'snapper' in the West Indies and off Chile. Barbot's 1678 journal records the catching of 35–40 *pargues* when one day North of Cabo das Barbas. He drew a *pargue* and a *capitaine*, and described them as follows: (*pargue*) 'its flesh is white and firm, it is three feet long and is enough for seven men. The Portuguese come here to catch this fish in the same way as our Ollonois go to Newfoundland', 'Captain. Its flesh is better than that of the *pargue*' (*1679*, pp. 258–9). The two *1679* drawings are repeated in *1688*, with two more, of a much larger fish labelled 'Sarde 1' and of a slightly larger fish labelled 'Sarde d'une autre sorte'; and all four reappear on *1732*, Plate 32 (p. 536), but the largest fish is now labelled 'A Large Pargue'. An additional drawing of a *sarde* labelled 'sardes à gros dos' has already appeared (*1688*, illustration no. 9), and reappears on *1732*, Plate 20 (p. 224). Barbot's *pargue* is probably *Pagrus pagrus* and his *capitaine* probably *Dentex filiosus* (Debien 1979, p. 386, ns. 69–70).

⁴ Cf. *1732*, p. 526/6, which adds – ''Tis a very diverting, but somewhat laborious sport, because of the great depth of the water it must be halled out from'. The additions in *1732* on fish and fishing off the Saharan coast include elements which may have been borrowed from Leguat 1708, p. 18.

[5] The term 'dorado' was used to denote both the cetaceous mammal, the dolphin (*Delphinus delphis*), and a fish, the dolphin-fish (*Coryphaena hippurus* or *equisetis*, Debien 1979, p. 386, n. 75). Since Barbot's references at certain points appear to apply to the fish, the translation hopefully presumes that he was consistent in using the term in this sense. For the drawings, see note 6 below.

[6] Barbot, with his particular interest in fishes, considerably expands this material in *1732*, pp. 526/7–527/4, which includes the Additional Passage on the dolphin-fish, and also a reference to a surgeon of St Malo who saw a dolphin-fish off Madagascar. Of the dog-fish (*chiens de mer* or *roussette*), Barbot adds that each female was 'big with two little ones shut up in a bag, fastened to the fish, by a pretty long ligament, through which the little twins were nourished by the substance of their dam, as the figure represents it. The bag was full of a gloomy yellow soft matter, which I suppose was to keep and nourish them till the time of being cast out by nature ... The skin of this fish being of the nature of shagreen, is useful to joiners, and other artificers, to polish wood, etc.' In *1679*, Barbot recorded the catching of a dolphin-fish ('de 3 pieds'), the sailors' name for it, its beauty, and his drawing of the fish, on 19 November 1678, not off the Saharan coast but after passing Cape Verde (*1679*, p. 260). He also recorded the catching of a shark on 27 November off Sierra Leone, a lengthy description being supplied as well as a drawing (*1679*, pp. 261–2). Both drawings appear in *1688* and reappear on *1732*, Plate 32 (p. 536), the dolphin-fish now labelled 'The Hen Dorade', and the shark labelled 'The Requin' (as referred to on *1732*, p. 225/8). A second drawing of a dolphin-fish, labelled 'Dorade 2me Espèce', is not in *1679* but is in *1688* as illustration no. (114); and also appears, labelled 'the Cock Dorade', on *1732*, Plate 32 (p. 536). A third drawing of a dolphin-fish, drawn by James Barbot in 1700, appears on *1732*, Plate 29 (p. 497). The dog-fish with its 'ligament' is not illustrated in either *1679* or *1688*, but appears, labelled 'The Seal fish als. Roussette', on *1732*, Plate 32 (p. 536), having been briefly discussed under that name (p. 262/1). On sharks, see the material in the Additional Passages to Letter 2/20 and note 26, above. Since sharks, whales and porpoises have been discussed earlier (at several points), Barbot's statements that he will refer to them later probably indicate that at one stage the Letters were rearranged and these statements overlooked.

[7] Cf. *1732*, p. 527/7, which begins 'Tho' we sail'd by this coast in November', a remark which fits both of Barbot's voyages; and ends 'but when north-east, we kept at night nearer the land', which may or may not correct the translation above.

[8] Cf. *1732*, p. 527/6, 'a large Panapana or hammer-fish'. The drawing in *1688* is repeated on *1732*, Plate 32 (p. 536), and a drawing of the head of this fish is added – 'the figure of the head of the Panapana I have drawn after that

which is in Gresham college in London; and have seen another at a house near the lanthorn tower in Rochel' (p. 527/6). Barbot's drawing does not seem to derive from an illustration of the same fish, here termed 'le Pantouf-flic', in Jannequin 1643, p. 47.

[9] Cf. *1732*, p. 527/5.

[10] The omitted sentences enlarge on the localities but contain no personal references and are most likely derived.

Cf. *1732*, p. 527/9–11, but Barbot adds references to two soundings 'we made', one off Otagedo South of Angra dos Cavallos, another off Olaredo, four leagues South of Rio do Ouro.

[11] Cf. *1732*, p. 528/9.

[12] Omission of three paragraphs on capes Carvoeiro and Blanc; cf. *1732*, p. 528/10–12, although Barbot adds a sounding for 14–15 leagues westward of the former cape.

[13] On the dolphin-fish, see note 5 above; and on the drawings of the dolphin-fish, see note 6 above.

[14] Accounts of equivalent although different ceremonies aboard contemporary French vessels can be found in Froger 1698, p. 5; Le Maire 1695, pp. 38–41; Gaby 1689, pp. 16–17; Leguat 1708, pp. 20–1. Barbot mentions the ceremony again (*1732*, p. 540/3 – see Letter 3/20, note 8, below).

[15] In November 1678, Barbot drew a profile of 40 km of the coast from Cape Barbas to Cape Carvoeiro (*1679*, p. 259, drawing not reproduced), drawn with the former cape ENE at 4–5 leagues, a long low coast with 'Pedra da Galla' (Pedra da Galé) in the centre. The drawing only loosely corresponds to the description and profile in *Africa pilot* 1967, pp. 252–3, 612. The drawing was omitted from *1688* but reappeared, somewhat carelessly copied, on *1732*, Plate 32 (p. 536), as 'The Prospect of the Coast of Libie ...'.

LETTER 18

Description of the Desert of Sara, according to modern geographers. [Locusts.] Arab Moors, etc.

[.../pp. 220–221/...][1] Here they are greatly afflicted by enormous swarms of locusts which like great clouds sweep across Arabia and Egypt into the deserts of Libya, Numidia and Barbary, and occasionally as far as Spain, from which, again occasionally, they travel further NE. I do not know whether the great swarms of these insects which ate up the crops in the province of Aunix in 1672 and which perished crossing over to Ile de Rhé represented a flight from that dreadful clime. They say that these insects leave eggs wherever they have been, and that after their departure the sun hatches out a species which cannot fly but which feeds on plants more rapaciously, and even on the bark of trees. This is what brings about all the great famines which these peoples regularly experience, and it also leads the Africans and Arabians to hate this insect. There are even some people who, out of hatred, eat them (they call them *jarat*). Apparently a large number of these insects crossed the Sahara in November 1678, for on the coast the sea was covered in many places with those the North wind had driven away from land. I took up several which were still alive. They were as large as a little finger, red all over, with a long body, and very ugly-looking. I kept one in a scrap of paper for three months, without it having access to air in the normal way. It died at Isle du Prince. I noticed that it fed on the paper in which it was shut up. I am ashamed of repeating to you such small matters, but my defence is that this is what you desire.[2]

[illustration no. (112), view of Fort Royal of Martinique, inserted after p. 220][3]

[.../p. 222/...][4] Very few among them [the Moors] trouble to participate in the trade in gum, which formerly they used to carry to Arguin, and nowadays carry to Terrier Rouge or Rood Land, on River Senegal.[5] [.../p. 223/...][6] This is the country which is the least penetrated in all of Africa, its vast deserts and the terror of the frightful monsters in them having always held back the steps of the most inquisitive. Or perhaps we should say that it is the lack of profit to be made there, since, in the burning desire for gain that nowadays reigns, not Libya nor the African desert nor /p. 224/ all the monsters there would stop those who love this world and seek renown in it. Were I possessed of this unfortunate passion, I would reduce it as much as I could, by persuading myself, as indeed I do, that a content mediocrity is worth much more than great fortunes earned at the expense of health and often of life itself, great fortunes which give satisfaction only in the anticipation of those who pursue them and those who judge matters only by outward appearance. Forgive this moralizing. I fell into it without thinking, having just received some letters from America which inform me of the deaths of two of my closest friends [*margin:* Messers Massiot and Fourestier], my travelling companions on my first venture to Guinea, who have paid

nature the price for a second visit to these lands.[7] I am compelled to
stop, in order to devote a few moments to their memory and my
sorrow. I will write to you again later more fully. I am, however,
Your etc.

NOTES

[1] Omission of eight paragraphs on the desert. In the final paragraph of
Letter 3/17, Barbot announced that Letter 18 would supply a description of
the Sahara desert, according to 'our modern geographers' and 'what the
Moors of Senegal say about it'. In fact the material is almost entirely derived
from Dapper, pp. 1/366–372, somewhat abbreviated, Dapper's material in
turn being largely from Cadamosto and Leo Africanus, sometimes via Marmol. Most of this Letter is therefore omitted. The material is repeated in
1732, pp. 533/3–534/12, with the addition of a list of tribes from 'a very
modern author'.

[2] In his journal Barbot noted that in November 1678 the sea off the
Saharan coast for more than 150 leagues was covered with large red locusts,
and that in March 1679, as his ship neared Príncipe, a locust, 'taken at Sierra
Leone' and kept in paper, died (1679, pp. 258, 353).
   Cf. 1732, p. 539/4–9, which enlarges as follows: 'When dead, I observed
the bottom of the paper full of the ordure of the insect. . . . In the year 1672,
a plague of these insects came into the province of Aulnix in France . . . and
being carry'd by the wind to sea from Rochel towards the isle of Rhee, I saw
a ridge of them dead, for several leagues in length, as they had been thrown
up by the waves, and left there at low water; which, with the heat of the sun,
it being then summer, caus'd a very offensive stench. And I remember, that
before they were thus drown'd, there was not a house in the province, but
what was pester'd with them; and I heard abundance of the people say, that
for some days they could scarce dress any meat, those insects falling so thick
down the chimneys into the fire. It was a dismal sight to behold the country
without any the least green left in it, as if all had been burnt up; whence we
may easily judge how much the land suffers which is so frequently infested
with them.' Finally, Barbot adds a digression on locusts in the Ukraine
(from Churchill 1704, I, 533) and concludes as follows: 'Whilst I was writing
this, I received a letter from Lisbon, dated July twenty-fourth N.S. 1710,
giving an account, that the crop in Portugal would have been generally good;
but that in the province of Alentejo, the best of that kingdom, the locusts
had destroyed most of the wheat, which had rais'd the price of foreign corn.'
Barbot referred to locusts and famines earlier (1688, Letter 1/7, p. 37 and
note 32), and his more general observations about the insect derive from
Dapper, p. 404/5. Locusts in Senegal were first reported by Europeans in

the 1450s (Cadamosto 1948, pp. 26/27–8). A plague of locusts affected central and southern Morocco in 1677–1678, the year previous to Barbot's voyage (Cigar 1981, p. 130). The term *jarat*, which is not in Barbot's vocabularies of Wolof and Fula, is unidentified.

[3] It is not clear why the drawing of Martinique is inserted at this point. It was drawn in 1679 (*1679*, p. 375) and is repeated on *1732*, Plate 34/2 (p. 570).

[4] Omission of one paragraph and most of a second, on salt caravans and the Moors.

[5] On the gum trade, see Letter 1/9 and notes 17–18.

[6] Omission of ten paragraphs, on the life-style of the Moors of the desert.

[7] Fourestier was a fellow *commis* of Barbot in 1678–9 and probably Barbot's senior, and his activities are very frequently mentioned in Barbot's journal (e.g. *1679*, pp. 262, 292, 322, 376). Massiot, on the other hand, is barely mentioned, and is difficult to distinguish from the Massiot who was Barbot's employer and who remained in La Rochelle (*1679*, pp. 256, 328, 331, 361, 363 – see the Introduction, note 20). The present reference clarifies that a Massiot did travel with Barbot, and it is likely that he too was a commercial agent. Barbot makes no further reference to these deaths, which must have occurred in a year between 1683 and 1687.

LETTER 19

Further course to navigate from Europe to Guinea, in the seas of Gualata. Cap Blanc. Description of the kingdom of Arguyn, and of the fort at Arguyn, its foundation by the Portuguese, its capture from them by the Dutch, and its demolition by the French. The trade of the Moors, the Moors in general and their intrepid nature. Further course in the seas of Genehoa, and the currents of the coast. Rules for anchoring a vessel in the roadstead of Senegal.

[...][1] Under the heading of Sahara, I have already discussed the kingdom of Gualata. Here I deal with Arguin and Genehoa. [...] The fort which the Portuguese built on the Isle of Arguin [... /p. 225/...][2] passed into the hands of the Dutch who strengthened it with works on the seaward side and kept it until 1678, when Sieur Jean du Casse, an agent of the French Senegal Company, took it by means of a formal siege, although he had only 120 men on three ships. He destroyed it, after removing from it and transporting to Senegal considerable booty, especially gum and slaves, and also two small vessels which an officer of his in an armed sloop had captured under the walls of the fort. The Company razed the fort in order to

attract blacks and Arabs more successfully to Senegal, especially
those who traded in gum arabic. The majority of these Africans had
carried their trade to the Dutch at Arguin as long as there was a fort
there, but nowadays most of them direct themselves to the banks of
River Senegal, so that the annual trade in gum in that locality has
risen to 400 *milliers*. This has not stopped the Dutch from sending
one ship along the coast almost every year, and a fairly large number
of *milliers* of gum is obtained in this trade.[3] [...] In the Bay of
Arguin there are other islands. [...][4]

The breakers extend as far as River St Juan. Some say that this
river is linked to River Senegal by Rivière des Maringouins. /p. 226/
They argue that the waters of the latter contain elements of salt water
and that these come from inland, where there is no river other than
River St Juan.[5]

From this last river to River Senegal I will conduct you rapidly,
there being nothing worthy of description between them to halt me.
There is only Penya, lying 44–45 leagues North of the Residence on
River Senegal, where the Dutch ship goes to conduct the trade in
gum with the Moors. The anchorage is within the sand-bank facing
the bay.[6] The coast of Genehoa from Arguin to Senegal is only
accessible to medium-sized vessels which can pass within Schey
d'elle Gaze. If you are coming directly to Senegal from Cap Blanc,
once you have passed the Schey delle Garze, keep towards the land
of Genehoa and in day-time coast along it within two leagues and
anchor at night. If you go this way do not be surprised, Sir, if you
suddenly find yourself in 17 fathoms. A sand-bank lies 17–18 leagues
North of Senegal road. Next you must look out for Mast-boom, that
is, Palm-tree, which is 16 leagues from it, and keep in sight of the
land at 1½ leagues until you see the turrets of the Senegal Residence,
which you will pass one league away. There is no danger at 1½
leagues, the coast being clean and sandy. The roadstead lies 4½
leagues South of the turrets. Pay attention also to all I said in my
sixth letter in Part 1, and you will find all you need to know about
this coast as far as Rio Grande. I will say only one other thing about
the Senegal coast. The sea breaks there with a terrifying noise, but it
breaks directly on the shore-line. You will see many trees along the
river banks in Genehoa, and a thick forest behind the Senegal
Residence, against which the turrets show up well.[7] Between Cap
Blanc and Senegal the currents are fast-flowing in summer and run
to the SE and SSE.[8] The land of Genehoa next to the sea is all sand-

dunes, like Holland. Scattered trees can be seen, and woods stretch further inland.

The Moors of this country and those of Arguin are powerful and robust men. Those from Gualata who were enslaved by Sieur Ducasse when he captured the fort at Arguin, to the number of 120, men and women, were put aboard a small vessel belonging to the Senegal Company, to be transported to St Domingue. Either out of nobility of spirit or because all African peoples have been gifted by nature with the capacity to brave death, in the course of their passage to America they decided that they preferred an honourable [death] to a shameful captivity. Having plotted against the crew, and having found the means one morning to break out of their irons, after laying hands on some axes and crowbars which they had secretly hidden away in the vessel they attacked the sailors unexpectedly and while part of them were sleeping, and some were then thrown overboard by the mutineers. But others with their captain, Sieur Pierre Guillet, escaped to the powder-chamber and shut themselves up there (although they were only four or five out of the original ten). They kept up such a fire on the savages, with seven or eight muskets they had, that several were left for dead on the deck, which made them lose heart. Finally, despairing of success in what they had undertaken, the most determined among them, some 40 men and women, /p. 227/ threw themselves into the sea. Turning on their backs and calling out that their deed should be witnessed, with sad despair written on their faces they let themselves drown, without making the slightest bodily movement, and thus perished in the sight of the others.[9]

Do not be surprised, Sir, at this act of fearlessness. Apart from the instances of the same I have given you in several of my letters, we have other instances among Orientals and Westerners, whereby some persons when they feel themselves incapacitated by old age require their own children to kill them, while other persons allow themselves to be burned alive on the pyre of their dead spouse, ceremonially and splendidly. You know that Calunus did just this before Alexander, and then Zinamare, an Indian ambassador, in the presence of Augustus, and then again Seevola.[10]

I have a headache which has been killing me for some months and I must say frankly that you are the cause, it having been brought on by the way I have applied myself to searching and reading accounts in order to supply you with the description you have been seeking

763

from me over a period of two years.[11] You can clearly see, Sir, from the number of letters I have written to you that I was right to hurry myself along, just as you were urging me to do before I set to work. And you could not have gained a better indication of my compliance! But in the last analysis I am not complaining, since with my whole heart I am, Sir, Your etc.

Additional Passages from *1732*

[p. 530/2–3, on the Brandenburgers at Arguin]

In the year 1685 the Brandenburgh African company settled a factory at Arguim, by consent of the *Caboceiros* or chiefs of the country, seeing the French had blown up the fort above-mention'd, and carried away with them the cannon, ammunition, merchandize, and all other things they found therein, insomuch that they left neither lodge nor house or cabbin, nor any body whatever belonging to France. The Brandenburghers taking it for a total abandoning of the fort, rebuilt it out of its ruins, and garrisoned it, to secure their own people and trade. The French Senega company, finding their Gum-Arabick trade lessen'd by this new settlement, pleaded a property thereof at the French court, as being their conquest, and within the bounds of their concessions; and did so much insist upon their suppos'd right, that the French plenipotentiaries at the conferences for peace at Ryswick in 1697, presented a memorial to the mediators on that head; which was fully answer'd by another memorial from Mess. Schmettau and Danckelman, ambassadors of his late electoral highness of Brandenburgh at the Hague, that it was found the French had forfeited their right to the country and fort of Arguim, by their forsaking it totally and intirely, as is above observ'd; and the property thereof devolv'd to the Brandenburghers, by rebuilding it so many years after. Thus they possess it quietly to this present time, according to the law of nations. This account is inserted in the book publish'd of the conferences for peace, held at Ryswick Anno 1687. / I have not been able to hear whether the Hollanders, since this possession taken at Arguin, and the French, do still trade there for gums, etc.[12]

[p. 532/1–2, on a ray and pilot fish, and on the course approaching River Senegal]

From about the latitude of Cape Branco being twenty degrees

thirty minutes, as has been observ'd, we set our course south and south by west, till in seventeen degrees forty minutes, and then south-east.[13] In this latitude we saw passing by the ship's side a fish of an odd figure, but prodigious large and black, of the shape and form of a thorn-back, as represented in the print [*margin*: Plate 19]; differing in this, that it has two fleshy horns shooting out at the head, which we judg'd to be above thirty feet in compass. Our sailors give it the name of the sea-devil: it is a gamesome fish, and we observ'd it once took a leap pretty high, and falling down again, tumbled over and over with great force, making a mighty noise; by which motion we observ'd, that it's under side or belly was as white as the back was deep-black; and that it had as large a mouth, in proportion to its bulk, as our rays or thorn-backs. This sea-devil, or Whipray, is always attended by three little fishes, about nine inches long, of the figure as in the print, striped all round with white and black almost of an equal breadth and largeness, which renders them very beautiful and remarkable; our French sailors call them the pilots of the devil of the sea. Those small fishes, as is suppos'd, guide this monstrous fish, and prick him as soon as they spy some fish near; at which this enormous fish launches away very swiftly. Commonly those little pilots keep playing about his head, and chiefly betwixt his horns, and sometimes under his stomach. This Whipray has a tail four yards long at least. 'Tis a very strong fish, by what I could observe of its gamesome motions and leapings.[14] Soon after that fish was gone, we were in thirty-six, and at night in thirty-five fathom water, black sand and mud, about four leagues from the land of Genehoa; exactly west of Penha, or Resgate beforementioned.

In the day-time we set the head south from this latitude, and at night south-south-west, sounding every two hours. The next day we found ourselves on a sudden fallen into seventeen fathom fine sandy ground, which caus'd us to lie by for a while; and found by the sight we had of land immediately, about three leagues at east-south-east, that we were got on to the bank of sand, which is eighteen leagues to the northward of Senega road; and exactly west of Ganar, and of Petit-Palmit: the former a village, the latter a remarkable palm-tree appearing on the downy shore, so named by the French; and by the Dutch, Mast-Boom, which usually serves as a land-mark to steer into the road aforesaid, at one league and a half distance from land, without crouding too much sail, for fear of overshooting the Senega road: the tide from about Cape Branco to that river, in the summer season, setting very swift to south-south-west, and sometimes to south-west, and the wind north-north-east and north-east, always a brisk gale.[15]

NOTES

[1] Omission of an introductory paragraph.

[2] The two omissions cover two paragraphs and part of a third, describing the coast between Cap Blanc and Arguin, the Portuguese fort at Arguin, and the Dutch capture of the fort in 1633, all taken from Dapper, p. 1/370/1–6. Cf. *1732*, p. 529/3–9, with some additions from a nautical guide.

[3] The Dutch surrendered their fort at Arguin to the French under Jean-Baptiste Ducasse in August 1678 (Le Maire 1695, pp. 46–7; Labat 1728, I, 73–5; Ly 1958, p. 140; Monod 1983, pp. 79–82). Barbot referred to the capture in his 1678–9 journal (*1679*, p. 259) and presumably obtained further information from Company informants in Senegal, possibly first-hand information. '400 *milliers*' is 4,000 cwt, hence in *1732* 'two hundred tons'. It has been stated that by 1687 the Arguin trade was again entirely in Dutch hands (Ly 1958, p. 282): this is not based on the source cited (Ducasse), but is probably correct, at least in the sense that the agents of both Dutch and Brandenburg interests were in fact Zeelanders (Monod 1983, pp. 85–92). French ships visited Arguin in 1682, 1686 and 1687 to attack Dutch traders and challenge Brandenburg plans to occupy the forts, and it was complained that Dutch trade there was contrary to the Treaty of Nimuegen (Gaby 1689, pp. 18–19; Le Maire 1695, p. 47; Thilmans 1976, p. 19; Monod 1983, pp. 83–4; Jones 1985, pp. 162–4). A detailed inspection of the site in 1686 showed that the Dutch fort had only been partially demolished (Monod 1983, p. 83; Jones 1985, p. 122).
Cf. *1732*, p. 530/1, slightly abbreviated, but adding that the Dutch trade is now in the bay of Penha (see note 6 below).

[4] The two omissions cover three paragraphs and part of a fourth, on Arguin and its vicinity, taken from Dapper, pp. 1/370/6–8. Cf. *1732*, p. 530/4–9.

[5] For previous discussion of this river, see Letter 1/6 and note 6, above. Cf. *1732*, p. 531/1–6.

[6] On his map of Senegambia (*1688*, Letter 1/11, p. 61, illustration no. 11), Barbot indicates that Pena is 'where the Dutch now trade for gum after losing Arguin': cf. *1732*, Plate A (p. 16). For French attempts in 1686 to stop the Dutch trading at Pena, see Gaby 1689, pp. 19–20; Cultru 1913, p. 122; Ly 1958, p. 198.

766

Cf. *1732*, p. 531/7–11, which enlarges slightly, from a nautical guide, on this coast and on Pena (later known as Portendic).

[7] The 1678–9 journal does not make it clear whether Barbot was able to observe the coast to any extent before reaching the mouth of River Senegal; hence probably not all the information in this passage is from personal observation. For his earlier references to the coast near the Residence, see Letter 1/6, p. 21, above.

Cf. *1732*, p. 532/1–533/1, where the directions are enlarged, partly from new borrowings (e.g, the Mortier map), partly from recollection – for the latter part, see the Additional Passage; and for a much enlarged account of the immediate approach to River Senegal, presumably from personal observation, see an Additional Passage to Letter 1/6 above. The mysterious 'Schey d'elle Garze' is re-read and achieves a form, 'Secca de Gracia', nearer its Portuguese original, as the name of a sand-bank.

[8] On the general southward current of this coast, see *Africa pilot* 1967, p. 40.

[9] The uprising and suicide of Moors captured by Ducasse at Arguin was briefly mentioned by Barbot in a marginal note in the 1678–9 journal (*1679*, p. 259). His story is confirmed by a manuscript report to the Senegal Company c. 1687, complaining of Ducasse's ill-faith in enslaving the Moors, with the result that they all died (Ly 1958, pp. 140–1 – Ly was unaware of the Barbot reference, hence of its indication that not all the slaves were lost). For the episode, see also Monod 1983, pp. 82–3.

Cf. *1732*, p. 530/10, with the following changes: ' . . .the captain and some others, who had shut themselves up in the forecastle and great cabbin . . . holding their mouths quite open, swallow'd down the sea water. . .'.

[10] The instances of individuals maiming or killing themselves to make a point (but not because of old age or on a funeral pyre) are from Arrian (*Life of Alexander the Great*, book 7), Cassius Dio (book 53, section 9, 'Zarmarus'), and Livy (book 2, the individual being Caius Mucius Scaevola). But probably Barbot found the names conjoined in a single reference in a moralizing secondary source.

[11] The period of two years is probably part of the epistolary fiction.

[12] The adoption of the Portuguese form, 'Arguim', was probably due to the use of the Mortier map. Brandenburg occupation of Arguin was proposed in 1684, the site was inspected in 1685–6, a treaty was made with the local Moors in December 1687, and an agent-general was resident by 1692 and perhaps earlier (Monod 1983, pp. 94–101; Jones 1985, pp. 8, 181). For drawings of the Brandenburg fort, see Ly 1958, p. 282; Monod 1983, plates 9–13; Jones 1985, plate 11. Barbot does not claim to have had any information about this fort later than 1697, not even from his relative who was in the Brandenburg service c. 1700 (*1732*, p. 431/1). For a lengthy account of the

fort, the French diplomatic claim, and the eventual French capture of it in 1721, see Labat 1728, I, 76–156.

[13] The course here described seems not to be that recorded in the 1678 journal and must therefore be the 1681 course; however, it is curious that none of the personal references appears in the *1688* text. The course appears to differ from the one described somewhat impersonally in *1688* (and repeated in the succeeding paragraphs in *1732*), in that it lies out of sight of the coast between Cap Blanc and Ganar.

[14] The fish is a giant ray. A drawing of the ray, labelled 'Le Diable de Mer', with two accompanying fish, and a drawing of one of these fish labelled 'un Pilote du Diable de Mer', are on *1688*, illustration no. (113), inserted after p. 229, and are repeated on *1732*, Plate 19 (p. 224), but with three accompanying fish, and a new drawing, 'the under Part of the Sea Devil'.

[15] This latter part of the course to River Senegal enlarges, in the first person, on the course given in *1688*, p. 226. On Barbot's map of Senegambia (Letter 1/11, p. 61), sea-depths near the coast are shown only from Ganar south. For a 1684 French map of the coast from Cap Blanc to River Senegal, see Ly 1958, opp. p. 282.

LETTER 20

Another course from Europe to Gold Coast or to Ardres direct. Brief description of the Islands of Cap Vert. Course to be taken when leaving Gold Coast for Europe direct, or from Gold Coast or from Juada [sic] or Ardres for the islands or mainland of America. How to approach land at Cayenne. The islands of S. Matieu, Ascension and Fernando de Noronha, which are near the equator. Birds and fishes that can be taken in equatorial waters. Other enjoyments of the passage. Maxims to be observed by those who direct ships, both to keep the ships seaworthy in these torrid climates, and to conserve the cargo of black slaves being transported. The best way to treat them, in respect of sleeping and feeding, and generally whatever can be done to keep them alive. The exemplary punishments that must be given to those who conduct mutinies. Course from Cayenne to Martinique. Description of the town of S.Pierre and of Fort Roial du Cul de Sac on the same island.

I have led you, Sir, to the roadstead of Senegal, and if you have to go further, to Gambia and along the coast of Nigritia to Rio Grande, and from there still further to Sierra Lione, you may conduct yourself according to your judgement and in keeping with the information I have given you in my [previous] letters. The route is easy and I have passed on to you all the knowledge of it I have, coast after coast, up to Cabo de Lopo Gonzals. But if you are travelling from Europe direct to Gold Coast or Ardres, after passing south of Cap Blanc your course will lie within 12–15 leagues of Cape Verde. In that latitude take care not to approach land, since the currents split into two, especially in the vicinity of Rio Grande, the first and stronger running westwards along the equator to the West Indies, and the other twisting around and developing between Cape Verde and Cape Mount and then continuing East along the coasts of Guinea, in such a way that it often happened, at the beginning of the present century, that ships going to the East Indies, in order to avoid being driven on to the coast of Brazil near Cape St Augustin, took a course too far East and were gradually carried on to the shoals lying between Cape Verde and Cape Mount, and other ships were driven into the Ethiopian Gulf. But if you follow what is said above and what I have told you in my letters on Sierra Leone, you will sight land at Cape Mount, and when you find that landmark North of you, you will coast as far as Rio Sestro, if you want to water and take on wood there; or if you want to proceed further, as is not uncommon, sail within sight of Sestre Paris in order to obtain some casks of malagueta pepper for your slaves. /p. 228/ You must also take sight of Cape Palmas, steering round it at 3–4 leagues distance to avoid its shoals, and from there, if you are bound for Gold Coast, you need not coast along Ivory Coast but should anchor off Isseny, or Assany, the first village on Gold Coast, and then proceed along the remainder of the course as befits your circumstances and following the instructions I have given you in my letters. But if you wish to go direct from Cape Palmas to Ardres, keep South until in the latitude of Cape Tres Puntas, which you should also take sight of and anchor off, in order to buy a special bar-canoe at Axim or Tacorary. This must be for 16–20 rowers. From there proceed at 5–6 leagues off-shore and you will presently reach Juda.[1]

You will find that the currents on this course generally run strongly to the East and NE between Cape Palmas and Ardres, and to the NW between Cape Verde and Cape Palmas. From Cap Blanc onwards, there is good fishing in the sea for sharks, dolphin-fish, 'blackies' (*neigres*), bonitos, tunny, flying-fish, *carangues*, sucker-fish, which attach themselves to the flat part of the head like lampreys, *machorans* and a host of other fish; and this fishing is a pleasant diversion for the crew.[2]

Sailing 20–25 leagues out from Cap Blanc, you will find the sea covered in many places with a green and yellow weed called *saragossa* or *sargaso*, which resembles the weed that grows in wells, or sea-parsley. It has seed-pods at its extremities and these have neither taste nor substance. It is difficult to say precisely where this weed originates, since even more of it is found 60 leagues out. In some spots it is so thick that it takes a strong wind to drive a vessel through it. There are those who think that it was this floating weed which prevented Sataspes, son of Theaspes, one of the Archimedes, from completing his journey around Africa, he himself stating that he had encountered some obstacle which halted him. As you know, Sir, Sataspes was ordered to perform this voyage by Xerxes, as a punishment for having raped the daughter of Zoppyrus, the son of Megabyze. It would certainly seem that these weeds come from the islands called the Hesperides or Gorgades, which lie 150–160 leagues off Cape Verde.[3] [.../p. 229/...][4]

On this course I also noted that when level with these islands a fog sometimes descended which was so thick and so reddish in colour that it looked like burnt sand. This clearly shows that the islands have very bad air, and the fog at this point often causes severe headaches, burning fevers and bloody fluxes.[5] [...][6]

Now we come to the courses that must be followed when leaving Gold Coast for Europe, and when leaving Juda and Ardres, either for the mainland [of America] at Cayenne and from there continuing to the American islands, or directly for the islands. These courses are so well-known and so simple that I am almost at fault in wasting time on them – your time in reading them, my time in writing them. But since you have asked me to leave out nothing that might be of any use for such voyages, you must be answerable to yourself for the time that we seem to waste in discussing a matter so commonplace that almost every schoolboy knows it. Forgive me this warning, but I always like to alert you beforehand.

[illustration no. (113), four named fish, inserted after p. 229]

[illustration no. (114), three named fish and a porpoise, inserted after p. 229][7]

Let us suppose that you are leaving Gold Coast (either from Cormentyn or Axim) for Europe, and that you have all the necessary

provisions for your voyage and do not need to call in /p. 230/ at any
of the islands in the Ethiopic Gulf or at Cap Lopo. Keep as close to
the wind as possible, in order to pass to the windward of St Tomé
(although this can only be done with difficulty, unless it is the season
of squalls from the NE). Otherwise you can reckon that you will not
sight this cape, because the currents bear strongly into the Gulf.
From there, Sir, you make directly towards Annoboan (or if you lack
provisions and stores, you can anchor and get them on this island).
From there, you make your way to 3½ or 4 degrees South, where
you pick up the SE wind, which very quickly sends you North of the
equator, which you will pass in the longitude of Cape Verde. Continuing northwards, you will gradually pick up the NE winds, until
almost level with the Azores or Ilhas Flamingos. There are some
who, according to the season, or as they find the wind when leaving
Cape Lopez, sail North and South of the equator, within one degree,
as far as the longitude of Cape Palmas. From there, it is very easy to
return to Gold Coast, if that is what is want (the small vessels trading
in gold do this), or if you are going to Europe you can easily find the
course. But the first route is the surest way of making a quick voyage
from this cape to Europe, since the experience of many has shown
that the neighbourhood of the equator is subject to calms, between
the two belts of SE and NW [read: NE] winds, which hold the ship
back for long periods. Some friends of mine took five months this
way, whereas others going further South took only two and a half
months. It is true that there are instances of ships reaching the
English Channel in 70 days by zigzagging North and South across
the line, but it is better, Sir, to follow the general rule. Almost all the
nations of Europe follow it, and in my view it is much speedier, since
a good ship can make 60–70 leagues each twenty-four hours on this
route, with a good sea and fresh winds.[8]

If, when leaving Juda or Offra for Cayenne or the Isles Antilles,
you have to call in at Isle du Prince, you will have great difficulty in
fulfilling your intention from windward, at least unless you have a
ship which is extremely good at sailing close to the wind. In these
districts the wind constantly blows from the South and SE and the
currents carry you rapidly ENE and ENE-by-East. You are obliged
to work along the coast of the Ethiopic Gulf in order to reach this
spot, which may take 20–30 days, because you have to anchor most
of the day and sail at night, in order to take advantage of the land
breeze. It is true, however, that I once went 50 leagues to the West

771

of Isle du Prince when leaving Juda, but this was in the season of squalls from the NE, and the ship was a brigantine extremely good at sailing close to the wind. Nevertheless, this course misled me, for I fell to leeward of the island, which I eventually reached by rowing into the currents which divide as they approach that landmass. One flows NNE, the other SSE.[9] It is still more difficult to get to St Tomé from windward if you set out from Ardres. Hence there is always very slow progress, especially [? worrying] when slaves are carried. This is why I advise you to furnish yourself with all that you can in the way of stores and provisions at Juda, where they are available in abundance, so that you can go directly to Cape Lopez to obtain water and wood, and then pass to Annoboan if you lack anything, since it will be in view.[10]

As for the rest of the course, if you have to go to Cayenne you will place yourself (as I /p. 231/ have said) in 3 or 3½ degrees South, to catch the ESE or SE winds, and then carry on West until you reckon you are 100 leagues short of the islets of Ponendo de Santo Paolo, which the maps put at 1°40'N and 352 degrees of latitude. From there make NW, then NNW, after which head WNW as far as 4° North, so that you bear towards Cap Casse-pourri (on the mainland of South America). [. . .][11]

This route from Cap de Lopo to Cayenne will take you 40–45 days, and you will have a good wind, smooth seas and very few severe storms, apart from some squalls near Cape Lopez and Anno-boan and some heavy showers off America, with very occasionally some water-spouts, otherwise known as 'dragons' tails'. As soon as you see one of the latter, take the precaution of furling the sails in time. Do not be stubborn on these occasions, for this has led to many serious disasters. You can tell these storms are coming, either by night or day, when you see a small black cloud shooting up on the horizon which in no time covers the whole hemisphere.[12]

During such an easy passage, there is pleasure to be had in fishing and taking sea-creatures, for apart from often catching bonitos, tunny, porpoises, sharks, dorados, flying fish and sucker-fish, you can often see thousands of whales and grampuses, which appeal by their slow and heavy movements. You can take many of the birds which the Dutch call *Meuvettes* and the French *Fous* [Fools], be-cause they let themselves be handled and so seized, when they perch on the yards and rigging in the evening to spend the night resting, which happens especially in the vicinity of the islands of St Matieu and Ascencion. Almost all of them come from the latter island. There are /p. 232/ two or three sorts. Some are as big as a young goose, with a large long beak and short legs shaped like those of a duck, and their cry is piercing. Here is what they look like.

[illustration no. (115), the Madcap bird]

Others are white and smaller, with red feet, and others again are small and very like lapwings. These creatures are found in great flocks on these seas, where they live on flying fish. I have sometimes had whole hours of diversion watching these birds prey like vultures on millions of flying fish, which the bonitos and tunny have forced to take to the air, out of their own element and into that of the birds, in order to save themselves. But as if the winged creatures were in collusion with the bonitos, both being enemies of these wretched amphibians, the birds force the flying fish to return to to the sea so that they become the prey of those they try to flee from, or else in flight they become the prey of the Fools and other birds that frequent these seas. However, this whole confused scene is diverting to watch. Since I know you like plenty of illustrations, I present you with a drawing I made on the spot, which I am sure you will find very interesting. [13]

[illustration no. (116), birds and flying fish] /p. 233/†

[illustration no. (117), flying fish][14]

[illustrations nos. (118)-(120), bonito fish and views of the coast of America and Cayenne Island, inserted after p. 233] [. . ./p. 234/. . .][15]

If you follow exactly the procedure I have set out you can be assured of a good passage and of not taking more than 50 days to reach the Isles Antilles, whereas if you stick too closely to the equator you will most frequently find yourself in the doldrums, which will greatly prolong your crossing and cause great loss, particularly if you are carrying large numbers of slaves. For the high mortality which we learn occurs on the ships of our nation, and their slow passage, derive, indeed, Sir, more from ignorance than from any other cause. Many of those who find themselves to leeward of Cayenne have attributed the error to the doldrums, but more often it is because they have not planned their route and have failed to pay close attention to the land from the time that they encounter the currents of the Amazon. Others have made unsatisfactory voyages not only because they have not held to a sound procedure in their navigation but also because they have not exercised enough care in putting their ships into good condition before leaving port. It is essential, Sir, and you must on no account overlook it but regard it as a guiding rule, that at the point of departure, whether this be Juda or Cap de Lopo, you set your shrouds and stays, and tar them as you do the lesser rigging, and also grease the pulley-blocks. If you are in a quiet locality, lay the vessel on its side as far as you can, in order to clean it below and give it a good coating of tallow or sulphur, so that it will sail more lightly.[16]

Further, you ought to take care during the passage to caulk the vessel regularly, in good weather on the outside, and in bad weather on the deck and on the inside. After that, have it scraped and tarred all over, to preserve it and give it an appearance that pleases the eye. This is very good for all and especially for the slaves, for whom you must also take particular care that the in-between deck is always clean and in good order. Certain of the crew should be required to attend to this only, and they should be given permission to select from among the slaves those they consider most suitable to help them in caring for their companions, since there are always some who are infirm and sick. Thrice a week you should heat cannon-balls and put them when red hot into buckets full of vinegar standing between the two decks, with the hatches shut, so as to improve the bad air that engenders there. Do this after you have had the deck thoroughly swept and washed down with sea water, and finally have several bucketfuls of cold vinegar thrown down; and leave the hatches open during the daytime, although you have to close them at night to keep the damp out. The men and women are usually separated, the men being placed in the forepart beyond the main mast, and the women towards the stern, with a stout barrier between them, otherwise there would be dreadful confusion.

Since these wretched creatures are themselves cannibals, at least most of them, they so strongly believe that we buy them in order to eat them in Europe, instead of eating animals, /p. 235/ that nothing can make them abandon this strange prejudice. It so alarms many of them that they refuse what is most necessary for life and allow

56. Birds and flying-fish

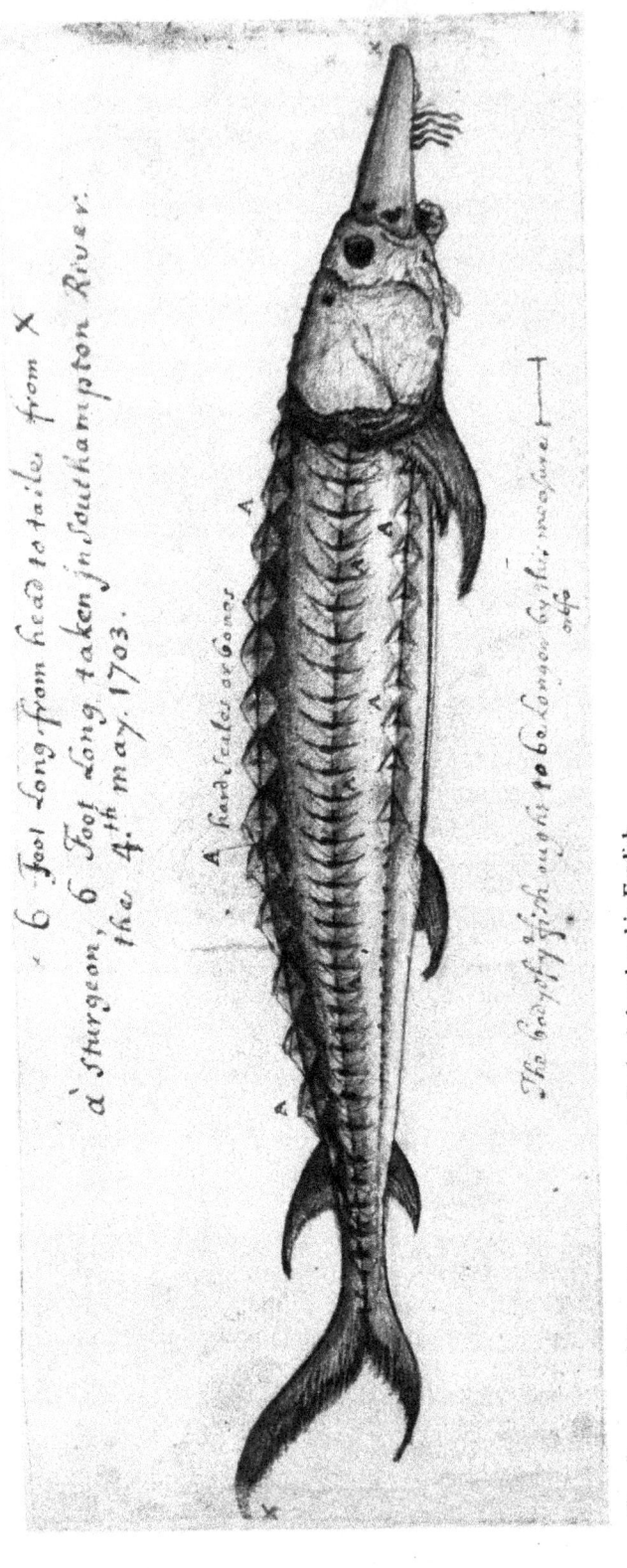

57. Sturgeon, 1703 – with a description in Barbot's hand and in English

themselves to perish miserably, so that if one puts them in irons, as some do, it increases their terrors and their melancholia and consequently causes greater loss. Instead, leave them free and let them go and come on the deck as they please, hence they can amuse themselves in company.[17] But in order that this liberty does not harm you, deprive them of all the means whereby they could raise a revolt. To that end, have as many of your crew as you can sleeping at the rear of the vessel, and keep all your weapons, fire-arms and others, in your cabin, with a sentinal on guard. Thus it will be difficult for them to have an uprising, but if one occurs, on account perhaps of their desperation or out of sheer mischief, spare no effort to repress their insolence and as an example to the others, sacrifice the lives of all the most mutinous. This will terrify the others and keep them obedient. The way of making it clear to them, I mean the form of punishment that scares Africans most, is by chopping parts off a living man (*couper un homme vif*) with blows from an axe and presenting the separated parts to the others.[18]

They are also sometimes brought to revolt when provisions are lacking, which almost always happens on ships which make a lengthy passage. Give them two meals a day and a full coconut-shell of water each meal. I made them eat, each sex separately, in a mess of ten, at 10 o'clock in the morning and 5 o'clock in the evening. Between meals, to keep them happy, they are given sometimes handfuls of maize, sometimes tobacco and pipes, and coconuts, and occasionally brandy. Above all, make them plenty of friendly gestures (*caresses*), and often jest with them and make them play various games, giving them freedom to sing and dance, especially the women. Further, give good treatment to the sick and wounded, and punish in front of their eyes those sailors or other members of the crew who do them any harm. They are also given a piece of thick wrapping cloth, and wooden spoons for eating beans and peas, their usual food, with a little lard and fat. Some feed them on maize, peas and grains, with palm-oil and maniguette pepper. I consider broad beans the best food of all. The outcome depends on how much care you take in the transaction.[19] [.../p. 236/...][20]

I am sure that you do not require of me a new description of the Islands any more than you require one of Cayenne. I will limit myself merely to giving you a map of the latter place, and a profile and plan of the town and Fort St Louis, together with a profile of Fort Royal and the borough of St Pierre de la Martinique which I have drawn very carefully. This also is the point at which I wish to conclude a work that has kept me in bondage for two years, the years during which you have begged me to labour on it. I have satisfied your curiosity as best I could, and I hope that you will give me credit for my compliance. I am, Sir, Your etc.

[illustrations nos. (121)–(123), map of the Cayenne district and profile and plan of the town of Cayenne][21] /pp. 237(blank)–238/

[illustration no. (124), a sturgeon][22]† /p. 239/

[. . .][23]

[illustrations nos. (125)–(126), a marine monster and a fish]

Additional Passages from *1732*

[p. 540/1–5, on navigating to Gold Coast]

I shall subjoin to the course to steer for the Gold-Coast of Guinea, the following observations, as deliver'd by the late Mr. Henry Greenhill, whom I have mention'd heretofore as my particular acquaintance, when he was agent at cape Corso castle, and ever since in England; being a very intelligent and experienced gentleman, commissioner of the navy at Plymouth and Portsmouth, and projector and builder of the royal dock at Hamozes.[24]

Winds on the Coast The coast of Africa from cape Palmas to cape Fermoso lies east and east by north; and near those points the land-breezes blow on that coast, which commonly begin about seven in the evening, and continue all night till the same time the next morning: during which interval we are troubled with stinking fogs and mists from shore, which by return of the sea-breezes upon the opposite points, are all driven away; and we have the benefit of them in a curious fresh gale, till about five in the afternoon. / And here let me note it for a general observation, that in these, and all other places within the tropicks, as far as ever I took notice, the wind is drawn by the land. For if an island or head-land were inclining to a circular form, the sea and land-breezes fall in diametrically opposite to that part where you are; so that if you are on the south-side, the sea-breeze shall be at south, and the land-breeze, when it comes in its season, at north. / In getting on the coast, we endeavour to fall in with cape Monte or cape Mesurado, which is about eighteen leagues to the east-south-east thereof; and after that, we double cape Palmas, whence, as aforesaid, the land tends away east by north, the current near the shore sets upon that point down into the Bight. The land-breezes between cape St Anne and cape Palmas are at east, blowing brisk four leagues off the shore. The sea-winds there are at south-west.

The tornados, says he, usually come in the beginning of April, and seldom leave the Gold Coast till June commences, and with frequent visits make us sensible of their qualities. We have sometimes three or four in a day, but then their continuance is but short, perhaps not above two hours, and the strength or fury not above a quarter of an hour; but accompanied with prodigious thunder, lightning and rain, and the violence of the wind so extraordinary, that it has sometimes roll'd up the lead the houses are cover'd with, as closely and compactly as possibly it could be done by the art of man. The name implies a variety of winds, but the strength of them is generally at south-east; and by ships that are bound for the coast, they are made use of to get to windward.

[p. 541/8, a course from New Calabar]

At parting from the New Calabar River, if the wind be west-south-west, we lay the head south by east, and with the south-west wind, to south-south-east; keeping as near the wind as is reasonable to weather the island of Ferdinand Po, distant thirty-six leagues from Bandy Point north-east by east; and having past to the windward of it, set the course for Cape St. John; and thence ordering the navigation, according to occurrences, as above related, if we design for St. Tome, to wood and water, and for provisions, we may very well, in the month of September, get our passage from Bandy Point to St. Tome's road in fifteen or sixteen days. At that time of year we find the weather commonly so cold, as we approach this island, though so near the line, and at the time of the equinox, that it may well be said to be as raw and pinching, as on the coast of Britany; especially in the night, every man aboard, though never so hardy, is glad to put on more clothes.[25]

[p. 544/8, on Noddy-birds or Madcaps]

They are a sort of sea-gulls; the Portuguese call them Alcatraces, and give this farther account of them. At night when dispos'd to sleep, they soar up as high as possible, and putting their head under one wing, support themselves for some time with the other; but because the weight of their bodies must needs force them down at last, as soon as they come to the water, they take their flight again, and often repeating it, may in a manner be said to sleep waking: it often happens that they fall into the ships as they sail. Those who know the nature of them add, that at a certain time of the year they always go ashore to build their nests, and that in the highest places, whereby they facilitate their flight. It has been observ'd, that being set at liberty upon the plain deck, they cannot raise themselves. Some English sailors call this bird a booby, and others a noddy. As they feed mostly upon flying fish, they taste very fishy; and if you do not salt them very well before you eat them, they will make you sick. They are so silly, that when they are weary of flying, they will, if you hold out your hand, come and sit upon it.[26]

[pp. 546/1-548/2, on the treatment of slaves aboard ship]

As to the management of our slaves aboard, we lodge the two sexes apart, by means of a strong partition at the main mast; the fore part is for men, the other behind the mast for the women. If it be in large ships carrying five or six hundred slaves, the deck in such ships ought to be at least five and a half or six foot high, which is very requisite for driving a continual trade of slaves: for the greater height it has, the more airy and convenient it is for such a considerable number of human creatures; and consequently far the more healthy for them, and fitter to look after them. We build a sort of half-decks along the sides with deals and spars provided for that purpose in Europe, that half-deck extending no farther than the side of our scuttles, and so the slaves lie in two rows, one above the other, and as close together as they can be crouded.

The Dutch company's ships exceed all other Europeans in such accommodations, being commonly built designedly for those voyages, and consequently contrived very wide, lofty, and airy, betwixt decks, with gratings and scuttles, which can be cover'd with tarpawlins in wet weather; and in fair uncover'd, to let in the more air. Some also have made small ports, or lights along the sides at proper distances, well secured with thick iron bars, which they open from time to time for the air; and that very much

778

contributes to the preservation of those poor wretches, who are so thick crouded together. / The Portugueses of Angola, a people in many respects not to be compared to the English, Dutch, or French, in point of neatness aboard their ships, tho' indeed some French and English ships in those voyages for slaves are slovenly, foul and stinking, according to the temper and want of skill of the commanders; the Portugueses, I say, are commendable in that they bring along with them to the coast, a sufficient quantity of coarse thick mats, to serve as bedding under the slaves aboard, and shift them every fortnight or three weeks with such fresh mats: which besides that it is softer for the poor wretches to lie upon than the bare deals or decks, must also be much healthier for them, because the planks, or deals, contract some dampness more or less, either from the deck being so often wash'd to keep it clean and sweet, or from the rain that gets in now and then thro' the scuttles or other openings, and even from the very sweat of the slaves; which being so crouded in a low place, is perpetual, and occasions many distempers, or at best great inconveniencies dangerous to their health: whereas, lying on mats, and shifting them from time to time, must be much more convenient; and it would be prudent to imitate the Portugueses in this point, the charge of such mats being inconsiderable.[27]

We are very nice in keeping the places where the slaves lie clean and neat, appointing some of the ship's crew to do that office constantly, and several of the slaves themselves to be assistant to them in that employment; and thrice a week we perfume betwixt decks with a quantity of good vinegar in pails, and red-hot iron bullets in them, to expel the bad air, after the place has been well wash'd and scrubb'd with brooms: after which, the deck is clean'd with cold vinegar, and in the day-time, in good weather, we leave all the scuttles open, and shut them again at night.

It has been observed before, that some slaves fancy they are carry'd to be eaten, which makes them desperate, and others are so on account of their captivity: so that if care be not taken, they will mutiny and destroy the ship's crew in hopes to get away. / To prevent such misfortunes, we use to visit them daily, narrowly searching every corner between decks, to see whether they have not found means to gather any pieces of iron, or wood, or knives, about the ship, notwithstanding the great care we take, not to leave any tools or nails, or other things in the way: which, however, cannot be always so exactly observed, where so many people are in the narrow compass of a ship. [28] / We cause as many of our men as is convenient to lie in the quarter-deck and gun-room, and our principal officers in the great cabbin, where we kept all our small arms in a readiness, with sentinels constantly at the door and avenues to it; being thus ready to disappoint any attempts our slaves might make on a sudden. / These precautions contribute very much to keep them in awe; and if all those who carry slaves duly observed them, we should not hear of so many revolts as have happen'd. Where I was concern'd, we always kept our slaves in such order, that we did not perceive the least inclination in any of them to revolt, or mutiny, and lost very few of our number in the voyage. [29]

It is true, we allow'd them much more liberty, and used them with more tenderness than most other Europeans would think prudent to do; as to have them all upon deck every day in good weather; to take their meals twice a-day, at fix'd hours, that is, at ten in the morning, and at five at night; which being ended, we made the men go down again between decks: for the women were almost intirely at their own discretion, to be upon deck as long as they pleas'd, nay even many of the males had the same liberty by turns, successively; few or none being fetter'd or kept in shackles, and that only on account of some disturbances, or injuries, offer'd to their fellow-captives, as will unavoidably /p. 547/ happen among a numerous croud of such savage people. Besides we allow'd each of them betwixt their meals a handful of Indian wheat and Mandioca, and now and then short pipes and tobacco to smoak upon deck by turns, and some cocoa-nuts; and to the women a piece of coarse cloth to cover them, and the same to many of the men, which we took care they did wash from time to time, to prevent vermin, which they are very subject to; and because it look'd sweeter and more agreeable. Towards the evening they diverted themselves on the deck, as they thought fit, some conversing together, others dancing, singing, and sporting after their manner, which pleased them highly, and often made us pastime; especially the female sex, who being apart from the males, on the quarter-deck, and many of them young sprightly maidens, full of jollity and good humour, afforded us abundance of recreation; as did several little fine boys, which we mostly kept to attend on us about the ship.

780

We mess'd the slaves twice a day, as I have observed; the first meal was of our large beans boil'd, with a certain quantity of Muscovy lard, which we have from Holland, well pack'd up in casks. The beans we have in great plenty at Rochel. The other meal was of pease, or of Indian wheat, and sometimes meal of Mandioca; this provided in Prince's Island, the Indian wheat at the Gold Coast; boil'd with either lard, or suet, or grease, by turns, and sometimes with palm-oil and malaguette or Guinea pepper. I found they had much better stomachs for beans, and it is a proper fattening food for captives; in my opinion far better to maintain them well, than Indian wheat, Mandioca or yams; tho' the Calabar slaves value this root above any other food, as being used to it in their own country: but it is not at certain times of the year to be had in so great a quantity as is requisite to subsist such a number of people for several months; besides that they are apt to decay, and even to putrify as they grow old. Horse-beans are also very proper for slaves in lieu of large beans: there is good plenty of them in Great Britain, which, as well as the other beans, will keep, if well put up in dry fats or casks.[30] / We distributed them by ten in a mess, about a small flat tub, made for that use by our coopers, in which their victuals were served; each slave having a little wooden spoon to feed himself handsomely, and more cleanly than with their fingers, and they were well pleased with it. / At each meal we allow'd every slave a full coco-nut shell of water, and from time to time a dram of brandy, to strengthen their stomachs. / The Dutch commonly feed their slaves three times a day, with indifferent good victuals, and much better than they eat in their own country. The Portugueses feed them most with Mandioca.

As for the sick and wounded, or those out of order, our surgeons, in their daily visits betwixt decks, finding any indisposed, caused them to be carried to the Lazaretto, under the forecastle, a room reserved for a sort of hospital, where they were carefully look'd after. Being out of the croud, the surgeons had more conveniency and time to administer proper remedies; which they cannot do leisurely between decks, because of the great heat that is there continually, which is sometimes so excessive, that the surgeons would faint away, and the candles would not burn; besides, that in such a croud of brutish people, there are always some very apt to annoy and hurt others, and all in general so greedy, that they will snatch from the sick slaves the fresh meat or

781

liquor that is given them. It is no way advisable to put the sick slaves into the long-boat upon deck, as was very imprudently done in the Albion frigate, spoken of in the description of New Calabar; for they being thus exposed in the open air, and coming out of the excessive hot hold, and lying there in the cool of the nights, for some time just under the fall of the wind from the sails, were soon taken so ill with violent cholicks, and bloody fluxes, that in a few days they died, and the owners lost above three hundred slaves in the passage from St Tome to Barbadoes; and the two hundred and fifty that survived, were like skeletons, one half of them not yielding above four pounds a head there: an oversight, by which fifty per Cent of the stock or outset was lost.[31]

Much more might be said relating to the preservation and maintenance of slaves in such voyages, which I leave to the prudence of the officers that govern aboard, if they value their own reputation and their owners advantage; and shall only add these few particulars, that tho' we ought to be circumspect in watching the slaves narrowly, to prevent or disappoint their ill designs for our own conservation, yet we must not be too severe and haughty with them, but on the contrary caress and humour them in every reasonable thing. Some commanders of a morose and peevish temper are perpetually beating and curbing them even without the least offence, and will not suffer any upon deck but when unavoidable necessity to ease themselves does require; under pretence it hinders the work of the ship and sailors, and that they are troublesome by their nasty nauseous stench, or their noise; which makes those poor wretches desperate, and besides their falling into distempers through melancholy, often is the occasion of their destroying themselves. /p. 548/ Such officers should consider, those unfortunate creatures are men as well as themselves, tho' of a different colour, and pagans; and that they ought to do to others as they would be done by in like circumstances; as it may be their turn, if they should have the misfortune to fall into the hands of Algerines or Sallee men, as it has happen'd to many after such voyages perform'd. They ought also to consider the interest of their owners, who put them into that employment; and, unless they have laid aside the sense of gratitude and credit, it may be an inducement to curb their brutish temper, and move them to a gentle humane carriage towards the poor slaves, and to contribute as far as in them lies, to keep them clean, healthy and easy; to lessen the deep sense of their lamentable condition, which many are sensible enough of, whatever we may think of their stupidity. These methods will undoubtedly turn to the advantage of the adventurers, their masters, and is the least return they can reasonably expect from them.[32]

It also concerns the adventurers in Guinea voyages for slaves, not to allow the commanders, supercargo or officers, the liberty of taking aboard any slaves for their own particular account, as is too often practised among European traders, thinking to save something in their salaries by the month: for experience has shown, that the captain's slaves never die, since there are not ten masters in fifty who scruple to make good their own out of the cargo; or at least such licence-slaves are sure to have the best accommodations aboard, and the greatest plenty of subsistence out of the ship's stock: and very often those who were allow'd to carry but two slaves, have had ten or twelve, and those the best of the cargo, subsisted out of the general provisions of the ship, and train'd up aboard, to be carpenters, coopers, and cooks, so as to sell for double the price of other slaves in America, because of their skill, etc. And such commanders, when return'd home, and required to account for such licentious practices, and to restore the product of such slaves so disposed of, allowing them their first cost, not only refuse to comply with so reasonable a demand, but knowing how many formalities the law in England requires, to compel them to it, which reduces it almost to an impossibility, they fall out with, and ungratefully abuse their benefactors and patrons. So that it were infinitely better, in lieu of such grants, to augment the salaries proportionably to the great fatigues and imminent hazards of life in such voyages, with this condition, that any person whatsoever transgressing in this point, shall forfeit not only such slaves as he shall presume to carry over without permission, but also all his wages, and pay a reasonable fine besides. All this rigorously executed would have a great influence, and deter many from their ill practices for the future. And thus I conclude the description of the coasts of North and South Guinea . . .

[p. 573/1, on the voyage of the *Jolly* from Whydah to Martinique in 1682]

. . . [We] came to an anchor, near our other companion of the Guinea voyage, the Jolly, who was arriv'd there twelve days before us, and inform'd me, that at his sailing from Whidah road in Guinea, with the Emerillon and the Pearl, as I have taken notice of in that part of the description of Whidah, he fell to the leeward of the islands Prince and St. Tome in the Bight of Guinea; and after several days spent in turning and tacking, at last reach'd the cape Lope, where having taken in wood and water, finding the officers and crew very sickly, and no refreshments at all on the said cape at that time, even not so much as a chicken, they had projected to sail for St Tome; but whether thro' ignorance, or design of the pilots aboard, could not compass it, and were necessitated to make the best of their way for Martinico, in the sorry condition they were in. But by a peculiar providence finding the trade-winds of south-east, at two degrees south of the line, they got their passage in forty-eight days, and had sold their slaves immediately... [33]

NOTES

[1] Cf. *1732*, p. 537/8–10, where 'you' becomes 'we', making it seem that Barbot did not call at River Sess, whereas he did in 1681 (see Letter 1/29, p. 151, above); and 'this century' correctly becomes 'last century'.

[2] On these fish, see Letter 2/20, notes 15, 18, 20, 22, 26, 31, 32, above. Cf. *1732*, p. 537/11–12.

[3] Cf. *1732*, p. 537/13, but 'samphire' instead of sea-parsley, and with the classical reference (originally from Herodotus, book 4) omitted.

[4] Omission of six paragraphs, except for the two sentences that follow, describing the Cape Verde Islands. Most of the information is extracted from a much longer (mainly navigational) account by Dapper (Dapper/ *Eylanden* 1668, pp. 84–90), but Barbot may be following an intermediate source, perhaps one of his 'modern geographers'. A few changes may be mere embroidery (e.g. goatskins produce Moroccan leather) or may be from an untraced source – Barbot notes the number of accounts of these islands already available in order to excuse the brevity of his description, and in fact very many earlier voyage accounts contained references to them (e.g. Ligon 1657, which Barbot does not appear to have seen). The version in *1732*, pp. 538/1–539/1, is rewritten and has additional material, especially on salt-making and tortoises, mainly from Dampier 1703, pp. 12–13, 19, 21–2, 25, with perhaps echoes of Leguat 1708, pp. 11–13. There is no evidence that Barbot or his relatives visited the islands – *1732* has no illustrations of them. Speaking of the large red asses bred on Sal, Barbot adds – 'when I was at Cayenne, a Dutch ship carry'd over thither sixteen of these asses for sale' (but this is not mentioned in *1679*); and speaking of Santiago, he adds – 'The

784

French took and plunder'd it in the year 1712' (in May 1712, see the Introduction, pp. xxxv–xxxvi, and note 107). Finally, he adds information obtained in 1681 in Senegal – 'To these islands the French agents at Senega and Goree send for provisions, when there is any scarcity in those parts of Nigritia, and have them in exchange for some few slaves, and all sorts of linen and wearing apparel for men and women. In the year 1681, when I arrived at Goree, there being a great dearth in that country, one of the company's ships was gone to the islands for provisions' – for this famine, see Letter 1/7, note 32, above. For the export of asses and horses to colonies in America, see Ligon 1657, pp. 3, 18, 58; Dampier 1703, p. 21; Phillips 1732, p. 188.

[5] The 'fog' described is the dust-ridden air brought by the harmattan wind from the Sahara, although this is more prevalent off the Saharan coast in the first quarter of the year than in November, the month Barbot passed through the area in 1678 and 1681.
Cf. *1732*, p. 539/3.

[6] Omission of two sentences – the brevity of comment on the Cape Verde Islands has spared Barbot 'leafing over many volumes'.

[7] The illustrations show seven fish and a porpoise: the porpoise, sucker-fish, and machoran had been drawn in 1678–9 (*1679*, pp. 260, 355, 359), the flying fish is not the one in *1679*, p. 355, and with the pilot fish, *diable du mer* (ray), balahou, and 'dolphin-fish of the second kind' must have been drawn in 1682. The drawings are repeated on *1732*, Plate 19 (p. 224).

[8] None of the Barbots is recorded as ever sailing directly back to Europe from Africa. Barbot himself sailed back to Europe twice, but each time from America, not from Africa; his brother, as far as we know, only once sailed to Africa and then he too returned by America; his nephew, travelling as far as we know on his first voyage, died in America. Barbot may have obtained additional information on the Africa-America passage from the journals of his relatives and their companions, Grazilhier and Casseneuve, but the sections of the journals presented in *1732* omit the return passages to Europe.
Cf. *1732*, pp. 540/6–541/4, which adds or enlarges at a number of points, as follows: 'It must be observed in this passage, that when once we are to the westward of the said cape Lope, and in south latitude, the current sets northerly, and the wind, to twenty degrees of latitude, is generally at east-south-east; as to the like number of degrees, on the opposite side of the line, it blows at east-north-east. Nor is there any change of the current observed, unless in the tornado season, when, during their blowing, they set to windward; tho' perhaps the moon, upon full and change, may have the like influence there, as in other places'. Crossing the equator at the longitude of Cape Verde is now said to be for the months May-August, but in September 'we may sail continually along the line'. However, 'at that time it proves so

cold there, at so small a distance from the line, that the sailors, who are commonly more hardy than other people, clothe themselves warm; the thick weather and fresh gales, wholly obstructing the heat of the sun, though it be then passing the line, and directly over our heads' – for more on the relative chill, see the Additional Passage. The vessels returning to Gold Coast are now described as 'the interlopers, and other Europeans who use a coasting trade in Guinea'. Finally, 'the custom of ducking, before-mentioned in speaking of the tropics, is observ'd by all nations in passing the line: the French use much pumping of them in a tub with salt-water, instead of ducking. There are many other sports used by sailors, which afford passengers good diversion. The ducking is by the French call'd the sea-baptism.' For the earlier reference to the custom, see Letter 3/17, Additional Passage.

[9] Although Barbot gives confident instructions, he only sailed from Whydah to Príncipe on this one occasion. We do not have the journal of the voyage in April 1682, but Barbot marked his course, day by day, from Juda to Santo António, 'in a brigantine of 15 tons', on his map of the Gulf of Biafra (*1688*, illustration no. (90)). Port to port, it took eleven days.

Cf. *1732*, p. 541/5, which adds the month of the voyage, and concludes more dramatically: 'It was with no small trouble that I reach'd the port of St. Antony; for when I came in sight of the island, though its southerly point bore east-south-east, and it was then very calm, the current drove us under the north point of it, and we had certainly miss'd it, and fallen into the Bight, had we not seasonably made use of six long oars we had aboard, and hands enough to hold it out rowing from morning till sun-set, notwithstanding the scorching vehement heat of the sun, and no air at all; and by that means coasting the west side of the island, gain'd the division of the current, one branch of it setting north-east as customary, and the other south-south-east round the land: so I made this passage in ten days from Whidah road hither, which is extraordinary.'

[10] Cf. *1732*, p. 541/7. For another voyage which had difficulty in leaving the gulf, see the Additional Passage (*1732*, p. 537/1).

[11] Omission of further instructions referring to making landfall in America: cf. *1732*, pp. 542/3–543/6. In 1679 Barbot's ship crossed the equator on days 11 and 41 of a 51 days voyage from Príncipe to Cayenne (*1679*, pp. 353, 358). In *1732*, p. 542/1–2, Barbot inserts material on correcting for compass variations during the passage, taken from the text of Halley's famous charts (Thrower 1981, p. 33, figs. 7–8).

[12] Barbot has discussed the waterspout earlier, see Letter 1/5, p. 18 and note 18, above.
Cf. *1732*, p. 543/7.

[13] In late March 1679, when North of Ascension Island, Barbot saw flying fish in large numbers and recorded *fous* being caught and eaten, but tasting

like sea-gulls (*1679*, p. 357). His reference to vultures swooping on their prey indicates Barbot's unfamiliarity with a bird which only scavenges. The drawing of the duck-like Fool (or Madcap) bird is not in the 1679 journal so was presumably made on the 1682 voyage: it was not repeated in *1732*. The drawing of flying fish under attack, also not in the journal and therefore presumably made in 1682, reappeared on *1732*, Plate 7 (p. 104), but with a waterspout added.

Cf. *1732*, p. 544/6–10, much enlarged, notably as follows. The fish – 'we take them fresh and fresh [sic] every day, especially the bonitoes and albacores, of which latter sort some weigh sixty pounds or more, being not only pleasant, but very useful and refreshing for travellers.' The cetaceans – 'lying still as if they were dead with their snouts above water, and sometimes playing about the ship, with a heavy slow motion and a great noise; and when in company of other ships, we visit one another by turns in our pinnaces or yauls, having commonly good weather and a smooth sea in this passage'. For a long passage on the sea-birds, see the Additional Passage (p. 544/8). For a contemporary reference to *fous* and for very similar descriptions of flying fish under attack, see Ligon 1657, p. 4; Leguat 1708, pp. 10, 82.

[14] The illustration shows a flying fish. But it is not the drawing of a flying fish which Barbot inserted in his 1679 journal (*1679*, p. 355), so presumably it was made on the 1682 voyage. Repeated on *1732*, Plate 19 (p. 224). For a similar drawing, see Leguat 1708, p. iv.

[15] Omission of five paragraphs, the first two on the island of St Matthew (an imaginary island) and the island of Ascension, largely from Dapper, *Eylanden*, p. 82; the remainder on navigation on the American side of the Atlantic, and on the island of Fernando de Noronha, off Brazil. Cf. *1732*, p. 543/8–544/5, 545/1–7, enlarged.

[16] Cf. *1732*, p. 545/8–10.

[17] Barbot enlarges on material in Letters 2/21, p. 88, and 3/2, p. 137, above. While Barbot was inaccurate when he repeated the common contemporary European belief that most Africans were 'cannibals', it is likely that many Africans equally believed that cannibalism was common in the world – a belief they held with some reason, since the practice was not unknown in Black Africa – and it is also highly likely that their fear of being eaten by the Europeans was correctly reported. Anthropophagy being normally for religious rather than gastronomic reasons, the horror of being eaten was not merely the fear of physical death but the additional dread that the soul of the victim would be consumed by the eater, extinguishing the survival of the individual in another world. As regards refusal to eat, Barbot earlier reported forced feeding (Letter 2/21, p. 89, note 30). For a comparable account of the arrangements aboard slave ships of the period, including

references to health precautions, the attempted segregation of the sexes, and slave suicides (allegedly 'in the belief that when they die they return home'), see Phillips 1732, pp. 218–9, 229–30.

Cf. *1732*, p. 546/5.

[18] Slave uprisings aboard ship were not uncommon, partly because of the small numbers of crew and the frequent disabling of the seamen from sickness when voyages were extended. This provides the context for Barbot's savage instruction. An English captain claimed that he himself 'could not be perswaded . . . [to] cut off the legs or arms of the most wilful', but on another English voyage a mutinous woman slave was 'slashed with knives till she died' (Phillips 1732, p. 219; Atkins 1735, p. 73). Extreme brutality to individuals as a form of communal deterrent, in Barbot's day common in Europe, Black Africa, and across the world (and today probably not greatly reduced overall), was in the past more openly accepted and acknowledged, implicitly as a lesser evil, reflecting perhaps both relative insensitivity to human physical pain, and greater frankness and realism. Ironically, a slave uprising occurred on Barbot's nephew's ship in 1700, partly because some of the slaves had been 'provided with knives', but if the account is to be believed the surviving ringleaders were only whipped (*1732*, p. 513/1). On James Barbot's 1699 voyage, there was quarrelling and fighting between slaves and some died, an aspect of slave ship conditions which it is curious that Barbot does not comment on (*1732*, p. 465/1). On security and uprisings, see Phillips 1732, pp. 235, 229–30.

[19] In 1678 Barbot was warned that a long voyage increased the melancholia of the slaves (*1679*, p. 280). This section on the treatment of slaves aboard ship is much enlarged in *1732*, pp. 545/10–548/2. Barbot enlarged partly from recollection and partly from the experiences of the voyages of his brother and nephew. The *1732* passage appears to be the earliest known account of conditions aboard slave-ships described in such detail (but Phillips' similar account, written slightly later, was published at the same time as Barbot's); hence Barbot's account has been much deployed by historians. Although the information is original, and in tone authoritative, Barbot's knowledge of these conditions must have been severely limited, given that he himself had only made two voyages, and some caution needs to be exercised in generalizing from his account. Nevertheless, the *1732* passage is so significant that the greater part of it is presented in an Additional Passage (pp. 546/1–548/2).

[20] Omission of two paragraphs, on navigation from Cayenne to Martinique.

[21] The map of the Cayenne district, unlike the other illustrations of Cayenne, is not in *1679*. Barbot obtained it from 'Monsieur de Ferolles, major of the place', apparently in 1682, and he 'caused [it] to be ingraved at

Rochel in a large sheet, for the use of the court' (*1732*, p. 559/1): it reappears on *1732*, Plate 33 (p. 543). Inquiries in France have not enabled the engraved map to be traced.

[22] Barbot affixed this drawing on a blank page. The inscription is in English and reads – '6 Foot Long from head to taile from X. a sturgeon, 6 Foot Long, taken in Southampton River the 4th May 1703'. Although irrelevant to the description of Guinea, the drawing reappeared on *1732*, Plate 26 (p. 462). Perhaps Barbot was influenced by noting that a fellow Huguenot refugee in England, whom he may well have known, included in his account of an overseas voyage – an account cited by Barbot – a 1702 drawing of 'A Bonito taken on the Coast of Kent' (Leguat 1708, pp. vii, 17– 19).

[23] The final page of the manuscript has a text written in French, apparently at the same date as the earlier pages, but with no relevance to Barbot's account. The text describes a number of episodes involving 'marine monsters'. The first episode occurred at La Rochelle in 1635, when a M. Béguin, *maître serrurier*, shot and killed a 'monster' which left foot-prints on the shore: the drawing perhaps indicates a sea-lion. Another 'like monster' was taken at La Rochelle in 1600. The large fish illustrated was taken at Chatelaillon in 1645: a similar fish was taken at St Martin de Ré in 1645. All these episodes occurred before Barbot was born, hence it is likely that the text and drawings were taken from a printed work – unless the skins of the creatures were preserved locally and he drew on oral tradition. Barbot added that he had seen a similar fish 'taken in the Thames about 1668, at Gresham College in London', patently a preserved specimen.

[24] For Greenhill, who died in 1709, see the Introduction, note 55. It is not clear how much of this passage is Greenhill and how much Barbot. For other metereological observations by Greenhill, see *1732*, p. 171/3.

[25] This passage is clearly based on the journal of the 1699 Calabar voyage, which Barbot tells us elsewhere sailed in early September from Bandy Point to São Tomé, the passage taking a fortnight (*1732*, p. 465/1). The experience of (relative) cold on this voyage seems to be the basis for the more general comment earlier (p. 541/1, quoted in note 8 above).

[26] It is possible that much of this passage is borrowed from an untraced source, very many voyage accounts containing such descriptions.

[27] Barbot, his brother, and his nephew appear to have had only limited contact with Dutch or Portuguese slave ships. But information about Dutch ships may have come from Grazilhier, who worked for the Dutch and slaved at Calabar in 1703–4 (*1732*, p. 464/7–9).

[28] Barbot probably has in mind the use of knives and 'billets' in the slave uprising on his nephew's ship in 1700 (*1732*, p. 513/1).

[29] The editors of Barbot's 1678–9 journal calculate that 14 out of about

380 slaves died on the voyage: Barbot himself put the loss at only seven (*1732*, p. 570/6). They conclude that 'the voyage was rapid and profitable, despite a less than adequate cargo, and mortality was low, not only among the slaves but among the crew, of whom only one died' (Debien 1979, pp. 251, 255). However, on arrival at Cayenne, 50–60 slaves were weakly and declining every day (*1679*, p. 362) – although Barbot later declared they were 'very hearty' (*1732*, p. 570/6). A list of slaves on a sugar plantation in Guiana in 1690 included six slaves who had crossed the Atlantic in 1682 on *La Perle*, a ship of Barbot's squadron: their ethnic orgins indicate that they had been bought (perhaps by Barbot himself) at Whydah (Debien/Houdaille 1964, p. 173). Two more slaves had been conveyed at an unstated date on *Le Soleil d'Afrique*: this was Barbot's ship in 1678–1679, but since one of the Africans came from Great Popo on Slave Coast and since this coast was not visited in 1679, it would seem that this slave, if not both of them, had travelled on a later (or earlier) voyage of the ship.

[30] On his 1678–9 voyage, Barbot recorded the purchase of *gros mil* (either sorghum or maize) on Gold Coast and cassava (manioc) meal and rice at Príncipe Island, as well as meats presumably for the crew (*1679*, pp. 250–1, 280, 285, 301, 314, 349, 351). On James Barbot's 1699 voyage, 'Indian wheat' was bought on Gold Coast, expressly because the 'horse-beans' brought from London were spoiled; yams and meats were bought in the Calabar district; and corn, peas and beans, cassava meal, and 'a hundred coco-nuts', together with a few live animals, were bought at São Tomé (*1732*, pp. 465/3, 6–7, 460/12, 18, 464/9, 11 – see Letter 3/12 above, Additional Passage). At Calabar in 1698, the *Dragon* bought 'forty baskets of plantains' and many yams; and at Anobom Island in 1701 Grazilhier's ship bought 'hogs, goats, tamarinds, Mandioca meal, Guiavas, oranges, lemons, etc', the fruit no doubt for the crew (*1732*, pp. 465/1, 5–6, 466/4 – see Letters 3/7, Additional Passage and note 24; and 3/13, Additional Passage, above). It is now recognized that the supply of provisions for slave ships was a significant factor both in the contemporary economy of the Guinea coast and in the procedures of the Atlantic slave trade. For difficulties in procuring sufficient yams at the growing season, see *1732*, p. 464/11 (in Letter 3/7, Additional Passage, 'An Abstract'). Barbot further remarks as follows. 'A ship that takes in five hundred slaves, must provide above a hundred thousand yams, which is very difficult, because it is hard to stow them, by reason they take up so much room; and yet no less ought to be provided, the slaves there being of such a constitution, that no other food will keep them; Indian corn, beans, and Mandioca, disagreeing with their stomach; so that they sicken and die apace, as happened aboard the Albion frigat, as soon as their yams were spent, which was just when it anchor'd at St Tome, after a fortnight's passage from Bandy-point, at Calabar' (*1732*, p. 465/1). Failure on the part of slavers to recognize the heterogeneity of Africans in relation to

their feeding habits, and in particular to their acceptance of certain staples and gastronomic and psychological rejection of others, undoubtedly contributed to slave mortality. Yams remain the staple of eastern Guinea, together with the more recent staple, the related tuber, cassava; and a diet of corn or rice would still be regarded as inappropriate. It is notable that c. 1680 cassava is obtained from the islands, implying that it had not yet spread widely on the Guinea mainland (assuming that the 'root' valued by Calabar slaves in Barbot's muddy sentence indicates the yam). For maize and horse-beans as slave food, see Phillips 1732, p. 245.

[31] On the *Albion* disaster, cf. *1732*, pp. 465/1 (included in Letter 3/7, Additional Passage, 'An Abtract').

[32] This paragraph sums up Barbot's moral approach to the Atlantic slave trade, which appears to be thoroughly representative of European opinion in his age. Although slavery is accepted as an inevitable social and economic condition within mankind, and although slaves are pagan and often stupid, they are to be treated as kindly as possible, both because they are unfortunate fellow human beings, 'tho' of a different colour', and because it is economically unsound to do otherwise. Barbot's *credo*, while of course neither that of an emancipationist, nor that of a latterday believer that slavery is a transcendant evil outside the normal balance of consequential morality, fails to support the current popular view that, because of their 'race' and their predominance in the surviving slave trades, Black Africans were in the past regarded by Europeans as non-human. Similarly, a contemporary English slave captain did not 'think there is any intrinsick value in one colour more than another', spoke of the slaves as being 'as much the works of God's hands, and no doubt as dear to him as ourselves', and said that the climate and their lack of true religion was 'their misfortune more than fault' (Phillips 1732, p. 235).

[33] Contrary to what Barbot states, in his account of Whydah there is no mention of the three ships leaving there or indeed of their visiting the port.

APPENDIX A

THE ATTEMPTED PUBLICATION IN 1689

[unn. page, inserted before the *Avis*]

Extract from a letter from the late M. Savouret, bookseller (*libraire*) at Amsterdam, which he wrote to me concerning my manuscripts which I had sold him in 1688.[1]

Amsterdam 8 April 1689

Your voyages are kept in my cupboard: I have only shown them to the author of the Bibliothèque Universelle, who seemed very pleased with them.[2] He shares your view that some revision should be done. He very much praises your modesty – when I told him that you agreed that I should have these voyages only on condition that I had them read again. A bookseller who is a friend of mine has also seen them and I believe that he will participate in the printing, but he says that a delay is necessary, because of the war.[3] We have calculated that printing them would cost about 8,000 livres, a frightening sum. I did not think that the expense of producing copper-plates would be so great. I leave it to you to say more about this when I am with you, which, please God, will be next month. etc

M. Savouret died on 18 April, ten days after writing this letter. His unexpected death and the war with France forced me to recover my manuscripts, and I will await a more peaceful and favourable time to have them printed at my own expense, however I propose to etch all the drawings and plans myself, to reduce the great cost.

NOTES

[1] Pierre Savouret published works, often of Protestant appeal, up to 1686 from La Rochelle, and then in 1687–1688 from Amsterdam, the works

793

including *Prières pour ceux qui voyagent sur la mer*. His widow published in 1689, also from Amsterdam, *Histoire des reformés de La Rochelle . . . depuis 1660 . . . 1685* (V. F. Goldsmith, *A short title catalogue of French books 1601–1700 in the Library of the British Museum*, London, 1969–1973). Patently Savouret was a Huguenot refugee and probably Barbot had known him at La Rochelle.

[2] The *Bibliothèque universelle*, issued in eleven volumes between 1686 and 1693, was edited at Amsterdam by two Huguenot refugees, Jean Le Clerc and Jean Cormand de la Croze. Barbot mentions reading a 1686 issue in December 1687: 1688, Letter 2/28, p. 145. Later in the letter Savouret contradicts the present statement, by noting that he has shown the manuscripts not only to this 'author' but also to a fellow bookseller-publisher.

[3] The War of the League of Augsburg, mainly between France on the one hand and Holland and England on the other, broke out in September 1688.

APPENDIX B

BARBOT'S FRENCH AND ENGLISH ACCOUNTS OF GUINEA COLLATED

The collation is only approximate since the Letters and Chapters seldom match exactly and certain passages were widely transferred.

1688			1732	
Letter Number	*First Page Number*	*Subject Matter*	*Chapter*	*First Page Number*
[unnumbered]		Avis		
Part 1			**Book 1**	
1–3	2	Nigritia, Guinea, general	Introduction	1
4	9	climate	[omitted]	
5	11	seasons, winds and weather	[dispersed, e.g. Book 2, chap. 12]	
6	18	SENEGAL, St Louis, Gorée, Rufisco	1	15
7	30	landscape, products, animals, plants, weather	2	27
8	37	blacks, character, costume, houses, food, children, arms	3	33
9	44	agriculture, trades, commerce	4	40
10	51	women's occupations, meals, languages, a feast, magic, funerals, kings and succession, religion	5	49
			6 (Islam)	63

Part 3   **Book 4**

In references in the notes the Letters of Part 3 are distinguished as 3/1, etc, but as the second pagination continues, the pages if cited separately as 2/1 etc.

APPENDIX C

ANALYTIC TABLE OF ILLUSTRATIONS

IN BARBOT'S THREE WRITINGS

The arrangement of the entries in the table is as far as possible geographical, the guiding order being that of the 1678–1679 journal, represented by the entries in the first column. Each entry refers to a single illustration, whose repetition or development is shown across the page. To correlate, the entries in the other columns are adjusted to those in the first column and therefore do not necessarily represent the order of the source. A gap indicates that the relevant source lacks a corresponding illustration. Where there is a gap in the first column, the additional entries in the second column are normally in the order of that source; and similarly, when there is a gap in both the first and second columns, the third column follows the order of that source.

Column 1
The illustrations in *1679* are numbered 1–71 in the table. (Barbot failed to number his illustrations, and the 1979 edition numbered only the selection reproduced.) Two page numbers are given, the first that of the manuscript (as numbered by Barbot), the second that of the 1979 edition. But when the edition only notes, but does not reproduce, an illustration, the second page number has added an †. When an illustration has an accompanying title or caption, this is given in the table, but sometimes shortened. Additional titles or explanations, supplied editorially, are given in square brackets [ ].

Column 2
Barbot numbered, and supplied a list of titles of, the illustrations of

800

the 'Première partie'; but failed to do the same for the other two Parts. Barbot numbered 1–51: the illustrations of the later parts have been numbered editorially (52)–(125). The page numbers are those of the manuscript (as numbered by Barbot). The first and second paginations (the latter covering both the later Parts) are distinguished as 1/ and 2/. (An occasional illustration has been noted in the present edition at a different page – this is indicated by the addition of [see p.].) When an illustration is inserted between pages, only the first page number is given, followed by an asterisk *. When an illustration has an accompanying title or caption, this is given in the table, but sometimes shortened. A few illustrations in the first Part which lack a title or caption are given the title shown in Barbot's list of titles. Additional titles or explanations, supplied editorially, are given in square brackets [ ]. (Note that the titles or captions accompanying illustrations do not always exactly correspond with the titles in Barbot's list.)

Column 3
The illustrations in *1732* were grouped on plates, except for a few large views of forts which take up the whole of a plate. The plates were given either the letters A–N or the numbers 1–34, 34(2), 35(2); but the grouped illustrations were not individually numbered. No list of illustrations was provided. In the present table, when an illustration forms only part of a plate the letter/number of the plate is followed by a cross +. A plate normally covers two facing pages which are not themselves separately numbered, but *1732* supplied on each plate the page number of the preceding text page, and this page number is given in the table. When an illustration has an accompanying title or caption, this is given in the table, but sometimes shortened. Additional titles or explanations, supplied editorially, are given in square brackets [ ]. The text of *1732* often makes specific reference to an illustration or a plate: such a reference is noted in the table, its page number being given in round brackets ( ).

Column 4
Items represented in the set of engravings of forts (of c.?1690) are indicated with an asterisk *.

Column 1 1679	Column 2 1688	Column 3 1732	Column 4
1. [frontispiece, map of Atlantic in roundel, winged figure, dividers, title]†	Première Partie, Frontispiece [Atlantic map in elaborate cartouche, with figures, scene, globe, title, in ribbon 'Estat present des costes de Guinée en 1682', and below 'Description des Costes d'Afrique; depuis le Cap Boiador jusques à celuy de Cap Gonsalvues']		
2. p. 1/256 [cartouche]			
3. p. 1/257† Cap Pinas [profile]			
4. p. 1/257† Cap Ortegal [pr.]			
Canary Islands to River Senegal 5. p. 2/258† Allegranca . . . l'Ancerota [pr. Alegranza . . . Lanzarote]	(105). p. 2/204* Veue des Isles Alegranca & l'Ancerota	31+. p. 523 The Prospect of Alegranga [sic] and Lancerota (p. 523)	
6. p. 2/258† Grand Canarie [pr.]	(104). p. 2/204* Veue de Grand Canarie	31+. p. 523 The Sight of Grand Canary (p. 523)	
7. p. 2/258† [pr. Fortaventura . . . Grand Canary]	(106). p. 2/204* Veue de Fortaventura	31+. p. 523 The South Side of Fortaventura (p. 523)	

Column 1 1679	Column 2 1688	Column 3 1732	Column 4
8. p. 3/258† le pic de Teneriff [pr.]	(108). p. 2/206* Veue du Pic de Tenerif	31+. p. 523 The Sight of Tenerif and Gomera (p. 524)	
	(107). p. 2/204 [pr. Lanzerote-Gratiosa]	31+. p. 523 The Prospect of Lobos, Lancerota and Gratiosa (p. 523)	
		28+. p. 492 The Prospect of the two small Islands, Las Desertas (in the NE of Madera) [drawn 1700 by James Barbot junior] (p. 523)	
		28+. p. 492 The Prospect of the Town of Funchal [drawn 1700, as above, p. 497] (p. 525)	
		28+. p. 492 The Prospect of the West Side of Gomera [drawn 1700, as above, p. 497] (p. 523)	
		28+. p. 492 The Prospect of the Island Palma [drawn 1700, as above] (p. 523)	
9. p. 3/259 [two fish, A unnamed] B Capitainne	(109). p. 2/217 [four fish, named-] Sarde, Capitaine	32+. p. 536 A Sarde, a Captain (p. 526)	

Column 1 1679	Column 2 1688	Column 3 1732	Column 4
10. p. 3/259† [pr., Cap Barbas … Cap Caroceira]		32+. p. 536 The Prospect of the Coast of Libia (p. 528)	
	1. p. 1/16 [see p. 1/18] Veue d'un Travados [very dark – storm, with ship leaning over]	7+. p. 104 [the leaning ship, as well as a waterspout, is added to a different sea scene] (p. 543)	
	2. p. 1/22 Veue de l'abitation du Sénégal du côté de la Mer [pr. St Louis 'que j'en ay tiré en passant de la mer']	1+. p. 18 The Prospect of the Habitation of the French Senegal Company [identifications omitted] (p. 18)	
	3. p. 1/22 Islet St Louis [plan of St Louis, 'que j'en ay eu d'un Architecte de la Compagnie']	1+. p. 18 The island St. Lewis [revised, and with additional identifications]	
Cape Verde 11. p. 4/259† terre de Gambie [pr., wrongly named, actually Les Mamelles, Cape Verde]		2+. p. 20 The Prospect of the Coastings about Cabo-Verde [redrawn, extended]	
12. p. 4/260† Cap de Verd [pr., mainly Gorée Island – 'Je l'ay eue d'un Hollandois']		2+. p. 20 The Prospect of C. Emanuel & of the Isle Goerée	

Column 1 1679	Column 2 1688	Column 3 1732	Column 4
	7. p. 1/26 Veue du Cap Verd [from SSW]	2+. p. 20 The Prospect of Cabo Verde ... SSW (p. 20)	
		2+. p. 20 The Prospect of Cabo Verde ... SSE	
	5. p. 1/24 Veue de l'Isle et du Fort V. de Goerée ... Xbre 1681 [lettered, with key]	3+. p. 24 The Prospect of the Island of Goeree [identifications omitted] (p. 21)	*
	4. p. 1/24 Plan de l'Isle de Goerée [lettered, with key]	3+. p. 24 A Plan of the Island Goeree [fewer identifications; enlarged plan of fort in separate drawing]	
		A+. p. 16 The Coast of Cape Verde Exactly Drawn [map of the cape]	
	8. p. 1/26* Profil du Bourg de Rufisco	2+. p. 20 The Prospect of the Negroes Town of Rufisco [identifications added] (p. 22)	
	6. p. 1/24* [see p. 1/23] Poule Pintado et Aygrette	B+. p. 28 An Aygrett, A Pintada Hen	

Column 1 1679	Column 2 1688	Column 3 1732	Column 4
	10. p. 1/37* Chameau de Nigritie [and an unnamed animal]	B+. p. 28 An unknown Animal, A Cabo Verdo Camel (the former described p. 28)	
	(omitted from Table des desseins), p. 1/33* Escaille d'un Poisson pris au Cap Verde	B+. p. 28 One of the Scales of a Fish taken at Cabo Verdo	
		3(2)+. p. 51 [costumes, etc – scene of figures, tents, camels, etc., copied from various sources, as follows – from Le Maire 1695, item D (pl. opp. p. 94), F (pp. 124–5), G (p. 95), H (p. 68); from Froger 1698, E (p. 45); from Dapper A and B (p. 407)]	
		3(2)+. p. 51 [birds, etc., copied – from Le Maire, O and P (p. 60); from Froger, K and L (p. 14), M and N (p. 46), Q and S (p. 40)]	
13. p. 4/260 [three fish –] dorade, [two] machorans	(110). p. 2/217 [two fish, including –] Dorade	32+. p. 536 [fish, including –] The Hen Dorade	

Column 1 1679	Column 2 1688	Column 3 1732	Column 4
	(113). p. 2/229* [four fish, including–] 8 Máchoran	19+. p. 224 The Cat Fish als Machoran of America (p. 468)	
	(114). p. 2/230–1] [three fish, and a porpoise, including –] Dorade 2me Espece	32+. p. 536 the Cock Dorade	
	(9). p. 1/33 [many fish, including –] Máchoran [different sort, two whiskers above head]	20+. p. 224 The Cat Fish of Cape Verdo (p. 648)	
	(9). p. 1/33 Divers Poissons 1 Espece de Barbeue 2 Lune du Cap Verd 3 Grondin 4 Ancornet 5 Soles 6 Sardes à gros dos 7 Raye Marcottée 9 Houmar	20+. p. 224 a Kind of Barbeue a Cape Verdo Moon (p. 224) a Grondin als. Grumbler An Ancornet als. Scuttle Fish A Sole of Cape Verdo (p. 224) a Sarde wrth. a Greatback The Stingray spotted A Sort of Cray Fish very large (p. 224)	
	10 Meulle	A Mullet of the Bay of Rufisco (p. 224)	
	11 Poisson à corne de grandeur naturelle	a Hornfish of natural bigness or Coffre de Mort	

Column 1 1679	Column 2 1688	Column 3 1732	Column 4
	[12 unnamed fish]	Unknown but is much like a large Pyke	
	[13 cuttlefish bone]	The only Bone of the Scuttle Fish [the Coffre de Mort different from that of plate 24]	
	11. p. 1/61* Carte des Pays entre le Sénégal et la Gambie, [near Arguin to Cape Verga, and far inland]	A+. p. 16 [coast and near interior only]	
		A+. p. 16 [plan of Fort James on River Gambia, with note of guns in 1695: plan from Froger 1698, p. 35]	
	51. p. 1/173 Carte des Isles Bissos [map of Bissagos Islands and mainland]	4+. p. 82 A Map of Cacheo River (p. 83)	
Gambia to Sierra Leone		4+. p. 82 A Prospect of the Portuguese Town of Cacheo (p. 83)	
14. p. 4/261† [pr. Cap Furnado]	[inset on 13] p. 1/85* [see p. 1/82] Veue du Cap Verga alias Furnado	C+. p. 94 Cape Verga als. Furnado	

Column 1 1679	Column 2 1688	Column 3 1732	Column 4
	12. p. 1/85* [see p. 1/82] Poissons et Productions Marines du Cap Furnado [taken from 'le Journal de mon dernier voyage', key explains fish, insect and luminescent growth]	C+. p. 94 [same items but key omitted]	
15. p. 5/261† [pr. Iles de Los, large island E by NE, with lettering and key]	14–15. p. 1/85* [see p. 86] 2 Veues des Iles Tamara [first view, one island and islet: no lettering]	C+. p. 94 The Islds. of Tamara als. Doles [lettering copied from 1679]	
16. p. 5/261† [pr. Iles de Los, several islands, two islets, with lettering and key]		C+. p. 94 The Same Islds, the Biggest ... [lettering less than in 1679]	
17. p. 5/261† [pr. Iles de Los, three islands: lettering and key]	14–15. p. 1/85* [see p. 186] 2 Veues [second view, with ship: no lettering]	C+. p. 94 The Same Islds. haveing the 2 Rocks ... [no lettering]	
18. p. 6/262 requin [shark]	(110) p. 2/217, as above, under (13) of 1679), Requin	32+. p. 536 The Requin (p. 225)	
19. p. 6/262† [pr. Sierra Leone Peninsula hills from sea: lettering and key]	16–17. p. 1/87 2 Veues de Sierra Liona [first, Veue de la Haute Terre: no lettering]	C+. p. 94 The High Lands of Sierra Liona [less lettering than 1679]	

Column 1 1679	Column 2 1688	Column 3 1732	Column 4
	16–17. p. 1/87 [second, Veue du Cap Tagrin, Cape Sierra Leone rising at left, northern peaks of hills]	E+. p. 99 The high lands of Sierra Liona [lettering added, and key, wrongly stating that a passage exists between Cape Sierra Leone and the land SE]	
20. p. 7/262† Carte de Rivière Siera Lionna A° 1678 [given to Barbot by an Englishman from Bunce Island]	13. p. 1/85* [see p. 81] Carte depuis le Cap Verge ou Furnado jusqu'à celui das Palmas [detail mainly between the Sierra Leone estuary and Cape Mesurado]	D+. p. 98 [with slight omissions of outline and text]	
	13. p. 1/85* [inset, map of the bays of the south shore of the Sierra Leone estuary]	D+. p. 98 [inset, with additions and omissions of labels]	
		E+. p. 99 A Prospect of the Road in the Bay of Sierra Liona [with lettering and key]	

Column 1 1679	Column 2 1688	Column 3 1732	Column 4
21. p. 9/264 Case de Jean Thomas, Tabac, Bananiers, Ris [huts with plants around; labelled]		E+. p. 99 [scene includes –] Captain Jno. Thomas's house [now with a Union Jack], Mille [same plant as Ris, tobacco plant not labelled]	
22. p. 9/264 comme ils fument leurs poissons [fish in smoke of fire]; Leurs grigris [head under conical roof]; Leurs sièges [stool]	21. p. 1/97 [the grigri only]	E+. p. 99 [scene includes –] An idol or Grigri [and a man kneeling before it: a stool is also shown but with a man sitting on it] (p. 104) E+. p. 99 [scene also includes a square house, with fire, children playing, a woman with baby on her back and men drinking and smoking, all labelled]	
23. p. 9/265 Leurs Cannotz [canoe, goods, three men seated, one smoking, two standing to paddle, woman on bank with baby on back, hut]	18–19. p. 1/93*, 2 Desseins du fruit cola	E+. p. 99 Negros going aboard Ships with Provisions in their Canoes [canoe, one passenger smoking, goods now cows, four paddlers, ships added: the cows perhaps from Marees pl.8] 5+. p. 107, The Cola, The same cut (p. 101)	

Column 1 1679	Column 2 1688	Column 3 1732	Column 4
24. p. 10/266 [six fish] Carangue Bannane Bequne Treshar [no name] Jaquine	20. p. 1/93* 13 Poissons [including –] Carangue Bannane Béqu'une Trezar [no name] Jaquine	6+. p. 101 (p. 101) Carangue (p. 224) Banana Bekune (p. 224) Trezhar Unknown Jaquine	
25. p. 11/267 [five fish] Bourse Moine Perroquet Vieille d'un pied Lune	20. p. 1/93* Bourse Moine Perroquet Vieille Lune	6+. p. 101 Bource The Monk the Parratt The Old Wife als. Vieille A Moonfish als. the Silver Fish	
26. p. 12/268 [2 fish] Vieille de 8 pouces, de 5 pouces	20. p. 1/93* [no name] Espèce de Sardine	6+. p. 101 Unknown a Sort of Pilchar	
27. p. 12/268† [pr. Turtle Islands]	22. p. 1/103* Veue des Iles de Tota	C+. p. 94 The Islds. of Tota als. Plantin Islds.	
	23. p. 1/104 Veue de R° de Galinhas	5+. p. 107 Rio Galinhas (p. 107)	

Column 1 1679	Column 2 1688	Column 3 1732	Column 4
Cape Mount to River Sess 28. p. 12/268† [pr. Cape Mount]	24. p. 1/106* Veue du Cap de Monte [missing from MS]	5+. p. 107 A Sight of Cape Mont [with lettering] (p. 108)	
	28. p. 1/128 Obsèques [burial scene – 'je l'ay copié de Mr. Dapper' – p. 2/23]		
	29. p. 1/133 Manière de donner le titre de Dondagh ['j'ay depouillé Mr. Dapper' – p. 2/37]		
	30. p. 1/136 Audience des Ambassadeurs Negres ('je prins encore dans Mr. Dapper' – p. 2/41]		
29. p. 12/268* [pr. Cape Mesurado]	25. p. 1/106 Veue du Cap Mesurado [missing from MS]	5+. p. 107 A Sight of Cape Mesurado (p. 109) 5+. p. 107 Cape Mesurado at E¼NE	
		5+. p. 107 Rio Junck (p. 110)	
	26. p. 1/110 Veue de R° Noel	5+. p. 107 Rio Noel (p. 111)	

Column 1 1679	Column 2 1688	Column 3 1732	Column 4
30. p. 13/269† [pr. Rio Corps]	27. p. 1/111 Veue de Rio Corso	5+. p. 107 Rio Corso als. Cors (p. 111)	
31. p. 13/269† [pr. River Sess, captain Woodfyn's ship shown]	31. p. 1/148 Veue de Rio-Sestro [a view from further out to sea, covering more coast than 1679]	H+. p. 137 The Coast of Sestro [as 1688]	
		F+. p. 128 Map of Sestro River [with inset –] Sestro Negro's in their small Canoes	
	32. p. 1/147* Poissons de Rio Sestro [three fish, not named]	F+. p. 128 Fishes at Sestro not seen in other parts of the Coast of Guinea [same, not named]	
	33. p. 1/150 Entrevue avec le Roi de Sestro	G. p. 130 [scene of visit to king, inset view of the lodge: added lettering and key]	
	34. p. 1/152 Nid d'oiseaux curieux [weaverbird's nest, and a large bird sitting on branch]	F+. p. 128 a Birds nest twisted by little Birds, the Sestro Pheasant	
	35. p. 1/153 Chenilles et fourmis [an ant, a centipede, and two worm-like creatures]	F+. p. 128 a Pismire of Natural Bigness, a Worm [and on an adjacent scene two more 'worms']	

Column 1 1679	Column 2 1688	Column 3 1732	Column 4
	36. p. 1/153 Mouton de Sestro	F+. p. 128 a Sestro Sheep	
	37. p. 1/154 Nègres malades [standing man, sitting man, both smoking pipes]	F+. p. 128 [men the same, added trees, woman: trees lettered but no key]	
	38. p. 1/157 Sacrifice au Fetiche	F+. p. 128 [in a scene] (p. 134)	
	43. p. 1/162 Arbre de Maniguette	F+. p. 128 The maniguetta or Guinea Pepper Tree [lettered, no key]	
		F+. p. 128 [remaining items –] The Banano Tree, a Monky, the Rice Plant, Sestro Houses	
	39. p. 1/158* [pr.] Cap das Baixos Svino		
	40. p. 159 Veue de Wappo [ship added]	H+. p. 137 The Land of Wappo [ship removed]	
32. p. 15/271† [pr. Wapo]	41. p. 160 Veue de Sestro-Paris	H+. p. 137 Sestro Paris [ship omitted]	

Column 1 1679	Column 2 1688	Column 3 1732	Column 4
Cape Palmas to Cape Three Points 33. p. 16/271† [pr. Cape Palmas]	42. p. 1/161 Veue du Cap des Palmes [two views, at NE, at SE]	H+. p. 137 The Cape das Palmas at N.E. The Cape das Palmas at E¼SE	
34. p. 16/271 [pr. Tabbo]	45. p. 1/163* Veue de la Coste de Tabo	I*. p. 139 The Prospect of the Lands of Tabo	
35. p. 16/270† [pr. Bereby]	47. p. 1/163* Veue de la Terre de Berby [ship added]	I+. p. 139 The Prospect of the Coast of Berby [no ship]	
36. p. 17/272† [pr. Druyn]	48. p. 1/163* Veue de Druyn-Petry	I+. p. 139 The Prospect of the Lands on the S. W. of Rio St. Andrew	
37. p. 17/373† [pr. River S. André]	46. p. 1/163* Veue de Rio St. Andero [dead tree removed]	I+. p. 139 The Prospect of the Land of Rio St. Andrew	
38. p. 18/274 [missing from MS: pr. Coetroe]	49. p. 1/165 Veue de Coetroe	I+. p. 139 The Prospect of Coutrou alias Coetro	
	50. p. 1/166 Fruit de Qua Qua		
	44. p. 1/163* Carte de la Côte depuis le Cap Palmas jusqu'au Rio da Sueiro da Costa		

Column 1 1679	Column 2 1688	Column 3 1732	Column 4
	Frontispiece, Seconde Partie [map of Atlantic in oval roundel, cherub, navigational instruments]		
39. p. 21/277† [pr. Cap St. Appollonia]	(53). p. 2/2* [see p. 23] Veue du Cap Sta. Appolonia [less labelling]	K+. p. 148 The Prospect of Cape Sta. Appollonia	
40. p. 25/282 [pr.] S. Anthonio d'Axem	(54). p. 2/4 S. Antonio d'Axim ou Achombeme [slight changes include the caption]	L. p. 149 The Prospect of the Fort St. Anthony at Axim	
	(55). p. 2/5* Fredericksburgh à Crema 1684 [note dated 27.3.1688 that drawing by 'un de mes Compatriotes' 1684]	11+. p. 173 The Prospect of the Danish Fort Great Frederick's Burgh [not the same, probably obtained from a relative of Barbot c. 1702, see p. 431: the caption should read 'Brandenburg', not 'Danish': two plans of the fort are added] (p. 11, wrongly)	
41. p. 26/282† [pr. Cap Tres Puntas]	(56). p. 5* Veue du Cap Tres Puntas	M+. p. 150 The Prospect of the First Point of Cape Tres Puntas	

Column 1 1679	Column 2 1688	Column 3 1732	Column 4
Gold Coast			
	(52), before p. 2/1 [map] Coste d'Or de Guinée	K+. p. 148 A Chart and Map of the Gold Coast from Rio da Costa to R°. da Volta [and inset –] A Particular Chart of the Coast of Mina and Cabo Corso [the main map derives from the *1688* map, but with many changes]	
42. p. 28/285 [pr.] Boetroe	(57). p. 2/6 Le Fort Badensteyn	M+. p. 150 The Prospect of the Fort Badenstyn at Boetroe	
43. p. 29/286 [pr.] Sama	(58). p. 2/8* Le Fort St. Sebastien	M+. p. 150 The Prospect of the Fort St. Sebastiaen at Sama	*
44. p. 33/290† [three fish, a swordfish and two small fish]	(81). p. 2/80 [four fish, including –] un Nègre, unnamed fish, un Crapaut de Mer [the two middle items from *1679*]	18+. p. 216 The Fetisso fish, The Kings Fish als. Negro Fish, Comendo Fish of the taste of Pilchard, A Comendo Fish, The Sea Toad, A Bonnito of the South of the Line (pp. 223–4)	*
	(82). p. 2/81 Poisson Fetiche [swordfish]	18+. p. 216 [apart from the fish listed above –] The Mad Bird, A	

Column 1 1679	Column 2 1688	Column 3 1732	Column 4
		Scorpion, A Pismire nest at Akra, Parroquet, Gold Coast doggs, A Sort of Eagle at Cabo Corso ['I have drawn the figure of a small parroquet ... I am sorry the engraver has not been nice enough in his cut, so to represent this bird as my drawing did', p. 220; anthill 'I drew at Accra', p. 222; but the dogs are copied from Marees, pls. 5 and 10] (dogs p. 216, eagle p. 218, parroquet p. 220, scorpion p. 221, anthill p. 222)	
45. p. 33/291 [pr.] Comendo	(59). p. 2/10 Petit Comendo	N+. p. 154 The Prospect of Little Comendo	
46. p. 34/292 [pr.] St Iago del Mina, St Georges del Mina	(60). p. 2/11 Veue du Bourg de la Mina [redrawn from 1679 with different details, titles of forts omitted]	N+. p. 154 The Prospect of the Town and Castle del Mina [as in 1679 but the left-hand fort now labelled Coenraedsburg]	

Column 1 1679	Column 2 1688	Column 3 1732	Column 4
47. p. 44/303 [pr.] Cabo Corse Castel	(61). p. 2/17* St. Georges del Mina, Coenraedsburg [reverse view to previous and redrawn in details, possibly influenced by Dapper, after p. 2/68]	8. p. 156 The Prospect of St. George's Castle at Mina [slight changes] (pp. 156, 157, 158, 267)	*
	(62). p. 2/25 Cabo Corso Castel	10. p. 169 A View of Cabo Corso Castle [a closer viewpoint than 1679, seemingly derived from the bird's-eye drawing of 1682 by Greenhill, see Lawrence 1963, plate 37] (canoes, p. 267)	*
48. p. 45/303 [pr.] Fredericburgh	(63). p. 2/25 [see p. 24] Fredericxburgh [very slight changes]	14+. p. 177 The Fort Frederiks'burgh formerly to the Danes and now Fort Royal English, at Manfroe (canoes, p. 267)	*
49. p. 47/306 [pr.] T'Fort Nassaw	(64). p. 2/27 Le Fort Nassau [differs in detail from the 1679 view]	12. p. 175 The Prospect of Fort Nassaw at Mouré ... I have here added this small Prospect to supply some Omissions in the other ... Fort Nassaw from the ENE [the main view is that of	*

Column 1 1679	Column 2 1688	Column 3 1732	Column 4
		1688, but the inset view seems to be a revised version of that of 1679, with perhaps traces of Bosman's view, here copied on plate 25, p. 446, below] (p. 175)	
50. p. 58/218 [pr.] Anamabou	(65) p. 2/29 (Le) Chateau d'Anamabou [totally different from 1679]	13. p. 176 The Prospect of the English Castle at Anamabou [version of 1688, showing 'the English castle, lately built, instead of an old house which stood there in 1679', p. 176]	*
51. p. 59/319 [pr.] T'Fort Amsterdam	(66). p. 2/31 Le Fort Amsterdam [different from 1679, 'les hollondois ont changé toute la forme de cette place en 1681 et 82']	14+. p. 177 The Fort Amsterdam at Cormentyn (p. 177)	*
52. p. 61/321† [pr.] Montagne du Diable	(67). p. 2/32* Veue du Cap Ruygehoeck ou Montagne au Diable [slightly extended from 1679]	15+. p. 182 Cape Ruygehoeck or Duyvelsbergh	
53. p. 71/332 [pr.] James' Fort	(68). p. 2/35 Le Fort James	14+. p. 177 The Fort James, English at Accra	*

Column 1 1679	Column 2 1688	Column 3 1732	Column 4
54. p. 72/333 [pr.] t'Fort Crevecoeur	(69). p. 2/36 Le Fort Creuecoeur [ship omitted]	15+. p. 182 The Dutch Fort Croevecoeur at Accra (p. 182)	*
55. p. 71/332 [pr.] Christiaenburgh	(70). p. 2/37 St. Franciscus Xavier ou Christiansborg [the second name added in handwriting]	15+. p. 182 The Danish Fort Christiaenburgh, at Accra (canoe, p. 267)	*
		25. p. 446 [views of nine Gold Coast forts, all copied from Bosman, first Dutch edition or English version, in the latter pp. 41, 45, 58, 67]	
	(71). p. 2/38 [see p. 39] Veue du Village et de la Côte de Lay (p. 186)	15+. p. 182 The Prospect of the Village and the Coast of Lay	
56. p. 74/335 [two fetish objects]	(86). p. 2/103 Figure de Fetishe [one object only]	7+. p. 104 [arrangement of –] Fetisso Tree, a Mountain Fetisso, Fetisso [last item as in 1688: tree from Marees, pl. 5] (pp. 104 wrongly, 230, 312)	

Column 1 1679	Column 2 1688	Column 3 1732	Column 4
		7+. p. 107 [arrangement of –] 1.2.3. other Sorts of Fetisso [no key: items largely from Marees, pl. 6]	
	(72). p. 2/51 [scene of plants, labelled Bananier, Figuier d'Inde, Mahys, Millet, and Ananes: copied, with improvement, from Marees, pls. 13 and 14]	17+. p. 202 [scene, whose items H, N, O and P are from 1688 or direct from Marees] (N p. 202; O p. 202)	
	(13). p. 2/52* [scene of hunting, of elephants, hares and deer, and a feline entering a trap, copied from Marees, pl. 11]	17+. p. 202 [scene, whose items E (trap), I, L and M are from 1688, or direct from Marees] (E p. 209; L p. 214)	
		17+. p. 202 [scene, many items copied: apart from those noted above, F is from Dapper (p. 2/102); G from Dapper (p. 2/33) – and not Gold Coast; R, distant figures perhaps gold-getting, if so from Dapper, p. 2/94; birds B and E resemble Bosman, pls. 13 and 14; but Q, 'my own drawing of this	

Column 1 1679	Column 2 1688	Column 3 1732	Column 4
		tree', p. 202] (A p. 210; C p. 214; E bird, p. 219; Q p. 202; S p. 217)	
	(74). p. 2/54 [scene of wild animals, elephant, leopard, etc. and anthill, labelled: animals copied from Marees, pl. 12]		
	(75). p. 2/58 [scene of gold-getting in a river, copied from Dapper, p. 2/94, despite – 'J'ay trouvé à propos de vous faire cette planche' p. 58]		
57. p. 77/339 Divers petits ouvrages qui servent à l'ajustement des femmes et filles [gold ornaments 'qui me sont tombées entre mains et que j'ai emporté avec moy']	(76). p. 2/64 [ornaments in gold, ivory, etc., and wooden combs: some items in gold from 1679, but often redrawn, others new, and additional combs, gold hatbands, manillas, rings, etc.: 'je vous fai éxprés une planche de ces petits bagatelles']	22+. p. 251 [gold and ivory ornaments and gold-weighing tools: a very few of the ornaments from 1679, many more from 1688, but often loosely copied, and other new ones: 'I have taken the pains to draw most of the pieces of both goldsmiths and black-smiths work', p. 262: key to the items, which are numbered or lettered in	

Column 1 1679	Column 2 1688	Column 3 1732	Column 4
		groups, p. 264] (p. 237, but reference in error to Plate 21)	
58. p. 82/344 Armes de guerre [bow, arrows, swords, spear, lettered with key, p. 83]	(89). p. 2/120 [weapons, more than in 1679 and those from there redrawn: no numbering or key]	22+. p. 251 [weapons, more than in 1688, with many the same and some redrawn: lettered, with key, pp. 263-4, but some descriptions in the key from Bosman, pp. 185–7]	
59. p. 83/345 Ustancilles [trumpets, drums, canoe, manillas, rings, combs, stools, spoon, pipe, violin, hats, lettered or numbered and key]	(76). p. 2/64 [as above, includes manillas, drums, from 1679]		
	(84). p. 2/87 [scales, beans, iron krakra]	22+. p. 251 [all the useful objects included: lettered, with key, p. 264] (krakra, p. 269)	
	(85). p. 2/93 [musical instruments, different from those in (59) of 1679]	22+. p. 251 [musical instruments, as in (85) of 1688 and not as in (59) of 1679; and combs, as in 1688, not as in 1679; lettered, with key,	

Column 1 1679	Column 2 1688	Column 3 1732	Column 4
		pp. 264–5, some descriptions from Bosman, pp. 138–140] (horns, p. 251; combs, p. 236, reference to Plate 21 in error)	
60. p. 85/437 [six heads, to illustrate hair-styles and face-decoration for Quaquaas, Corso and Acraa]	(77). p. 2/65) [three male figures: 'Voilà ce que j'avois à vous dire pour achever le portrait de ces Africains. Je va travailler à celuy des femmes, après vous avoir desseigné quelques figures de ces Mores': in fact copied from Marees, pl. 2] (78). p. 2/66 [three female figures, copied from Marees, pls. 3, 16]	21. p. 237 [six male and seven female figures: references pp. 236–7 to Barbot drawing this plate himself seem to refer instead to plate 22: all the figures are from Marees, pls. 2, 3, 6 and 16: one male figure is closer to original than in 1688]	

Column 1 1679	Column 2 1688	Column 3 1732	Column 4
	(79). p. 2/78 [scene, coast from Cabo Corso to Manfrou, canoes carrying slaves to a ship: the main canoe and persons aboard are largely copied from Marees, pl. 8]	9+. p. 156 Negro's Cannoes, carrying Slaves, on Bord of Ships att Manfroe [different coast, more ships, main canoe as in *1688*]	
	(80). p. 2/79 [scene, coast from Mina to Mourée, fishing canoes: canoes from Marees, pl. 9]	9+. p. 156 Fishing Cannoes of Mina [same coast, ships, more canoes, lettered: most canoes from Marees, pl. 9, despite 'I was so pleas'd with the sight that I could not forebear representing them in the print', pp. 156–7, which gives a wrong reference to pl. 8]	
	(83). p. 2/82 Diverses Manières de Pêcher ['Je vous ay desseigné cette planche', p. 81: but the scene is largely copied from Marees, pl. 9 (bis) 'La pescherie de nuict']		
	(87). p. 2/105 ['une planche que j'ay desseigné pour vous faire mieux comprendre comment les Mores se comportent en leurs		

Column 1 1679	Column 2 1688	Column 3 1732	Column 4
	devotions de fetiches': copied from Marees, pl. 5]		
	(88). p. 2/108 [burials: copied from Marees, pl. 17]		
River Volta to Luanda	(90). p. 2/129* [map of the coast from River Volta to Cape Lopo Gonsalvez, with Barbot's 1682 voyage from Whydah to Príncipe shown]		
	(91). p. 131 [map of Popo lagoon]	7+. p. 104 Papo's Bay als. Tary [with alligator] (p. 322)	
61. p. 90/353† escaille curieuse		26+. p. 462 [miscellaneous objects including some sea-shells and three iron weapons: the items lettered but no key: item C perhaps from 1679 – cf. 23+ below] (p. 462 – collected by James Barbot in 1699)	

Column 1 1679	Column 2 1688	Column 3 1732	Column 4
62. p. 91/355 [flying fish and porpoise]	(113). p. 229*, as above, under (13) of 1679 [other fish –] Le Diable du Mer, un Pilote du Diable de Mer, Poisson volant [the last different from that in 1679]	19+. p. 224 [other fish, etc –] The Whipray als. The Sea Devil, A Porpoise, A Flying Fish, A Boneto of the North of the Line, The Pilote, A Balahow, A Flying Fish [all except the flying fish as in 1688 – the bonito of 1679 is the Bonnito of the South of the Line on plate 18, see under (44) of 1679] (ray, p. 532; porpoise, pp. 226,497; flying fish, p. 227)	
65. p. 93/358 [fish –] bonnite		32+. p. 536 [fish, including –] The Remorafish als. Susset [two views] (p. 227)	
66. p. 94/359 [fish –] suscet [two views]	(114). p. 2/229*, as above, under (13) of 1679 [other fish, etc –] Marsouin, Balahou, Susset – latter two, two views – and the porpoise as in 1679] (117). p. 2/233 [flying fish different from that in (113) above and that in (62) of 1679] (118). p. 2/233* [a fish, 'bonnie', different from that in (65) of 1679]		

Column 1 1679	Column 2 1688	Column 3 1732	Column 4
63. p. 92/356 [two fish –] orphie, coffre de mort	(101)–(102). p. 2/181 two fish –] une Orfie, Le Coffre de Mort	24+. p. 400 [includes two fish –] Orfie, Cofre de Mort [latter different from that on plate 20 above] ('I drew them as near the life as my skill would permit', p. 402)	
	(111). p. 2/218 [one fish –] le Marteau	32+. p. 536 [fish, including –] The Panapana als. hammerfish [with drawing of head] (p. 527)	
	(92). p. 2/140 [see p. 142] [salutations, copied from Dapper, p. 2/117, but with the figures relocated and the addition of a river, the prow of a European vessel, a man smoking a pipe, and a cannon]	27. p. 463 A New Correct Mapp of Calbar River ... drawn ... in the Year 1699 by several Pilots Jointly (p. 463)	

Column 1 1679	Column 2 1688	Column 3 1732	Column 4
	(93). p. 2/174 [inhabitants of Gabon, copied from Marees, pl. 20]		
		23+. p. 395 The sight of Cape Iopo gonsaluez (p. 395)	
		29+. p. 497 [maps of Bay of Cabinda and entrance to River Congo]	
		30+. p. 523 [map of coast around Luanda]	
Príncipe and other islands 64. p. 88/351† [pr.] l'ille du Prince [from 20 leagues ESE]			
	(99). p. 2/180* [two views –] Veue de l'Isle du Prince 18 à 20 lieues E¼SE [this reverses 1679]	24+. p. 400 Princes Island at E¼SE distant abt. 18 leagues [as 1679]	
		24+. p. 400 The Prospect of the Bay and Town Sto. Antonio in Princes Island	
		24+. p. 400 The Map of Princes Island	

Column 1 1679	Column 2 1688	Column 3 1732	Column 4
64a. p. 89 in margin [overlooked in the edition: Ille du Prince ENE 6–7 lieues: profile lettered and with key]	(100). p. 2/180* Veue de l'Isle du Prince de 2 lieues étant à ESE	23+. p. 395 The Sight of Prince's Island at E.N.E. about 6 leagues distance 23+. p. 395 The Prospect of Prince's Island abt. 3 Leagues distance, being at E.S.E. [both views appear to be clumsy versions of (64a) of *1679*]	
	(97)–(98). p. 179 [two views –] Veue de l'Isle du Prince de [blank] Lieues au [blank] Veue de l'Isle du Prince de [blank] Lieues au [blank]		
	(94). p. 2/176* [three views –] Veue de l'Isle Annobon de 7 Lieues au N.N.O.	23+. p. 395 Large Muscles [two sides of a sea-shell: outside may be that of (61) in *1679*, perhaps duplicated in 26 above] (p. 402)	

Column 1 1679	Column 2 1688	Column 3 1732	Column 4
	(95). p. 2/176* Veue de l'Isle d'Annobon de [blank] Lieues au N.E.		
	(96). p. 2/176* Veue de l'Isle Annobon de [blank] Lieues au N.	23+. p. 395 The Sight of Annoboan at N.N.W. abt. 7 leagues	
		23+. p. 395 The South Star…as seen from about Annoboan Island (pp. 402, 411)	
	(103). p. 2/183 Isle St Tomas	23+. p. 395 The Prospect of the Island St. Tomé (p. 404)	
	(115). p. 2/232 [bird, a Madcap –] Fou		
	(116). p. 2/232 [birds diving on flying fish]	7+. p. 104 [leaning ship and waterspout added, see above, under 1 of 1688]	
		29+. p. 497 [four fishes –] The Sea Sun, A Dorado, A Germon, Sea Hogg, als. Porpoise [the	

Column 1 1679	Column 2 1688	Column 3 1732	Column 4
		dorado and porpoise are different from those in plates 19 and 31: all four drawn by James Barbot junior 1700] (dorado, porpoise, p. 497; sea sun, p. 499)	
		26+. p. 462 The English Isld. Redonda [in the Caribbean, p. 654]	
		30+. p. 523 [three sea creatures, one a sea-cow or mermaid: lettered but no key]	
	(109) p. 2/217 [fish, apart from those entered above, under (9) of 1679 –] Sardes Pargues, Sardes [two fish]	32+. p. 536 [fish, apart from those entered above, under (9), (13), (18), (63) and (66) of 1688 –] a Large Pargue, a Pargue, The Seal fish als. Roussette [the pargues are the same as in 1688] (pp. 226, 526, 527)	

Column 1 1679	Column 2 1688	Column 3 1732	Column 4
America and Europe 67. p. 95/360† [pr.] Cap Cassepourri	(119). p. 2/233* Veue de la Côte ferme de l'Amérique aux environs d'Wia-poco	33+. p. 543 The Prospect of Cape Cassepoury (p. 543)	
68. p. 95/360† [pr.] Veue de la Terre de Cayenne	(120). p. 233* Veue de l'Isle de Cayenne [lengthened]	33+. p. 543 The Prospect of the Island Cayenne (pp. 543, 555 [read 33 for 23])	
69. p. 99/366 Veue de la ville et du fort de Cayanne dessignés [sic] le 4 May 1679 [numbered and with key]	(122). p. 2/236 Profil du Bourg et du Fort de Cayenne de la Rade 1679 [lettered and with key]	34. p. 555 The Prospect of the Fort and Town of St. Lewis in Cayenne [canoes added; lettered and with key]	
70. p. 99/366 Plan de la ville et fort de Cayenne ['la figure en plan cy-attachée, que j'ay eue d'un amy, qui l'avoit tirée dès la reprize qu'en fit Mr. le comte d'Estrées': lettered and with key]	(123). p. 2/236 Plan du Bourg [very small]	33+. p. 543 Town and Fort St. Lewis att Cayenne [lettered and with key]	
	(121). p. 2/236 [map of Cayenne district]	33+. p. 543 A Map of the Island Cayenne	

Column 1 1679	Column 2 1688	Column 3 1732	Column 4
		16. p. 200 A Serpent of 14 foot, at Cayenne, Anotto Flower and Anoto Seed, Papay Trees, a Sugar Cane, The Mangnoc Tree, The Millet Plant, The Palm Cabidge Tree, The Patato Plant, Ginger root, The Ananas Plant, the Frigott [bird], The Paile en cu [bird] (pineapple p. 200; pawpaw p. 201; manioc p. 401; snake p. 559, anotto p. 561; birds p. 648)	
(71) unnum. p. between 104 and 105/375 Veue en profil du Fort Royal de la Martinique dessigné de 31esme Juillet 1679 [lettered and with key]	(112). p. 2/220* Veue du Fort Royal de la Martinique	34(2)+. p. 570 The Prospect of Fort Royal of Martinico [numbered and with key]	
		34(2)+. p. 570 The Sight of Part of the Isld. Martinico	
		33+. p. 543 A Mapp of the Harbour of the Cul de Sac Royale in the Island Martinico	

Column 1 1679	Column 2 1688	Column 3 1732	Column 4
		35(2)*. p. 647 The Prospect of the Town and Fort St. Peter in the Isld. Martinica [numbered and with key]	
		7+. p. 104 The Lamentyn Female alias The Manatee or Sea Cow, The Chitote of the Island of Anjuana, Sapajous of Cayann, Parokeets of Cayanna (pp. 560, 563 – the chitote was seen in a shop in London)	
	(124). p. 2/238 A Sturgeon taken in Southampton River the 4th May 1703	26+. p. 462 A Sturgeon … Caught in Southton River	
	(125). p. 2/289 [two monster fish taken in France in 1637 and 1644]		

BIBLIOGRAPHY

Works cited only in the Introduction and in full there are not included.

ABBREVIATIONS:
ARB   *Africana research bulletin* (Freetown)
BIFAN   *Bulletin de l'Institut français/fondamental d'Afrique Noire*
HIA   *History in Africa*
HS   Hakluyt Society
JAH   *Journal of African history*

EARLY (PRE-1800) SOURCES

The date of the short title is that of publication, not that of completion, some early works not being printed until after 1800.

*   A source employed certainly or almost certainly by Barbot
⟨*⟩   Barbot's reference/s to the source (when frequent, only the first reference, then 'etc.')

ACARETE DE BISCAY 1664   *Voyages and discoveries in South-America . . . The first . . . by Christopher d'Acugna . . . The second . . . by Mons. Acarete . . . The third . . . by M.Grillet and Bechamel,, London, 1698 [each account separately paginated] [Translation of 'Relation des voyages du Sieur Acarete de Biscay dans la rivière de Plate', in Melchisedech Thévenot, *Relation de divers voyages*, t. 2, Paris, 1664, separate pagination] ⟨*1732, p. 48⟩
ACUÑA 1641   *Voyages and discoveries [see ACARETE above] [Translation of Christoval de Acuña, *Nuevo descubrimiento del gran Rio de los Amazones*, Madrid, 1641, French translation *Relation de la rivière des Amazones*, Paris, 1688] ⟨*1732, p. 563, etc⟩
ALMADA 1946   André Álvares d'Almada, *Tratado breve dos Rios de Guiné*, ed. L. Silveira, Lisbon, 1946

ALMADA 1964   André Álvares de Almada, *Tratado breve dos Rios de Guiné do Cabo Verde*, ed. A. Brásio, Lisbon, 1964 [A slightly shorter text than that in ALMADA 1946: also in BRÁSIO 1964, pp. 229–378]

ALMADA 1984   André Álvares de Almada, *Brief treatise on the Rivers of Guinea* (*c. 1594*), ed. and trans. P. E. H. Hair, with additional notes by Jean Boulègue, 'interim edition, issued for the use of scholars from the Department of History, University of Liverpool', 2 vols, 1984

ÁLVARES 1617   Padre Manuel Álvares, 'Etiópia Menor e Descrição Geográfica da Província da Serra Leoa', unpublished manuscript of Biblioteca da Sociedade de Geografia, Lisbon, English translation by P. E. H. Hair of a transcript prepared for the late A. Teixeira da Mota, 'issued for the use of scholars, Department of History, University of Liverpool', 1991 [The undated manuscript was probably worked on up to the author's death in 1617. For a short section of the translation, annotated by P. E. H. Hair, see *ARB*, 11, 1981, pp. 92–140]

ANALECTA 1915   'Documenta ad historiam Missionis Guineae spectantis', *Analecta Ordinis Minorum Capuccinorum*, 31, 1915, pp. 327–30, 357–9 [Letters from Father Celestin de Bruxelles from Dieppe 1681 and Whydah 1682]

ANGUIANO *c*. 1690   see CARROCERA 1957

ASTLEY 1745   *A new general collection of voyages and travels*, 4 vols, Thomas Astley, London, 1745; reprint 1968

ATKINS 1735   John Atkins, *A voyage to Guinea, Brasil, and the West-Indies . . .*, London, 1735

AVEZAC 1845   [M. A. P. d'Avezac de Castera-Maya], 'Dictionnaire des langues françoise et nègres dont se sert dans le concession de la Compagnie royale du Sénégal', *Mémoires de la Société ethnologique*, 2, 1845, pp. 205–67

BAIDAFF 1929   Léon Baidaff, ed., 'Extrait d'un voyage fait en 1707, 1708, etc., aux costes de Guinée en Affrique et à Buenos Aires . . .', *Boletin del Instituto de investigaciones historicas*, 8, 1929, pp. 289–97

BARROS 1552   João de Barros, *Asia, primeira decada*, Lisbon, 1552, English translation of West African section in CRONE 1937

BAUDRAND 1701   *Michel Antoine Baudrand, *Dictionnaire*

géographique universel, Paris, 1701, translation of *Lexica geographica*, Paris, 1670 ⟨*1732, p. 4⟩

BEAULIEU 1664   'Mémoires du voyage aux Indes-Orientales du Général Beaulieu [1619–20], dressés par luy-mesme' in Melchisedech Thévenot, *Relation des divers voyages*, t. 1, pt. 2, Paris, 1664

[Annotated translation of the Sierra Leone section, by P. E. H. Hair, in *ARB*, 4, 1974, pp. 41–56]

BEAUPLAN 1660   *abridged translation in CHURCHILL 1704, 1: 541–71, of Guillaume de Vasseur, sieur de Beauplan, *Description d'Ukraine*, Paris, 1660 ⟨*1732, p. 539⟩

BECHAMEL 1674   see GRILLET 1674

BEGIN 1645   [Isaac Commelin], *Begin ende voortgangh van de Vereenighde Nederlantsche Geoctroyeerde Oost-Indische Compagnie*, Amsterdam, 1645 and 1646; reprint, 4 vols, Amsterdam 1970, with an introduction by C. R. Boxer

[Each voyage account having a separate pagination, citation is by the name of the main commander of each]

BOSMAN   *William Bosman, *A new and accurate description of the Coast of Guinea*, London, 1705; reprint 1907; reprint, with notes by J. D. Fage and R. E. Bradbury, London, 1967 ⟨*1732, p. 433, etc.⟩

[Translation of Willem Bosman, *Nauwkeurige beschryving van de Guinese Goud-, Tand- en Slave-kust*, Utrecht, 1704: corrections to the translation, not cited separately, are from Albert van Dantzig, 'English Bosman and Dutch Bosman: a comparison of texts', eight instalments in *HIA*, 2–11, 1975–84]

BOULÈGUE 1967   Jean Boulègue, 'Relation du port du fleuve Sénégal de João Barbosa, faite par João Baptista Lavanha (vers 1600)', *BIFAN*, sér. B, 29, 1967, pp. 496–511

BOYLE 1692   *Robert Boyle, *General heads for the natural history of a country*, London, 1692, originally published in *Philosophical transactions of the Royal Society*, 11, 2 April 1666, pp. 186–9

BRÁSIO 1955, etc   António Brásio, *Monumenta missionaria africana: Africa ocidental*, 20 vols, Lisbon, 1952–88

[Individual volumes are cited by date, as follows: BRÁSIO 1955, 1st ser., vol. 5; BRÁSIO 1960, 1st ser., vol. 8; BRÁSIO 1964, 2nd ser., vol. 3; BRÁSIO 1968, 2nd ser., vol. 4; BRÁSIO 1979, 2nd ser., vol. 5; BRÁSIO 1985, 2nd ser., vol. 6.]

BRUN 1624   Samuel Brun, *Schiffarten*, Basel, 1624

[Annotated English translation of part in JONES 1983a, pp. 46–96]

BURTON 1686   R[obert]. B[urton]., *A view of the English acquisitions in Guinea and the East-Indies*, London, 1686

CADAMOSTO 1937   G. R. Crone, ed., *The voyages of Cadamosto and other documents on Western Africa in the second half of the fifteenth century*, HS, London, 1937

CADAMOSTO 1948   [Damião Peres, ed.], *Viagens de Luís de Cadamosto e de Pedro de Sintra*, Lisbon, 1948

CADAMOSTO 1966   T. G. Leporace, ed., *Le navigazioni atlantiche del veneziano Alvise da Mosto*, Il Nuovo Ramusio 5, Venice, 1966

[Barbot does not appear to draw directly on Cadamosto's text, available in his day in many editions and translations, but on references in secondary sources]

CARNEIRO 1642   see FIGUEIREDO 1614.

CARREIRA 1983   António Carreira, *Documentos para a história das Ilhas de Cabo Verde e 'Rios de Guiné' (Séculos XVII e XVIII)*, Lisbon, 1983

CARROCERA 1957   Buenaventura de Carrocera, ed., *Misiones Capuchinas en Africa, II, Misiones al reino de la Zinga, Benin, Arda, Guinea y Sierra Leona*, Madrid, 1957

[Prints the text of an account written *c.* 1716, but largely the same as material in Mateo de Anguiano, *Vida, y virtudes del Capuchino español, ... Fr. Francisco de Pamplona*, 2nd ed., Madrid, 1704. See LEITE DE FARO 1959]

CARVALHO 1635   A. Viegas, 'Roteiro da Costa da Guiné (1635)', *O Instituto*, 70, 1923, pp. 97–102; and in translation, G. Thilmans and N. I. de Moraes, 'Le Routier de la côte de Guinée de Francisco Pirez de Carvalho (1635)', *BIFAN*, sér. B, 32, 1970, pp. 343–69

CASTELO BRANCO 1970   Fernando Castelo Branco, *Actas da Câmara de Santo António da Ilha do Príncipe, I (1692–1777)*, Lisbon, 1970

CHAMBONNEAU *c.* 1675   see RITCHIE 1968

CHOISY 1687   Abbé de Choisy, *Journal du voyage de Siam*, Paris, 1687

CHURCHILL 1704   *[Awnsham and John Churchill, publishers], A collection of voyages and travels*, 4 vols, London, 1704, enlarged to 6 vols, 1732; reprint 1746, 1752 (enlarged to 8 vols)

[Barbot's account forms most of vol. 5]

CIGAR 1981   N. Cigar, ed., *Mohammed al-Qadriri's Nashr al-mathani, The Chronicle*, London, 1981

CLUSIO 1964   Carlos Clusio (Clusius), *Aromatum et simplicium aliquot medicamentorum apud Indos nascentium historia, 1567* [a Portuguese translation], Lisbon, 1964

COELHO 1953   Francisco de Lemos Coelho, *Duas descrições seiscentistas da Guiné* [1669, 1684], ed. D. Peres, Lisbon, 1953 [For a French translation of the Senegal section, see MORAES 1973a.]

COELHO 1985   P. E. H. Hair, ed. and trans., *Francisco de Lemos Coelho, Description of the Coast of Guinea (1684), vol. 1*, 'issued from the Department of History, University of Liverpool', 1985

CORDEIRO 1881   Luciano Cordeiro, *Memórias do Ultramar. Viagens, explorações e conquistas dos Portuguezes*, Lisbon, 1881; reprint in 3 vols, Lisbon, 1935–6

COULON 1648   le sieur Coulon, ed., *Les Voyages fameux du sieur Vincent le Blanc*, Paris, 1648

CRONE 1937   see CADAMOSTO 1937

C. S. P. COLONIAL 1661–1668/1669–1674   *Calendar of State Papers, Colonial, America and West Indies*, 1661–1668, ed. W. N. Sainsbury, London, 1880; 1669–1674, ed. W. N. Sainsbury, London, 1889

CULTRU 1913   P. Cultru, ed., *Premier voyage du Sieur De La Courbe fait à la coste d'Afrique en 1685*, Paris, 1913

DAMPIER 1703   *William Dampier, A voyage to New Holland*, London, 2 vols, 1703, 1709, and later editions; reprint of 1729 edition, ed. J. A. Williamson, London, 1939 ⟨*1732*, p. 545⟩

DAPPER   *Olfert Dapper, *Naukeurige beschrijvinge der Afrikaensche gewesten* ... , Amsterdam, 1668, 2nd ed., 1676; French abbreviated translation *Description de l'Afrique*, Amsterdam, 1676, of which the sections on Black Africa are reprinted in *Objets interdits*, Fondation Dapper, Paris, 1990, with notes (mainly on the translation) by Albert van Dantzig, pp. 85–374; English translation *Africa. Being an accurate description of the regions ... Illustrated with notes ... by John Ogilby* [Dapper's name does not appear], London, 1670 ⟨*1688*, p. 19, etc⟩ [Page citation is of the Dutch 1676 edition, which is more commonly available than the 1668 edition, and from which it differs only in pagination and very minor details such as changes in spelling. The 1676 version has two paginations, but since most of the material on Black Africa is in the second pagination, only the first is here distinguished, as Dapper, 1/ (page number)/(paragraph number). To convert from the cited 1676 pagination to the 1668 pagination, for first pagination pp. 1/328–428 substract 59, 60 or 61, and for second pagination pp. 1–11 add 368, pp. 12–55 add 369, pp. 56–68 add 370, pp. 69–86 add 371, pp. 87–115 add 372, pp. 116–36 add 373, pp. 137–9 add 374. For an annotated edition of the material on Senegal, see THILMANS 1971; and for Dapper's sources, see JONES 1990 and 1990b]

DAPPER/*EYLANDEN* 1668   *Olfert Dapper, *Naukeurige beschrijvinge der Afrikaensche eylanden*, Amsterdam, 1668, often bound with previous item; a French translation within the 1676 work above ⟨*1688*, p. 2/204, etc.⟩

DAVENANT 1709   *Charles Davenant, *Reflections upon the constitution and management of the trade to Africa*, London, 1709 ⟨*1732*, p. 446, etc.⟩
[Page citations from *The political and commercial works of Charles D'Avenant*, 5 vols, London, 1771, vol. 5]

DAVID 1744   see DELCOURT 1974

DAVITY 1643, 1660   Pierre d'Avity, *Description générale de l'Afrique*, 2nd ed., Paris 1643, 3rd enlarged ed. by J. B. de Rocoles, Paris, 1660
[Davity was a major, but largely uncited, source for Dapper]

DE LA COURBE 1685   see CULTRU 1913

DE LA CROIX 1688   *[P. de la Croix], *Relation universelle de l'Afrique ancienne et moderne*, 4 vols, Lyon, 1688 ⟨*1732*, p. 467⟩
[Essentially a paraphrase of DAPPER, at least in the relevant sections]

DE MAREES   see MAREES

DELAFOSSE 1913   Maurice Delafosse, *Chronique du Fouta Sénégalais*, Paris, 1913

DELBÉE 1671   *'Journal du voyage du Sieur Delbée ... en l'année 1669 et la presente ...' and 'Suite du journal du Sieur d'Elbée' in J. de Clodoré, ed., *Relation de ce qui s'est passé dans les isles et terre-ferme de l'Amérique ...* , 4 vols, Paris, 1671, 2: 347–558 ⟨*1688*, p. 2/132⟩

DELCOURT 1974   André Delcourt, ed., *P. F. B. David: Jour-nal d'un voiage fait en Bambouc en 1744*, Société française d'his-toire d'Outre-Mer, Paris, 1974

DESTIVAL 1951   see MAUNY 1951

D'ESTRÉE(S) 1670   see *RELATION* 1674 and THILMANS/
MORAES 1977

DONELHA 1977   André Donelha, *Descrição da Serra Leoa e dos Rios de Guiné do Cabo Verde (1625)/An account of Sierra Leone and the Rivers of Guinea of Cape Verde (1625)*, ed. A. Teixeira da Mota and P. E. H. Hair, Lisbon, 1977

DONNAN 1930   Elizabeth Donnan, ed., *Documents illustrative of the history of the slave trade to America*, 4 vols, Washington, 1930–35

DOUBLET 1883   C. Bréard, ed., *Journal du corsaire Jean Doub-let de Honfleur*, Paris, 1883

DRAISE DE GRANDPIERRE 1718 see GRANDPIERRE 1718

D.T.V.Y. 1619   *[Pierre Davity], *Les Estats, empires, et principa-litez du monde . . . par le sieur D. T. V. Y.*, Paris, 1619 ⟨*1732, p. 285⟩

DUBOIS 1674   *Les voyages faits par le sieur D. B. aux Isles Dauphines*, Paris, 1674

DU JARRIC 1614   Pierre du Jarric, *Histoire des choses les plus mémorables . . . de ce que les Religieux de la Compagnie de Jesus y ont faict*, t. 3, Bordeaux, 1614
[Translation of GUERREIRO 1611]

DU PLESSIS 1700   *D. Martineau du Plessis, *Nouvelle géog-raphie, ou description exacte de l'univers*, Amsterdam, 1700; 2nd ed., 3 vols, The Hague, 1733 [edition seen] ⟨*1732, p. 4, etc.⟩

DURAND 1802   J. B. L. Durand, *Voyage au Sénégal*, Paris, 1802

DU VAL/DUVAL 1670, 1685   *Pierre Du Val, *Le Monde, ou la géographie universelle*, Paris, 1670, translated as *Geographia uni-versalis: The present state of the whole world*, London, 1685 ⟨*1688, p. 159⟩
[Barbot appears to have used, at least at times, the English translation]

DU VAL 1676   *P. Du Val, *Mémoire géographique de tous les pays du monde*, Lyon, 1676,

ENGLISH PILOT 1701   J. Seller and C. Price, *The fifth part of*

the general English Pilot ... the West Coast of Africa, London, 1701
[The text is basically a new translation of the text of ROBIJN/ ROGGEVEEN 1685, with minor changes]

FARIA Y SOUSA 1698   Emanuel de Faria y Sousa, *The history of Portugal*, London, 1698 ⟨*1732*, p. 85, etc.⟩
[Translation of Manoel Faria y Sousa, *Historia del reyno de Portugal*, Madrid, 1616]

FARO 1945   L. Silveira, ed., *Peregrinação de André de Faro à Terra dos Gentios*, Lisbon, 1945
[Annotated translation of slightly abbreviated text in HAIR 1982]

FENTON 1959   E. G. R. Taylor, ed., *The troublesome voyage of Captain Edward Fenton, 1582–1583*, HS, London, 1959
[For a fuller version of some of the material, see MADOX 1976; and for an analysis of the Sierra Leone section, HAIR 1978b]

FERNANDES 1951   Valentim Fernandes, *Description de la côte occidentale d'Afrique (Sénégal au Cap de Monte, Archipels) (1506–1510)*, ed. T. Monod, A. Teixeira da Mota and R. Mauny, Centro de estudos da Guiné portuguesa, Bissau, 1951

FIGUEIREDO 1614   Manuel de Figueiredo, *Hydrografia ... com os Roteiros de ... Guiné ...,*, Lisbon, 1614, 1625
[No copy of an alleged earlier edition, of 1608, can be located; and an alleged French translation of 1614, by Nicolas Le Bon, has not been traced. The information on Guinea is copied exactly in António de Maris Carneiro, *Regimento de pilotos ...* , Lisbon, 1642, 1655, and almost exactly in Luis Serrão Pimentel, *Arte prática de navegar ...* , Lisbon, 1681; it is the major source of the Mortier maps of Guinea c. 1700]

FRANÇOIS DE PARIS 1682   see THILMANS 1976

FROGER 1698   *F. Froger, *Relation du voyage de Mr. de Gennes au détroit de Magellan / Relation d'un voyage fait en 1695, 1696 et 1697, aux Côtes d'Afrique, Détroit de Magellan ...* , Paris, 1698, English translation, London, 1698 [with some illustrations omitted] ⟨*1732*, p. 424⟩

GABY 1689   [F. J. B. Gaby], *Relation de la Nigritie*, Paris, 1689
[See C. Becker, 'A propos d'un plagiaire: le père Gaby', *Notes africaines*, 133, 1972, pp. 17–21]

GOLDEN COAST 1665   *The Golden Coast, or a description of Ginney ...*, London, 1665

GONZALEZ 1902   'Relation abrégée du voyage des Pères de
l'Ordre des Frères Prêcheurs missionnaires en Afrique et en
Guinée . . . par le Supérieur de cette mission, le Père Gonzalez
François [1688]', *L'Année Dominicaine*, 14, Sept. 1702; reprint
Lyon, 1902, pp. 462–75
GRANDPIERRE 1718   Draisé de Grandpierre, *Relation de di-
vers voyages faits dans l'Afrique, dans l'Amérique et aux Indes
Occidentales*, Paris, 1718
GRILLET 1674   *Voyages and discoveries* [see ACARETE
above], translation of 'Journal du voyage qu'ont fait les Pères
Grillet et Bechamel dans la Guyane l'an 1674', in *Relation de la
Rivière des Amazones*, Paris, 1688 ⟨*1732, pp. 550, 556, etc.⟩
GROEBEN 1694   Otto Friedrich von der Groeben, *Guineische
Reisebeschreibung*, Marienwerder, 1694
[Text and annotated English translation of part in JONES 1985,
pp. 23–57, 220–49]
GUERREIRO 1605, etc.   Fernão Guerreiro, *Relaçam annal das
cousas que fizeram os Padres da Companhia de Jesus nas partes da
India Oriental, e no Brasil, Angola, Cabo-Verde, Guiné . . .*, 5
parts, Lisbon, part 2 [1602–3] 1605, part 3 [1604–6] 1607, part
4 [1606–7] 1609, part 5 [1607–8] 1611; reprint, 3 vols, Coimbra,
1930–42
[French translation in DU JARRIC 1614; also contemporary
translations in Latin and Spanish. Annotated English translation of most of the material, by P. E. H. Hair, in *ARB*, 5/4,
1975, pp. 81–118; 6/1, 1976, pp. 45–70; 6/3, 1976, pp. 34–60; 8/
2–3, 1978, pp. 64–108; 12/1–2, 1983, pp. 55–96; the transla-
tions with additional material in HAIR 1989]
HAIR 1975a   P. E. H. Hair, 'Sources on early Sierra Leone: (5)
Barreira (letter of 23.2.1606)', *ARB*, 5, 1975, pp. 81–118
HAIR 1975b   P. E. H. Hair, 'Sources on early Sierra Leone: (6)
Barreira on Just Enslavement, 1606', *ARB*, 6, 1975, pp. 52–74
HAIR 1978b   P. E. H. Hair, 'Sources on early Sierra Leone: (14)
English accounts of 1582', *ARB*, 9, 1978, pp. 67–99
HAIR 1979   P. E. H. Hair, 'Sources on early Sierra Leone: (10)
Schouten and Le Maire, 1615', *ARB*, 7, 1979, pp. 56–75
HAIR 1981b   P. E. H. Hair, *Sierra Leone and the English in 1607:
extracts from the unpublished journals of the Keeling voyage to the
East Indies*, Occasional Paper 4, Institute of African Studies,
University of Sierra Leone, 1981

HAIR 1981c   P. E. H. Hair, 'Sources on early Sierra Leone: (18) Barbot 1678', *ARB*, 11, 1981, pp. 46–60

HAIR 1982   P. E. H. Hair, trans. and ed., *André de Faro's missionary journey to Sierra Leone in 1663–4*, Occasional Paper 5, Institute of African Studies, Freetown, 1982 [Translation of most of FARO 1663]

HAIR 1989   P. E. H. Hair, trans. and ed., *Jesuit documents on the Guinea of Cape Verde and the Cape Verde Islands 1585–1617*, Department of History, University of Liverpool, 1989

HAKLUYT 1589   Richard Hakluyt, *The principall navigations ... of the English nation*, London, 1589; facsimile reprint, ed. D. B. Quinn and R. A. Skelton, HS, London, 1965

HAKLUYT 1598   Richard Hakluyt, *The principal navigations ...*, 3 vols, London, 1598–1600; reprint Glasgow, 12 vols, 1903–5 [Cited by the original pagination, which appears in the reprint.]

HALLEY 1702   *[text from a chart reprinted in] N. J. W. Thrower, ed., *The three voyages of Edmond Halley 1698–1701*, HS, London, 1981 ⟨*1732, p. 542⟩

HARRIS 1705   John Harris, *Navigantium atque Itinerantium Bibliotheca, or, A compleat collection of voyages and travels*, 2 vols, London, 1705 [Although the collection contains summary extracts from several of Barbot's minor sources, e.g. MARMOL, LUDOLF, DAMPIER, there is no evidence that Barbot used this work]

HEMMERSAM 1663   Michael Hemmersam, *Guineische und West-Indianische Reißbeschreibung de An. 1639 biß 1645 ...*, Nürnberg, 1663 [Text and annotated English translation of part in JONES 1983a, pp. 97–133, 356–83]

HILLIER 1697   *'Part of two letters from Mr. J. Hillier dated Cape Corse, Jan. 3. 1687/8 and Apr. 25. 1688 ... giving an account of the customs of the inhabitants, the air, &c., of that place, together with an account of the weather there ...', *Philosophical transactions of the Royal Society*, 292, 1697, pp. 687–708 ⟨*1732, p. 443⟩

HOUSTOUN 1725   James Houstoun, *Account of the Coast of Guinea ...*, London, 1725

JANNEQUIN 1643   Claude Jannequin, *Le Voyage de Lybie au Royaume de Senega*, Paris, 1643; reprint Geneva, 1980

JOBSON 1623   R. Jobson, *The golden trade*, London, 1623; reprint Weymouth, 1904

JONES 1983a   Adam Jones, *German sources for West African history 1599-1669*, Wiesbaden, 1983
[Includes texts, with translations and notes, from HEMMERSAM 1662 and ZUR EICH 1678, and annotated translations of part of BRUN 1624 and all of MÜLLER 1673]

JONES 1985   Adam Jones, *Brandenburg sources for West African history 1680-1700*, Stuttgart, 1985
[Includes texts, with translations and notes, from GROEBEN 1694 and OETTINGER 1886]

JOSEPHUS 1957   Josephus, *Jewish antiquities*, vol. 1, trans. and ed. H. S. J. Thackeray, London, 1957

JULIEN 1948   C.-A. Julien, *Les Voyages de découverte et les premiers établissements (XVe-XVIe siècles)*, Paris, 1948

JURIEU 1704   *Pierre Jurieu, *Histoire critique des dogmes et des cultes*, Amsterdam, 1704, translated as *A critical history of the doctrines and worship of the Church*, London, 1705 ⟨*1732, pp. 309, 318, 345, etc.⟩

JUSTEL 1674   see *RELATION* 1674

LABAT 1728   Jean-Baptiste Labat, *Nouvelle relation de l'Afrique occidentale*, 5 vols, Paris, 1728

LABAT 1730   Jean-Baptiste Labat, *Voyage du Chevalier des Marchais en Guinée, isles voisines, et à Cayenne, fait en 1725, 1726, et 1727*, 4 vols, Paris, 1730

LAVANHA c. 1600   see BOULÈGUE 1967

LE BLANC 1648   see COULON 1648

LEERS 1665   Arnout Leers, *Pertinente beschryvinge van Africa*, Rotterdam, 1665

LEGUAT 1708   *François Leguat, *A new voyage to the East Indies*, 2 vols, London, 1708, French version, *Voyages et avantures de F. Leguat*, 2 vols, London and Amsterdam, 1708 ⟨*1732, p. 560 – 'if they deserve any credit'⟩
[The two versions were published simultaneously, allegedly edited by Maximilien Misson, like Leguat and Barbot a Huguenot refugee in England; and significantly Barbot once cites the work as by Misson (p. 306/8). The English version was reprinted, with annotation, in Pasfield Oliver, ed., *The voyage of François Leguat*, 2 vols, HS, London, 1891: the pagination of this edition is cited]

LE MAIRE 1695   *Les voyages du Sieur Le Maire aux Isles Canaries, Cap-Verd, Sénégal et Gambie, Paris, 1695, translated as A voyage of the Sieur Le Maire ..., London, 1696 [lacks some illustrations]
[A later translation, Voyage to the Canaries, Cape Verde and the coast of Africa ..., trans. E. Goldsmid, Edinburgh, 1887, silently omits sections]

LEO AFRICANUS 1956   A. Épaulard et al., transs and eds, Jean-Léon l'Africain: Description de l'Afrique, 2 vols, Paris, 1956 [The best edition of a work first published in RAMUSIO 1550: a major source of MARMOL 1573 and DAPPER, but not of their material on the Guinea coast]

LIGON 1657   Richard Ligon, A true and exact history of the Island of Barbados, London, 1657

LINSCHOTEN 1934   Jan Huygen van Linschoten, Itinerario, deerde deel, ed. C. P. Burger and F. W. T. Hunger, Linschoten Vereeniging, The Hague, 1934
[An edition of Jan Huyghen, Beschryvinghe van de gantsche Custe van Guinea ..., Amsterdam, 1596]

LOYER 1714   Godefroi Loyer, Relation du voyage du royaume d'Issiny, Paris, 1714
[Reprinted in ROUSSIER 1935]

LUDOLF 1684   *Hiob Ludolf, Nouvelle histoire d'Abbissine, ou d'Ethiopie, Paris, 1684
[French translation of Historia aethiopica, Frankfurt, 1681; English translation, A new history of Ethiopia, London, 1682] ⟨*1688, p. 183 'la nouvelle traduction'⟩

LY 1964   Abdoulaye Ly, ed., Un Navire de commerce sur la côte sénégambienne en 1685, IFAN, Catalogues et documents 17, Dakar, 1964

MADOX 1976   Elizabeth Story Donno, An Elizabethan in 1582: the diary of Richard Madox, HS, London, 1976
[For related material, see FENTON 1959, and for an analysis of the Sierra Leone material, see HAIR 1978b]

MAREES   *P[ieter]. D[e]. M[arees]., Description et récit historiale du riche Royaume d'or de Gunea, Amsterdam, 1605 ⟨*1688, p. 18, etc.⟩
[Translation of P. D. M., Beschryvinge ende Historische Verhael vant Gout Koninckrijk van Gunea, Amsterdam, 1602; reprint, ed. S. P. l'Honoré Naber, Linschoten Vereeniging, The Hague,

1912; it is unlikely that Barbot ever used the original Dutch version. English translation, Pieter de Marees, *Description and Historical Account of the Gold Kingdom of Guinea (1602)*, eds. Albert van Dantzig and Adam Jones, London, 1987. Citations are of the foliation of the Dutch version, this being indicated in both the reprint and the English translation. The annotation of the English translation is cited as MAREES 1987]

MARMOL 1573   see MARMOL 1667

MARMOL 1667   *L'Afrique de Marmol ... enrichie des cartes géographiques de M. Sanson ... Avec l'histoire des Chérifs traduite de l'espagnol de Diego Torres*, trans. Nicolas Perrot, sieur d'Ablancourt, 3 vols, Paris, 1667 ⟨*1732, p. 5, etc.; Torres, p. 50⟩ [Translation of Luis del Marmol Carvajal, *Descripcion general de Affrica*, pt. 1, 2 vols, Grenada, 1573; vol. 1 reprint, Madrid 1953; pt. 2, Malaga, 1599; with an added translation, in vol. 3, of Diego Torres, *Relacion del Origen y Sucesso de los Xarifes*, Seville, 1585. Annotated English translation of the section of Marmol relating to the Guinea coast, by P. E. H. Hair, in *ARB*, 9, 1979, pp. 70–84]

MAUNY 1949   Raymond Mauny, 'Un Plan de Gorée de la fin du XVIIe siècle', *BIFAN*, sér. B, 14, 1949, pp. 18–19

MAUNY 1951   Raymond Mauny, 'Relation du Sr. Destival 1672', *BIFAN*, sér. B, 13, 1951, pp. 1298–1301

MISSON 1691   François Maximilien Misson, *Nouveau voyage d'Italie fait en l'année 1688, avec un mémoire contenant des avis utilisés à ceux qui voudront faire le mesme voyage*, The Hague, 1691

MONTAUBAN 1698   *Relation du voyage de sieur de Montauban capitaine de filibustiers en Guinée, en l'année 1695. Avec une description du Roiaume du Cap de Lopez, des moeurs, du coûtume, de la religion du pais*, Amsterdam, 1698

MOORE 1738   Francis Moore, *Travels into the inland parts of Africa, containing a description of the several nations up the R. Gambia ...*, London, 1738; reprint, London, 1968

MORAES 1973a   Nize Isabel de Moraes, ed., 'La Petite Côte d'après Francisco de Lemos Coelho', *BIFAN*, sér. B, 35, 1973, pp. 239–68

MOUETTE 1711   *Travels of Sieur Mouette* [1710] in [John Stevens], *A new collection of voyages and travels*, London, in parts 1708–10, in 2 vols 1711

[Translation of *Relation de la captivité du Sr. Mouette dans les royaumes de Fez, et de Maroc*, Paris, 1683] ⟨*1732, p. 79 'translated into English in the two quarto volumes of monthly travels'⟩

MÜLLER 1673   Wilhelm Johann Müller, *Die africanische auf der guineischen Gold Cust gelegene Landschafft Fetu*, Hamburg, 1673 [Annotated English translation in JONES 1983a, pp. 138–259]

N * * * 1719   Mr. N * * *, *Voyages aux côtes de Guinée et en Amérique*, Amsterdam, 1719

NAVARRETE 1676   *Domingo Fernandez de Navarrete, 'An account of the empire of China', in CHURCHILL 1704, I, 1–424 ⟨*1732, pp. 210, 312⟩ [Abridged translation of Domingo Fernandez de Navarrete, *Tratados historicos ... de la monarchia de China*, Madrid, 1676]

NEWTON 1764   John Newton, *An authentic narrative ...*, London, 1764, many later editions, consulted in *Forty-one letters ... [and] the narrative ...*, London, 1822

OGILBY 1670   see DAPPER 1668

OETTINGER 1886   Paul Oettinger, ed., *Unter kurbrandenburgischer Flagge. Nach dem Tagebuch des Chirurgen Johann Peter Oettinger*, Berlin, 1886 [Text and annotated English translation of part of Oettinger's 1692–3 Guinea voyage in JONES 1985, pp. 180–98, 291–305]

PACHECO PEREIRA 1956   Duarte Pacheco Pereira, *Esmeraldo de situ orbis: Côte occidentale d'Afrique du Sud Marocain au Gabon*, ed. R. Mauny, Centro de estudos da Guiné Portuguesa, Bissau, 1956

PHILLIPS 1732   Thomas Phillips, 'A journal of a voyage made ... in 1693 ... to Africa' in CHURCHILL 1704, 6, 173–239 (1732 edition, but pp. 187–255 in 1746 and 1752 editions)

PRINS 1666   Jeurian Prins, *Journael van de reyse gedaen ... onder ... Admirael Michiel A. de Ruyter*, Amsterdam, 1666

PULGAR 1943   Fernando del Pulgar, *Cronica de los reyes católicos*, ed. Juan de Mata Carriazo, 2 vols, Madrid, 1943

PURCHAS 1625   Samuel Purchas, *Purchas his Pilgrimes*, 4 vols, London, 1625; reprint 20 vols, Glasgow, 1905–7

RALEIGH 1650   *Walter Raleigh, *Judicious and select essayes ... upon the first invention of shipping ...*, London, 1650 ⟨*1732, p. 42⟩

RAMUSIO 1550, 1554   [G. B. Ramusio], *Navigationi et viaggi*, vol. 1, Venice, 1550; 2nd ed., vol. 1, Venice, 1554

RASK 1754   Johannes Rask, *En kort og sandfaerdig Rejse-Beskrivelse til og frå Guinea*, Trondheim, 1754, ed. J. Øvrelid, as *Ferd til og frå Guinea, 1708–1713*, Oslo, 1969

RATELBAND 1953   K. Ratelband, ed., *Vijf dagregisters van het kasteel São Jorge da Mina (Elmina) aan de Goudkust (1645–1647)*, Linschoten Vereeniging, The Hague, 1953

RECUEIL 1702–6   *Recueil des voyages qui ont servi á l'établissement et aux progrès de la Compagnie des Indes Orientales*, 5 vols, Amsterdam, 1702–6; with partial translation, *A collection of voyages undertaken by the Dutch East Indies Company*, London, 1703

[Abridged translation of BEGIN 1645]

RELATION 1674   'Relation du voyage fait sur les costes d'Afrique aux mois de Novembre et Décembre de l'année 1670, Janvier et Février 1671, commençant au Cap Verd' in H. Justel, ed., *Recueil de divers voyages faits en Afrique et en l'Amérique qui n'ont point esté encore publiez*, Paris, 1674

RITCHIE 1968   Carson I. A. Ritchie, 'Deux textes sur le Sénégal (1673–1677) [by Louis Moreau de Chambonneau]', *BIFAN*, sér. B, 30, 1968, pp. 289–353

ROBBE 1685   *Jacques Robbe, *Méthode pour apprendre facilement la géographie*, 2 vols, Paris, 1685, later editions 1697, 1703 ⟨*1732, p. 4, etc.⟩

ROBIJN/ROGGEVEEN 1685   *Jacob Robijn [maps by A. Roggeveen, 1668], *De nieuwe groote zee-spiegel*, pt. 5, Amsterdam, 1685, English version J. Robbyn, *The fourth part of the new great Sea-Mirrour*, Amsterdam, 1687, this version reprinted as Jacob Robijn and Arent Roggeveen, *The burning fen, second part*, Amsterdam, 1687, with introduction by I. C. Koeman, Amsterdam, 1971

[Barbot probably used the 1685 Dutch original (but see VAN KEULEN 1683), hence the date of the short title: the editors have used the reprint of the 1687 work, reputedly an exact translation of the text and a reproduction of the maps. The translation is in almost incomprehensible English and the translation in *ENGLISH PILOT* 1701 is to be preferred]

RØMER 1760   L. F. Rømer, *Tilforladelig Efterretning om Kysten Guinea*, Copenhagen, 1760

ROOK 1666   [Lawrence] Rook, [directions for a long voyage],

Philosophical transactions of the Royal Society, 8 January 1666 = 1 (1665–6), pp. 139–43
[Summarized in CHURCHILL 1704, 1, lxxiii-iv]

ROTEIROS 1952   D. Peres, ed., *Os mais antigos roteiros da Guiné*, Lisbon, 1953

ROUSSIER 1935   Paul Roussier, ed., *L'établissement d'Issiny 1687–1702: Voyages de Ducasse, Tibierge et d'Amon ... et ... Relation de Loyer*, Paris, 1935

RUITERS 1623   Dierick Ruiters, *Toortse der zee-vaert*, Vlissinghen, 1623; reprint, ed. S. P. l'Honoré Naber, Linschoten Vereeniging, The Hague, 1913
[Citations are in the form 1623 foliation/1913 pagination. For a French translation of the section on Senegal, see THILMANS/ROSSIE 1969]

RUYTER 1961   P. Verhoog and L. Koelmans, eds., *De reis van Michiel Adriaanszoon de Ruyter in 1664–1665*, Linschoten Vereeniging, The Hague, 1961

RYSVIC 1697   *Relation de ce qui s'est passé devant et dans la negotiation de la paix à Rysvic*, 2 vols in one, The Hague, 1697
⟨*1732, p. 530/2 'the book publish'd of the conferences for peace, held at Ryswick Anno 1697' – perhaps this book⟩

SAINT OLAN 1695   *François Pidau de Saint Olan, *Relation de l'Empire de Maroc*, Paris, 1695, translated as *The present state of the Empire of Morocco*, London, 1695 ⟨*1732, p. 71⟩

SANDWICH 1703   *Edward Montagu, Earl of Sandwich, *Hispania illustrata ... in letters from the Earl of Sandwich*, London, 1703 ⟨*1732, p. 48⟩

SANSON 1656   Nicolas Sanson, *L'Afrique en plusieurs cartes nouvelles et exactes et en divers traictés de géographie et d'histoire*, Paris, 1656

SANSON 1667   *Nicolas and Guillaume Sanson, *Tables de la géographie ancienne et nouvelle*, Paris, 1667, 2nd ed., 1679 ⟨*1688, p. 2/215 'la Nouvelle Géografie de Samson fils', *1732, p. 4⟩

SCHOUTEN 1945   W. A. Engelbrecht and P. J. van Herwerden, eds, *De ontdekkingsreis van Jacob le Maire en Willem Cornelisz Schouten*, 2 vols, Linschoten Vereeniging, The Hague, 1945
[Annotated reprint of *Journal ofte beschryinghe van de wonderlijke reyse ghedaen door Willem Cornelisz Schouten ... inde jaren*

1615, 1616 en 1617, Amsterdam, 1618, and *Spieghel de Austra-lische navigatie door . . . Jacob le Maire*, Amsterdam, 1622; for an annotated English translation of the Sierra Leone sections, see HAIR 1979]

SCHÜCK 1889   Richard   Schück,   *Brandenburg-Preußens Kolonial-Politik unter dem Grossen Kurfürsten und seinen Nach-folgern (1647–1721)*, 2 vols, Leipzig, 1889

S. LÔ 1637   Alexis de S. Lô, *Relation du voyage du Cap-Verd*, Paris, 1637

SENEGAL VOCABULARIES c. 1700   see AVEZAC

SMITH 1744   William Smith, *A new voyage to Guinea*, London, 1744

SNELGRAVE 1734   William Snelgrave, *A new account of some parts of Guinea and the slave trade*, London, 1734

SPRAT 1667   Thomas Sprat, *History of the Royal Society*, London, 1667

STRUYS 1676, 1684   J. J. Struys, *Drie aanmerkelijke en seer rampspoedige Reysen*, Amsterdam, 1676, English translation, *The voyages of John Struys*, London, 1684

SYSTEMA 1690   see WILKINSON 1690

TEIXEIRA DA MOTA 1969   Avelino Teixeira da Mota, 'Un document nouveau pour l'histoire des Peuls au Sénégal pen-dant les XVème et XVIème siècles', *Boletim cultural da Guiné portuguesa*, 24, 1969, pp. 781–860, also Série separatas, no. 56, Agrupamento de estudos da cartografia antiga, Lisbon, 1969

[Pagination cited is that of the offprint]

TEIXEIRA DA MOTA 1987   Francisco Leite de Faria and Ave-lino Teixeira da Mota, 'Novidades náuticas e ultramarinas numa informação dada em Veneza em 1517', *Memórias da Aca-demia das ciências de Lisboa, classe de ciências*, 20, 1977, pp. 7–75, also Série separatas, no. 99, Centro de estudos de cartografia antiga, Lisbon, 1977.

TELLEZ 1711   *Balthazar Tellez, *The travels of the Jesuits in Ethiopia*, 1710, in [John Stevens], *A new collection of voyages and travels*, London, in parts 1708–10, then in 2 vols, 1711 [Translation of Baltasar Tellez, 'L'Histoire de la Haute Ethiopie', in M. Thévenot, *Relation de divers voyages*, Paris, 1696, separate pagination] ⟨*1732*, p. 8 'in the quarterly collec-tion of travels in two volumes'⟩

THEVET 1558   André Thevet, *Les Singularitez de la France antarctique*, Paris, 1558; reprint, ed. P. Gaffarel, Paris, 1878

THEVET 1575   André Thevet, *La Cosmographie universelle*, Paris, 1575

THILMANS 1971   G. Thilmans, 'Le Sénégal dans l'oeuvre d'Olfried Dapper', *BIFAN*, sér. B, 33, 1971, pp. 508–63

THILMANS 1975   G. Thilmans, 'Les Planches sénégalaises et mauritaniennnes des 'Atlas Vingboons' (XVIIe siècle)', *BIFAN*, sér. B, 37, 1975, pp. 95–116

THILMANS 1976   Guy Thilmans, 'La Relation de François de Paris (1682–1683)', *BIFAN*, sér. B, 38, 1976, pp. 1–51

THILMANS/MORAES 1972   G. Thilmans and N. I. Moraes, eds, 'La Description de la côte de Guinée du Père Baltasar Barreira (1606)', *BIFAN*, sér. B, 34, 1972, pp. 1–50

THROWER 1981   see HALLEY 1702

TILLEMAN 1697   Eric Tilleman, *En liden enfoldig beretning om det landskab Guinea*, Copenhagen, 1697

TORRES 1585   see MARMOL 1667

TRUE STATE 1710   *A true state of the present differences between the Royal African Company and the separate traders*, London, 1710

URING 1727   Nathaniel Uring, *A history of the voyages and travels of Capt. Nathaniel Uring*, 2nd ed., London, 1727; reprint, London, 1929

VALLE 1650–63   **Viaggi di Pietro della Valle il Peregrino ... in 54 lettere familiari ... mandate in Napoli all' erudito e ... di molti anni suo amico Mario Schipano ...*, 3 pts in 4 vols, Rome, 1650, 1658, 1663; French translation, 4 vols, Paris, 1661–6; English translation 1664 ⟨**1688*, 'Avis'⟩

VAN DEN BROECKE 1634   K. Ratelband, ed., *Reizen naar West-Afrika*, Linschoten Vereeniging, The Hague, 1950
[Edition of a partly independent manuscript version of Pieter van den Broecke, *Korte historiael ende journaelsche aenteyckeninghe*, Haarlem, 1634, with additional material]

VAN KEULEN 1683   **Jan van Keulen, De nieuwe groote lichtende zee-fakkel*, pt. 5, Amsterdam, 1683
[The text of this work (written by Claas Janszoon Vogt and sometimes referred to under his name) was borrowed by ROBIJN/ROGGEVEEN 1685, and the maps are very similar. Barbot may have used this work rather than Robijn/Roggeveen,

but because the latter is available in a modern reprint it has in most instances been cited rather than Van Keulen]

VASCONCELOS 1639   see VASCONCELOS 1641

VASCONCELOS 1641   *Augustin Emanuel et Vasconcelos, *Histoire de D. Jean II*, Paris, 1641 ⟨*1732*, p. 27, etc.⟩ [Translation of Agustín Manuel y Vasconcelos [Agostinho Manuel e Vasconcelos], *Vida y acciones del Rey Don Juan el Segundo, Decimotercio de Portugal*, Madrid, 1639]

VEGA 1609–1617   *Garcilaso de la Vega, *The royal commentaries of Peru*, London, 1688 ⟨*1732*, p. 375, etc.⟩ [Translation of Garcilaso de la Vega, *Historia general del Peru*, Cordova, 1617]

VILLAULT [1669]   *[Nicolas] Villault, sieur de Bellefond, *Relation des costes d'Afrique appellées Guinée; Avec la description du pays, [des] moeurs et façons de vivre des habitans, des productions de la terre, et des marchandises qu'on en apporte, avec les remarques historiques sur ces costes*, Paris, 1669; translated as *A relation of the coasts of Africk called Guinee* . . . , London, 1670 ⟨*1688*, p. 17, etc.⟩ [On Villault's voyage, see THILMANS/MORAES 1976]

WATTS 1672   *[John Watts], *A true relation of the . . . barbarous murders of negroes . . . committed on three Englishmen in Old Calabar*, London, 1672 [Reprinted with slight changes in B. R., *A view of the English acquisitions in Guinea and East-India* . . . , London, 1686, 2nd ed. 1700, pp. 51–7 – probably Barbot's source]

WILKINSON 1690   W. Wilkinson, *Systema Africanum; or a treatise discovering the intrigues . . . of the Guiney Company* . . . , London, 1690

WINTERBOTTOM 1803   Thomas Winterbottom, *An account of the native Africans in the neighbourhood of Sierra Leone*, 2 vols, London, 1803; reprint with an introduction by J. D. Hargreaves and E. M. Beckett, London, 1969

ZUR EICH 1678   Hans Jacob Zur Eich, 'Africanische Reißbeschreibung in die Landschaft Fetu . . .' in Johann W. Simler, ed., *Vier löblicher Statt Zürich Verbürgter Reißbeschreibungen*, Zurich, 1677–8, 2: 91–175 [Text and annotated English translation of part in JONES 1983a, pp. 261–8, 383–90]

B: MODERN SOURCES AND STUDIES

AFRICA PILOT 1967   *Africa pilot, Vol. 1 (Cabo Espartel–Calabar River)*, 12th ed., Hydrographer of the Navy, London, 1967

AFIGBO 1973   A. E. Afigbo, 'Trade and trade-routes in nineteenth century Nsukka', *Journal of the Historical Society of Nigeria*, 7, 1973, pp. 77–90

AKINJOGBIN 1967   I. A. Akinjogbin, *Dahomey and its neighbours, 1701–1818*, Cambridge, 1967

ALAGOA 1972   E. J. Alagoa, *A short history of the Niger Delta*, Ibadan, 1972

ALAGOA/FOMBO 1972   E. J. Alagoa and A. Fombo, *A chronicle of Grand Bonny*, Ibadan, 1972

ANSTEY/HAIR 1976   Roger Anstey and P. E. H. Hair, *Liverpool, the African slave trade and abolition*, Historic Society of Lancashire and Cheshire, 1976; reprint, with additions, 1989

ARDENER 1968   E. Ardener, 'Documentary and linguistic evidence for the rise of the trading polities between the Rio del Rey and Cameroons, 1500–1650' in I. M. Lewis, ed., *History and social anthropology*, London, 1968, pp. 81–126

ARGYLE 1966   W. J. Argyle, *The Fon of Dahomey*, Oxford, 1966

BAESJOU 1988   René Baesjou, 'The historical evidence in old maps and charts of Africa with special reference to West Africa', *HIA*, 15, 1988, pp. 1–83

BAL 1979   Willy Bal, *Afro-romanica studia*, Albufeira, 1979

BARRY 1972   Boubacar Barry, *Le Royaume du Waalo*, Paris, 1972

BARTH 1862   Henry Barth, *Collection of vocabularies of Central African languages*, Gotha, 1862; reprint London, 1971

BAZIN 1906   H. Bazin, *Dictionnaire Bambara-Français*, Paris, 1906; reprint Farnborough, 1965

BECKER 1985   Charles Becker, 'Routiers anciens, cartographie et connaissance de la vallée du Sénégal a l'époque de la traite Atlantique', paper presented to Colloque international sur la traite des noirs, Nantes, 1985

BERBAIN 1942   Simone Berbain, *Le Comptoir français de Juda (Ouidah) au XVIIIe siècle*, Dakar, 1942

BLAKE 1937   John W. Blake, *European beginnings in West*

Africa 1454–1578, London, 1937; reprint 1971, and, with additional preface, as *West Africa: quest for God and gold 1454–1578*, London, 1977

BOAHEN 1964   A. Adu Boahen, *Britain, the Sahara and the western Sudan 1788–1861*, Oxford, 1964

BOOTH 1960   A. H. Booth, *Small mammals of West Africa*, London, 1960

BOUCHER 1977   Bernadette Boucher, *La Sauvage aux seins pendants*, Paris, 1977

BOULÈGUE 1972   J. Boulègue, *Les Luso-Africains de Sénégambie XVIe–XIXe siècles*, Université de Dakar, Département d'histoire, travaux et documents 1, Dakar, 1972 [Revised as BOULÈGUE 1989]

BOULÈGUE 1987   Jean Boulègue, *Les Anciens Royaumes Wolof (Sénégal) Vol. 1. Le Grand Jolof (XIIIe–XVIe siècles)*, Blois/ Paris, 1987

BOULÈGUE 1989   Jean Boulègue, *Les Luso-Africains de Sénégambie*, Lisbon, 1989

BUCHER 1975   Henry H. Bucher, 'Mpongwe origins: historiographical perspectives', *HIA*, 2, 1975, pp. 59–89

BULL. SOC. HIS. PARIS 1911   *Bulletin de la Société de l'histoire de Paris*, 38, 1911

BURTON 1864   Richard Burton, *A mission to Gelele, King of Dahome*, 2nd ed., London, 1864

CARREIRA 1968   António Carreira, *Panaria Cabo-Verdiano-Guineense*, Lisbon, 1968

CESINALE 1873   Rocco da Cesinale, *Storia delle Missioni dei Cappuccini*, Rome, 1873

CHRISTALLER 1933   J. G. Christaller, *Dictionary of the Asante and Fante language called Tshi (Twi)*, 2nd ed., Basel, 1933

CHURCH 1957, 1980   R. J. Harrison Church, *West Africa*, 1st ed., London, 1957, 8th ed. [revised but omitting the Gulf islands], 1980

CLARKE 1966   J. I. Clarke, *Sierra Leone in maps*, London, 1966

COLE/ROSS 1977   Herbert M. Cole and Doran H. Ross, *The arts of Ghana*, Los Angeles, 1977

CULTRU 1910   P[rosper] Cultru, *Histoire du Sénégal du XVe siècle à 1870*, Paris, 1910

CURTIN 1975   Philip D. Curtin, *Economic change in pre-colonial*

Africa: Senegambia in the era of the slave trade, 2 vols, Madison, 1975

DAAKU 1970   Kwame Yeboa Daaku, *Trade and politics on the Gold Coast 1600–1720*, Oxford, 1970

DALBY/HAIR 1964   D. Dalby and P. E. H. Hair, '"Le langaige de Guynée": a sixteenth century vocabulary from the Pepper Coast', *African language studies*, 5, 1964, pp. 174–91

DATTA/PORTER 1971   Ansu K. Datta and R. Porter, 'The *Asafo* system in historical perspective', *JAH*, 12, 1971, pp. 279–98

DAVIES 1957   K. G. Davies, *The Royal African Company*, London, 1957

DAVIES 1974   K. G. Davies, 'The living and the dead: white mortality in West Africa, 1684–1732' in S. L. Engerman and E. D. Genovese, *Race and slavery in the Western hemisphere: quantitative studies*, Princeton, 1974, pp. 83–98

DEBIEN 1979   Gabriel Debien, Marcel Delafosse and Guy Thilmans, 'Journal d'un voyage de traite en Guinée, à Cayenne et aux Antilles fait par Jean Barbot en 1678–1679', *BIFAN*, sér. B, 40, 1978 [published 1979], pp. 235–395
[The text of Barbot's 1678–1679 journal supplied in this publication is cited in the present work as *1679*, but the scholarly apparatus in the publication is cited as DEBIEN 1979]

DEBIEN/HOUDAILLE 1964   G. Debien and J. Houdaille, 'Les Origines des esclaves aux Antilles, no. 32: sur une sucrerie de la Guyane en 1690 ...', *BIFAN*, sér. B, 26, 1964, pp. 166–211

DeCORSE 1989   Christopher R. DeCorse, 'Beads as chronological indicators in West African archaeology: a reexamination', *Beads*, 1, 1989, pp. 41–53

DE JONGE 1871   J. K. L. de Jonge, *De oorsprong van Neerlands bezittingen op de kust van Guinea*, The Hague, 1871

DELAFOSSE 1901   Maurice Delafosse, *Vocabulaires comparatifs de plus de 60 languages ou dialectes parlés à la Côte-d'Ivoire*, Paris, 1901

DU CASSE 1876   Robert du Casse, *L'Amiral du Casse (1666–1715)*, Paris, 1876

EHRLICH 1987   Martha J. Ehrlich, 'Early Akan gold from the wreck of the *Whydah*', *African arts*, 22, 1987, pp. 52–7, 87–8

FAGE 1980   J. D. Fage, 'A commentary on Duarte Pacheco

Pereira's account of the Lower Guinea coastlands in his Esmeraldo de Situ Orbis and some other early accounts', *HIA*, 7, 1980, pp. 47–80

FALLOPE 1988   Josette Fallope, 'Contribution de Grand Lahou au peuplement afro-caribéen (Guadeloupe-Martinique)' in S. Daget, ed., *De la traite à l'esclavage: Actes du Colloque international sur la traite des noirs, Nantes*, 2 vols, Nantes/Paris, 1988, 1: 9–24

FEINBERG 1974   H. M. Feinberg, 'New data on European mortality in West Africa: the Dutch on the Gold Coast, 1719–1760', *JAH*, 15, 1974, pp. 357–71

FEINBERG 1989   Harvey Feinberg, *Africans and Europeans in West Africa: Elminans and Dutchmen on the Gold Coast during the eighteenth century* (= Transactions of the American Philosophical Society, vol. 79), Philadelphia, 1989

FIELD 1937   Margaret J. Field, *Religion and magic of the Gã people*, London, 1937

FITCH-JONES 1933   B. W. Fitch-Jones, 'The Ruyter Stone', *Sierra Leone studies*, 19, 1933, pp. 158–61

FROIDEVAUX 1898   Henri Froidevaux, 'La Découverte de la Chute du Félou (1687)', *Bulletin de géographie historique et descriptive*, 2, 1898, pp. 300–21

FYFE 1962   Christopher Fyfe, *A history of Sierra Leone*, London, 1962

FYFE 1964   Christopher Fyfe, *Sierra Leone inheritance*, London, 1964

GADEN 1914   Henri Gaden, *Le Poular: t. 2, Lexique poular-français*, Paris, 1914

GAMBLE 1957   David P. Gamble, *The Wolof of Senegambia*, London, 1957

GARRARD 1980   Timothy F. Garrard, *Akan weights and the gold trade*, London, 1980

GARRARD 1984   Timothy F. Garrard, 'Figurine cults of the southern Akan' in Christopher Roy, ed., *Iowa studies in African art, 1*, Iowa City, 1984, pp. 167–90

GARRARD 1989   Timothy F. Garrard, *African gold*, Munich, 1989

GAULME 1981   François Gaulme, *Le Pays de Cama*, Paris, 1981

GOLDIE 1874   H. Goldie, *Dictionary of the Efik language*, Edinburgh, 1874; reprint Farnborough, 1964

GRAY 1940   J. M. Gray, *A history of the Gambia*, London, 1940

GROTTANELLI 1965   Vinigi L. Grottanelli, 'Leben, Tod und Jenseits in den Glaubensvorstellungen der Nzima' in Dominique Zahan, ed., *Réincarnation et vie mystique en Afrique Noire*, Paris, 1965, pp. 69–86

HAIR 1964   P. E. H. Hair, 'An early seventeenth-century vocabulary of Vai', *African studies*, 23, 1964, pp. 129–39

HAIR 1967, 1968, 1969a   P. E. H. Hair, 'An ethnolinguistic inventory of the Upper Guinea/Lower Guinea coast before 1700', *African language review*, 6, 1967, pp. 32–68; 7, 1968, pp. 43–73; 8, 1969, pp. 225–56

HAIR 1969b   P. E. H. Hair, 'The earliest vocabularies of Cameroons Bantu', *African studies*, 28, 1969, pp. 49–54

HAIR 1974   P. E. H. Hair, 'Barbot, Dapper, Davity: a critique of sources on Sierra Leone and Cape Mount', *HIA*, 1, 1974, pp. 25–34

HAIR 1978a   P. E. H. Hair, 'Hamlet in an Afro-Portuguese setting: new perspectives on Sierra Leone in 1607', *HIA*, 5, 1978, pp. 21–42

HAIR 1981a   P. E. H. Hair, 'A note on Jean Barbot (1655–1713)', *Proceedings of the Huguenot Society*, 23, 1981, pp. 295–308

HAIR 1984   P. E. H. Hair, 'The Falls of Félou : a bibliographical exploration', *HIA*, 11, 1984, pp. 113–30

HAIR 1990   P. E. H. Hair, 'The Spanish Capuchins in Sierra Leone' in Adam Jones, P. K. Mitchell and M. Peil, eds, *Sierra Leone studies at Birmingham 1988*, Centre of West African Studies, University of Birmingham, 1990, pp. 21–4

HAIR 1992   P. E. H. Hair, ed., *Barbot's West African vocabularies of c. 1680*, Centre of African Studies, University of Liverpool, 1992

HAIR/KENWORTHY 1987   P. E. H. Hair and J. Kenworthy, 'Observations of the weather at Sierra Leone by sixteenth century mariners' in Adam Jones and P. K.Mitchell, eds, *Sierra Leone studies at Birmingham 1985*, Centre of West African Studies, University of Birmingham, 1987, pp. 51–65

HARGREAVES 1965   J. D. Hargreaves, 'Assimilation in eighteenth century Senegal', *JAH*, 10, 1965, pp. 177–84

HAZEWINKEL 1932   H. C. Hazewinkel, 'Twee attestaties over de Nederlandsche kolonisatie aan de Goudkust', *Bijdragen en mededeelingen van het Historisch Genootschap*, 53, 1932, pp. 249–61

HAZOUMÉ 1938   Paul Hazoumé, *Le Pacte de sang au Dahomey*, Paris, 1938

HENIGE 1973   David P. Henige, 'Abrem stool. A contribution to the history and historiography of southern Ghana', *International journal of African historical studies*, 6, 1973, pp. 1–18

HENIGE 1975   David Henige, 'Adom/Supome and Jabi/Yabiw: cases of identity in a period of shifting paramountcies', *Transactions of the Historical Society of Ghana*, 16, 1975, pp. 29–46

HENIGE 1977   David Henige, 'John Kabes of Komenda: an early African entrepreneur and state builder', *JAH*, 18, 1977, pp. 1–19

HENIGE 1982   David Henige, 'Truths yet unborn? Oral tradition as a casualty of culture contact', *JAH*, 23, 1982, pp. 395–412

HECQUARD 1855   Hyacinte Hecquard, *Voyage sur la côte et dans l'intérieur de l'Afrique occidentale*, Paris, 1855

HOGENDORN/JOHNSON 1986   Jan Hogendorn and Marion Johnson, *The shell money of the slave trade*, Cambridge, 1986

ISICHEI 1973   Elizabeth Isichei, *The Ibo people and the Europeans*, London, 1973

JEEKEL 1869   C. A. Jeekel, *Onze bezittingen op de Kust van Guinea*, Amsterdam, 1869

JEFFREYS 1935   M. W. D. Jeffreys, *Old Calabar and notes on the Ibibio language*, Calabar, 1935

JONES 1956   G. I. Jones, 'The political organization of Old Calabar' in Daryll Forde, ed., *Efik traders of Old Calabar*, London, 1956, pp. 116–60

JONES 1963   G. I. Jones, *The trading states of the Oil Rivers*, London, 1963

JONES 1983b   Adam Jones, 'The Kquoja kingdom', *Paideuma*, 29, 1983, pp. 23–42

JONES 1983c   Adam Jones, *From slaves to palm kernels: a history of the Galinhas country (West Africa) 1730–1890*, Wiesbaden, 1983

JONES 1987   Adam Jones, 'Cannibales et bons sauvages: stéréotypes européens concernant les habitants de la Côte d'Ivoire, 1600–1750' in D. Droixhe and K. H. Kiefer, eds, *Images de l'africain de l'antiquité au XX siècle*, Frankfurt, 1987

JONES 1990a   Adam Jones, 'Olfert Dapper et sa description de l'Afrique' in *Objets interdits*, Fondation Dapper, Paris, 1990, pp. 73–84

JONES 1990b   Adam Jones, 'Decompiling Dapper', *HIA*, 17, 1990, pp. 171–209

JULIEN 1948   Ch.-André Julien, *Les Voyages de découverte et les premiers établissements (XVe-XVIe siècles)*, Paris, 1948

KEA 1982   R. A. Kea, *Settlements, trade, and polities in the seventeenth-century Gold Coast*, Baltimore, 1982

KEA 1986   R. A. Kea, '"I am here to plunder on the general road"; bandits and banditry in the pre-nineteenth century Gold Coast' in D. Crummey, ed., *Banditry, rebellion and social protest in Africa*, London, 1986, pp. 109–32

KOELLE 1854a   S. W. Koelle, *Polyglotta africana*, London, 1854; reprint, with introduction by P. E. H. Hair, Graz/ Freetown, 1963

KOELLE 1854b   S. W. Koelle, *A grammar of the Vei language*, London, 1854; reprint, Farnborough, 1968

KOEMAN 1967   I. C. Koeman, *Atlantes neerlandici*, 5 vols, Amsterdam, 1967–71

KROPP DAKUBU 1985   M. E. Kropp Dakubu, 'Notes on the linguistic situation on the coast of Ghana during the nineteenth century', *Institute of African Studies research review* (Legon), n.s. 1, 1985, pp. 192–202

KUP 1955–6   A. P. Kup, 'Instructions to the Royal African Company's factor at Bunce 1702', *Sierra Leone studies*, n.s. 5–6, 1955–6, pp. 44–53, 71–80

KUP 1961   A. P. Kup, *A history of Sierra Leone 1400–1787*, Cambridge, 1961

KUP 1975   A. P. Kup, *Sierra Leone: a concise history*, Newton Abbot, 1975

LATHAM 1971   A. J. H. Latham, 'Currency, credit and capitalism on the Cross River', *JAH*, 12, 1971, pp. 599–605

LATHAM 1973   A. J. H. Latham, *Old Calabar 1600–1891*, Oxford, 1973

LAW 1977   Robin Law, *The Ọyọ empire c. 1600–c. 1836*, Oxford, 1977

LAW 1982   Robin Law, 'Jean Barbot as a source for the Slave Coast of West Africa', *HIA*, 9, 1982, pp. 155–73

LAW 1983   Robin Law, 'Trade and politics behind the Slave

Coast: the lagoon traffic and the rise of Lagos', *JAH*, 24, 1983, pp. 321–48

LAW 1986   Robin Law, 'Early European sources relating to the Kingdom of Ijebu (1500–1700): a critical survey', *HIA*, 13, 1986, pp. 245–60

LAW 1987   Robin Law, 'Problems of plagiarism, harmonization and misunderstanding in contemporary European sources: early (pre–1680) sources for the 'Slave Coast' of West Africa', *Paideuma*, 33 [issue entitled *European sources for sub-Saharan Africa before 1900: use and abuse*, eds Beatrix Heintze and Adam Jones], 1987, pp. 337–58

LAWRENCE 1963   A. W. Lawrence, *Trade castles and forts of West Africa*, London, 1963

LEE 1835   Mrs R. Lee, *Stories of strange lands*, London, 1835

LEITE DE FARO 1959   [review of Carrocera 1957], *Studia*, 3, 1959, pp. 298–308

LINTINGRE 1971   Pierre Lintingre, 'Le Vénérable Père Seraphin de Léon, apôtre du Sénégal et de la Sierra Leone', *Collectanea franciscana*, 41, 1971, pp. 87–130

LY 1953   Abdoulaye Ly, 'Retour sur la fondation au XVIIe siècle du comptoir français d'Albreda', *BIFAN*, sér. B, 15, 1953, pp. 1262–77

LY 1958   Abdoulaye Ly, *La Compagnie du Sénégal*, Paris, 1958

MASSING 1985   Andreas W. Massing, 'The Mane, the decline of Mali, and Mandinka expansion towards the South Windward Coast', *Cahiers d'études africaines*, 97, 1985, pp. 21–55

MATTIESEN 1940   Otto Heinz Mattiesen, *Die Kolonial- und Überseepolitik der kurländischen Herzöge im 17. und 18. Jahrhundert*, Stuttgart, 1940

MAUNY 1950   Raymond Mauny, 'Les Prétendues Navigations dieppoises à la côte occidentale d'Afrique au XIVe siècle', *BIFAN*, sér. B, 12, 1950, pp. 122–34

MAUPOIL 1943   Bernard Maupoil, *La Géomancie à l'ancienne Côte des Esclaves*, Paris, 1943

McCASKIE 1986   T. C. McCaskie, 'Komfo Anokye of Asante: meaning, history and philosophy in an African society', *JAH*, 27, pp. 315–39

McCASKIE 1990   T. C. McCaskie, 'Nananan Mpow of Mankessim: an essay in Fante history' in David Henige and T. C.

McCaskie, eds, *West African economic history: studies in memory of Marion Johnson*, Madison, 1990, pp. 133–50

McCULLOCH 1950   M. McCulloch, *The peoples of Sierra Leone Protectorate*, London, 1950

METTAS 1978   Jean Mettas, *Répertoire des expéditions négrières françaises au XVIIIe siècle, 1: Nantes*, ed. S. Daget, Paris, 1978

MONOD 1983   Théodore Monod, *L'Ile d'Arguin (Mauritanie): essai historique*, Centro de estudos de cartografia antiga, Lisbon, 1983

MORAES 1972   Nize Isabel de Moraes, 'Le Commerce des peaux à la Petite Côte au XVIIe siècle (Sénégal)', *Notes africaines*, 1972, 134, pp. 37–45; 136, pp. 111–6

MORAES 1973b   Nize Isabel de Moraes, 'Le Commerce des tissus à la Petite Côte au XVIIe siècle (Sénégambie)', *Notes africaines*, 1973, 139, pp. 71–5

MORAIS-BARBOSA/FERRAZ 1975   Jorge Morais-Barbosa, 'Cape Verde, Guiné-Bissau, and São Tomé and Príncipe: the linguistic situation', and Luís Ferraz, 'African influences on Principense Creole' in M. F. Valkhoff, ed., *Miscellânea luso-africana*, Lisbon, 1975, pp. 133–64

NARDIN 1988   Jean-Claude Nardin, 'Que savons-nous du chevalier des Marchais?', in S. Daget, ed., *De la traite à l'esclavage: Actes du Colloque international sur la traite des noirs, Nantes*, 2 vols, Nantes/Paris, 1988, 1: 325–45

NØRREGARD 1966   Georg Nørregård, *Danish settlements in West Africa 1658–1850*, Boston, 1966

NORTHRUP 1978   D. Northrup, *Trade without rulers: precolonial economic development in South-Eastern Nigeria*, Oxford, 1978

OPPER 1989   Marie-José and Howard Opper, 'Diakhité: a study of the beads from an 18th-19th century burial site in Senegal, West Africa', *Beads*, 1, 1989, pp. 5–20

PARKES 1886   [J. C. E. Parkes], *Information regarding the tribes*, Freetown, 1886

PATTERSON 1975   K. D. Patterson, *The northern Gabon coast to 1875*, Oxford, 1975

PEEL 1987   J. D. Y. Peel, 'History, culture and the comparative method: a West African puzzle' in Ladislav Holy, ed., *Comparative anthropology*, Oxford, 1987, pp. 88–118

PERSON 1975   Yves Person, 'La Toponymie ancienne de la côte entre la Volta et Lagos', *Cahiers d'études africaines*, 15, 1975, pp. 715–21

PETERSON 1969   J. Peterson, *Province of freedom: a history of Sierra Leone 1787–1870*, London, 1969

PICHL 1963   W. J. Pichl, *Sherbro-English and English-Sherbro vocabulary*, 2 vols, Freetown, 1963; reprint Pittsburgh, 1967

PORTER 1968   R. Porter, 'English chief factors on the Gold Coast, 1632-1753', *African historical studies*, 1, 1968, pp. 199–209

POSTMA 1973   Johannes Postma, 'West African exports and the Dutch West India Company, 1675–1731', *Economisch en sociaal-historisch Jaarboek*, 36, 1973, pp. 53–74

RATTRAY 1923   R. S. Rattray, *Ashanti*, Oxford, 1923

RATTRAY 1927   R. S. Rattray, *Religion and art in Ashanti*, Oxford, 1927

RATTRAY 1929   R. S. Rattray, *Ashanti law and constitution*, Oxford, 1929

RAWLEY 1981   James A. Rawley, *The trans-Atlantic slave trade*, New York/London, 1981

ROBINSON 1975   David Robinson, *Chiefs and clerics: Abdul Bokar Kan and Futa Toro 1853–1891*, Oxford, 1975

RODNEY 1970   Walter Rodney, *A history of the Upper Guinea coast*, Oxford, 1970

ROUSSEAU 1925   R. Rousseau, 'Le site et les origines de Saint-Louis', *La Géographie*, 44, 1925, pp. 116–28, 282–301, 429–38

RYDER 1969   A. F. C. Ryder, *Benin and the Europeans, 1485–1897*, London, 1969

SANTAREM 1849   Visconde de Santarem [F. M. de Barros e Sousa de Mesquita de Macedo Leitão e Cavalhosa], *Atlas*, with accompanying *Essai sur l'histoire de la cosmographie*, Paris, 1849 [Readings of toponyms on some of the maps reproduced (by redrawing) in this work are given in A. Anthiaume, *Cartes maritimes chez les Normands*, 2 vols, Paris, 1916, but the toponyms were not all reproduced correctly]

SIEVEKING 1937   Heinrich Sieveking, 'Die Glückstädter Guineafahrt im 17. Jahrhundert. Ein Stück deutscher Kolonialgeschichte', *Vierteljahrschrift für Sozial- und Wirtschaftsgeschichte*, 30, 1937, pp. 19–71

SMITH 1970   Robert Smith, 'The canoe in West African history', *JAH*, 11, 1970, pp. 515–33

STONE 1924   T. G. Stone, 'The journey of Cornelius Hodges in Senegambia', *English historical review*, 39, 1924, pp. 89–93

SUMNER 1921   A. T. Sumner, *A handbook of the Sherbro language*, London, 1921

TEIXEIRA DA MOTA 1950   A. Teixeira da Mota, *Topónimos de origem portuguesa na costa ocidental de África*, Bissau, 1950

TEIXEIRA DA MOTA 1969   A. Teixeira da Mota, 'Un Document nouveau pour l'histoire des Peuls au Sénégal pendant les XVème et XVIème siècles', *Boletim cultural da Guiné portuguesa*, 24, 1969, pp. 781–860, also Série separatas no. 56, Agrupamento de estudos de cartografia antiga, Lisbon, 1969 [Pagination cited is that of the offprint.]

TEIXEIRA DA MOTA 1971   A. Teixeira da Mota, 'D. João Bemoim e a expedição portuguesa ao Senegal em 1489', *Boletim cultural da Guiné portuguesa*, 26, 1971, pp. 63–111, also Série separatas no. 63, Agrupamento de estudos de cartografia antiga, Lisbon, 1971 [Pagination cited is that of the offprint]

TEIXEIRA DA MOTA 1974   A. Teixeira da Mota, *As viagens do Bispo D.Frei Vitoriano Portuense à Guiné e a cristianização dos reis de Bissau*, Centro de estudos de cartografia antiga, Lisbon, 1974

TEIXEIRA DA MOTA/CARREIRA 1966   A. Teixeira da Mota and António Carreira, '*Milho zaburro* and *milho maçaroca* in Guinea and in the Islands of Cape Verde', *Africa*, 36, 1966, pp. 73–84

THILMANS/MORAES 1974   G. Thilmans and N. I. de Moraes, 'Un Moulin à Goerée au XVIIe siècle', *Notes africaines*, 142, 1974, pp. 48–51

THILMANS/MORAES 1976   G. Thilmans and N. I. de Moraes, 'Villault de Bellefond sur la côte occidentale d'Afrique. Les deux premières campagnes de l'*Europe* (1666–1671), *BIFAN*, sér. B, 38, 1976, pp. 257–99

THILMANS/MORAES 1977   G. Thilmans and N. I. de Moraes, 'Le Passage à la Petite Côte du vice-amiral d'Estrées (1670)', *BIFAN*, sér. B, 39, 1977, pp. 36–80

THILMANS/ROSSIE 1969   G. Thilmans and J. P. Rossie, 'Le "Flambeau de la Navigation" de Dierick Ruiters', *BIFAN*, sér. B, 1969, pp. 106–19

THOMPSON 1852   G. Thompson, *Thompson in Africa*, New York, 1852

TOOLEY 1969   R. V. Tooley, *Collector's guide to maps of the African continent and southern Africa*, London, 1969

TREATIES 1892   *Treaties with native chiefs on the West Coast of Africa*, Confidential Print (West Africa) 411, Colonial Office, London, 1892

VAN DANTZIG 1978   Albert van Dantzig, *The Dutch and the Guinea Coast 1674–1742: a collection of documents from the General State Archive at The Hague*, Accra, 1978

VAN DANTZIG 1980   Albert van Dantzig, *Les Hollandais sur la Côte de Guinée à l'époque de l'essor de l'Ashanti et du Dahomey 1680–1740*, Paris, 1980

VERGER 1968a   Pierre Verger, *Flux et reflux de la traite des nègres entre le Golfe de Benin et Bahia de Todos os Santos du XVIe au XVIIIe siècle*, Paris, 1968

VERGER 1968b   Pierre Verger, 'Les Côtes d'Afrique Occidentale entre "Rio Volta" et "Rio Lagos" (1535–1773)', *Journal de la Société des africanistes*, 38, 1968, pp. 35–58

VOGT 1979   John Vogt, *Portuguese rule on the Gold Coast, 1469–1682*, Athens, Ga., 1979

WELMAN 1930   C. W. Welman, *The native states of the Gold Coast. II: Ahanta*, London, 1930

WIGBOLDUS 1986   Jouke S. Wigboldus, 'Trade and agriculture in coastal Benin c. 1470–1660', *Afdeling agrarische Geschiedenis Bijdragen*, 28, 1986, pp. 299–383

WILKS 1957   Ivor Wilks, 'The rise of the Akwamu empire, 1650–1710', *Transactions of the Historical Society of Ghana*, 3, 1957, pp. 99–136

WILKS 1979   Ivor Wilks, 'The Golden Stool and the elephant tail: an essay on wealth in Asante', *Research in economic anthropology*, 2, 1979, pp. 1–36

WILLIAMSON 1927   James A. Williamson, *Sir John Hawkins*, Oxford, 1927

MAPS

Maps within cited modern works are not included.

1629 MAP   manuscript map of the Gold Coast dated 25.12.1629, in ARA, Leupe 743; printed, with some misreadings, in K. Y. Daaku and A. Van Dantzig, 'Map of the regions of the Gold Coast in Guinea', *Ghana Notes and Queries*, 9, 1966, 14–15; see also JONES 1983, fig. 2; MAREES 1987, xxii.

ADMIRALTY CHART   West Africa – 600 'Cacheu Point to Iles de Los'; 601 'Iles de Los to Sherbro Island'; 689 'Cape Sierra Leone to Turtle Islands'; 1172 'Cestos Bay to Grand Butu Point'; 1173 'Grand Butu Point to Great Nifu'; 1363 'Sherbro Island to Cape Mesurado'; 1365 'Baffu Bay to Grand Bereby'; 2478 ' Manna River to Junk River'; 3648 'Junk River to Cestos Bay'
[Although there have been more recent surveys of the sections of coast represented in these charts, the base surveys were carried out in the first part of the nineteenth century, hence their toponymy provides useful evidence on earlier forms]

ATLAS IVORY COAST 1979   *Atlas de Côte d'Ivoire*, Abidjan, 1979

BEAURAIN 1695   'Carte tres détaillée des pais compris depuis le Cap Blanc jusqu'à la Rivière de Serelione ... Par le Sr. de Beaurain', on reverse, 'par M. de la Courbe vers 1695', PBN, Collection D'Anville, Ge DD 2987, port. 119, no. 8138 (for a slightly altered copy, redrawn perhaps for engraving, see no. 8099), reproduced in part in TEIXEIRA DA MOTA 1974, fig. 7

BLAEUW 1659   'Novissima Africae Descriptio', reproduced in MCA, p. 1151 and WMC, 3:73

DANVILLE 1728   'Carte générale de la concession du Sénégal dressée par le Sr.d'Anville ...', enlarged in 'Carte générale du cours de la Rivière de Senegal', 'Carte particulière du cours ... depuis Le Desert jusqu'à la mer', 'Carte particulière du Senega comprenant les Isles du Morfil et de Bilbas', 'Carte particulière du Senega depuis Le Desert en remontant jusqu'à l'Isle du Morfil', 'Carte de la Rivière Falemé ...', in LABAT 1728, passim.
[Only the first two maps carry Danville's name, but all are related and form a set]

CARTA 1961   'Carta da Província da Guiné 1:500,000', Ministério do Ultramar, Lisbon, 1961

DAPPER (1676)   'Africae Accurata Tabula', 'Nigritarum Regio' (Arguin-Benguela), 'Guinea' (the maps prepared by J. van Meurs)

DELISLE 1700/1707   Guillaume de l'Isle, 'L'Afrique dressée sur les observations de Ms. de l'Académie royale des sciences .... 1700', revised 1707; English version, [John Senex and] C. Price, 'Africa corrected from the observations of the Royal Societies at London and Paris ... 1711'

DELISLE 1707   Guillaume de l'Isle, 'Carte de la Barbarie, de la Nigritie et de la Guinée ... 1707'

DE WITT 1675   Frederick de Witt, 'Tractus littorales Guineae a Promontorio Verde usque ad Sinum Catenbelae', not dated, but in *Orbis maritimus ofte Zee Atlas*, Amsterdam, [1675], and Witt's later atlases

ENGLISH PILOT 1701   see List A

FISHER 1773   R. Fisher, 'A plan of the River Sherbro ... 1773', 1789; also in *The African pilot*, London, 1799

FITZHUGH 1684   Augustine Fitzhugh, manuscript map, 'Guinea ... 1684', PBN, Dépôt, III.2.11 (the greater part reproduced in DONELHA 1977, fig. 6)

JANSSONIUS/JANSSON 1638, 1641   Johannes Janssonius (Jan Jansz.), 'Guinea', in *Nieuwer atlas/Le nouveau théâtre du monde*, pt. 3, Amsterdam, 1638, 1641 [the editors consulted different editions]

LUÍS TEIXEIRA 1602   'Effigies ampli Regni auriferi Guineae ... per Lodovicium Texeram', in MAREES (1602, 1912) (reproduced in part in DONELHA 1977, fig. 3; see MAREES 1987, pp. xxiii–xxv)

MCA   [F. C. Wieder and] Youssouf Kamal, *Monumenta cartographica Africae*, tome 5, fasc. 1, Cairo, 1951

MORTIER 1700   Pierre Mortier, 'Carte particulière des costes de l'Afrique qui comprend le Royaume de Cacheo, le Province de Gelofo, etc.', 'Carte ... qui comprend une partie de la Guinée et partie de Mina, etc.', 'Carte ... depuis Cabo Corso jusques à Omorro' in *Suite de Neptune françoise*, Paris, 1700

'PASCAERT VAN SIERA LEONA'   'Pascaert van Siera Leona vertoonende de Zeecust van Cabo Verga tot Rio Nuno' [probably *c.* 1660], manuscript map in Atlas Blaeu/Van der Hem, Österreichische Nationalbibliothek, Vienna

'PLAN OF SIERRA LEONA 1794'   'Plan of Sierra Leona and the parts adjacent 1794', in *Report of the Sierra Leone Company 1794*, London

PMC   A. Z. Cortesão and A. Teixeira da Mota, *Portugaliae monumenta cartographica*, 5 vols, Lisbon, 1960–62

ROBIJN/ROGGEVEEN 1685   see List A – the relevant maps are 'Paskaert van de kust Genehoa en Rio de Senegael', 'De cust van Gambia tusschen Rio Senegael en Rio Cazamansa', 'Pas caert van Gambia', 'De zee cust van Melegette en Melly tusschen C.Roxa en Rio Serbera' (inset 'Pascaert van Siera Liona'), 'Pas kaert vertoonend in twee deelen de Greyn en Tandt-Cust', 'Pas-caert van de Gout-Cust in Guinea', 'Paskaert van de Gout Cust en Boght van Benin', 'Pas-caert vertoonende alle de zee custen van Biafra, Fernando Poo, en Ilha de Prince, streckende van de Ruyge hoeck tot Rio Corisco', 'Paskaart van Gabon, Loango en Congo'

SANSON 1655   Nicolas Sanson, 'L'Afrique ou Lybie ... La Coste des Nègres et Guinée ... 1655', in *Cartes générales*, Paris, 1658

SANSON 1656   Nicolas Sanson, 'La Guinée et pays circomvoisins 1656', in SANSON 1656 (List A), and *Cartes générales*, Paris, 1658

'SIERRA LEONE 1666'   'De Rivier van Siera Lions ... 1 Maij 1666', manuscript map in Atlas Blaeu/Van der Hem, Österreichische Nationalbibliothek, Vienna, reproduced in WMC, 5: plate 102

SANTAREM 1849   see List B

SELLER *c.* 1670   John Seller, 'A chart of Guinea', in *Atlas maritimus*, 1675, and *The third book of the English pilot*, 1675

SENEGAL COMPANY *c.* 1700   'Carte de la Coste d'Afrique contenant partie de la concession de la Compagnie royale du Sénégal, depuis the Cap-Blanc jusques au Bissaux', undated and anonymous, PBN, Collection D'Anville, Ge DD 1987, port. 119, no. 8140 (reproduced in part in TEIXEIRA DA MOTA 1974, fig. 26)

SMITH 1727   William Smith, *Thirty different drafts of Guinea*, London, [? 1727]

THILMANS 1975   see List A

THOMPSON 1787   'A survey of the entrance of Sierra Leona River, by Captn. Thompson, of His Majesty's Ship Nautilus',

Laurie and Whittle, 1794, and in *The African pilot*, London, 1799

VAN KEULEN 1683   see List A – the maps cited are 'Nieuwe paskaert van de kust van Genehoa als mede een gedeelte van Gambia', 'Pas caarte van Rio Gambia van C.Verde tot Rio de Serraliones'

WMC   F. C. Wieder, *Monumenta cartographica*, 5 vols, The Hague, 1925–34

WOODVILLE 1777   W. Woodville, 'The volcanic islands named Ilhas dos Idolos ...' inset on 'A new survey ... from Senegal ... to Cape St Ann ... 1797', in *The African pilot*, London, 1799

MANUSCRIPT SOURCES

AANAO   *Aix-en-Provence, Archives nationales, Archives d'Outre-Mer*
Dépôt des fortifications des colonies: Côtes d'Afrique, MS 104, 'Relation du Royaume de Judas en Guinée ... [1691]'

AGA   *Amsterdam, Gemeente Archief*

ARA   *The Hague, Algemeen Rijksarchief*
(papers of the Dutch West India Company)
OWIC (Oude West-Indische Compagnie)
WIC (West-Indische Compagnie, i.e. post–1674), especially Aanwinsten 1. Afdl., 1898 XXII, journal of Louys Dammaert 1652–1656, cited as ARA, Dammaert journal
Radermacher no. 587, report of Heerman Abramsz to Assembly of Ten 23.11.1679, cited as ARA, Abramsz 23.11.1679
Leupe 743, map dated 25.12.1629, cited as 1629 MAP

BL   *London, British Library*
Add. 28788 Jean Barbot, 'Journal d'un voyage de Guinée', published in DEBIEN 1979 and cited in the present edition as *1679*
Add.19560 Des Marchais [= Jean Pierre Thibault], 'Journal de navigation du voyage de la coste de Guinnée ... [1704–1706] Par le sieur Des Marchais'

COP   *Copenhagen, Rigsarkivet*
(papers of the Danish West India-Guinea Company)
Vestindisk-guineisk kompagni, cited as COP, V-gK

ESA   *Emden, Stadtarchiv*

872

(papers of the Brandenburg African Company)

KITLV   *Leiden, Koninklijk Instituut voor Taal-, Land- en Volkenkunde*

MZS   *Merseburg, Zentrales Staatsarchiv*

(papers relating to the Brandenburg African Company)

OBLR *Oxford, Bodleian Library*

    Rawlinson Papers (Royal African Company) C.745–747 (letters to Cape Coast 1681–1699), consulted in the microfilm with index prepared by David Henige, *Correspondence from the outforts to Cape Coast Castle, 1681–1699: a guide to Rawlinson C.745–747* (Cooperative Africana Microform Project: Madison 1972)

PAN   *Paris, Archives nationales*

    C6/25 'Mémoire de l'estat de Pays de Juda et de son négoce'

PBN   *Paris, Bibliothèque nationale*

    Collection D'Anville (various maps)

    Collection Arnoul, Nouvelles acquisitions françaises 21393, 'Mémoire [by de Monségur] contenant quatre feuilles pour la guinée et angola . . . 1692'

PRO   *London, Public Record Office*

    ADM 7/830 Jean Barbot, 'Description des côtes d'Affrique depuis le Cap Bojador jusques à celui de Lopo Gonzalves', cited as *1688*

    T/70 (Royal African Company, various)

    HCA (High Court of Admiralty)

INDEX OF PLACES AND PEOPLES

Variants, which are often in the forms of several languages (and often corrupted), are listed. Descriptive terms, being often in varying language forms (e.g. Cape/Cap/Cabo, River/Rio, Point/Pointe/Ponta/Punta), are ignored, as are the linking terms often found in non-English forms (e.g. de/du/des/da/do/dos/das). The English term 'Saint' and its equivalents in other languages are abbreviated as S. – uniformly.

For capes, islands, forts, rivers and points, see the lists under those headings. Toponyms applying to more than one category of locality are, however, to be found in the general listing, being signalled in category lists by (see). In these items, I indicates island/s, F fort, R river, P point. Certain terms given as African names and titles, and listed in the Index of Persons, may also be toponyms.

The following terms appear too frequently to be listed: Africa/Africans, Guinea, Blacks/blacks/whites, Europe/Europeans, France/French, England/English.

882

883

INDEX OF PERSONS

African individuals are described where possible; African titles are listed when the title denotes an individual. For generic titles see the Index of Subjects; for authors of publications and maps see the Index of Authors. Note that certain terms given as African names appear to be also, or more correctly, toponyms.

INDEX OF AUTHORS

For full names, see the Bibliography or notes to the Introduction.

INDEX OF SELECT SUBJECTS

Entries are of two kinds: topics (in *italics*) and keywords. Entries for topics list only significant references in the Introduction and Barbot's text, but suggest relevant keywords (within asterisks). Keyword entries list all references to specific select terms throughout the edition. For further guidance on broad topics, see Barbot's own analysis of his text (List of Letters, pp. cvii–cxvii).

913